AMAZING GRACE

BOOKS BY LAURA KNIGHT-JADCZYK

The Secret History of the World
The Noah Syndrome
High Strangeness: Hyperdimensions and the Process of Alien Abduction
9/11: The Ultimate Truth
The Apocalypse: Comets, Asteroids and Cyclical Catastrophes

THE WAVE SERIES:

Riding the Wave
Soul Hackers
The Terror of History
Stripped to the Bone
Petty Tyrants
Facing the Unknown
Almost Human
Debugging the Universe

Laura Knight-Jadczyk

AMAZING GRACE

Red Pill Press
www.redpillpress.com

Copyright © 2012 Laura Knight-Jadczyk.

ISBN 978-1-897244-81-4

Design & layout: © 2012 Quantum Future Group, Inc., The Fellowship of the Cosmic Mind, Inc.

No part of this publication may be reproduced, stored in a retrieval system, or transmitted in any form or by any means, electronic, mechanical, or otherwise, other than for 'fair use', without the written consent of the author.

For my husband Arkadiusz, who gave me the strength to BE.
For my children: Aletheia, Arianna, Jason, Amelia and Arielle,
who gave me the will to Be, and for whom I made the choice to BE.
If I can do it, so can they.
For my beloved grandparents who protected me,
and most especially my grandmother.
She loved me as I was; and because of her, I had faith that I could BE.

Laura & Ark by Cherie Diez,
St. Petersburg (FL) Times.

CONTENTS

Introduction	11
CHAPTER ONE: The Face at the Window	15
CHAPTER TWO: The Lost Boys and Girls	19
CHAPTER THREE: Another Window Opens on Strange Connections	45
CHAPTER FOUR: Dead Babies and Iron Skillets	55
CHAPTER FIVE: Jane Eyre Redux	63
CHAPTER SIX: Violets and Bulls in the Graveyard	73
CHAPTER SEVEN: Trapezes and Dog Days	79
CHAPTER EIGHT: The Farm	85
CHAPTER NINE: The Standoff	93
CHAPTER TEN: Shrinks and Rebels or Being Fifteen is an Awkward State	105
CHAPTER ELEVEN: Graveyards, Psychopaths, Psychics, and Meetings on the Bridge	117
CHAPTER TWELVE: Dr. Jekyll and Mr. Hyde	131
CHAPTER THIRTEEN: Oysters on the Half Shell	143
CHAPTER FOURTEEN: Pearls in the Oyster	159
CHAPTER FIFTEEN: Blitzkrieg	177
CHAPTER SIXTEEN: Dances with Sunlight	191
CHAPTER SEVENTEEN: Mirror! Mirror! On the Wall ...	203
CHAPTER EIGHTEEN: The Wolf and the Dove	215
CHAPTER NINETEEN: The World's Most Beautiful Baby	225

CHAPTER TWENTY: Minks and Turkey Basters   237
CHAPTER TWENTY-ONE: Parties, Mosquitoes, Hives, Hypnosis,
    and Fishing Boats   247
CHAPTER TWENTY-TWO: The Devil in the Details   261
CHAPTER TWENTY-THREE: In the Forest   265
CHAPTER TWENTY-FOUR: The Poisoned Apple   279
CHAPTER TWENTY-FIVE: The Boat Ride to Damascus   295
CHAPTER TWENTY-SIX: Another Face at the Window   313
CHAPTER TWENTY-SEVEN: The Noah Syndrome or The Lost Love   323
CHAPTER TWENTY-EIGHT: The Ark in Montana   347
CHAPTER TWENTY-NINE: The Dream   365
CHAPTER THIRTY: A Knight in Armor   383
CHAPTER THIRTY-ONE: The Cleft in the Rock   399
CHAPTER THIRTY-TWO: Moving to Montana   409
CHAPTER THIRTY-THREE: Synchronicity City   425
CHAPTER THIRTY-FOUR: That's Hollywood!   435
CHAPTER THIRTY-FIVE: The Crane Dance   447
CHAPTER THIRTY-SIX: Hailing the Universe   455
CHAPTER THIRTY-SEVEN: Missing Child, Missing Time   475
CHAPTER THIRTY-EIGHT: Flying Black Boomerangs   487
CHAPTER THIRTY-NINE: Flying Black Boomerangs Redux   499
CHAPTER FOURTY: Aliens, Demons, and Vampires   517
CHAPTER FOURTY-ONE: Aunt Clara   529
CHAPTER FOURTY-TWO: Green Slime   545
CHAPTER FOURTY-THREE: Hungry Aliens, Stinky Demons,
    and the Return of Keith   561
CHAPTER FOURTY-FOUR: Comets and Cassiopaeans   583

Acknowledgments   612

She dwelt among untrodden ways
Beside the springs of Dove;
A maid whom there were none to praise,
And very few to love.
A violet by a mossy stone
Half-hidden from the eye!
Fair as a star, when only one
Is shining in the sky.
She lived unknown, and few could know
When Lucy ceased to be:
But she is in her grave, and O!
The difference to me!

— William Wordsworth, "The Lost Love".

My grandmother, Lucy Young, at about age 18.

INTRODUCTION

There are, at present, fundamental problems in theoretical physics ... the solution of which ... will presumably require a more drastic revision of our fundamental concepts than any that have gone before. Quite likely, these changes will be so great that it will be beyond the power of human intelligence to get the necessary new ideas by direct attempts to formulate the experimental data in mathematical terms. The theoretical worker in the future will, therefore, have to proceed in a more direct way.

—Paul Dirac.

I grew up in the deepest South, the Gulf Coast of Florida, and our family history here goes back over a century before my birth. The old tintypes and yellowed photographs of our ancestors were displayed proudly by my grandparents. Everywhere we went, there were places that "used to be" like this or that, where some memorable event occurred in the days when horses and buggies were the only means of transportation. There was a sense of belonging here.

And as I grew up, sheltered within the vibrant green canopy of my grandparents' farm, sheltered in its turn within a primeval landscape, a time that has now passed by forever became my own home and held my own history.

With almost inexpressible poignancy, I think back to cruising Florida coast roads during endless summer nights, driving down the center line on two-lane blacktop in my brother's '57 Chevy with the top down; our headlights were the only lights in the onrushing wind and darkness. We drove on, enchanted by this salty and balmy air, the fields of brilliant stars above us, nothing on either side of the road for miles but salt marsh and the Gulf of Mexico in the distance.

This fragile time was not to last. The northern developers came down and bought up the land in a dispossession of the old homes of so many people. Our original family home is gone with that time, when the world seemed simpler and the constellations shining above our heads were the only lights in the velvet blackness of the night.

This is the beginning of my story, and how the Cassiopaeans came to be a part of my life. Their channeled messages, based on the concept that knowledge protects and ignorance endangers, have drawn the attention of intellectually advanced, yet spiritually hungry people from all over the world. The Cassiopaeans came to initiate me into the realm of self-knowledge and cosmic truth only after a long and arduous struggle to comprehend the deeper realities of the world around us, and only after I asked—repeatedly and fervently.

I've spent much of my life trying to find reasonable explanations for complex and mysterious events, struggling to fit my experiences into ordinary life, shoving my own observations under the rug of the mundane world. Once the veil of that matrix illusion has been pulled back and we see a glimpse of truth, there's no choice but to tear it away completely and expose all.

I had been relegated to the quiet corner of marginalization all my life. My feelings of self-worth had been repeatedly savaged with every anomalous experience I had shared with the people in my life most important to me. There's nothing more devastating than to realize there's no one with whom you can share all, and by whom you can feel valued no matter what you think, do or say. And to have this arena of my life and experiences fenced off from revelation, for the simple reason that it may be considered trivial, abnormal, or even sinful, is devastating to the soul.

Like many, many people, I never asked for strange things to happen in my life. I most definitely fought a losing battle to pretend they weren't happening. How many other people in the world had suffered because their deep realities had been ridiculed? At the most extreme end are people considered insane because their perceptions are different. But there are also vast numbers of people who have had many odd experiences who are afraid to speak of them, who hold them close inside, wondering daily if they're losing their minds, or perhaps even whether they are being subjected to some sort of demonic torment.

The story of the reality of spirit, of the play of forces that exist as a subtext to the lives of all human beings, can be told as a journey toward knowledge and understanding. My search for the existence of truth about our reality forced me to recognize the validity of perceptions beyond those of materialism. I learned to challenge my own beliefs and suffer the agony of surrendering my own dearly held reality constructs.

My life may be deeply rooted in one geographic location, but my work has led me to friends across the world. And ultimately, it led my husband Ark, a theoretical-mathematical physicist, to join me in a new venture to discover the underlying fusion between science and mysticism.

Ark was born in Poland and spent his academic life at big accelerators, universities, and research centers. In Wroclaw, Poland, he created the Division of Nonlinear Dynamics and Complex Systems, the new domain of physics that came into being after the computer revolution enabled him and his colleagues to attack the problems of "self-organization," the reason for order that we see in the universe without and the universe within.

Recently we watched the wildly popular film, *The Matrix*, on the recommendation of our teen-aged son. He declared to us that it was a "totally awesome metaphor" for all the information we had been receiving from the Cassiopaeans, as well as the work we had been doing in both theoretical and practical ways. Naturally, we were skeptical that such a young person could really grasp the nature of our work and our thinking, but we were surprised to discover just how accurate his description was.

The experience of viewing this film was, to put it mildly, stunning. It is one thing to be thinking certain things and to be working in those directions with real physics and math, and another to see a presentation of so accurate an analogy that even a high-school student could appreciate its subtleties.

There were, of course, some slight variations in the presentation, but overall, it was so startlingly close to our own speculations—including the most amazing reference to déjà vu as a "change in the program" (for us, evidence of a time-loop), that we were left with our mouths hanging open.

The major analogy of the movie was that the "real now" was a control system that produced a "programmed dream of reality" experienced by those "trapped in the Matrix." The Matrix Reality was based on the way things were in the past, before a terrible event had occurred to destroy the World-That-Was. After that cataclysmic event, everything came under the control of computers that had become sentient and needed to utilize human beings as power sources or "food."

The difference between that view and our own was that we were proposing a theoretical para-physical realm as another layer in the structure of space-time from which our own reality is projected, looping over and over again in endless variations. This para-physical reality is inhabited by beings of both positive and negative polarity who have "graduated" from our reality, although not necessarily in the sense of "dying" and going to a strictly ethereal realm, as many seekers into metaphysical truths have attempted to understand this concept. These beings exist, effectively, in a world of the future that creates our present by projecting itself into the past. But if we think about the future in terms of probable futures, or branching universes, then what we do now, whether we wake up from the Matrix or not, determines what kind of future we will experience, individually and collectively.

These very ideas were presented to us from the contact with the Cassiopaeans, who have told us: "We transmit through the opening that is presented in the locator that you represent as Cassiopaea, due to the strong radio pulses aligned from Cassiopaea, which are due to a pulsar from a neutron star 300 light years behind it, as seen from your locator. This facilitates a clear channel transmission from 6th level reality to 3rd level reality."

But that was to come later, and I am getting ahead of myself.

This is the story of the beginning of my search. I am telling not only the story of my own experiences, but also the greater story of the potential that exists in every woman and man. We have the potential to discover the genuine existence of spirit and the play of the archetypal forces in our world, and to connect with them in a dynamic way. Amazing Grace can become an immediate reality in our lives and in our hearts.

CHAPTER ONE

THE FACE AT THE WINDOW

I am awake and I am cold.

In the first few moments of awareness, this is all I know. Waves of shudders pass through me, and in a single spasm of deep shock, I open my eyes. I don't know where I am or who I am. The surroundings are unfamiliar and something is terribly wrong.

Through eyes that seem to be mine, I examine my condition, my situation, my environment.

Nothing makes sense.

I am in a bedroom, lying on a bed with a blue and white cover. I think for a moment that I would like to move and get under this cover because I am so cold. But something else attracts my attention with paralyzing immediacy: a sound, a faint movement from outside. My eyes are drawn to the windows opposite.

There are two windows, side by side. I am possessed of a preternatural awareness that something is approaching and I am in mortal peril.

Where does this awareness originate? I am unprepared for the sensations flooding through this body in which I find my consciousness. The heart beating in this chest seems to have vaulted to the interior of the head, thudding in my ears. My eyes water from the intensity as I watch the windows. It seems hard to catch my breath. The icy air sharpens its edge on my skin.

I am confused to discover this body is a child's.

I can hear a crunching sound on the gravel under the eaves of the house. Someone approaches along the back of the building toward the windows. I know I must do something now. My confusion intensifies. How do I know this? I don't even know who I am and where I am.

I catch the sound of heavy, raspy breathing. Terror vaults in me and I am sure my heart will explode. My eyes are the only things I can move, and they rapidly scan the room for a route of escape.

The closet door is only a few feet away. I try to get up and cross this small space, but I find that I cannot command these limbs. Why is there a world of distance between me and safety?

The cat-footed approach is closer now, more immediate. What must I do? Can I master this unfamiliar body enough to get under the bed? But anyone looking in the window could easily see me there. If I get up, cross the floor, crouch directly under the window, I won't be seen. But that will put me in reach of whatever approaches. I know that something will appear at the window in the next instant. They will know where I am, wherever I hide.

If they touch me I will die.

It was, inevitably, too late. The Face appeared at the window.

These lungs are gasping for air in the grip of terror and disorientation. My tongue slips backward into my throat, threatening to suffocate me. How good it would be to close my eyes and recede back into the darkness, but I cannot.

My eyes burn and water, magnetized by some unseen force emanating from that face. Those eyes are swirling pinwheels of glowing green, spirals encircled by an aspect so unnaturally white that it seems to glow in the deepening gloom outside.

Me at about the age of the "Face at the Window". We are still living in Orlando, I've got chocolate milk on my upper lip and am holding a new toy broom. My brother is obviously NOT happy to have to sit in the same chair with me for a photo.

Laura aged 4, dressed for church.

THE FACE AT THE WINDOW

It speaks.

Not with audible words, but words carried on a different wave, a rhythm that contacts my consciousness and paralyzes it, a wave that invades my innermost thoughts and opposes them with emanations, penetrating the furthest and most private reaches of my mind, probing and seeking within the recesses of my being.

I am receiving data.

Images and impressions and forms of horror incomprehensible to my mind. But I cannot assimilate them. I refuse. My act of refusal paralyzes my mind. I am an immovable object confronted by an irresistible force.

And finally, it withdraws. But the withdrawal brings rage and sickening disappointment and frustration. Words lash out like the blows of a whip slicing through the air. A deep internal pressure accompanies the sneering words:

"You can't hide. No matter where you go or what you do, when the time comes, we will find you! We will come for you!"

Its laughter slashes furiously down on my awareness and my mind reels under the damage being done in this struggle. Under the impact, my soul leaps upward and my consciousness recedes to that still, quiet place of rest.

* * *

The Face at the Window that came when I was four years old is a memory as clear today as if it had just happened. I have examined this memory with great care, as though it were an unknown and incomprehensible object kept in a locked box, only to be contemplated in private. For years I told no one about it. I tried to convince myself it never happened at all except in my imagination, or merely in a Halloween prank of neighborhood kids, misinterpreted by my child's mind. I tried every way I could to fit it into a normal category of experience. If other events had not occurred in my life, perhaps I would have been able to keep it there.

This was the primary formative event of my childhood. After it happened, I never again felt safe. There was a Hound of Hell pursuing me, and I could hear its panting and feel its breath on my heels.

But to understand this event in its proper context, some details of my early life need to be shared.

CHAPTER TWO

THE LOST BOYS AND GIRLS

Families are somewhat like planetary systems. In a certain terrain and atmosphere, the members develop and evolve based on the resources available. It seems to me, after all these years, that it's impossible to understand the deep inner nature of anyone without understanding these elements of the family "planet."

My parents were divorced when I was a baby. Actually, they were separated before, and my father's family talked my mother into going back with my father, even going to the extent of offering her financial security for life if she did so.

My father had been one of a set of adored and indulged fraternal twins: Jack and Fred. Jack, my father, had black hair, olive skin and dark eyes. Fred had red hair, pale skin and blue eyes. Their parents were well-to-do, established in the drug business, and involved in politics to some extent as various family members held assorted offices, backed often by my paternal grandfather's money. Keeping the family "face" was an important issue even if there were rumors that Tom Knight had made most of his money running rum from the Bahamas during Prohibition.

However he made his money, he spent it liberally on his children. And, judging by the letters and documents I inherited when my father died, he also spent a great deal of time with his children. There are endless pictures of them on family outings, hunting or fishing, dressed in their matching sporting or riding clothes, or standing with displays of long stringers of huge fish.

One rather infamous story about the twins and their escapades provides insight into the forces at play in their development. Accompanying this story is a series of newspaper clippings, because it involved a prank truly larger than life, just like my father.

The first, from a local paper, is headlined "Seven Boys Rescued From Florida Swamp Tell Story of Torture By Three Men." The competing newspaper printed a similar story headlined "Harrowing Experience: 7 Lost Boys." The lurid writing style is more like what we've come to expect in weekly tabloids, but the story it relates is truly hysterical:

"Scores of Plant City citizens spent Sunday recuperating from an experience that but few have had to endure. They had spent the greater part of the previous night wading and sloshing about in the treacherous swamps of the Hillsborough River, seeking rescue of seven Plant City boys ranging in age from ten to near thirteen years. ...

"The youngsters were members of a Sunday school camping party who spent Friday night on the north border of the great Hillsborough river swamp ... and the story relative to their predicament was of such nature to at once arrest the attention of anyone. The search lasted until 6:15 o'clock Sunday morning, when one of the posse came upon the youngsters reclining on a long log two miles from the nearest road and more than a mile from the outer recesses of the great swamp, so dense in this particular region that only the pioneer, or old-timer accustomed to penetrate it, could be expected to 'pass inside its portals' with reasonable expectations of getting out without assistance.

Fraternal twins, Fred (left) and Jack (right) Knight, with their father, Big Tom, in front of one of the family businesses.

"The seven lost boys were Jack and Fred Knight, twin sons of Mr. and Mrs. Tom J. Knight [the other boys were listed].

"They, with ten other boys, were guests of Justice of the Peace Garland M. Branch, the outing being tendered by Mr. Branch in recognition of their good attendance at Sunday School.

"All went fairly well until Friday night, when [one of the boys] met with an accident. [He] stumbled while being chased by some of his camp-mates and fell partly into one of the campfires, sustaining painful burns on the wrists and chest. Mr. Branch immediately brought the lad home, where he could receive medical attention ...

"It had been planned that the party would break camp near noon Saturday, and with that end in view, Mr. Wells [the Sunday School worker left with the boys while Mr. Branch was in town with the injured boy] departed for home, in a Ford car, about 11 o'clock, bringing four of the smaller boys. Soon after that, Mr. Branch, in another car, left for Plant City bringing three other lads, the understanding being that the nine still at camp would remain there until a truck arrived to bring in the tents and other paraphernalia, and the nine boys were to return on the truck.

"Within a few minutes after Mr. Branch departed, three young men who had been camping at a small house about a quarter of a mile away, where the Plant City party had secured water during their stay in the woods, approached the boys. The men had been drinking, it was said, and had a rifle and some revolvers which they removed from their car when they stopped at the boys' camp-site. The men were decidedly boisterous, it was said ...

"The youngster and his companions were ordered into the open at the point of pistols and then told to dance. When one of the youths stopped from sheer exhaustion, the men shot at his feet and demanded that he continue. After dancing for some time, the youth was seized and a bottle containing what he thought was whisky was pressed against his lips and he was forced to swallow. Attempts were made, young Knight said, to force liquor into the mouths of the other boys.

"Fred Knight, his brother Jack [and the others] were forced to flee into the swamps because they feared for their lives ... leaving a note 'Gone to Plant City, Fl, Threatened' behind."

As you might guess, subsequent accounts were equally melodramatic. The next one, headlined "Men Who Drove Boys Into Swamps Known, Will Be Prosecuted," had this gem in it:

"While medical aid was being administered to the seven boys of the First Baptist Sunday School of Plant City who, Saturday night, were driven into the dense swamps around Lake Thonotosassa by the threats of drunken revelers ... the fathers of four of the youngsters were in conference with Sheriff L. M. Hiers ... the men said to have threatened the boys are said to have had their identities established, and warrants probably will be sworn out for their arrest today on charges of having liquor in their possession."

Now, remember, this was during Prohibition. Never mind that he might have made money on liquor, my grandfather was outraged that his own children would be assaulted by anyone and forced to drink "demon rum"! As it turned out, of course, he had to eat a lot of crow. The men were arrested with the following headline: "Arrest Is Taken As Joke By Youthful Trio Accused Of Attacking Boy Campers."

"Smiling and apparently unconcerned at charges filed against them, three of the four young men implicated in an alleged malicious assault on a group of Plant City boys ... were placed in the Hillsborough County Jail late yesterday afternoon.

"The prisoners, C. Hill, H. Bryan, and H. Hill ... were taken into custody yesterday. ... Upon their entrance in the jail the youths regarded the matter as a joke and did not appear worried by their plight. They submitted to a search in a jovial manner and expressed surprise when they were led to a cell. It was their first experience behind bars, they said, and it was not until they had been in confinement several hours that their jubilant spirit waned and smiles were replaced by troubled brows and tear-dimmed eyes."

At this point, the newspaper accounts end, because the truth came out. What really happened: the innocent boys, led by ringleaders Jack and Fred, had set up the whole plot. They maneuvered to be "left behind," having made arrangements to buy whiskey from the three men during one of their trips to get water for the campers. They had dreams of being the new Tom Sawyer and Huck Finn.

The rapscallion twins with their hunting dog, Frank.

Of course, they didn't expect to get found so quickly, lolling in their drunken state on a log in the swamp. And, they most certainly did not expect two hundred people, who searched for them in the muck, in the rain, all night, to get so serious about it all that they'd actually demand to arrest the fellows who had been their source of liquor!

Finally the boys told the real story, and apparently provided proof they'd been paid for the liquor out of the well-lined pockets of my father and his equally rapscallion brother.

This was just a precursor to Jack's later escapades. As he grew older, my father was devoted to proving that he was the champion drinker of the county. He was also dedicated to driving faster than anyone in his crowd. In his early twenties, home on leave (he was a chemist in the Navy), his arm was broken so badly in a car crash that numerous operations were required to reassemble it in normal conformation. He recovered from other, nearly fatal, injuries, but during the course of these surgeries and intermittent recovery periods, he became addicted to morphine.

Remember: his father was in the drug business.

Well, dear old Dad, not to miss any opportunity, decided to "reform" his life, use his Navy training, and go into the drug business with his father. And the addiction was covered up for a very long time.

My mother Alice enters the scene at this point. She was quite a bit younger than my father. The heroic figure he presented as star football stud of the county school system was part of the charm he used to seduce as many young girls as possible. As a freshman, Mother thought he was the hottest and most dangerous guy in town, but by the time she was out of high school, he was in the Navy, out of sight and mind, and Mother married someone else.

One day, after his recovery from many surgeries, they literally ran into each

Jack Knight at about the time he married my mother. Notice how he kept his hands in his pocket to minimize the damage to his shorter and wasted left arm. My mother said he looked like Clark Gable and the resemblance is there!

other, crossing the street in opposite directions. Apparently, it was a stunning event for both of them, because they immediately decided to go to a nearby cafe for lunch, and by the time they finished dessert and coffee, Mother had agreed to divorce her husband and marry my father.

And she did.

This may seem either very romantic or very foolhardy. But it brings us back to the idea of families as planetary systems. My father's family was rather proud, claiming (as many do) to be descended from royalty. In later years, when searching for clues to my own internal make-up, I discovered that one of the Knight men had married a woman descended from the noble De Ferrieres. This was the only provable link. But I also discovered something else: the Knights, along with a select group of other families, were frequently consanguineous, marrying cousins to cousins, uncles to nieces, and so forth down through the generations. It was almost as though they had a kind of internal mandate to combine and recombine their bloodlines, with an occasional infusion of "new blood" from time to time. Some theorists would suggest this was a risky practice. Perhaps so. But, by and large, they were powerful personalities, pioneers, with many successes to their credit even if few of them ever managed to become more than a big fish in a little pond. Genealogy articles I've discovered about some of my forebears in this line say things like: *"Mr. and Mrs. Knight became the ancestors of a large and influential family connection of South Florida where most of the Knight children lived and died. Samuel Knight was an influential man in his day."*

This Samuel was my great-great-great-grandfather. About his son, it was written: *"Jesse Knight was a local preacher in the Methodist Church, and did much work in this section in establishing and developing churches."*

Another, written on the death of my great-grandmother, Martha Collins Knight, tells us:

Alice Meadows on her graduation day.

"The passing of Martha Ann Collins Knight removes one of the few remaining links between the present and the long-distant past when the lives of the pioneers were silhouetted against the rugged skyline of frontier days.

"She was married to William Samuel Knight ... in what was one of the most elaborate events of the time ... Mrs. Knight was fond of recalling that more than 100 persons, nearly everyone in the area, attended. ... The young bride and groom moved into the ancestral home in 1872, and there began to rearing of their family of 11 children ..."

One of these eleven was my grandfather, Thomas Jefferson Knight. The article fails to mention that William Samuel's grandfather was Martha Ann's great-grandfather. He married his niece.

The American progenitor of this line of Knights apparently was a Quaker who came to the New World in 1682 with William Penn. God, Freedom, Intelligence and Courage were highly valued in this pioneer, mini-empire-building milieu. They went from Pennsylvania and Quakerism to travel to Virginia, where they paused to fight in the Revolution; and then southward, generation by generation, acquiring land and producing large families, usually at the expense of the women of the line, who died in childbirth with alarming regularity.

My father, Jack Knight, was undoubtedly one of the most talented of his line. He was a voracious reader, a gifted artist, and could discourse with brilliance on many subjects. His best friends were doctors, judges, and politicians, many aided in their careers by my grandfather. But Jack became an addicted, self-indulgent playboy who ran through his inheritance until he was left to live on the charity of the family. They continued to pay for his excesses, hoping that no one would notice him. With every advantage of brains, family, resources, and connections—the terrain of the family planet—he ended his life drunk and practically homeless.

Tom Knight with his mother, Martha Collins Knight, shortly before her death in 1950.

What went wrong? What noxious vapors did he breathe that stunted his potential?

I had many conversations and written correspondence with him in the last few years before his death. I found him to be entirely contemptuous of those who live their lives on the surface. To him they were hypocrites and liars and bombasts. Was his retreat into addiction as much a reaction to some realization about the world that was too painful to bear, as a need for relief from physical pain?

Today, I can only conjecture. At a crucial time when events could have played out one way or another, my mother had a strong presence in his life. There are some people who are so toxic that when you are in their presence you really need to put on a hazmat suit for handling noxious materials. Mother was such a one. But, as always, even in her case, there is a reason for such twisted growth.

My mother's family planet was quite similar in terrain, but with an altogether different "atmospheric mixture." This "air" we breathed was the product of several converging lines. Each contributed something to the mixture that became, in a sense, psychic poison. Those who breathed it either died psychically or mutated to adapt. And, as geneticists know, while mutations may be beneficial, they are more often detrimental.

The first records of the Meadows line appear in headright grants by the governor of the Jamestown Colony, dated 1636. The name was "Meades" originally, but years of spelling as pronounced in various accents produced two lines: the Meadows and the Meadors.

In 1694, John Meadows married his stepsister, a daughter of Henry Aubrey, creating a rift in the family, which suggests that the Meadows' perspective was not so accepting of consanguinity as the Knights. Most children of this union left Virginia, moving gradually westward to Iowa, some making the trek to Florida in search of more land and opportunity. Earlier generations converted to Quakerism; some were penalized for refusing to fight in the Revolution. In Iowa, one branch split from the Quakers, going west and becoming converts to the Church of Jesus Christ of Latter-day Saints, the Mormons. The other branch became Methodist and traveled to Florida. My great-grandfather followed the family tradition of becoming a minister of the Gospel by attending a Methodist seminary.

There must have been at least a brief sojourn in Georgia, because Great-Grandpa married Leila, a daughter of the Georgian Hugh Murdoch of Clan McRae, a legendary family of fierce fighters who never had a clan chief because no single branch would submit to any other in terms of ascendancy.

Curiously, Leila was descended on her mother's side from the same Knights of my paternal ancestry. And maybe that's a clue, because something was unusual about Leila—a tendency to depression. The record from the *Florida Conference Archives of the Methodist Church* tells the story rather coldly:

"Schuyler Grant Meadows admitted into FL Conference on trial (probationary membership) in Jan 1891; was ordained a deacon and admitted in full connection in Jan 1893; ordained an elder Jan 1895. In 1899 transferred to South Georgia Conference and was appointed to Bibb [County]. That same year he was tried for immorality and expelled from the conference."

What in the world happened?

It took many years of hearing faint rumors and patiently piecing together the evidence to discover that Great-Grandpa sinned in a way that was unacceptable to his society and time, and the noxious vapors that were produced had a profound effect on the family atmosphere.

Assigned to a new church in Georgia, SG, as some of the family refers to him, left his wife and four children in Florida while he went to establish a new position and a new life for his family in Georgia. What he didn't count on was coming face to face with a different destiny.

Great-Grandpa, a solid, righteous, and dedicated minister, essentially ran off with the choir director, Mary Alice Wimbish, of his new church. Did they have an affair as rumored, or did SG attempt to maintain two families at once, or did he ask his first wife for a divorce? We don't know. But Leila either put a gun to her own head or hanged herself (I have heard two versions of the story). She left four little girls motherless, and the event and its results cast a long shadow of secrets over three generations.

Mary Alice Wimbish, scanned painted photo miniature.

As it happened, the four little girls would soon be fatherless as well. The legendary McRae Clan descended upon SG with all the fury of the Highlands from which they had departed only two generations before. They took the children, but left SG alive, with a warning that if he ever tried to contact his girls again, they would take his life as well.

Four lost little girls, tainted by adultery, lies, and violence.

What could SG and Mary Alice have felt about this ending to their adultery? How does a person deal with such guilt? How do they face a world that has collectively consigned them to a realm beyond the pale of acceptable society? Did SG blame Mary Alice for the destruction of his life and career? Did she blame him for the hardships suffered in the loss of social cachet? Were the fires of passion extinguished in the icy water of cold, hard reality?

We don't know the answers to those questions because the social cover-up dynamic went into operation. But it seems that, even though they moved to a new "neighborhood," the rumors followed. In this atmosphere, my grandfather was born: first child of the defrocked preacher and the disgraced choir director; a child born of condemnation and adultery, ever after to bear the burden of this shame. (Curiously, Mary Alice was a distant cousin to Leila, also connected through the Knight lines.)

In later years, Great-Grandpa was partially reinstated into the Methodist Church. He was given a church, but never an official "appointment." One family member noted about him:

My grandfather, Wilbur Wimbish Meadows at about 8 months old.

Rev. S. G. Meadows, with two of his brothers, in his orange grove.

"He was a wonderful man, respected in the community, and preached fiery sermons accompanied by pounding on the pulpit to make his points. When he prayed, it was lengthy and sometimes another sermon. He was tall and lean with gray hair and a handsome gray mustache. He taught the adult Sunday school class at Riverview church when I was growing up there. I remember during the service at prayer time he always rested his head on his arms on the pew in front of him.

"... Behind [his] house was a magnificent garden which, with his nurturing care, produced enough fresh vegetables to supply many friends and relatives.

"Half a mile down the road was his orange and grapefruit grove. He tended it by pruning, hoeing around each tree and fertilizing at the proper time. He was a very hard worker in his fields, toiling from dawn to dusk. He was an equally hard worker in God's fields, nurturing and harvesting people for Jesus Christ. ... At Sunday dinner after church, he insisted on taking the chicken wing and neck, saving the choice pieces for others. Humbling himself was his way of life."

I try to imagine the environment of guilt, secrecy, shame, and self-abnegation in which my grandfather and his two brothers were brought up. It is pretty clear from later evidence and observation that my great-grandparents spent the rest of their lives trying to live up to an impossible standard of moral rectitude as atonement for their sins.

* * *

In 1944, Great-Grandma died of uterine cancer, twenty-two years after giving birth to a Down's syndrome child who lived only four years. My grandmother, who attended her in the final days, told me that Great-Grandma had often been mean and vindictive toward Great-Grandpa, and that she had "paid for it" with unimaginable suffering at the end. (God only knows what atmosphere she breathed as she grew up.)

The point is: my maternal grandfather was probably conceived in an act of adultery by two people who were deeply inculcated in the faith of their church and the society of their time. It's possible that a pregnancy, incontrovertible proof of infidelity, triggered the suicide of Leila. If so, it is not hard to imagine the atmospheric pressure placed upon my grandfather as he grew up. The first three years of a child's life are crucial in establishing a sense of relationship to the world and all within it. Those three years in the life of this child, after such a series of events: what must they have been like?

Yet his two younger brothers, born three and thirteen years after the scandalous events, experienced an entirely different atmospheric pressure. There was a sense that my grandfather, for some inexplicable reason, was not quite part of the family. He unconsciously took the role of scapegoat, the sin-bearer on their behalf.

Grandma also grew up breathing poisonous vapors. Her grandmother was a Pearce, descended from Henry "Hotspur" Percy of Shakespearean fame. This great-great grandmother of mine was actually the product of two very long royal lines that had intertwined consanguineously so many times that it's a wonder that any of them were sane. Lots of them weren't. The epithet "Hotspur" could have applied to many. The Pearce family left Rhode Island due to a scandal involving a rich and merry widow, made their way to North Carolina, then settled in Georgia.

The role of genetics in the development of the personality complex is comparable in importance to early environment. Historic accounts of my forebears have illuminated the internal make-up of my immediate family as well as my own. There is little difference between "royal" families and all others, except for a certain force of being that manifests from time to time. And when it does, you can find a great Saint or the most heinous of Sinners. In researching these family histories I soon realized Sinners far outnumber Saints. To claim distinction by virtue of descent is problematical at best. For the most part, they are people I would be embarrassed to know, and most definitely would not invite into my home.

In Georgia, a union between the Pearces and another interesting line, Mazel, produced my great-great grandmother. The family moved to Florida to escape the censure of yet another scandal in which a young man was beaten to death by the "Mizelle and Pearce boys." God only knows how many family skeletons I have yet to uncover!

My grandmother was virtually orphaned at the age of five when her father died of tuber-

My grandmother's great-grandmother, "Grandma Pearce", born Mary Mizell in Georgia, 1811, married to John Pearce, 1 Dec 1831. Since my grandmother remembered her, she must have lived to almost 100 years old.

culosis. Her mother, Laura Eugenia (after whom I am named), under the influence of "modern thinking" inspired by Florence Nightingale, sought her independence as a trained nurse after her husband's death. My grandmother was left in the care of "Aunt Lizzie," Laura Eugenia's sister.

Aunt Lizzie was the archetypal wicked stepmother. She put my grandmother to work to "earn her keep" as a servant in her house. I rather doubt that she let her sister know this was the state of affairs. Grandmother was so grief-stricken at the death of her beloved father and the break-up of her family, she never wanted to burden her mother with tales of woe on the rare occasions they were together.

My grandmother was a beauty who matured early, and Aunt Lizzie perceived a threat in such an attractive and "biddable" young woman in her own household. So she hatched a plot to get rid of her. Yes, I know this sounds like a Victorian melodrama, but it really happened. On one of Aunt Lizzie's frequent New York shopping excursions, to maintain her fashionable image as the wife of a prominent architect and 33rd-degree Mason, she kindly invited my grandmother along.

Aunt Lizzie had been working on my grandmother in a manipulative way to convince her the right thing to do for her family would be to go into a workhouse in the city. Aunt Lizzie knew a man who owned a china factory, and this was where my grandmother was "put out to work."

She was to be trained to paint designs on expensive dishes. I actually have a piece that she painted for practice during this episode of her life. She was only twelve years old. The story is a bit unclear because it was too painful for my grandmother to talk about casually. Yes, Aunt Lizzie left this child in New York City alone to make her own way. I never thought to ask what cover story Aunt Lizzie told when she returned sans Grandma, but knowing Aunt Lizzie, it was a doozie!

But it's sometimes ironic how such plots get exposed.

Apparently my grandmother attracted the attention of a German gentleman named Mr. Ernst, who was touring the china factory art

My grandmother, shortly before her father died.

department with the owner. I don't think he realized how young my grandmother was, and I don't think that she realized how young she was either, at least not in legal terms.

Nevertheless, Mr. Ernst took Grandma under his protection and, as far as I can determine, may even have arranged a marriage with her, however illegally, and brought her back to Florida to visit her family. And there all hell broke loose.

Aunt Lizzie's perfidy was exposed and she was disgraced; her husband, Uncle Fred, the high-level Mason-with-connections, took charge of the situation. It turned out Mr. Ernst was connected to the German Kaiser by blood, and there was a strong anti-German sentiment in America at the time. Using his influence, Uncle Fred made sure that Mr. Ernst was taken into custody as a possible spy. The marriage was annulled and Grandma was returned to the bosom of her family, a lovely but now-tarnished rose.

A few years later: enter my grandfather.

Grandpa was another who was physically mature at an early age. Inspired by the call to arms at the beginning of World War I, he lied about his age and joined the army. He was assigned to E Company of the 314th Engineers. He was a veteran of the St. Mihiel Offensive, an intense three-

Aunt Lizzie at far right, my grandmother, Lucille Young, next to her, then Minnie Colson Strassner and Bessie Buchanan Colson at left.

month period of combat that included the Battle of Verdun, forcing the German line across the Meuse River and the takeover of the railway that ran from Metz to Mezieres.

This historic offensive dealt a paralyzing blow to German forces and essentially ended the war. On the morning of the eleventh day of the eleventh month, at the eleventh hour, the time set for the cessation of hostilities arrived.

I have read lengthy accounts of the amazing work of Grandfather's army engineering unit and I can barely comprehend how he survived with his sanity intact. Perhaps he did because he had someone to come home to: my grandmother. His cards and letters to her from Europe during the war reveal deep love and hopes for their future together.

But is love enough?

The experience of war had a profound effect on Grandpa, as it does on any man who has marched away, smiling with patriotic fervor, to kill their fellow human beings. Men may look the same when they return, assuming they haven't lost any limbs or other body parts, but they are never the same again. How could Grandma, with her own narrow view of the world, as well as her own scars of the soul, have the capacity to heal him? And how could they heal each other when both were so wounded?

Wilbur W. Meadows smiling in the army. After the war, he almost never smiled.

My grandparents during their WWI courtship.

Grandpa suffered all his life from the physical and psychological effects of this journey to hell and back. But his war experience gave him compassion, even though it was difficult for him to express his kindness in words. After he died, I found dozens of letters among his papers, many from unknown people writing to thank him for his sponsorship of their endeavors, his gifts of cash or material goods that helped them over a difficult time, as well as requests for him to stand as godfather for half a dozen or more babies. I have the idea that he tried to help others as a vicarious way of trying to save himself.

After the war, Grandpa applied for veterans' assistance and obtained a loan to open a mechanic's shop.

He studied engineering at night school, earned a degree and certification, and ultimately gained recognition in his field, employed by some of the largest corporations in the United States.

In the Depression, while my father was cooking up his Tom Sawyer escapade in the local swamp, Grandpa was the backbone of his own family as well as the family of his in-laws. He was unstinting in generosity to others who would not have had food on their tables except for his willingness to forego luxuries for his own family, to ensure there would be enough for all. But he never talked about his gifts. I found the cancelled checks and bank drafts of those days to testify to his generosity.

I try to imagine how two people with such deep scars interacted in the early days of their marriage. Obviously, Grandma needed a father and emotional attention that Grandpa was unable to give. He was so psychologically stunned that he could function only within the framework of hard work habits instilled in him as a child. His parents had turned to work to assuage their guilt; so Grandpa worked to ameliorate his pain.

This was the atmosphere into which my mother was born. Her

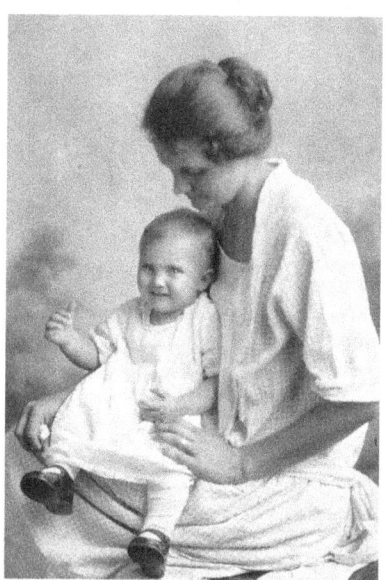

My grandmother and my mother as an infant.

mother was emotionally needy, her father was emotionally switched off, and she became, in effect, psychological food for both of them.

As I mentioned in reference to my maternal grandfather, the first three years of a child's life are crucial, and the first "earthquake" on this specific family planet occurred when my mother was only two years old.

My grandmother was in labor with her second child and everything was wrong. The baby was too big to be delivered naturally. Its head emerged, but the shoulders were too large and it was too late to do a Caesarian section. It's not an uncommon story for women throughout history; in similar situations, millions have died. In later years, only one could be saved: the child or the mother. To give life to the infant, the mother must be butchered; to save the mother, the baby must be decapitated, the body removed in pieces with a meat hook. That is really no choice at all.

Yet the doctor presented it to my grandfather. And he chose.

The dead baby had weighed fifteen pounds.

Even though she was given anesthesia, Grandma knew enough of nursing to know what had been done. She nearly lost her mind. And she never regained her health. One day, fifty years later, she told me what had really happened. The doctor had listed this as a "live birth," and the family was told that the baby lived one day and died. "What else are you going to say?" my grandmother told me with resignation. Today's ideas on malpractice would have given her at least some compensation. But back then, you just didn't do things that way.

The poison released into the family atmosphere by this event made my mother an emotional orphan. Well, maybe not completely: she had her grandmother Laura Eugenia, the nurse, who became more of a mother figure than her own natural parent was able to do. In fact, she called her grandmother "Mama" and never addressed my grandmother with this affectionate term.

But, the tectonic plates of this family planet kept shoving against one another until the next small shift resulted in a nonlinear "pop" that produced a major cataclysm.

When Mother was four years old, her grandmother Laura Eugenia remarried after twenty years of widowhood. The groom, Mr. Reed, solemnly vowed to love, honor, and cherish Great-Grandma Laura till death. In the midst of family secrets and lies, this at least was true. Two years was all it would last.

Enter Aunt Lizzie, arriving for regular visits with the couple for the duration of their brief marriage. No one knows what sick and destructive gossip Aunt Lizzie the manipulator may have whispered to Mr. Reed.

"On June 13, 1927, Mr. George M. Reed shot his wife, Laura Eugenia, while she was peeling peaches in the kitchen, and then turned the gun on himself."

My mother was not quite six years old.

My mother's beloved "Mama"—Laura Eugenia Colson Young—who was cruelly murdered in 1927. I am named after her.

No one could tell her what happened, to explain the loss of her mother, the most important person in her life. The entire family was inculcated into habits of keeping secrets. How does a child who needs love and affection and a feeling of security and stability respond to the lack of all of these? Parents cannot give this love and feeling of security when they are emotionally shut down, because all their own experiences of love end in tragedy and disaster.

I would imagine this child could believe that she was, of all things, not worthy of love. And then, she might feel that giving love was a very dangerous thing, and decide that she must never love anyone again. Further, she might believe that she had been very, very bad, that she was in some way responsible for the loss of love and attention in her world. The only way to atone for her guilt would be to seek out situations where she could be "punished" by others.

When the family atmosphere is so thin because it exists on a high mountain of scars and wounds and lies and secrets, there is little possibility of healthy emotional development. A human being is like a tree in this sense, and on very high mountains, trees cannot grow. All is stunted and deformed.

And so it was. Another lost little girl.

What happens to such a child? She has material goods, freedoms and privileges too bold for her age, too much responsibility too soon. Her parents compensate this way because they cannot show love.

* * *

We see Jack and Alice at the lunch counter, laughing and talking. They've found each other. Soon they will plan their marriage made in heaven.

My mother Alice knew Jack's bad reputation for being a wild one. Now he's learned his lesson through tremendous pain and suffering. He has changed his life; he's in line to take over the family drug business. All of that "bad boy glamour" packaged into an up-and-coming figure of the local social scene. What a catch! Thrills and chills and excitement ahead.

My mother, Alice Meadows, standing beside her paternal grandmother who is holding her baby sister, also named Laura. This was taken not long after the death of her beloved "Mama".

They had great fun for a few years. When my brother Tommy was born, as Jack told me in later years, "I was a changed man when I became a father." The old photographs actually show him with a stunned look on his face. But Mother, in our baby pictures, just looks lost.

Mother told us that Jack refused to quit drinking and be a parent. And for years that was all I knew. But his version, revealed to me later, was quite different. He claims that he tried to get himself off the morphine and to quit drinking, but every time he did, Mother would throw a curveball, and all his good intentions would go out the window. How do two people relate when one is wounded by loss and abandonment and the other by indulgence?

Maybe the addict always has a reason that he "didn't have a chance." There is a very complex and subtle two-step dance in the psychology of addiction, with two partners fully involved. But the family dynamics of

My brother as an infant with my lost mother and stunned father.

addiction are merely a background noise in this family.

What did Mother want?

Studying her patterns of behavior and manipulation in later years, it is rather clear that she unconsciously set Jack up for a fall so that he would abandon her; that was what she knew. He never knew what hit him. He never married again, and you could even say that he probably drank himself to death from a broken heart. I can guess that Mother pushed all of Jack's emotional buttons, manipulating him into situations where overcoming his addiction was doomed to failure, all the while making sure that everyone could see what a martyr she was for putting up with this kind of situation. What is saddest of all is how she manipulated the two families.

I am still asking why, and the only answer I have ever managed to find is that, on the surface, she just had two main requirements: avoidance of boredom and abandonment. I think that the former was closest to her consciousness and manifested in selfish manipulations to get her way in all things, even if pretending that she was making a great sacrifice. The abandonment part was more unconscious, and was the inevitable result of all her actions. No matter what she said or thought consciously, when anything positive manifested in her life, she made decisions that destroyed it and drove people who loved her away. Perhaps it was fear that if she got too close, someone would die as her Mama did.

Unfortunately, those who loved her, or were connected to her in any way, suffered as well. Perhaps they were the only ones who really suffered, because Mother never seemed to suffer at all. She made the same mistakes over and over again. For a long time, I wondered if she was mentally deficient, like an idiot savant who seemed intelligent but had some serious deficiency in mental processes. But I finally realized that unconscious need to be abandoned was the inner driver of her make-up.

She set Jack up to be the drunken, drug-addicted fall guy, took her baby, and left.

This is where we came in.

The whole family wanted to cover it up and definitely did not want the scandal of divorce, the small town social and political implications, the prominent memberships in churches, lodges, and clubs at risk on both sides. An enormous amount of pressure was put on Mother to return to her husband, and try to "make a go" of it. Strings were pulled, visits and negotiations were made, and, in the end, she agreed to give it another try. This didn't last long, but nevertheless, I was the result. And Mother won the martyr role for her efforts.

Mother was a master of working with the tools at hand. She'd named my brother Tom after both of his grandfathers (and father), and then made much of the fact that I was "almost" born on my maternal grandfather's birthday. So she had the perfect means of getting whatever she wanted: grandchildren. With great care she inserted us into our grandparents' lives like anchors, and I can't say I regret that. Without them, there is no way to imagine what life with Mother would have been like.

Later on I imagined what life would have been like if the ties to our father and paternal grandparents had not been so effectively cut by Mother. Because, of course, we had two sets of grandparents. It is clear that grandchildren for the Knights meant contact with my father and so Jack and his parents must be cut out of the picture at all costs.

The first photo of yours truly in the arms of my paternal grandmother at The Farm. My grandfather is holding my brother, Tommy. They sure look proud and happy.

I know that my grandparents went to their graves believing my mother had told them the truth about the Knights. They acted based on what they believed: whatever Alice told them. They had to believe what she told them because they had a vested interest in believing. Alice made sure of that.

What my grandparents were told, and what my brother and I believed for most of our lives was this: since we were the only grandchildren of the paternal grandparents, they were determined to try to control our upbringing, if not obtain outright custody. Mother had convinced Grandpa that the Knights would even steal us if they could. At the same time, she created an environment of extreme concern on the part of our maternal grandparents regarding our safety in the care and presence of our addicted father. Jack, drinking in despair at the break-up of his marriage, didn't realize he was playing exactly the part that Mother had scripted for him. We must be protected from the evil Knights at all costs!

Naturally she didn't create such a complex situation all at once. It required a couple of years of careful, slow manipulation. I have only a few memories of the times we were able to spend with our father and his parents.

The first memory is of my father coming to take me somewhere. I was sitting in my high chair. Jack sat down and began to feed me, and I can still remember the love in his face as he sailed the spoon through the air toward my mouth.

My paternal grandparents had a huge Great Dane named Dutch. I was both frightened and fascinated by this big dog. My father would take my hand and let me walk up to Dutch, pet him, and sit on his back. I never felt afraid as long as my father was with me.

So, there we were: two little kids at the center of what could turn into an ugly legal battle. After consulting an attorney they decided

My brother and I with our father and grandmother. I'm obviously pretty happy.

that, in this case, possession was the proverbial nine-tenths of the law, and my maternal grandfather wanted us to be removed to a place where we were safe from any alleged legal maneuvers of my father's wicked family.

Grandpa was a consultant for Georgia Iron Works in Augusta, Georgia, so we three moved in with my grandparents there. My grandfather's connections helped my mother get a post as secretary to the Chairman of Georgia Pacific.

While Mother worked at Georgia Pacific, she met a man who was often present in her boss's office doing "business." This man owned thousands of acres of orange groves in Florida and other business interests.

Then Mother's boss died suddenly. What the details are, I don't know, but Mother was singularly obstinate in her refusal to talk about this. One of the outcomes of the death of her employer was that Mother left Georgia Pacific to go to work for this other man. We were moved into a house in Kissimmee, near Orlando.

Being back in Florida meant, of course, that our father could visit us. And he did, regularly.

There is an old photograph from this time of me in a little Western outfit consisting of a "cowgirl" skirt, hat, and vest. In the photo, I am wearing my Mary Jane shoes, but I originally had a pair of very snappy boots to go with the outfit.

My father had taken me out to buy this outfit, and a complete Western suit for my brother as well. I remember I was so happy! I loved those boots. They were shiny and smelled good and felt just right on my feet. They also made an important sound when I walked. After buying them, I was allowed to put them on right away and I walked down the street with my father in my new boots and

In my cowgirl suit, leaning against my grandfather's car, behind our house in Kissimmee.

cowboy hat and I just knew I was special. Holding my father's hand, I was somebody. And that is how my father made me feel.

Sometime later, I lost one of the boots at the house where we lived with Mother. When my father came to pick us up, I wanted to wear them. He helped me look, but the other boot was nowhere to be found. I began to cry because I was absolutely sure that I had put them away in the closet. He picked me up and told me not to cry, that we would go right out and get another pair, but my mother became very angry when he said this. I had to be "taught a lesson." She later made me throw the other boot in the trash.

I cried bitterly for those boots.

Soon after, the first really strange event occurred. By this time, I was three years old. It was 1955. The story, according to the adults of the family: I was put down for a nap, and my mother was doing her chores around the house. She went in a bit later to get me up, but I was not in my bed where she had left me. She thought I'd gotten up and was playing or hiding, so she searched the house. Nothing. Next, she went outside and searched, calling me repeatedly. Nothing. Next, she went to the neighbors, who came and re-searched the house with her. Then they all went outside to search again, widening the area of examination. Nothing.

I was nowhere to be found.

They decided the sheriff's department must be involved as well as all the neighbors. After all, a three-year-old child was missing. A massive search for the next hour yielded no result. At the time, there was a large ditch dug in one side of the street where storm sewer pipes were being laid, and after a rain the pits were about half full of water. The idea came to all these folks that, obviously, I had fallen into this big hole of water and had drowned. They were so sure they were going to find me there, and didn't want my mother present when they brought up the body, that one of the neighbors took her into the house to wait with her there. Mother went to my room where she was going to sit wringing her hands waiting. I'm sure she worked this situation for all it was worth.

And there I was, asleep on the bed exactly as she had left me some hours before.

What do I remember?

I remember only being drawn outside to a field of tall grass behind the house. At the back of this field was a grove of trees. I was lying in this grass, watching butterflies and dragonflies. I was acutely conscious of myself and my surroundings. And then, someone came to me, from the grove of trees, beckoning me to follow them, and that's all I remember.

* * *

My mother was introduced into a certain social circle by her new employer, and this "set" was in the habit of frequenting certain nightclubs to hear music and dance. We might even think that the promise of an exciting social life was the reason Mother left Augusta and the stern eye of my grandfather. Who knows what she was promised, or thought she could achieve, by leaving a stable situation to dive into the unknown with the two of us in tow?

Orlando has a significant Navy presence in the form of a base and training installation, and these same clubs Mother's crowd frequented may also have been the haunts of Navy personnel out for a night on the town. A certain Cecil Bryan became part of the social circle, though Mother can't remember precisely when or how he arrived, who invited him, or how he was introduced. Nevertheless, he was there, and for a time she paid little attention to him since she and another man were the star performers on the dance floor.

Dancing was Mother's claim to fame. It's true that when she got on the dance floor with a good partner, everyone else would soon stop and just gape in awe. Ginger Rogers or Cyd Charisse had nothing on my mother's skill and style.

When I was trying to talk to her about this strange and darkening time, she kept going off on tangents to talk about this or that club, this or that dance, this or another particular night when the lights were brighter and the applause from the crowd of watchers loudest.

Apparently, she had found the dance partner of her dreams. So how to explain that Cecil Bryan, who she admitted couldn't do the two-step, got her away from this guy?

Eventually, however, he made his presence known and persuaded her to go out with him. Now she says she can't even remember anything remarkable about him at all, and she was really quite attached to the other man, her dance partner. She claims this whole period is pretty much a blank. Yes, she does remember agreeing to marry Cecil.

And here is where there is a mystery. Only Mother had the key and she's gone now.

On her deathbed, my grandmother said she never believed my mother would turn against her as she had done. This betrayal is years in the future, and we will come to it soon enough. My grandmother could not understand it, especially after all my grandfather had done for her "in Orlando, taking care of that awful mess."

I asked her: "Grandma, what do you mean? Did Mother do something in Orlando?"

And Grandma only would say: "I vowed I would never tell a soul, and I won't. Some things happen and should never be talked about. That was one of them. Your mother has done some terrible things in her life, and that was the worst. But you don't need to know it."

And she sighed deeply and looked so sad that I thought: *Maybe she really wants to tell me; I only need to do a little persuading.*

But apparently not. She said: "I should never have mentioned it."

She only did so in a moment of weakness and sadness at how everything had turned out in the end.

Well, of course that is exactly the kind of thing that would drive a person crazy with curiosity. I tried every way I could think of to get my grandmother to tell me what had happened in Orlando. It must have been really bad, because Grandma shared things with me that I am sure she never told anyone else.

But she took it to her grave, literally.

CHAPTER THREE

ANOTHER WINDOW OPENS ON STRANGE CONNECTIONS

Now I wonder if this mysterious event in Orlando that my grandmother would not even talk about on her deathbed drove Mother to take up with a new protector. As soon as Cecil entered our lives, we moved, first to a different house in Orlando, and very soon after to Jacksonville.

I didn't see my father again until I was twenty-five, just a few years before he died. For a long time I pretended he was coming to get me every day. I had to face the reality that he wasn't going to come. But it was years before the hope died completely.

Cecil very quickly became attached to me. He was very attentive and, as hard as I have tried to remember if there was anything suspicious about this, I can remember nothing inappropriate about his conduct toward me. He was fatherly and proud of everything I did. At first, I was put off, because I was still waiting for my father. But after a while I accepted his attention and soon came to be fond of him. This wasn't strange, since I rarely received any special attention from my mother. Curiously, Cecil disliked my brother, and was unable to conceal it. When I discussed it with her, my mother remarked that this had been a "painful" realization.

Cecil apparently had a job offer in Jacksonville, and we moved into a house close to the beach. It was 1956. There are three Navy bases near this city. The Navy, and the bases, were to play a part in my story. It was in Jacksonville at the house near the beach when the Face at the Window came.

I was four years old.

Life was certainly strange on the planet of Lost Boys and Girls. And it was going to get even stranger.

In later years my mother and grandmother told me about these events. Yes, I have my own memories, but I was not included in adult policy conversations. Also, I was protected from the knowledge of certain events around me. Working on this book, when I asked my mother about this period, she deliberately evaded important issues and refused to help me uncover the true sequence of events. And, unfortunately, there are no photographs from that time; if there ever were, Mother must have destroyed them.

"There are many things that ought to be forgotten," she liked to say.

Maybe that's true in some cases, but in this instance, every clue could lead to understanding of a very great mystery.

With help from my husband Ark and my brother Tom, who also questioned her at various times, I've been able to put together the idea that early in the marriage, Cecil started to exhibit bizarre behavior. Yet the details Mother was willing to give us were peculiar. The strange, ritualistic way Cecil handled his food when he ate; the unusual way he used his knife and fork; how he would be meticulous and finicky one day, and a completely different person with hideous personal habits and language the next. She seemed to be describing someone with multiple personality disorder or some form of schizophrenia.

Mother said she came home one day and found Cecil huddled in the closet in a fetal position, crying, talking crazy about "Them."

"Just all kinds of paranoid ravings. I don't remember," my mother told us. "He was convinced that something or someone out there was trying to control him or get to him in some way."

In the next strange episode, she smelled smoke, went to investigate and caught him building a fire under the fuel tank outside the house. This was followed by a horrific suicide attempt.

Cecil was standing at the bathroom sink slashing his wrists over and over with a razor blade. Blood was everywhere. Cecil fought violently against her attempts to get the razor away from him. She wrapped towels around his arms and called an ambulance. She emphasized that her main concern at the time was to prevent me and my brother from being exposed to this sort of thing.

Cecil was admitted to the hospital. In the course of a police investigation into the incident, Mother had learned there was an ugly secret that he and his family had been hiding from her. Cecil had been discharged from the Navy for psychiatric reasons. Mother recalled being told that

ANOTHER WINDOW OPENS ON STRANGE CONNECTIONS

he had spent much of his time in the years before she met him in a veterans' hospital in Augusta. (Yes, curious that mention of Augusta!)

This turned into a rather tricky situation. Although he had been released, he had never been declared cured. The validity of Mother's marriage to Cecil was in question. He was considered to be legally incompetent to enter into a contract. Not only that, he had a first wife from whom he had never been legally divorced for the same reason.

After a short while in the hospital at Augusta, where he had been sent after the suicide attempt, Cecil begged my mother to come for him. Even though there was a big question about the legality of their marriage, apparently no one but my mother could sign him out. He was also calling his family, so they soon began pleading with Mother, promising they would take responsibility. She was reluctant until one of the doctors told her that Cecil was "ready to be released" if she would come and take care of the paperwork.

Now this is singularly strange. Supposedly she is not even legally married to him, yet she is the only one who can sign him out of the hospital? And the doctors asked her to do it also?

Mother drove to Augusta, where the doctors assured her that anything he had ever told her about his experience in the Navy was simply untrue and that she was not to believe a word; it was all fantasy. She vaguely recalls that Cecil had talked about being in places and doing things that she could only describe as "out of a spy movie" or "it was just crazy stuff." She claims that the last time she saw him was after checking him out of the hospital.

I was almost five years old then.

Mother had suffered for years from debilitating headaches that left her completely unable to function for up to a week at a time. During one of these episodes, a neighbor had come over to help her get my brother and me settled for the night. But I remember hearing quiet conversation in the next room even though my mother swears that she was in her bed.

My bedroom opened off a small hallway that opened into the dining room so that a shaft of light came in through the door left slightly ajar. I was lying in the bed listening to the grown-up voices murmuring in the background and drifting off to sleep when, for some reason, I looked at the window. Something had caught my eye. Something wasn't right.

Of course, after the previous window event, I didn't trust windows at all. But it also seems there was some particular tension in the air that I cannot describe or define. I do recall lying in bed, starting to fall asleep, and suddenly watching that window as though I expected something to show up there.

To my horror, I noticed the window slowly opening.

I called my mother. She came in, told me there was nothing there, shut and locked the window, and went out of the room. I was still upset and kept watching that damned window. Sure enough, it started easing open once more. Again I called Mother.

She shut and locked the window again. I kept watch. And, for the third time, it started opening, so slowly that I was not sure that I was seeing it. But when it opened an inch or so I called Mother again.

As it happened, she had been standing in the hall, peeking through the crack in the door to catch me "playing a trick." She had my feet in view, and saw clearly that I hadn't moved from the bed. So, when I called this time, she knew I wasn't the one opening the window, and it became a serious matter.

As she told us later, the neighbor lady called her son, who came over with a loaded gun and investigated the premises inside and out. I was also told that the neighbor's son was stationed in a chair with his gun in my darkened bedroom to wait for the next occurrence, but I certainly don't remember that part of it.

After a while, the window began to open again. The story becomes garbled at this point. Someone went out the back door and someone else went out the front door to trap the culprit. In the earlier version of the story, Mother said she and a friend went out the front, but later she claimed she did it alone. Nevertheless, as soon as they reached the corner of the house a "white figure" went flying past across the street and into the nearby woods. It happened so fast that, to this day, she can't say what her real impressions were. She was convinced that it was Cecil playing tricks and, believe it or not, didn't consider this a serious threat.

No one figured out how the locked window unlocked itself three times in a row. After she claimed she locked the window each time, I asked her how she could explain this problem of a magically unlocking window. A glazed look came into her eyes. She looked trapped. She then declared that she was sure there was no lock on the window at all, so she must have been mistaken. Yes, that was it. There was no lock. Cecil was just "playing a trick."

Isn't it amazing how desperate we are to "normalize" things?

ANOTHER WINDOW OPENS ON STRANGE CONNECTIONS

One day, rather soon after this, I was sitting on the porch playing with my toys. Mother was inside, perhaps making lunch. Cecil came up to the house. He told me he missed me and my mother and he was coming home for good very soon.

I was happy to see him because he had always been attentive and kind to me. He told me not to tell my mother that he had been to see me because she would be mad at him. He was trying to make her understand that he loved all of us and he wanted to bring her a nice surprise. It would be a "secret." Would I like to go for a ride one day soon? I had some idea I wasn't supposed to do this, so I said no. But then, for some reason, I told him I would only go for a ride if it could be in a new yellow and black convertible like I had seen in a picture in a magazine. Why I was so taken with the idea of this yellow and black car, I'm not sure.

The next day, I was out playing on the porch again when Cecil drove up in a brand new yellow and black convertible exactly like the one I'd seen in the magazine. He hopped out and said he had bought it just for me.

I wasn't exactly dressed to go for a ride since I was playing in a tee shirt and my underwear. Cecil reassured me that it would be just around the block. Nobody would see me and no need to tell Mother, because we would be back before I was missed.

I agreed, got in the car, and off we went. And it wasn't just around the block! We drove and drove and drove. I began to get very unhappy and said I wanted to go home. He told me: "Soon, soon! There are some people who really want to meet you. Just a few minutes and you can meet them, and then I'll take you home!"

We drove on. Out of the city, down along two-lane blacktop road through a forest. I realize now this was a plantation pine forest because all the trees grew in straight rows. Finally, we turned to the right onto a side road that was just a track cut through the trees. He drove probably a couple more miles until we came to a large, perfectly square clearing in the middle of this massive forest of tall, thick trees. Everything was cleared; not a single tree or shrub in sight. But right smack in the middle was a small white building and an outbuilding resembling a tool shed or large pump house to the rear.

Two or three men dressed exactly alike in light tan pants and shirts were standing on the steps along with a woman dressed all in white. They smiled at me, and my stepfather nudged me toward them. They murmured comments like "So here she is! We've wanted to meet you!

How adorable you look. Oh, we've waited so long for you to get here!" and so on. It was the usual overdone adult way of talking to a small child, and I recall being put off by it immediately.

I was ushered into the house. They indicated a chair at a dining room table where I was to sit. I sat and they sat. We were sitting all around this table looking at each other. I wondered what I was doing here. One of the men began to ask me questions in a condescending voice, though I really can't remember what these questions were. All I remember saying is that I wanted to go home, that my mother would be missing me.

They acted hurt and repeated how special I was and how long they had waited to meet me. I was becoming more and more uncomfortable. I repeated that I wanted to go home. I remember them looking at each other and my feeling that something had changed subtly. The woman in white more or less took over.

"We will certainly take you home right after your nap," she told me. "Your mother knows you're here with us. She wants you to have your nap."

That seemed reasonable. It was my usual nap time.

I was led into a bedroom toward a shiny metal crib with very high sides.

"This room has been prepared just for you," said the woman in white. "How happy we are that you've come to see us."

I really wanted to go home. I wanted to get this nap over and done with so I could leave.

I was too old for a crib, I thought to myself. These people must not know much about little girls as grown up as I was. And this made me suspect maybe my mother didn't know I was there with these people after all. But they were so happy to see me and had worked so hard to prepare a special room for me, and they promised I could go home after the nap. So I resolved to say nothing, to be a "good girl," and not to be rude.

After I was settled into the crib, the woman said: "Oh! You need a bottle! It will help you sleep better!" And she left the room. I remember thinking to myself: *These people don't even know that I am too big for bottles!* But, being a good girl, I wasn't going to be rude and say so. Let's get the nap over!

When she returned with the bottle, I took it rather awkwardly and stuck it in my mouth while she watched me anxiously. I figured she was just trying to be nice, so I dutifully began to suck on the bottle, feeling extremely embarrassed to be doing something so babyish. And that's the last thing I remember—a blank spot in my mind—until …

ANOTHER WINDOW OPENS ON STRANGE CONNECTIONS

I am in the car with Cecil and we are going very fast down a road with red flashing lights of a police car behind us. He is driving crazy, dodging cars, driving up into people's yards, zigging and zagging around trees and along sidewalks. And then, suddenly, up a steep sloping lawn and dead-on into a palm tree.

I flew forward. My face hit the dashboard and blood was running into my eyes. A group of policemen came up to the car. Several took my stepfather out on one side of the car and handcuffed him. I was taken out the other side of the car by another policeman, who took me to his car to drive me home.

Now, that is from my memory. The other side of the story was filled in by my mother in recent years after I'd shared my memories with my brother. We decided to ask her about it. Apparently, there was something about this incident that was unusual, even though I believed I had simply been taken by my stepfather to visit his family. Perhaps my mother had hoped I wouldn't remember this incident at all. When she realized that I had, she told me "the rest of the story," but the parts she still wouldn't talk about are troubling.

According to my mother, when she began to search for me, a neighbor told her that I had gotten in a car with Cecil. Mother called the police. Embarrassed to say that Cecil was a mental case, she told the police she was worried because Cecil might have been drinking. The police told her the law gave him the right as a stepfather to take me if he wanted. And as for the drinking, unless he broke the law they could do nothing.

She tried to wait it out, thinking that Cecil was only going to scare her a little bit. But as the hours passed with no sign of me, she called my grandmother in Tampa.

My grandmother, a veritable tiger when it came to protecting me, sent a telegram to my grandfather, who was on an out-island in the Bahamas on a consulting job. The telegram had to be flown out to him in a small company plane. Grandpa flew back to the main island, caught a flight to Miami, then another to Tampa, got in his car, and drove to Jacksonville. All this took several days.

I was still missing.

Once Grandpa arrived in Jacksonville, he apparently put on some pressure to activate the manhunt. Mother is vague on what he actually did, but when Grandpa wanted something accomplished, he had ways of getting it done.

So, with the neighbor's description of the car, the police were looking for Cecil. It seems that he was on his way to "return" me when he was spotted. But we can't really know that for sure.

Cecil was taken into custody and put in the drunk tank overnight. The next day, my grandfather took my mother down to the police station to sign the papers to press charges against him.

But Cecil was already gone.

Mother recounts that my grandfather was furious and demanded to know why they had let him go. Grandpa was taken aside privately and told that the police could do nothing. Grandpa gave Mother a brief, edited version of the conversation afterward. A representative from the Navy had come to get Cecil. They were able to do this because their authority "superceded civilian jurisdiction." The police had no choice but to release him to the Navy.

That was the end of that.

Cecil could have called his family, who then could have requested that someone from the veterans' hospital go to pick him up. But such action suggests a reaction time beyond the ordinary case of a veteran with mental problems on the loose in the civilian world. To send representatives from Augusta to pick him up overnight is fast work, for sure. Of course, with all the local Navy presence, it would have been just as easy to send someone from one of the bases. But why was this done so quickly, before any formal charges could be filed? Finally, if Cecil was just an ordinary nutcase, why didn't they just leave him there to be dealt with by civilian authorities?

No record of the event existed.

My grandfather immediately moved us to a small house in Tampa near his own. We were there for a just a little while. I had

Immediately after the kidnapping: My brother and I in the "Tepee Motel". My grandparents took us from Jacksonville back to Tampa and left my mother to pack up the house and move. This is one of only two photographs from that time.

my tonsils out, and started school. Mother could not divorce Cecil because he was incompetent, and at the same time could not be legally married to him for the same reason. She said she did not receive any cooperation from the Navy or the veterans' hospital in trying to sort through this process.

Then Cecil called Mother at work one day. He was out of the hospital and he was coming to get me. She left work, went straight to the school for Tommy and me, and left town immediately under the protection of a family friend. We went to a fishing resort some fifty miles away, where we stayed till my grandfather could come back from the Bahamas again.

First grade. The dog is named "Mike" and he was amazing. We are holding gifts Grandpa brought us from the Bahamas. I obviously didn't.

For me and my brother, being set free from school was a lot of fun. Living in a resort cabin on the water, fishing, going for boat rides, and eating in restaurants was a great adventure.

We had no idea there was a madman on the loose trying to get to me, and that the forces behind him, thwarted in one way, would begin taking another approach.

In retrospect, it is clear now that someone wanted to get their hands on me very badly, and someone else had an equal interest in preventing this.

Who would win?

CHAPTER FOUR

DEAD BABIES AND IRON SKILLETS

Grandpa decided to arrange for Tom and me to stay with Aunt and Uncle, my mother's brother and his wife, in Sarasota. In this way, Mother could keep working on legal problems and we would be "safe."

My aunt put us back in school, I contracted chicken pox, and we lived a normal life. It is to my aunt's credit that she was infinitely kind and fair to my brother and me, who were at the time virtually abandoned due to a difficult situation.

Aunt was only seventeen when she fell in love with my uncle. They met in Miami, where he worked after Navy service in the Pacific in World War II. She and my uncle decided to get a house and have everything arranged when she approached her mother about getting married. They talked to my grandfather and he agreed to give them the down payment on a house as a wedding gift. They bought the house and decided that they didn't want to wait until she was eighteen to marry. My aunt's mother said that if they wanted to get married without waiting, they would just have to go to Georgia to do it.

They did.

They visited the rest of the family on their way back from the wedding in Georgia. For my mother and her brother's wife, it was hate at first sight. My aunt remembers that when they were introduced, Mother ignored her completely and remarked to my uncle: "Well, son, you've really done it now!"

Mother had a habit of feigning little confidences, no matter if the topic was of any importance or not. "Let's go for a walk and talk," she'd suggest, or "Let's go in the other room. I have something to discuss." The one who was singled out for "confidences" naturally felt special, and the

My uncle and aunt, around the time of their marriage. The photo is damaged, but it is the only one I have of them from that time. This is how I remember them. My uncle passed away in February, 2010 at 85 years old.

one who was excluded naturally felt resentful. My mother would exclude my aunt even in her own house.

As soon as her divorce was final, Mother came to Sarasota and took over my aunt's house as though it were her own. My grandfather was under the impression, obviously conveyed by my mother, that we were not being well treated by my aunt and that it was urgent for Mother to do something right away to rectify the situation. In this way, the onus of the decision was placed on him. That was her way. She set him up to give her advice, leaving out or twisting the most critical details, and this made him feel responsible when inevitable disaster struck. He would reach into his pocket for more money or more gifts or more efforts on her behalf. And then she would end up with what she really wanted.

In a letter from this period, Grandpa wrote to her:

"... *Glad to hear that you are all clear of court, etc. Now about your question of what to do, I cannot answer firmly on acct. of various conditions, but one thing I am sure of—you should not let the existing condition continue with the kids—enough damage to them has been done.* [God only knows what kind of story she told him. Her letter to him has not survived.]

"*As you suggested, you might hurriedly go to Sarasota and see if you can find a place to stay and job so as not to move the kids from school—if so let them finish there—if not I would not hesitate a minute in bringing them to Tampa.*

"*They may or may not be able to re-enter school there—believe the damage to them would be greater, and do more harm than the good from 6 weeks of school. In fact I believe they may as well have missed this term for all the good they will receive—as against the upset that has occurred. [This last clearly is a reference to the whole Cecil episode, including the kidnapping.]*

"I know you had no alternative at the time—but now you have a chance to try and correct some of the difficulties. You are perfectly welcome to stay there with Mother—job or no job—as long as you wish—and all parties congenial.

"At any rate, I think you should let your brother out of the responsibility and make a final agreement of settlement for all their expenses—if you can't pay now let me know what is due."

Grandpa was clearly being put on the spot in this one. It seems that Mother's suggestion to move to Sarasota was obviously what she intended to do from the start. She didn't want to live in Tampa with my grandmother while my grandfather was away on business, because she couldn't go out with men as freely as she liked. It was also her way to precipitate a crisis, which put Grandpa on the spot so that he had to hurriedly send her a big chunk of cash rather than submitting her bills to him to handle directly.

It never occurred to anyone to ask us how we felt. Were perfectly happy. Our lives were stable and "normal" for the first time in our experience, we had cousins to play with, and honestly, we didn't miss Mother much at all.

But Mother moved in. My grandfather, to ease what he knew was a potentially explosive situation, invited my aunt to come to the Bahamas for a week or two. She flew over with my baby cousin, leaving my mother to look after my other two cousins, my brother, and me. Mother was supposed to find a job and a place for us to live.

One night I awoke as though I had been thrown off a cliff, with the images of a very clear, powerful, and terrifying dream washing over me.

I was sleeping with my head by a window. With my experiences of windows, it's surprising that I could sleep at all this way. I actually felt as if I had been thrown through the window back into the bed, and as I hit the bed, that water had been splashed on me. This sensation of water flowing over my skin, the coldness and wetness of it, came at the exact moment that the well pump outside the house switched on, as it did whenever anyone opened a faucet or flushed the toilet. But I could hear no movement in the house to indicate that anyone was up using any water.

My heart thudded wildly in my chest. I lay there trying to orient myself. I had a paralyzing sensation that there was, indeed, something outside, but I was unable to move.

My dream was clear, and I struggled to deal with concepts that were far beyond the capacity of my child's mind.

In the dream, I saw the sky full of smoke and flames as if cities were burning. People were screaming and running down the streets in terror of huge reptiles stomping all over the place, silhouetted against the glowing red smoke pouring up from the landscape around me.

Now, this was before Godzilla movies came out, but the imagery was pretty similar. In the dream, I knew I had to do something to save my family and get away. As I ran to sound the alarm, men who were more like creatures in uniform appeared in my path and grabbed my arms to stop me. They ordered me to come with them because there was something they wanted to show me.

In the dream I am taken into a grove of trees. Silently the men point to a patch of loose soil. I frantically dig the soil away with my hands. The first thing I uncover is a baby's foot. I begin crying, gently moving the soil away to uncover the baby. I nearly collapse in horror to see that the baby is dead. Hands and feet had been cut off and placed in the grave alongside the body in reversed position. I pick up the little hands and feet and reposition them as they ought to be, crying desperately. The men look at me coldly and I understand the message: "This is what will happen to you and those you love if you tell."

* * *

After her vacation at my grandparents' home in Nassau, my aunt flew back to Miami and spent a few days with her own family. She took a bus back to Sarasota with my baby cousin, asking the driver drop her off at the end of the road to her house. She walked with the baby the rest of the way in the afternoon heat, tired after a 300-mile bus ride.

When she got home, nothing had been picked up or put away. She found popcorn scattered all over the furniture and floor, dishes on the table caked with dried food, unwashed pots piled on the stove, unmade beds, and a pile of laundry in the bathroom several feet high.

My aunt knew she needed to be calm and find out why the house was in chaos. She also needed a cup of coffee. She walked into her kitchen and opened the cupboard for a cup. None were there. She opened cupboard after cupboard to discover that her entire kitchen had been "rearranged."

Mother had decided that my aunt didn't know the best way to set up her own kitchen and took it upon herself to change everything around. After all, if she was going to live there, things ought to be convenient for her, right?

We will pass with silence over the ensuing scene between my aunt and my mother. My aunt got pretty hot and said some choice words, but Mother, as usual, facing the results of one of her manipulations, remained cool and calm, the only one in the room "in control" of the situation.

The result of the confrontation: we were homeless. But not to worry! Since Mother had found a job and could not possibly be expected to abandon it and go to Tampa, Grandpa was expected to fund a new living situation in a hurry. A large chunk of cash was dispatched to Mother, and she happily set about finding a place, getting us moved in, and settling down, free of parental control. Not only that, she had managed to provoke my aunt to a display of temper that "justified" all the mean things Mother had been saying about her.

* * *

Sarasota was an artists' haven even back in the Fifties. A sculptor and woodcarver named Charles lived next door to our new rented house. He worked every day in a converted barn, leaving the big double doors open to let in the light. Naturally, this was a big attraction to a couple of bored little kids, and we gravitated to the spot to peek in and watch him cutting and carving wooden models, chiseling stone, creating molds, and casting objects of amazing grace and beauty. He had created, literally, a miniature Ringling Brothers' Circus. (His work is still on display at the Ringling Museum in Sarasota.)

Charles was clearly gratified with our big-eyed, open-mouthed awe. We noticed he never seemed to have anything to eat, so we urged Mother to fill an extra plate. We took dinner to Charles and had an excuse to inspect all the interesting things in his studio while he ate. Naturally this led to a growing bond, which culminated one day in a most daring plan.

We decided that it would be a perfect solution to everyone's situation if Charles and Mother were married. We persuaded Mother to invite Charles for dinner. We set the table with candles in place and wildflowers for a centerpiece. We could hardly contain ourselves in our excitement to execute the plan. All through dinner Mother and Charles kept asking us what we were up to, and we just collapsed in giggles. Finally, dinner was over and it was now or never. My brother took a deep breath.

"Mother," he blurted out, "you won't be alone any more and Charles will have a good dinner every night if you both get married!"

Well, there were a few moments of resounding silence, and then Charles and Mother both burst into laughter.

The only thing was, they did it. (Not immediately, but not too long after.)

They had a good time for a while, going out to Mother's favorite clubs and restaurants. Then Charles wanted Mother to settle down and take care of the family so he could concentrate on his work. Mother wanted to go out with her friends and apparently was doing just that whether Charles liked it or not.

Charles, in his frustration, began to drink, and then they began to argue. I remember him shouting at her that she dressed up for other men, but couldn't even give him the time of day. What she replied, I have no idea, but it exploded into violence.

I remember the first time. As the sounds of blows and overturning furniture escalated, I crept from my bed in terror and peeked through a crack in my bedroom door. It was knock-down-drag-out, Mother giving as good as she got. I noticed the expression on her face as she wrestled and fought with him; it seemed she was enjoying herself.

Her lip was bleeding, but Charles seemed to be in worse shape with a swollen eye and red marks and scratches all over his face and neck. The neighbors called the police. Mother rapidly straightened her dress, smoothed her hair, and wiped her face before answering their knock at the door.

The policeman asked, "Any trouble here?" I was completely shocked to hear Mother say, "No. Everything is fine, officer. No problem."

My brother and I didn't realize our mother was probably as much a participant as a victim in this struggle.

Until then, even with so many strange things going on among the adults around us, we had never been exposed to any cursing, shouting or overt violence. After one or two of these sessions of Mother going out, Charles drinking and storming, my brother and I again came up with a plan. (We were creative if nothing else.)

We decided to sleep with iron skillets under our beds so the very next time Charles started to rage and rant, we'd jump up and hit him over the head with our frying pans, grab Mother, and make our escape.

Having a plan is one thing, but we lived in dread of having to execute this one.

We were in our beds sleeping when the shouting and slapping began. I woke with a start. I don't know about my brother Tommy, but I was lying there with my heart pounding, knowing I was committed to a course of action. Come hell or high water, I was not going to back off.

Tommy slipped into my room to see if I was awake and ready. I was. I got up, put on my bathrobe, and we stood by the doorway with our iron skillets in our hands. I was seven and Tommy was eight. We were going to rush in and subdue a large man who was drunk enough to be dangerous but not drunk enough to be stupid.

As we stood shivering, we realized discretion is the better part of valor. We conferred in whispers. Since our grandfather was visiting at Uncle's house nearby, we'd slip out of the house and call him and let him handle this lunatic. But we had to pass through the living room to get to the door. Charles might stop us.

My brother told me to be ready to run on his signal, and I concentrated all my thoughts on holding my body ready to spring into action while he watched for the opportune moment.

When it came, he whispered, "Run!" and we dashed to the door, tore it open and flung ourselves madly in the direction of the neighbor's house as if veritable demons were pursuing us. Gasping for breath, certain of imminent doom, we rapped frantically on their window in a cacophony of cries: "Help! Let us in! He's going to kill us!" We really did think Charles would kill us for running away to tell on him.

The neighbor came quickly to the door to let us in and we poured out our story, begging her not to let Charles in because he would surely beat us. Sure enough, in a few minutes he was pounding at her door. She told him he'd better run away quick because the police were coming.

At our house in Sarasota. We weren't very big, but we were creative and courageous!

Dressed for church.

Only it was worse than the police: it was Grandpa!

My grandfather was a man of few words, but when he did speak, everyone listened. And when he said a thing was to be done a certain way, it was done that way and no other. I can't explain even today what quality in him produced this effect in family, acquaintances, and strangers alike, but there it was. I don't know what he told Charles that night. But we never saw Charles again.

We spent the night with our aunt and uncle. My aunt reports that my grandfather asked her if she would take us in for one night, even though he knew there was bad blood between her and my mother, and she kindly agreed that she would do anything for us kids, but nothing for my mother. I can't blame her. The next day, we were packed up and taken with our grandparents to Tampa, and life returned to some semblance of normalcy.

Grandpa was pretty disgusted with Mother. His letters from this time often pose the question to my grandmother: *what are we going to do about Alice?* It's clear in retrospect that he was beginning to get an idea, after four marriages, repeating violence, and family crisis, that something was wrong with Mother.

Finally they set some rules she had to obey to continue to live on their bounty. Yes, she could work—in fact it was required—and yes, Grandma would take care of us; but no going out with men for the time being because, obviously, she simply had no judgment. No nightclubs, no dancing, no dates. Time to settle down and make some sense of your life.

What did Mother do under these restrictions?

She got religion!

Yes indeed! Church was the answer, because, you see, how could my grandparents object to her going to church three times a week? And remember, churches are places to meet men, too.

But churches can also be dangerous places for little girls who see faces at the window.

CHAPTER FIVE

JANE EYRE REDUX

Mother's new religious zeal was fine with me. I loved Sunday school, the stories the teacher told with illustrations on the felt board, singing, and just the whole feeling. I was reading the Bible (in bits and pieces), and God was taking care of us now for sure.

Because of my grandmother's constant presence in the background of my life, and despite my mother's hedonistic lifestyle, I was brought up in a very Christian environment.

As a small child I heard Great-Grandpa preach. He was an impressive figure of a man, with a booming bass voice that carried to the very last pew without a PA system. He once took me on his lap and held my hand up to my mother and grandparents, saying: "There's more holiness in the little finger of this hand than in the rest of us in this room."

I was impressed. I was unaware, of course, that this remark concerned little children in general, and not my own state of spirituality. But, I took it to heart and vowed to strive to make it true.

The questions raised in my mind by the Face at the Window drove me to discover a haven of safety in the arms of God. My quest became to find God. I felt the Hound of Hell at my heels. Our experiences of Mother's manipulations and self-centered behavior damaged our sense of security. My internal operating system demanded a source of stability, and God was the logical choice.

I was avid in my Sunday school studies and devoted in my prayer life. I spent many hours writing songs and prayers and decorating them with drawings of vines and flowers, tucking them here and there for God to "find" them. But early on I became aware of contradictions and discrepancies in "standard religion." The anomalous events of my life were inexplicable. I constantly prayed for guidance and support.

At the same time, I was keenly aware of pain and suffering all over the world, and it seemed I was cursed with the burden of acutely tuning in to this cosmic pain. I could sense the sorrows of people behind their words.

This was distressing, because what was inside them seldom matched their words or expectations. Someone said, "Oh, I'm fine!" and I could tell clearly that they were not. Someone talked happily about their plans, and I felt a sudden heavy sensation of gloom. At times this feeling of gloom had presaged tragedy in their lives. I suffered with every starving child, every grieving parent and pain-racked victim. I prayed constantly for the world's pain to be ameliorated because I needed my own pain to end. But everywhere I looked, there was suffering now, or suffering to come.

My great-grandfather, Rev. S. G. Meadows, at left with his son, my grandfather, and my uncle and cousin. Four generations of Meadows Men. This is how I remember my great grandfather; I was born two months after this photo; he died 7 years after this photo was taken.

In retrospect, I wish this profound empathy had extended to "reading" those with negative intentions. But whatever the source of this ability, I was denied a useful self-protective application and manifested one that was crippling.

I could perceive the pain of the disenfranchised soul, but I could not read the thoughts of the mind.

Where was God?

I believed in the literal truth of all we were taught in Sunday school. All my life I heard about God talking to people, bringing revelations, answering prayers. When anyone said: "I prayed about it and God showed me," I believed that God had really spoken audibly, or had produced a real, visual image, or some other equally miraculous event of guidance. And this led to a problem: why, if I prayed to God and waited in silence for an answer, I never heard one.

If God wasn't answering, there must be a reason. I asked the Sunday school teacher. The reply concerned original sin. I was told that if I had faith I could overcome this sin, and Jesus would save me and God would most definitely answer my prayers. But what is this thing called Faith?

I was told this meant "belief in God."

Well, heck, I had a lot of that! No problem.

I kept praying to a God in whom I believed literally and completely, but I still received no answers—and no changes in the situations I was praying about. I asked God to explain why He wasn't giving the help I needed.

Silence. God wasn't talking.

Why did God speak to everybody else and not to me?

Clearly it was because of the Face at the Window. I was contaminated in some way. I was bad. That's why my father didn't want me. That's why Mother couldn't keep a husband. Somehow they always found out a darkness existed because of me.

But I didn't want to be in darkness. I loved God! And I needed God to tell me how to make the Face at the Window go away forever. Then God would know I loved him, and He would love me too.

Since God seemed to be hiding, I determined to find out how to get to Him.

Finding contact with God became my overweening goal. He was, after all, my Father too, wasn't He? Didn't I have a right to his love and attention like all others who claimed to have a hotline to heaven? Did I need to pray more? Sacrifice something I liked? I would willingly give up what little I had just to feel the touch of God's breath on my cheek. How about just a little, teensy, tiny sign to assure me that YOU exist? Something to hold on to? A straw, for God's sake! I am drowning here!

But God never answered me.

Then I began to wet my bed at night. This mortally embarrassed me. Not drinking a single drop of water from about three in the afternoon didn't work. All the folk remedies my grandmother came up with didn't work. The instant I fell asleep signaled my bladder to let go. On cold nights, I woke up immediately, wet and freezing and miserable. I didn't know, of course, and

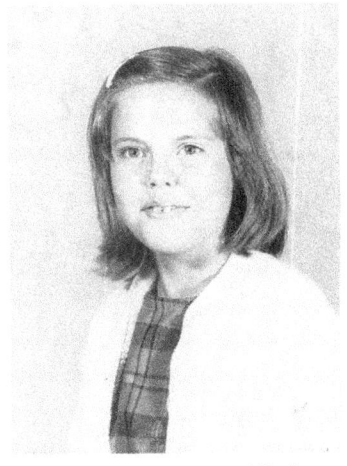

School picture taken in the fall of 1960.

neither did anyone else, that this was one of the early symptoms of the autoimmune disorder that would almost destroy me.

At my grandparents' house I slept in one bed with my mother, and Tommy had his own bed in the same room. My mother's solution to my lack of nightly bladder control was to lie awake until I was asleep. The instant she felt wetness spreading, she'd start slapping me to wake me up in a state of pain and shock. I spent many nights trying to stay awake so that wouldn't happen.

Soon, not surprisingly, Mother met a nice elderly widower at church, a successful businessman named Ed who traveled a great deal. He had a teenage son and the appearance of a kindly and devout father figure just waiting to enfold us all in his loving embrace.

All Mother's new church friends favored her marriage to Ed, so she launched into an exciting time of shopping and preparing for a "real" church wedding. But Tommy and I were excluded. The children of the bride were not invited to be members of the wedding party. We were not even allowed to attend the ceremony. As soon as the honeymoon was over, we were informed that we would soon be sent away to a boarding school in the Carolinas.

Mother assured us that boarding school was a favorable opportunity. Only children of rich families could attend. In later years, I discovered

Early summer of 1961 around the time of my mother's marriage. We had been told we would be sent away to school in the autumn and here, I am with my grandparents visiting a family friend.

the new stepfather was actually a conniving cheapskate. Ed used his connections in the church to get us accepted to a school primarily set up for missionaries' children unable to accompany their parents to wild and forbidding posts among the heathen in deepest, darkest Africa or wherever. It was, in short, a "charitable institution." Talk about your basic Jane Eyre drama.

In all fairness, I can't say that anyone at the school was harsh or cruel to us. It was a lovely school in a beautiful location, with excellent staff. But I was a nine-year-old girl separated from my family and especially my brother, who'd been my hero and constant companion. I was left in the care of strangers unable to give special attention to one child of twenty-four in their charge.

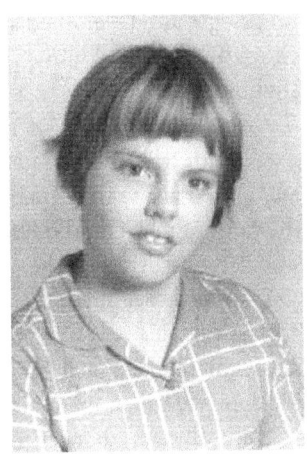

This is the school picture taken right after school officials ordered my hair cut. As you can imagine from the previous photo taken in early summer, by autumn, it had grown quite long.

School discipline was modeled on military basic training sans the exercise routines and drills. We did everything by the clock and marched everywhere in straight lines. Boys were separated from girls. I saw my brother only on occasion and at a distance. This was a cruel separation for me. Tommy had been the only constant I was able to trust with any degree of certainty. And now, even the small sense of security that he'd be there the next morning was lost.

Little girls who see faces at the window need a lot of protection.

I was not to receive it. Immediately, I was shorn of my long hair. I couldn't take care of it alone and no one had time to help, so it had to go. I wept as the teenage girl assigned to the job sliced through my hair with heavy scissors, joking all the while that my hair was so thick it was like a horse's tail. I was still a child who cried at night clutching a toy bear. And wetting my bed, of course, made me the brunt of many cruel remarks.

Once a month we marched down the mountain in double rows to the little movie house in town. We paid a nickel to see the latest amours of Elvis Presley. Older girls wore poodle skirts and saddle shoes. "The Lion Sleeps Tonight" was soon to be their number-one song.

Every Sunday we went to the Baptist or the Presbyterian churches. I tried both, settling on Presbyterian because it was built of such beautiful granite and resembled some ancient medieval cathedral. I sang in the choir, but not too loudly. I didn't want to be noticed. Once, I forgot my shyness, singing the very moving phrase in "The Holy City": *"Me thought the voice of Angels From Heav'n in answer rang ..."* The word "voice" reaches for that lovely E-flat. The choir director stopped waving his wand and stared at me in surprise. I didn't realize I'd given so much power to the hymn that I could be heard above the choir. I lowered my voice and warbled on with the other girls.

I stopped singing in the choir after that, even though I received many messages that I was missed and would I please come to practice. It didn't occur to me that I had a pleasant voice. No one had ever said so. Mother had given me attention only when I did something wrong.

Naturally, my demon problem went with me to school. The feeling grew that I'd been sent to this place because other people, especially my mother, could sense in me some contamination, the same way I could sense the pain behind their words. I was a person to be shunned and sent away from the family. Perhaps my mother's marriage would work for the very reason that I was not present.

I kept my eye on the window in my room and cried bitterly for God to rescue me from my utter aloneness. But God wasn't talking.

Mother and the new stepfather were traveling at Christmas time and weren't coming to see us. It seemed, for a time, that we would be the only two kids still at school over the holidays. All the others were making happy preparations to go home to celebrate.

So my grandfather put Tommy and me on a bus to Tampa, traveling by ourselves for the first time in our lives. When our two-week vacation was over, Grandma packed our suitcases with care and precision, tucking in small gifts and goodies. I cried miserably, dreading the return to school.

Grandpa promised us if we could stick it out till the end of term, he'd see that we didn't have to go back again. I think Grandpa was already getting a clue about this "good Christian" my mother had married. He definitely wasn't pleased to see us so unhappy.

Back at school, my tenth birthday was approaching. I felt depressed because there would be no cake, no ice cream, no gifts, nothing but just another winter day. Sure, I would get a card with money in it from my mother, and maybe the same thing from my grandparents, and later, the housemother would probably take me to Asheville to spend my birthday money on new clothes. I was growing out of the wardrobe I'd brought to school. My knees stuck out below my dresses, the waistlines hung halfway to my armpits, and several inches showed between the cuffs of my sweaters and my wrists. I felt gangly and badly turned out.

I was sitting morosely in the common room on my birthday night, reading a book. It was snowing outside. I doubted we would have classes the next morning. It would be too treacherous to venture down the mountain. A knock came at the door and one of the girls went to answer it. The wind blew in, the snow swirled across the polished floor, and someone called my name.

Mother!

Standing there in the doorway, with the stepfather behind her, wrapped in a magnificent coat, wearing elegant fur-topped boots, was my beautiful mother. And oh! how much at that moment I loved her. How happy I was to see her. I was not forgotten. I was loved. She had come!

But only for a few hours.

She'd persuaded the stepfather to go a little out of their way to stop by the school. She told me later that Ed complained this would put him off his travel schedule, but she'd threatened that if he didn't take her to see her children, she'd find her own way there and he could travel on alone. Nothing and nobody could stop her from seeing her children.

Mother had already spent a couple of hours with my brother, and now we had a little time together before they had to leave. They were on their way back to Florida to stay, Mother said. When we finished the term, we would come home to a new house, and we would all be happy together.

It sounded too good to be true, but I held on to the hope. I was so happy to be held by my mother that nothing else mattered. I was safe, I was loved, I was wanted, and God had answered my prayers. Maybe he hadn't spoken to me, but everything was going to be fine now.

She hadn't brought me a birthday present, but she gave me her fur-topped boots to keep my feet warm. I had outgrown my own. And, since she was returning to Florida, where she wouldn't need them, she also gave me her sweaters, her snowsuit and her heavy coat. I was so proud to wear my mother's boots, coat, and sweaters, even if they fit badly. It was proof she loved me.

The mysterious events after this hit-and-run visit could reasonably be attributed to emotional and psychic trauma. God only knows I have thought it all over many times, trying to plumb the depths of meaning that may lie hidden in symbols of memory so easily distorted.

I remember waking up one night and seeing a bright light outside shining in through the window. The residence I lived in was built high on a cutaway flat place on the side of a mountain. There was less than fifteen feet between the back of the building and the vertical slope that went up about thirty to fifty feet. The driveway provided just enough room for the housemother to park her car and have room for passengers to get out on either side. The only way a light could shine in the window would be if the back lights of the building were on, or if someone were standing on the drive with a strong light. I figured that it was the former, disregarding the fact that the building lights were off to the side and didn't shine in my window when they were on. With that explanation, I dismissed any other and went back to sleep. Whatever it was, it didn't seem to concern me.

The next thing I knew, I woke up with my body on fire. I was so hot that I couldn't breathe. I threw off my covers and thought about all that nice snow outside that was so very cool. I got up and went to the window, a tall affair much like French doors, opened it and stepped outside. I walked in my bare feet along the back of the building, past the housemother's car, to a place where the snow was piled up nice and deep. When I lay down it felt like a cool feather bed. And that is the last I remember until I woke up shivering and shaking in my bed.

The housemother went from room to room turning on all the lights (the usual morning procedure) and singing out "rise and shine!" into every room. I knew I didn't feel quite right, but I must have been too young to realize there was something very wrong. I had seldom been sick in my life.

I struggled through the process of dressing myself, pulling on two layers of clothing, working my way into my snowsuit and boots. In a daze, I followed the other girls in the darkness, down the side of the mountain to the dining hall. I slowly took off my snowsuit, hanging it on my peg in the foyer with all the other students milling around and hanging their snow gear up, too.

When I entered the dining hall, the brightness of the lights and clatter of dishes and voices was shocking and seemed completely foreign.

I found my way to the assigned table and sat down like an automaton, unable to lift my head or look at anyone until the table monitor began to pile food on my plate, encouraging me to "eat up!" I looked around at tables crowded with people enjoying the wonderful breakfast the school provided so generously. I didn't recognize a single thing. I looked back at my plate, piled with eggs and bacon and hot buttered biscuits, and wondered what I was supposed to do with all this food.

The voices at my own table had fallen quiet. Everyone was staring at me. I took my hand out of my lap, picked up my fork, and took a small bite of egg. The instant I did, I experienced a sensation that can only be compared to being hit in the stomach by a sledgehammer. As though I were watching from a distance, I saw my body go into a convulsion and fall from the chair onto the floor. It was heaving and vomiting like an animal struck by a car. Chairs were thrown back as several people gathered around me, watching helplessly as my body convulsed and emptied itself with such violence that I thought my eyes would be ejected from their sockets. Finally, someone helped me to my feet, wiped my face, and asked if I was going to be okay.

That reminds me of the joke about the guy who falls from a tenth-story window. He's lying in the street with every bone in his body broken. A passerby runs up and asks, "Are you hurt?"

Only when I laugh.

Well, what do you think? Was I okay? Well, heck, I wasn't even connected to that body, so naturally I said yes.

At this point, the clean-up crew arrived. I knew I'd be required to clean up the embarrassing mess I had made, so I tried to take the mop, but they told me to let someone else handle it because I needed to go to the infirmary. I said that I just needed air. I couldn't breathe in that heat and light and noise. I made my way to the foyer and struggled into my snowsuit in the semi-darkness. No one came to see if I was managing. I seemed to be forgotten. I opened the door and went out into the snow. It was barely daylight outside. I don't remember walking to the infirmary. But then I was aware of the sharp smells of Lysol and rubbing alcohol as I collapsed just inside the door.

I remember waking up at odd times of the day or night with so much pain in my head that I immediately went unconscious again. I drifted in and out for days. Finally, the intense, blinding pain was gone, and I awakened to a dull throbbing and the feeling of warm wetness all around my face and in my hair. I lifted up my head to see my pillow soaked with blood.

A nurse washed my face and cleaned the side of my head where blood and fluids were draining from my ear. She changed the pillow and gave me something sweet to drink in a little paper cup. I was so exhausted I immediately went back to sleep. Days passed this way.

One morning I woke so early that the sun had not yet come up from behind the mountain. The light was clear, but muted. And everything was in black and white. I felt something unusual about the way the light appeared in the high windows of the infirmary, so I got out of the hospital bed, crossed the room to the windows against the far wall, and climbed onto an empty bed to look outside.

The world had been transformed. It must have been snowing for a long time because it was deeper than anything this Florida girl had ever seen, and we had already had a lot of snow that year. All the leafless shrubs wore fluffy hats, like little clouds scattered here and there.

Across the way the trees in the apple orchard looked like they were connecting puffy little clouds to the bigger one on the ground. There was one glorious tree centered directly opposite the window, so perfect in proportion and shape that I could only stare fixedly at it with a certain sense of an inner meaning to such perfection.

There was not a mark or a track or sign of any living thing anywhere. The entire world, as far as my eye could see, was clean and white. It was like waking up in the clouds.

I couldn't stop looking, as if hypnotized by the scene. And as I gazed in breathless wonder at this amazing display, it began to transform before my eyes. The sun emerged behind the distant mountain, and golden rays of light were probing and feeling their way through the tops of the trees, gradually moving down the trunks to the ground. This living light turned what formerly looked like puffy clouds to masses of glistening gold and silver, with sparkling diamonds studded everywhere. With the slow, but detectable movement of the sun, the earth came alive with light, sparking like electricity, dancing and leaping in rainbow colors. I don't know how long I stood there. The spell was broken when a bird hidden in the branches of the tree suddenly took flight, scattering snow illuminated by the rays of the sun like a halo in the air drifting slowly to the ground.

I forgot pain and suffering and the misery of the past weeks, and felt a surge of longing to dress and go outside and dash around and explore this magical landscape. The resilience of childhood, hope for a better world, a new adventure, and life itself was alive and well inside me.

This time, the Face at the Window was mine.

CHAPTER SIX

VIOLETS AND BULLS IN THE GRAVEYARD

After my long illness, deep changes in my metabolism emerged and the beginning of life-long health issues started to manifest in full force. For the next three decades, I seldom felt completely well again. This is typical for people with autoimmune disorders, as I have since learned. Nowadays, I control it completely with diet, eliminating all gluten, dairy, and most carbohydrates, but back then, everything I ate did nothing but further inflame my body.

Spring in the Blue Ridge Mountains is definitely a magical time. The variety of flowers and ferns and mosses growing in the mountains simply enchanted me. I spent many hours at school creating a sort of magic garden of my own, and thinking, thinking, thinking.

My life had two bright spots and one that was very dark. The housemother of my residence had taken an extreme dislike to me. I am not sure why. I can think of no significant interaction between us that created such a situation. Maybe it had to do with a girl at school, whose real name I can't remember, but I will call her Flossie because of her amazing blonde curls.

This little girl was one of three others sharing a room with me. We had our own closet and dresser space and were required to keep everything clean and neat at all times. Flossie was not inclined to do anything for herself, and because of her great beauty—she literally looked like a doll—she managed to get away with many infractions of the rules.

Mrs. McNeil, the housemother, doted on this little seven-year-old. She often took her shopping or to her own home for special sleepovers. Whatever Flossie wanted, Flossie got. Except from me.

There was another little girl in our room, a shy and withdrawn child who often lapsed into sign language to communicate out of long habit (both her parents were deaf). Flossie made fun of the signing, and I was in a constant state of war with her to leave the other girl alone. It is very likely because of this ongoing conflict with Flossie that I came to be the brunt of rather unnecessary cruelties from Mrs. McNeil.

The two bright spots were my classroom teacher, Mrs. Evelyn, and a little mountain girl named Norma. In class, and away from the residence, I was the favored one. I can only say that Mrs. Evelyn played a guardian angel role in giving so generously of her time and attention. So to some extent my misery was balanced with intellectual challenge and success.

I was placed in advanced classes, spending several hours a day studying with high-school juniors and seniors who were rather curious how they became afflicted with a ten-year-old.

Norma, a local day pupil whose family lived in the backwoods of the mountains, and whose clothes were little more than rags, was so curious and open-minded that we formed a friendship that I have never, in all these years, forgotten.

Many girls in my dormitory adopted the housemother's attitude toward me and thought of me as a teacher's pet. Norma was an exception. She was quick and bright and laughed a lot in spite of her obvious poverty. We sat under a crab-apple tree at the side of the playground during recess talking about our lives and hopes for the future. Naturally, my greatest hope was to go home, so we turned our minds to plotting.

We decided that something very wicked had to be done to be sent home; but what might this be? I don't think we had any real concept, though we had certainly been exposed to wickedness in our short lives. I thought about this for a few days while picking wild mountain violets to put in bottles of hot water with the idea that it would make cologne.

While I was filling my bottles of violets with hot water in the residence bathroom, the idea came to me. I knew what I could do to get sent home. I outlined my idea to Norma during recess the next day. She didn't think it would work, but she was loyal and would help me. We agreed to meet during free time on Sunday afternoon. She knew that, as a day pupil, she wasn't allowed on the school grounds on weekends, but she was willing to risk it.

On Sunday afternoon, we gathered flowers; lots of flowers; bushels of them. I filched some pillowcases from the linen room at the residence and we stuffed them full of every kind of flower we could get our hands on, mostly violets. Then, we climbed up the slope to the big concrete dome covering the school well, removed the cover, and one after another emptied the pillowcases of flowers into the water.

My idea was that the water would be spoiled and undrinkable, and they would just have to close the school and send everyone home.

So, I waited. I was sure that the "bad water" would be discovered at any moment. An investigation would begin, the water would be declared "unfit," and home was just a few days away.

As the days passed and nothing happened, I began to worry that maybe the water would not be spoiled, but that the deed would be discovered nonetheless. I would be forced to confess the wicked deed and be sent home in disgrace. Well, I wanted to go home, but not in disgrace.

Nothing happened. Nobody noticed anything. Of course, I drank lots of water every day, constantly testing to see if the effects of all the flowers we had dumped in the cistern were noticeable yet.

Pure, clear mountain water flowed in copious quantities from the taps, disappointing me with every drop.

I never did figure out what went wrong with my plan.

Time for plan B. If I couldn't get sent home, I'd run away. But Norma wasn't able to help me with this one. I thought I would just do it alone. As it happened, I had an unexpected companion and ally.

Another girl at school, just as anxious to go home, was a city slicker from Boston, the object of much teasing because of her "citified" ways and funny accent. Janice and I decided the best time to make our escape was at the start of Sunday free time so we could get as far as possible before our absence was discovered.

On the designated day, we both stuffed extra bacon and biscuits in our pockets at breakfast to have "traveling food," and pretended to be sick so we could skip church and make the rest of our preparations. We packed bundles of clothes to a hiding place in the forest at the edge of the school grounds. After church, we were accounted present at lunch. The instant we were released from supervision, we hurried to our bundles to make our getaway. We set off through the forest in the opposite direction from town.

Now, traveling in mountains is not quite the same as walking down the street in a flat landscape. Going down can be downright treacherous. After a few exhausting climbs and a precipitous plunge down a steep slope blanketed with slick pine needles, we came to a large meadow. In the center was a fenced graveyard.

Well, I wanted to have a look. We'd started blithely across the field when we noticed the bull. We ran. Of course the bull ran too. Just in time, we made it to the graveyard and threw ourselves over the fence in panic, panting and gasping for breath, our hearts pounding in our throats.

At last the bull became bored with keeping us hostage and wandered away. I'd had enough of this adventure. A nice dinner and a place to sleep away from bulls seemed just the ticket, so I was ready to give up on running away for now. But Janice wouldn't budge. She was so terrified of the big black bull that she was utterly incapable of even thinking about going back over the fence. I pleaded, reasoned with her, told her we could get back in time for dinner and no one would even miss us, but nothing penetrated her stubborn fear of that bull.

Well, heck, I didn't like the bull either, but I knew that if we kept our eye on him until he wasn't looking, we could get half-way across before he would even notice us. And then, we could probably outrun him the rest of the way.

No dice. Janice wasn't buying it.

I told her that if she was too scared to come, then I would have to just leave her there and send someone to get her and we would both get in trouble. She sobbed and blubbered that she didn't dare go over the fence, because the bull would get her, and demanded that I not leave her alone in a graveyard.

I was pretty disgusted with her. If she couldn't get up the courage to cross the meadow, and she didn't have the courage to stay there while I did it, what were we going to do? Sit there and rot? Getting chased by a mad bull was better than sitting there moaning and groaning. But that was exactly what Janice was doing.

Finally, I couldn't take it any more. I told her that she could come or not. I was going. But she grabbed hold of my arm, pulling me back, crying and begging hysterically for me not to leave her there alone. I kept trying to pull away and peel her hands off my arm. Finally, in exasperation, I slapped her face with my free hand.

She was so stunned she immediately stopped crying and carrying on like a lunatic, and for the moment that she was silent, I looked her in the eye and said: "I'm going. Come with me or stay; I don't care what you do. You're nothing but a big baby!" And I was over the fence.

Well, Janice wasn't far behind me, and I found our way back to school. It was too late for dinner, and we were grounded for a week for that infraction, but fortunately, we managed to hide and retrieve our bundles and return everything to normal with no one the wiser.

Janice held a grudge against me after that because I'd slapped her. I should have left her for the bull and the ghosts in the graveyard. She was sent home in disgrace not long after that for stealing money from another student. I don't think she needed the money, so I can only guess that this was her way to get home. I just never could do it that way. There is being sent home in disgrace, and there is real disgrace. And, after I watched the way Janice was "taken into custody" like a criminal, how her name became anathema among the students, and the whole serious deal that she was put through to get home, I lost interest in the project myself. Besides, June wasn't that far away. I could live until then.

CHAPTER SEVEN

TRAPEZES AND DOG DAYS

Needless to say, I was ecstatic to go home at the end of the term, and I was confident my grandfather would keep his promise to see that we didn't have to return. But I wasn't prepared for all the changes in the year we were away. A year is a long time when it's one tenth of your whole life.

During the last months of school, Mother had loomed large in my consciousness as the beautiful fairy coming in from the snow on my birthday. I longed desperately to be embraced in her welcoming arms, nurtured, and restored to life after my long ordeal.

The reality was a bit different. Coming home to an unfamiliar house, a mother who seemed a stranger, and a new stepfather, presented certain adjustment problems. Fortunately, we had fascinating neighbors just next door.

They were members of a Hungarian circus family who had achieved some fame in their specialties of the high wire and trapeze. They happened to have a little girl exactly my age. She had a long, unpronounceable name, but I just called her Hetty.

A large, empty lot between their house and ours, owned by Hetty's family, was used for their off-season practice. A trapeze was set up there, and two complete high-wire arrangements: one about three feet high, the other at standard height for actual performances. The low one was for experiments and practice, and the high one to further refine the act.

Hetty was being groomed to be a child performer of great skill and daring. Every day I sat and watched as her father and older brothers supervised her routine. They were very kind people, and they decided it would help Hetty to have more enthusiasm if she had a companion in her drills. I was soon included in the instruction process.

At this age, I wasn't a very good subject for hypnosis!

I was having a great time learning to walk on a steel cable, jump rope on it, climb up and down the "webbing," balance, slide and hang dramatically from my ankles on the trapeze (conveniently low to the ground!) and various other fun activities. I was thrilled to be shown all of Hetty's gorgeous costumes—handmade, sequined, and beaded by her mother—and to stand in front of the shrine in their home dedicated to several relatives whose lives had been lost in the pursuit of their art. I was fascinated by the food they ate, the delicious smells that permeated their house at dinnertime, and the fact that they spoke their native language with as much ease as they spoke English. In short, I was having a ball, until Ed the stepfather discovered what was going on.

You see, not only were they "foreigners," they were Circus People; and worse than that: they were Catholic. I was forbidden to associate with, or speak to, Hetty.

Now, Ed, a widower when my mother married him, had a seventeen-year-old son, Devin. We overheard our grandparents telling our mother that Devin's mother was dead was because Devin himself had shot her. It had been an accident, but we kept our distance from him nevertheless. I mean, how do you talk to someone who shot his own mother?

Devin was a senior in high school, the drum major of the school band, so he had a lot of activities going on. He became interested in hypnosis and had several books on the subject. He wanted a subject to experiment on, and I was selected since my brother thought the whole thing was too stupid even to consider.

I dutifully sat in a comfortable chair and tried to relax, though I was not altogether sure what "relaxing" meant. Devin dangled a pocket watch on a chain in front of my eyes while reading a script from his hypnosis book in a sonorous voice.

I was watching the watch, then watching his face. He looked serious and prim. I had a vision of him in his drum major Indian outfit, a huge feather headdress trailing down his back, leaping and dancing, wearing brown make-up to cover his pale skin.

Devin's roles of serious hypnotist and leaping wild Indian struck me as too funny and I started to giggle.

"Shush!" he said, and went back to reading his text while swinging the watch furiously in front of my eyes. I just completely collapsed in laughter and he slammed the book shut and stormed out of the room in disgust.

He definitely avoided me after that.

Meanwhile, the stepfather began showing his true colors. Despite the probable dangers our mother had exposed us to, her cold and selfish ways, she had been the only person ever to strike us for serious misdeeds (in her opinion). But Ed's staunch Christian tenets demanded a thick leather razor strop because sparing the rod spoiled the child. He also had a heck of a backhand. While he lived with us, my lips were regularly split and bloody.

Ed's formerly successful business was failing, and Mother often borrowed money from the grandparents to pay the bills. He was under a lot of pressure.

Ed's decision to implement such modes of discipline on two kids who had never experienced any such thing up to that age was probably not the wisest thing the guy ever thought up. You have to remember the incident of the iron skillets to figure out how fiendish the two of us became under this regime. My grandmother called us perfect hellions.

By this time, I was eleven, my brother was thirteen, and we were just getting warmed up.

We quickly figured out the one disagreement between Mother and Ed centered on the issue of dogs. Mother had been raised with dogs,

My brother with our little dog on the lawn of the house where we lived with "Ed"—the wicked, dog hating, step-father.

she loved dogs, and we always had a dog that was part of the family. Ed detested dogs.

The current dog had lived with the grandparents while we were away at school. We decided now we were at home to bring our dog back also. Mother, to our surprise, agreed with us immediately. But my grandmother wasn't too pleased to give her up, making remarks about people who didn't like dogs. "You can always tell about people by whether or not a dog likes them," she muttered. Mother assured her that Ed was a good person, so he would naturally want the dog back too.

Well, Ed wouldn't admit he didn't want the dog because that would make him look bad. The dog could come, but had to be kept outside. This, of course, eliminated the issue of whether or not the dog liked him.

We weren't worried. We would work on getting her into the house later.

Of course the dog got pregnant staying outside. Florida is pretty steamy in the summertime, and the poor little pregnant doggie was suffering miserably in the dog days. We pointed out to Mother how hot it was and how much the dog was suffering, and she agreed that the dog should not suffer and we ought to bring her onto the screened porch.

So, here is the set-up: the dog is not precisely inside the house, and not precisely outside either. She is pregnant and miserable. In the door walks the stepfather. The first thing that meets his eye after a long, hot day at work, and a ride home in the blistering heat, is a dog inside his house. Even if she is not technically "in the house."

I was sitting there reading when I heard him shouting about dogs in the house and how this particular one was going out this very instant. Something inside me snapped at that moment; like the bull-in-the-meadow situation.

Better to do something, anything, than to do nothing. I was going to wave the red flag and distract the bull. I told my stepfather piously that since my grandfather was paying the bills, his rules had precedence, and his rules consisted of kindness to defenseless animals. I knew a major backhand was coming, or possibly even the strop. I didn't really expect him to open the door and kick my little dog through it like a football as hard as he could.

She sailed through the air, yelping and crying in pain, landed on the pavement outside the door writhing and whimpering. Ed didn't expect a berserker eleven-year-old to launch herself out of the chair and tackle him like a wildcat with tooth and nail and kicking feet that hit the mark, bringing him to his knees in an agony I only hoped was equal to that experienced by my poor little dog.

By this time Mother made it to the porch to discover what all the racket was about. I am sure she never expected to see me with balled fists, blazing eyes, telling my stepfather through clenched teeth that if he ever touched my dog again I would kill him. I really meant it. I was literally panting from fury and exertion.

Ed struggled to his feet, clutching his crotch. "Aren't you going to do something with her? She struck me!"

I was really expecting doom to fall on my head in a big way. And I was ready to accept it. I had taken my stand, and even if all the fires of hell had been the consequence, I wasn't going to take it back.

"She only did what I would have done if I had been here," my mother said. She turned her back on him and walked into the house.

With those startling words, Mother's fifth marriage ended. There was icy silence all that evening, and Tommy and I decided it was the better part of valor to keep the dog out of sight completely. She was all right, but it could have been a disaster.

The next day, after Ed left for work, Mother announced it was time to pack. This was Ed's house, and she wouldn't stay in it another night. Where were we going?

To The Farm.

CHAPTER EIGHT

THE FARM

Everyone in the family called it The Farm with capital letters. An old Florida Cracker-style farmhouse already a century old when my grandparents bought it in the Great Depression of the 1930s, it came with eleven acres, a tidal spring or "bayhead," and half a dozen huge grafted pecan trees of several varieties.

The Farm was situated nearly three miles from the nearest neighbor, on a stretch of the Old Dixie Highway bypassed when the new Highway 19 was built a mile or so to the east. The house faced the Gulf of Mexico with a shaded front porch a hundred yards away from the lime-rock road. On the opposite side of the road a broad expanse of tidal flats stretched away to the Gulf for about a mile, dotted by little islets of cabbage palms and cedar trees and palmettos. It was a setting entirely appropriate for a brontosaurus to graze.

The bootleggers of Prohibition times ran their illicit trade along the Old Dixie Highway. About five miles to the north of The Farm was a little town called Aripeka, named (supposedly) after a semi-legendary Indian chief. Aripeka is "The Town Time Forgot."

A little bit north of Aripeka once stood an elegant resort, raised up in the middle of nowhere, which extended regular hospitality to such luminaries as the great Babe Ruth and "Scarface" Al Capone.

The Farm was the greenest and lushest place I have ever seen. Along with pecan trees, there were several tall cedar trees, cabbage palms, a camphor tree, orange and tangerine trees, fig and pear trees, and a wide variety of semi-tropical shrubs scattered over three acres of thick green lawn. Climbing roses and honeysuckle grew up a big trellis on one side of the porch, and wisteria meandered on another trellis to the north of the house.

The only photo of The Farm taken from the road, looking down the driveway. It is winter and the pecan trees are bare.

The house had no electricity or indoor plumbing, but there was an outhouse to the back of the barn, and a big iron hand pump in the backyard. The whole place, except for the long front drive, was surrounded by pinewoods. It was, quite literally, paradise.

My grandparents bought the house as a vacation home, and it was furnished with no-longer-stylish, too-treasured-to-be-thrown-away antiques and cast-off furniture from various family households. The cupboards were stocked with stacks of odd dishes from many times and places, and a special shelf held the row of kerosene lamps always ready for duty.

The key was hidden on a rafter on the back porch, and if you used anything in the house, you replaced it and you always left it cleaner than when you arrived.

For years, various relatives and friends of the family had enjoyed the use of The Farm, and with all the coming and going, and an occasional

We were spending holidays at the farm from the time we were born. I am about a year old in this photo.

hired helper, a large garden was kept year after year in the black muck adjacent to the bayhead in the back. The Gulf high tide pushed through the porous lime rock against the shallow aquifer, and fresh groundwater rose and watered the garden faithfully twice a day. Grandpa kept his garden like his mind, carefully planned and geometric, growing excruciatingly straight beds of highly prolific things like okra and squash. Rutabagas grew big as pumpkins and collards big as palm fronds. Grandma was able to indulge her obsession for "putting food by" and canned endless bushels of pickles, corn, peas, beans, beets, and more.

The bayhead was a slow freshwater spring that rose and descended with the tides also. When Grandpa waded in to clean it out, intending to make a fish pool and lily pond, he found an old polished chunk of limestone with a name and two dates carved into it. It was obviously a gravestone. The bayhead was thereafter allowed to grow wild. This became for the kids—my brother, cousins and myself—a challenge to our courage, a place of mystery and foreboding known as "The Spring." The gravestone was placed as a curio on the hearth in front of the fireplace, joining a gigantic turtle shell big enough to cover the entire fireplace opening.

Rattlesnake skins from "big ones" killed by Grandpa hung on either side of the door to the dining room. The still-attached rattles rustled slightly every time you walked through that door, whispering softly: "Watch out!"

My brother poking our temporary pet alligator, "Pokey" with our dog, Mike, in the background, at The Farm. This was taken on a holiday a few years before we moved there to live with our mother.

There were, of course, some little drawbacks to the place: the above-mentioned rattlesnakes, cottonmouth moccasins, and mosquitoes. Grandpa solved the mosquito problem to some extent by installing screens on all the windows, and screening in the porch, but life with mosquitoes is just something that a person learns to deal with in Florida.

Sitting on the front porch in the expansive shade of those massive old pecan trees, listening to the rustling of the cabbage palms and the droning of mosquitoes outside the screen, watching the sun descend the last quadrant of the sky to set behind the distant, silhouetted bayheads, is a memory of inexpressible poignancy. Sometimes an entire day would pass without the sound of a single automobile. And if we heard a car in the distance, it was usually someone we knew on their way to The Farm.

The Old Dixie between The Farm and Aripeka was empty of any other dwelling. There had been a couple other houses up the road, old farmsteads still in use during Prohibition, but they had long since burned down.

At the time we moved to The Farm, the "parent house" still stood about 300 yards to the south. The Farm had been built by the owner of this larger house as a wedding gift for one of his children. The big house was a rather grand plantation-type affair with a detached kitchen connected by a covered walkway. It was a glorious and mysterious place. We spent many days wandering slowly through it, savoring the ghostly atmosphere, straining to catch the echoes of life and laughter that must have permeated its walls. But we heard only the rustling palms, droning insects, and the calling of an occasional distant bird. The grounds surrounding the house always seemed to be cloaked in a preternatural stillness that added to the thrill of exploration.

Later on, when we were no longer living at The Farm, the big house burned to the ground. I felt deeply the loss of its history and meaning and essence. In later years, I heard rumors of the wild boys who bragged about burning that gracious old home. I was sickened and sad. What poverty of soul must exist in those who would derive satisfaction from such wanton destruction?

Because of the machinations of my mother, I was forced to sell The Farm in 1989. It broke my heart. But, it's just as well. Nowadays, the sunset view from the porch is blocked by nearly a mile of identical houses built on man-made canals carved out of the prehistoric salt marsh. The honking of horns, squealing of tires, the drone and stench of a sewage treatment plant, have replaced the rustle of cabbage palm, buzz of insects, and silence of that clean, balmy air we breathed so long ago. Even the greenness of the place has faded. But, for the time we were there, it seemed to have the same effect on me that it had on all the other living things there: growth.

The Old Dixie Highway was, for a while, a time warp, frozen by the spirits of bygone days—some gracious and beautiful, some violent and twisted, some narrow like the road where they lived and moved. The whippoorwill no longer sings at my grandfather's farm and the woods where we once hiked and hunted is a golf course now. U.S. Highway 19 is the world's longest parking lot. Take a number and get in line!

Time flows on.

The house was rather primitive. We had only the fireplace for heat, and an old gas range in the kitchen that required bottled gas on a regular basis, but after all of the events of the past years, getting settled down in the old house was truly like coming home. It was familiar. Every object settled in its precisely correct place according to the designs of my grandfather. A barn full of interesting items waited to be explored: an old "woody" station wagon, a big diesel engine. The tool shed held sets of tools for every design and purpose. The storage shed contained an old Victrola, boxes of magazines from the '20s and '30s, trunks full of old clothes, and jar after jar of old coins among the treasures.

There were also boxes of books. In one, I found a book with a rather off-putting title, seemingly about politics, a subject in which—up until the assassination of John F. Kennedy—I had no interest.

I was eleven years old and in my sixth-grade classroom when the news of John F. Kennedy's assassination was first broadcast. Up to this point in time, I thought about evil as something that was personal, local even, not some sort of global juggernaut stalking whole societies. John Kennedy's assassination was the event that changed all that. Even though I was not able to fully comprehend it then, years later I was better able to articulate the raw, horrifying face of evil I had seen on that sunny November day in 1963. I didn't know then that Kennedy himself had already seen it and described it: *"For we are opposed, around the world, by a monolithic and ruthless conspiracy..."*

So, there I was, poking around in the shed with the disturbing events of that November heavy on my mind and heart, and there it was: *The Story of a Secret State* by Jan Karski. I picked it out of the box and opened it to read a page or two.

"On the night of August 23rd, 1939, I attended a particularly gay party. It was given by the son of the Portuguese Minister in Warsaw, Mr. Susa de Mende ..."

For some reason, I continued to read with inexplicable fascination. I realized I was holding my breath. I read on.

"On the night of September 1, around 5:00 a.m., while the soldiers of our Mounted Artillery Division tranquilly slept, the Luftwaffe roared through the short distance to Oswiecim undetected and, perched above our camp, proceeded to rain ablating shower of incendiaries on the entire region. At the same hour, hundreds of the powerful and modern German tanks crossed the frontier and hurled a tremendous barrage of shells into the flaming ruins.

"The extent of the death, destruction and disorganization this combined fire caused in three short hours was incredible."

My heart was pounding painfully in my chest, but there was no way I was going to put this book down. I'm sure I must have had dinner or something, but since I always had the habit (deplored by my grandmother) of taking my books to the table and reading while I ate, it's a certainty that I wouldn't remember it. I was no longer at The Farm because I was over there: in Europe, in Germany, and most of all, in Poland.

By the time I had finished Karski's book, I was certain that the only person I could ever marry would be a Pole.

The heroism and fortitude and sheer guts of those in the Polish resistance were extraordinary. My mind was dazzled. I admired courage, intelligence, and creativity more than anything else. I believe this inspired me to hold these qualities as conscious ideals.

A child's goals and perspectives in life are formed at crucial stages of imprinting. Perhaps this was one of those times when my mind was open and waiting for seeds to be planted, only to bloom many, many years later.

Perhaps this could have been the awakening of a certain awareness sleeping fitfully since the time of my birth. One thing is certain: the thread of events in Nazi Germany, both tragedy and hope, wove themselves through my life like a ribbon of darkness and light.

The nightmares began again. I dreamed of endless vistas of dead bodies in cratered landscapes. Planes flying ceaselessly overhead in smoking red skies. Soldiers, terror, and tears. Rivers of tears, where serpents writhed, flowed across the land. I had lost my balance internally and at the same time I had found the first firm footing of my life.

Now nothing interested me at all except to try to understand how so great and terrible an event as the Holocaust could happen on the face of the earth if there was a God in heaven. Indeed, it diverted my attention from the present evil that led to John Kennedy's murder, but somehow, I felt that if I could understand the Holocaust, any and all other evil would be comprehensible.

CHAPTER NINE

THE STANDOFF

The Farm gave me the best environment to ponder the nature of evil and how it came to exist. Yes, I had been taught that man sinned in Eden because Eve was tempted and passed the temptation along to Adam. But this simple story did not answer the question of so great an evil as the Holocaust. I needed to understand the problem of evil and its relation to God and man.

The most sacred dogma of my childhood affirmed that the Bible was the Word of God. I intended to read the Bible more carefully than ever before, in a systematic and studious way. Surely the issue of evil would be made clear.

I read the standard King James Version from start to finish. I noted considerable contradictions, but, in a standard way, I sought answers to these puzzles from the local theological community. Their answer: the Bible was not contradictory. I simply did not understand it properly.

I needed to gain a deeper understanding to resolve these conflicts. So I read books that explained the Bible, the history of the times, the customs, the people, the archaeology, and so forth. I limited my reading to books by Christian authors, reasoning that only Christians could write about Christianity, as only Christians could "understand" the Bible. After all, this was pretty much a doctrine of faith. But nothing was satisfactory. All the purported answers, when deeply considered, did not satisfy some deep essence that I could not quite articulate.

The way I understood it, from a notebook I kept later:

"*Suppose your innocent five-year-old is given a special treat. A playroom is prepared, containing all the delights of childhood. Every imaginable toy and activity is there. A table spread with every delicacy to please the eye and bring pleasure to the palate. But, for some sick reason, you decide to place a huge frosted cake in the center of the table and forbid the little one to even touch it, much less taste it. You point out that everything else is there for his pleasure and use. Now, also imagine you are a knowledgeable parent, one who understands that any child is likely to want the very thing he has been forbidden. But you issue your warnings and step out of the room.*

"*The child, wanting to be obedient, begins to play and eat as permitted. But wait! That nasty little kid from next door—the one who tortures cats and pulls wings off flies—comes over and you send him in with Little One. Immediately, Little Nasty tells Little One that the wonderful cake has got to be the ultimate yummy! And, furthermore, Nasty tells Little One that it doesn't make sense for Mom and Dad to have forbidden eating the cake, since it is so obviously a wonderful treat! Little One thinks about this for a bit and acknowledges that Mom and Dad are good to him and he can see no rationale for not taking a little taste. So, not knowing that Little Nasty is Nasty, he accepts the reasoning that surely Mom and Dad would not put something truly Deadly within his reach. So, being curious, innocent and Tricked, he takes a bite!*

"*IS THIS THE BIG ONE? Do Mom and Dad now come in and toss Little One out on his ear and take all his goodies away? Do they further toss him out WITH Little Nasty to continue his education in Nastiness?*

"*Is that what you would do?*

"*Where and how did the 'flaw,' the 'evil,' the 'fly in the ointment,' originate—the influence under which Little Nasty operated—and why does the 'Punishment' seem all out of proportion to the crime?*

"*If Little One is bad, will you punish all his little friends and his children as well? For millennia? And, if Little One was, in fact, perfect—that is, having an adult appreciation of his error—would he have done it? And, if Little One was sorely tempted by a situation YOU created, wouldn't you admit that there were mitigating circumstances, accept part of the blame, get rid of the cake and Little Nasty, and take better care of Little One?*"

In my pondering over the problem in this way, the Judeo-Christian concept of God and the nature of evil came off looking pretty puerile. It boiled down to the fact that, first, we are taught that God is All Powerful, Omniscient, Perfect and Loving. Second, we are told that man was created "in the image and likeness of God." But temptation arrives in the form of a "fallen" angel who, we must assume, was also created by this same "Perfect, Loving, All-Knowing God." The "perfect man," created in the image of God, succumbs to the trials of temptation offered by his fellow creation and "falls." Ever afterward, all of mankind suffers the repercussions of this event.

In my simple-minded way, I realized there was something seriously wrong with this concept. I tried to break it down to see if there might be some way I could excuse God. But the more I thought about it, the worse the problem became. If man is created in the image and likeness of God, he must, of necessity, possess the attributes of God. Well, we know what man is and, if he is subject to temptation as this story clearly states, then we must assume that God is also subject to temptation.

At the same time, if the fallen angel was also a created being, as it must have been, what was the model for its creation? Further, if God is All Powerful and Perfect, how could any creation of His, be it angel or man, possess attributes of evil of any kind unless the creator Himself possessed those attributes? That was a terrifying thought. An All-Powerful God with human whims or evil proclivities? Perish the thought!

Even the explanation that man was given free will to choose God, which was the answer I was given to this question, didn't satisfy me because in the implied image of God, man's free will would lead toward perfection and good in all cases.

If God were, in fact, an all-knowing creator, perfect in knowledge and foresight, He would have known the outcome of His act of creation. If that is the case, and He did it anyway, then we are merely playing pieces in a great cosmic game—a joke—with mankind as the punch line.

It amounts to this: if God is, in fact, the Loving Father of All, then many humans are better parents than He, for they would certainly know better than to place their children in a situation fraught with temptation, unprepared and unwarned. And, furthermore, had such a scenario unfolded, the loving parent would certainly not inflict punishment out of all proportion to the offense.

The Sunday school teachers tried to explain to me that "man was warned!" Well, that's all fine and good, but he was not warned against subterfuge and trickery. He was supposedly a perfect man, set down in a perfect creation, but it was not truly perfect because evil was allowed to exist in it. And that point really grabbed me. We never are informed why this evil happened to be there; it is as though it was part of the creation from the beginning. Nevertheless, this evil was able to trick the perfect man and woman, and, as a result, countless billions of human beings have suffered untold miseries—both rich and poor, strong and weak, old and young—year after miserable year for countless centuries.

Is that the best God can do in his role of Perfect Loving Father?

Now, you have to realize that I was pretty distressed by the fact that I was even questioning God. In the faith of my family, the role was "God said it, I believe it, and that settles it!" It was a closed, comfortable system with no ambiguities, and I could see that, in principle, the system was a good one: it taught people to be kind, honest, sacrificing of personal comfort for others, loyal, and so forth. Devotion to these values, even if actual practice of them was sometimes problematical, was a hallmark of the faith along with confidence in the "rightness" of our belief. But, as I struggled with this issue, it was becoming increasingly clear that nothing could be allowed to challenge the system.

This troubled me. Was it so fragile that it couldn't withstand questions and challenges? What was being hidden from me? Why was everyone so evasive when I started asking my questions?

The next problem concerned different versions of this belief system. As it happened, my aunt—the one who married my mother's brother—was Catholic. At some point in my early childhood, my other aunt—my mother's sister—had converted to Catholicism. This was considered to be a great blow to the family, steeped for generations in Protestant theology.

My mother constantly remarked on my aunts' Catholicism as though it were demon possession. I had been forbidden to play with Hetty, my circus friend, partly because she was Catholic. It was obvious that others in the family also held Catholicism to be some sort of major doctrinal error that could lead directly to damnation, though they were not as vocal about it as Mother was. At the same time, during all of my interactions with my cousins, I was repeatedly informed by them that Protestants were the damned ones because Catholicism was the one "true religion."

This produced some confusion because, as I have said, my aunt was always very kind to me, and even though I loved my mother and grandmother, I could see their treatment of my aunt, or, at the very least, their attitude toward her, was less than Christian. Her attitude toward them was far more Christian, even though she was the one who was supposed to be damned! All I could do was observe. And question.

I plunged into a frenzy of prayer intended to extirpate these questions from my mind. According to doctrine, the fact that one questions the

Bible is evidence of satanic influence—a mind that questioned God was a curse—and doubt was the wide road to hell.

I pleaded with God to show me the answer to this problem, but all was silence. I was left with my question. And it burned like a smoldering volcano.

I was carrying a pretty heavy burden. The conflict between my thinking and my faith led to some very serious cognitive and emotional difficulties.

Because of those questions raised in my mind at the age of eleven, I began systematically reading everything I could get my hands on that might provide a clue to the solution of the Great Mystery—mainly history. By now it has become literally thousands upon thousands of books. The closest conservative estimate I can make is somewhere around 10,000 volumes. And I pretty much remember everything I read, where I read it, and who wrote it. This has been a blessing because it has enabled me to make connections and draw inferences that would have otherwise been impossible.

If there were some historical evidence that man was to blame for all his own miseries, this would let God off the hook. And I was most definitely trying to find the way to do that. I realized pretty quickly that this was not going to be a simple path. One event depended on another; start at any point, go in any of hundreds of directions, and never run out of material. With the naiveté of the child, I thought I could just jump in and reinvent the wheel, solving problems that have occupied philosophers and theologians for millennia. What hubris!

I went through all the useful books in the school library rather quickly. We went to Tampa almost every other weekend to visit the grandparents so I managed to get to the big library there. The librarians finally got used to seeing me take 15 to 20 books out at a time, to return them promptly after two weeks and take another stack.

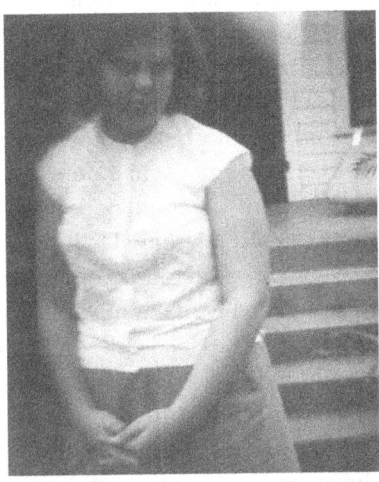

Me at age 13, in front of my grandparents' house in Tampa.

I went through the next few years of school in a constant daze. I can remember very little about junior high and high school because I constantly had my nose in a book. For me, the rest of the world basically didn't exist, except in the picture I was trying to put together in my mind from the pieces in all the books I was reading.

While I was learning about the world of history, I was also learning about Mother. When I think back about Mother's decision to move to The Farm, I realize part of our excitement was the hope that we could now have our mother to ourselves. My brother and I had very little relationship with her, and she was, essentially, unknown to us. We'd spent our time in the care of others. When we had been with our mother, she had been either working or out dancing. She was emotionally absent even when she was at home. Naturally, we blamed this on the constant presence of the stepfathers. Now, with no one to distract or worry or hurt her, she could be her "natural" self and we would be happy and loving all the time.

Before we moved to The Farm, I remember being allowed to watch Mother get ready to go out. She had beautiful clothes, silks and satins and taffeta evening gowns, and shoes in every style and color. She enjoyed quite an elegant social life before we moved to The Farm. So what seemed to be a delightful situation to us seemed dreary and boring to her. And Mother couldn't stand boredom.

In her role as a mother she was materialistic and controlling. Emotions were to be suppressed, repressed, or totally done away with. Emotion was weakness. Don't cry, don't feel, and don't talk about things that cannot be dealt with in a practical way.

Mother almost never spoke to us except to direct us to do something or to criticize all we had done. No matter what I did to please her, she found a flaw. She could not say: "You did a good job." Instead, she would say: "You did it wrong. Do it my way."

My clearest memories of my mother: endless days of the silent treatment. When I tried to find out what I had done wrong: "If you don't know, I'm not going to tell you!" And usually, I didn't know. So, the only thing I could suppose was that my very existence was a burden and that my being was repellent to her.

For Mother, anyone who did not submit to her manipulations was a threat, not only to her, but also to my brother and me. The answer to questions about my father: he had been a terrible alcoholic who refused to give up his drunken ways to keep his family. No mention of morphine addiction or the reasons behind it. His parents were evil because they condoned his behavior toward us and wanted to steal us from her, so they were also the enemy.

My aunt and uncle were enemies too. Well, actually, her brother was an enemy by default: he was married to my Catholic aunt, the chief enemy of the entire family. Yet Mother managed to avoid listing her Catholic sister as an enemy. That troubled me. The list of enemies to our safety and well-being grew with each passing year. The only real topic of conversation in our house, other than being told what to do or how we had not done it right, was a recapitulation of all the wrongs that had been done to Mother and all the wrongs being planned against Mother. Of course, the way she presented it, all these wrongs that had been done to her were the cause of our suffering too. The reason we didn't have anything, the reason we couldn't go anywhere or do things like other kids, was because of all the wrongs done to Mother. Everyone was wrong, and Mother was just the most misunderstood, selfless, and giving human being on the planet. The problem was, my observations did not support what was being told to me. This led to many conflicts with Mother because I had a mouth on me!

She told me how awful and manipulative all these other people were. They were all out to get her. My aunt, especially, had designs on my grandparents' property, so we must all band together to prevent her wicked Catholic hands from taking what was rightfully ours. Never mind that our cousins were legitimate heirs to the grandparents. It seems that Mother's goal, at this point, was to cut all of them out of any inheritance. And we were going to help her.

I can see now that she was simply doing all the things she accused others of doing, to justify her own negative actions against the family by dehumanizing and reviling them. But, of course, I could not see this then. For the most part, I truly believed that Mother was telling the truth. She would support her version of events with claims that our grandparents agreed. It never occurred to either of us to go and ask Grandpa or Grandma. We took it for granted they agreed, and that added weight to Mother's arguments. To my great regret, I supported her for years in her campaigns against enemies that existed only in her own mind.

It was on the occasions when I did not agree that major conflict between us developed. Every once in awhile I would see through her in a small way. And when I did, I was compelled to say so, because I had the idea that if I could heal these family rifts, Mother would be able to be happy.

Nice idea, yes? Did it work? Nope.

In fact, it led her to move me toward the margins of the family. The slander against me began with my brother, extended to my grandparents, and only in later years did I discover what a thorough and complete job she did of blackening my name in the most subtle and insidious ways imaginable.

Questioning Mother's views, decisions, and dictates was verboten.

My brother had a very quiet and methodical nature. Tom didn't seem to want or need to seek out other people to talk and exchange ideas. He also didn't seem to want or need affection and closeness as I did. As a result, he developed a different way of coping with Mother. He agreed with everything she said, performed as required of him, and then did as he pleased behind her back.

I wasn't able to do this. I had a high need to be myself openly and honestly, to do away with secrets. I wanted to be loved and accepted in a desperate way. Mother was not able to give love or acceptance of anything or anybody that was not strictly under her control. To get along, it was necessary to agree with her completely, to do exactly as she said.

I couldn't do exactly as she said in many instances because it contradicted my perception of what was right. I'm not talking about issues of parental authority, where a child needs rules to abide by because they have a valid basis in fact. I am talking about arbitrary rules that enforced isolation and restriction of a child based on a view of the world that was twisted and hurtful to others.

There was no discussing anything. She would simply exert her parental control to completely override anything I thought and said. The unfairness of it, the blind stupidity of it, would literally send me over the edge. The more upset I felt, the colder and calmer she became in the act of crushing the spirit of her own child. I was convinced that she hated me.

I was obviously the one with a problem because I was the one who was out of control! And, of course, I would get even more out of control and end up screaming at her that she was a cold, unloving mother and I hated her and I was going to do as I damn well wanted to whether she liked it or not.

And then came the strop.

THE STANDOFF

She had kept the razor strop that Ed had used on us. She raised the strop high, bringing it down again as I tried to deflect it with my hands or curl up to minimize the amount of exposed flesh. To this day I cannot remember a single clear instance of why I was being whipped, other than the fact that I disagreed with Mother. If being whipped was supposed to "teach" me something, it was singularly unsuccessful.

She complained to my brother. "There's something wrong with your sister ..." accompanied by praise that he at least remained her stalwart supporter.

Everything wasn't dark, though. We had some very good times sitting around the fire on cold winter nights, reading and reciting poetry, singing in the dark before going to sleep. I can still hear my mother singing some of her favorites from the '30s and '40s. My favorite was "Old Man River" and she did a bang-up job on it too. Mother was also a very good cook and she liked to be creative in the kitchen, so we had marvelous meals with exquisite desserts.

My job was the ironing for all of us, every week. And back then, everything had to be ironed. I had to use the old heavy irons that you heat on the fire and I can tell you that I got burned plenty of times. To this day, I hate ironing, but I'm darn good at it!

It was difficult to live in such a primitive old house and go to school with others who lived in modern dwellings with electric lights and flushing toilets. We had a two-mile bike ride to the bus stop and a fifteen-mile bus ride to school. I used the time to read and think.

After a few years had passed, the local electric company installed power lines within a mile and a half of the house. My grandfather contacted them about running the lines all the way up to the house so we could have lights, and they agreed if he would pay for the poles. He did, and we soon had electricity.

I now had a new venue of experience: music. I could listen to the radio and play records. There were stacks of old 78 rpm records in the shed with the old Victrola that didn't work. I hauled them out and Mother bought me a little record player at a thrift store. I became familiar with songs that most people my age have never heard. At night I stayed in touch with the real world by listening to WLS in Chicago on the radio until I fell asleep.

Mother stayed on her religious kick for a few years because, really, it was the only social life in town. But, as a divorcee, she was not quite acceptable in that small community, and she soon got tired of the sly looks and whispers and simply stopped going.

By this time, however, it didn't matter, because God and I were at a standoff.

I still kept my eye on windows. Aside from the war dreams, the all-consuming loneliness, and conflict with my mother, no more weird stuff happened and I was left in peace with my books.

As I read, the problem of evil seemed to grow larger. It was pretty evident that man was cut off from God. Yet the environment we lived in presented so much beauty that it was hard not to see God everywhere. How could I reconcile this beautiful, natural world, full of splendor and glory, with the presence of evil?

Design and purpose was everywhere apparent. For me, the very fact that a single atom existed was a matter of such wonder that I would be swept away in amazement. The vastness of the sky and wonder of stars, the wind and storms; lightning was fabulous to me. I observed birds and small creatures and tried to understand what Will inhabited them that compelled them to live and breathe and have being.

On clear nights during cool weather, I went outside to sit and gaze at the sky. The rarefied atmosphere of the winter sub-tropics, still and cold, gave such dimension to the pulsing and throbbing of the stars that it seemed as though each possessed fingers of light, dancing and teasing the velvet blackness of the earth.

I tried to imagine what answer would dispel the cosmic void that enveloped the planet as it spun ponderously toward its rendezvous with dawn—yearning in all its parts for eternal union with the life-giving light.

What if someone, some thing, were watching everyone, waiting, knowing that at some precise moment, all the lights would go out?

I would shake loose from the icy mirror of such thoughts and focus my eyes and mind on that amazing black expanse of nothingness dotted with billions of worlds for which no rational explanation existed.

What could possibly be outside of the space in which we exist? Where was God? How could I find Him? Was He aware of me, this pathetic, suffering speck of matter that dared to try to imagine Him? To question Him?

On the occasions when we went out to the lonely jetties of lime rock to fish, I'd stand on the shore and try to imagine the depths and vastness of the waters and all the life within.

But because of this question of evil, the pleasure of life was denied to me, except as an observer. I could not enter into it if I did not understand it. I needed to find God in a personal and definite way. I needed to know in all my cells that this will and purpose of existence included me. I wanted God to acknowledge me, to notice me, to love me, and to protect me from faces at the window.

And that always led me back to the problem of evil.

CHAPTER TEN

SHRINKS AND REBELS OR BEING FIFTEEN IS AN AWKWARD STATE

Rumors about aliens and flying saucers flooded the school the year I went into eighth grade. First there was a story about a man who lived up on Highway 50 near Weeki Wachee. John Reeves claimed he'd been taken up in a spaceship by aliens landing in the woods behind his house.[1] He built a model of the saucer right there on the side of the highway. It became a rite of passage for county kids to work up the nerve to go talk to Reeves. Of course everyone thought he was touched in the head.

Next, a rumor spread that aliens were going to make a mass landing and take away all children between the ages of 12 and 18. Everyone talked about it excitedly, making plans to be the first to get aboard, and laughing gaily at the prospect of freedom from parental restriction.

Could it be true? I clearly remember the day this "alien rapture" was supposed to occur. Sitting in my algebra class, one chair removed from the window behind me, I kept glancing backward through the window at the sky about every five minutes.

I felt relieved when the appointed hour passed with no sign of aliens. Everyone else was disappointed. But I started watching the sky out the window every night, trying to detect any strange lights moving in an odd way. Can't say I ever noted any, other than ordinary planes. Good! I didn't want to know anything about aliens.

Back in 2000, around the time of my high school class reunion, I talked to one of my companions from those days about this "UFO fever"

---

[1] For an account of his claims, see: http://ufoexperiences.blogspot.com/2007/03/john-reeves.html

that we had experienced as kids. She told me about an event that happened to her at about the same time. She had been riding in the car with her mother driving; they were taking one of her girlfriends home after a sleepover. Up ahead on the side of the road, there appeared to be two children waving at their car. As they approached, they also saw a bright light in the woods some distance away. Her mother asked in an upset way: "What are those little kids doing out at night on this road?" (It was a lonely, lime-rock road through the woods). She started to slow down, and my friend said she suddenly panicked and started crying and begging her mother not to stop. As she was telling me this part of the memory, she burst into tears and could not continue. I asked her: "Well, what happened?" She could only shake her head and say: "I don't know, I don't know. I just know that every time I think about it I get scared and start to cry." Then, she wouldn't talk about it anymore.

Very strange.

* * *

The only photo that exists of me at 14, with my little dog, Pixie, in front of my grandparents' house in Tampa.

I was fourteen years old. I began to feel acutely "displaced." I woke up at night on several occasions not knowing who I was or where I was. I got out of bed, so unfamiliar with the room that I bumped into things. A sensation of panic accompanied these bizarre episodes: I needed to find someone, but I didn't know whom. It was disorienting, to say the least. This happened when I woke from deep sleep, and the feeling only lasted for a short while. Did everyone experience similar disorientation when they woke up in the night?

I tried to ask Mother if this had ever happened to her.

She told me thinking about such things was silly and a waste of time.

"Don't let your wild imagination run away with you," she said. "Don't you have chores to do?"

I tried to talk to my brother, but he was preoccupied with girls and cars. He had no time for me.

I began to feel out of time and out of place at home and at school. One day I sat in science class with a book on medieval history hidden behind my textbook when suddenly a flying blackboard eraser bounced off my head.

"Laura," the teacher asked in a dry voice, "do you think that book is going to earn you an A in my class? Let's take a good long look at this girl," he told everyone. "A perfect example of the waste of a good mind."

I wasn't being deliberately bad. The class lagged so far behind what I already knew, and my mind raced far ahead of the others. The real questions of life waited to be solved, with so many clues to follow, and I felt I had no time to spend on the life cycle of a frog. I could not forget that at every moment, someone was in pain, some child had lost a parent, some husband was gazing upon the face of his wife for the last time.

All the history accumulating in my head seemed like the biography of the Devil. Humanity was powerless against cosmic catastrophes, military onslaughts, social injustice, personal and familial misfortunes, and a host of other assaults against existence too numerous to list. Death and destruction come to all, both rich and poor, free and slave, young and old, good and evil, with an arbitrariness and insouciance that, when contemplated even momentarily, sears the soul with terror. People have seen their fields and cattle laid waste by drought and disease, loved ones tormented and decimated by illness or human cruelty, a life's work reduced to nothing in an instant by uncontrollable events.

The rapacious movements of hungry tribes, invading and conquering and destroying in the darkness of prehistory; the bloodbaths of the crusades of Catholic Europe against "infidels"; the stalking "noonday terror" of the Inquisition, where martyrs quenched the flames with their blood; the raging holocaust of modern genocide; war, famine, pestilence: all produced an intolerable sense of indefensibility against the evil that clearly exists in our world.

As I contemplated the facts of history, I came face to face with a dreadful reality, forced to look at the evidence that human beings are in the iron grip of an existence with no real care or concern for pain and suffering. I could write until the end of the world, using oceans of ink and forests of paper, and never fully convey the Pain and Terror I felt at facing this fact of arbitrary evil. For me, it was personal. For me, it was related to the Face at the Window and the Hound of Hell at my heels.

I really needed an answer. Because if I didn't find it, I was sure that the Face would return, and the Hound would run me down and destroy me.

I began to have recurrent dreams of another life when pain had reached a summit of intensity: landscapes laid bare by violence, skies of destruction, bloated bodies floating in pools of blood, and serpents everywhere. And me, in the dream, in a small boat paddling for dear life to find a place of rest, an Ark of safety.

* * *

My brother had a job after school, doing yard work for an old man who lived up in Aripeka. This gentleman often drove my brother and his bicycle home after a hard day trimming trees or hauling brush. He was lonely and liked to visit a bit with us, and sometimes Mom would invite him to stay for dinner. He was so appreciative. He soon became aware that I was a reader. He had an extensive library of old and rare books and invited me to come to his house to read them, though I would not be allowed to take them out.

What a treasure trove!

Books lined every wall of the front room.

The old fellow's mother had been an early twentieth-century occultist, acquainted with many of the movers and shakers of the British Society for Psychical Research. She'd collected proceedings, research, analyses—everything related to the mysteries of the occult imaginable. Volumes of case histories of poltergeists, apparent hauntings, magic practices from around the world, Hawaiian Huna to Haitian Voodoo. Studies of mediums and old photographs of ectoplasm produced from their bodies. Cases of psychokinesis, telepathy, clairvoyance. And they weren't just stories, they were investigated, annotated cases with long analyses, giving insight and assessments of how such events could be explained in scientific terms.

In one large book on miracles of Catholic saints, the same rational analysis was applied. Christianity stood alone in declaring that, if anomalous events occurred outside approved Church doctrines, they were Satanic delusions and imitations.

I compared descriptions of "holy" miracles of Christianity to "demonic manifestations." I had to admit there was little difference except what a group of people decided to believe. I kept thinking I'd find smoking-gun evidence that Christianity was right, and all other views were wrong. But I never found it.

Even Jesus himself was accused, by officials of the standard religion of his time and place, of casting out demons by the power of Satan. His answer, that a "house divided against itself cannot stand," pretty well established the idea that a miracle is a miracle no matter what the context.

So, the "Satanic Delusion" theory of the casting out of demons didn't hold water. On the other hand, I noticed that Jesus did label other kinds of miracles as "lying wonders" of false prophets in the desert claiming to have dibs on Jesus. With a sense of shock, I saw that many ideas of Christianity could be attributed to "false prophets in the desert," since their main claim to fame was that "Jesus is here and nowhere else." I began to see that many of the religious teachings of my childhood were fraudulent.

I felt that I had reached the end of the line. None of the religions, none of the occult studies could answer my question about human suffering, the nature of evil, or why evil existed in the first place. This question was so compelling, and so generally ignored, that I simply could not comprehend how humanity could continue to exist without an explanation for this problem. No one could explain to me how a child who had essentially done nothing wrong could be terrorized by a Face at the Window and pursued by the Hound of Hell.

People around me believed firmly that evil would never enter their lives. Evil was something that happened to others. I couldn't grasp how easily they avoided the question, how they could say, "The Lord gives and the Lord takes away, Blessed be the name of the Lord." Didn't they see this impossible contradiction? God, as he was described and promoted, could not possibly be responsible for the things attributed to Him. Or worse, if he was responsible, then we had a serious problem, because it meant that God himself was capable of evil.

In Tom French's article about me in the *St. Petersburg Times* (Feb. 13, 2000),[2] he makes much of the idea that in the extremity of my despair over this problem I decided to climb a tree to face the power of a raging hurricane.

---

[2] http://www.sptimes.com/News/webspecials/exorcist/

"Think of it as a love story like no other. ... For Laura Knight, it started ... several decades ago, when she was a child growing up on the west coast of Florida. Even then, she lived on curiosity. That is where it really began: with Laura's monstrous, breathtaking, epic curiosity. From early on, she refused to believe in randomness. She was sure there were cosmic blueprints, an underlying grid of meaning, and she wanted in on it. She devoured libraries of books. She immersed herself in particle physics. She pored through Freud and Jung. She studied Greek to aid her reading of the New Testament. She longed to understand the matrix of the tides, the language of the periodic table, the seductive progression of Beethoven's Moonlight Sonata.

"But understanding these things was not enough. Laura hungered not just to comprehend, but to experience.

"So one day she climbed into the storm.

"It was 1966, and Hurricane Alma was spinning cartwheels in the Gulf of Mexico. At the time, Laura was 14 years old and living with her family on a farm in northern Pasco County, outside Hudson, less than half a mile from the coast. She had heard on the radio that Alma was generating mountainous waves, and she wanted to behold their ferocity for herself. She asked her mother to take her to the beach, but the answer was no.

"As Laura recalls it, she made her move late that afternoon. Her mother dozed off while working on a crossword puzzle—all these years later, Laura is still astonished that the woman actually labored over something so mundane in the middle of such a spectacular day—and Laura grabbed binoculars and slipped outside. She headed for her favorite tree, a towering camphor she had often climbed to gaze out into the gulf, ideal for what she had in mind now. Slowly she fought her way toward the tree, leaning her body against the wind and the rain, walking unsteadily through a sea of mud and debris. Around her she could smell the unmistakable ozone perfume—earthy, pungent, almost sulfurous—of Alma, making her presence known. [Not a bad description for how it feels to walk in a hurricane.]

The camphor tree I climbed in a hurricane is in view here between the cedars and behind the century plant.

"When Laura finally made it to the tree, she climbed until she reached her usual vantage point, a three-branch fork that formed a natural cradle near the top, some 30 feet off the ground. [It was probably more like 15 feet.] Wedging herself in, she took her place in the heart of the maelstrom. The camphor pitched violently; the wind whistled and cried; the rain pounded into her, pushing against her eyelids and into her mouth. Peering westward through the rain-splattered binoculars, she could just make out the black, seething expanse of the Gulf. [It was actually very dark gray.]

"Inside, Laura willed herself into stillness. When she had stepped out of the house, a part of her was afraid. But now she had ascended to a place above fear. As the hurricane rocked her in her cradle, engulfing her and the rest of the visible world, she was transported into a heightened state of both perfect calm and absolute exhilaration. She had become the eye of the storm, the consciousness inside the chaos. She was not afraid to die.

"In that moment, the questions of Laura's life—questions that would run through all the years stretching before her—announced themselves once and for all. Was it brave of her to venture out into the hurricane? Or was it foolish? Was it proof of something wonderful inside her, or an early sign of something not quite right?"

I'll spare the reader the part about "riding the storm in ecstasy." My object here is to clarify that the act Tom saw as the great symbol of my life process, was merely another in a constant series of interactions with the natural world that I sought in order to come to some understanding of God. It was probably a little foolhardy, but no more so than many acts of many other kids my age who had more guts than good sense.

"Was it ... an early sign of something not quite right," as Tom asks?

Well, that depends. From my perspective, people around me claimed to talk to God, to get answers from God, to be guided by God, and to be absolutely certain that God existed in a personally interactive way.

Many Christians claimed to hear God, Jesus, or the Holy Spirit, but I did not—at least not in any way I could accept as being provable and not imagination, corruption, or deception. I saw increasing proof that Christian teachings promulgated in the faith of my childhood were definitely not supported by external evidence. These religious beliefs seemed delusional to me.

The diagnostic manual of mental disorders consulted by psychiatrists, known in the trade as the DSM-III, defines delusion as *"false belief based on an incorrect inference about external reality."* A delusion is firmly sustained, despite *"incontrovertible proof to the contrary."* The belief that one interacts with spirits is defined as a *"delusion of being controlled, in which feelings, impulses, thoughts or actions are experienced as being not one's own, as being imposed by some external force."* Sounds like someone who's got religion. But religious context is excluded from this definition: *"This does not include the mere conviction that one is acting as an agent of God."* One has to wonder why "mental health" professionals believe it is acceptable to be deluded by religion, but that it is pathological in any other context.

I was coming to the idea that a delusion was being imposed on humanity, and I didn't like it.

I observed, I read, I searched. I was determined to make the connection so that I could hear God speak to me. I had been calling for years, and I needed to know I was heard. I needed an answer.

What I was really doing in that tree was calling out to God.

* * *

I was not happy to give up my faith or to think that all I'd been taught was a lie. And I was putting forth the effort to give this God every chance to give me a single clue.

Was the child crazy who saw that the emperor was naked?

This search had a profound effect on me. At first, I had straight A's, consistent scores in the top percentile on every test, awards for essays, and regular contributions to the school newspaper. I gradually became a withdrawn, angst-ridden rebel without a cause who refused to participate in class or turn in homework. I was failing in school. My teachers were concerned; the principal was concerned; my mother was advised I had a problem. At their conference they agreed I should be tested and interviewed by a psychiatrist to resolve the dilemma—this "waste of a good mind."

In the doctor's office in Tampa, I was sullen and uncommunicative. But in the testing room, they presented me with intriguing puzzles and tests. Well, of all things I do like, puzzles and tests are pretty much at the top of the list. Any kind of challenge of mind, skill, or speed of solution is fun for me. I never could understand "test anxiety," because I especially liked to take tests cold, without studying. I liked to compete against my own personal best, because I never even considered outdoing anyone else. I'd made up my mind to be uncooperative, but I couldn't resist such fun.

Next, we looked at inkblots. Well, heck, that's fun too! I liked seeing images in clouds, too, and this was just a variation on that pastime. I was having a great time. This was certainly more fun than sitting in a boring classroom hearing the teacher endlessly droning on about topics that meant nothing in the great scheme of the universe.

I took an MMPI, a personality inventory, then several versions of IQ tests, word associations, you name it. I worked for about eight hours at a time, three days in a row. At the end, I had a long interview with the psychiatrist (he's famous now, but back then, he was just getting started). We got along just fine, shared philosophical views, bounced literary allusions off one another. This turned out to be the first intelligent conversation I'd ever had. Finally, he set up a meeting with my mother, the school counselor, and me.

The counselor arrived looking smug. He had really shiny, slicked-back hair and a squatty face like an Addams Family grandpa. I'm sure he was expecting a list of corrective actions and remedial tutoring to implement, so he was practically wringing his hands in anticipation. It was the first year we even had a school counselor, and he was anxious to prove that his position was extremely important. For months he'd sidled up to students, suggesting if they had "any problems at all, come see me! I'm always available!" Most kids didn't know what to make of the idea of a school counselor. We unanimously thought he was creepy. But state law mandated that we have one, and in a small school in a small town, I don't think we had too many applicants.

Mother was, of course, embarrassed to be in this position. I'm sure she thought this reflected badly on her mothering. Maybe her own lifestyle contributed to The Problem, so there was surely some guilt. I can't say if she felt guilty because she truly felt bad, or if she felt guilty because she'd been "caught."

From my point of view, the whole human race was screwed, and nothing mattered anymore. On the other hand, I was a little nervous that this doctor, who I liked very much, had penetrated my shell and discovered the tracks of the Face at the Window, and that he would betray me. He was, after all, a member of the "adult world."

The shrink looked at the counselor, my mother, and then me. He sighed and opened the folder on his desk, and began to list all the tests and resulting scores, assessments, and so on. The numbers were nonsense to me, but I did notice the counselor's puzzled look. Finally, at the end of this recitation, the doctor closed the folder. "Mrs. Knight, your daughter's only real problem is that she's smarter than her teachers, and probably smarter than all of us here in this room."

Mother looked confused. The counselor was dumbfounded. I felt a little sorry for him.

The unfortunate result of this little episode was to confirm my idea that going to school was a complete waste of time. It also didn't do much to improve my opinion of teachers who were doing their best, and were, indeed, perfectly adequate for the majority of students. And finally, it put the last brick in the wall between me and other kids my own age. It drove home the point that I was too different to fit in. Being a "brain" did not make me feel special. It made me feel awful. And the fallout was not long in coming.

One day soon after, my brother's friends were discussing King Arthur's knights, about which they knew nothing. I interjected a comment, just trying to be helpful, and my brother snapped at me, "Go away. Nobody likes a walking encyclopedia."

It was true. Nobody did. Except on test days when the seats near me in class became very popular.

So began the long years of alternating between acting dumb and trying to be normal, or being a rebellious and sarcastic know-it-all.

Of course, the idea that I was "smarter" made me even less tolerant of the controls my mother attempted to impose on me. The conflict between us intensified. One day, when she took out the strop, I took it away from her.

"If you ever try to use that on me again," I told her, "I will use it on you."

Fortunately, at about this time, I was given a piano.

I'd taken lessons at boarding school. I detested practicing, but rapidly picked up enough basics so that now, with a piano and no worries about disturbing any neighbors, I could play all I wanted. A teacher came once a week and I made rapid progress. She was an elderly lady, very pleased to have an easy student. After she died, I played on alone. I didn't like drills and technical exercises, so I worked my way through complicated pieces a little at a time, often having to make up my own fingering because my fingers were short.

I spent as much time as possible in a fantasy world of marvels. As I played my piano, I dreamed of The One who would be passing by and hear the distant strains of music. He'd pause and listen with enchantment, compelled to seek out the source of such magic. He'd know me instantly as The One he was looking for. Together we could solve the problems of God and the universe, and most especially why very bad things happen to innocent people, including a little girl who saw a Face at the Window and was kidnapped, and couldn't remember that whole part of her life.

Then, I would go to the mirror and come back to reality. There was my plain face, my shapeless and lumpy fifteen-year-old body, and the extreme unlikelihood there was any handsome prince out there waiting to rescue that damsel.

I wrote in my notebook: Being fifteen is an awkward state; too old for toys, too young to date …

CHAPTER ELEVEN

GRAVEYARDS, PSYCHOPATHS, PSYCHICS, AND MEETINGS ON THE BRIDGE

My mother, always mindful of beauty and appearances, decided to do something about my weight.

She believed that how I looked reflected on her, and she disliked being accompanied everywhere by a chubby child. So she told the pediatrician to prescribe a diet for me. Well, he did better than that: he prescribed diet pills! They were the very latest; everyone raved about how well they worked. They eliminated my appetite and increased my energy. But I had no idea of their real cost. The pills introduced me to a way of life that would ultimately nearly destroy me.

My performance as a "worker" for my mother, who had decided that keeping house was completely my job, definitely improved. Mother was funny about this. She kept all her drawers absolutely immaculate, with everything perfectly folded and her underwear in plastic bags. But her habits of order were nonexistent. She never made her bed; she tossed used tissues on the floor. She never put anything away except her underclothing. I spent most of my time following along behind her picking up the clutter she generated.

Well, if a parent is working, perhaps it's reasonable for the child to keep house. That would be fair if the child had an enjoyable social life, but this was not permitted. Mother actively discouraged my friends and activities. I needed to be available to her to carry out the next order she might issue.

My brother was allowed to go where he wanted and do as he pleased with his friends, but I had housekeeping chores and yard work to keep up. What made things really bad was that I never felt well. I was always exhausted and repeatedly afflicted with ear infections and viral-type illnesses.

As I said, Mother had given up going to church and now she began dating again. As a business school graduate, she was able to start a bookkeeping and tax preparation service. Years later, I learned that most of her dates were married clients of her service. To my great humiliation, she had an affair with the grandfather of one of my classmates, a girl who was universally liked by everyone, including me.

When the man left his wife of many years, upsetting his extended family, and my mother was named as correspondent, the humiliation I suffered in school from being the daughter of the "other woman" was crushing.

Every day, I needed to walk or ride my bicycle two miles to the bus stop and back, and when I came home I started on the housework. When I was finished, I was expected to stay home, miles away from anything or anybody, until Mother came back, even on Friday and Saturday nights, when most kids my age were allowed to go to the movies or skating, or even to visit each other's homes. Sometimes she didn't come home until very late, so I was alone out in the middle of nowhere, with no neighbors, surrounded by the eerie night sounds of the Florida backwoods.

Finally, I rebelled. My close friend Dana was responsible for her four brothers and sisters. She was even expected to do all the cooking for her family. Together, we devised ways to sneak out of the house at night and ride around with our friends until two or three in the morning. Our brothers, Tom and Jerry, were both the same age and hung out together. They shared an interest in souped-up jalopies, so we often persuaded them to take us out when they didn't have dates. Though they were obliged to complain loudly to save face with other buddies, they did take pity on us occasionally and take us to the drive-in with them.

In rural Florida in the mid-to-late 1960s, options for getting in trouble were pretty limited. We could go out to the waterfront at night and snatch mullet; build a fire and cook the fish; drink beer that someone had "appropriated" from the family refrigerator; and maybe drive madly through the orange groves with the lights of the car turned off, seeing how many oranges we could pull from the tree limbs without slowing down and getting completely stuck in the sand. There were lime-rock pits to swim in at night, and a friend of a friend was a band singer at a roadhouse, so we often went there to listen to country-and-western music.

One night we had the idea we ought to have a séance at a graveyard. Since I was the "occult specialist," I was elected to be the one who knew what to do. I didn't, but I wasn't going to say so.

We all piled into two or three jalopies and headed down the road to the Tarpon Springs cemetery.

It was a good size, with many old graves and big marble monuments glowing eerily in the moonlight. Someone brought a bottle of whiskey and we decided that it would be appropriate to have a few drinks before engaging in our project of calling up the dead. We found a nice marble slab over some poor soul's last resting place, sat down, and passed the bottle around. For kids accustomed to nothing stronger than a can of beer, it was a fast buzz.

After we finished the bottle, we gathered around the grave in a circle, held hands, and began to concentrate. I thought I ought to say a few appropriate words, and I started with something really lame like "Oh spirit come forth and speak ..." or similar nonsense.

At that very moment, horrible moans and clanking sounds issued from some bushes behind the large statue at the head of the grave. We all froze. My heart jumped into my throat, the hair stood up on my head, my skin practically crawled off my body, and everyone bumped into each other in the dark trying to get away. It was every man for himself.

We were off and running, hollering and yelling at each other, "Come on! Run!" and other appropriate words that I will pass over in silence. Down the graveyard lane we flew as though the very fiends of hell were pursuing, to get to the cars and get the heck out of there!

As it happened, some of the graves had little "fences" around them consisting of short metal posts with chains looped from pole to pole. At the last instant, in the dim moonlight, I tried to make the leap but didn't quite gauge the height correctly in the darkness. The chains caught me right below the knees and I went down like a rocket-propelled stone. Fortunately, my face hit the dirt and not the marble, and I had a mouthful of grass and other nastiness rather than a broken nose and a mouth emptied of teeth. I was too full of adrenaline to let a little thing like possibly smashing every bone in my face stop me. I scrambled back to my feet and heard peals of laughter behind me. The laughter sounded awfully familiar, so I paused to listen. Panic was replaced by a slow burn of mortification.

Sure enough, our brothers, Tom and Jerry, were half running, half staggering with hilarity behind us, gasping out between paroxysms of roaring guffaws, holding on to each other to keep from falling to the ground: "Stop! Stop! It's only us!"

Me at 16 or 17.

I was going to get them.

Dana's brother Jerry collapsed on a grave slab, laughing so hard he could barely hold up a tow chain they had snuck out of the car while the rest of us were drinking whiskey and talking about ghosts. They'd slipped behind the bush while everyone else concentrated on our occult endeavors. We'd all been had.

I never forgot how easy it was to produce an effect when people are in a suggestive and expectant state, and to make them believe whatever you wanted them to believe. What's more, I realized how easy it would be to control people and cause them to do things they would not do under any other circumstances. I also realized that fear was an absence of knowledge, and when you gave into it, and acted without thinking, you very often ended up getting hurt.

If nothing else, I was good at getting the essence of a situation and transforming it into a lesson.

I was about to experience one of the most devastating experiences of my life.

* * *

During the several years of journalistic investigation by Tom French for his article about me and my life and work, I was interviewed dozens of times, and very often, the same questions were being asked over and over again. I didn't realize it then, but this was standard journalistic "truth testing." The journalist will ask the same questions in different ways at different times in order to ensure that the interviewee is telling the truth.

My thoughts about allowing my life and experiences to be made public were rather mixed. On the one hand, I valued my privacy highly (I still do). On the other, I realized that there were many other people who had experienced similar things, and who had been similarly marginalized. The issue became: was I willing to speak publicly for the sake of others? With an enormous sensation of dread, I agreed finally to do if it would help others. I could see no other value to my life at that point in time.

The reader who has also read the Times article knows how differently it all turned out from the way it began. That, of course, led to its own set of problems. It was one thing to be just a housewife with unusual interests and hobbies; it became an altogether different thing when I married a career scientist with a reputation to consider.

At this point, there was an item that Tom French investigated that he decided not to write about for several reasons, not the least of which was simply the space he was allotted in which to tell the story.

However, once his article was published—and possibly even in reaction to it—and as I was initially writing this more in-depth account to balance what Tom could not include, the omitted item came back to haunt both of us. Initially, it was used as an attempt to blackmail me (and by extension, my husband) by individuals who will appear later in this story.

In this book, the name "Frank" is given to one of the main players. The reader can, of course, easily discover that individual's real name in the St. Pete Times article. It was Frank—in partnership with a man named Vincent Bridges and his associate, Jay Weidner—who was ultimately responsible for the attempt at blackmail, coercion, and extortion. Thus, to completely remove this horrifying episode of my life from the hands of those who would try to use it to coerce or control me, it is being set out here in detail.

Some may think that Tom French should have included the incident and subsequent fallout because the fact that women are sexually assaulted, or taken in by psychopaths, with alarming regularity gets far too little attention as it is. But, as noted, his decision was based on the amount of space he had to tell a particular story that interested him, and considering that, his choice to omit it was correct.

When Tom interviewed me, I did tell him everything, even though I was very reluctant to talk about something so distressing. As every other woman who has ever been through a similar experience will agree, it was so unpleasant that I have spent the rest of my life trying to forget it. After consulting with the attorney who acted for me at the time, Tom agreed with us that it ought to just be left in the past.

In the end, that series of events from the past that I am about to recount was rather similar to what Frank later attempted to do: coerce,

The only photo I have of myself taken while I was in Tallahassee. It is cut out of a group photo of classmates.

extort, blackmail and control. As one reader noted: "Anyone who would attempt to blackmail you with this incident falls into the same category as the person who committed the initial assault. Such people view others as prey. They assess all those that they wish to prey upon as vulnerable and methodically proceed to search for a weak point and then attack." And sometimes they take years to do it, as is proven in the case of Frank. But some people are covert aggressors, as Frank was and is. They just manipulate and agitate behind the scenes, passing confidential information to full-blown pathologicals like Vincent Bridges and Jay Weidner to utilize on their behalf. Or, the pathologicals worm the information out of weak and wounded people like Frank; it's hard to tell without being able to get inside their heads.

Anyway, on with the story:

As I noted, my mother was a bookkeeper who had contracted with several local businesses to do their books. One of these businesses was owned by a man who was also something of a local politician. He ran for a state office and was elected, so spent much of his time in Tallahassee, the state capital. Mother ran his business for him. He was sort of like a local bigwig who had a home in the county and an apartment in Tallahassee. When he was in residence here, he would come to the house and discuss the business with Mother, drop off and pick up the accounting and checks and deposits, and so forth.

During this time, I was spending many hours a day practicing the piano. I would practice in one room while they would spread out papers on the table in the other room. One day, Mother announced that this man had expressed an interest in me and wanted to send me to school in Tallahassee where he could oversee my advancement. She thought this was wonderful and a great opportunity.

It was agreed that this plan would be put into action, but I had to wait until my eighteenth birthday. At that point, the plan was that I would go to Tallahassee and finish high school there in an accelerated class, and then be enrolled at the university. So, in January I went.

An apartment had been reserved for me in the same building this man lived in when he was there doing his legislative duties, whatever they were. Everything had been arranged. So, I went to school, met new people, and things were fine for a few months—through April. The apartment building had a nice pool, and I enjoyed studying by it ... or, for me, at least reading. Dana came to stay with me because I was lonely and her mother also knew this man and thought this would be fine for her as well.

One night he came to our apartment and asked me to come down so he could talk to me privately, since he had something very special to tell me and it was a surprise. So, in an hour, when I was done with my homework, I walked down the outside walkway and knocked on the door. He answered wearing a robe and smoking a cigar and with a glass of liquor in his hand.

To make a long story short, it became clear that the man expected "payment" for his help. I was so dumb that I actually thought that he was just being a nice guy with a fatherly interest in me. But that wasn't the case.

When I said no, he got rough. When he got rough, I fought back. When I fought back, he became enraged and started choking me. Since we happened to be standing in the kitchen, and I was being pressed back against the counter and was starting to lose consciousness, I threw my hands back to grab the counter to keep from falling. When I did, my hand landed on a heavy object with a handle. I grabbed it and hit him with it. He loosened his hold momentarily, but then started squeezing again and I hit him again, only harder this time since I had been able to get a breath. I hit him again in the head, and it was sort of a nightmare where he was totally enraged and I was totally determined to hit him until he let go of me. The reader might want to remember the incident with my little dog and my stepfather. If the guy killed me, I wasn't going to go down without a fight.

At this point, he was bleeding on me, still refusing to let go, so I hit him again. I think I must have landed about four or five good ones before he let go to try to protect his head from another, and when I realized he was no longer restraining me, I ran like hell. I was sure that he was after me, and I made it to my apartment, banging wildly on the door for Dana to let me in. She did and was utterly horrified. We were both just hysterical.

Dana was frantically trying to get all the blood off of me to see where I was hurt, and I was trying to explain that it wasn't my blood. It would be almost impossible to try and describe my state of mind. I was crying, shaking, terrified of further assault, completely stunned by such betrayal, and horrified at my own response, even though I knew I had been as close to being murdered as anybody ever comes and survives. I wanted nothing so much as to get this horrible blood off of me and make the whole nightmare disappear. Neither of us knew what to do. Dana was certain that he was going to appear at the door any second and try to force his way in, and the only thing we could think of to do was to keep him out until we could escape. Dana was insisting that I take my bloodied clothes off and take a shower while she guarded the door. She was going to faint if she had to look at the blood any longer.

While I was in the shower, still shaking with the thought that the man could force his way into the apartment, Dana came to the door and announced in hysterical tones that police cars and an ambulance were in the parking lot outside. Apparently, the man had crawled (walked? He was still standing when I ran away) to the balcony and called, and someone heard him and called the police. I was dressed and shaking violently when the knock came at the door. He had made a statement to the emergency crew that I had attacked him for no reason after coming on to him sexually!

I went with the policemen to the station and told the whole story right there and then. They were satisfied but told me not to go anywhere for a while until they investigated further.

And, seemingly the incident was closed. But, three days later, I was called out of my English class to find a message that the police department wished to ask her a few more questions. So, after school, I took the bus to the police headquarters. When I walked in, expecting to answer questions, handcuffs were immediately placed on me and I was arrested for "Assault with a Deadly Weapon with Intent to Commit Murder."

And I was taken and locked in a cell.

There is no way to describe such a transition. None. If a person is of a nature that they deliberately break laws, there is some idea in their mind that this could be a result. But, for a person who has, essentially, done nothing wrong but be stupid and naive, someone who has been betrayed by someone she trusted, who has been viciously attacked, and then, instead of anyone realizing that I was the victim, I was put in jail on the word of a psychopath and charged with trying to murder him! All women who have suffered this way understand that such an event is in a class by itself, especially when the realization comes that Grandfather cannot fix it, Mother cannot fix it, no one can fix it.

A week later I was taken, in handcuffs, to court and stood before a judge who read the formal charges. I was just eighteen years old, and I had to walk down a public street, between two policemen, in chains.

The judge asked me if I had legal counsel. I started to cry and said no. He started the process of assigning a public defender, and a man sitting in the row of attorneys jumped to his feet, came forward, and said: "Yes she does, your honor. I am offering my services." He then asked me if I would accept him as my attorney and I said yes. So that was settled. I had an attorney. His name was Brian T. Hayes. He was assisted by a really neat and funny private investigator, Joseph Aloi, and both of them were knights in shining armor as far as I was concerned.

What these two (attorney and PI) discovered about my "benefactor" was shocking. It seems that I had been the prey of a very sharp operator who had been trying to gradually draw me into a very ugly operation of prostitution, pornography, and extortion aimed at government officials. My instinctive refusal to be used had saved me, though it had also plunged me into a somewhat serious problem, as it has repeatedly in my life. The Powers of Darkness don't like it when you resist their attempts to control you or draw you into their plans. It is the same now as it has ever been.

All of the evidence of this little "business" that my benefactor had going on was discovered by Brian and Joe, who had the presence of mind to view a few of the movies discovered hidden in a bottom drawer of the benefactor's apartment while the guy was still in the hospital desperately trying to lie his way out of the mess that was coming to light. He even tried to get the charges dropped by changing his initial claim that I had assaulted him for no reason; he was desperate to avoid scrutiny. But it was no go.

Once the state decides to prosecute, it doesn't matter if someone who formerly claimed to be a victim has now changed his mind. The state is a juggernaut, and the trial did take place.

Well, the bloodbath in the courtroom was actually worse than the one at the time of the incident in some ways. His attorney, in concert with the prosecutor, worked very hard to keep the topic of his little "side business" out of the trial. He had a secret camera set up in an A/C vent and he apparently had a string of "girls" he used to make movies. These movies would then be used to extort money and favors, and probably even for a special brand of "lobbying." In fact, in retrospect, it almost seems as though there was agreement that the state would put on a very weak prosecution; the defense had plenty of evidence of his perfidy without going into the tapes and hidden cameras, and the only reason I can see for this is that some of those tapes must have included highly compromising information about high-level officials. The guy, like all true psychopaths, lied himself black in the face, even when confronted with hard evidence of his intention, his actions, his perfidy—in his own writing—even if it appeared to me that he wasn't very enthusiastic about his lies. He obviously had so much to hide that he just put on a show of testifying and actually allowed himself to be led into admission of unsavory intentions. The end result was a resounding return of the verdict of "Not Guilty by Reason of Self Defense."

* * *

I went to live with my grandparents; I no longer trusted my mother, and neither did they. Repeatedly, her choices in regard to my welfare had been disastrous.

Naturally, since I was working for a photo studio, I had a portrait made. This is one that I "colored".

My grandfather had retired and was declining rapidly. I could finish school and be there to drive them to do their errands and help my grandmother with the house. Both my grandparents doted on me. They gave me practically anything I wanted or needed, and my grandmother was always cooking things that she knew I especially liked. In Tampa, I was also closer to the doctor who prescribed the diet pills and I went to him for another prescription. My grandmother's house was pretty spotless as a result.

GRAVEYARDS, PSYCHOPATHS, PSYCHICS, AND MEETINGS ON THE BRIDGE

I did spend some time with my mother and, while there, did some babysitting for a local artist. In addition to her painting—which didn't bring in much money—she had a sideline coloring portraits for a well-known photography studio in Tampa. It looked like fun and she taught me to use the transparent oil colors to transform sepia photographs into color portraits. In just a few days I mastered the technique. She was so proud of me that she sent samples to the studio and the studio art director called to ask if I would be interested in doing this for money. Well, it was fun and easy and it sounded good to me, so I said yes and there I was, with my first "real job." At eighteen years old, in 1970, I was making $20 an hour.

I was rich!

A few blocks down the street from the photo lab, a big sign advertised a gypsy palm and card reader. Now that I had money to spend on whatever I liked, I decided that it was time to do some in-the-field research.

I had read enough literature about various fraudulent mediums of the past, and how they did "cold readings," to know that clients usually give information away by their responses, facial expressions, or body language. Even where no fraud could be detected, some other element of deceit might be involved. Now I could test it myself. At the same time, although many psychics were playing on the gullibility of hurt or lonely people, I did think real talent existed somewhere. I wanted to find out who had it. But my search for true psychic ability all over central Florida for the next few years had abysmal results.

I deliberately misled the psychics to see how far they'd go. If they suggested a jealous blonde or dark stranger in my life, I'd nod vigorously. They built on every response I gave until, in the end, they were pronouncing advice on a situation that bore no resemblance to my life at all. Of course, in nearly every instance, my "problems" were declared to be a curse put on me by someone jealous. For a few hundred bucks in cash, small bills please, wrapped in newspaper, I could be freed of this dire situation. Naturally, failure to remove this curse would result in even more dreadful consequences.

I never let on what I was doing because I most definitely did not want the word to get around. I was utterly shameless in this activity. But I kept thinking that eventually I would find someone who was truly psychic.

* * *

People my age were getting married and starting families. My brother joined the Navy and married soon after, and I found myself drifting alone again. No one encouraged me to think of college. Having a job and taking care of my grandparents seemed to be the limit of my horizons. Everything was fine on the outside, but something was stirring inside.

I compared the lives of my former schoolmates and felt overcome with emptiness and sadness. I wanted a husband and family, too. I yearned to be like everyone else, simply to be normal. But I could relate to no one at a deep level, much less form a relationship that might lead to marriage. Heck, what am I saying? I had never yet met anyone in my milieu to have a real conversation with unless I dumbed myself down. What in the world was wrong with me?

In late 1970, my grandmother was diagnosed with breast cancer. A radical mastectomy was performed. This was, in the plainest of terms, a butcher job. The surgical wound extended from about halfway up the inside of her upper arm, all the way to her navel. They had taken everything, including most of the muscle tissue of the upper inside arm, and everything on the chest right down to the bones. She suffered terribly and it was months before she was healed. She was never able to wear a prosthesis because the sensitivity of her scar tissue remained for the rest of her life.

My grandmother shortly before her cancer diagnosis. Always cooking or working with her plants.

I couldn't understand the mechanics of this issue of cancer. Why was it that the most loving and giving of people were stricken?

In October of 1970, a terrible thing happened in New Port Richey, the town where I attended school, and it cut very close to home. The brother of one of my classmates was murdered by some guy who picked him up hitchhiking. The murderer had apparently just left a local restaurant, Dorn's Hideaway (where my mother used to go with her friends), and where he had murdered four people, including the owners of the restaurant, one of the waitresses, and her husband.[3]

Richard's death, and the fact that mass murder had come to the quiet small town, was shocking in the extreme to all of us. Many of the kids I grew up with had been quite accustomed to hitching rides because, generally, someone you knew stopped to pick you up. But it was clearly no longer safe to do so—to assume that people were friendly and, for God's sake, NOT a mass murderer.

I drove aimlessly at night that winter. I turned on the car heater and drove with the windows down and the cold air hitting my face, not knowing where to go or what to do. This silly habit resulted in an almost deadly case of pneumonia. I was unconscious for almost a week and woke up considerably reduced in weight, which was okay by me!

I drove up to Aripeka and sat on the bridge and stared at the water flowing underneath, and then I drove home again.

There was another person who was there regularly, apparently doing the same thing. He had a huge, droopy mustache and was smoking a pipe and sitting on the bridge rail. Eventually, we struck up a conversation. What a surprise! He was well read and interesting to talk to. And I was starved to talk to someone about my real interests, shoved to the background in all my relationships.

His name was Tom. We became good friends, played tennis once a week, and he never seemed inclined to cross the line of brotherly relations. I remarked one day that I wished that ten-speed bicycles had been made when I was a child (I thought of the serviceable second-hand one I'd had to ride to the bus stop all those years living at The Farm). For my twenty-first birthday he gave me a white one. No one had ever given me such a gift without expecting something in return, so it was quite a puzzle to encounter a person who was simply interested in me because I was me. We discussed philosophy, religion, politics, science, history, and all the subjects that were loaded into my mind, just waiting for discussion and comparison.

I also kept in touch with my friend Dana and the old crowd from the cemetery-haunting days. But most of them were drifting away—moving to distant places. After Richard's murder, nothing was the same.

---

[3] You can read more about it here: florida-issues.blogspot.com/2008_01_01_archive.html

One night I was driving home from a visit with Tom very late along a back road with my usual excessive speed. A car approached me flashing its lights. I had no idea this was a warning of trouble on the road ahead. I passed a wide turn, traveling now at about eighty miles an hour. Directly ahead was a vehicle stalled right in the road. There were deep ditches on both sides, and coming toward me in the other lane was a big truck. I had absolutely no options. I would crash going into the ditch, I would crash hitting the stalled car and kill the people standing there, or I could move into the oncoming lane and hit the oncoming truck. No matter what, I was going to die.

I felt something shift inside me with the realization of what was coming. I think I said "Oh shit!" and found myself past the stalled car ... driving in the correct lane, and the oncoming truck had disappeared even from the rearview mirror.

That put an end to fast driving, but I have never figured out what happened there. One thing we can observe is that it is the intent and not the words of the prayer that count!

Tom was also a science fiction fan. There were several authors whose stories he admired greatly, among them a certain Keith Laumer. One day, he excitedly announced to me that he had discovered not only that this esteemed person lived in Florida, but also that he lived near The Farm in the wilds of Weeki Wachee. Further, Tom had driven over to visit him and had been invited back; did I want to come?

I never really cared to read science fiction, but I agreed to go because it seemed like a sort of holiday outing, and I was curious to meet a real writer.

This meeting signified the opening of the door to a series of profound, life-changing events. And twenty years later, another meeting with Keith—though he would then be on "the other side"—opened the door to the most profound experience of all.

But at the moment, Keith Laumer was my introduction to a real Dr. Jekyll and Mr. Hyde.

Clowning around with Dana in the sporting goods department.

CHAPTER TWELVE

DR. JEKYLL AND MR. HYDE

Keith Laumer had retired from the diplomatic corps to write, and had achieved some success and a reputation as a prolific science fiction novelist. Keith was pleased to have sold movie rights to a book adapted for the screen with a starring role for Michael Caine (*The Peeper*, based on the book *Deadfall*). But he had recently suffered a stroke that paralyzed the left side of his body. He was a tall man, emaciated by ill health. His body, though gaunt, appeared normal, but his left arm and leg were terribly still.

Tom was Keith's great fan, but I tried to avoid notice on our first visit. I didn't want to admit that I had never read any science fiction, so I pretty much kept my mouth shut. Keith was a real raconteur and was obviously having a good time regaling us with his adventures in the diplomatic service in Burma. Keith was brilliant and charming or sarcastic and vulgar by turns. He seemed hell-bent on destroying himself. More than anything, he seemed starved for companionship.

At last he turned his attention to me. "Such a quiet mouse," he said.

"I've never been anywhere," I blurted. "And I haven't read any science fiction."

I rather expected a sarcastic or derogatory comment, but Keith turned on the charm.

"Honesty is a virtue," he declared. "And such an abysmal lack is certainly one that can and must be rectified immediately. Follow me!"

He summoned us to a large pantry off his kitchen toward a wall of shelves containing extra copies of all his books. I was impressed. Selecting a half-dozen or so, he piled them into my hands. We returned to our places by the fire. Tom asked when Mr. Laumer would write his next book. After such a charming and pleasant reaction, when I had expected censure over the fact that I was not a fan, I was completely taken aback by the instant shift in his mood. He literally erupted into rancorous violence and malevolent self-deprecation.

"There will be no more books! How can a cripple write?" His face got red; blood vessels bulged on his neck; the paralyzed arm and leg jerked spasmodically as he visibly swelled in rage. Flecks of foam flew from his mouth as he denounced every member of his family, starting with his brother. "He defaced my house installing hand-rails for a CRIPPLE! And my mother! She dared to suggest that I might benefit from a long-term rehabilitation center for CRIPPLES! They have all abandoned me because I am now the most disgusting of all creatures: a CRIPPLE! More than that, to add insult to injury, my vile bitch of an ex-wife married a CRIPPLE, after abandoning me, the most excellent specimen of manly vigor on the planet, and now I am reduced to this!"

The language he used to vilify these people (and more I can't even remember) was relentlessly malevolent and sufficiently rousing to peel the chrome off a car bumper. I had never witnessed anything like it in my life. It sure gave new meaning to the term "conniption," which I had never really understood before.

Then Keith turned on a dime. The raging fit stopped in an instant, and he gazed down at his good hand lying still beside him. I think I was even more stunned to see a tear trickle down his cheek than by the vehemence of his bitterness and self-loathing.

He lamented quietly and mournfully that he was no longer a man.

But the drama was not over. Keith reached between the sofa cushions and drew out a pistol. My heart skipped a beat. I was sure he was going to murder us. But, no, he pointed the gun to his own head and said dolefully, "Here's the proof I'm no longer a man! I don't even have the courage to put a period to my own miserable existence!"

He warmed up with rage again. I was afraid he'd reach another peak of violence and actually do it right there in front of us. I was so alarmed that I began to plead with him. "Mr. Laumer! Please don't do such a terrible thing! Your life surely is not over. As long as you're alive, there's hope!"

He began to cry. "I have no reason to live. I've been abandoned by the world because of my disgusting, repulsive, damaged body! Even my own family can't bear to look at me." He wept bitterly.

I assured him that this could not be true. I firmly took the hand holding the gun and removed the pistol gingerly, wondering if it had one of those hair triggers you see in Western movies. I leaned far to the right of the sofa and put the gun out of his reach. Keith grabbed my hand and kissed it, thanking me profusely for my assurances that he was not the most despised of human beings.

Talk about a scene out of a movie!

Tom added his assurances to mine. "We'll help any way we can," Tom said. "You have only to ask. You're not friendless any more!"

I was completely overcome with sympathy for this tortured soul, and I guess he could see it in my eyes. He told us that, yes, perhaps he might make it with such friends. If we would not turn against him like everyone else had, he would have the heart to go on. We all began to plan how we were going to make sure that he could continue turning out his books, how he could regain his health, how he could find joy in life again.

I couldn't leave my grandparents alone, but I promised to help him with his manuscripts a few days a week. He was downcast to think that I could not just move in immediately. He seemed so pathetic and grateful for a few words of kindness that it was difficult to leave him alone there.

When I got home, I explained Keith's situation to my grandparents. They thought if I went to work for Keith, he could help me learn to write—a valuable skill—so they were willing to make sacrifices. They also thought his house was too far to drive every day. They could manage if I could come home on weekends.

So I gave notice at my job and soon was off to help Keith get his life back together.

First, I needed to get some decent food into him. Next, clean the house. He had been so verbally abusive to his regular cleaning lady for the infraction of moving an object on his desk that she refused to come back. Now, layers of dust, mold, and mildew multiplied everywhere.

His lakeshore home was a lovely modernistic structure built of red

The only photo I have during the period of time with Keith.

brick with an entire glass wall that soared fifteen feet high, overlooking the water that surrounded the house on three sides. River-stone terraces ran toward the banks, and tall pines sheltered the house from the wind. It really was a pleasure to put all to rights again.

When I was ready to go home at the first weekend, Keith sniffled and made dolorous remarks about how difficult it would be to survive until I returned. When I did get back after two nice and peaceful days with my grandparents, I found that Keith had eaten absolutely nothing and had survived on bottles of beer.

This was appalling. Without me to watch things, he'd go down the tubes! I could hardly bear to see so brilliant a man disintegrated by suffering. As weeks passed, it became progressively harder for me to leave on time.

I organized his schedule, devised ways he could write in comfort, typed his manuscripts, made him eat regularly, and protected him from the outside world. Brain damage from the stroke included disruption of the emotional centers. Keith could go from a pleasant conversation to raging lunatic frenzy in seconds, foaming at the mouth, his paralyzed limbs jerking and twitching. And his language could have sent hell demons fleeing. But he didn't show anger toward me—at least not in the beginning. Keith lashed out at himself, other people, or inanimate objects instead.

He read and studied, obsessed with regaining the use of his paralyzed limbs. It didn't matter if a promising therapy was halfway around the world—he was off to try it immediately. I made endless reservations, packed his bag, and drove him to the airport over and over again. He left with such anticipation and hope. And when I went to pick him up, he insisted he felt much better, even if neither of us could gauge any external difference. He was sure his efforts were cumulative; one day he would wake up and the nightmare would be over. His self-image was so completely tied up in physical prowess that nothing short of total recovery would be satisfactory.

Since he had been a regular distance runner before his stroke, he decided that running would be one way to retrain his body, which would then reprogram his brain. He marked off a measured distance on his long circular driveway, and each day we would go out while he ran the distance. He wanted to shorten the time it took by one second each day until he could get back to his old pre-stroke time.

Calling what Keith was doing on that track "running" is really stretching it. His left leg was in a metal brace to keep the knee joint from bending backward and the ankle joint from collapsing entirely. It was more of a series of hops and drags than an actual run. He gamely gave it all he had until he was perspiring profusely. It broke my heart to see him torturing himself this way while I stood there holding the stopwatch, urging him on.

Keith loved opera—Puccini, mostly—and every waking hour, literally. He had a phonograph that was in the living room with the fifteen-foot ceiling, and he turned up the volume as high as it would go without distortion to hear his favorite arias throughout the house.

He also had numerous eight-track tapes of Puccini and whenever we went anywhere in the car, the volume was turned up as high as it would go without causing physical pain. This did distract me if I was driving, but not as much as the leg-jerking, mouth-foaming fit I'd encounter if I suggested we turn it down a bit. I grew to detest operatic music. There was no escape from Puccini and his arias, except when we went for walks. Nowadays, of course, he would have taken a portable player with a playlist along.

I enjoyed our long walks to search for fat lighter pine in the woods surrounding his home. With three fireplaces in the house, and Keith's habit of keeping a fire going at all times, even in summer, we needed a lot to start the daily fire. On our walks, he confided details of his life, ideas, his studies, his work, and taught me all he knew about science, which was a lot. He was brilliant, and his knowledge in many areas was vast and profound, so I was challenged constantly to keep up with him.

But Keith didn't have a very high opinion of women. This was as much cultural as experiential. Like many men, he viewed women as objects not worthy of engaging in serious conversation. However, at this point in his life, it was me or nobody. Yes, Tom came out to visit once in awhile, but I became Keith's constant companion, and little by little, the subjects open to discussion expanded until we engaged in lengthy philosophical debates. He was not used to having conversations with a female on such subjects, and he naturally would dismiss some of my arguments without any consideration at all. But, if I refused to speak anymore until he at least acknowledged that my thoughts had some merit, he soon learned not to reject an idea just because a woman said it.

At some point, he remarked that I was the most intelligent conversationalist he had ever known—for a woman. Well, I wasn't going to push it, so I took it as a compliment.

As I helped him to regain his life in many respects, he was helping me to obtain a much wider view of the world and the cosmos. I encouraged and calmed him. And he began to thrive. He challenged and taught me, and I had the chance to sharpen my thinking with one of the brightest men I have ever known.

Keith was absolutely certain he did not believe in God or any kind of consciousness except as a by-product of evolution. He utterly rejected the concept of a soul. I did, of course, believe that there was consciousness beyond matter, though at this point I was not precisely sure in what context I believed. This was a topic of endless discussion between us, and I found that I was being challenged to look at the matter in a new way: pure science.

Keith had an extensive library with a great many science texts. I had neglected strict scientific inquiry in favor of social and historical explorations or metaphysical applications. A fundamental question took shape in my mind: Does consciousness exist independent of matter at all? This question went well beyond trying to solve the problem of evil in a universe purportedly created by an all-wise and loving Perfect Creator. According to Keith there was no God to consider, evil was simply an evolutionary stage in the development of mankind (who was, by the way, the most sublime and perfect product of chance mutation and survival of the fittest). Consciousness was merely a by-product of mindless evolution.

Even if I now doubted the existence of God in the terms of any particular religion or philosophy, I never doubted the value of the human being as consciousness, whether that consciousness existed as a by-product of matter or not. Keith disagreed. He repeatedly expressed views of eugenics popular among many Darwinists. Only human beings who were superior, both mentally and physically, should be allowed to reproduce. All children who were less than perfect in any way should be euthanized. People who were a burden on society by virtue of age, infirmity, or some catastrophic physical damage, needed to be done away with humanely. Of course, that brought him to the inescapable conclusion that he was no longer worthy to be allowed to draw breath. And this was at the very root of his rage and self-denigration.

He had even married his first cousin so their children would be of the same "superior lineage." (His wife had left him some years before his stroke.) This subject was something of a hot issue between us, and one day I told him the story of my friend Sammy.

Sammy was a Thalidomide baby. He lived two doors away from my grandparents' house. We were best friends for many years. Sammy had no arms and one leg was a vestigial "flipper." The other leg was normal. But he was a genius, with a delightful personality and an assertive, no-nonsense, ambitious nature. There was no question that he was in charge in our relationship! I spent a lot of time executing his wishes, building things, setting things up, fetching and carrying—just generally being his arms and legs. I'll never forget the year he decided that Christmas trees ought to have a use after Christmas, and we were going to create a "magic forest." It was my job to go up and down the streets of our neighborhood and retrieve all the trees set out for the trash collectors. I had to drag them back, many of them bigger than I was, and set them up according to Sammy's specifications. In the end, we had about fifty trees. It was quite a sight to behold. His parents probably weren't terribly happy to see such an assemblage of items that would need to be disposed of eventually, but they good-naturedly let them stand until they were bare of needles before finally having them hauled away.

I never thought much about the fact that Sammy was "different" when we were very little. I was four and he was two when we were plopped into a sandbox together for the first time. All of his development took place before my eyes, for the most part, and seemed natural. He could do just about everything with his feet that I could do with my hands, including using scissors and playing the organ. When he came over to our house to play and have a snack, he sat on a special stool the same height as the table so he could use his feet to eat. Once he was situated, my grandmother would wash his feet for him.

As we grew older, however, I often accompanied him and his mother on a trip to the market, a department store, or a movie. I became aware that other people stared and moved away from him, and so I came to realize that his difference was really different. I was already so accustomed to his difference

My brother with "Sammy", 1965 in Tampa.

being acceptable that I thought the people who stared had very bad manners. It was only when I grew up that I learned that Sammy was the way he was because a doctor gave his mother some pills for morning sickness.

I never, ever forgot that a doctor—acting in good faith—had done this. Like I said, I was good at extracting the essence from a situation and understanding it as a lesson to be learned from.

As I told Sammy's story to Keith, I knew that Sammy was attending college at that very moment. I knew he'd been valedictorian of his high-school graduating class. Sammy had a wide circle of friends, and clearly a great deal to offer humanity, both from his amazing intellect and his super personality.

"Should such a person, who did nothing to be guilty of such an affliction, be euthanized?" I asked Keith.

"Yes," he said, and walked away, ending the discussion.

I could not believe it. To suggest that my adored Sammy had no right to live was so revolting a thought that I couldn't plumb the depths of a mind that could conceive this view of humanity. My feelings toward Keith changed at that moment. I could see how totally fitting his own condition truly was. If there were evidence of consciousness independent of matter, Keith's own experience of being forced to face this issue was very practical proof (to me) of higher purpose.

I realized that I played a role in Keith's life similar to the one I had in Sammy's, but with a big difference between the two individuals. What was the nature of the evil that brought affliction on Sammy and Keith alike? In a sense, they were both stricken seemingly without reason. The real contrast was in their reaction to their situation. Sammy accepted his life and saw everything as perfect under conditions that would have crushed some people. Keith, with so many years of physical perfection to be thankful for, could now do nothing but revile the universe and seek constantly to change everything to conform to his view of perfection. I never felt pity for Sammy. But I now had nothing but pity for Keith. And not for his condition; for the poverty of his soul.

I think Keith felt the change in my feelings toward him. The anger in him began to shift subtly in my direction. Up to this point, we had interacted very much like companions helping one another: teacher and pupil, nurse and patient. Now he began to respond to me more like a man to a woman. This was not good news. To him a woman was an object that was owned.

I had already heard the story of why his wife had left him. As he explained it, she just didn't understand that it meant nothing when he had affairs. How dare she run off to Spain with an artist and leave him with the children in England? (He had three beautiful and talented daughters.) Well, figure it out!

Little by little, Keith put me under a jar where I could neither breathe nor move without his scrutiny or control. This became unbearable. Along with this increasing interest in controlling me came a disturbing tendency to test me; to act out and see how far he could go before I reacted.

One day he couldn't find a bottle opener in the drawer where it belonged. It was in the sink to be washed, not two feet from the drawer. He went into a rage, pulled out all the dishes in the cabinet, and started throwing them at me. They smashed against the wall. Slivers of glass and china were bouncing all over the place. I was in a corner and managed to get away, but by this time, he had broken nearly every dish in that cupboard.

I was so furious with him that I went directly to my bedroom and began to pack my bag to leave.

He came to the open door, saw what I was doing, and meekly apologized. I didn't even speak to him. I didn't want to hear any apologies. When he saw how disgusted I was with his behavior, he broke down and cried. He begged me not to go and promised he would never take his frustration out on me again.

"You know that with all I have to bear that the least frustration is intolerable," he wept. "I'm so painfully aware of how inadequate I am as a man! You deserve so much better than me. I'm just a broken down wreck!"

I felt alarmed that he was thinking of me this way. But at the same time, concerned that he should not be hurt, I swallowed my anger, made light of it, and went to the kitchen to clean up the broken china.

Not too long afterward, making a call to his agent in New York, he was shouting at the telephone operator in vibrantly colorful language that escalated to a new altitude of violence. Then he bashed the phone against the stone fireplace as if he wanted to do this to the poor woman. Now, the old telephones were pretty sturdy instruments, but nothing could have withstood that. The phone flew to pieces as though a bomb had exploded inside it. Naturally, I cleaned up the mess and called the phone company with a fabricated excuse why he needed a replacement.

This next incident plays a significant role in events years later, during a second "meeting" with Keith twenty years later, when he had already passed over.

I had driven Keith to a specialty butcher shop to pick up a large order of meat for his freezer. He examined the packages of frozen meat, neatly packed in boxes, and noticed right away that the sirloin had been cut into steaks, not ground into burger as he had instructed. He began shouting at the butcher and working himself into another foaming-at-the-mouth frenzy. I was shocked nearly out of my senses when he began throwing the packages of frozen meat at the poor man's head. I tried to calm Keith down, to plead with him to behave, to defend the butcher, but every word I said only seemed to inflame him the more. I didn't know what else to do except turn and walk out the door.

I got in the car and waited, shaking, certain that a police car was going to drive up any instant. I wanted to be away from the action so they would know I was not the one who needed to be arrested. Keith came out with a jaunty air, thumping the ground with his cane, and got in the car. He turned to me and said, "I showed him, didn't I?!" and smiled a crooked smile of self-satisfaction, looking like a puppy dog seeking a pat on the head.

I was speechless. He clearly did not feel one bit of remorse, and he obviously thought his behavior was perfectly justified. I realized he simply had no concept of consideration for others. Besides, it was my turn to have a fit.

"I will never, ever, get in this car and go out in public with you again unless you promise, swear on your life, that you will never do such a thing again."

He was astonished. Then abashed. "I promise," he said meekly. And we drove home.

Keith's trips around the world to try new therapies now became a welcome relief. One day, after a week's absence, I went to pick him up at the airport. As I passed a bar in the terminal, I thought to myself: *I need a good stiff drink before Keith gets off the plane!* I literally stopped dead in my tracks right there in the airport and thought: *What are you saying? You need a drink?*

I knew at that moment that I was disintegrating. I had to get away from him. But I couldn't just abandon him. I had to do it in increments. I still cared for his well being and wanted to see if he could be encouraged to do things for himself.

The Farm was only about fifteen miles from Keith's house, and was unoccupied most of the time since Mother had finally, after quite a long spell, remarried and moved to the East Coast with her new husband. I decided to create some space for myself. I told Keith that I needed to be there to watch the house. I'd stay during the night and come early in the morning to see to his needs.

Keith cried and raged, but I was firm. He did persuade me to agree to put in a telephone so that he could reach me during the night if he needed me. That didn't seem like too much to ask, so I said I would.

What a small decision it was. Agreeing to order a telephone doesn't seem like a life-changing choice, does it? My restless drives to Aripeka where I met Tom, his interest in science fiction—such odd things that led me to Keith. What if I hadn't realized I needed to get away from Keith? What would have happened if I had decided that I would marry him? He certainly was sending signals that this was an agreeable idea. Would he have murdered me in one of his violent fits? Or would he have become more content and gentle as a lamb with a wife young enough to be his daughter?

We will never know, because I decided that I could not fix him. The only way I could continue to interact with him at all would be with some distance and time to myself. And then I made a small decision to order a telephone as he requested.

The seeds of disaster were sown. I almost didn't survive it.

CHAPTER THIRTEEN

OYSTERS ON THE HALF SHELL

I ordered Keith's telephone and went back to The Farm.

Late September nights were cool and the days warm, sunny, and dry. The house had been closed for almost a year. My brother was in the Navy and had married. Mother had remarried and gone to the East Coast to live. Now she and her sixth husband moved back to Tampa to be near my grandparents.

First, I headed to the backyard pump for water, priming from the sealed jugs on the shelf left for that purpose, working the handle until the water ran cold and clear. Then I wandered around the place, inside and out, meeting ghosts from the past at every turn. A deep silence settled here, except for droning cicadas and an occasional bird calling. No more Puccini blasting in the background. No more air conditioner humming night and day to keep the house cool with a fire burning constantly in the fireplace. Most of all, no sounds of Keith calling for attention.

Just the silence.

But the silence was rich with memories. In the kitchen, I could see my mother, grandmother, and aunt washing dishes by lamplight after a big dinner of fried fish caught on a family fishing trip. In the dining room, around the huge oak table with braces carved like a crouching lion, and legs like lion's paws, I could see the family in all their accustomed places, enjoying feasts of fresh vegetables from the garden, and rabbit stew from Grandpa's hunting expeditions.

In the bedrooms, I could hear all of us children settling down in the big iron bedsteads, giggling and talking, while the grown-ups talked back and forth between the bedrooms, until Grandpa called out, "It's time to go to sleep!" And then only the rustling of the palm fronds outside the window in the breeze that blew constantly from the Gulf, and the occasional slapping of an errant mosquito that had slipped past Grandma's insect-killing pump gun.

The years all flowed past me, awakening ghosts of the voices of the past as though I could really hear them now. This effect was so strong, in fact, that I had to shake my head to dispel the sensation that I was actually hearing whispers and faint echoes of years gone by.

At first this sensation seemed comforting, but as days went by, it became oppressive.

I swept and dusted and took clean linens down to make the bed, wondering if I was going to be able to live there alone after all. The sensation of being watched as I moved from room to silent room was unnerving. I spent most of the time until dark working to ignore it by staying busy.

But every evening, as twilight turned to dusk, it would not be ignored.

It was too late in the season for the whippoorwill, but owls of all varieties hooted and screeched alternately, and all the sounds of the backwoods Florida night were amplified by the simple fact that I was alone. The weak light from the kerosene lamps didn't do much to dispel the darkness. (I did not bother to order the lights to be turned on.) In a way, I felt more vulnerable because all that darkness "out there" was not illuminated. I was in the circle of light and could be seen, but could not see.

I put out the lamps and sat in a chair by the open window. Gradually, my eyes became accustomed to the dark. I was absolutely certain that I was not alone. I listened and looked, scanning the part of the yard I could see from the window and the part of the house I could see from my chair. I absorbed all the night sounds, the creaking and cracking of the old house as it settled down to sleep for the night. I gradually came to feel that the house itself was alive, probing me to see how I had changed since I had last been there.

Finally, when I could sit up no longer, I went to bed and the Gulf breeze through the palm trees sighed me to sleep.

I had to stay at the house until the phone was installed, having promised to call Keith the instant it was operational. I overslept. After sitting up over half the night, I was exhausted.

I was dreaming fitfully about an evil old woman sitting on the front porch in one of the rocking chairs, when I was awakened by a pounding at the front of the house. It was like swimming to the surface from the bottom of the ocean to come awake, and as I got closer to the top, I became more confused about who I was, where I was, and what I was doing there. When I finally opened my eyes, it all came back to me: the phone guy!

Through the window I could see the phone company truck.

I wasn't sure how long the guy had been knocking at the door. I most certainly didn't want him to give up and leave, so I called out "Just a minute!" just to let him know that there was someone at home. I struggled into my robe as I stumbled to open the door. I was sure that I didn't look my best, but since it was just a serviceman, I wasn't too concerned. My hair by this time was long, mussed, and falling in my eyes, and I went to the door feeling pretty much like death warmed over.

Standing outside the screen door of the porch was a tall, blond, blue-eyed guy with the build of a wrestler and the face of an angel. I opened the door and mumbled something incoherent about having been sleeping and "Sorry, the place for the phone is thataway." I held the door open, waiting for him to enter. But he just stood there looking at me with the most amazed expression I had ever seen on anybody's face. He seemed to be unable to speak for a few moments, and then managed to say that he was there to install the phone. Well, we already knew that, and I wondered if my nose had turned green or something.

I let him in, showed him where I wanted the phone, and went to the kitchen to make coffee. Since there was really nothing else to do, I returned to watch the hole being drilled in the wall. It must have been hard to install the phone and stare at me at the same time, but he did, and I began to feel more than a little uncomfortable. He must have realized this because he started to talk, asking questions about the old house, and why I was there and what did I do. He told me his name, which surprised me because it was Grant, a traditional name in my family, and not very common. He then volunteered the information that he was Polish, his

Me not long after the "phone guy" came.

father having escaped from Poland during World War II. He said that he was working for the phone company so as to save money to go to school to be an electrical engineer.

He sure hit all the right buttons. But I was not biting. He was, after all, a complete stranger, and was only there to install the phone. I was relieved when he finally left.

Later that day, Keith came to take me to lunch at our favorite seafood restaurant up the coast. Usually I drove, but on this day he insisted on driving himself. He was driving so fast and recklessly that I suggested he take more care. This set him off on a foaming-at-the-mouth rant. How dare I criticize his driving! I demanded that he stop and let me out of the car. Well, that set him off even more. How dare I insult him by implying that he would stoop so low as to put me out on the side of the road! Of course, if I were determined to abandon him, he would not stop me. So, he slammed on the brakes, squealed the tires, turning the car around and nearly putting us in the ditch, and drove me home. When he pulled up in the drive and stopped, he switched to his poor-pitiful-me role, and begged me not to leave him.

But I couldn't give in any more. Over and over again he had pulled the "Dr. Jekyll and Mr. Hyde" maneuver, and I knew as long as I kept giving in, he would keep it up. I told him I didn't believe that he would never do it again and I needed time. He was practically in tears as he drove away.

And so was I.

I knew he was not rational. He'd suffered brain damage; it was unreasonable of me to expect him to control himself. He was drowning in his suffering. But he was drowning me too. All my sympathies and Christian upbringing said that I should disregard all the negative and nurture the good in Keith. But the negative was growing and the positive was diminishing.

It seemed that I should just pack up and go back to my grandparents' house, which would mean that I had failed. At the same time, I couldn't afford to live on my own without a job of some sort. I was struggling with myself over whether or not to call Keith and tell him all was forgiven when I heard a car coming up the driveway. He must be really sorry to get out and navigate all the heavy grass and the steps up to the porch with his paralyzed leg. I waited. A knock came and I went to the door expecting to see Keith.

It was the phone installation guy.

"Hi! I just got off work. I just wanted to come back and make sure everything was working okay!"

He looked at me with the kindest, most sympathetic blue eyes I had ever seen. I was at one of the lowest points ever. The contrast between Keith's violence and this obvious kindness undid me. I invited him in, glad to talk to somebody normal.

And we did talk—for hours! The floodgates opened and I poured out the story of Keith. He listened attentively, and when I began to cry, he wiped my eyes with a tissue from a pack in his pocket, and even helped me to blow my nose.

I finished talking and crying and said, "So that's it! Sorry to talk your ear off. It's really not as bad as I make it sound. I'm sure it will look different tomorrow. So now it's only fair that you can tell me some of your problems." I don't know what I expected when I said this, but it most definitely was not what I got!

He looked at me so strangely, took a deep breath, and just launched into the craziest series of words I had ever heard. He told me that he had never, ever, had the feeling before that he had when he first laid eyes on me. He had tried to just go on about his job the rest of the day and forget it, to go home and push it away, but it was so overpowering, so compelling, so unbelievably immediate and intense that he thought he was going to have a heart attack. He was risking everything, but he had to say these things: he was in love! Totally, completely, unbelievably—he knew it was crazy and none of it made any sense, but there it was. Seeing me had ignited a fire in his soul that simply was raging out of control and he was helpless.

Wow! Talk about being speechless. I was stunned. I didn't know what to say. I mean, what do you say when a perfect stranger practically falls on their knees in front of you and declares you to be the most beautiful, incredible, and marvelous creature on the planet?

It's sort of hard to think of a snappy comeback to that one!

The first thought that passed through my head was that this guy was really off his rocker. Better to run back to the safety of the known madness of Keith than to walk into what was so obviously a trap. Sure, he was an attractive guy, he was Polish, he was intelligent—but no instant fireworks on this side. (In retrospect, I really should have listened to my instincts on this one.)

I guess he could see the shock and doubt on my face, because he immediately backed up and explained that he knew how unsettling his words probably were, but would I please give him a chance? Would I please give myself a chance?

I thought that I had a reasonably fair estimation of my looks and sex appeal. On a scale of one to ten, I was maybe a four. On a good day, with make-up, I might rate a five. But only if I kept my mouth closed to conceal my crooked teeth. I was most definitely not Helen of Troy with a face to launch a thousand ships. I wasn't even sure I could launch a toy boat!

I simply did not trust the idea of love based on looks. All my experiences in junior high and high school showed that the good-looking kids were popular, but less than stellar in personality, kindness, and brains. And they definitely did not become attracted to people like me. I had learned through painful experience that good looks did not equate to being good inside.

So how could this guy know he was in love with me when he didn't even know me?

Yet, from another point of view, I had spent most of the last year with a highly intelligent man who had all the potential to be lovable, but was stunted and twisted emotionally. I realized intellect didn't necessarily equate to emotional depth either.

It was certainly true that I felt an attraction to Grant of some sort. But I really had no experience with this thing called "being in love," and for all I knew, reports from other people regarding love were the same as the reports that God had answered their prayers. Maybe my search for true love would end up like my search for the voice of God. And, in that case, I would probably be alone all my life, and such a prospect was not very pleasing. I was tired of being alone. Very, very tired. My objections crumbled like sand on a beach.

My thoughts, taking such an unexpected turn, left me confused. I must have said something, but all I remember is that he was slowly moving toward me with his arms extended, and in the next moment I felt those arms go around me with tender gratitude, drawing me close. It was a shelter from the storm and I felt that a long battle had come to the end. He turned my face up to his and kissed me.

Too soon he had to leave, promising that he would return. Surely this was a dream. All that evening I kept touching my lips that had never been kissed in such a way.

And, he did return. So we began. When Keith called to get me to come back, Grant took the phone and told him in a very firm voice that

I was not able to take his abuse anymore, and Keith stopped calling. I was grateful for the shield, though it hurt to think how it must have affected Keith.

Grant and I talked about our future. He came every day and we talked on the phone almost constantly. At work he tested new phone lines by calling me. I cooked our suppers on the old gas range. We ate at the old oak table by the light of the kerosene lamps and made love to the sound of the whispering palm trees and shrieking owls.

My life felt like supernatural bliss. I was living in the place I loved. I was loved completely and without reservation. There was only one thing I really couldn't understand: why Grant couldn't stay with me at night. Every night he came, and every night he left before midnight.

But I brushed my concerns away as we kept planning our future. And, of course, one of the things I wanted most was a family. To be normal.

When I brought this up, Grant seemed troubled. He looked away or changed the subject. But instead of feeling warned, I brushed it aside. We were happy now. Time enough to think of such things. And the palm fronds whispered and the owls shrieked.

We drove to Tampa one Saturday to meet my grandparents.

Grant was charming, understanding, and patient with my grandfather, who sometimes acted confused due to the medications he was taking. I announced that we were going to get married and Grandma hugged me. Grandpa gave Grant the third degree about his occupation and plans, and grudgingly admitted that he sounded like a likely prospect for marriage.

When he took me back to The Farm that evening, Grant stopped his car in the drive.

"We need to talk."

I was startled by the serious tone of his voice. "Whatever you have to tell me, we ought to go inside."

"I'm already married," he said.

The long story that emerged was that he'd married young, had a child, and discovered he had nothing in common with his wife. He was starving for spiritual and mental union.

"I'm so sorry to be hurting you, but the fact that I'm married shouldn't make one bit of difference," he told me. He would get a divorce. We could continue as we were until then.

I was so stunned I couldn't even speak. He had made all those professions of love to me night after night, and had then gone home and slept with another woman. And she was the one who had the most right to feel betrayed. I was outraged for both of us.

My heart felt as though it had turned to stone. As long as he was married, there was a wall between us. I asked him to leave. He pleaded to allow me to just let him visit, to remain friends, to not abandon him to spiritual death.

I felt my heart break. "Go," I repeated again. I couldn't see him or speak to him without wanting him, and wanting him was a sin I would not commit again.

He left.

And then the internal questions started. Who did I think I was? What did I have that was so precious? Did God create me in a new and better mold than other women? I had spent years taking in stray animals and feeding them. What was different about a man suffering from a much greater hunger? Why did I feel that the payment was more than I could give?

Grant called the next day. "I'm desperate to hear your voice," he said. I hung up the phone. But Grant simply could not accept that I wouldn't talk to him. He came to the house every morning and parked in the drive in front and just sat there for an hour, staring at the house with a miserable, woebegone expression. When it was time for him to head for work, he'd drive away, only to reappear after work to sit for another hour.

I felt like a prisoner in my own house.

One afternoon, my good friend Tom, the one who'd introduced me to Keith, came to see me.

I explained the situation to him. I knew I couldn't hold up under this kind of emotional pressure for very long. Tom suggested that I go away for a little vacation. Just simply disappear.

This seemed like a pretty good idea, so I called my brother and told him I was coming for a visit.

After a few days of relaxing enjoyment of my nephew and baby niece, seeing what sights there were to see in Brunswick, Georgia, I was sitting idly on the sofa in my brother's house while my sister-in-law was starting dinner. Suddenly, we heard a car pull up next to the house. I looked casually out the window and nearly had a heart attack. It was Grant.

I wanted to run and hide under the bed, but my brother told me to relax, that he would take care of it, and he went out to talk to him. Apparently the conversation was long and emotional, because, after it was over, my brother came in and said, "Sis, the guy is sincere. He really loves you, and just wants to talk to you. Why won't you talk to him? Give the guy a break!"

I knew that refusing to even talk to him after he had driven over three hundred miles to see me would make me look incredibly selfish. So we went for a drive down the coast to Jekyll Island, to the beach.

Jekyll Island, the perfectly named place for Grant to take me.

We walked on the beach while Grant made declarations of the purest undying love ever before known to man: the sun rose and set at my command; he worshipped me and would never hurt me; without me he simply could no longer find a reason to draw breath.

"I'm getting a divorce," he said finally.

I stopped walking. "I object," I told him. "I grew up without a father because my parents divorced when I was a baby and I never want to be responsible for contributing to that kind of suffering for anyone. Forget it."

I turned away; he took hold of my arm. "I don't want to hurt my wife. But it's unfair for her to live with someone who can't love her. If I let her have her freedom, she might find someone who loves her as much as she deserves to be loved. Don't you see?"

Slick logic, right?

And, in a funny way it is really true, though it was being used to manipulate me. I fell for it.

I packed my bag and Grant drove me home. Along the way he explained how he went to see my grandparents, thinking I would be there. He persuaded them to tell him what town my brother lived in and then got the address from the phone book. Very enterprising, yes? Nowadays they would call it stalking.

Just because I fell for his story doesn't mean I was entirely brain-dead. I had been lied to once, and I wasn't going to risk being lied to again. He would have to prove himself to me now. The situation itself

My grandparents at about the time I moved back home after working for Keith Laumer. My grandfather didn't have long to live and it showed on his face.

provided the needed parameters. Since I couldn't live at The Farm without a job, I packed my things and moved back to my grandparents' house.

After all the mental stimulation of the time I spent with Keith, I knew I could no longer just drift along. I decided that I needed to go back to school. This idea also worked well with the needs of my grandparents. Grandfather's condition was rapidly deteriorating. A few hours of classes were just enough to give me something to do, while still leaving me available to look after their needs. The county had voted funding for a new community college, and it seemed like just the thing to get my feet wet before heading out to a four-year school. Until the new buildings were constructed, classes were being held in the old airport building. I drove out to sign up.

I decided to begin with basics: math, psychology, biology, sociology. Another seed of fate was planted.

In that psychology class, I met Eva and Carol, two women who would soon play supporting roles in my life drama; one as a heroine, the other as the most fiendish of villains, though it was only accidental that she was the villain of the piece; she was as wounded as everyone else.

That first day in class, I saw the most amazing woman in a row across from me.

Eva literally looked like the legendary bust of Nefertiti. Her black hair, cut in the Egyptian style, naturally played up the resemblance. She wore huge dark glasses. She took them off to look at me. We both smiled. Eva and I clicked immediately.

After class we made a dash to the girls' room

"I'd love to have hair the color of yours," she told me.

Well, I couldn't tell a lie. "You could certainly have it for a few dollars at the drug store!"

We practically collapsed laughing.

We talked all the way out to the parking lot. I found it amazing to be with someone who could actually finish my sentences exactly as they were being formed in my own mind. I had never experienced the feeling of really knowing someone so well while being certain we had never met. I commented on this and it opened the door to the fact that we were both avid students of metaphysics and had actually read most of the same things.

Eva was quite a bit older than I was, a housewife with nearly grown children who had decided to go to school to ease her transition to the empty nest. But she most definitely did not look or act her age. By the time we left in our respective cars, we knew we were going to have a good time in this psychology class.

And we did.

I was thrilled, once again, to have someone to talk to with whom I didn't have to act dumb. We talked every day at school, and frequently on the phone. We had lunch together and soon began to attract a sort of circle of other interesting people.

For quite a while, I was too busy to pay much attention to another girl in class who kept watching us with birdlike eyes: Carol, the brilliant little troll. Carol wasn't ugly, she was just "symmetrically challenged." She, too, had an Egyptian-pageboy bob; but on her it looked like a 1930s cartoon character come to life. She had a round body and short legs and arms that gave the overall impression of one of those old Kewpie dolls. She wore shapeless sack dresses, to hide her extreme rotundity and lack of any feminine curves, and Mary Jane shoes. She blinked constantly as though someone were going to strike her down at any instant.

I kept finding her watching me during class with those sad, birdlike eyes. God only knows, I had spent enough years as an outsider to know how it felt. That I was rapidly becoming the center of many discussions before, during, and after class was gratifying; I certainly never wanted to forget what it was like to be on the outside. So, I reached out and drew her in and discovered a mind that was amazing in its acuity and attention to detail.

She was not only well read; she was a thinker, even if her thinking tended to run in an almost mirror image parallel to Keith's. He had been focused on an almost Nazi-like belief in white supremacy. Carol, on the other hand, was equally devoted to racial equality and blending of the races for the new Superman. But both of them were certain that Darwin was the true God.

We were taught by a professor with deep insight and grace—Rose Frank—an amazing woman. We spent more time in free-for-all discussions than hearing lectures, and the class seemed to bond into more of a club than anything else. The issues of God and consciousness that I had been pursuing for so many years were now very proper subjects for discussion. This was the heyday of humanistic psychology. There was Eric Berne and *Games People Play*, Alex Comfort and the radical *Joy of Sex*. We talked about giving and getting "strokes" and assured each other that we were "OK." We talked to our "inner child" and tried to rewrite the "scripts" that we lived. It was heady stuff. So what if humanity was the product of mindless evolution; we had a mind now, and it could be whatever we chose to make it. Let's play man and make God in our own image!

One day Eva called me excitedly to say there would be a three-day training seminar in hypnosis over in Clearwater the next week. Well, I had always been interested in hypnosis since the episode with the stepbrother, and had even experimented a bit with it in high school. The subject came up in the girls' room one day. I mentioned that I had read a little about it. They began to ask questions and one girl insisted that I should try to hypnotize her because she wanted to see what it felt like. Since I was being put on the spot, how hard could it be?

Well, there we were in the girls' room and the only available chair was a toilet, so she sat on the toilet and I began to "talk her down." I was completely freaked out when she really did go into a trance. One of the girls panicked, thinking that this hypnotized girl was going to die, but I counted her up and she woke up just fine. So, I knew I could do it—I just figured I'd better not try it again until I knew more.

Here was my chance. "Of course I'll go with you!" So we signed up, paid our money and waited expectantly for the first day of the course.

We had to drive to Clearwater. There's really only one direct route there—across Tampa Bay on a long bridge.

There is something very strange about the drive across the Bay Bridge that Eva and I made on the day we attended the first session of the hypnosis seminar. To this day, what both of us remember is starting across the bridge, and coming off the bridge, but nothing in between.

It was as though we spent no time at all on that bridge. Sure, that's pretty normal for most people, but it wasn't normal for either of us.

Quite a large crowd signed up for the course and we took our seats about halfway back. I was determined to figure out this hypnosis business. The lecturer had everyone stand up and asked us to do a series of actions including holding out our arms, closing our eyes, touching our nose with our fingers while our eyes were closed, and so on. It was all pretty silly, but I went along with it while continually peeking at what everyone else was doing.

At this point, with our arms extended out to the side, the instructor asked us to pay close attention to how our outstretched arms felt. Well, heck! Holding your arms out in the air for any length of time is a pain. Then he said that they felt extremely light and that no matter how hard we tried, we would not be able to drop them to our sides.

Naturally, my arms did not feel light, and I was perfectly able to drop them to my sides. In fact, I was glad to do so. I looked around me and I was pretty surprised to see quite a number of people struggling to drop their arms, and obviously completely unable to do so! What was going on? Why did it work on them and not on me?

We were soon to find out.

The instructor, a professor of psychology, explained to us that when he had asked us to do the little nonsense actions at the very beginning, it was actually a form of hypnosis. When people obey a request or suggestion, thinking it is just a more or less reasonable request, or a game, that they are basically giving up their will to the person making the request and that this is, in its most basic form, a type of hypnosis.

Some people are more susceptible. Once they have agreed to do the simple requests, they come completely under the power of the person making the request. When the next suggestion is made—that their arm is light and they cannot bring it back to their sides—they have no effective will to counteract this "belief" that has been imposed on them by their own consent.

We were told that this was a common test performed by stage hypnotists before they begin their act. They are looking for those who have very little will, or are most suggestible, from the audience members, and only those will be the ones called to the stage, seemingly at random, to be hypnotized and cluck like a chicken or bark like a dog.

Many people have the idea that the state of being hypnotized consists in passing out and becoming comatose. Nothing could be further from the truth.

Everyone passes into a state of hypnosis occasionally throughout any given day, whether it is induced by their environment or their own attention, reading a book or watching television. This professor believed that dancing was a form of self-hypnosis. If you watch people dancing, you may see a complete lack of expression on their faces. They don't talk at all. I had the passing thought that maybe people who were good dancers were also highly suggestible.

I knew now that I was not very suggestible, and I certainly couldn't dance worth a hoot!

Priests and witch doctors have long taken advantage of this fact, using chanting, dancing, music, and rhythmic drumming to put their followers into trance, better to inculcate them with prescribed beliefs.

Hypnosis is not a state of unconsciousness. It's more a state of hyperconsciousness with a very narrow focused awareness. It can be described, but not precisely defined. Though the conscious mind is still present, depending on the subject and the level of hypnosis, the mind of the subject is more or less *en rapport* with the hypnotist to an extreme degree. He wants to do what is suggested to him because, in a certain sense, he has willingly identified himself with the hypnotist.

That, of course, leaves the question open of what people are *en rapport* with when they are dancing or participating in other activities that produce trance states.

Then the "yes set" was explained. This is when a hypnotist puts people under hypnosis in a very sly way by asking them a series of questions to which he is sure that they will answer yes. Generally, by the time a person has answered yes to three questions in a row, their brain has shifted into rapport with the hypnotist, because the pattern of affirmation is interpreted by the subconscious mind as agreement with the person asking the questions. The subject feels a sort of unity with that person and will then, most likely, agree with everything that the hypnotist—or politician, or preacher—says after the hypnosis has been induced by the yes set.

Well, just hearing that made my hair stand on end. I realized that this was standard practice in every church I had ever attended—all the services that had begun with the preacher standing at the pulpit and asking the congregation urgently, "Do you need more happiness in your life? Do you need more peace in your life? Do you want a richer, fuller life?" And, of course, with each question, the congregation answered "Yes! Yes! Yes!" and followed commands for standing up, sitting down, opening the hymnal, and all the instructions of the service.

The essence of hypnosis—to give one's will over to the control and direction of another—was actually what was happening all over the world at this very moment, somewhere, under some circumstance, and most often in churches.

What a racket!

There were morning and afternoon classes. In the mornings, we learned theory; in the afternoons, we watched demonstrations. And, of course, at the end of the course, we were offered the opportunity to elect a private session if we wanted it.

I did.

So, I scheduled a session with the psychologist, and Eva scheduled one next to my time slot. I wanted to learn about my own level of suggestibility. I decided to enter the experiment with complete willingness to be hypnotized. I realized that the only way to know was to be completely honest with myself. This meant that I couldn't go in with an attitude that "I can't be hypnotized." Besides, it would be a waste of money.

It was a waste of money.

The poor guy did everything he could. I did cooperate and follow the directions. But it just wasn't happening. It seems that I was, after all, not hypnotizable. Dr. So-and-so was pretty flustered, mumbling that he had never encountered such resistance. Well, heck, I wasn't resisting! I was trying to "get into it!" Maybe it had something to do with having two left feet on the dance floor ...

But, it didn't matter, really. Eva and I had a new toy to play with. We went home anxious to try it out on everybody we could rope in to experiment on.

What a great time I was having! Things to do, places to go, interesting people to do things with, and the whole world was my oyster.

Well, sometimes you find pearls in oysters, and sometimes you die from toxic ones. Which was it going to be?

CHAPTER FOURTEEN

PEARLS IN THE OYSTER

Shortly after my introduction into the field of hypnosis, I went to dinner with Grant on Christmas Eve 1973. A few days earlier, he had announced that his divorce would soon be final. He was monstrously depressed over it. At dinner, he seemed distraught that his little boy didn't realize their last Christmas in a whole family was already over. I thought of my own father and how desperately I had longed for him to come and take me away from the life with Mother. I remembered walking down the street, holding his hand, in my important-sounding boots. How special I felt! My heart ached for all of them. The guilt nearly suffocated me.

I had asked Grant not to do this. We ought to be strong enough to put aside our own wants for the sake of others who were innocent. But if I reminded him now, he would feel even more depressed and morose because I was not "giving him full support." I couldn't win.

My guilt grew until it became a powerful sensation of unreality closing around me, separating me from all the other people around us, the tables full of talking, eating, laughing people, the bustling waiters, the music, the clatter of dishes and flatware. I couldn't hear Grant's voice anymore. I was swept back to the time I was a little girl waiting for her father to come home and hold her. But he never came.

Children tend to blame themselves for the absence of a beloved parent. They take on the role of sin-bearer for their family. All the guilt becomes theirs alone.

So, I was guilty. And now, I was double, even triple guilty.

Grant must have noticed my distance and changed his tactics to draw me back. Now he seemed happy to be with me, gazing at me across the table with glowing eyes in a deep, sensual way with a nearly supernatural intensity. I seemed to be listening to something speak that was not quite human. I felt confusion and tried to look away several times, but I was repeatedly drawn back to his eyes as though they were powerful magnets I could not resist.

There actually seemed to be two of me. In our months together, even when I was sure I was in love and announced to my grandparents that we wanted to marry, I had still held some reservation, some part of myself inviolate and reserved. Even when Grant repeated that it was fate, it was destiny, for us to be together, I had always held myself back. When he had enumerated the strange synchronous things that were, for him, "signs from God," that we were soulmates, I always had some small doubt niggling at the back of my mind. Grant asked how I could explain the fact that his name was a traditional name in my family or that his military ID number was the same number as my grandparents' telephone number.

And the unspoken evidence: he was Polish.

Now, these two parts of myself came into open conflict under this massive and overwhelming guilt. There was an inner "push" of images, impressions. I could turn away now and drown in my guilt, or I could yield and be at peace. I felt a brief echo of my former resistance: "No! Danger!" But I brushed it aside under the hypnotic intensity of his gaze.

Looking deep into my eyes, he said: "You have the most beautiful eyes I have ever seen."

Yes, a hope of redemption! I realized that Grant had paid a deep price to love me. He had sacrificed his family. The only way to save us both was to hand myself over to him body, mind, and soul. The moment I yielded, I felt immediate relief from guilt and a deep conviction that what he had done was right, and that it was indeed a Grand Destiny for us to be together.

Romeo and Juliet had nothing on us! Heloise and Abelard were amateurs at love in comparison.

At that moment, all my senses came alive in the riot of sounds, odors, colors, and movement in the room around me. My skin tingled and felt more alive than it ever had before. Everything was permeated with the consecration of love, and I was full of pride and awe to be so privileged. I was renewed, at ease, and calm. Sensations flooded through me, animated now by a new sense of purpose and being that I had never known. Everything had become a sacrament of beauty and I gazed in awe at

Grant, feeling an enthusiasm and passion for him that I had never known before.

He had rescued the Princess in the Tower. And a princess pays her debts: usually with her heart.

*   *   *

A few months earlier I had met a girl about my own age while out bike riding along the river a block from my grandparents' house. Paula was working in a nursing home while attending nursing school and was very bright and lively. We had become instant friends though I didn't see her often due to her heavy schedule. As it happened, as Grant and I were leaving the restaurant, walking across the parking lot, I heard a horn honking and Paula was slowing down on the street to wave at me. I ran over to say a quick hello, and she urged me to drop by and see her for a few minutes because she was alone on Christmas Eve.

I felt immediately sorry that she was all alone on the holiday. In my new state of cosmic bliss that mandated I love everyone, I urged Grant to stop by Paula's for a few minutes before he took me home. He agreed, and we drove from the restaurant to her apartment.

Paula had some supermarket eggnog and a bottle of rum, so we toasted the holiday, each other, school, my hypnosis certification, and whatever else we could think of. Pretty soon, I was unburdening myself to Paula about how difficult it was for Grant and me without our own place to be together.

Well, Paula had the solution to that. She quickly produced an extra key to her apartment, and presto! Problem solved. Since she was so seldom home, we were invited to make use of her digs any time we liked.

Grant had an even better idea. Since he was still working in the next county and had not been given a transfer yet, he proposed that he would pay half the rent if he could have a space to keep some of his things, and a place to bunk on the weekends. This way he could come to Tampa on Friday night and stay until Monday morning, and we could spend more time together if he had a sort of base that was close by.

Paula liked the idea because of the financial considerations, and they settled it right there and then. Somehow I managed to shove the uneasy feeling I was getting under the rug. After all, Grant was doing this to be with me, right?

I was really riding on a fast horse with all my new friends, new ideas, and new activities. After years of painful isolation, it was truly culture shock. But I liked it. And I wanted everyone else to be happy too. I wanted to bring all the people I loved together into one big, happy group so that no one would ever be as lonely as I had been for so many years.

My particular concern was Carol. Her life had been almost as bleak as my own. She seemed fragile and needed a lot of attention. I invited her over at every opportunity and we had lunch together frequently. We went shopping together; to the library together; to lectures and symposia. She began to blossom and became involved in all kinds of activism. I wasn't too much into being an activist of any kind, but I observed it and enjoyed her successes vicariously.

I'd decided to go heavy on the science courses and signed up for biology, anatomy, and physiology. Soon I found a work-study job as an assistant in the biology lab. I did double duty as curator of the lab and tutor to other students.

Carol was working as an assistant to one of our psych professors, and on moving day a group of us showed up to box up the files and get Dr. Frank moved. We formed an assembly line. I was in charge of taping boxes as they were set in front of me. I was taping in the usual particular, painstaking way that I did everything when Dr. Frank came to stand beside me and watch. After a few minutes she made a comment that I have never forgotten: "You know, there are some things that aren't worth doing perfectly."

I was pretty shocked by this remark because somehow I had come to the idea that anything worth doing was worth doing as well as one could. The idea of conservation of energy for important things had never occurred to me.

The new campus was right in the heart of Tampa's Latin Quarter, Ybor City, and had attracted a comprehensive staff of outstanding art instructors and the art department rapidly became the central focus for an Ybor City subculture of bohemians and artists of all kinds. The area was a bona fide historic district with charming Cuban-style architecture rather similar to the famous French Quarter in New Orleans.

Many of these buildings were converted to restaurants, clubs, artists lofts and studios, sandwich shops, second-hand book and clothing stores, all the shops that seem to spring up overnight to serve a good-sized student body and numerous academics.

Eva was into art more than anything else. I took an art course with her: printmaking. I loved the physical work that went into operating old printing presses, but the art part of it didn't interest me overmuch. I had always been able to draw about anything I saw, accurately and stylishly, but it seemed to be a useless talent and I wasn't interested in spending any study time doing it. Eva was talented in the same way, and we soon found ourselves at the center of many art discussion groups either on campus, or in one of the local clubs or restaurants. And, somehow, many of the professors, the art instructors, and the resident poets all ended up gathered around our table, talking excitedly and laughing gloriously.

A sample of my drawing—a quick sketch of my son.

Naturally, in artsy circles, the conversations were often about metaphysics, psychology, consciousness, art and perception, art and expression, and so on. I was surprised to discover that, actually, I wasn't radical enough! I hadn't yet declared that God was entirely dead nor had I admitted that man was the product of this marvelous, though definitely accidental, universe.

Carol, of course, embraced the death of God with fervor, and constantly cited the proofs and evidence that it was so. I remember riding with her in her car one day down the Avenida Republica de Cuba while she declared that she simply could not believe that I still held on to the idea there was consciousness that existed in a purely ethereal state. Clearly, consciousness was only apparent and not actual: it was the result of evolutionary processes. The mind was a vague "something else" that interacted with itself in a social contract sort of way that had evolved from the survival of the fittest of the individual cells. Those cells that could gather together and work together survived, and their inter-

My sketch of Ark.

actions and communications with one another were what we perceived as our consciousness.

I decided not to argue the issue because, of course, nothing I said would have been considered proof. Every example I gave was countered with a reason it was clearly just a result of evolutionary variables. Carol's arguments of the time were based on theories that were later more fully developed in the books of Richard Dawkins, such as *The Selfish Gene* and *The Blind Watchmaker*. They are, indeed, very clever and convincing, with only one real problem: the idea that a single atom exists at all is completely inexplicable in these terms. No matter how cleverly these arguments are constructed, and how far back into our evolutionary history they go, they can never, by their very nature, go beyond the instant in which the first atom of matter came into being. (They, furthermore, cannot explain the leap of the gap between dead matter and life itself, in the simplest form.)

Dawkins and other proponents of this idea glibly slip past this point with the assertion that physics, or explaining the existence of atoms, is not in their purview. Either they fail to fully grasp the implications of this issue, or they know their own limitations and won't touch it with a ten-foot pole. The end result: their arguments are built on no foundation at all.

And that was my point. The only problem with my point was that I wasn't sure that there was any real evidence for consciousness that was conscious; maybe this consciousness of the universe was just a geometry of space that accidentally gave rise to atoms without intent. So, does consciousness exist as consciousness, in any kind of structure (albeit an ethereal one), beyond matter, after the death of the body?

That question troubled me. Yes, I had read endless case histories that seemed to demonstrate the existence of consciousness. But I also knew there were other explanations. Even if these other explanations did not follow Ockham's razor as the simplest, they did follow it as the most material, assuming a strictly material universe.

I realized that I could do some little investigating on my own.

After our hypnosis training, Eva and I were curious to test the limitations of the mind with this new tool. I have to laugh when I think about our experiments, because they are really quite silly in retrospect. We figured that if the body is a manifestation of thinking, whether in esoteric or physiological terms, we ought to be able to produce some obvious, measurable change. For instance, experiments had been done in increasing breast size and they'd seemed to work. Eva and I didn't happen to be interested in that particular process, but I was drawn to the idea of "enhancing" eye color. Could we use hypnosis this way?

We tried. We read the literature on the subject and obtained standardized suggestion protocols to use. We had no shortage of volunteers from among our acquaintances willing to be our guinea pigs for these prescribed therapeutic routines. I can't say we had any significant results, though several of the subjects did call and tell me that they were certain there was a difference. I looked and looked, but never could see any.

It was then only natural to extend this type of experimentation to issues of the mind itself. I obtained as much material on these things as I could and, again, there was no shortage of volunteers for the past-life therapy. Amazingly, many people were willing to pay!

I'll never forget the day I was working with one fellow who wanted me to hypnotize him out of being in love with a particular girl who had no interest in him whatsoever. He was sure it was a past-life attraction, and if I would just take him back to it, he felt certain he could resolve it and be free of his obsession.

Everything was going fine. He went to a "past life" where he was able to identify the same dynamic with the soul of the same girl. And, yes, sure enough, she was treating him with disdain. Well, I kept encouraging him to go forward so that we could get a complete handle on the scenario before we did any therapeutic work, and soon he described himself as walking into his study. (He was a Victorian gentleman of some means, naturally.) I asked: "What are you doing now?" His response, "Putting the barrel of the gun in my mouth," nearly gave me heart failure!

Fortunately I was able to bring him back to ordinary consciousness with no harm done.

Having dealt with more complex issues in the years since, I can affirm this is really a minor situation in hypnotherapy, but it was most definitely disturbing the first time I encountered it. It's one thing to read cases about people who describe their early life, previous lives, and even death, while under hypnosis, but quite another thing to be in the presence of such drama with only a manual and a script as a guide.

Carol was curious about these experiments, even if she didn't believe for one minute that real past lives were being experienced. She wanted me to try it on her. I didn't think she would make a good subject because she was so skeptical of anything mysterious. But, curiously, she was a somnambulist. She went immediately into a very deep trance. Actually, over the years I have learned that those who are very narrow in their views tend to be the most easily hypnotized. Perhaps it is a part of their narrow and limiting realities that they are literally hypnotized into them by their environments and training.

Under hypnosis Carol described a life as an African shaman storyteller. She even spoke in some strange other language that may or may not have been an actual African tongue, but I have no way of knowing for sure. (I do still have the tape!) She then moved into another life during the time of William the Conqueror and said I had been there with her, only as a Norman, and she was only one of the local Gauls. Apparently, there was some deep resentment of me in that time, as she told it, that still affected her in the present life. I was quite surprised by this because I had no inkling that Carol had any negative feelings toward me at all. I truly had come to adore her and to really enjoy our many stimulating discussions on so many topics, even if we never fully agreed with each other.

Grant, of course, wanted to get in on the action. He produced several interesting past lives including one as a Native American warrior left behind by his tribe to die, seriously wounded in a battle with the white man. In another, he was a Revolutionary War soldier who languished in a hellhole of a prison, tormented by British soldiers until finally he escaped. His last life had been as a soldier killed in the Civil War, and on that one he was able to give names and dates and truly graphic descriptions that impressed me with their accuracy.

Was all this real, or was it an artifact of something else? I didn't know. I couldn't swear one way or the other.

In the middle of March 1974 I awakened in the night terrified and with the old feeling of having been thrown off a cliff. My heart pounded and I was drenched in sweat. As I lay there, trying to orient myself, feeling that something was terribly wrong, I heard a car pass on the street outside. There were only Venetian blinds on the windows, and whenever a car passed at night, I could watch the movement of the lights across the room, filtered through the blinds. There had been no light. Not only that, but there was no light from the street lamp outside. I was blind. Literally.

Well, I didn't want to get into a panic. Maybe the car didn't have its lights on. The street lamp could be burned out. That was also possible. So, I reached over and turned on the bedside lamp. Nothing. I was still in total and complete darkness. I thought: *Perhaps the electricity is off. That would explain why the street lamp is off.*

I got up and groped my way through the house to the bathroom and turned on the light switch. Nothing. Complete darkness. I went to the window and pulled aside the curtain. Nothing. Total blackness. No ambient light at all. Even on the darkest nights, there is some ambient light from the city, the stars, from somewhere! But I was in complete blackness.

I called my grandmother and asked her if the lights were on. She assured me they were. She was very upset when I told her that I could not see, but somehow I persuaded her that I was not in any pain, and it would be better if we just waited until morning to see the doctor. She got me back to bed, and I went immediately to sleep. In the morning I awakened with my sight restored, but I was violently sick—sick beyond anything—and every morning after for days.

My grandfather was even aroused from his drugged stupor to notice my mad dashes to the bathroom early in the morning. I had no idea what was going on, but somehow I think Grandpa knew. He suggested that I had better go to the doctor right away.

I did. I was pregnant.

I was alternately terrified and thrilled. On the one hand, it might be a little inconvenient, but babies are so wonderful that inconvenience is a small price to pay for something so precious. It wasn't like I was only 16 and facing a major disaster; I had a fiancé and we had plans to marry. This only meant that we might do it sooner. And that wasn't such a bad thing either. Being married and having a family and maybe going back to school to finish after the baby was a little older—sure!

I could do that.

I wish I could remember the conversation I had with Grant about this, but for the life of me, I can't. The only thing about it that I can remember was that the idea of a baby plunged him into the most awful depression imaginable, and all the feelings of guilt in me bubbled back to the surface. He reminded me of all the suffering he had gone through already; that he had already had a family that he had given up. Somehow I got the impression that a family was a burden that kills love, and if I was a burden to him, with a baby, he might give me up too. Again, I gave in to him to relieve this internal pressure.

Carol helped me make the arrangements for an abortion.

I cried myself to sleep and dreamed of little babies with fat knees and pudgy little hands and soft hair and sweet breath. I got up the next morning and let Grant take me to the hospital where a doctor and nurses were waiting. This was before such procedures were easily available in walk-in clinics, and it was going to be done under general anesthesia. I held in my tears and pretended I was wise in these things. I let them put the needle in my arm and I went to sleep. March 28, 1974.

I woke up hearing one nurse talking to another. "There was no baby. I can't imagine who told her she was pregnant."

What?! What did she mean "there was no baby?"

Where did the baby go? Did it mean that I didn't kill my own flesh and blood? Was I safe from this evil? But, no, I must be crazy. I went back to sleep, and later Grant took me home. In retrospect, my symptoms of pregnancy may easily have been due to the fact that I had a cyst on my ovary, but I didn't know that then. All I understood at the time was that I had at least intended to have an abortion.

Of course, I couldn't tell my grandparents what I had done. I had only Grant to comfort me for a few hours until he had to go. He reassured me that, when all his affairs were straight, when he had time to recover from the trauma of his divorce, we would marry and have a baby. It just wasn't the right time.

Of course he was right. And I wanted what he wanted. I was being foolishly emotional.

In a day or two I was up and about my daily routine. I went to school. Eva noticed I was pale. She asked. I told her. Her eyes got tight and her jaw clenched, but she said nothing except to hold me and tell me I must have done the right thing because it was the thing I did. Eva was having her own problems. She, too, was getting a divorce.

Carol came to the rescue. She nursed me, talked to me, comforted me, and encouraged me to get out and back into my usual activities. But it was difficult. For some reason, I was not healing. Day after day I continued to bleed. It was spotty sometimes, and sometimes it was heavy. I had constant pain in my lower abdomen and in my lower back. The doctor gave me pills that were supposed to stop the bleeding, but all they did was make the back pain worse. It did slow down, and I had the idea it would get better gradually. It just takes time.

* * *

My pediatrician had started me on diet pills when I was fourteen. By now, I had been taking them pretty steadily for over seven years. Yes, they kept my weight down, but it was obvious I was paying a high price. As my body had adjusted to the dosages, I had required more and more amphetamines to sustain the effect. I was now seeing four doctors, none of whom knew about the others, keeping myself medicated with four different prescriptions. All were the highest dosages available.

The medical profession was becoming aware that maybe diet pills weren't all they were cracked up to be, but this information had not yet been released into the public domain. So, I was literally an addict and didn't fully realize it. My nerves were terrible. My hands shook, I couldn't sleep well at night, my digestion was a complete wreck, and everything I ate made me sick. So, I was given a prescription for Seconal to help me sleep, Donnatal to help my stomach, and Valium to help my nerves. There were other pills I don't remember, all prescriptions from these different doctors, all of them hard narcotics.

But, somehow I managed to keep going. I could take a take a pill to wake me up, calm me down, help me eat, and put me to sleep. As long as my supply of pills held out, I was okay.

I wasn't the only one being drugged by the medical profession. Grandpa had been diagnosed with high blood pressure. So, the doctors, in their infinite wisdom, prescribed tranquilizers, muscles relaxants, and diuretics. Valium, Meprobamate, and Lasix. Of course we had faith in the doctor's good judgment.

Grandpa had been rapidly deteriorating since he began taking the pills prescribed by the doctor. He would sit in a chair in his bedroom for long hours, leaning forward with his hands dangling in front of him, occasionally drooling and his eyes completely blank. I was extremely distressed by this and repeatedly suggested that his medication was responsible, but no one would listen to me. And, eventually I became convinced they were right. It was just the fate of old people to become like zombies.

Mother's current husband was a building contractor. The Farm had reverted to weekend use and needed some maintenance, so Mother and the new husband were going to take Grandma up there for a week. I was left to take care of Grandpa. I got him put to bed that Friday night before Grant arrived, thinking that we would just stay around the house and watch TV. I didn't think that I ought to leave Grandpa alone.

But, when Grant arrived, he wanted to go out. I was nervous about leaving Grandpa alone, but Grant assured me that he would be okay for just a few hours. I worried the whole time, and Grant kept telling me that I was ruining his evening.

But I couldn't help it. He finally gave up on me in disgust and took me home.

When I got back, as soon as I came into the house, I could hear Grandpa calling me weakly. He had fallen inside the door to his bedroom, against the door, and there was no way I could open it to get inside. I went outside, found an unlocked window, climbed up on the fuel oil tanks, and came in that way. After a month of bleeding, I found that I wasn't strong enough to pick him up.

There was another door from Grandpa's bedroom that opened onto the porch. I went back out through this door, came back into the house, and called an ambulance. The EMS people came and got Grandpa onto the stretcher and took him to the hospital. I called my mother at The Farm to see if there was anything else I ought to do. She said she'd call the hospital and find out if it was necessary for them to come back right away. After about an hour, she called me back, telling me to go to bed and not worry about it. Grandpa had only suffered a cracked rib and he was going to be fine.

The next morning, Mother called to reassure me that Grandpa had been in the hospital with his high blood pressure before and this was just another similar episode. They'd give him medication, bring his blood pressure down, and everything would be fine. He must have just gotten a little dizzy when he got up to go to the bathroom, and the only damage was the cracked rib. He'd be fine and home in a couple of days. I was enormously relieved.

Since it was a weekend and Grant was bunking at Paula's, I asked him to come stay with me since I was alone in the house with Grandpa in the hospital and Grandma at The Farm with Mother. I thought he would jump at the opportunity for us to be completely alone together, and was surprised when he tried to excuse his way out. In the end, he had no real reason except some vague thing about having already made plans to do his laundry. I pointed out that he could easily do it here at the house, and he reluctantly agreed to come as soon as he "got his things sorted out."

I felt an intense stab of fear race through me. I had a sudden vision of Grant and Paula being intimate, but I quickly erased that thought. Paula had been a good friend to both of us, and I was certain of Grant's love. Hadn't he given up everything for me?

Well, sure. But for some reason he couldn't give up getting his things "sorted out."

Grant didn't show up until later in the afternoon. I wanted to go up to the hospital, but he had accepted a dinner invitation from a friend on our behalf. He kept telling me everything was fine and that I should not be so upset over what was clearly just a very small issue. He then pointed out that it was completely unfair for me to be irrational and to spoil his weekend with my unreasonable fears for my grandfather.

Again the guilt. I was making him unhappy after he had sacrificed so much for me. I agreed to go to the dinner and tried to push my fears away. I had made it clear that I was going to the hospital to see my grandfather that evening after dinner whether Grant came or not. He grudgingly agreed and after dinner, we headed for the VA hospital at the north side of town.

When we got to the hospital, I went into my grandfather's room and didn't recognize him. I was completely shocked. In just two days he had changed so much that I didn't know him. At first, I just simply thought it wasn't him, that I had mistakenly walked into the wrong room. So I called out softly: "Grandpa?" He opened his eyes and as soon as he saw me there was some sort of transformation. The light came back in his eyes, the animation of the face came back, and it was him again.

His oxygen mask had slipped so that it was across one of his eyes, and I tugged on the straps to straighten it. Both his hands were strapped to the side of the bed and I was positively and completely horrified to see my brilliant, strong, incredible, wonderful grandfather tied to his bed like an animal.

Grandpa grabbed my hand with his poor, dear hand with the missing finger, and it was still so strong. He was clutching my hand as if drowning and I was the only lifeline there was. He said to me: "You'll take care of Grandma, won't you? She needs you." And I promised.

Then he said: "Take me home, Lolly. Take me home."

But I couldn't. How can you just take somebody out of the hospital without going through a whole deal of refusing medical advice and so on? This wasn't like other times when I had snuck deviled crabs into the hospital because he complained about the terrible food. Not only that, I did not have authority to take him home. So, I tried to be cheerful and make a little joke about his cracked rib, and how it was really going to be stiff when he got home in a day or two.

In the next instant, a hunted look came into his eyes and he asked me to untie his hands so he could get to the bathroom. I told him I couldn't do that because the nurses would be after me.

"I'll call." I pushed the button for the nurse, and we waited. And waited. He obviously had to go, and it seemed only reasonable to me that when a person has to go, and they need assistance to do so, that someone should see to it that it gets done. The idea of an elderly person being subjected to the humiliation of wetting themselves because no one was going to help them never occurred to me.

I went out into the hall, tagged the next passing nurse, and said we needed some help in here. Pretty quickly a nurse arrived and the first thing she did was bustle around telling me I had to leave because visiting hours were over. Clearly my interference was not wanted.

I kissed Grandpa on the cheek and told him he would be okay until he got home. We would have deviled crabs to celebrate. And I was hustled out.

And suddenly, as we were standing in the elevator, I knew I would never see my grandfather again.

I began to cry uncontrollably. I cried all the way down the elevator, out of the building, across the parking lot, all the way home in the car, and into the house. I was shaking and sobbing and just couldn't stop.

Grant kept telling me there was absolutely no reason for me to be in such an irrational state to carry on this way. I kept trying to stop crying, struggling and gagging on my own tears. Racking sobs were erupting out of some deep well inside me. Over and over again he told me that everything was going to be all right. I had nothing to worry about. But it wasn't working. I was rapidly becoming hysterical with grief even against my own will and inclination. I had never in my life felt this way.

I went into my room and, with shaking hands, managed to open the bottle of Seconal and take two. My eyes were so full of tears that I couldn't see. I felt completely foolish, completely out of control, and I knew that my behavior was illogical.

How could I know that I would never see my grandfather again? That was nonsense! I needed to get a grip on myself.

Grant agreed to sit with me until I was ready to go to sleep. So, he sat on the edge of the bed and I gradually began to calm down a bit as the Seconal started working.

We were talking when suddenly Grant said, "Shush!" I froze and listened. I heard a sound. Someone was rattling the doorknob on the side door of the house. We heard the sounds of the deadbolt coming undone, and the door creaked open—it had a very notable and particular squeak in the hinges. All thought of crying ceased. My heart was beating ninety miles an hour. Someone was breaking into the house.

Grant got up to search my room for a weapon.

Suddenly I realized what I was hearing: I heard my grandfather walk into the house. I heard it as clearly as I have ever heard anything. He had a very distinctive walk, and there was no mistaking it. And Grant heard it too.

We felt relieved because we didn't have to face a burglar, but we were still in a panic. How to explain to my grandfather why Grant was in the house, with me, in my bedroom?

Obviously, somehow, Grandpa had gotten out of the hospital and had taken a taxi home. Grant was ready to slip into the closet at any moment. We expected Grandpa to come to my door and tell me he was home.

But apparently Grandpa had other ideas. I heard the cupboard door in the kitchen, the one that backed against my bedroom wall, creaking open. Grandpa was fumbling around in the china. I could hear the cups and saucers rattling. The cupboard shut with a dull thump and I could hear pots and pans being shuffled and the water running. I realized that Grandpa was making a cup of coffee. I had heard the same series of sounds every morning, for so many years, and had witnessed the coffee-making ritual so many times I could predict the next sound.

Well, that was a relief. We decided that while Grandpa was busy in the kitchen, we would sneak Grant out the side door. We crept out through the living room to the dining room where the door to the kitchen was on the left and the door to the porch was on the right.

But something was wrong. There was no light shining across the dining room from the kitchen. How could Grandpa be making his coffee in the dark?

Puzzled, we tiptoed to the kitchen door. All was silent and dark. The sounds of the coffee ritual had ceased. We switched on the light. There was no pan on the stove, there was no cup and saucer on the table. There was no one there.

How could that be? Had we completely lost our minds?

Grant whispered, "It's a burglar, he's hiding in the room off the kitchen." Looking around for a weapon and finding nothing, Grant picked up a big cake pan from the sideboard to use as a shield. He approached the door into the adjacent room, my grandmother's bedroom. He suddenly leaped through the door, flinging it back at the same instant, spinning around to look in all directions as quickly as he could.

No one was there.

Not to give up so easily, he picked up the walking cane from the corner of Grandma's room and went through the entire house, turning on every light as he went. He opened and shut closets, peered behind doors, under beds, and literally everywhere that anyone could hide.

Meanwhile, I stood shivering in the kitchen clutching a knife I had taken out of the drawer. If the burglar slipped back in there while I was alone, I was going to be ready. As I stood there, I glanced up at the clock on the kitchen wall—a very fat chef with a clock in his huge belly—and saw that it was just then five minutes after one o'clock in the morning.

Grant finally gave up after he had searched the house three times, and besides, it was time for him to leave. But that was okay with me. I didn't need to cry anymore because I knew. Grandpa wanted to come home. And he did. He just didn't bother to bring his body with him.

* * *

In the morning the phone rang. A hospital official asked to speak to my grandmother. I explained that she was in the country and could I take a message? After verifying that I was a member of the family, the person said that they were sorry to have to tell me that my grandfather had passed away during the night. I only asked: "What time?" Around 1:00 a.m. was as close as they could come. It was May 19, 1974.

I still grieved over my almost baby, whether there was a baby or not. But that is not terribly unusual or special. Yes, I had a huge burden of guilt that Grandpa had fallen while I was out. I also felt guilt because I was certain that if I had taken him out of the hospital, if I had stood up to the system, he would still be alive. But that is also fairly normal.

The one thing out of the ordinary was the fact that my grandfather had "come home" at the time he died. More than that, I had received forewarning even though Grant had tried to convince me that it was nonsense. What is more, the phenomena had been experienced and witnessed by another person.

Was this proof of consciousness?

It was most definitely different from reading about cases that were written up in dry, technical language. Even if I had come to some conclusion in my subconscious mind that my grandfather was going to die, based on some physical clues, how could I then explain the auditory effects we both heard? Was the fact that a third party had, in my presence, also experienced this visitation any kind of evidence?

It was as though I had asked God a question and he had permitted me to receive an answer at the same time my grandfather died.

To bring me some small comfort ...

Grant was very good to me through the funeral arrangements and even agreed to be a pallbearer, so a very difficult time was gotten through with the least amount of difficulty. I found that if I took extra diet pills, I could work harder, and if I was working, I became exhausted, and if I was exhausted, I didn't cry so much. But that can only go on so long. Eventually, my hands shook so badly and my nerves were so taut that I had to increase the tranquilizers just to be able to talk coherently. I could barely keep any food down; I hadn't stopped bleeding for a single day in over three months.

I was, in short, a wreck.

I didn't know how truly dire my condition was. I have always had this ability to keep working, to keep going, to keep doing no matter how sick I am, right up to the moment of total collapse.

When an animal in the wild is weak and wounded, the vultures begin to circle, waiting for the imminent end. Sometimes they land and begin to tear at the flesh of the still-living creature, thus hastening death. Just so, the predators moved into my life.

CHAPTER FIFTEEN

BLITZKRIEG

After my grandfather's death, family dynamics shifted dramatically. For years my grandfather had managed my mother, knowing something was significantly wrong with her approach to life. He could limit the damage she did to others by supervising her. But all that was changed now.

When I was nearly fifteen, and we'd been living at The Farm for several years, Mother made a great show of following Grandpa's instructions for managing the property in every detail. At the time, a rather infamous land developer bought up all the salt flats across the road with plans to build a housing project. The flats were underwater twice a day when the tide came in, so he planned a dredging operation to form a network of canals and fingers of land. This unscrupulous developer made many futile offers to buy my grandfather's prime real estate. Then he bought all the land around us to make us miserable. Part of the misery came in a rapid rise of property taxes nearly impossible to pay.

Under the Florida homestead exemption a primary residence qualified for a tax break. But Grandpa owned two houses in Tampa and a block of city lots, so he needed a way to ease the tax burden. He called a family meeting to discuss the situation. My aunt and uncle already owned several houses they leased out for income. My grandfather decided to deed The Farm over to Mother, who owned nothing, so she could file for the tax exemption. He sat at the dining room table and laid out the rules. Mother needed to understand that this property was the inheritance of the grandchildren, and put into her care with that intent firmly established. She was never to mortgage it, or to make substantial changes without consulting the family, and she was never to sell without the family's agreement. She must also keep the taxes paid. As long as she lived, she had a home. But she must make arrangements to leave the property in her will to the six grandchildren, who might someday wish to build homes there.

Mother solemnly agreed to carry out my grandfather's wishes. He signed the deed. The notary summoned to the house for the occasion affixed his signature and seal. It was done.

Several years later, after I'd moved to Tampa to live with my grandparents, they decided the house in Tampa would be mine after their deaths. Grandfather designated the land on The Farm where the house stood to go to my brother, the remainder apportioned to our cousins. Additionally, the block of city lots would pass to my uncle and aunt to be divided among their children. It was a financially equitable solution. Grandpa believed that his wishes would be carried out. He was hesitant to tie these bequests to paper, not wishing to hamper any future situation that might come up for my grandmother.

I can only think my grandfather's mind was beginning to lose hold on reality when he made the arrangements as he did. He depended on my mother to keep her promise, and he depended on his son, my uncle, to see that she did.

My uncle had never stood up to Mother in his life.

Since childhood, Mother had worked to manipulate what she wanted from Grandpa, living as she pleased on his generosity. Now that he was dead, a whole new ballgame started. She immediately took the role of uxorious daughter, taking charge of Grandma's life. Grandma needed rest and recovery from all the years of caring for Grandpa. Grandma must be coddled and entertained and her every whim satisfied. Therefore, Grandma must come and live with Mother and her sixth husband. Naturally, this meant that Grandma's income came to live with Mother, too.

Since the house in Tampa was to be mine eventually, Mother decided I should most definitely begin to take care of it myself. It would still be Grandma's house, but I was the assigned heir. That made me the responsible party. Never mind that my job paid just enough to meet incidental needs and I was going to school full time. I was so devastated by my grandfather's death, physically and emotionally, that I could barely function. Never mind all that. Time for you to stand on your own, my mother told me. Grant and I should get married. We'd have a house of our own right away, and his job transfer to Tampa had come through.

But Grant had shocking news for me.

"I'm just not ready to get married again," he told me. "Of course I still want to marry you! Just not yet." We could live together for a while, but I was to understand right up front this was only a "test situation" and he was doing it "for me." In essence, I was held to a very high standard, and I'd better not fail.

Well, nothing like starting out with the idea that you are being measured for the "right fit!" What happened to "the sun rises and sets in your eyes" and "I can't live without you?"

In those days, "living together" was becoming quite popular, even if it was not yet acceptable in my family. But Grant convinced my mother and grandmother that he had tremendous love and respect for me. Living together was a temporary situation "until he was sure of his career potentials." Somehow, he made both of them believe he was just the cat's meow and ideal son-in-law material.

So Grandma went off to the East Coast with Mother. Grant and I settled into the house.

The next day I woke up with Grant beside me. I was completely ecstatic. Finally, a full night together—a foretaste of endless days of bliss to come!

Naturally, Grant wanted to make all kinds of changes. His idea of "preventive maintenance" meant going through everything and tossing out what he considered to be trash. He simply could not bear to live in a house where years of accumulated mementos cluttered the rooms. He needed to feel "in control" to be comfortable in his environment. I had to make it clear that the house still, technically, belonged to my grandmother as long as she lived. I stood firm that none of my grandparents' possessions would be touched. Besides, I was perfectly happy with the house. Well, maybe new drapes and fresh paint, but nothing major.

Grant began to act in a way that truly baffled me. First, he went outside and cleaned out my car. He came in with a whole bag of trash to berate me for being such a pig. Well, sure! When I have trash while driving, I don't toss it out the window. I'm not a litterbug. And I do, eventually, clean it all out; it just hadn't gotten to the point it bothered me. But I was very glad that he was taking such an interest in my affairs. He obviously loved me very much.

Next, there was the issue of his basket of dirty clothes. I was pretty surprised to see that they were all neatly folded. He actually folded his dirty clothes! I had never known anyone who folded their laundry before they washed it. I remembered what Rose Frank had said about not needing to do everything perfectly, but I remained silent.

While I was happily doing his laundry and trying on the wife role, Grant went to check out my car as a proper husband should. After a bit he came in and asked me when was the last time I had changed the oil. I have to admit that changing the oil in the car had never occurred to me, so I looked at him blankly and asked: "Should I?"

Grant rolled his eyes in amazement and said: "It's probably too late." He snorted in disgust and left the room. After a few minutes, I went to find him. There he was with my purse dumped out on the table, going through all the junk, sorting it into piles. He told me to sit down and began to lecture me about how preventive maintenance extended to all things in life, and how bad at it I was. He was even sure that I didn't keep my checkbook balanced and began to look through that, too.

Well, no one had ever taken such interest in my activities so I was very happy, even if I did get a stern lecture for my failings. Soon, the purse was put to rights and then he went back outside. I decided it was time to make a nice "wifely" lunch and was busy for a little while before I went to see what he was doing.

What I saw horrified me.

My grandparents had a huge, ancient philodendron growing beside the side porch of the house, a tropical plant often grown indoors as a potted plant. When it is allowed to grow outside, each year it sends out supporting roots that hold up the constantly extending trunk which grows at about a forty-five-degree angle from the ground. Grant had cut away all the support roots and the fifteen-foot trunk had collapsed on the ground. He was desperately trying to prop it up with concrete blocks, but it was ruined.

"What are you doing?!" I asked in shock.

"It was messy looking so I cut all the roots away."

"I can't believe you couldn't see that there was a reason for those roots!" I said.

As much as I loved him, I couldn't bear to see what he had done to my grandmother's beloved philodendron. I turned and went back inside the house.

Apparently, it was okay to criticize me, but not to criticize him. All the rest of the day Grant treated me with cool, but distant, courtesy. I was so upset over the plant that I was just as glad that I didn't have to talk to him overmuch. I decided that the less we said about it, the sooner things would return to normal, though I wasn't too sure what normal really was. God only knows, I had experienced precious little "normal" in my whole life.

* * *

I could not come to terms with the loss of my grandfather. A death is like a wound. For me, the death of the one person who had effectively given me the only mainstay of security in my life felt like having a major body part amputated. People take for granted that physical wounds take time to heal, but in those days emotional wounds were dismissed with comments like Grant's "get over it and get on with it." As evidence for his view, he repeatedly told me how he had found his own father dead. Yes, it had been a terrible shock, but since he needed to be strong for his mother, he was able to handle it rationally. Never mind that his father had been horribly abusive and both he and his mother were glad he was dead. Such comparisons were useless to Grant. Death was death.

I realize now that my grandmother's absence, my mother's abandonment, and Grant's "get a grip" attitude contributed to my deep depression. I was truly convinced that something was significantly wrong with me because I just could not stop crying. Every decision seemed overwhelming. I found myself asking Grant what to do about the smallest thing. This irritated him to no end.

When I drove home from classes, as I approached the house, all the memories of my life with my grandfather came rushing back. He had always been there waiting for me to come home. Now he would never be there waiting at the door to let me in again. Inside the house, as I came into the kitchen, my grandfather's favorite coffee cup sat on the counter. Everywhere I looked I was reminded of him.

"What are you crying about now?" Grant asked me. "If you don't get over it, I'm going to have to move out. It's too depressing. I have problems too! What about me?" He'd lived through his own trauma of divorce, and I should realize Grant's loss was far worse than anything I had ever suffered.

I found some relief by increasing doses of Valium during the day and Seconal at night. As much as I loved Grant, I could only make him angry and resentful that I was unable to devote all of my attention to him and his needs. There was just so little inside me to give. His demands were impossible for me to meet.

Carol began coming over every day, engaging Grant in long conversations that kept him happy and entertained. He decided to sign up for some evening classes. Carol was friendly with a number of people in the school administration; she volunteered to find out what kinds of special funding and scheduling would work to get Grant back in school.

Eventually, between his job, union meetings, and classes, he was often absent. When he was at home, our conversations were distressing. I was "invading his space." I was being too "dominant." If I didn't express concern over his complaints about his job or his schedule, I was ignoring his "inner child." If I was busy with something of my own, I wasn't giving him enough "strokes," and if I wanted to do something together with him I was "violating his right to do what he wanted." I didn't know anything about keeping a budget and I most definitely didn't have a clue about the "real world." The only way to cure this, as well as my depression, was for me to get a "real" job.

I knew that Grant had been psychologically overwhelmed by his experiences in Vietnam. He had survived two tours as an ordnance expert. He constantly reminded me that he was living on borrowed time because none of his friends had survived. At this point, he brought out the tape. One night during the Tet offensive when his unit was under a devastating attack by the Viet Cong, he'd left his tape recorder running during the ensuing battle. When he returned, he found that the tape had captured all the sound effects of the assault. He brought the tape home; it had become one of his most treasured possessions.

Grant became obsessed with playing this tape and demanding that I listen with him. He would describe in gruesome detail what was happening with each terrifying blast or series of mortar rounds. At one point I heard an almost endless series of explosions, screams, inarticulate voices, and cries. The munitions dump blew up, killing a whole list of his pals. He named them all, talking about what they had done the day before their deaths, how they had chatted or exchanged jokes. It was macabre, depressing, and emotionally numbing.

How could I help him? Grant insisted that I needed to become self-sufficient, that I couldn't depend on him. He arranged with friends to find me a waitress job at a sandwich shop, where the patrons were blue-collar workers who made vulgar comments and rude suggestions. I had no experience in dealing with such men. My grandfather had always protected me, so I thought this was the proper role for a man to take for the women in his life, whether they were wives, daughters, or girlfriends. I expected Grant to be outraged and to agree this was really not the proper work environment for me. But his response was to laugh uproariously that I was finally getting a taste of the real world. It was good for me and I had better get used to it! Because now he no longer wanted to be committed to a future together.

Grant told me he needed far more time to work through his own psychological issues before he would be able to commit himself to another person. He not only needed more time, he needed more space. He had decided, at the end of three months, that he wanted to move out on his own.

At the same time, he didn't want to give me up. He wanted me to be there for him at a distance. He told me how beautiful I was (never mind that I never believed that one!), how much he loved me, but that he needed to do this for both of us, for our future happiness. He needed to work through his confused emotions. It didn't make any sense. I suggested that we go to a counselor and try to find what was the root of the problem. I made an appointment. We went. The counselor told me Grant just wanted to do his thing, so why was I so obsessed with preventing him? Just let the guy go!

When we came home, Grant shook out a couple Valiums and gave them to me with a glass of water. After a bit I was able to control my shaking and sobbing. I got up to try to make him some dinner. He told me not to bother. He was going out to eat. But first he had something to tell me.

"I need to confess to you that I've been seeing other women."

He listed them—it was quite a list—from the beginning, starting with Paula. Some were women at his job, some were women for whom he installed telephones, just the way he'd met me. Of course, none of these women "meant anything" to him. This behavior was just "evidence" that he really needed time to sort himself out.

He didn't know why he did the things he did. He couldn't control his impulses. And this was why he was making full confession to me, and only to me. He loved me too much to continue to lie to me. I would just have to accept the fact that he needed to do these things until it was "out of his system." And if I would just be patient, he would soon get over it and we could pick up where we left off. Besides, it wouldn't be so painful for me if I didn't love him so much. Clearly, my suffering was my fault because I had made the mistake of loving him.

Something exploded like a bomb inside me. How dare he blame my pain on me! I never wanted to love him; I had resisted in every way possible, even running away from him. He had maneuvered, manipulated, and pursued me, broken down all my defenses—for what?

And what about the risk to me? How could I know that the problems I had with healing after the abortion weren't because of his loose morals and lowlife habits? And I just went berserk.

A three-foot-tall model of a Rodin statue, The Kiss, stood on a pedestal near the door. Grant had given it to me. The Kiss was the perfect symbol of Grant's lies and my stupidity for believing him. I picked up this heavy statue as if it weighed nothing and aimed it at his head. He ducked. The statue hit the screen door, knocked it open and went sailing across the porch, landing on the sidewalk and shattering into a hundred pieces.

That felt pretty good. How about a stereo?

Grant had given me a stereo too. I rushed over and grabbed the receiver, the speakers dragging along behind me. "Get out! Go! I can't stand to look at you! You disgust me!" I heaved the stereo and speakers out the door to land beside the shattered statue on the sidewalk. I looked around for something else to throw at him, but didn't want to debase any of my grandparents' things, so the only available object was a chair. I picked up the chair and hefted it up to my right with the intention of swinging it at him. Grant grabbed it by the legs and wrestled it away from me.

Grant tried to grab me by the arms. "I'm sorry! I'm sorry! I had to tell you the truth!" I guess I was on some sort of adrenaline autopilot because I just spit in his face and told him to take his filthy hands off me.

His hands dropped. He started to go around gathering up his things and loading them in his car.

I sat at the table and watched his every move as he packed and loaded. He looked utterly forlorn and bereft. But, in that moment, I was in icy control. I never spoke a word until he had finished. Then he came, stood at the door, and tried the long "looking in the eyes" maneuver, telling me how much he truly loved me and how fate was acting on him in such a tragic way. Would I please just give him one last kiss? He moved toward me, holding out his hand.

I simply could not believe the nerve. A kiss? I remembered that I had on a pair of earrings he'd given me. I reached up and jerked them out, not caring if I tore my ears to shreds, and slammed them into his outstretched hand.

"Get out of here before I call the police and have you arrested. You disgust me."

He gave me one last lingering, grieving look and said, "I love you, you know."

I was exhausted. And the Valium was taking full effect. I closed the door behind Grant. I went to bed and cried myself to sleep.

When I woke up alone some hours later, the cold isolation of my position became clear. Of all times that I needed my grandfather, it was now. But he was gone, because I hadn't been home, and I hadn't been home because I was with Grant. Insult to injury. I had been out with a slimeball and my grandfather was dead as a result.

But wait ... after so great a trauma as Grant's abused childhood, his experiences in Vietnam, his divorce, I expected too much of him too soon. My own needs, my grief for my grandfather, for my abortion, were more than he could bear. I had driven him to seek emotional support from other women because I had been inadequate to heal him. It was, indeed, my failing that was at the root of the situation.

I decided that a couple weeks of space would help him sort things out. And, fortunately, Carol was looking out for Grant for me. Carol was the one who held and rocked me in my grief. Carol, my dear friend, assured me that in time everything would work out.

I quit my waitress job and went back to work at school. It was nearly impossible to concentrate, to keep my mind on my work, on my studies. I tried to talk to people, to act normal, but I knew I was doing a really poor imitation. I lost more weight. When I looked in the mirror, I realized that I looked positively skeletal. My eyes had an unnatural, feverish glow. I barely recognized the gaunt person looking back at me.

A photo taken from around this time showing how gaunt I was looking.

Waking up with diet pills, keeping my nerves calm with Valium, settling my stomach with Donnatal, and going to sleep with Seconal, I decided to let Grant know I still loved him. I would be there for him and when he was ready to come home, I'd be waiting.

Carol was watching out for Grant on my behalf; she told me he'd found his own place. A light touch would work best: a brief visit, a thoughtful housewarming gift, and no pressure. She offered to come along for moral support.

We pulled up to an old Victorian house converted to apartments. I could see Grant inside the lighted windows of the ground-floor unit, carrying boxes, putting things away. He answered our knock at the door.

"Hi!" I smiled, holding out my gift.

"Thought you could use ..." and a woman's voice came from the room behind him. "Who is it, Honey?" A blonde in a housecoat came up behind him and Grant began to stutter.

"It's not what you think, Babe ..."

I just turned around and walked away.

Grant came tearing after me. "Wait, wait! She's just a friend helping me move! Stop! Let me explain!" And he reached out and took hold of my jacket to slow me down. I just shrugged out of it and kept walking, leaving him there in the moonlight holding the empty garment. I think he knew there was nothing he could say to explain this perfidy. I heard a terrible howl of grief and turned to see him sunk to his knees in the dirt, clutching my jacket to his face, sobbing. Can you believe the drama?

I got in the car and said, "Let's go."

A few days later Carol brought me a message. I was to come to Grant without delay, because he would be dead soon. I dropped everything, found someone to fill in for me in the lab at school, and signed out. I rushed over to his apartment. He came to the door looking fine. "What's wrong? Has something happened?"

He sank wearily into a chair, his head hanging down. "Yes. I'm at the end. I can't go on. I'm destroying you. And that is destroying me. I don't know what I am doing anymore, or even who I am. I know you can never forgive me. I can never forgive myself. I'm the scum of the earth. I'm nothing."

What happened to the woman who had been there with him? Why wasn't she the one he called on for help?

"She's gone. I told you she meant nothing to me. She was just a friend."

Well, sad to say, I bought it. Only I could save him. I sank to my knees beside him. "What can I do? I love you! I'll do anything to help you!"

Grant truly felt that his experiences in Vietnam had done something terrible to his mind and he simply could not be responsible for his behavior. He loved me to distraction, but he could not control his compulsions to hurt me. He hated himself for being alive while all his friends were dead. It was too big and terrible a wound to heal. He knew it. There was only one solution. We must die together. We were soulmates, but it simply was not possible for us to deal with the problems of this life. We could only be happy in another life, and the surest way to bring this about was to die together—to make a pact.

I didn't want to die. At least not right then. It took a few hours to talk him out of his suicidal plan.

Saving Grant became my reason to live.

The idea that we were doomed lovers, like Romeo and Juliet, preyed on my mind. Yes, maybe we were doomed. If he died, I would want to die too. And if I couldn't be with him, I didn't want to be with anyone.

Strangely, now that he had me back in the palm of his hand, the next time I saw him he was determined to keep me out of his life. To make it sink in, he had clearly decided that overt cruelty was the way to go. He told me he wasn't going to see me anymore, that I must not call him or come to see him. He smiled wickedly and said: "Payback is hell, isn't it?" I was stunned. What was he talking about?

These whiplash scenes of "yes I want you, no I don't" were breaking me in pieces. I needed somebody to talk to. Dear Carol. Always there to pick up the pieces and help me put myself back together.

But Carol had her own problems. Her marriage was crumbling because her husband was tired of being both mother and father to their two children while she went to school, worked, and kept up with her activist groups. She sent messages back and forth between me and Grant, keeping the modern-day Romeo and Juliet together. Grant called Carol, she rushed over, patted his back while he wept for his cruelty to me, and then came to my house to shake out another Valium and pour me a glass of water. Sweet Carol. Rocking me while I cried and patting my back and cooing like a mother. I don't know how I would have survived without her.

When she asked me to watch her children for a few hours, it was the least I could do. But her husband came by to pick them up early. So, with the evening ahead of me after all, I decided that I'd drive by Grant's apartment and maybe, depending on how I felt, I would stop in. I was hungry to hear his voice, to look into his eyes, and see just how the land lay at the moment. I was surprised to see Carol's car in his driveway. She was supposed to be at some sort of planning meeting.

Grant had left the door open and the screen unlatched. I wondered if they had gone somewhere to walk, so I decided I would just go in and sit and wait for them to return. I walked in and, as soon as I did, I was able to see through the bedroom door. There, through that door, was his bed. And there in the bed was a monster, a monster with four legs. Two of those legs were short and stubby, kicking in the air, while a most familiar backside heaved and humped and two voices joined together in moans of desire and declarations of eternal union.

I froze and stared in stunned fascination. Watching the swaying motion was like watching a cobra dance. A cobra. One must move away from danger slowly and carefully. I backed out the door, trying not to make a sound, but something bumped and the two bodies froze. The flushed and sweating faces looked at me and there was fear in their eyes. I turned and walked out, leaving the door hanging open. I got in my car and drove home.

The house was utterly silent and empty. I went into my bedroom and sat down on the bed, dry eyed for a change and numb with shock. I had destroyed Grant's marriage and the future happiness of his family. By loving him, I had conceived a life. I had destroyed this unborn child to prevent further damage. By loving Grant, I had caused the death of my grandfather. And, by the death of my grandfather, I had ruined my own potential to give support to Grant when he needed it most. By failing him, I had forced him to seek support elsewhere.

And through my most grievous fault, my own choices had destroyed so many lives. I must surely be guilty of something even greater for Carol to betray me. We had been closer than sisters. We had shared our deepest secrets. She had been my one source of strength and confidence that truth and honor and beauty existed in this world. I had come to see her as one of the most beautiful people I had ever known. I had long ago stopped seeing the awkward structure of her physical vehicle and only saw what I thought was a true and honorable and courageous soul.

But all that must have been a lie. And the fault was in me.

There was no "true love" anywhere. Not from Mother or Father, not from Grant or Carol. If my grandfather had been the only one who truly loved me, what good did it do? He was dead. Love could die.

I wanted no part of such a world. I could conceive not one single reason to continue to draw breath.

I can't say how the idea occurred to me. Perhaps I had been haunted by the same ghosts that were attached to Keith and Grant. The ease with which it came to the surface suggests an unacknowledged presence. Now, it pushed its way out with the unremitting pressure and torment of giving birth. The idea emerged with an anguished cry from the depths of my being into my consciousness fully formed.

In the peaceful silence of my room, moonlight filtering over the bed through the slats in the blinds, I realized that it would be very pleasant to have such peace in an absolute way. Forever.

Again, as in the moments when I yielded to Grant, there seemed to be two of me. And again, these two parts of myself came into conflict in my massive and overwhelming guilt. I knew I could turn away now, and drown in my guilt, or I could yield and be at peace.

I yielded.

The moment I did, tremendous relief and a sensation of a "presence" embraced me, emanating a sudden ease and overpowering calm that flooded my being. I could do nothing to heal my own pain, but I could certainly free many other people of the source of their pain: me.

Once I had yielded, this presence took over, as if operating under remote control. With new eyes I saw all the little bottles on the dresser—the ones that helped me get up, go to sleep, stay calm, digest my food—and there was a carafe of water. I began to empty the bottles one by one into my hand, pouring each little pile into my mouth and swallowing them down with water dripping from my mouth and chin. One by one. All of them. Then I lay down and began to make patterns in my mind out of the dots in the acoustic tiles of the ceiling.

After a while, I thought happily that I would just go to sleep and wake up where Grandpa was. I hadn't been able to bring him home, but now I could go to him and everything would be all right again.

My eyes were closing and consciousness was fading; I was floating—almost there—but the damn phone beside me was ringing and ringing and ringing. Disturbing the peace.

I tried to ignore it. I thought about just knocking it over, but a voice whispered to me that I had better get rid of whoever it was. If I just knocked it off the bed, or took the receiver off and said nothing, someone would get suspicious.

It was Eva. "Hi! Eva! Whatcha doin'? Jest gonna sleep a liddle here ..." and I couldn't hold the phone a second longer. It fell to the floor with a clatter.

Eva. Two strange men. Rolling through the side doors on a magic carpet into the cool night air. Noises. Engines. Voices. Someone holding me in their arms—a strange man saying over and over: "Come on baby, come on ... come back ... you can do it!" Tubes in my throat and nose, needles in my arms. Feeling a horrible shock and a sensation like a rubber band that is snapped across the room. Nothing else, just that. September 28, 1974. My mother's birthday.

It had been almost exactly nine months since I yielded to Grant on Christmas Eve. Seeds of destruction had been planted in the fertile womb of my soul, and in due time, had been born. What child was this?

CHAPTER SIXTEEN

DANCES WITH SUNLIGHT

What do you do when you wish to die and the Universe obviously has other plans? Argue?

Several days later I woke up in the hospital. My mother was there. I realized, to my horror, that by my own hand I had confirmed every negative opinion she had ever pronounced about me and my flawed character. I had given the whole world evidence that Mother was correct: Laura was "not quite all right."

I knew I would not be released from the hospital as long as there was any indication I might finish the job. I also knew enough about psychology to convince the doctors that it would be safe to release me to my mother. Since I hadn't died, I wanted to get on with things.

At home, I found Mother, the stepfather, and Grandma all back in residence at the Tampa house. Their whispering stopped instantly when I came into a room. Artificial conversation was spoken in tones a bit too loud and forcefully "normal." I was being "handled." Adult rights and privileges were revoked. I was to be treated like a small child who could barely dress herself, a damaged child who could not be told the truth about anything. Everything said to me was carefully weighed to avoid setting me off. Most significant of all, pills of every kind were removed from the house. There wasn't even a bottle of aspirin. Well, they didn't know about my secret stash in my dressing table. But I opened the drawer, looked at the bottles, and decided it was now or never. I took them in the bathroom, opened them one by one, pouring the contents into the toilet, flushing, and dropping the empty bottles in the trash.

I was about to experience cold-turkey withdrawal after eight years of amphetamine dependence.

Withdrawal is similar to the worst case of influenza imaginable. None of us knew this, and we simply assumed that I was sick.

My body was alternately racked with shaking chills or raging fever. I felt voraciously hungry, only to lose everything I ate after a mad dash to the bathroom. I was bent double by abdominal cramps as the system that had functioned so long on artificial support struggled to right itself. All I wanted to do was sleep, but often sleep would not come for hours that seemed interminable. Then exhaustion overcame me with a sleep full of nightmares, soaked in cold sweat. I lay in bed listening to my heart speed up and slow down, sure that it would either burst in my chest or stop completely.

I felt utterly cast aside by God. Weary of life, I prayed to be delivered from my existence. Another attempt by my own hand was unthinkable. If I failed, my position would be even more desperate. My life seemed to consist of blunders, misdeeds, lost opportunities, inadequacy, guilt, and now humiliation at being unable to "do the deed" in a competent way.

Nothing in nature lasted. All turned to dust in the vast blackness of the universe. Riches, fame, love, youth, health: all vain illusions. My heart entombed itself in a chilly vault of despair.

I had believed for so long, against all evidence to the contrary, that love and kindness and benevolence were our birthright. The realization that humanity could do little but "fail with good grace" was insupportable. I was inconsolable at the possibility that everything good, noble, clean, and pure was, in the end, merely ephemeral. I recalled Poe: *"And the angels uprising, unveiling, affirm, that the play is the tragedy, 'Man,' and its hero the Conqueror Worm."*

Day after day, with no relief, I suffered this intolerable desolation. After years of seeking God, all I had known had been the evil of the world disguising itself as good. When I looked ahead, I saw far more pain in life than happiness and long years of agonizing struggle until the grave.

My interior strength had been annihilated. I cannot say that I wanted to end my own life any longer, but the desire to be out of this world was now more present than my former desire to engage the world in order to learn about it. I agreed with Tolstoy: *"What is truest of life, there is nothing even funny or silly in it; life is cruel and stupid, purely and simply. ... What will be the outcome of what I do today? Of what I shall do tomorrow? What will be the outcome of all my life? Why should I live? ... Is there in life any purpose which the inevitable death which awaits me does not undo and destroy?"*

These questions are buried deep in every soul. In some, the question grows inside until it emerges and demands an answer. And, without an answer, it is impossible to go on. But an "observer" part of myself watching these mental torments offered one idea: there may be a pool of water beyond the next dune of sand in this endless desert of burning thirst.

Hope had not died.

At last the physical symptoms receded. Such disillusionment is like tasting of the fruit of the tree of the knowledge of good and evil. Everything was now a burden to be borne. I, like every other being on the planet, was accursed. Sacrifice and atonement were required to achieve the living water that was promised. *"Come unto me all ye that labor and are heavy laden and I will give you rest ..."*

How desperately I needed that rest!

* * *

Eva was the only one who was allowed to visit me. One day she told me that after the hypnosis seminar, she'd received an announcement in the mail of an upcoming appearance of an important new psychic, Al Miner. His abilities to give spontaneous channeled readings in deep trance similar to Edgar Cayce's work had rapidly developed, and his fame in the psychic underground had spread.

Al soon became involved in research conducted by the Association for Research and Enlightenment, the Cayce group known as A.R.E. Of a large group of other psychics tested for accuracy, Miner received the highest scores. He was appointed to the advisory board for Atlantic University, a sister organization of A.R.E. and The Edgar Cayce Foundation.

This was interesting, indeed.

Eva's brochure explained that Al's spiritual contact, called Lama Sing, was not a single entity, but a group. They needed no names or titles. Information came through Universal or God Consciousness, by a group of souls dedicated to the service of God and humanity. They were able to transmit this information through Al because he was a member of the soul group, the last one still incarnate. When he departed the earth, the entire group would move to higher levels and be no longer accessible for communication. Someone remarked that the voice sounded very much like an Eastern monk he'd met named Lama Sing, and the name stuck. So the entities became known as "Lama Sing."

Al had been given the "A.R.E. Seal of Approval," and Eva thought perhaps he was the new Edgar Cayce. Outstanding psychic ability is rare, so I didn't want to spend money for a reading with this guy. But I did encourage Eva to check him out. A few days later, Eva invited me to go to her appointment with Al Miner just to keep her company. I agreed, and we were off to Clearwater again.

It seemed like centuries since I'd been out of the house. Driving across the bay bridge with the windows down and the brine-scented air blowing our hair felt invigorating. The almost-fluorescent blue of the clear Florida sky shimmered with the dazzling sparkle of sunlight on the water of the bay. The atmosphere danced in a surreal way. I had a strong sensation of something teasing at the edge of my mind but when I focused, it slipped away. The hollow inside me seemed to recede.

Al was staying at the home of friends who were also active in the A.R.E., the Cayce group in Virginia Beach, and they made everything available for his comfort and the reception of his clients.

We were greeted at the door by a smiling, buxom blonde who cheerfully invited us inside. There were no trappings of weirdness that I had come to associate with the psychics I had visited: no dark drapes, icons of the Virgin, crystal balls, or long, flowing robes. On the contrary, this house was very ordinary, and this woman wore jeans and a Western shirt.

Apparently Al was already in trance, and Eva went directly into a small bedroom set up for this purpose. After a half hour she came out with a look of total amazement on her face.

"You must have a reading," she whispered urgently. "I'll pay for it if you don't want to spend your money!"

I was skeptical as all get out, but the appointment time was available, so I agreed. This was really a perfect setup for a valid test. I had not even made an appointment myself, so there was no way the guy could have collected any information about me in advance. And I had definitely mastered the art of asking questions completely ambiguously. After a quick consultation between Eva and our hostess, I went into the little room.

It was just an ordinary bedroom, but almost completely bare, with a frosted glass window without drapery and plain white walls. A tape recorder and small lamp on a cheap card table stood next to an army cot. Al was lying supine, covered by a light blanket, a hand towel over his eyes to block the light. His hands rested on the cot, extended at his sides. During the entire reading, the only part of him that moved, other than his lips, was one little finger, which sort of vibrated every time he spoke.

I wanted to open with a really ambiguous question to do a reality check. Controlling my voice to give nothing away, I asked for a general health commentary. I was prepared to mislead if he made vague statements assuming nonexistent health problems.

But I was surprised by that inert man who had no way to read anything about my expressions or body language. His voice was a deep, gravelly baritone, with a peculiar accent that was sort of British East Indian. In sonorous tones he inquired:

LS: *Is there a specific area in your body that concerns you? We note about you now a generalized condition that seems to be relating not only to your bloodstream, but seems to be affecting somewhat the assimilating of foodstuffs, and seems to be causing somewhat of an imbalance in your body. We note that the indications of the bloodstream in terms of the lymph cells and productive secretions thereof are of such a nature then to indicate a minor infection ... Also we note that the white cell count is somewhat erratic, but seems to be consistently higher than is normal. The red cell count seems to be weakened and somewhat diminished in terms of the elemental carrier conditions of the body's reservoir system ... it means concisely that your body is not dispersing properly foodstuffs, do you see? Now, lymph reaction seems to be due to inflammatory condition on uterine walls. We find somewhat of a tilted condition of some of the internal ... one moment, please. [long pause] Have you recently been with child?*

That certainly took my breath away. I answered yes.

LS: *Well, you are still bearing some conditions in regard to this. We find somewhat of the distension on the wall structure of the uterus. We find this to be due to ... [long pause] Did you have a difficult delivery?*

Obviously, this guy was right there inside my body looking at things. I couldn't figure out why he didn't know that I didn't deliver at all, but maybe his ability to access information was based on the structure of the question. So, I answered: "No, I had an abortion."

LS: *Very well then. This perhaps is the reason for this then. We see that there was an irritant along the uterine wall. We find this to have caused an inflammatory condition here. This seems to have caused a secondary infection causing discharge, causing also some natural production from lymphoid tissue. ... There seem to be several of the capillaries here that are very irritated, and there is indication that they are, from time to time, erupting.*

That was certainly true. I had been bleeding off and on, mostly on, for nine months or so. Lama Sing, speaking through Al, then went on to prescribe corrective treatments and dietary adjustments very much like the old Cayce readings.

Okay, he could do a physical reading similar to Cayce's, and he was on the money in that regard.

"I would like to ask about my association with an individual named Grant?" Is that ambiguous enough? I thought so. And that is why the response was so interesting.

LS: *There seems to be some confusion here in terms of this relationship. It does not seem as though you have both placed each other in harmony here. (That was an understatement!) There seem to be some aspects of this that you are not telling one another. If you would seek to make this a lasting relationship, it would require that you both express yourselves more completely. And to keep the expressions of an honest nature, so that there are no items that are hidden and no barriers to hide behind. Here there can be a lasting relationship if it is chosen. But it seems that there is not, indeed, a true choice here.*

That pretty much summed it up. I wanted to see if he could just come right out and tell me: who was lying? Who was choosing and who was not?

"You say that something is not chosen. By me or by him?"

LS: *Well, it is almost as though both entities are somewhat reserved in certain areas. Now, you know yourself, my child, that you do not seem to be totally releasing self.*

It was certainly true that I had spent all my energy hiding myself, suppressing myself, and feeling at fault for everything that had happened.

"Yes."

LS: *And this seems to be forming a cloud here around this relationship, you see. The clouds must be dissipated.*

Sure, I knew that. "How?" I asked.

LS: *By becoming quite honest and forthright with one another. To be vague and to be of a nature then, which is evasive and elusive in terms of your confidences, you shall have then a relationship which is of that same nature: elusive. You will find often there are times where you could become more open by saying what, truly, my friend, you feel about this or that, or by stating what you truly wish for the future in regard to this.*

It was certainly true that there was no honesty in the relationship, and I didn't see how I could convince Grant to be honest when he had clearly chosen not to be. That seemed to be the central issue. Since Grant had not "chosen" the relationship, and had said he couldn't, I figured that I would try to discover the source of his confusion. I asked, "Why is Grant so confused?"

LS: *The great confusion, as it is defined here, is merely a lack of defining self and then accepting that which is defined. He is not in confusion, he is being confused by those incidents, guidance, lurings and temptations that surround him. He dwells too heavily in what has been, and listens to the words of others as guidings and temptings from without. This causes certain balancing factors in his body to become askew. It makes him weary of mind and body, and tends to cause pains both mental and physical. These imbalances also drain his energy and make him despondent to the point of non-functioning. His mental body has no means of expressing itself. This is the normal course of events, as sadly is seen in the earth, when entities have no identity established within self. They seek for those false identities and attention and concern from others who do have an identity. Past persecutions are seen here for this entity was on the earth during the time when profession of faith was an act worthy of demise of the body.*

That was interesting.

Did it mean that he was afraid to commit because he remembered commitment as being dangerous? Maybe I had persecuted him in some way, explaining his need to hurt me so much. I asked, "What was our relationship in that time of persecution and how does it relate to our present day situation?"

LS: *Here we find this was an opportunity for some greater strengthening to wisdom and knowledge which could, at the emotional and mental level, be passed from you to him. But confusion should be avoided here as well. This relationship should not be drawn to ... one moment, please, comments are forthcoming ... [long silence] We are advised of several matters here which are quite pertinent to this situation. Do not be confused. Do not confuse matters of mind and spirit with matters physical. For any relationship which can be found on the earth plane will have, at best, a short duration when it is based upon physical relations. Grant must learn to find meaning behind the mental and spiritual aspects of all those with whom he dwells. In terms of interaction with you, my child, this could have been a possibility, though seems to be passing.*

I didn't want to hear this. I desperately wanted to know something that would give me hope. I wanted a clue to enable me to change fate, to turn back the clock, to make it end differently. "What is the purpose for Grant's incarnation in this life, then?" I asked.

LS: *The purpose of this incarnation is among the clearest we have seen in these many readings. This entity is struggling to relieve himself of a karmic bond which is saddening and binding to a level which is not proper. He struggles very desperately in the spiritual sense to convey to an outward expression of a physical being, that All that Is continues throughout time and should not be eradicated to the point of transcending common sense and common judgment. Briefly stated: heavily laden with karmic debt.*

I was stunned. I had never heard so dire a pronouncement in any of the literature I had read on psychic readings and channeling. It almost sounded as if Lama Sing was saying that Grant was either possessed or deliberately evil. It was like a diagnosis of terminal cancer. What could I do? How could I save him? I needed more details. I asked, "Can we look at the situation that brought about this condition? What is the explanation for this?"

LS: *Very easily done. We are viewing this at this time. Here there is domination by those from the East, the Romans. We find the entity as a professed follower of the Master. A large group of others as well, who we see encaptivated at this point of time we are now viewing. Given the opportunity to affirm or deny the association with the Master, and thus save the physical life, we find the entity, Grant, denying same, thus saving his body. A depth of sadness cannot be conveyed to you in words relating to this effect upon this entity's soul remembrance. But mark you, it bears a heavy imprint. This should be viewed in no different light than one whom walked with the Master and held firmly to his tenets and teachings. For all are equal in God's eyes. It should be viewed as an opportunity to expand and grow to the proper position with God.*

So that was it! Indeed. I must have been involved in some way that hurt him dreadfully. That was why I felt so great a guilt when I was around him, why I felt it was so essential for me to help him. It was only natural for me to compensate for a wrong done in the past. I needed to know more. "How did I relate to him in that time?"

LS: *You were one of the leaders of this group. Yes, indeed!*

"I don't understand."

LS: *A leader of the group following the Master's teaching; a companion of Paul on his journeys. You were a teacher of teachers among those who taught in those days. Yes. Met your death at the hands of these opponents. Some died from beasts, and some from the mere pleasure of sport at the hands of other men. Look at the entire grouping of souls around you. It bears the mark yet of the entire scene we have just described. Some of those you interact with, including your mother, were among those to be found seated in the Coliseum, not to be found following the Master. Again, being mindful not to judge on that basis. You are seeking to find again that same motivating belief that was ever present then. It is no further distance away from you than a mere thought. Only your own will can separate you from God.*

With stunning clarity I saw a flash vision of that death I had experienced as Lama Sing described. I had wanted to know that, somehow, all my suffering was deserved, not that I was a victim lifetime after lifetime. If being a martyr for Christ had not conferred upon me some special grace, if it was still necessary to struggle and suffer, what was the point?

I asked for a comment on Carol to discover if I had possibly committed some terrible act against her in another time to cause her to betray me in this life. I most definitely was looking for excuses for the behavior of others, and justification for their actions. After all, I was the one who was being pursued by the Hound of Hell. Regarding Carol, Lama Sing had this to say:

LS: *Yes, we find involvement here. One occasion involving three entities currently prominent in your experiences. We find this in the tenth or eleventh century following the entry of the Christ consciousness to the earth plane in that land now known to you as Languedoc. We find the relationship here that of the feudal system; that involving serfdom, the dominance of families with power, and land and wealth, having governing ability.*

That was certainly interesting. Not only that, but it rather confirmed the hypnotically recalled past life Carol had described; she'd accused me of being a privileged "Norman" while she was merely a lowly "Gaul." I asked, "What was my relation to Grant in that time?"

LS: *Seems to be one of blood relationship, yet very close to the current relations as we view this. But there was controversy here. Seems to have been in regard to matters of protocol or custom. There seems to have been a reaction between you in terms of what your place was and what his place was, and a seemingly endless discussion in this regard. The female you have mentioned was a very close companion of yours but died at a very young age in that lifetime and the relationship perhaps never did reach its fullest point, but was one treasured well in that time, but abruptly ended.*

It caused you some sadness in that time. We find your mother in higher stature in that life, having governing control over all of you, having the say of where you went, what your future was to be. Hence, there was always an attempt to maintain good favor with her and to attempt to ploy her with various ways to obtain what you wanted. Some reluctance between you and her in that lifetime in terms of what pathway you should have followed, and we find that this seems to have repeated itself again in this lifetime.

This was getting more interesting by the minute. I wanted to know about more of my lifetimes. In childhood I'd once been attracted to the idea of living as a Native American. Now I wondered if that had been an impression of an actual experience in that milieu. I didn't quite know how to ask it without leading, but managed to fumble out "What about a life as, perhaps, an American Indian?"

LS: *Yes. Well, we noted that very quickly when we greeted you. It was one which was very strong for you. In fact, several of the entities with whom you dwell now dwelled with you in that time also.*

"Grant?"

LS: *Yes. It seems that you had a high position here involved with religious practices and healing. We find your position in the gathering to have been of honor. The entity Grant, you have mentioned, seems to have been a comrade, though not of your standing. You would call him a warrior in that time. The female entity ... your ally in this lifetime ...*

"Carol?"

LS: *No ...*

"Eva?"

LS: *Yes. Well, we find her here as well. We find her as a maiden again, and there seems to have been a fondness between you and she, though you did not accept marriage in that incarnation. There was a great fondness here. We are finding this to be in the Northern and Eastern segment of your country.*

So that was why Eva and I seemed to know each other so well. Ha! It was funny the way Lama Sing worded it: almost as though suggesting that we had been married in another life that was not being described.

At last I decided to ask just exactly what caused my recent "depression." I most certainly didn't want to say that I had nearly taken my own life, so I asked, "Could you give me some insight regarding my present psychological or spiritual progress?" Is that not a very clever open kind of question? I thought so. I was trying very hard not to lead in any direction.

LS: *There is deep sadness, then, as defined here. There is that loneliness that comes from a weary heart; one who seeks only one to share with in this lifetime those joys, those sadnesses, and that part of life which is fulfilled only by having those about self with whom can be shared a complete and fulfilled portion of love. Do you see? This is wanting in you at this time.*

You feel, at this time, that your life has brought you to a point of what you would call stagnation. This point should not be assessed in this way, but rather that self has been brought to a point wherein you can search carefully within. Develop and flower into that which is truly within you.

It matters not what the vehicle of your being is, but what is contained within that being. For it is to be said very learnedly that that which is seen in its outer appearance to be of glistening, of glimmering radiance in terms of earth plane desirability, may oftimes, upon closer evaluation, be not that at all. A true beauty is vivid from within that entity once it is fulfilled in confidence and the knowledge that God is alive within self. Respect that temple within that is of the living God. Call upon that, learn to be with that, and you will find that outwardly your body will change, your skin will change, your body structure; all that which is a living part of your physical body will change. As long as this is not recognized, there must be, no doubt, sadness here and the body not responding as you would like it to.

And how difficult it has been to change your body. You have tried and tried. Yet seemingly nothing seems to work. But is it not, my child, perhaps you begin at a point here that is not at the beginning? You are working on the result, rather than seeking the cause. And it is not a serious cause, dear child. You must know that you are loved dearly, and know that this love comes to you because we are with you eternally. Your dwelling on the earth plane is to expand your soul's experience and expression. It is to have that opportunity to develop, to find that which is truly of love and beauty and to allow that to lie fallow, then to grow and become an example for others, do you see?

A departure from the earth plane, then, should be discussed here, we see.

(This remark was a shock.)

One can say that it is easily done to depart from the earth plane. One can merely will it to be so and find that, after a time, the body responds to the mind's command and you become ill of body and depart. But what do they find upon that departure? That they, themselves, are studying those very things that they had seen as a cause to want them to depart, you see?

Only in this plane, or from this aspect, it is done with a joy and some small, shall we say, relationship to humor here. But it is not done with the seriousness of your minds on the earth plane, but just as one would evaluate their ability to do this or do that as an actual deed on your plane. Not in a hardness or critical sense, do you see? After that, then, the entity ultimately will decide to return to the earth plane, or one similar to this, to experience and to develop and strengthen itself.

What is your greatest desire? That should be your goal, see? We are slightly humored for we find that you know the solution to what you consider to be your problem. But you are just a bit, shall we say shy, in order to pursue it. Dear child, you must know at this point that, as your mind builds, and as your heart feeds to that thought which lovingly is your desire, so does it become manifest. Not with anticipating, but in a loving, kind and willing way, know in the comfort and silence within self, that as you desire and as it is beneficial to you, so is it given. Fare thee well, then dear one. We depart.

And that was that.

It was a huge amount of information to assimilate. Driving home with the tape of the session in my hand, all I could really remember was that this man had suggested I had been a Christian martyr, and they thought it was humorous that I couldn't figure out what to do.

Well, I wasn't laughing, but I was, at long last, thinking.

And the sun danced on the waters of the bay as we sailed home across the bridge.

CHAPTER SEVENTEEN

MIRROR! MIRROR! ON THE WALL …

It's amazing how our emotions can drive our thinking. Grant was my soulmate and I'd never be happy with anyone else. That's how I interpreted the reading by Lama Sing through Al Miner. But we'd both apparently screwed up in some way. Until Grant unburdened his karmic debt, there was no hope for our life together. And I needed to learn to express my emotions honestly, so I read *When I Say No, I Feel Guilty*, and *Your Erroneous Zones*, trying to find the key to unlock the secret self, to activate Lama Sing's principle: "As it is beneficial to you, so is it given." I needed to really work on myself to make it "good for me" to have Grant in my life. Never mind that it would have been pretty clear to anybody else (and was) that he wasn't, and never would be, good for me.

But, Lama Sing had said: "What is your greatest desire? That should be your goal, see?"

My goal was Grant.

Of course, I mailed the reading to Grant to provide impetus for his own transformation. If we both just stayed away from each other, and worked on clearing away the clouds, everything would soon be right for our "destined" love to manifest fully. Until then, I had visions of noble sacrifice and suffering.

As Lama Sing noted, I sought only that One with whom I could share All. Nothing less would do. He had to be Polish, and Grant was, and there had to be a connection to WW II, and Grant had that through his father, so it was all clear.

The first Christmas of my life without my grandfather came with no celebration. I'd avoided any real interaction with my mother's husband because he annoyed the heck out of me. When he was home, I stayed in

A photo taken from around this time showing how gaunt I was looking.

my room reading or went out with Eva. Now he was constantly present and we faced a family sit-down dinner together.

Everything about Christmas reminded me of my grandfather. He had always made Christmas fun for us. I think he loved playing Santa, an alter ego who didn't have to be serious and gruff all the time.

On this Christmas I felt a building tension of agonizing grief and irritation at the presence of this pusillanimous man in my grandfather's house, posing as the man of the house. If Buck had been at all competent in any way, it might have been endurable. But, to put it plainly, he was an idiot. I wondered how he managed to dress and feed himself, much less keep a job as a building contractor.

What my mother saw in him was a mystery. But he was probably physically attentive and a faithful dog at her heels, all she required as an ageing belle.

We sat down for dinner. It was the first time in my life I had ever eaten a turkey that had not been cooked by my grandfather. Even if every other part of the holiday feasts were in the hands of the women, Grandpa always did the turkey: his specialty. Every dish on the table was part of family custom, the foods my grandfather liked.

Buck sat in my grandfather's chair at the head of the table. I didn't look up from my plate. Tears silently dripped onto my hands. I mumbled responses to overly cheerful queries or to pass a serving dish, and avoided lifting my eyes. I didn't want any pity at our family Christmas dinner. I knew that I couldn't eat a single bite, but I didn't want to upset my grandmother, so I pushed my food around a bit to seem interested. Meanwhile, the conversation had taken an unseemly turn.

"We can make a good profit using other people's money," Buck was saying. "It's standard operating procedure for all wealthy people. That's how they build their fortunes! And I have plans for us to be rich too!"

Well, fine, you old bore. Go for it.

"First we sell Grandmother's house. Of course, we'll make sure she has a home all her life. We'll use this as seed money. With other people's money, we subdivide the property, build houses and sell them."

Right there I froze. What was he talking about?

"Where did you come up with the idea," I asked him, "of selling my house and the property that belongs to our family? Just who do you think you are to come in here and sit in my grandfather's chair and make grandiose plans with the hard-earned property of my grandfather, who clearly had other plans for his life's work than handing it over to a slick-talking nitwit!"

Now, lest you think I was making a snap judgment, Buck was a guy who'd left a wife and seven children, scheming ways to avoid paying child support. He refused to help his son pay college tuition. "I never had a college education," he'd say, "and you don't need to go thinking you are better than your old man!"

My mother fixed me with the look of a sharpshooter taking aim. "Considering recent changes in the situation, you can just give up your expectations of this house little, Missy!" she said. "After all, I am the one taking care of Mother now! And in case you haven't noticed, Buck is taking care of all of us, including you!"

"Not any more!" I said. I stood up so fast my chair tipped over backwards. I wanted to pick up my plate and throw it in her face, but managed to restrain myself. I got my bag and keys and was out the door.

On the way out I heard my grandmother protesting, "Well, Alice, I don't think it's very nice for you to be making these plans without consulting me. I'm not dead yet!"

After a few hours at the riverside park, I went back home. Mother gave me the silent treatment with frozen hate in her eyes. Buck was nowhere to be seen. Grandma came to talk to me while I packed. We sat on the bed and held each other and wept.

"I don't know what to do about your mother," she told me. "Don't think that I'm behind this scheme, and don't think that I'll go along with it either. I know too much about Alice and her shenanigans, and as long as I still own this house, I'll dispose of it the way Grandpa and I already decided. You just try to keep your own head on straight, and we have to keep our eyes open. You're mother's up to something, I can feel it."

I felt it too, but I didn't have enough confidence in myself to take action. When we were growing up, my brother had a favorite sibling insult. He liked to tell me, "For somebody who's supposed to be so smart, you sure are dumb." Well, sometimes it seemed to be true.

Being a smart person who did dumb things was the self-fulfilling self-image that grew in me primarily as a result of my mother's projections. Because of her own feelings of rejection, which were decisions she had made about herself as a small child, she had no internal values of self-esteem at all. This is intolerable to the psyche. When one part of the mind is convinced there is nothing about the self to love, there seems to be another part, fueled by the need to be loved, that builds walls against any criticism.

In recent years, after reading the book *Trapped in the Mirror* by Elan Golomb, I finally began to understand the dynamic with my mother. Mother was a narcissist who had become one in self-defense. That's rather different from someone with narcissistic personality disorder (NPD), but just as problematical. She had created a disguise, a false self who was never wrong. In a sense, this false self was like the Queen in the story of Snow White: "Mirror, mirror on the wall, who's the fairest of them all?" And her mirror always told her: "You are." The emotional food for a narcissist is admiration and approval. But this creates an almost impossible inner conflict because the part of the self convinced that it is unlovable simply must act in ways that generate rejection in order to be right. The part of the self that needs continuous approval must get it by any means necessary.

The narcissist solves her dilemma by subterfuge and enormous trickery and deception. The part of self that drives her to perform badly must be "made right," to blame all the failures on someone "out there." This is essential, because to admit to one failing, to acknowledge a mistake, even a simple human error of judgment, would be to open the door to the deep internal lack within.

Such feelings of worthlessness are like an ocean being held back by a fragile dyke. The illusion of perfection, maintained by projecting faults onto someone else, is a barrier to be constantly tended, mended, and shored up. To admit any feelings of deficiency would be the equivalent of poking a hole in the dyke, an event to be feared as a total disaster.

To disagree with Mother was equivalent to striking her carefully constructed shell of grandiose fantasies about her own perfection. Any opposition to her views could plunge her into a black hole of inconceivable emptiness, jealousy, and rage generated by this fear of the breaching of the dyke. Anyone who tried to breach the shield had to be extinguished.

Because her entire perception of the world was organized to deny her own feelings of worthlessness, she needed to force others to go along with her views. In her deepest self, she felt her ultimate survival depended on this. People who live with narcissists have no other choice but to agree.

I became Snow White in this archetypal drama—the sin bearer. Not that I was beautiful or had Snow White's attributes. I was the mirror that kept suggesting there was some imperfection in the Queen. I became the threat to the carefully constructed and maintained dyke that held back the ocean of unworthiness that had been created in my mother as a consequence of the death-abandonment she suffered as a child when her beloved Mama was murdered. As long as I "lived," the mirror kept pointing out that the Queen was not the fairest of them all. In this way, Mother projected onto others the blame for anything that went wrong in her own life.

If I had realized the true state of affairs at the time, perhaps I would not have resisted her so vigorously, keeping myself in a constant stew, or regularly turning up the heat on the hot water I was in. Any move toward a separate identity was treated as betrayal, and I was made to feel that my seeking independence would "kill" her. And, above all things, I did not want to kill my mother!

Mother wanted my constant adoration and approval, a carbon copy of her illusory self-image.

She had certainly been a beauty, a potential sister to Ingrid Bergman or Grace Kelly. She had a fine figure, good teeth, and great hair. She was a marvelous dancer, social, outgoing. She craved action and excitement.

I was plain, pudgy, had crooked teeth, two left feet, and liked nothing better than to be left alone with a good book. When I was four or five, and still blonde and "cute," she spent time dressing me up and showing me off. When I turned six or seven, and began to morph into myself, I became her supreme disappointment. She magnified and commented on every imperfection with fiendish frequency.

I struggled against her projections throughout my childhood and adoles-

My mother in her twenties.

cence. This is at least a testimony to my will. But I still felt bad, wrong and confused. After all, Mother had to be right, didn't she? I was damned if I did, and damned if I didn't.

My brother caught on to the game more quickly than I did and became the mirror of perfection in her eyes, feeding her with approval and assisting her in crushing any resistance in me that made the mirror suggest she might not be perfect. Like the woodsman who took Snow White into the forest, my brother lacked the courage either to deny the Queen's wish or to do the wicked act of murder. He would figuratively take me to the psychological woods and abandon me, but he wasn't cruel in a deadly sense. He participated in this process by duplicating my mother's views of me. He learned to suppress any doubts that Mother was right and even his own perceptions, because he knew that to get along, he must agree with her in all things. I can't say I blamed him; he was sensitive and didn't like upsets, so it was easier for him to just go along and get along. Above all, the child of the narcissist is trained to be giving, to not be selfish, to be a mirror of the Queen. On those occasions when his needs become internally demanding, he follows his usual path of taking Snow White to the forest and leaving her there, returning with the heart of a pig in a box. Deception is his mode of survival. But, I wasn't made that way. I was constantly at war with what I perceived as wrong.

Conditional love hung like a pall over my environment. In every instance of self-expression as a child, I was rejected by my mother—abandoned—as her own childhood wounds were transferred to me. The death of her beloved grandmother and the cruel demands of her parents were crimes against her essential self. She was not accepted as herself, so she could not accept me. Because I was also her only girl child, she identified with me more strongly, was more demanding of me, and consequently more deformation was assigned to me as the scapegoat.

Every day I was evaluated and found lacking. I came to believe there was no support for my inner self, no right to exist as myself. Hopeless and paralyzed, I sought refuge in the only port I could see in the storm. It was years before I was able to begin the work to undo the illusions under which I was brought up, and which were part of my experiences in the "real" world.

The pressure from my mother to conform to her labels and expectations was like an invisible force in my life, so uniform and relentless and omnipresent that I was hardly aware of it. Like a fish in polluted water, I was able to survive, but only barely.

It is difficult to confront such painful experiences in which I was as guilty as any other participant. Sadly, until I woke up, I did the same with my own children.

I recently bought a book called Toxic Parents. In the first chapter the author blames parents for all the toxicity of a person's life. Parents are to be confronted and held responsible for the results of their actions. I closed the book right at that point and returned it to the store and got my money back. That is about the most ignorant and useless advice I have ever read. Anybody in a similar situation knows what I mean. Confrontation and attempts to engage in dialogue, unless both parties have achieved some self-awareness, can only perpetuate the dynamic of the child trying one more futile time to get love, and being rejected one more futile time.

I am not blaming here. I do not believe that my mother was responsible or aware of the damage she created in our lives. She was like a broken porcelain doll with shattered perceptions of the world around her. The burden of awareness is on me.

Any blame can be directed at the social and cultural systems that give rise to the false beliefs holding us captive. If I blame my mother for what was done to me, shall my own children not find it necessary to blame me for what I have done to them out of my own wounds and illusions? And then, what shall their children do? And their children's children?

A child who is told that "for being so smart, you sure are dumb" over and over again, will inevitably fulfill that prophecy. Such lack of faith in the intrinsic self puts intolerable pressure on the person to conform to this expectation by acting out submission to the wishes of the parent. And those wishes are for the child to be the scapegoat, the bearer of the sins of the parent, the one who is unloved, the one who fails, the one who screws up and who is to blame for every negative occurrence.

In some subconscious way I came to accept the opinions of my mother and those in the family conscripted to her point of view. Even though my grandmother loved me unconditionally, when she was under the manipulative influence of my mother, she would accede to Mother's view: "Whistling girls and crowing hens always come to no good end."

As a female with intelligence, I was being programmed to screw up, and screw up royally.

In retrospect, I realize that I was also programmed to be manipulated by authority figures and to fall prey to seduction where love was promised for surrender. I found myself repeatedly involved with friends who needed my uncritical acceptance. My role was the supplicant at their feet, listening in rapt awe, while nothing I said was ever heard. It was my job to laugh, but never to tell the joke. I called but was seldom called in return. I arranged my life around the schedules of others.

I was compelled to win Mother's love vicariously from other people. Naturally, many were narcissists. I was unable to put any need of my own at the top of the list—that was selfish. Love meant giving without resentment, competitiveness, or jealousy. Young women in our society were trained to believe the only way to be loved was to give love, to make others happy by surrendering our selves, our ideas, our values, our goals and objectives, and even our very thoughts. The only way we knew how to get love was to give up ourselves completely.

The idea of intelligence as a useless commodity was almost a tenet of the Christianity of my childhood. Brains would get you nowhere if you weren't "saved." It was a waste of time to read any book except the Bible, because all anyone needed to know was right there. Additionally, I was a girl. I was doubly damned, and disaster was sure to follow.

* * *

Grandmother and I both knew I was not going to be able to keep my mouth shut around Buck and Mother. Neither of us could deal with Mother when she was "with a man," as Grandma put it. Grandma gave me what cash she had to tide me over and I left for The Farm.

The time-warp quality of The Farm seemed to have intensified. All the memories of my standoff with God flooded back within hours of my arrival. I went about getting settled, putting fresh linens on the bed, hauling in water and all the usual tasks of opening up the house. But for some reason, the unearthly silence of the place unnerved me.

Everywhere I looked there were memories with a new meaning now. I looked over the land and realized, with full import, that I would never again see a garden of my grandfather's making there. I wandered through the house and saw everything organized according to his design and purpose, and I knew that the mind behind that purpose was now absent from this world.

How fleeting it all was. The few happy moments of my childhood were mostly memories of days at The Farm. I looked back over them, like a collection of photographs in a box, and saw how small was the ratio of happiness. Memories of my year with Grant descended on me in full force.

I had been at The Farm for a couple days when I decided I wanted some fresh fish to eat. I drove down to the little fish market we'd patronized for years when we wanted fish other than the kinds we could catch off the bank. I was surprised to discover that it had changed hands. A friendly, stylish blonde woman named Myrna stood behind the counter. We exchanged pleasantries. Her husband was retired from the Air Force and they had bought the fish house and a shrimp boat, trying their hands at living out their retirement dream. I commented that I would love to buy some shrimp, but unless I found a job locally, which wasn't very likely, I would have to go back to Tampa as soon as I ran out of money. She wanted to know where I lived. I told her we owned the old farm a few miles up the road. She had passed the house and wondered who owned such a terrific old place.

A few days later, Myrna drove up to the house in her snazzy convertible and waved at me sitting on the porch. "I have a proposal for you," she hollered as she got out of the car. "I know it's not like a real job or anything, but Rob's helper quit, and we need somebody to go out on the boat with us. You don't suppose you'd be interested in a low paid but interesting job on a shrimp boat? You get to take home all the shrimp you can eat, too!" Her enthusiasm was hard to resist even in my state of abyssal melancholy.

Work on a shrimp boat? Well, heck! Why not?

"We go out at about five o'clock," she said. "So, come on down and we can have a little fun. You'll see. It's not as bad as some people think it is!"

Out on the Gulf of Mexico at night, a stiff sea breeze blowing salt spray from the prow of the chugging little shrimp boat back on Myrna and me, working in the bright lights on deck, it seemed like being in a different world. Myrna and I talked non-stop while we picked and sorted shrimp from the big net bags her husband Bobby regularly dumped on the wooden tray in front of us. It was hard work, but in retrospect we had a lot of fun.

Myrna was interested in metaphysical subjects, and her latest idea was to experiment with miniature pyramids. We bought big sheets of heavy poster board in different colors and followed the instructions to make a bunch of little pyramids. I took mine home and carefully aligned them under the bed and on various tables around the house. I also began to practice meditating with a little pyramid perched on top of my head. I'm sure I looked perfectly silly, but I really did feel an enhanced energy flow.

Their experiment in living the retirement dream of owning a commercial fishing boat was not turning out well. Myrna and Bobby had given it a specified period to prove a worthwhile occupation, but the time was up with negative results. They decided to move back where they came from.

There was now no one to talk to but God.

I was soon out of money and down to canned food and instant coffee, but I was unwilling to give up my plan. I decided to make my supplies last longer by extended periods of fasting. The grounds of The Farm also needed a lot of attention, and since my grandfather would never again be there to oversee the work, I decided that the responsibility was now mine.

I established a meditation and work schedule. I mowed, trimmed trees and shrubs, cut fallen limbs into firewood, and cleared several acres of high, thick weeds and volunteer tree saplings by hand that we normally hired a man with a tractor to handle. It was grueling labor. I stopped only for water and pushed on till dark.

Day after day I worked, pleading with God for understanding. I spent hours in various meditation postures. I focused, concentrated, repeated mantras, cried, emptied my mind, and mostly, I simply waited and listened.

Nothing.

Perhaps, in some unknown way I didn't understand, I belonged to the creature that appeared as the Face in the Window of my childhood.

Such a thought was insupportable.

Again, I saw no way out. This time nothing would go wrong. Practically no one knew where I was, and most certainly, no one had been to visit me for several weeks.

I found a long piece of flexible rubber hose, much larger than a water hose, and affixed it with a clamp to the exhaust of my car. Methodically, I arranged the mechanism of my release. When I was finished, I examined my handiwork and was satisfied. What to do now?

Well, let me have just one last cigarette, I thought, and I sat on the steps of the back porch. One cigarette, and that was it.

It was the strangest cigarette I ever smoked. The first couple of puffs hit me like a ton of bricks. I was suddenly unable to keep my head erect or my eyes open. I struggled against this feeling of overwhelming sleepiness without success.

Okay, I told myself, *I will have a little nap first.*

I thought briefly about just getting into the car for my nap, but found my limbs heavy as lead. I could not even get up. I simply stretched out right there on the porch in the sun and fell asleep as suddenly as if I'd been drugged.

The next thing I knew, a horn sounded. I struggled out of a deep abyss of sleep in confusion and puzzlement about that crazy noise.

Eva was racing up the driveway, honking her horn as she came.

So it seemed that even under the most ideal circumstances to accomplish the deed, I couldn't put a period to my own existence. Somebody was watching out for me and was strangely able to exert some influence in the world of matter. Either that, or it was my own inner self. It was hard to say, but it was equally hard to ignore the implications.

CHAPTER EIGHTEEN

THE WOLF AND THE DOVE

The bizarre synchronicity of Eva's appearance, for the second time, on the scene of my imminent demise is, of course, a curious matter. I am reminded of Lama Sing's description of her as my "ally in this life."

When Eva saw the hose in the tailpipe of the car, she told me there must be a God. She believed that God had clearly put the idea into her mind to come to see me right at that particular moment. In fact, she had been over twenty miles away having her car serviced. The urge to talk to me became so overwhelming that she did something that was quite out of character: she drove to the general area of The Farm, trusting that she could get specific directions from the locals once she had arrived in the vicinity.

This idea, that prayer is answered by the events of our lives, struck me rather forcefully. All this time I had been expecting to hear a voice!

Eva proposed that since she was lately divorced, I should come back to Tampa and stay with her until a door opened. I didn't like being obligated to anyone for so much, but Eva was absolutely sure that I could help her adjust to her new life as much as she could help me.

Eva was quite a bit older than I was, and her eldest son Alex was only four years younger than me. He had suffered many difficulties Eva attributed to his poor relationship with his father. Alex's father had high expectations for his eldest son. But Alex was as much his mother's child, and his artistic sensitivities clashed with his father's harsh mold of "keep a stiff upper lip and be a man." Alex's father treated him like a shabby failure who "didn't have what it takes."

Because he loved his father, Alex internalized this hateful attitude. He resisted his father's pressure to conform to directives that would have obliterated him as a person. After his parents' divorce, Alex felt devastated. He began to demonstrate violent, self-destructive behavior, which Eva desperately wanted to resolve.

Admittedly, I was so raw and wounded inside when I arrived at Eva's that I really didn't know how to react. My entire life, up to that point, had been spent observing those around me and trying to find out what they wanted or needed in advance so that I could provide it and thereby be accepted. I found myself slipping into this mode rather quickly.

As part of her divorce settlement, Eva's husband paid her tuition toward her degree in nuclear medicine. She had a heavy class load, so I filled in as "older sister" for her three boys. It was a little odd being in the middle in age—being a sister-friend to the boys, and sister-friend to Eva—but somehow it worked. It was really like being a glorified au pair. I cooked and helped keep up with laundry and housework. We went to their family lake house for weekend swimming and boating. All of them were wonderful athletes, in excellent physical condition, and they tried to teach me to ski and play games and throw a Frisbee, but I was horribly gauche and inept in any physical pursuit whatsoever. It was better if I just drove the boat while they skied, or sat on the dock and watched, or cooked burgers when they were hungry.

On one weekend retreat, Eva's boys had a group of friends who joined the lake-house parties. Three were sons of a high-profile local judge. One day, when supplies had run low, the eldest of the three boys volunteered to make a run to the nearest supermarket for more snacks and drinks. He didn't want to go alone and, since I was the only one at the moment who was not in a bathing suit, he asked if I would come along. I said "sure!" and climbed into his big, fancy four-wheel-drive vehicle and off we went.

It was about five miles to the nearest store along a winding country road flanked by occasional farms and seemingly endless cow pastures. "Bobby" was driving a bit too fast to suit me. I tried to make a joke about it. At least if we got stopped by the police, neither of us was drinking. I had to shout over the wind in the open vehicle.

He shouted back that we'd better not get stopped because he was higher than a kite on some prescription drug he swiped from his mother and if his father found out, he was dead. I shouted back that, in that case, he'd better slow down. He looked at me and grinned fiendishly. I didn't need to worry about a thing because he had "everything under control, baby!"

At that instant we went around a curve and the knobby back wheel of the vehicle slipped off the pavement onto the soft shoulder of the road, grabbing the mucky soil and jerking us sideways. We spun into the barbed-wire fence along the cow pasture, mowing down fence posts like dominoes.

Bobby jerked the wheel to get us back to the road, but the barbed wire wrapped around the axle. Our forward momentum was transferred to the rear of the vehicle, swinging it out sideways like an object on a tether, to smash resoundingly and finally against a telephone pole on the driver's side, just behind the seats.

Both of us were ejected sideways; Bobby cleared the pole and landed in the soft grass, and I felt something like a flamethrower on my chest and abdomen as the trajectory of my body was slowed and shifted by dragging across the elongated gearshift lever. This spun me around so that, as I was flung out, my back slammed solidly against the telephone pole. I slid to the ground in a daze.

Well, my adrenaline was pumping like crazy. If Bobby's father discovered he was stealing his mother's prescription drugs, he was in big trouble. Above all, I wanted to protect Eva's boys—and their friends—from any backlash.

I saw a man on a tractor way across the cow pasture, heading in our direction. I rolled over onto my knees and crawled to the vehicle, pulling myself up by holding on to it, and managed to get into the seat. The engine had died under the strain of the barbed wire wrapped around the wheels, and I turned the key off and back on to see if it would start. It did. "Get in!" I shouted to Bobby, and dropped the lever into four-wheel action, slammed it in reverse, and felt it jumping and bouncing as the wheels dug into the dirt, pulling against the obstacle of the fence wire wrapped and tangled around the wheels and axle.

Just as Bobby made it into his seat, we broke free with a sudden lunge backward and shot back onto the pavement. I slammed the lever into first gear and off we went, dragging a fencepost behind us that soon fell away in the distance as we roared down the road.

Bobby told his father about the accident, leaving out the part relating to his state of chemical intoxication, and his father gave a generous check to the farmer to pay for the replacement of the section of fence that had been uprooted. The incident was closed.

Except for one thing: I was seriously injured in a way that was to affect me for the rest of my life.

Because I couldn't feel anything broken and didn't have any open wounds, I thought I'd just get over it. A horrendous black and blue and purple and green streak, about five inches wide, extended from my breastbone to my lower abdomen from the raking action of the gearshift lever as my body dragged across it when I was flung out on impact. My back was stiff and sore and I couldn't move at all without pain. My left leg was numb and the skin felt like somebody was constantly pouring scalding water on it. But I thought I'd just take it easy, have a few soaks in Epsom salts, and just basically let the body heal itself.

Eva urged me to contact Bobby's father and inform him that I needed medical attention. If he had paid for the farmer's fence, he most definitely ought to pay for my injuries. Finally, I agreed to see a spine specialist.

After an exam and x-rays, the doctor told me that disks in my lumbar vertebrae were severely compressed. Without surgery, which might include removing the disks and fusing the bones, I would be in constant pain for the rest of my life. But surgery might also result in significant impairment of my ability to walk.

Well, swell! Either way, it was lousy news. I'm gonna suffer if I don't have surgery, and I'll probably suffer if I do. From my perspective, at least I was still able to walk and appear normal, even if I was in pain, so the choice was easy. No surgery.

Eva's second son had back strain from playing the tuba in his school band, and chiropractic treatment had helped him. She thought chiropractic adjustments might help me, also.

After chiropractic work, I was able to function again, though for some reason they never would "hold" for very long. Any stressful activity, lifting heavy objects, or sudden moves in the wrong way sent severe pain signals again. I started down a path of learning to tolerate pain at levels most people never dream of.

* * *

In our spare time, Eva and I continued our experiments with hypnosis. We had more readings from Lama Sing, and with Eva's Ouija board, we soon had lengthy and fairly complex conversations with purported discarnate entities. I decided to test them in the same way I'd tested the local psychics. I was really getting into this project when Eva became bored with it. Unfortunately, it didn't work nearly as well with anyone else, so I gave it up too.

I occasionally heard news about Grant. He was running with what sounded like a rather wild crowd of bikers, and I was desperate to know that he was all right. I decided to call him and a female voice answered the phone. I asked to speak to Grant, and gave my name hesitantly, sure that it would mean nothing to her.

"You have a lot of nerve calling after what you've done to him! How dare you!"

In a flash, it was clear. I was the new excuse for Grant's troubles. Whatever I was supposed to have "done" to him was his new sympathy hook. Now he was vilifying me.

"I don't know who you are, or what you think," I said between clenched teeth, "but I have no idea what you are talking about."

"For your information, I'm Grant's wife. We were married two weeks ago, and you are some bitch with nerve to call him after what you did."

Controlling my voice in an effort to sound as pleasant as possible, I asked, "Do you mind telling me what it is I'm supposed to have done?"

"You know what you did. And you know how damaged he is. It will probably take the rest of my life to undo what you've done."

Suddenly, I felt cold. I knew that Grant was lost to me completely. "I hope you have a good time for as long as you can, because I guarantee you it won't last!" I hung up.

Eva's oldest son, Alex, was sitting in the next room watching me through the doorway.

"Are you okay?" he asked.

"Yes," I lied.

I went into another room to pull myself together. Tears streamed down my face and I tried to stop them because I didn't have a tissue to blow my nose when Alex came in quietly and sat down beside me. He offered me a tissue and I blew my nose. The next thing I knew, he was holding me and saying, "You don't deserve to be treated that way. I wish I could help you." A very strong bond formed between us. I was just a wounded person being comforted by another, similarly wounded, human being.

As time went by, I noticed Alex watching me constantly. Every time I looked up he was looking at me. I was more than ordinarily vulnerable, so I made every effort to not be alone in a room with him. The more I did, the more I realized he wanted to make sure I was alone with him. I was in a condition of siege, though it was gentle and subliminal. This went on for months. I tried going out on several blind dates Eva suggested, hoping that Alex would lose interest in me, but it only seemed to upset him. This inevitably resulted in more self-destructive behavior on Alex's part.

I was in a very painful position. Eva was the best friend I'd ever had. Forming an attachment to her son that was more than sisterly would amount to a betrayal. At the same time, I was painfully lonely and Alex was always there.

Eva's concerns for Alex's lack of career-oriented enthusiasm prompted her to have a long talk with his father. They decided to enroll him in a wilderness trek organization designed for exposure to the perils of basic survival in the wilds. I don't remember how long he was gone on this mountain-climbing expedition, but when he returned, the result was shocking.

Alex had contracted a parasitical infection, probably from drinking the water in one of those pure mountain streams. He had lost about twenty pounds from his already lean frame, and he was to lose even more before the parasite ran its course. He needed full-time nursing.

Eva was still working on her degree, so I cared for Alex. It was difficult for me to observe the cruel results of this "experiment" in molding another human being. He needed to get away from the influence of his parents, but he could not break free.

I spent the second Christmas after Grandpa's death with Eva and her boys. Mother and Buck had taken Grandma back to the East Coast with them. I moved to Grandma's house and took a secretarial job with a company that installed and managed security systems.

And I bought a piano: a gorgeous baby grand with glorious sound.

I spent hours playing and dreaming, transported back to the days I had dreamed of The One who walked all over the city frantically looking for his own Love and finding me at my piano. I realized gradually that Grant appeared less frequently in these fantasies. I was growing past the pain.

* * *

George, the business owner where I worked, wanted to move back North and arranged to sell out to the store manager. David was young, good looking, and personable. He played piano and sang in a gospel quartet at church. He confided in me that his parents had mortgaged their house to lend him the money to buy George's business. I wasn't sure that was a good idea, but I was agreeable to stay on and run the office.

I went through the contracts to get things organized for the coming push to increase sales so David's loan could be repaid as soon as possible. My work included delivery of contracts to several banks and loan companies. The procedure was to finance a deal if the buyer didn't pay cash, and then to "sell the paper."

When I took them to the bank, I was informed that new state regulations on this kind of sale made all the contracts in my hands virtually worthless. It seemed pretty apparent that George had known that his contracts, written under what was now considered to be duress or high-pressure scare tactics, would no longer be accepted by the various lending institutions. George had gotten out of the business before anyone else knew this. Naturally, the very large sum he made in selling the business to David was based on exactly these kinds of sales, which were now illegal. The inventory for which David's parents had mortgaged their home was worthless paper.

I tried to soften the blow, to comfort David in his despair at putting his parents in this position. I assured him we could reorganize and make things legal. He pulled himself together and agreed that everything would be all right. When I left work Friday night, I was confident David could formulate a new plan.

On Sunday morning, the phone rang. Our office receptionist told me that David had apparently driven his new Lincoln out to the airport and parked on the shoulder of the road at the end of a runway where high-school kids liked to go to watch jets take off over their heads.

David put a gun in his mouth and blew his brains out.

Somehow, I think his parents would rather have lost their house. After all these years I still think about David occasionally. He had so much to live for, so many talents, so much personal charm and appeal, all gone in an instant. He had been bitten by a shark and had not survived the encounter.

I felt something evil had passed very close, blowing on the back of my neck with icy breath.

I spent several hours going over that last conversation with David, but not a single thing had been evident to make anyone think he would take his own life. Maybe he had not made the decision yet. Maybe he decided only after telling his parents the bad news. For all I knew, he had parents like my mother who would have most certainly made him wish to kill himself rather than to admit failure.

The bottom line was, now I needed a job. I learned fast and was a good worker, but I had no technical skills, degrees, or certification. I'd been attending college classes for over two years, but I couldn't even type. Among columns of job ads in the Sunday paper, however, my eye stopped on one: "Assistant to physician. No experience necessary. Will train. Please write in longhand describing your background, interests and experience …"

Well, that was about the strangest advertisement I had ever read. Let me get this straight: a doctor wants an assistant with no experience? Well, heck! That's me! Besides, I had great handwriting when I tried. What did I have to lose?

I composed a letter and admitted all my lack of skills and experience. I certainly didn't want to be put on the spot having to type for anybody. I added that I really did well in my science courses and I most definitely could learn anything fast.

I copied my letter in my best formal script (I'd earned the calligraphy prize at boarding school), walked to the post office and dropped it in the letterbox before I had a chance to chicken out and change my mind.

I was surprised to get a phone call a few days later for a personal interview.

The physician turned out to be a well-known Italian-American surgeon with family connections rumored to have mafia connections. In Tampa, that didn't mean the wrong side of the tracks; it meant the movers and shakers of city government and society. Doc was a prominent diplomat of the "Good Ole Boy" network.

We had a nice conversation, if a bit surreal, that didn't have anything to do with the job at all. He was more interested in my family background and personality. His main concern seemed to be whether or not I had good nerves and could be counted on in any kind of stressful situation. His last question was "Are you religious?"

"Well, actually, no."

"Good!" he said. "I think we will work very well together!" And I understood I was hired.

Well, I thought I was just the cat's meow! I could dig out my old waitress uniforms and wear white stockings and shoes and pretend I was a nurse. I envisioned scenes as Florence Nightingale, giving merciful benedictions to the suffering masses, who would gaze at me with eyes of wonder and gratitude as I soothed their fevered brows and brought succor to the wounded.

The reality was different, needless to say.

Doc, who is no longer living, was a good teacher. He introduced me to procedures gradually. As soon as I had mastered one, he moved on to the next. We started with the patients he saw in his office in a steady stream. He had four examining rooms and a room reserved for office surgery procedures. All the rooms were kept occupied at all times. I began by coordinating this flow of bodies, making sure their charts were filled out with blood pressure, temperature, symptoms, and so forth. I learned to write medical shorthand and to ask the right questions so that Doc could have an immediate handle on everything in a quick glance.

The whole operation ran like a clock. It only got a little hairy when he began to include me in the minor surgeries he performed in the office. Fortunately, I was able to be objective about the blood and messes, though I most definitely didn't like it when anyone was in pain.

After a certain period of training, I discovered that I was expected to assist Doc in major surgery at the hospital. I soon enough learned that "real" nurses didn't like Doc because he would have little to do with them and only put up with the operating room staff at the hospital because he had to. I was his right hand, and my presence was resented. I must have been good, though, because he rarely had to say anything to me at all. I knew what was needed, and we worked like a well-oiled machine.

I loved my job.

In the early months working for Doc, I noticed that he had an unusual relationship with the other girl in the office. It didn't take me long to figure out that Aline was his mistress. Fine with me—it wasn't my business so I didn't worry about it. Later, Aline confided in me that her child was Doc's. Well, that was a sticky situation, but it still wasn't my business.

Doc's office was closed Wednesdays, but Aline and I took turns working, to answer the phone and sterilize all the instrument packets. I was trying to stay busy by dusting a bit and arranging the magazines in the reception area when I heard someone unlocking the back door and just figured it was Aline coming in to see how I was doing. It was Doc. After greeting me he kept standing there watching me work. The air was heavy and I became increasingly nervous. I just knew he had something on his mind, and I was afraid to know what it was.

"What do you do on the weekends? Do you have a boyfriend? Do you go out?" he asked.

"No. I just work at home. I like to garden. Or I read or play the piano. Sometimes I have friends over, but nothing special." I didn't want it to sound like I had no life, even if that was pretty much the case.

"Do you ever get lonely?" he asked.

Well, what kind of question was that for an employer to ask an employee?

"Not really," I lied. "I manage to stay busy."

The situation was becoming more awkward by the moment. When there was absolutely no other magazine to line up and not another speck to dust on any of the tables, I knew I had to walk back into the office and he seemed to have no intention to move out of the doorway. I decided to brazen it out and took a few steps toward the door. I almost made it.

Doc was a big, powerful man who played tennis and sailed his own yacht. I'm not a small woman, even when thin, but I was no match for his strength.

And he most definitely had something on his mind: me.

Thanks to romance novelist Rebecca Brandewyne, I am spared the task of describing my interaction with this man. The difference is that in her novel, Ms. Brandewyne's heroine is most gratified to be the object of such long-suppressed lust. I was not.

"Without warning, Wulfgar reached out, taking Rhowenna unaware as he grabbed her and possessively jerked her to him. A slow, deliberately wolfish smile curved Wulfgar's lips as he stared down at her, his eyes dark, unfathomable. Before she realized what he intended, he roughly yanked her head back, and abruptly crushed his mouth down on hers—hard, hungrily."

I was horrified, mortified, and extremely anxious to extricate myself from this situation, which I did by wrestling myself away and sputtering something about him being a dirty old man old enough to be my father.

Doc didn't take rejection lightly. It was a personal insult.

I was out of a job.

CHAPTER NINETEEN

THE WORLD'S MOST BEAUTIFUL BABY

Nowadays sexual harassment on the job is grounds for legal action and could bring financial advantage to the woman who wants early retirement. But when I worked for Doc such options were still on the horizon. The incident with the doctor made me wonder again just exactly what was wrong with me.

I was friendly with my neighbor across the street, and she noticed I was home during the day and not going to work. So she dropped in for coffee. When I told her about Doc, her eyes got big and round. "Aren't you flattered that he wanted you?" she asked in breathless amazement. "What would it have hurt to go along with him? I mean, he's a doctor, right? He's rich, right? Are you crazy? You could have been fixed for life!"

She thought I was hopelessly old-fashioned if not downright prudish. People my age looked on sexual relations as natural and uncomplicated. They thought women were entitled to orgasms—"the more, the better." For good health a person ought to have proper portions of the major food groups every day, a daily bowel movement, and, most definitely, regular orgasms. If you can't be with the one you love, then love the one you're with. In this case, love meant sex.

I simply did not feel the urge to have sex for the sake of having sex. For me, sex was far and away more significant than satisfying a bodily urge to maintain good "physical balance" or "sexual hygienic homeostasis." Unfortunately, I couldn't explain why. I had no counter-arguments to stand up to the mechanistic view of the human being. Maybe I was just not normal.

Finding a job was my top priority at the moment, but again, it seems the Universe had other plans. Not too long after my neighbor's visit, I awakened to face a new day of reading employment ads only to discover that I felt unusually tired. I dragged myself out of bed and ran a bath to wake up and get going. I sank down into the hot water and reached up to rub my stiff neck. I was horrified to feel what seemed like hundreds of knots.

Well, maybe not hundreds, but there sure were a lot of them. I had Rubella. German measles.

Ordinarily, Rubella runs a fairly mild course in a few days, but for some reason this particular case was extremely hard. I was alone in the house, truly sick and barely able to get myself a drink of water or make it to the bathroom.

When Eva's son Alex discovered how sick I was, even though I protested that Rubella was contagious, he came to help me. He moved into the house and took over the nursing, just as I had helped him during his own illness. More than that, he helped me pay the bills and generally took on the role of knight in armor rescuing damsel in distress.

He wanted the relationship to be more permanent. I wasn't so sure.

In my weakened and desperate state, I wanted Alex to stand up for himself and, by default, for me. But Alex needed to confront his own conflicts with his father and his own self-abnegation before he felt ready to provide a protective framework for a relationship between us. In short, he wanted to be with me, but he wanted it to be kept a secret.

This created such severe anxiety that I became paralyzed with guilt and feelings of worthlessness. And so, I ended the not-really-there relationship.

My neighbor across the street began to try to set me up with different men by inviting me to dinner along with a selection of her husband's friends and co-workers (she and her husband both worked for a major airline). One night, there was a hit with enough synchronicity to rivet my attention. The man in question was Cuban-American and had been born on the same day I was, in the same hospital; in other words, we had been in the same nursery together when we were born, and here we were, twenty-five years later, meeting over the dinner table in my neighbor's house. Though I initially thought that it was a destined thing, my relationship with Alfredo couldn't last. I just couldn't deal with the Latin-male complex. Heck, I had enough problems dealing with a Southern, French-English-Welsh set of complexes of my own. I broke it off after a very short time, and we parted friends. Not long after, I discovered that I was pregnant.

Being pregnant changed everything and nothing. When Alex learned I was determined to have the baby he pressed me to allow him to take on the responsibility. I put him off. If Alex and Eva were drawn in, I could see only heartbreak and suffering and, above all things, I loved them too much to allow that. By whatever means necessary, I needed to save them from a fate worse than death—a life with me.

Finally Alex joined the Air Force in desperation and left for basic training, leaving me in a fantasy world of dreams that a baby would bring nothing but love and harmony into my life, all wounds magically healed.

But this pregnancy, following so soon after a serious illness, was taking its toll. I realized I was not going to be able to work at all. I wanted my mother and grandmother to help and advise me. I called Mother and told her I was sick and needed her. She and Grandma arrived a few days later.

I was terrified to be roundly criticized when I revealed the true situation. Surprisingly, Mother and Grandma seemed quite in agreement that I was handling the situation in the best way. Both seemed just as happy to welcome a new baby as I was. They agreed with my decision not to marry Alex and understood the need to conceal the fact that he was to become a father (or so I thought).

Mother and Grandma decided to close up the Tampa house and go to The Farm to save on expenses. Mother didn't seem particularly anxious to return to her husband on the East Coast. Grandma told me privately that Buck was not doing as well in business as he had claimed. Mother felt increasingly cranky because he had nothing but excuses, the world was "out to get him," and he did little to change his situation.

So, the three of us went to The Farm.

For the first time in my life, in the presence of my mother, I began to feel a sort of contentment. She was loving and attentive. All the years of emotional and psychic neglect seemed to fade into the background. After all, a baby was on the way. It never occurred to me that she had an agenda: that she was already planning to live vicariously through my child since I had turned out to be such a disappointment.

The three of us settled down to make baby clothes in great quantity and variety. We focused on layettes for either a boy or a girl, but I was certain that the baby would be a girl. It was several weeks before I decided to visit an obstetrician. When I gave the doctor the estimated date of conception, he looked at my swelling abdomen and lifted his eyebrows. During the exam, he seemed concerned and grave, and told me to see him in his office. He didn't sound very optimistic, and my heart began beating in terror that something was wrong with the baby.

He told me that I was not pregnant. He suspected instead a pre-cancerous condition called a *hydatidiform mole*. To confirm this, he ordered a sonogram.

I drove to the hospital in a complete daze. How could it be that my precious little baby, whom I already loved, did not exist? What had I done wrong to be struck with such a blow? Was it because I had lied to Alex and Eva? Was it because I was being selfish to want a baby to love?

The next day I presented myself to the doctor again. The sonogram had confirmed his diagnosis. My uterus was rapidly swelling because it was filling with fluid in reaction to the presence of this "mole," which was, as he explained, possibly a fetus that had died and had never been expelled. He ordered an immediate and complete hysterectomy. In fact, he was free tomorrow. Yes, it most definitely needed to be done that soon. Who knows? It might already be cancer!

I was completely in a state of shock. I didn't have health insurance. The nurse informed me that, to schedule the surgery, I had to give a payment of two thousand dollars up front, and make arrangements with the hospital to pay the rest later.

Well, I didn't happen to have two thousand dollars in either my pocket or my bank account. In terror of dying right there on the spot, I mumbled that I was sure I'd be able to get the money from my family. I was desperate, but the nurse was firm. No money, no surgery. Never mind that I was supposed to be dying of cancer here!

At home, my mother and grandmother agreed that we would all just have to do the best we could and Grandma would dip into her savings. After all, my life was at stake. It was too late to do anything that day, but we planned to go to the bank and then to the doctor's office the next day to pay the deposit and schedule the surgery.

The Universe had other plans for the next day.

I called Eva to tell her the news and explained that I was soon to have a hysterectomy and there would be no baby now or ever. She was completely aghast at this turn of events and not as willing to accept the diagnosis as I was. A second opinion was in order when one is contemplating such a serious, life-changing move as a complete hysterectomy at the age of twenty-five.

As it happened, Eva had recently obtained her degree in nuclear medicine and was now working for the head of the nuclear medicine department at the medical school in Tampa. Her idea was that her boss should be the one to give this "second opinion." She would make the arrangements and call me back.

It turned out that this doctor–professor was quite gracious and willing to use all the up-to-date equipment of his department to verify that I'd received a correct diagnosis. At lunchtime the next day he would handle everything himself—gratis.

The doctor spent several hours with me, taking a history, asking many questions, examining, and doing sonograms. In the end, he pronounced that with my history, something was definitely amiss, and it certainly did look as though it could be a hydatidiform mole. But he was not convinced the uterus was full of fluid. It looked like a semi-solid mass on the outside, something growing in the abdominal cavity in front of the uterus. He wanted colleagues to have a look and sent me right over to the teaching hospital to meet with this other professor and his entourage of star residents who were doing rounds at that very moment.

I drove to the hospital and, sure enough, I was expected. It seemed the cachet of Eva's boss cast a long shadow. I met with six or seven doctors and their professor. All the same questions I had already been asked were asked again, and dozens more.

Then it was time for the exam.

Now, having a gynecological exam done by a single doctor with a nurse present is one thing. Having one done by a team is something else altogether. I was fighting to keep my emotions under control and humor seemed to be the best defense. As they took turns poking, prodding, pushing, and invading my private parts, I kept up a dialogue with them, answering their questions with dry one-liners that soon had them all laughing. Finally, it was over and the professor asked them, "Well, what's the verdict?" All of them described their technical observations and the standard teachings of what those observations must suggest. Finally, one of them said, "I don't think it's that simple. What if she actually is pregnant?" And they all looked at each other.

"Only one way to find out," the professor said. He described a new type of sonography that employed real-time moving pictures. Only one doctor in the area had such an advanced piece of equipment in his office—in the same building as the doctor I had worked for! It gave me a very funny feeling to be there, and I crossed my fingers that I wouldn't run into anyone I knew. I lucked out and slipped in unnoticed.

Again, I was taken right in with no waiting. The exam was handled by the doctor himself rather than the tech. The nurses and technicians gathered around, aware of the details of the case. As soon as the wand was applied to my abdomen, moved and shifted around, suddenly, there on the monitor, in real-time, real-life pictures, was a baby.

And, what's more, the baby was alive and well and had a beautiful, strong heart. Everyone in the room burst into cheers and applause. I cried tears of relief.

But, at the same time, based on the new age of development of the baby, given by accurate measurements of the sonogram, I knew it was not Alex's—it was Alfredo's. That solved one problem. It also made me aware of the bizarre synchronicity of two people, born on the same day, in the same hospital, coming together just long enough to conceive a child.

But there was still a problem: the rapidly growing semi-solid mass that was apparently somewhat frightening in terms of the rate of its expansion. I was sent back to the hospital and the team of doctors with the results of the sonogram in hand. They very much wanted to supervise the situation because it was, as they put it, such an interesting and challenging case.

This meant, of course, that I needed to be in Tampa to be close to the doctors and the hospital. Mother and Grandma didn't want to leave The Farm, but, as it happened, my brother was sent to a special school by the Navy, worried about his wife left alone during his duty assignment. The solution seemed obvious: his wife and baby would come to Tampa to live in the house. We could look after each other.

It promised to be an ideal situation.

I had to go to the hospital for a sonogram every week for two months for the medical team to monitor the growth of both the baby and the mass. At a certain point, it was decided that the mass had to be removed because it was expanding frighteningly fast. When the baby was mature enough to survive the surgery, it was scheduled.

The day before surgery, the bed across from me had been occupied by a young girl in great pain who began to stir and moan and cry out for relief. Since she was barely conscious, I pressed the call button and the nurse came to give her an injection. The nurse resented the summon to relieve this girl's pain and muttered balefully about girls who "dance to the music" and then cry when they have to "pay the piper." I wasn't too sure what she was talking about.

A man came to visit this young girl. I had never seen a pimp up close before, but they'd been pointed out to me by a friend as we drove down a street in a certain neighborhood once. This guy was obviously a pimp. I now began to understand the attitude of the nurse who had been so uncaring earlier in the day. I overheard some muffled, disjointed, and somewhat incoherent conversation between this girl and the man who came to visit her.

He was very anxious for her to get well and back to work because she had "customers" asking for her. She, on the other hand, was just crying for relief and begging him to not expect her to do anything soon because she needed to rest. She began to cry in the pain again, and the man went to summon the nurse.

Again, there was an "attitude" from the nurse toward the girl, and most especially toward the man. She was not just rude to him, she actually snapped at him that it was men like him that put women in such conditions. He told her to "be cool, mama!" and she snarled back that he'd better not call her "mama" again or she would have security come and remove him. "I'm leaving anyway!" he said, throwing up his hands and laughing as he strolled out the door.

The next morning, the girl was gone. When I asked about her I was told she had died during the night. When I asked what in the world she had died from, the answer was that a gynecological infection had invaded her entire system and that was what happened to prostitutes.

What a terrible way to die. Surely, she was someone's daughter, someone had loved her. Where were they when she died? Did they know she was sick? Did that horrible man who just wanted her to get well so she could make more money for him care at all about her suffering and dying alone in the care of nurses who looked on her with disdain?

I never forgot that poor girl and her suffering.

My own surgery was scheduled for early that morning. Despite the drugs given to me to relax before I was taken to the operating room, I was wide awake and sitting up on the stretcher when the doctor arrived: a woman, the star surgical resident of the medical school. We joked a little about how I was so curious that I would really like to be able to watch what was going on and how unfortunate it was that I had to be asleep through the whole thing.

I was wheeled in, my arm strapped out to the side, and the drug administered. Slam! I was gone. The next thing I knew, I was being moved to a stretcher from the operating table feeling pretty much like I had been hit by a truck. The surgeon had removed a very large mass that had apparently begun as a blister on my left ovary and weighed over eight pounds.

My first child would be born almost six months to the day later, but the rest of my pregnancy would prove to be stressful and eventful.

My grandmother's cancer had come back. The doctors advised admitting her for radiation and chemotherapy where she could be constantly monitored. This was a terrible ordeal for her and for all of us. Her hair fell out and her skin peeled in thick sheets as though she had been horribly burned. She lost weight and became so frail that a strong gust of wind would have knocked her over.

Mother saw no need to join us at the house in Tampa. She could drive to the cancer center a couple of times a week to keep tabs on the situation. We didn't realize there was an agenda behind this decision, but it soon became apparent. Left alone at The Farm, Mother welcomed her erstwhile husband back into the fold. She probably had financial motives when she did so, because he had, again, come knocking at the door with claims of great prosperity.

Meanwhile, my brother finished training school in the Navy, and his wife rejoined him. Shortly afterward, Grandma's cancer was in remission and she came home to the house in Tampa.

Mother planned to come back to look after us, but she'd slipped and fallen on the steps while carrying a tub of peaches and hurt her back. Her husband brought her to Tampa anyway, and I was left to take care of both my mother and my grandmother while waiting out the last days before the baby came.

Pregnancy was a dreadful ordeal for me in many ways, mostly due to my weakened back. The pressure on my lower spine produced all kinds of strange effects from day to day. Some days I was fine, and others I just couldn't walk at all from the pain in my left leg. On several occasions, when I felt okay and was just walking along in a normal way, something would suddenly shift, and it wasn't just pain that hit me, but a sudden nerve impulse that caused my leg to collapse completely. I would find myself without support at all, falling to the floor.

It was a terrible, hot spring. There was a drought that lasted for an unusually long time, and I was beyond miserable in the heat. We didn't have

THE WORLD'S MOST BEAUTIFUL BABY

air conditioning, and the humidity hit daily record levels. It was a struggle to keep Grandma comfortable and Mother was cranky with pain. I was in the bathtub a half-dozen times a day just to rinse off the sweat. I watched the sky anxiously for rain and knew, somehow, that if it rained, the baby would come too.

And so it was. Finally, a day full of lowering clouds and a freshening breeze. When the first cold drops began to fall, labor began. As we drove to the hospital, the wipers on the car couldn't go fast enough to keep up with the sheets of rain.

Before I even made it to the hospital door, my first *real* pain hit me. There was a mailbox in front of the building just waiting for someone like me, in that condition, to grab on for dear life until the contraction passed. As soon as it was over, I looked around quickly to make sure no one had seen me in my moment of extremity, and then I casually walked in the door in my straw hat and rope sandals.

I was terrified.

Yes, I had read a dozen books on baby- and child-care during my pregnancy. I had read uplifting books and listened only to classical music the entire time. I watched my diet carefully, faithfully swallowed vitamins and ate extra vegetables to ensure the baby had the absolute best possible nutrition. But I had never managed to get anyone to explain to me exactly how this process called "labor" actually worked.

I had visited with friends who already had children, and, without exception, I had listened to stories of unparalleled delivery-room horrors. No one, however, would divulge the secret. I was told knowingly that when it was time, it would happen.

The books I had read all talked about "pushing" and "bearing down." Dilation of the cervix I understood, but there was something elusive in the execution of this matter. I was most curious to find out what it was.

An orderly helped me to a wheelchair and made his way toward the ob-gyn section of the hospital when the most god-awful, blood-curdling scream I have ever heard in my life issued forth from behind a set of double doors.

Not a good sign.

The orderly pushed a button on the wall and, as it happened, my doctor came to receive me at the gates of what seemed to be hell. As he took over the wheelchair and pushed me through the doors, another horrifying moan built rapidly to an ear-splitting shriek and I said, "I don't think I want to do this. I think I want to go home!"

"Sorry," he told me. "Once you start, there's no way out but to do it!"

"There's gotta be a better way," I suggested as another scream drowned out all other sound.

"I wish," he said.

I was set up in a labor room to wait until I had dilated. Well, I had no idea how long that was going to be, and I thought I knew what a labor pain was. I didn't. I was soon to find out, though.

The poor girl in the next room was really having a rough time of it. I had some idea of what labor was, but I certainly didn't think it was sufficiently painful to cause me to lose my dignity and start screaming like that poor soul. She was blubbering and crying over and over, "I'll never do it again! As God is my witness, I'll never do it again! Oh, Mama! Mama! Help me, help me!"

When the nurse came to check on my progress, I had to ask her what was going on next door, and she just shook her head sadly. The girl was only thirteen and had been in labor since the day before. "They need to do something for her," she said. Doctors and nurses were coming and going from that room where the screams never let up and one had to wonder just how much strength a human being had to withstand that kind of suffering.

The next thing I knew, the screaming had stopped and the girl was being pushed across the hall into what I later learned was a surgical delivery room. Whatever was happening was going very fast because they didn't shut the door. I leaned up on my elbow to see what I could. People in green outfits gathered around a table and somebody was rolling up a sheet that was completely saturated with blood and tossing it onto the floor in a hurry. This person looked up briefly, saw me watching and, quickly shut the door.

The girl lived, but her baby died. She had been left too long before the decision was made to do a Caesarean.

But what would a thirteen-year-old do with a baby?

When my own turn came to be moved into the delivery room, I nearly had a heart attack. What, in the name of God, was that contraption in the middle of the room? It looked like some sort of medieval torture device.

It was the delivery table.

Not only that, but I was suddenly in the grip of a new pain—and I had barely taken a break since the last one. Gads! This was getting intense.

"Get on the table!" I was ordered.

What do you mean, "get on the table?" I can't move here! I'm having a pain here, can't you see? It's impossible to move. My whole body is in a state of tetany and you want me to move?! Get real!

Somehow, I was moved onto the table, though I can promise that it was with very little assistance from me.

I was shocked speechless to feel leather straps being closed over my wrists and ankles. *Dear God! What kind of thing is going to happen that requires that I be restrained like some kind of wild beast?!*

"Uh, what are those for?" I asked in a panic.

"That's so you won't hurt yourself or the baby," was the reply.

Well, how about so I don't kill the doctor by kicking his teeth in? I thought.

The next pain hit like a speeding train and the nurse urged, "PUSH!"

"What, precisely, do you mean by push?" I asked in the most normal conversational tone that could be managed through clenched teeth. "Exactly what muscles do you wish for me to employ?"

The startled nurse looked at me with surprise and answered, "You know, just like having a bowel movement."

Oh. So that was the big secret. *Bizarro!* I thought.

Okay, here comes the next one! I'm gonna push!

And I did. Well, that is until I ran out of air and stopped pushing to catch my breath.

"What are you doing?!" the nurse demanded.

"I'm breathing!" I replied with some resentment that she couldn't realize that the human organism did require oxygen to function.

"Don't breathe! PUSH!" she shouted.

Oh. Okay. So it's like that, is it? Well, you asked for it. When the next one comes, get ready.

The next one came almost immediately. I took a deep breath and did the deed.

There she was. I had a brief glimpse before they popped her into a little heated box on a cart and whisked her away. I was so excited I wanted to jump up and follow the person pushing the cart.

When that beautiful, utterly perfect little being was placed in my arms for the first time, I was so overcome with emotion that I could hardly believe I could feel so much love and still be in the world. It seemed to me that such transcendence could only be experienced in the heavenly

The World's Most Beautiful Baby—objectively.

spheres. She looked at me and I looked at her and I told her: "Oh, Sugar baby! Mommy's here. Mommy will take care of you."

I meant it with all my soul. And with all my soul now, I wish I could have fulfilled that promise.

My baby was so beautiful, with her curls and perfect nose, lips, and face, that in a nursery which was occupied by thirty or more babies, when visitors gathered at the big glass window to look at the babies, it was my baby they all oohed and aahed over. She was constantly held in the arms or laps of the nurses because she was so beautiful they could not bear to put her down. When the clerk came to take orders for the newborn photographs, he said: "Oh! You're the mother of that absolutely gorgeous baby!"

She was. And is.

Not only that, but she was perfect in every imaginable way. She was never fussy; she was contented. She began to sleep through the night when she was about two months old, and the older she got, the more beautiful she became. People on the street or in stores would stop and stare at her with their mouths open. Little children would point to her and say: "Mommy, look at that beautiful baby!" Neighbors and friends vied to give her gifts of beautiful clothes and adorable toys, obviously pleased to see her dressed up in an outfit they had chosen, or holding a toy they had given her.

And to my mind, everything she did was perfect.

But I was perfect when I was born, too. And God help me, what was done to me, I did to her. And now I can understand my own mother. The only difference between us is that I woke up from the dream. Mother never did. And whether my daughter will overcome it, only time will tell.

CHAPTER TWENTY

MINKS AND TURKEY BASTERS

Within a few weeks of the baby's arrival, Mother and Grandmother decided to go back to The Farm. I didn't want to go, because I couldn't stand to be around Mother's husband. Buck was such a whiner and sniveler that within ten minutes of being in his presence, I felt nearly mindless rage at his abyssal ignorance and hubris. He repeated stories of uneducated rubes who managed to pull a fast one on anybody with brains or education, where dumb luck and foxy cunning came out on top. He was intimidated by intellect, most especially in a woman, so these stories were always directed at me. It completely baffled me that Mother couldn't see through him.

After two months of rest, I knew I'd have to go back to work. Mother most definitely was not going to let go of Grandma (and her bank account) even if she wanted to be with me and the baby. I knew that Grandma wasn't well enough to help with a baby yet, and it was better if she wasn't tempted to put too much strain on herself. Yet, she wanted to be with the baby, and I knew she didn't have many years. So I needed to move back to The Farm too. There was no way I'd leave my baby in the care of strangers, and Mother was most willing to take care of her while I worked. On Mother's own terms, of course. But, beggars can't be

My baby at the farm with plastic roses and a big hat!

choosers. I closed up the house in Tampa, found some friends willing to move my piano, and back to The Farm I went.

* * *

Even though I had some experience and two years of college, the job choices were limited. I ended up taking a position with the State Department of Health and Rehabilitative Services as an interviewer and certifier in the local welfare office.

While I waited for the job interview, I noticed several welfare workers parading back and forth behind the counter, looking me over. Years later, one of them told me why they'd been checking me out. "You didn't look too bright," she told me. "Didn't look like you'd make any trouble. So we all voted to tell the supervisor to be sure to hire you!"

The Farm was in rural Pasco county, and the State Offices only employed about a hundred people on the west side with all the departments in one place: Social Services, Child Welfare Protective Services, Food Stamps, Aid to Families with Dependent Children, and a few other odds and ends. West Pasco County had half a dozen small communities along the main coastal Highway 19, and they all blended together with a few traffic lights separating them.

My own unit consisted of about a dozen people, six of whom were certifiers, and we all shared a couple of clerical workers to handle the phones and filing. Our boss, John Dear, was a retired military base commander with a gruff way about him, very big on morale and chain of command, but also very fair minded. All of us adored him.

My co-worker Nancy was married to the mayor of one of the little coastal towns. She was petite and funny and always brought a big bowl of sugar-free chocolate pudding with a two-inch layer of whipped topping for lunch. She was counting carbs, and it really worked for her.

Sabrina was divorced from a wealthy doctor who was slow to pay her alimony, but she still dressed to the nines. She was gorgeous, too, decked out in the latest fashions in a backwater welfare office, sitting across the desk from the often dirty and poorly dressed clients who came for assistance. She had a good heart, though.

Tim was a retired New York City policeman working on a second pension, and after all his experiences, nothing fazed him. He was out the door at break time, lunchtime, and time to go home no matter what else was going on. He could forget it and walk away. He never did one thing more than was required by the job description.

Jody was the wife of a raging drunk she described as an alcoholic. She attended Al-Anon meetings regularly and the philosophy she exuded was pretty much "what, me worry?" She didn't, but she drove everyone else nuts. She could criticize with the best of them, but she never did anything wrong herself!

Finally, there was Sandra, a big, beautiful Sicilian princess from New York. Sandra believed anything could be cured by a plate of pasta and a heart-to-heart talk. She organized monthly "secret pal" days, set up potluck dinners in the lunch room, brought decorations for every holiday and supervised their arrangement. Nothing made her happier than getting everybody together like a big family to cook, eat, laugh, and fulfill some ideal she had of love and kindness and good manners. You can probably figure out that her home life lacked all of these things.

Both the clerical workers were retirees who decided to take jobs to keep from falling into a decline. Of course, this meant that wherever they worked, the decline went with them. Ellen was the bane of our existence. She had worked many years for a firm of attorneys in Boston before retiring to Florida. Ellen couldn't remember anything for two minutes, where she put a phone message or left a file folder, but we were expected to make due obeisance because she was a "real" secretary. She resented ordinary clerical functions and expressed her disdain by being so incompetent that we would all think twice before asking her to do anything again.

I really tried to be patient and understanding with Ellen because of her age and related failings, but it was hard. My patience came to an end one day after I caught her falsifying a document to cover up the fact that she had screwed up a case, causing extreme hardship for an entire family who went without food and shelter for almost a month as a result, while she kept lying to cover up the fact that she couldn't remember where she had put the documents that were supposed to be in their file. As much as I had sympathy for her, I railed against the fact that allowances were made for her incompetence at the expense of others.

Ellen's daily screw-ups were a regular topic of discussion. Unfortunately, the union and the tenure system for state employees, making us feel secure in our jobs, also kept incompetents like Ellen in theirs. None of us wanted to see Ellen lose her pension. We just wanted the state to find a place for her where she could really fit. Finding ways to get Ellen to apply for a transfer to another unit became a primary occupation.

* * *

I had some mink heads and tails made into clasps for sewing projects, and one day I brought them in to show to Sandra. We looked at each other, looked at the little desiccated head with glass eyes and gleaming teeth, and then the idea occurred to both of us at the same time. We inserted them into a file folder in a drawer so it looked like a rat was peering up out of the masses of files. The head was at one end, the tail stuck up at the other. Then, we closed the drawer.

After lunch, when Ellen had just come back (thirty minutes late as usual) from her favorite restaurant, Sandra called her on the intercom and requested a file from the drawer. I was holding my breath to keep from collapsing in laughter when ... nothing happened. Ellen couldn't remember the file number long enough to get to the correct drawer.

Sandra wrote it down on a slip of paper and Ellen diligently went looking. She opened the drawer and extracted the file and still nothing happened! It took us a bit to figure out that the file, which should have been behind the mink head, had been misfiled by Ellen by chance. And with Ellen's crazy system of file hunting, she'd found it by chance without ever pulling the drawer all the way open.

Well, we were not going to be denied. I slipped over to the file cabinet, opened the drawer, and took note of a file that was most assuredly behind the mink head. I went back to my office to call Ellen on the intercom to ask for it.

There was a long silence.

Finally, I could stand it no longer and went to the door to peek, only to find Ellen rummaging through the wrong drawer! Sandra came along and nonchalantly asked what file she was looking for and pointed out the correct drawer. Ellen had pulled a bundle of files out of the drawer to go through them, including the one with the mink head, and was shuffling them in her arms when the head fell forward onto her chest. Screaming and throwing her hands up to grab at the monster that was leaping toward her throat, Ellen managed to throw about fifteen or twenty files so high into the air that all the contents came raining down. Ellen shrieked, stomped, jumped and babbled, and finally ran out the door into the hallway, tearing at her dress and hair as though some creature had her and wouldn't let go.

Tim came out of his office to see what the fuss was all about, saw me and Sandra crying and laughing over the little fuzzy mink head and tail on the floor, and realized what we had done. He shook his head in disgust and went out after Ellen to tell her it was only a joke. Sandra and I finally pulled ourselves together enough to begin picking up and re-assembling the files scattered all over the office.

Ellen never liked us after that. I wonder why ... She also dug in her heels and refused categorically, no matter how tempting the offer, to apply for a transfer to any other office.

The unit next door was AFDC. Most state offices are staffed with people who have useless liberal arts or psychology degrees and can't find any other way to use them. Employees of AFDC had to have a four-year degree. Food Stamp certifiers needed a two-year degree, so naturally they thought they were far superior to us and that none of the Food Stamp certifiers had the brains to assemble and manage an AFDC case. Never mind that very few of them could manage to fulfill the simplest of agency requirements in verification and documentation for the Food Stamp portion, or that we invariably had to do their paperwork over when it was passed to our office.

At some point, the state allotted two more positions to the AFDC office, and they were filled by two women who transferred in from another district. It didn't take us long to realize that they were lesbians, they lived together, and wore matching wedding rings.

Well, that's fine; nobody cared but the loving couple. At first, they shoved lesbianism and gay rights issues in our faces, so we called them the Prickly Pair, Linda and Leila. After awhile, they settled down and realized we didn't judge their lifestyle. Soon they became as much a part of the office scenery as anyone else.

One day the cashier went home early and I was tapped to help count all the food stamps for the daily report. There I was, in the bankers' cage, counting thousands of dollars' worth of food stamps when a clerk from the AFDC office—Barbara—came to the window. She had a funny look on her face, so I stopped counting and waited for the news I knew was coming. One of the Prickly Pair, Linda, was pregnant!

"Hmmm! I guess she likes guys after all! Wonder what Leila thinks about this?"

But my friend, Barbara, said right away, "They used a turkey baster!"
"What?" I couldn't quite figure out what she was saying.
"You know, a turkey baster! Somebody gave them a supply of sperm and they just explained to everyone in the office how they used a turkey baster to deposit it. That's how Linda got pregnant!"

I guess I was more speechless over the fact that such an intimate item of information was being so openly discussed than I was over the fact that Linda was pregnant, or even the method used to produce the condition. I had to start my count all over again.

Everyone was happy for the couple and we planned a baby shower.

Linda must have really wanted to get pregnant because she began wearing maternity clothes right away. I'm sure her jeans weren't even tight yet.

A few weeks later, Linda was absent from the office and the word raced around the building that she had had a miscarriage. We were all very upset, almost as if we had lost the baby ourselves. When she came back to work, she was depressed for a long time.

Leila ended up abandoning Linda for a nurse she had met at the hospital and Linda married a guy, so I guess she did like guys a little.

Not long after all this happened, a new fellow came to work down in the Protective Services unit. He was tall, good looking, and such a sharp dresser that all the women were just swooning over him. His name was Alfonso with about half a dozen other names following behind, and he was an exiled Cuban aristocrat. His father had been a diplomat and his mother was a psychiatrist. He was cultured, well educated, urbane, and sophisticated. Our backwater office had never seen anything like him. He naturally had his pick of the single ladies employed by the agency, and I noticed quite a stream of them (even a couple of married ones) "going out to lunch" with Alfonso and returning looking more like they had been wrestling a bear than a burger.

At about the same time, a new girl was hired to run the copy machines. She, too, was a very snappy dresser and had a face and figure to knock your eyes out. There was only one problem: when she opened her mouth to speak, we could barely understand a word she said for the thick backwoods South Carolina accent. Not only that, her grammar was atrocious. Being a Southerner myself, I am not unused to the many and varied accents of the South, my favorite being the cultured, molten tones of Augusta, but this accent was utterly impossible to comprehend. For this girl, there was no such thing as "bread." It was "laaht bray-uhd." (I think that this meant "light bread," as opposed to biscuits or cornbread.)

As fate would have it, the Southern Belle and the expatriate Cubano fell in love and decided to marry. I had a little difficulty understanding what they might have in common because I knew that she aspired to be a country-western singer and he was fond of opera. But, you just can't tell about these things.

We held a shower for them and the lovebirds made out like bandits with all the goodies. We were invited to their elegant church wedding and the bride looked like an angel. (She managed to maintain that illusion as long as she didn't speak.) Off they went on a honeymoon cruise and we all waited breathlessly for their return, to bask in the glow of their happiness. Those who had aspired to romance with Alfonso could vicariously experience the fruition of such a dream.

Well, they returned, but it was more like an icy north wind sweeping through the building. To this day, no one knows what happened, because neither of them ever revealed even a clue to anyone. The upshot of it was that she left him on the wedding night, went home to her parents, and received an annulment.

Now, what in the world could Alfonso have done to set off that South Carolina wildcat? I suspect he decided that he'd teach her to "speak properly." Either that or he was a pervert and she wasn't going to put up with that sort of nonsense! Who knows. It's one of those mysteries of life that provides hours of enjoyment with endless speculation.

They both kept coming to work in the same building, but neither ever spoke to the other again except to conduct business. They also never returned any of the wedding gifts.

I was happy in my job and, after a while, we were all like one big, dysfunctional, but mostly happy, family.

Working in a welfare office is very stressful. All day long I interviewed people who were at the end of their rope. Most of them were women who were tired

Me during my first year working for HRS. The puppy's name was Weegee.

and hungry and had no means of feeding their children. Most were abandoned by their husbands, boyfriends, or families, and most had no employable skills. Many were abused, bruised, sick or disabled, or mentally retarded. The chief feature they had in common was abysmal ignorance.

There were exceptions, of course, but so few.

My work entailed a great deal more than just filling out forms and signing endless documents, and the state provided an ongoing series of classes in psychology, interviewing techniques, stress management, and assorted others designed to help state workers help the clients so we didn't burn out completely and become clients too.

I started keeping little packages of peanut butter crackers and fruit in my office for children facing a long wait. Some parents figured that if their children cried we'd put their case ahead of someone else just to get them out of there. I fell for this maneuver a lot in the beginning. I was working like crazy to get everyone seen and out of there just so I didn't have to hear another crying, hungry child. After a while, Sandra came over and had a little talk with me.

"You have to slow down," she said firmly.

"I can't," I said.

"Don't you realize how they are playing on your sympathy? You're going to burn out so fast that you'll be in a hospital if you don't get a grip!" She recounted stories of other workers who'd just gone off the deep end.

I was refusing breaks, eating lunch at my desk, coming early to finish up cases left from the night before, and staying late to see additional, unscheduled clients. I was drinking about two pots of strong coffee a day, and my stomach had a hole in it already. Since I couldn't turn off my sympathy for the children, I simply out-maneuvered the parents by feeding them crackers and fruit.

Not only was I working during the day, I was continuing to develop my skills as a hypnotherapist in the evenings. Sandra was excited and intrigued by this and wanted to encourage me to continue this kind of work. She would never agree to be hypnotized herself, but she decided to become my "publicist" and contacted several professionals in the psychological counseling field, whose offices had begun to spring up in the neighborhood of the state office building. (Not a surprise!) I formed a working relationship with a couple of the more open-minded ones, and was called in on cases where it was deemed desirable to employ hypnosis. As time went by, I also began to get private referrals from these interactions.

Sandra also decided that I must teach some of the things I had learned. She organized classes where I taught hypnosis, relaxation techniques, and guided meditation. In a sense, it could be said that I sought to solve problems for others because I could not solve the most basic problem of my own existence. No matter how hard I studied, what I tried, or where I turned, I could not find satisfaction for this empty feeling inside that I perceived as a need for God, for meaning and purpose, to be able to establish faith and be content in my faith and my life.

I soon decided that I needed a "real" career. The state would help me through nursing school, while allowing me to work part-time. I applied, took the entrance exam, passed, and was accepted. Needless to say, it was a crushing schedule, but I knew it would only last for two years, and I could work for the state in a new capacity that would pay a lot better and give me more satisfaction overall.

So, while everything about my life seemed to following a positive path—I had a beautiful baby who brought joy to all of us, and I was happy being of service in some significant way—there was unseen pressure being exerted in other areas of life that would, ultimately, lead to total disaster.

There are many kinds of death.

CHAPTER TWENTY-ONE

PARTIES, MOSQUITOES, HIVES, HYPNOSIS, AND FISHING BOATS

The main authority in my life was the district manager of the state offices, a Burt Reynolds type in looks and attitude. Charles was a Florida native like me and he had the same last name (I've given him a different first name for privacy). Some of my co-workers suspected we were related, but he didn't come from any branch of our family as far as I knew. He'd suddenly developed an intense interest in the Food Stamp office, and he liked staring at me, boldly and lazily. A divorced guy with some interest in a single girl—that seemed all right. But you may recall my extreme vulnerability and almost total lack of social skills in dealing with predators. And Charles was a predator, the kind you wouldn't suspect.

Whenever he spoke to me, I felt tongue-tied and intimidated and couldn't think of a thing to say. But the night of the Christmas party, in the private dining room of a popular restaurant, things changed. I had a great red velvet dress—just the color for Christmas—and a sweater with a rabbit fur collar. As I was getting ready to leave, my friend Tom (from the bridge) stopped by and insisted on taking a picture of me, so I clowned for the camera.

At the restaurant, when Charles arrived a dozen voices called out to him to "come and sit here!" but he kept looking till he spied me and made a beeline for the chair beside me.

I was feeling a little out of place. No one from my work unit was there, and drinking and dancing had never been my forte in any event. While Charles chatted casually for a few minutes I had a glass of scotch that I decided I ought to drink so I could stop being so stiff and formal. And then I had another. There was a very nice band playing and Charles

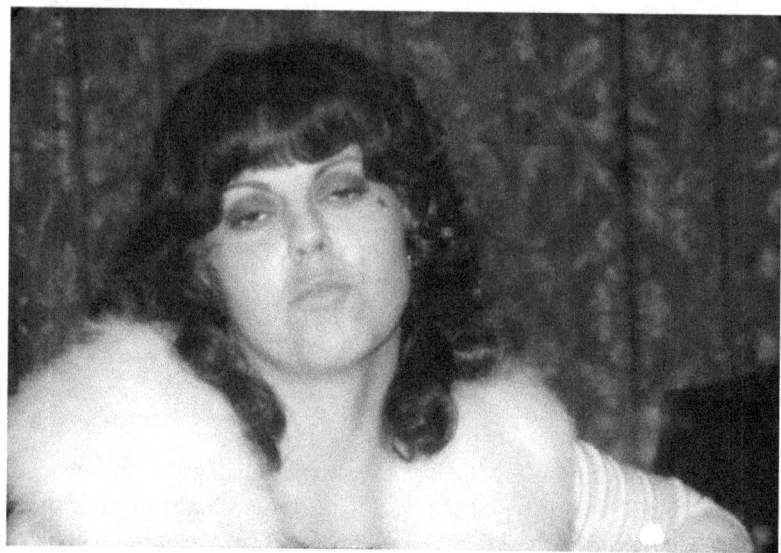

Me clowning for the camera.

wanted to dance. Well, I most definitely did not want to demonstrate my two left feet, so I declined. "Can't dance," I said. "Try the lady in the pink dress!"

He did. And he proved to be a dancer like my mother, amazing to watch, and I was quite breathless at the display. When the dance was over, he sent the lady off to her corner and returned to sit by me. So I decided I needed another glass of scotch. The room got a little blurry. "Let's get out of here," Charles told my left earring. "Let's go somewhere we can talk."

"Where," said I.

"Why, my place, of course," said Charles.

"Why not?"

I felt like a fifth wheel with all the bopping and bumping going on. Why not go where we could just listen to some quiet music and talk in a civilized way? My normal inhibitions and cautions had disappeared with the third scotch. It might be fate that we had the same name, and who knows? It might be destiny. A romance might develop. He might turn out to be The One. I'd never know till we got better acquainted. And, if I decided he was not on the level after we talked awhile, I could always put a period to any further advances, right?

PARTIES, MOSQUITOES, HIVES, HYPNOSIS, AND FISHING BOATS

Wrong.

I vaguely remember driving ten or more miles, following him as he exceeded the speed limit dangerously. I was most definitely not sober enough to be behind the wheel. But, somehow, we made it to his house.

Charles did all the talking. He lied about how deeply moved he was by my presence, my "mystery," or some such blather. I was nearly asleep from the effects of the alcohol when he started pawing my dress.

"No! I need to go home!"

"Well, obviously, you wanted it," he said, "and you're going to enjoy it a lot better if you just relax and stop fighting me." The next thing I remember is waking up, pre-dawn, in this man's bed, in a complete panic to get home.

I slipped into my clothes, ran my fingers through my hair, and knew that I was going to catch it from Mother for being out so late. When Charles woke up, he was not the least bit apologetic.

"You have to forget this ever happened," he said. "I have too many responsibilities and obligations." He fixed me with a stern, authoritative eye. "If any word slips out, it will be very unpleasant."

Okay. I understood. It was a mistake on both sides. He had too much lust built up, and I had too much scotch. We're adults here. I can handle this.

The term "date rape" hadn't been invented yet.

I started vomiting in the morning a few weeks later. I just could NOT figure out how it could happen. Just ONCE, for God's sake! Just one lousy slip, one error in judgment, one encounter! What was I going to do? The problem was so huge that I felt paralyzed just thinking about it. I liked my job, I had a future, and I had screwed up again, and royally!

I argued back and forth with myself. I could have the baby, never say a word about who the father was, and just go on with my life with two children. I could tolerate all the whispers and rumors; I could finish school, pregnant or not; I could work out all the logistical details and everything would be fine.

But I knew I was kidding myself. Having the baby would ruin any chance of finishing school and making a future for myself and my daughter. I needed to act and act fast.

But I wasn't sure I was thinking clearly. At work I decided to confide in Madge, who had a very good working relationship with Charles. He looked on her as almost a mother. Her son was one of his fishing buddies. I figured that, since she was an insider with Charles, she would know best whether I ought to notify Charles before I took this serious step.

"Yes, you ought to notify him," said Madge. "And he ought to pay the bill!"

"But ..."

"And," said Madge, "you ought to tell him yourself."

"That," said I, "is a most terrifying thought."

"Charles is not really an ogre, even though he acts like one," Madge told me. "You must not be afraid of the truth."

* * *

It was a terrible ordeal, more painful than I care to remember. I was accused of lying because, of course, how could *one* mistake have such consequences? Surely someone else was responsible and I was just trying to blame it on him for purposes of getting money or advancement. I was simply trying to tell the truth and deal with a difficult situation in an honest and fair way for us both. That he was so contemptuous and dismissive was excruciatingly painful.

I fled his office, went to Sandra, and poured out the story to her. She was furious with Charles. Her advice was to have the baby and "stick it to him." I didn't want to do that. I just wanted to take care of the problem and be assured I could keep my job without harassment and get on with my life.

After my previous experience with the emotional fallout of such a procedure, I most desperately did not want to do it. It was, in the end, the only choice that was unselfish and truly loving to all concerned. That Charles had only to pay the bill and forget about it was clearly a little unfair, but I wasn't focused on that issue. I just wanted to get through it.

Madge made the arrangements, drove me to the clinic, and brought me home afterward.

A week at home resting and recovering was just what I needed.

Meanwhile, during my absence, my supervisor, John Dear, had a confrontation with Charles, resigned his job, and left. Jody was appointed supervisor.

Back on the job, I was overwhelmed with feelings of being dirty, guilty, and definitely *persona non grata* in Charles's eyes. Maybe it's my imagi-

PARTIES, MOSQUITOES, HIVES, HYPNOSIS, AND FISHING BOATS

nation, maybe not, but it seemed that Jody spent an inordinate amount of time closeted with Charles. Then she marched into my office and delivered an entire list of failings on my part about the way I was doing my job.

Cases were piled on my desk that were claimed to be full of errors. I went through each one, finding no errors according to manual procedures, and returned them to Jody with memos explaining my justifications.

"Oh," says Jody. "Well, I'm just learning this job! Be patient with me!"

And then she delivered another stack of cases with no errors, bogging down my time so that I had to go through every one of them, writing narrative memos, getting more and more behind in my daily caseload taking care of this nonsense.

Of course, when I was behind with my caseload, Jody asked me with a sneer, "Plan to take any appointments today?" As if I were sitting there doing nothing but filing my nails! Never mind that I was struggling like crazy to finish the stack of case reviews she was frivolously piling on my desk almost daily.

I would have had to be blind not to know the deliberate pressure cooked up between Charles and Jody.

Perhaps my resistance was low because of this stress, perhaps it was fate that intervened, but the next event was another step down into the pit.

As it happened, Easter week that year was accompanied by strange weather. A southwest wind had been blowing for days and the mosquitoes were suddenly out en masse. Mosquitoes are part of living in Florida. Their cycles and types were well known to me, but this was something new. We even joked about these particular mosquitoes that they were kamikaze suicide bombers. My grandmother said they were "salt marsh" mosquitoes and must have been blown in with the southwesterlies.

Well, one of them must have come from a marsh in Central America because the result of her biting me was that I contracted dengue fever. Dengue is also called breakbone fever because one of the initial symptoms is that all the bones in your body, especially in the back, feel like they are broken. It is accompanied by a high fever, bone-rattling chills, a crushing headache, and basically total prostration. My fever went so high it felt like my eyeballs were roasting in my head and I couldn't bear to open them because the light was too painful. My very skin was in agony at the contact of the bedclothes.

When it was over, my heart was damaged. I certainly did not feel like myself ever again.

I had used up all my sick leave, all my annual leave, and had to go back to work as soon as possible. Of course, that meant the pressure from Jody had to be faced. This intensified daily. At one point, I testily remarked that I really didn't think it was necessary to keep on finding non-existent errors in my cases since, over and over again, she'd been wrong about any errors at all.

"It's clear to me that you're being put up to this attack," I told her.

She smiled sweetly. "I have no idea what you're talking about! Maybe you need to take some more time off until you can handle your job!"

I was not going to let that woman get to me. Or to let that absurd man with his paranoid ego problems put so much pressure on me that I'd quit my job. By this time, other workers were aware that something was going on, but I kept quiet. Only Sandra and Madge knew the truth, and we all knew that we couldn't prove anything. Jody had been given her supervisor's position because she had agreed to do the deed. I even think, in retrospect, that the confrontation between Charles and John Dear was manipulated to get him to quit. He'd been my ally and would have never tolerated anyone treating me that way.

Sandra counseled me to just hang on until we could gather enough evidence that Jody was an absolute incompetent. They were watching her and she knew it. Our office staff, known for our outstanding efficiency and high morale under John Dear, had become a snake pit of jealously, rivalry, and backstabbing. And I felt like I had created the situation with my single act of indiscretion.

At this point, the hives kicked in. About midmorning every day, my skin started to itch. My arms, my neck, my face, my thighs, my belly, and back—the itching was unbearable. I was clawing myself until I drew blood. Sandra suggested that I see an allergist. He gave me a shot of cortisone and everything was fine for a few days. Then the itching began again. Another appointment with the allergist and another shot of cortisone.

After about half a dozen visits and shots, the doctor told me, "You need to see someone else for this problem. I've done every test possible and there is nothing physically wrong with you. I cannot, in good conscience, continue to give you these shots. Cortisone is good for emergency relief, but it is not a long-term solution. It has serious side effects and you have to stop now."

PARTIES, MOSQUITOES, HIVES, HYPNOSIS, AND FISHING BOATS

I didn't know what to say. "Who do you suggest I see?" I asked with a sinking heart, knowing what was coming.

He wrote a name and number on his prescription pad and handed it to me. A psychologist.

Maybe just knowing that the hives were psychosomatic would help me deal with it. Maybe I could do a little self-hypnosis on myself and that would take care of it. I mean, after all, I could help other people with similar problems, why couldn't I do it for myself?

Between working, going to school, hypnotherapy work, dealing with demands at home from Mother and Grandma, and spending as much time with the baby as possible, I fell into bed each night exhausted and dragged myself out of bed each morning to start the same routine over again.

Later that week, Jody came into my office with another of her barely veiled sneering mandates that I shape up or she was going to be forced to write a negative evaluation for that period. I kept a private list of all my cases and actions. My caseload was triple that of everyone else's, competently managed, and done by the book. John Dear wrote as much in a letter of reference he gave me some years later when I wanted to return to working:

"During the period [Laura] worked for me she displayed loyalty, integrity and devotion to duty rarely seen in other employees. She has tact and intelligence and she applied these qualities to her work. ... She constantly outperformed other workers with consistent high quality results."

I visited John Dear at his retirement home a few years back. We talked and laughed over the old times, and he chuckled when he told me, "The best day's work I ever did was when I hired you."

Jody's complaints were categorically unfounded and deliberate harassment. But I refused to give up my job.

* * *

Mother's husband, Buck, put pressure on Mother to use our properties to provide money for his "ideas." Basically, he still wanted to subdivide The Farm and build and sell houses. Sure, it was probably a good moneymaking idea, but this property had been transferred into Mother's name so she could take care of it as an inheritance for the grandchildren and so she would always have a place to live. I called on my brother for support, and we persuaded Mother it was not morally proper to take such a step in contravention of Grandpa's wishes. But we learned that she and Buck had already, on the sly, sold half the undeveloped property in Tampa that was to go to my cousins. It had passed into Grandma's name, and Mother was supposed to ensure the taxes were paid every year, but she didn't. Several of these lots were on the verge of being sold for back taxes. Using this "emergency situation" as an excuse, Mother persuaded Grandma that they ought to be sold right away. Grandma, not realizing that she had other options, signed over the deeds.

So, that property was gone. What about the money Mother and Buck got for selling? I wish I knew.

I raked Mother over the coals.

"No earthly reason the taxes on this property were left unpaid," I told her.

"Well, we needed new ..."

"Do you intend to turn the proceeds over to your brother? For his children's inheritance the way Grandpa wanted?"

"Well, they hadn't paid the taxes and they hadn't taken care of a thing. So they don't deserve anything," Mother said.

It was useless to point out that this happened only because she worked so hard to keep it all a secret and exclude them. But I was beginning to see there was something not quite right in the way Mother handled business and affairs of trust. What I saw disturbed me greatly.

Since I brought the spotlight on her from my brother as well, and we threatened to notify my uncle what she had done, Mother's solution to this intolerable, but accurate, criticism, was to blame everything on Buck. Buck had to go.

Mother was again without a husband, her only support my job and Grandma's income. This really put her in a situation she disliked, though it is only in retrospect that I can see this. I was perfectly happy to work and pay the bills for the three of us. With Grandma's pension and savings for extras, we certainly weren't suffering.

But Mother liked to be in control. I can see now the charge that ignited her next explosion of manipulation, but at the time I sure didn't see it coming.

Because I was always working, I had a joint bank account with Mother. I put the money in the bank and she could take care of the bills, do the shopping, buy what we needed. What set me off was the income tax return.

PARTIES, MOSQUITOES, HIVES, HYPNOSIS, AND FISHING BOATS

When I filed, I discovered to my delight that I had a nice refund coming, enough to do some maintenance on my car and buy some desperately needed new outfits for the baby and me. I especially had my eye on certain toddler toys a little more expensive than my weekly salary could afford.

Well, the check came, my mother deposited it into the joint account without saying a word to me, and then wrote herself a check for nearly the full amount and spent it on God only knows what. I was so furious at the time that I can't even remember now. She owed money for a long time, which she had never mentioned, and there was just enough in this check to cover it. It was gone. It was a done deal. There was no getting it back.

I blew up again and told her that if she had owed this money for so long, why hadn't she told me about it so that I could be putting money aside to take care of it instead of just stealing my tax refund without a word to me?! I closed the joint account and opened one in my name only, denying Mother control of my money.

Again, she was in an intolerable situation and the only person who could be blamed for this one was me. All these shenanigans drew me back to the idea of the psychologist. If he couldn't talk me through the stress, at least he could refer me for a tranquilizer!

I went to my first appointment. I sat in the waiting room and observed all the many diplomas and certificates arranged on the wall. Among them were several that related to hypnosis, and I realized this was the obvious solution to my problem. A little hypnosis and I would be right as rain. And surely, being so highly educated and accredited an individual, he would be the one who could do the job.

I was ushered into the consulting room by the plain receptionist, and when I was finally face to face with the man, he looked at me long and hard.

"Forgive me for staring," he said, "but I feel like we've met before."

We hadn't, but as I looked into his intent turquoise eyes, I was overcome with the strangest sensation of déjà vu I have ever experienced. His name was Dr. Richard.

I explained my situation, my problem, my own analysis of it, and my belief that hypnosis—if it could be effectively induced in me, which I doubted—would resolve the problem rather quickly. Surprisingly, he agreed to set up appointments to begin the process of trying to condition me to effective hypnosis.

The first few attempts achieved only a mild trance state. I was very relaxed, but fully awake and aware. I began to better understand why hypnosis is really only a question of compliance in giving up the will. After several sessions of pleasant "guided imagery" activities, I began to feel better, but I was still having the problem with the hives.

I just simply did not trust anyone enough to give up my free will to them.

I discussed this problem with Dr. Richard, and he agreed it would take time. Maybe we should just not worry about the hypnosis sessions at the moment and concentrate on a project that he had been considering since he met me.

Dr. Richard wanted me to work with him on some difficult cases. I was flattered to no end that he thought so highly of my skills and opinions and, even though I was doubtful that my insight could equal his, I was happy to oblige. My consultant status with the doctor soon led to a new shift in our relationship. We had many long philosophical discussions. He was happy to explain complex psychological theories with examples from his cases over the years. He would outline a case and ask for my opinion, delighted that I'd seen the diagnostic clues. "Oh, if only I had met you long ago; if only I weren't so much older than you! What a team we'd have made!"

Another brilliant older man in my life. Soon my sympathetic feelings and intellectual rapport turned toward affection. But I was cautious, even though I'd become comfortable in his presence and impressed with his skills and benevolence toward his patients. Still, I was sure he'd take good care of me under hypnosis.

And this is where it gets really strange. I'm sorry to even have to write this, but I can't do otherwise than tell what I remember, even if what I remember sounds a bit crazy.

Apparently I really went under. Actually, I thought I had just gone to sleep because I was so overworked and tired, and when I woke up I stretched and yawned and apologized for going to sleep on him. Dr. Richard assured me that I had not gone to sleep, that I was really deeply under. He said he had been able to give me life-changing suggestions. "Everything will be fine from now on," he said. There was some mysterious implication in these words.

I felt a frisson of fear because, while "asleep," I had a very strange dream.

PARTIES, MOSQUITOES, HIVES, HYPNOSIS, AND FISHING BOATS

In my dream, he had driven me to a local beach and we were just sitting in the car talking and watching for meteorites. The dream was so real that I could feel the fresh breeze from the Gulf. Suddenly, there was a very bright light flashing across the sky. It was huge and lit up the water below and … the dream had shifted and I was in the back seat of the car. Dr. Richard was zipping his pants and I could tell what had just happened, though I was completely baffled because I could not remember a single thing about how I got in the back seat, how the deed was initiated, or anything at all past that bright meteor flashing across the sky.

For some reason, I didn't want to tell Dr. Richard about this dream. I realized that I didn't know very much about him. From our talks I knew he had family in Chicago and spent a number of years in Central America, where his wife's family lived. He spoke fluent Spanish and had been educated in England.

But that was about all. I didn't even know where he lived, precisely.

We walked out to the parking lot together. Dr. Richard waited until I started my car before he got into his own car. That is the last time I ever saw him.

The next time I went to his office, a notice on the door said "Closed due to illness. Patients should contact Dr. … until further notice."

This was extremely puzzling.

Back in my office, I called information to ask for Dr. Richard's home number. Well, it was not just unlisted; no such number existed. I called the psychologist whose name was posted on the door, but he knew nothing about Dr. Richard at all. He wasn't even aware that he was the designated one for patients in need to call.

I called the allergist who had referred me to Dr. Richard. The allergist had received a letter announcing the opening of a new psychiatric practice and he had made the referral as a courtesy.

I tried to think of any other approach to find out what had happened, but I came up with no solution to the mystery. But, as things turned out, Dr. Richard's strange disappearance was forgotten in new developments at home, though it would come back to haunt me not long afterward.

* * *

I went home that day to find something very strange going on. Mother was deep in discussion with an old friend. At that time, the developer who had bought up all the salt flats across the road had begun the dredging project that turned the prehistoric marsh into fingers of land that gradually, over the past few years, had become crowded with rows of tract houses, each with its own dock and access to the Gulf. It was a popular way to deal with Florida wetlands then, impelling Buck's desire to divide and develop the farm in a similar way. I hated it. Every time I drove past those houses, that rape of the land, I was sickened.

But, ten years previously, when the land was being initially developed, a crew of men were there every day with large cranes, bulldozers, and other equipment. One day, since we were the only house in the area, they came to ask us for a refill for their water cooler. This man talking to my mother, Larry, had been one of the workers on the land-developing crew from Miami. Larry liked the area, so after the job was finished he bought land himself and stayed on.

As a native Floridian, Larry really loved The Farm and often came by to visit through the years, occasionally doing some little job for us when we were in residence there.

Larry seemed quite intelligent and was interesting to talk to, with good stories about geography, history, and natural history. But he talked a lot, and very fast. Larry was older than me by ten years. I first met him when I was sixteen, so he seemed to be quite ancient. Now, he was more "my age" since I was grown up. But he was still irritating because of his rapid and assertive speech.

Larry sat at the dining room table in deep conversation with Mother. She looked at me in a hostile way when I said hello, so I went to find the baby, playing under the watchful eye of Grandma. I picked her up and went back to the dining room to sit and visit with Larry. Right away Mother informed me that she was discussing "business," and it wasn't mine!

Well! Aside from being extremely rude, I couldn't imagine what "business" she needed to discuss so privately since, after all, I paid the lion's share of expenses for all of us. I was embarrassed at her dismissal of me as if I were a snoopy child. But I went into the other room to see if Grandma knew what Mother was up to.

Grandma sighed and said that she had no idea what was going on. Mother had been repeatedly going out during the day for hours, leaving her alone with the baby, and there was just no telling what kind of plans she was making. Neither of us liked it one bit.

PARTIES, MOSQUITOES, HIVES, HYPNOSIS, AND FISHING BOATS

As soon as Larry left, I confronted her and demanded answers. Mother's behavior was actually bizarre. She was bright, cheerful, and smiling, gaily and playfully telling me "all our worries will soon be over!" When I pressed for a serious answer, all she would say was "you'll see!"

Well, I was to see sooner than I expected. Just a couple days later Mother told me we needed to talk. Apparently, the situation had shifted and I was now to be included in her confidence. It seems that Mother wanted "us" to go into business.

"What kind of business?"

"Well, you'll never believe it. A commercial fishing boat!"

Yes, indeed. Mother had become friendly with a woman who owned a fish market, and this woman convinced her that commercial shrimping was a great income-producing line of work, adventurous, "distinctive"—because women rarely own commercial fishing boats—and she just happened to have one she wanted to sell.

Well, isn't that amazing! Such a deal.

And where were we going to get the money to invest in this project?

Well, there were property lots left that hadn't been sold for taxes. And we had to move fast if we wanted to get in on the ground floor of this opportunity. We were most definitely going to be rich if we made our move now, and Larry knew all about running commercial boats and would teach us everything we needed to know. All Mother needed from me was agreement that I'd help her in the business.

Well, why not? I had had a ball years before helping Myrna on her boat. What could there be to running a big fishing boat? The idea of independence was definitely appealing, especially considering the present job situation. But was it such a good move to unload perfectly good real estate for speculation in the fishing industry? Mother assured me that, once I discussed it with Larry, I would have all the assurance I needed.

Larry soon convinced me this was a plan that could not fail. Mother assured me that Grandma was in support of the plan, and that she, Mother, would take care of everything. Quitting my job meant giving up funding for school, and I really felt bad about doing that. But I was soon cheered up by thinking of all the money we would soon be making, and I'd be free of Charles and Jody and their manipulations. I thought it was entirely appropriate that my monthly period should start on my last day at work.

Never mind that it was an anomalous period which only lasted two days; that was due to all the excitement.

As good as her word, Mother handled everything. She and Grandma went off to Tampa one day to sign papers with a real estate agent to handle the sale. The lots were hot properties, and she soon had a buyer. They went back to Tampa to close the deal. We had the money, and it was time to go to work. What a relief to be free and independent!

I didn't realize the trap had been set and I was already in the steel jaws. It would be sixteen very long years before I would fight my way out of this one.

CHAPTER TWENTY-TWO

THE DEVIL IN THE DETAILS

Larry began teaching me about boats and the commercial fishing business. After I quit my job, we were together all day inspecting the boat, a worn-out old tub that ought to have been sunk, and getting equipment either repaired or replaced. We rapidly developed a good working relationship. I admired his physical prowess and mechanical skills and his keen observations about life.

Larry was a fundamentalist Christian. Issues of God and salvation, the saved and the unsaved, became a main topic of our conversation. He had reasonable arguments and I was curious because he was, indeed, always in a good mood, always positive, and seemed to just glow with strength and good will.

As we talked and sweated in the heat, I started thinking maybe I had not been quite fair to God. I had asked too much. Larry agreed a change was overdue in my life. I really needed to give my life to Jesus. If I did, it was a certainty that everything would change for me. Happiness was just around the corner.

I was physically and mentally tired. I was bruised and battered psychologically and spiritually, and I most definitely needed someone to help me with my burden. "Come unto me all ye that labor and are heavy laden and I will give you rest ..." Those words were the sweetest I had ever heard.

Larry invited us to go to church with him the following Sunday. It would be nice to take the baby to a clean and wholesome place, full of promise for a better life for us.

Sitting in church beside Larry that Sunday, I watched as he bowed his head and prayed devoutly and opened his hymnal and sang eagerly with the congregation. The fact that he was a little off key only made his innocent faith that much more appealing.

It was good to be working with someone who was so clearly in God's favor. He was strong, hard working, and his faith was like a mighty oak on which I could lean. Even if I had little faith, his would protect me by virtue of association. More than that, I was becoming increasingly aware that my little girl needed a father. It was painful to think of her growing up with no strong and secure male presence. She had no one but three women who doted on her. Was that enough? She adored Larry and followed him around wherever he went. And he clearly loved children.

Larry thought my courage in not having an abortion when I had been in such a situation was commendable. He was the first person who had ever expressed such a thing to me. But, as he pointed out, abortion was murder of an innocent child.

I was stricken by this remark. Remorse and guilt flooded through me. In trembling words, I told Larry what I had done. He took me in his arms and assured me that my sorrow and grief were signs of repentance. God had already forgiven me. But now that I understood that to interfere in the will of God was the reason I had suffered so much, I must turn my life around and endeavor to act according to God's will in all things. And, God willing, he would be there to help me if I needed him.

There was only one insurmountable difficulty: Larry was married. We could only be friends.

As the days passed, Larry and I became closer. He told me how he had been repeatedly thwarted in his efforts to live a life of faith and independence. His life had been a litany of failures until he found God. The more I listened, the more I felt that he was like me, struggling to live a life of deep commitment to what was right, but blocked or diverted at every turn. And it seemed that one of the chief blocks in his present life was his wife.

Dina was an alcoholic. She constantly made fun of his religion. She was sexually insatiable and Larry was sure she'd gone elsewhere for satisfaction. He'd helped her raise her two children from a previous marriage, but now that they'd both left home, she'd become a drunk who had nothing to say to him. When she did speak, her vile and filthy language offended him to his core.

Hearing him describe his life was so upsetting that I was almost desperate to help, even if only to be there to listen to his problems.

THE DEVIL IN THE DETAILS

One morning the sickness hit as soon as I moved my head from the pillow. Oh, God, no! How could it be? I hadn't done anything! As God is my witness, I had not been touched by a man since the disastrous Christmas party almost a year before.

Or had I?

My mind raced back to the hypnosis session with Richard and the "dream." I suddenly realized it had not been a dream. I was stunned by the import of what I was thinking. Richard had betrayed me. He had used me. He had violated my trust.

And then he had disappeared. Why?

When I was able to function I went to the kitchen to make coffee. What was I going to do? I went to the telephone and went though the whole routine again. His office phone had now been disconnected and there was no trace of a home phone listing. How could I find him? What should I do? How, in the name of God, could I be in this situation again?

I paced and fretted and finally sank into a chair and began to pray as I had never prayed in my life.

I looked up to see Larry coming up the drive.

I knew what to do. Larry would be happy, my little girl would have a father, and the new baby would come into the world never knowing she had been conceived in an act of betrayal of trust. There would be no more abortions. Acting according to God's will would be the new plan for my life, and God had just answered my prayers.

And that is truly what I believed. I didn't realize that the Devil was in the details. The trap closed, and I almost didn't get out alive.

CHAPTER TWENTY-THREE

IN THE FOREST

Religion is like a garment. One has to know how it fits before one can take it off.
—Sufi saying.

I was now proposing to myself that I should put religion on as an adult. I knew that it was necessary to do it fully and completely, and to do this I needed to submit my mind to the authority of the Bible.

Does this mean I had stopped thinking?

All my life I have been a seeker of truth and meaning because it is essential to me. Some people are content to not know; but I have never been content. My curiosity burns at a white-hot heat almost constantly. And behind it is a driving force that makes me unable to truly rest until I have discovered all I can about the nature of existence.

But my personal choices resulted in pain or disaster over and over again. Looking back, I could have held firm against Grant. I could have seen through his machinations and avoided a painful experience. I could have seen through Carol, not a true friend. I could have seen through Charles and refused to get in a situation where my judgment was impaired. I could have seen through Richard and refused to be betrayed by one who was supposed to be helping me.

Most of all, I could have sought out and extirpated that deep lack inside that seemed to be at the root of my intense sensitivity and which seemed to amplify each emotional blow so that my experiences were so utterly devastating. Never mind that, in all my seeking, that is precisely what I was trying to do.

Of course, doing all of these suggested things would have meant that I needed to "see through" things that happened to me during my formative years which conditioned my perceptions and reactions. In the end, the same can be said for everyone.

William James, in his *Varieties of Religious Experience*, asks: "What is human life's chief concern?"

Thomas Jefferson spelled it out in the Declaration of Independence: "Life, Liberty and the Pursuit of Happiness." It is, essentially, the inner motivation of everyone: how to obtain, keep, or recover happiness.

I was most definitely seeking all three.

It has been promoted throughout the millennia that religion is the mode of success in such endeavors. Each religion has the inner path to supernatural happiness. Members of every religion regard the "happiness" they experience within the fold as the proof of the truth of their own religion. Religions teach that the "nearness of God's spirit" is the source of this happiness.

We are told that this is the proof of the reality of God.

Some people can experience all kinds of dreadful events but, for some reason, they refuse to feel it in any deep way as something "wrong." They may have hardships and struggles, but it doesn't faze them one bit. It also doesn't seem to matter what religion they are born into: if there is a sinister theology in their environment, they can ignore everything that doesn't mesh with a basically pagan "union with the Divine." For them, God is the giver of all good things, and evil has no sting. The foundation of their thinking seems to be that God and nature are absolutely good. They are full of enchanting innocence and can think no ill of anyone or anything. God is neither judge nor ruler but merely the animating spirit of a beautiful and harmonious world: benevolent, kind, merciful, and pure. If they are involved in a religion, they seem to go to church more out of a need to socialize than to obtain salvation because, essentially, they have no consciousness of any burden of sin from which they need to be delivered.

There is another interesting thing about such people: they have no metaphysical tendencies and do not "look at themselves" at all. They accept themselves and their own imperfections totally. What's more, they accept others "as they are."

It seems to me that such people are children who were taught very early that they are "God's children," and this was exemplified in their caregivers in terms of acceptance and freedom and love. They are not told that they were born in wrath and wholly incapable of being worthy of God's love.

Well, clearly that was not the case in my experience. However, it seems that the initiating event of my "soul sickness" was well outside of the control of anyone with influence over my early development and experiences. And how many millions of others have suffered such battering of the soul at so young an age that no free-will choice of such events could possibly be considered to have been available? In such cases, what does that make of the "All-Powerful, Loving God?"

The twisting of society and culture that warps minds and brings about destruction of souls is at the root of what we call evil. From the humanist or Darwinian-evolutionary point of view, the evils of society are created by religion. Religion creates the disease of acute guilt, prescribes the cure, and sells it like a snake oil salesman.

But there was the Face at the Window to consider. A strange series of events in my life were simply not explicable in ordinary, coincidental terms. I sought to explain them in rational and normal ways, but the undercurrent of disease kept emerging: There was something evil out there, and it was after me, and I needed protection.

At every turn I had been sidetracked, slammed to the ground, or otherwise shown by experience that, at the very least, I needed a safe harbor in the cultural milieu in which I existed. My experiences taught me that in a man's world, for a woman who had no wish to compete with men or anyone else, I needed to compromise a bit and find an environment safe from male predation. The promise of spiritual safety that Larry held out was an additional lure impossible to resist.

Awakening in the night to the barely articulated thought reverberating in my mind, *Where is he?* repeated at odd intervals. The darkness gave no answer.

I was utterly lost and bereft. I very desperately needed to find out what might be wrong with me that I felt such an absence in my life no matter how I sought to fill it with activity, family, and all the accoutrements of modern society. No matter what I did, no matter who I was with, I felt alone. Repeating dreams that circled around a theme of tragedy and loss were a puzzle as well. I awakened from these dreams soaked in cold sweat, my heart pounding, crying in soul-deep grief.

After the battering I had taken for twenty-eight years, my hopes of finding The One had faded. I'd bought into the psychological interpretations of my tendre and became convinced that I must "be happy" if I expected to find happiness.

I shoved my dreams under the rug and married Larry (after his divorce), securing my life to an anchor that I thought would normalize and stabilize me. More than anything, I was tired. I was tired of searching, tired of fighting, tired of being used. I put away my books on mysticism and metaphysics, gave up my classes in meditation and hypnosis, and focused on going to church and devoting my attention to learning how to be a born-again Christian under the tutelage of my chosen partner.

Larry was chosen not because of love or lust, but simply because I was too tired to fight anymore.

Believing that he was going to be a father (yes, I engineered relations in time and I lied), Larry left his wife without much more than a second thought. In retrospect, I see that I was as good an excuse as any other for him to do what he wanted to do anyway. But there was something more subtle and destructive in operation here: the fundamentalist nature of the religious upbringing he had been exposed to.

Even though I needed him more than she did, two innocent babies also needed him, and his wife was a millstone about his neck with her drunken ways and rejection of God, Larry still felt guilty because he was also doing something that gave him pleasure. He wanted me physically, and that was, in his mind, the sin. And so I had to be punished. He was willing to fulfill his duty, but it must not be enjoyed. When he found himself enjoying it, he had to punish himself and that other participant in his happiness: me.

Larry's parents, despite their indulgence, also crushed his natural self with threats of hellfire and damnation and demands that he perform to a certain standard that was, I can assure you, completely unreasonable and even inhuman. So he felt a lack of motivation and enthusiasm that soon became emotional paralysis. As he grew up, he began to identify with God and his parents—the oppressors—and his mode of action was to treat himself and others in a harshly judgmental way. His religion would not allow him to be overtly abusive; there had to be a "righteous" reason. He was full of anger at God and his parents for not accepting him as he was, but terrified of the possibility of unleashing this rage. It was easier to just turn off emotions than to have to deal with the truth. He loved his parents, he loved God, right? His parents and God must be right, right? So, how could he be angry?

Well, he was. But he could not express it overtly, so he managed to express this anger by his inertia: this emotional and psychological paralysis. He was a master of passive aggression. He could not allow himself to succeed at anything, whether it was a career, a marriage, or even a fairly simple task, because that would have given his parents something to be proud of. Larry didn't care what other people thought or expected. He was a rebel. But he was truly a rebel without a cause.

I saw it as my job to heal him.

Larry was not a self-starter except in activities that would most assuredly not lead to success. Of course, once his engine was turned on—in an activity that was not a threat to his need to be a failure—he could work like a machine. I never saw anyone who could work so long and so hard at something that was almost completely useless. Larry could put in a shocking amount of time to very little effect. He didn't seem to know why some work is valued more highly than other work. Because of his religious training, he did believe that you're supposed to work and not be lazy. So, he kept himself constantly occupied. He seemed to be doing it just to say that he was working, to get admiration and establish his power. After all, if he was working so hard, the family must honor that! Yet, over time I noticed that when he worked, he didn't really pay attention to what he was doing. He seemed to prefer the easy way at every turn, with the end result that he managed to be a workaholic and extremely lazy at the same time. Larry measured his work only by how much time he spent on it, not by what he produced. He sought my praise and approval for the fact that he exerted the effort and could never understand why I valued results, not energy expenditure.

Larry seemed to know the price of everything and the value of nothing.

There was another aspect to his workaholic behavior. It often seemed that he held himself to a grinding work schedule to make himself unavailable to others' emotional needs. If he was tired from working, he could not be expected to give anything of himself to others. Not only that, he derived no pleasure from his work at all. More than that, he derived no pleasure from life. Any time I urged him to work at things he was good at that could have produced success, his response was "Why should I do something that I don't enjoy just because I'm good at it? It would kill me to have to do that!" So, he could commit to nothing.

He did, however, have grandiose dreams. As a boy, Larry had experienced a sort of double life. At home, he was subjected to the obsessive control of his mother. Because she was so afraid of hellfire and damnation, she wouldn't allow him to do anything for himself. He had no responsibilities or obligations and, as a result, never experienced any consequences. He loved his mother because she always provided, and he hated her because she demanded his freedom and absolute loyalty and adoration in return.

Larry's stepfather kept his mother in line. She was treated like a porcelain doll to be petted, admired, and displayed on demand. This, of course, included her prowess as a cook and housekeeper and mother. Perfection was expected because, after all, her husband provided her with a nice, new home with a swimming pool, two cars, yearly vacations, and the obligatory pearls to be worn while vacuuming. Her home was her domain, but only to the extent that her husband was satisfied when he arrived home from his job.

Weekends were, naturally, a man thing. Leaving his wife to keep the home fires burning, Larry's stepfather went hunting and fishing at every opportunity with his brothers, friends, and Larry in tow. The freedom from his mother's obsessive control (and she had to be obsessive to please her husband!) on these extended and repeated trips to the Florida Keys and into the Everglades were, in Larry's mind, paradise. Objectively, no one can say that it wasn't true. The result was, however, that he became stuck in this fantasy of life in the wilds, free from all constraints and controls and obligations of all kinds. This idealized Huck Finn character dominated his dreams and fantasies. His life was focused on this dream image and away from the real world and its practical needs.

It would have been different if his dreams had not been static, stuck in this single scenario of the glorious freedom of a boy in the wilderness with only his fishing rod and his gun (and maybe his airboat). His fantasies were tableaux or scenes, fixed stage sets that he believed reflected his true self. He couldn't see himself doing anything but this. The only room for any other person in this fantasy was someone who adored him at a distance for living in the wilderness, totally free from responsibility.

It was easy enough for me to vicariously share this fantasy and to admire the pure soul that produced it. My error was in thinking that it was just a nice memory—here was the real world, so let's put it away and get to work. Larry didn't see this image as either a memory or something that might come to pass in the future. For him, it was the way he wanted to be seen right now. He was the very model of the perfect woodsman, free in nature. Anything that caused a ripple in this image was resented, and the person who tried to pull him back into the real world was violating his divine image. Because, in the end, it was interpreted in his mind as the way God intended man to live. It was, therefore, "right."

The rightness of his ideal was the standard by which he measured all others. The role his mother played in his life was projected onto me. The role he had played, as Huck Finn to his stepfather's Tom Sawyer persona, was projected onto our son when he was born. He was unable to accept that his son had a different personality, different interests, different talents, and even different inclinations. Because his own physique was powerful and well developed, he was contemptuous of anyone who did not match this ideal.

Every night of our years together, Larry stood in front of the mirror and spent ten minutes or so flexing his muscles as "exercise," and I was naturally expected to admire him. Larry's role as a child who never had to do anything, who had no duties or responsibilities, he projected onto all the children, and all of us were weighed and measured according to this static dream world.

In the end, his dreams of success all centered around this wilderness fantasy. His application of the idea to anything remotely resembling a career was to engage in fish farming, or aquaculture. But, even here, his ideas of application were completely irrational. Just like my mother and her husband, he soon began to talk about making money with "other people's money." I cringed when I heard these things, but I felt that, with love and devotion, he would soon learn to channel his efforts into successful activities.

Part of acting out the "free man in the wilderness" fantasy seemed to include the idea that Larry must never give what he knew I wanted. It could also have been an aspect of the "control the little woman" dynamic, but whatever was at the root of it, he wanted me to do what he wanted because he wanted it and not because I wanted to do it. This was horribly puzzling for a long time. I carefully observed him to try to find out what he wanted and needed. As soon as I thought I had it figured out, he would become angry at my presumption and all the rules would shift again. I wanted to work beside my husband, helping him and supporting him, and the instant I did, he found some reason to get angry and quit whatever we were doing; and it was usually my fault. Even projects he talked about in glowing terms—as soon as I became interested and wanted to support him and help to make it a reality, he didn't want it anymore. In the end, what he could not ever share was himself. And, in the end, that was the only thing I needed.

As he now had a mate and children—one present and one on the way—he began to recreate the household of his own childhood with us as the occupants. He was captain of the boat and we were the crew whose job it was to jump to fulfill his whims and who must endeavor to fulfill his perfectionist standards of behavior, most specifically in religious terms. He pounced on minor crimes and infractions of his rules, which were never clearly defined or consistent, and he had something critical to say about most everything. To this day, I cannot remember ever producing a meal that received a compliment that was not delivered with a series of instructions about how to do it better next time.

Larry also liked to mock people. He did it in what he thought was a gentle and helpful way. He teased me and the children about fat, the way we walked, looked, acted, dressed, and, most especially, our spiritual state. All of us were under this constant, judging scrutiny, and it produced feelings of unbearable self-consciousness. Larry's jokes were mostly directed at the egos of the children. He liked to play practical jokes that were designed to humiliate them. When I objected, I was, of course, the wicked witch for criticizing such loving family fun. He was contemptuous of my view that teasing was a form of abuse. He had a completely dismissive attitude towards my (and the children's) feelings, wishes, needs, concerns, standards, property, and even work. If anybody else did it, thought it, said it, felt it, or wanted it, it was worth nothing to him. He had absolutely no empathy for any other human being unless they were in total agreement with him, and I don't think you can really call that empathy.

Even though he constantly teased me and the children, he had absolutely no sense of humor. Larry berated me for having no sense of fun when I protested against his practical jokes. He was, indeed, a specialist in sarcasm about others, and he thought this was witty. He was incapable of irony, which to me was true humor. He could make fun of others, repeat jokes he had heard others laugh at, and laugh at jokes that were essentially the kind that ridicule weaknesses in others. He just never knew that knowing how to make people laugh is not necessarily the same as having a sense of humor.

Larry also had no sense of time. Living in his fantasy world of perfection, he would often underestimate the time it took to do something.

This wasn't just a slight miscalculation but a consistent pattern that caused a great deal of misery to a lot of people. If he said it would take an hour, it would really take about five hours. But to ask him to postpone doing something until adequate time was available was tantamount to an insult. He would complain that no one ever supported him and this was why he had so many failures in his life: no one had faith. No one loved him.

Of course, this was the hook designed to focus my attention on the immediate need of loving and supporting Larry. Having lived my entire life doing for others in order to be loved, I was in total empathy with such a remark, and I fell for it every time.

In these ways, he made victims of all of us by imposing his will, his views, his opinions, and his beliefs. He criticized and demanded perfection, but with no defined parameter in which to operate. His demands were based on his moods, and none of us ever knew what mood he was going to be in, or whether his demands would tend in this direction or another.

I decided if I worked to fulfill these standards, to direct the children in ways that would elicit praise from Larry, winning approval for myself as a good and faithful wife and mother, then maybe Larry could relax a bit. He'd begin to accept us and know that he was truly loved.

Larry did honor helping others. He'd drop everything to go help a friend—or even a stranger—fix or build or move whatever. He'd go out to do an errand and run into someone who had a problem. He'd listen for hours and offer advice, forgetting his own task. He gave away his time and energy, and when he worked for anyone, he always undercharged them. But then, this did fit with his Huck Finn fantasy image of himself.

He constantly gave advice to everyone, solicited or not. Friends tried to make him understand that he was overbearing in this respect. Many put up with his overbearing intrusiveness because they were charmed by his generous, compassionate, and self-sacrificing mask. Larry was considered a good ole boy who would literally give you the shirt off his back. Why not? It proved what a great guy he was!

In the end, he walked away from applying himself to life in a successful way because it "didn't interest him." Worldly things were not important to Larry because they were transitory and meaningless. He was a talented and compassionate man to outsiders only and, in this way, created a life for himself without internal meaning in order to both fulfill the demands of his God and his parents, and to punish them, himself, and now me.

At the time, however, I simply saw his willingness to help others as proof of his goodness and purity of heart. All I had to do was figure out how to support him properly and all his good works for others would, in the end, act in beneficial ways for his family. After all, if a person does good works, he is promised to be taken care of by God. Doesn't the Bible say "The race is not to the swift nor the battle to the mighty, but God rewards those whom he loves"? If we loved God, and demonstrated this love by helping others, we would be loved back by God, right?

I think that the reader realizes at this point that I had, figuratively, married my mother.

Yup. I was so sure that I wasn't going to repeat the mistakes of my mother and marry anyone who drank or was violent or who would not be a good parent. I had proof that Larry would not abandon me or the children, because he had raised the children of his ex-wife faithfully and dutifully, right? Being convinced that Larry was the right one because it was God's will, and because he was a righteous, church-going, non-drinking, hard-working man, I was sure that I had managed to score a coup here. I had avoided the mistakes of Mother. What is so gruesomely ironic was that I simply replaced her with Larry in my life. They were like two peas in a pod. Only I didn't see it then!

Children do have a powerful tendency to grow up and marry the kind of person who is similar to the parent of the opposite sex. Girls "marry their fathers," and boys "marry their mothers." I was on the lookout for that one. What I didn't realize was that this was not necessarily a hard and fast rule. We marry a person who reproduces in our life the conditions of our childhood.

Every child loves their parent, no matter how abusive that parent is. We love our parents even if all we can remember from our childhood is pain and suffering. We also begin to associate this pain with the occasional moments of love that we experienced from the parent, and most definitely, we associate this pain with our own love for them.

If our beloved parents never kept their promises to us, we marry someone who forgets their obligations to us. If our parent made a slave of us and did not help with the work, we marry someone who leaves the lion's share of the work to us. If we felt constantly insecure and unanchored by a parent who did not provide for us financially or materially, we are attracted to mates who cannot or do not earn sufficient income to take care of us. If our parent was not one who touched us in sincere affection, we marry someone who only touches us for sex, never for simple affection. In the end, we weep for our suffering childhood and cannot see that we have recreated it in our present. We block out the fact that we love our mate because he or she mistreats us in exactly the ways we have come to associate with love. We can't see the fact that we have chosen a partner who exactly duplicates the conditions in which we did not receive love and nurture as a child, to continue to try to find the way to get that love from the parent. In the end, the most terrible realization is that we have married someone not because we really love them, but because we need to get them to love us in order to get love from our rejecting parent.

As a child, every time my overtures to my mother were met with coldness and rejection, there was a feeling produced in me that somehow I was to blame for these responses. The fact that I had also felt abandoned by my father, even if the true conditions of this event had not been truthfully communicated to me, added to the idea that I wasn't lovable, nice, acceptable, or pretty enough to be admired, loved, and respected. This psychological abandonment became my model for love, and the actions of the child who constantly watched and sought ways to get close to the parent were focused in an obsessive and addictive way upon Larry. My goal was, as with my mother, to love enough, to give enough, to sacrifice enough, to turn Larry into a loving, giving, and available husband and father. I kept trying, and the worse it got, the harder it was for me to stop trying.

When we discussed our future together, Larry promised me the sun and moon. I discovered he expected it from me! I fell into a pattern of asking for change in a tentative way. I had to get up very early to figure out ways to talk to Larry that would not set off his rejecting diatribes, which included all the faults I was known to possess. These were, according to him, the reason for his own behaviors and even his failures. His rejection mode was like a stick of dynamite that could go off at any moment, and I had to think hard and choose my words carefully not to light the fuse.

Larry demanded attention and consideration from all of us, as our family grew, but seldom gave any back unless it was in the specific context of what he wanted to do. I used to joke that he was "strategically helpless," but it was a constant oppressive burden to deal with his lack of interest in the practicalities of life. He denied this, pointing out how hard he worked in his garden to grow fresh vegetables for us to eat, and how he caught fresh fish for the family on his many fishing expeditions. Wasn't that "for us"? Couldn't I see how much effort he was putting forth "for the family"?

Well, fine. Now, go out and make enough money so we can pay the bills and I don't have to lie awake all night worrying how I am going to keep a roof over their heads, clothes on their bodies, and shoes on their feet. That would be a real help! I could send him to get milk for the children, and he would return hours later, having stopped to pick up a hitchhiker whom "God directed him" to drive to his destination instead of putting him out where their routes diverged.

As a child, Larry was bailed out of his problems by his mother. In a sense, I became his mother. Larry was like a baby holding on to me for dear life. Like an infant, he was unavailable when I needed him, and uncooperative when I tried to get him to face the facts of the real world. He hid in his religion, leaving the management of real life to God, his preacher, and me. Fishing and hunting were good enough for him, so it should be good enough for us, too.

The only material thing that really concerned Larry was that the children and I should be right there, available to him, at all hours of the day or night. His reason for this was that the world was so dangerous a place that we could not be allowed to go anywhere or do anything at all. The terrors of the "outside" world were described to us in graphic detail. Satan lurked around every corner. Corruption was in everyone we would meet, so best not to meet anyone. Of course, none of this applied to him. He joked regularly and repeatedly about the possibility that I would meet someone and Satan would take hold of my mind, and I would leave him. Women had to be guarded and suppressed because, of course, they were the reason for the fall of man from grace. Any pleasurable activity for a woman meant that she was a "delicious woman," and that was only a euphemism for a whore.

My perceptions of Larry in the beginning were that he was also a rebel against the empty and meaningless life. I was deceived by his seeming ability to survive in unconventional ways. I was so oppressed myself that his defiance against the world and its oppressors, couched in religious terms, made me think he was like me. By attaching myself to him, I'd have a champion to stand up for me, protect me, and most of all, love me as I was, with all my perceived flaws, even though I had been pursued all my life by a Face at the Window.

In the end, I had grown the way I was bent. Because I loved my mother, and she was incapable of loving me back, I was conditioned to continue to try to get blood out of a stone. Sure, you can't—but I was trained to keep trying. I think I felt that by bonding with Larry, I could somehow cure my Mother. If I could find the key to his heart, I could heal my mother also. I learned to love people who could not love me back. And I was conditioned to tolerate and even actively work to maintain a relationship with someone no healthy person would have tolerated for one minute.

At the same time, to Larry, love was weakness, a trap. When I said, "I love you," I was essentially asking to be hurt. Larry never trusted me, and our relationship was a continual test of my total devotion. If I did not submit to his ideas and will, the threat of being discarded as no good was dangled over my head. If I persisted in disagreeing with him or resisting his demands, he said, "I give up on you, you are worthless," and he stormed out. I was required to agree with his opinions, spiritual positions, or treating the children like little automatons who should never have a thought or feeling of their own. As time went by, his regression into ever more bizarre and paranoid fundamentalism made these demands on our minds not only outrageous but also impossible to fulfill.

One day he was courting me and wanting me and swearing devotion to me and my child and the coming baby. We discussed it reasonably and made our commitments to one another. The next day—and I am not joking here—he informed me that no woman was going to dictate anything to him, not even so much as a gentle suggestion that he tuck in his shirt to go to church.

My expressions of love and concern actually triggered these nasty reactions. Larry was aware that I was emotionally attached to him, so he expected to be able to use me like an appliance.

In the end, he even added the children to his nasty and insulting diatribes, but only the ones who had the courage to stand up to him. Like all women who "love too much," my own blind spot was unknown to me. I fell into the hands of an angry, narcissistic rebel looking for revenge. And I had a child and another on the way.

Well, it's a fine mess I got myself into—again.

There was my mother, conditioned to fail at whatever she did, always on the lookout for someone to blame. And now Larry, the angry rebel who needed to screw up so he could punish his parents for their oppression. In the middle there was me, Grandma, and my little girl, all trying to give love and support to these two. What do you think was going to happen?

CHAPTER TWENTY-FOUR

THE POISONED APPLE

Mother was quite unhappy that I should shift my loyalties to Larry, and he was equally determined for his demands to be served through me. That is to say, my mother wasn't going to tell him what to do since, at this point, it was obvious that she didn't have a clue what she was doing.

Mother, of course, let us know that her money was running the show and put me on the spot to force the decision where my loyalties were: with Mother or Larry.

The baby was due in only a few months. Larry went out to help a friend cut down some trees. I protested that he really didn't have time to do this, but he shut me up by telling me that I was being very un-Christian not to help this man who had done him a favor on some occasion in the past.

Several hours later, Larry came racing in the driveway, got out of his truck, and came staggering in the house. He was injured. He clutched the back of the chair and weakly asked me to help him to bed. His face was ashen.

He had been cutting up a huge old fallen cypress tree. When he'd cut through most of the trunk, the root portion of the tree, where he'd been standing, had snapped away, throwing him into the air. He flipped over and came crashing down on the jagged edge of the broken trunk.

He had a series of cuts on his lower back, as if a giant cat had clawed him deeply, but none were deep enough or bleeding badly enough to require stitches. I bathed the wounds, applied antibiotic ointment, and bandaged them. He was in pain, but it looked like something he would live through. By morning, the injury had swelled to the thickness of a football covering the area of a large serving platter. It did not look good.

Me, pregnant with my second child in late 1980 at the farm.

After several days of pain and swelling that would not go down no matter how I treated it, we decided that a visit to the doctor was in order. Larry had ripped all his muscles away from their anchors to the bony structures of the lower back. A bursa had been formed that was full of fluid, and unless this was drained, he would not heal properly and would never have effective use of these muscles again. This meant surgery. It was supposed to be a fairly simple procedure, though it had to be done under general anesthesia.

We scheduled the operation and I anxiously sat in the hospital waiting room for news that I could go in and tend to my husband. He'd need my attention immediately. The surgeon had encountered complications: a spider-like tumor was growing on Larry's spine. It wasn't cancerous, just fibrous—nothing to worry about. The tumor was removed, but Larry was an uncooperative patient.

Mother's response was understandable: somebody had to run the business. My brother was "elected." Mother went up to Jacksonville, where he was stationed, and tempted him with grandiose plans of all the extra money in store. She'd foot the start-up bill, so he was willing to give it a try. He came down to get the boat and haul it up there (a major undertaking, to say the least).

Naturally, Mother had to be right in the center of things, giving orders, now the expert on all things nautical. She managed to fall off the boat while stepping onto the dock and broke her shoulder. She was an even worse patient than Larry.

So, again I was due to have a baby and had two injured people to take care of. Grandma, thank heaven, though frail, was doing all she could to help me. I was exhausted twenty-four hours a day, and my back and leg felt like someone was holding a flamethrower against them constantly. But I wasn't allowed to have pain or rest.

Mother demanded meals cooked to mush so that she could eat them (having recently had all her teeth pulled and dentures made). Larry, on the other hand, would not eat anything that was even a tiny bit overcooked. No matter what I cooked or how I cooked it, no one was satisfied. Mother even threw her plate of food at me in a truly unusual display of temper. She then yanked her dentures out of her mouth and threw them at me too, shattering one of the plates. She did not handle pain well at all. It was immaterial to her that I was almost ready to have a baby and was in constant pain. I was still expected to cater to her demands with no effort on her part to help in any way. She had to be bathed, because she could not manage to get in and out of the shower, unsteady from pain-relieving drugs. And no matter how careful I was to avoid hurting her, she'd snap and snarl and accuse me of deliberately causing her more suffering. I had to stand there, almost ready to pass out from the pain in my back. If I tried to get some rest by sitting down on the adjacent toilet, she'd rage that I was torturing her by not standing in the proper position to be able to assist her. She would not tolerate any pain during her bath.

After several weeks of recovery for both of them, Mother demanded that Larry should go up to Jacksonville and help my brother. Larry was, of course, feeling that he was on the guilty end of the stick and was suitably subdued from his own ordeal. Mother had convinced all of us that if Larry hadn't screwed up and had to have surgery, she would not have had to break her shoulder! Knowing he couldn't work elsewhere in his condition, Larry dutifully packed up and drove to Jacksonville to stay with my brother and his wife to salvage what could be saved from the mess. Of course, I protested that I needed help to manage the house but Mother was determined to see that I was isolated from any help at all.

Almost immediately after Larry left, the baby arrived. Labor came on so fast in the early hours of the morning that I was unable to drive myself to the hospital. Mother couldn't drive, of course, so I called an ambulance to take me to the hospital.

I delivered my second daughter with no one nearby but the hospital staff.

This baby was not immediately plopped into an incubator and rushed away, but placed in my arms immediately, even before the cord was cut. Apparently disoriented by the sudden lack of restriction to her arms and legs, she squirmed to feel the enclosure that had been her home for so many months. I held her close, and her eyes tried to focus on mine. My heart just melted with love and pity for this helpless little child brought into the world by such mysterious circumstances.

Again, I had produced an incredibly gorgeous child. She was fair and perfect in every way, with evidence of truly great beauty in every feature. Of course, I could instantly see her likeness to Richard. This terrified me. I was sure my sin would be evident to all. But these particular features—the shape of her face, her fair skin, and beautiful lips—were also similar to my grandmother's. I was desperate to forestall any possibility that Larry would notice she was nothing like him or any member of his family. When he finally arrived at the hospital late that evening, I immediately pointed out the similarities to Grandma. He agreed that she was perfect and tried to hide his disappointment that she was not a boy.

Even though Larry, as a "good Christian," loudly proclaimed his joy and satisfaction with a perfect, healthy child, there was an undertone of feeling that somehow I had failed by not producing a son. I was also a failure because I didn't bounce back from this delivery as quickly as I had from the first. My old back injury had taken a severe beating with all the work I had done throughout the pregnancy, and there were prolonged and severe pains. I was so tired and depleted from months of taking care of everything and everybody that all I wanted to do was sleep.

But I couldn't. There was a baby to take care of. Not only that, but this baby was quite different from the first. While number one had been content and easy from the first day, this baby was fussy and demanding; she needed holding and cuddling. I was happy to hold her and nurse her for extended periods as I had with my first, but this baby did not ever want to be put down. If I fed her and rocked her and sang to her and she finally went to sleep, the instant I put her in her bassinet, she stiffened like a wooden doll and began to scream in terror. After a week of this, I took her to the doctor who said that she was colicky, but there really was no medical basis for colic. Some babies were just that way. "Hypertonic," he said, "and likely to become hyperactive." Best to get her on medication right away. He prescribed a barbiturate liquid that I was supposed to put in her bottle.

I had rather different ideas about why babies might come into the world with certain dispositions. Even though I had put away my metaphysical practices, the idea of reincarnation still seemed a distinct possibility. If so, the soul connected to this baby had most definitely suffered something truly terrible.

Later, when she was about three years old, she often had nightmares and would wake up crying. One night, she woke up screaming "Mommy! Mommy!" in absolute terror and I quickly ran to her and picked her up, speaking to her, trying to soothe her terror. Her eyes were wide open, but it was clear that she was neither seeing nor hearing me. She was in some other reality where she was fighting and kicking me as though I were some terrible monster attacking her. I kept saying over and over: "It's okay, Mommy's got you! It's okay, Mommy's here!"

Suddenly, she became perfectly still for an instant, focused on my face, screamed "You're NOT my mommy!" and began screaming "Mommy! Mommy!" and kicking and crying again.

I was totally unnerved. What did this tiny child mean when she looked at me and screamed, "You're not my mommy"? I was the only mommy she had, the only one she had ever known—in this life, that is. I wasn't perfect, but God only knows, I loved my children with every breath in my body. The only answer could be that something truly terrible had happened to her in a previous life, and the memory held her in a death grip.

In any event, the idea of drugging my baby was objectionable to me, and fortunately, Larry was willing to walk her and hold her so I could snatch a little sleep now and then. It was a very little, of course, but any was better than none. The baby was comforted, and I had some rest. I was thankful to Larry for that. He was actually a very good parent as long as the children were little and adoring. When they got older and began to have thoughts of their own or—horror of horrors—disagree with him, it was a different story.

Time passed and my brother became disillusioned with Mother's enterprise. Larry had to go back to Jacksonville and haul the boat back down.

Larry and I struggled to make the business work for a long time. Our son, my third child, was born while we were still trying to swim against the current in an overpriced, under-equipped boat that literally ate money. Sure, there were times when we made a lot of money in a single three- or four-day trip, but it never balanced out what we spent in fuel, ice, and repairs over the long term. Marine parts are prohibitively expensive. It wasn't long before we had maxed out all our credit cards in an effort to salvage Mother's dream. It clearly was going to kill us before we made a killing in the commercial fishing business.

I tried talking to Mother about selling the boat, cutting our losses. I was rapidly wearing out going on the boat with Larry and then coming home and having all the housework to catch up because Mother felt that it was her fair contribution to take care of the children. Doing laundry and keeping the house tidy never was her strong suit. If I wanted it done, I had to do it myself.

There were other disturbing aspects to the situation that gradually became apparent. Grandma confided in us that she was worried about Mother. Mother's behavior had become so erratic that Grandma was actually becoming frightened of her. She was certain her bank account was being rapidly emptied. If she so much as questioned Mother about checks she wrote, Mother became enraged and browbeat her. She told my grandmother that she'd ruined Mother's chance for a happy life. If Grandma didn't cooperate with her activities, then she could damn well find somebody else to be her slave and lackey.

Grandpa had asked me, just before he died, to "take care of Grandma," and I had promised. I was beginning to see what he knew then about Mother. She needed handling somehow, but was evidently competent enough that no judge would declare her incompetent. Yet the evidence of her life demonstrated a strange inability to see things as they really were and to learn from her mistakes.

The obvious solution: let Mother find someone else to run her boat. Larry and I would take Grandma and move to Grandma's house in Tampa. There, Larry would be better situated to work, I would be able to find work part-time, and Grandma could help in small ways with the children.

Then we discovered the full extent of Mother's perfidious destruction. We couldn't move to the house in Tampa because Mother had sold it.

Yes indeed. When she took Grandma to the realtor to sign the agreement to sell the lots, and then later, to sign over the deeds, among the big pile of papers being shuffled around on the table were the papers that sold her house.

Mother had tricked Grandma into signing away her own house.

At least that explained how Mother had so much money to pass around to get other people to do her bidding. And why she was so desperate to make everything work. She had bet the ranch.

Grandma was devastated. She could not believe Mother's deceit and betrayal. I was equally crushed. My own mother, knowing the house in Tampa had been intended to go to me, never to be sold as long as Grandma lived, found it in her heart to do such a terrible thing. It was not the greed and manipulation that hurt, but the total lack of consideration for anyone else in any way, shape, form, or fashion.

My mother sat there in front of me and claimed she had sold Grandma's house because I wanted her to do it; that I had been in support of the plan; that I had been the one to suggest that she do it behind Grandma's back. Nothing of what she was saying was even remotely true. But what was crazy was the conviction and sincerity with which she said it, as though she really and truly believed it.

Every similar crazy-making experience I had ever had with my mother now came back to me in stunning clarity. I had been screwed by this woman—my own mother—royally, all my life. And I was just now seeing it for the first time.

She accused me of lying, of making this whole thing up. I was the one who needed help. After all, I was the one who had tried to kill myself, wasn't I? I was the one who had had a child out of wedlock, wasn't I? I was the one who had found it necessary to see a psychiatrist, wasn't I? More than that, at this very moment, I was the one who was shouting at her and she had not even raised her voice. What more proof was necessary that I was the crazy one and she was the innocent party who had been subjected to my horrible, selfish, self-centered, and greedy manipulations?

It was at this point that the full impact of my mother's illness hit me. I can remember struggling for control, trying to explain to her the situation from a reasonable point of view. Half way through it, I knew that one of us was crazy, and I was pretty sure it wasn't me.

My mother was never neurotic, psychotic, or emotionally disturbed in any apparent way. She never displayed a violent temper, nor was she ever materially destructive such as having fits or breaking things. In social situations, she was always outgoing, charming, and verbally proficient. Most of all, she has always been calm and collected, even when angry. Even when everybody else was upset, she was always able to convey the impression that she was everything under control. But I was observing her closely now, and was seeing with complete horror that this apparently sane behavior was really a deep manifestation of a personality that was callous, manipulative, massively selfish, and routinely untruthful.

Mother was never a pathological liar who lies compulsively—getting caught because they tell lies that are unnecessary. I was seeing now that she just lied convincingly and consistently to get what she wanted. It was devastating to realize that, above all, she was a consummate actress. She had spent years pretending to feel, or rather making me think that she was feeling, whatever emotion was necessary in order to get what she wanted. At this moment, I understood with stunning clarity that it was just an act.

Mother wasn't a criminal in the ordinary sense of the word; most of my mother's "crimes" had to do with having no true regard for her family or children. She could set up events clearly designed to avoid monotony in her life. She went through relationships like some people wear out flip-flops. She constantly stirred the pot or added gunpowder to the fire, but she could talk herself out of trouble in nothing flat.

When Mother carried on a conversation, it seemed, on the surface, like it was a two-way discussion even if there were weird and undefined overtones that were hard to pin down. Now, I was understanding that her constant interruptions of others, the zigging and zagging into unrelated tangents and irrelevant subjects, were an example of her mental landscape; she actually believed she was communicating coherently, that she understood what others were thinking and saying. She never did. Not only that, she literally didn't seem to hear all the words said to her, because she could only hear words that referenced her. What I was realizing, in horror, was that it wasn't just habits of speech or just her way of talking; it was literally a cognitive deficiency.

Mother was a master of logically inconsistent statements and phrases, non-sequiturs, and half-formed sentences that somehow conveyed the impression of great depth and meaning. And she always got away with it because she could be so charming. But at this moment in time, I was not going to be charmed or manipulated. There were facts, dreadful facts, that needed to be explained and understood.

Just as your life passes before your eyes in moments of extremis, my interactions with my mother over all my life ran like a horror movie through my brain.

In the years since this event, I have come to realize that true loyalty, warmth, and compassion were foreign, incomprehensible concepts to Mother. The deep affection felt by most people for spouses and children was too complex for her. I even think she believed such deep emotions were a vague and unimportant concept. She seemed to have no need to give or receive love. She really had no desire to maintain familial contact unless it was useful to her.

Something inside Mother had died back when she was little and her Mama was murdered and she was effectively abandoned by her own parents in their struggles to come to terms with that event. Whatever was real and essential in Mother had either died then and there, or gone to sleep and never grew past that point. Effectively, my Mother was locked inside a shell; the surface was there, the exterior curves and lines and colors, but whatever was inside couldn't get out. In hours of conversations I had with her, to discover the wounds and heal her, I found to my great sadness that when she said she understood an event, and perhaps even expressed regret, she never really did.

Of all the crushing blows of my life, this was the worst.

My mind was literally staggering at the realization of what my mother really was. And the only thing I could think in response to this understanding of her true nature was that I obviously hadn't made it clear how much I loved her and how much I wanted to help her and support her, especially now, when she was clearly cornered.

My heart was broken at the realization that it was utterly impossible that I would ever, ever, in this life, receive real love from my mother.

I looked at her, took a deep breath, and told her as calmly and clearly as possible: "No, Mother. I'm not the one who's crazy here. And you aren't going to play that game with me anymore. All those years I believed in you, believed everything you said. Now, I can't believe anything you say ever again. YOU are the one who needs help. I love you and I will help you if you'll let me, but you have to realize that you DO need help. For all our sakes, I hope you decide to get it." And I turned and walked away.

Now, normal people can behave irrationally under emotional stress. They can be confused, deny things they know, get a little paranoid, or whatever. Normal people also come to their senses within an hour or two, or a day or two. When you are dealing with normal people, your expressions of love and concern for their welfare will be taken to heart.

Not so with Mother. With Mother, you either saw things entirely her way, or you were banished from her. Mother could not see that she had a problem. With Mother, it was always somebody else who had the problem. This was an immutable law. She didn't want to change. She wanted the world to change to suit her.

I realized that it was possible to have a relationship with Mother only by giving her whatever she wanted or needed whenever she asked and to not expect any reciprocation at all. I understood that I could never expect her to show the slightest interest in me or my life unless it was predicated on serving her ends. I could never expect her to be able to do anything that I needed or wanted. I could never expect her to apologize or make amends or show any consideration for my feelings at all unless she was giving it lip service in order to get something she wanted.

Mother was able to manipulate new people into serving her all the time because she was so good at maintaining a conventional persona in superficial associations. She would flatter and smile and laugh and bat her eyes if she thought you had something she could use or if she needed you for some reason.

I suddenly saw that one of the reasons she was never able to keep a job had nothing to do with anyone ever actually acting against her; it was because she always cut corners and cheated wherever she thought she could get away with it. More than that, she alienated people with her arrogance, lies, malice, and constant complaining. Throughout my entire life I observed the fact that everyone that Mother had close contact with seemed to go away mad.

At this point, as I confronted Mother with the evidence of her criminal activity in defrauding Grandma of her house, Mother was faced with a situation that could have been disastrous to her carefully constructed persona. Her response was a power move of such devious cunning that the entire family was nearly destroyed.

Grandma felt that we ought to do something. I agreed to take her to an attorney to see if anything could be done, but the advice was rather bleak. Sure, we could sue Mother, but it wouldn't get Grandma's house back, and if Mother didn't have any money left, there really wasn't any point. In retrospect, of course, we should have taken some action to compel Mother to sign over The Farm.

But neither of us ever expected that her self-destructive behavior would lead her to risk The Farm. After all, it was her home. Surely she had learned something from these experiences?

We would both, very soon, regret the assumptions that Mother had any ability to reason and learn from her mistakes. I didn't fully comprehend the most important implication of my mother's cognitive impairment: her terrible errors in judgment. She could not understand that when she abused or exploited other people, they would very likely retaliate. She couldn't see another person's point of view no matter how much she claimed she did. It was as though the entire world "out there" was blocked from her view by a huge, encircling mirror.

I felt I had as much right to live at The Farm as Mother did. And Grandma certainly had the right to a home there since Mother sold Grandma's house. It had been, in effect, as much my house as Grandma's and whatever Mother had bought with the money was ethically mine as well. Unfortunately, it would have taken the force of law to establish this. We felt that the best thing to do would be to find a place of our own and move out, let Mother figure her way out of her business problems with the boat, and step in to help with the taxes on the place.

Larry found a job with a construction company and, until we had enough money to make the move, we were all in an uneasy situation. Even though she had become very quiet and secretive in her behavior, we could see that Mother was not going to easily give up her grandiose ideas of being the owner of a fleet of fishing boats. Never mind that we had done nothing but pour time and money into the project and it had not paid back even one tenth of the amount invested. I used every opportunity I could to remind her. Somehow, I thought all my exhortations that she should sell the boat, invest the money in something safe like bonds or CDs (assuming she could get anything!), was getting through to her. I had the idea that, perhaps, her excursions "out and about" might, hopefully, be a result of these ideas; that she was seeing about selling the boat and behaving reasonably.

I was wrong. She was looking for a new slave to do her bidding.

Of course, slaves are expensive. This meant that Mother needed more money. How to get it? Well, her new potential slave, a man she met God knows where or how, suggested the obvious: she was the legal owner of a fairly large and valuable tract of land; why not mortgage it?

And that is what she set about doing. Unfortunately, she discovered that, at her age, and with no significant credit history, you can't just borrow a large amount of money. The bank wanted a co-signer who was younger and employed to guarantee repayment of the note.

There was only one solution: my brother. She turned the charm on him without my knowledge, and he hadn't been there to witness what she had been doing for years now, so he was just as vulnerable as I had been for years.

He showed up one day, ready to go out with Mother to "take care of business." Of course, I was not allowed to know what this business was.

After it was done, Tom informed me he had cosigned on a note with Mother. The Farm was now heavily mortgaged and Mother had the money she needed to buy a new slave. Tom also went home with money in his pocket: Mother basically bribed him.

How could my brother do this?

Didn't he see what she had done with all the property so far? What in the world was wrong with him that he couldn't see what Mother was doing?

Angrily, my brother echoed all Mother had said: I was a liar.

I was doing the manipulating, because I wanted to have everything myself.

I didn't care about the family. I was the one behind the sale of Grandma's house.

Larry and I were the ones who had spent all the money.

I was utterly helpless in the face of Mother's manipulations. Grandma tried to talk to Tom, to explain to him that Mother was not in her right mind; but he wouldn't listen. He couldn't listen. He had the money in his pocket and just like in the fairy story used as an example of narcissism, he had committed himself to take Snow White into the forest and cut out her heart.

The situation could only get worse. And it did.

With all the money from the mortgage in her pocket, Mother packed her things and moved to stay with a newly acquired friend. This was a woman from the church Larry and I attended. Mother went to church with us several times and became chummy with this woman. At the time, I was glad to see her with a new friend. At this point, I could see that she had an agenda and it wasn't long before we discovered what it was.

Not long afterward, I was helping Grandma with her bath and she pointed out a lump on her chest in the area of the mastectomy scar. It didn't look good. We made an appointment with the doctor and the news was as bad as it could get. It was too late for surgery. Without immediate radiation and chemotherapy, Grandma had maybe six months to live. Grandma wanted no more surgery or chemo. She said to me: "I just want to go now. I've suffered enough." I understood, though I could hardly bear to contemplate a future without her.

A few days later I learned I was pregnant with my fourth child. On the same day, a registered letter from an attorney arrived addressed to Larry and me. It was a notice that we were being sued by Mother to vacate the house. Mother had made good use of her borrowed money.

Unfortunately, the order of eviction did not give Grandma time to die in peace. Grandma refused to stay there if we left, and it was impossible to move her in her condition. Larry and I decided that we really needed the advice and possible help and intervention of the pastor of our church on this matter.

Mother had already thought of that. The pastor had been having regular dinners with Mother and her friend. He had become another mirror declaiming loudly that Mother was the fairest of them all. It was clear that he thought Larry and I had defrauded and abused and slandered Mother, and eviction was a small price to pay. Mother had even managed to convince him that Grandma was crazy too, or that she was hypnotized by me and would say anything I wanted her to say. When she tried to explain to him exactly what Mother was capable of doing, her words fell on deaf ears. He pontificated to my dying grandmother that she ought to submit herself to the care of her most uxorious daughter who clearly had her best interests at heart and was utterly devoted to her.

As for me and Larry, we should thank God for such a wonderful woman as my mother, so patient and understanding and willing to forgive if we would all just submit ourselves to her glorious plans for our futures.

I was practically foaming at the mouth in fury.

There was only one thing left to do: we called my Uncle, hoping that he would be able to have some influence on Mother to at least persuade her to back off until Grandma was buried. He had been estranged from us for some years now. Uncle, like the rest of us, lived under the illusion that Mother was normal if only a bit quirky. Worse yet, we discovered that she had blamed all the cruelties she had directed against him on my grandparents. She had led him to believe that she was only acting the way they dictated she should act.

When he arrived with my aunt, they had shocking news for us. Their youngest daughter had died. And my grandmother's youngest child, my mother's youngest sister, was killed in an accident out west. Her name was Laura, too. I think she was the only one in the family who saw, a long time ago, what Mother really was. When she couldn't get anyone to believe her, she moved away and cut off all contact with the family except my grandfather's brother.

Grandma blinked her eyes rapidly as she received this information. She put her hand on her breast, over the cancer, as if to hold her heart still. She breathed a deep sigh and said: "Well, that does it." I knew what she meant. She could take no more.

My uncle went to see my mother. Then he came to tell us that Mother had agreed to drop the eviction suit if we would promise to move as soon as Grandma was buried.

The next weeks were impossible. I had three little children, two of them still in diapers, and a fourth on the way. My beloved grandmother was dying. All of us were being evicted from the home we loved by the person into whose charge it was given to ensure that none of these things ever happened.

I was in constant pain from a kidney infection as well as the onset of gestational diabetes.

Night after night I sat up with Grandma, holding her upright against my shoulder so she could sleep. The cancer had moved into her lungs. She couldn't breathe unless she was leaning forward. As I held her, I wept. She patted my arm gently. "I don't know what's going to happen to you when I'm gone," she said. "I've loved you all your life, and I tried to protect you from your mother, but she has won, and it breaks my heart to see things end this way." And I wept even more.

Grandma was not afraid to die; she welcomed it. She had truly suffered enough.

After two months, Grandma could no longer even walk. I couldn't lift her and it became apparent that she had to go to the hospital.

At this point, we discovered that Mother lied to my uncle. Not a surprise. Because Mother had said that she did not plan to prosecute the eviction case, we did not present any defense. Mother obtained a judgment by default. The order of eviction was delivered by the sheriff.

We had thirty days to vacate or be put forcibly on the street.

It became increasingly difficult to cope with taking care of the children, my pregnancy, and the daily visits to the hospital. I should have followed up on this legal matter, but I hadn't in the maelstrom of events around me.

I realized that by failing to present a defense, I lost my chance to have these issues brought up in court. I wrote a letter to the judge to explain the situation, asking that eviction be deferred at least until my grandmother was buried.

But I never needed to mail it. Grandma died five days before her birthday, fifteen days before the expiration of the eviction notice.

THE POISONED APPLE

Mother was called on (as eldest child of the deceased and next of kin) to make funeral arrangements. She feigned poverty and ignorance and called my grandfather's brother to help, since he knew the funeral director and was in charge of the family burial plot. She asked him to co-sign a note for the funeral expenses. He did. Many years later I learned that she told him I was the one who had Grandma's money and would pay the bill. She never paid a cent.

Larry owned a parcel of land that we discussed selling to have money to make the down payment on a house. This was where his wilderness fantasy took over, however. He thought he could build a house for us and we could keep the land and end up with something far more valuable.

I was still certain that, with love and support, my husband could do anything he put his mind to. I agreed to his plan. In a week, he nailed up a little twelve-by-twenty-four-foot "house." We moved into it with our three children, a baby on the way, and my piano.

The Queen had sent the poisoned apple, and I had bitten.

CHAPTER TWENTY-FIVE

THE BOAT RIDE TO DAMASCUS

By now the reader knows that I cannot write all of this in strictly chronological format since there are always several threads weaving through a person's life. For the sake of clarity, I'm separating those threads both thematically and chronologically. Most of what is in this chapter was running along at the same time as the events of the last chapter, though at a different level.

Larry had been brought up Baptist and I had been raised Methodist. Both of us were after a more intimate relationship with God. That was, after all, promoted as a producer of peace and happiness. Above all, I needed peace. Or so I thought. I realize with hindsight that Larry's motivations must have been completely different from mine.

I wanted to try again the "faith of my fathers" and enter into submission to this mode of life in a complete and dedicated way. Any critical reservations would produce a barrier. All doubts and fears and questions had to be left at the door I now proposed to enter. Perhaps the faith of my childhood hadn't been mature enough to activate the results of living a full Christian life in every aspect, every hour of every day.

Larry and I decided to find the "right" church, one where this intimacy with God was present and evident. The only problem was: how do you really determine this?

We visited churches in a search for this communion with God. In the charismatic churches, speaking in tongues, dancing in the spirit, miracles, prophecy, and other manifestations of "gifts" delineated in the Bible were believed and practiced as the "fundamentals" of the Christian faith. The parishioners absolutely believed in the truthfulness and morality of the Bible. Principles derived strictly from the Bible were "rightly understood and interpreted in their intended sense." It is necessary to maintain one's faith unswervingly in all these things. Fundamentalism preached an absolute certainty in a solid rock all the way down.

Well, that sounded like the ticket to me! I saw they obviously had "something" that "filled them to overflowing," and they believed it was the Holy Spirit. Who was I to question that judgment without having tried it myself?

Fundamentalist charismatics strive to obey the law, and a very high value is placed on the experience of being "born again," engendered by a person's obedience and evidenced by receiving the gift of tongues.

Now, naturally, I was not deaf, dumb, and blind. I realized, early on, there seemed to be an inverse ratio of intellectual achievement and fundamentalism. But to receive the peace I sought, I had to acknowledge there might be truth to the idea that the hearts of intellectuals are hardened. This prevents them from perceiving the "foolishness of the Cross of Christ" which is "wisdom unto salvation." You had to become "as little children" to have your heart melted. This was the way to peace. (Not much different from the New Age schtick about "heart knowledge vs. head knowledge.")

Larry and I finally joined a congregation of the Church of God denomination, where we were impressed by the happy enthusiasm of the members, the seeming erudition of the pastor, and the observable dedication of his talented family in providing angelic music for every service. Surely, such devotion within a single family was evidence of God's grace upon them. That grace would naturally benefit their parishioners, including us, right?

In the early days of this experience, I remember sitting in the pew at the back of the church feeling my separation from joy with painful acuity. I watched as the congregation sang so joyously and with such obvious sincerity. I observed the depth of the prayers, the devoted and intense supplications to God, and the resultant "descent of the spirit" as the members, one by one, were overtaken with such "joy unspeakable" that it seemed as if their bodies simply could not contain the effects. They felt the need to dance and babble in tongues to express this Divine proximity.

As a trained hypnotist, a part of my mind, of course, also observed the hypnotic procedures that were in place prior to these activities, but I simply dismissed it because, even if it was hypnosis, it was being done for the "right" reason.

How I longed for that joy! How I wanted to be filled with the Holy Spirit and to experience the "peace that passes understanding."

I made an appointment to talk to the pastor about it and was told that it would come, that if I sincerely prayed, as soon as I was in a right relationship with God, I would receive the gift. Of course, he added, it would have to happen through the laying on of hands of others who already had the gift, so I needed to submit myself at the altar next Sunday for them to pray for me.

The following Sunday, I overcame my shyness and went forward at the altar call. All the deacons of the church gathered around me and placed their hands on my head, shoulders, back, and arms. A mighty outpouring of prayer began on all sides from a dozen or more voices, all calling on the spirit of God to come upon this "dear sister" who so desperately needed God's grace.

Nothing happened.

The praying intensified, and I heard members of the congregation breaking out into tongues as they gathered around to add their voices to the uproar. A general melee of dancing was going on all around and the emotion was building like a volcano.

Nothing happened.

One of the deacons grabbed my jaw and hissed into my ear that I should just "let it go, Sister!" and he began to work my jaw spasmodically as if to force the utterance of tongues. Several more of the deacons chimed in with their demands that I just "let it come; give in to God," and so forth.

Nothing happened.

I really felt like maybe I ought to just fake it to make them feel as though they had accomplished their mission, but I couldn't do anything to contaminate my experiment.

Eventually, the excitement of the congregation peaked and all were babbling in tongues or dancing in the spirit or interpreting the pronouncements of the tongues. Except me. Meanwhile, the preacher's wife kept on playing the piano in the background. When the people reached a certain point of near exhaustion, she launched into a stirring hymn and all joined in singing with the rich baritone of the pastor leading from the pulpit.

I returned to my seat, chastened and disappointed. Why was God giving these experiences to all these people and not to me? What was wrong with me?

I became a bit obsessed with this matter of receiving the gift of tongues as evidence of the infilling of the Holy Spirit. I began to study it in my usual way. I also began to ask questions. I wanted to know how it felt, what signs showed it was about to manifest, and so on. I guess that once a seeker and questioner, always a seeker and questioner.

I was told that once it happened to you, it happened, and there was no other experience that could compare. One day, we visited fellow parishioners. While Larry conducted business with the husband, I decided to ask the wife my questions. She was one of the more prominent members who had the gift of tongues and interpretation for years.

"How does it feel physically?" I asked.

I'll never forget what she said: "Well, you know, some people would say it's sort of carnal. But they don't understand."

"What do you mean by 'carnal'?" I asked.

"You know ..." she said, obviously embarrassed. "It's like ... well, carnal."

"I don't understand," I said. I was truly puzzled.

"Well ... you know, when you are with your husband ... that sort of thing. Carnal," she said. And she was evidently not going to say any more.

Did she mean that it produced an orgasm? I didn't dare ask that, but I believe that this was the event to which she was alluding.

The whole thing troubled me greatly. In reading the passages on which this doctrine was based, it was clear that the intent was never to suggest that tongues was the only gift of the spirit, nor was it the definitive one. The apostle Paul wrote: *"If I speak in the tongues of men and of angels, but have not love, I am only a noisy gong or a clanging cymbal. ... Eagerly pursue and seek to acquire this love. Make it your aim, your great quest; and earnestly desire and cultivate the spiritual endowments, especially that you may prophesy: that is, interpret the divine will and purpose in inspired preaching and teaching. For one who speaks in an unknown tongue speaks not to men but to God, for no one understands or catches his meaning ... He who speaks in a tongue edifies and improves himself ... Now I wish that you might all speak in tongues, but more especially to prophesy ... He who prophesies is greater than he who speaks in tongues. ... Thus tongues are meant for a sign, not for believers but for unbelievers ... So, earnestly desire and set your hearts on prophesying and do not hinder speaking in tongues. But all things should be done with regard to decency and propriety and in an orderly fashion."*

Reading these two chapters in I Corinthians (13 and 14), put a whole different light on the matter. The issue of tongues might not be the proof that a person was born again or had been filled with the Holy Spirit, as the doctrine of the church proposed. This proof was right there in the Bible. I naturally made an appointment to discuss this with the pastor.

The answer to the question I was raising was that the original interpretation had come from the infilling of the Holy Spirit in certain leaders of the original denominational movement. They got it straight from God, so to say. Also, the very fact that I was questioning those in authority was evidence that Satan was working on my mind!

It was very troubling to me when I realized it was merely a denominational interpretation that the initial infilling of the Holy Spirit was signified by the gift of tongues. I really needed to understand this issue, so it was back to the books. Of course, these books were strictly Christian books, written by Christian writers.

As I read, I discovered to my dismay that the vast realm of disagreement among theologians on how to interpret difficult passages was, in many respects, a linguistic problem. When one reads the King James Version of the Bible, one is reading something translated from Hebrew, Aramaic, or Greek into old Latin, and from the Latin of the Vulgate translated into the English of the 1600s, read by an English speaker in modern times.

I remember a particular incident that really drove this point home. A rather famous radio minister of the Church of God denomination was preaching a sermon based on Acts 28:13 where the KJV says, starting with verse 11, *"And after three months we departed in a ship of Alexandria, which had wintered in the isle, whose sign was Castor and Pollux. And landing at Syracuse, we tarried there three days. And from thence we fetched a compass, and came to Rhegium: and after one day the south wind blew, and we came the next day to Puteoli ..."*

Well, this particular pastor decided to use this last verse as a metaphor for the Christian needing to have the "compass of God" in order to find one's way when the winds of life threaten to buffet the faithful. He kept driving home the point about how the apostle did not rely on his own direction, but bought a compass, and the reason for this story to be in the Bible was to set just this example.

I wondered about this passage, so I did some research. I discovered that the real meaning of "from thence we fetched a compass" was "from there we made a circuit" or sailed in a circle, following the coastline.

This was an Elizabethan nautical term that had absolutely nothing to do with the little gadget that points north which today we call a "compass."

It upset me greatly that this preacher had, in my mind, made a mockery of God to those outside the church by formulating this interpretation of the passage. This, of course, created a new problem in my mind. If the Bible was the Holy Word of God, ought we not, as faithful believers, discover precisely what those words meant, in the deepest way, according to the author of the words, so that we would not fall into errors of understanding? This seemed pretty simple and logical to me.

I brought the issue up with the pastor and was set down in a pretty firm manner. I was told that, in the first place, the Holy Spirit "reveals" the truth to the faithful if they will only pray for guidance, and in this particular case, the guidance was given to use this passage in this way. Further, I was told, it was not necessary to be "informed as to the vagaries of translation," for this very reason. And if a person begins to question their pastor or teachers of the faith, that's tantamount to questioning the Bible. This is clear evidence these questions were being stimulated by Satan and, consequently, I was in grave danger and needed to do a lot of praying to save myself from falling into this pit!

I searched my conscience and carefully monitored and examined every thought and feeling, searching for the inroads made by Satan. I prayed diligently and fervently. I read the Bible feverishly, looking for clues, and the more I read, the more I realized that somebody was having a lot of trouble understanding the difference between subjects and verbs, and other parts of speech. I heard sermons preached using text from the Bible in a manner exactly opposite to the way the passage actually read. To be absolutely certain, I obtained a Greek lexicon and the Amplified translation of the Bible and diligently compared the texts in question to discover any possibility that my understanding of the grammatical structure of the sentences was in error. After all, if the worlds come into being by the Word of God, those words must be pretty darn important!

This process only led to more amazing discoveries about the translations of the Bible. I was convinced that the true believer ought to search out these things to come to a better understanding of what God intended us to know.

But nothing could be allowed to challenge the system, so fragile that it could not withstand questions and challenges. Was I suffering from a blind spot preventing me from seeing satanic influences in my studies?

I plunged into a veritable frenzy of prayer and fasting intended to extirpate these questions from my mind if they were in error. I was told a mind that sought knowledge was a curse, and doubt was the wide road to hell. At the same time, I was discovering richness in the text to which other members of the congregation, including the pastor, were oblivious.

I had become very comfortable with this congregation and, little by little, I was losing my shyness and feeling more at home with the other ladies, active in the many social events and fund-raising activities. To be branded a heretic and suffer exclusion from the congregation was a frightening thought.

* * *

It is at this point that I realized that the business enterprise we were involved in with my mother was failing miserably. Even if we were making a lot of money, we were spending a lot more than we ought to on maintenance and other overhead costs, and we were dealing with weather variables that often proved to be mini-disasters. If God was in favor of our enterprise, and we were acting as good stewards, it seemed only reasonable to think that the weather, which was directly under God's control, would be mitigated for us. Right? After all, this was what we were supposed to believe.

I was doing the work of a man, side by side with my husband, going through three pregnancies and keeping up all the housework. My heart had been damaged in the bout with dengue fever. The physical labor to manage a home and three children, caring for my aged grandmother, and a now failing business, put so much strain on my heart that I was near collapse.

Of course, being committed to the path of fundamentalism meant that the only interpretation for this challenge in my life was a test of my faith. Not being a quitter by any stretch of the imagination, I wasn't going to let such things stand in the way of my faith! Things like deteriorating physical health or financial disaster after financial disaster were not going to stop me. No sir! I fasted, prayed, and assiduously schooled my thoughts and emotions. My sole direction was "going for compassion and purity of passion and will ... aiming towards a feeling of fullness and unification of all ... following of the love in the present moment, of opening the heart to that present moment and the love in it."

The more things came against me, the more I suffered, the more I was attacked from within and without, the more my resolve strengthened. For a long time I even refused to even ask the obvious question, why. I read the book of Job to comfort myself that, at least, I was not alone in my suffering. I used the opportunity to "experience vicariously the sufferings of Christ on the cross." By comparison, nothing I experienced could possibly be considered suffering. I took no offense at offense, whether intended or not; I forgave and loved and comforted my hurts by transforming them in the crucible of my suffering to pure and passionate love for God, for Jesus, and for all mankind.

It was at this point that I had what I call my "Boat Ride to Damascus."

We had suffered so much bad weather that half a dozen working trips in a row had cost more than double what we made. We had also experienced more than usual mechanical breakdowns, and the repair costs had eaten up all our reserves. I knew we were dancing close to the edge of disaster, but we really had no options. Mother was demanding money, our creditors were demanding money, we needed to pay the tuition on my daughter's private Christian pre-school, and, at the most basic level, we needed to keep food in the house. I prayed long and hard over the matter, we consulted with our pastor, and the consensus was that God was just testing our faith. So, faith it was. We used our credit to cover our expenses and made arrangements for the next working trip.

As a rule, when we took the boat out, we would be gone for up to a week at a time. We worked at night and slept during the day. It was a rough schedule to keep, since even when you sleep on a boat, you can't really relax because there are all kinds of electronics that have to be regularly checked to make sure everything is running right.

This trip was the disaster of all disasters.

On the first day out, I was just sitting there steering the boat when I noted a strange wallowing feeling when I moved the wheel even slightly. I called Larry and asked him to check the bilge pump and nearly died when he shouted at me to throw the engine into neutral and help him bail. The water was halfway over the engine, which, thankfully, continued to run. The bilge pump wires had been corroded by the salt water and we had been running for God only knows how long with no pump. Ordinarily, this wouldn't have been a problem, except that a fitting on the propeller shaft had vibrated loose. The shaft had begun to slide out, taking the fitting (called a packing gland) with it, unsealing a hole about three or four inches in diameter at the bottom of the boat. The wobbling of the shaft was what I had felt as a wallowing feeling when adjusting the wheel.

We bailed with five-gallon buckets like crazy until we were no longer in danger of sinking. Larry had to make the repairs while I kept bailing on my own. I was rapidly exhausted but, under such circumstances, exhaustion doesn't even bear consideration. You perform or you die.

It was not an auspicious beginning to the trip, to say the least. Well, my point of view was that we had managed to overcome this difficulty, so we had experienced all the bad luck for the trip in one fell swoop. Things could only get better, right?

Wrong.

The weather had been a bit iffy, which was normal for March in the Gulf of Mexico. "Iffy" was soon to change to downright dangerous.

After a night of modestly successful trawling, we anchored out. We had been in contact with a friend by radio during the night and agreed to have breakfast together. They anchored a few hundred yards away from us in the darkness, and we all stowed our equipment and turned in for a few hours of sleep. It was a huge relief to shut down the eternally thrumming diesel engine and take a shower in the cabin and collapse in the bunk to be rocked and lulled to sleep by the gentle swells and waves lapping at the sides of the boat.

I woke up after being asleep only a short while and immediately felt that something was wrong. It took me a few minutes to figure out what the problem was: it was utterly silent outside. There were no lapping waves, there was no rhythmic rolling of the boat with the swells; just preternatural silence and semi-darkness at a very late hour.

I got up and looked outside: thick, pea-soup fog everywhere. It was even impossible to see our friends only a short distance away. I got on the radio to see if I could raise them, and soon they cranked their engines and began to move slowly toward us. When they emerged from the fog, Larry caught their lines and held the two boats close while they climbed onboard.

They were a younger couple who ran their own boat together the same as we were, trying to make the business work against the high expenses, the weather, and the newly imposed fishing restrictions mandated by the state and federal management agencies. The fellow took the lines from Larry as soon as he was onboard and tied them off on a cleat at the stern. For some reason, the fact that he allowed a long section of the rope to dangle in the water caught my eye and bothered me, but since I was no expert on these matters, I said nothing. I went into the galley to fry the bacon and whip up some pancakes.

As I was cooking, I noticed we were beginning to roll in such a way that the fat in the pan moved slowly from one side to the other to the point of danger that it would spill over the side. I couldn't really feel any waves or swells because they were so long and slow, so I didn't think in terms of danger. I just finished cooking and we all sat in the main cabin to eat.

We noticed that the wind was picking up rather quickly, and the swells were no longer so long and gentle, but were becoming higher and shorter. Larry commented that we had better finish up and batten down the hatches. It looked like it was going to blow.

We didn't have time to finish eating.

A terrific gust of wind hit us almost like a tornado. In almost no time at all, the swells had become huge, crashing waves. A window in the main cabin suddenly blew open so violently that it was nearly torn off its hinges. At the same instant, our boat lifted on the crest of a huge wave. The other boat tied up at our rear dropped its bow underneath our stern, and the dangling rope caught around our propeller.

I grabbed all the plates and stowed them, syrup and all, in a pan in a locker. Every unsecured item in the cabin went flying through the air as we pitched and tossed. Larry rushed out with our friends to take care of the disaster in progress.

The wind was actually roaring by now. In the next moment, another massive wave rolled under us. This time, it lifted our friend's boat up, straining the rope wrapped around our propeller to the max. The bow came crashing down on our stern, knocking a hole in their boat about the size of a dinner plate.

Something had to be done quickly to separate the two boats. I clung to the side rail and watched in horror as Larry barked instructions. Our guests scrambled onto the bow of their boat, barely missing being dumped in the water. Larry stripped off his pants and shoes and, clenching a knife in his teeth, went over the side, holding onto the rope that yoked the two boats together. I was certain that in the next moment he would be crushed between them.

The next wave crashed under us, lifting the other boat high on its crest. Larry, still holding on the rope, was lifted up with it. When the bow of the other boat dropped, Larry was plunged back into the water.

I could barely breathe, and my heart was pounding from the adrenaline flowing.

Nothing I could do but watch helplessly, sure that I was about to become a widow.

Somehow he did it. Larry cut the rope and the other boat was free. By this time, our friends had their engine running and, when they saw that the rope was cut, they slammed it in reverse and backed away rapidly. I tried to get to the back of the boat to help Larry get back in, but another crashing wave made it more of an airborne maneuver than actual walking. We managed to get him in, and both of us set about tying all the equipment down to ride out the storm.

The wind kept building in force. We were anchored in sandy bottom, being blown backwards toward the coastal rock piles and islands.

Larry put the boat in gear and we kept accelerating the engine with our bow in the wind. Soon it was clear that even that was not going to work. We were still being blown backward, dragging our anchor. We kept hoping the anchor would catch in rocks.

A quick check of the charts didn't give us hope for a rocky bottom between us and disaster.

I decided to try to find out what I could about this freak storm on the radio. It seemed that it had struck at a very bad time when there was a sort of regatta a few miles up the coast. Many boats were being swamped, and the Coast Guard was out in force hauling people out of the water. This news came from another friend who happened to be out at the same time, and he was getting it from the television he had in his cabin. I explained our situation and he suggested that we ought to come over to his anchorage and tie up behind him. His boat was so big that he anchored with a big ship anchor on a chain and he was sure he could hold both of us to the big rock pile he had found for the purpose.

It was a tricky maneuver in that storm to find him, then approach with our bow in the wind in exactly the right way. Then, I could step from our boat onto the bigger one in a sort of "eye" of stability. Somehow, I managed, and Larry and our friend got the lines fixed so our boat was securely tied.

Actually, at that point, I wouldn't have cared if it had broken free and disappeared in the crashing waves.

On this truly huge boat, it was almost a different world. With its broad beam construction, the bow in the wind, anchored to a rock pile, we hardly noticed the storm raging outside. We sat in the lounge and watched television and wondered how there could be so drastic a difference between the weather a few miles offshore and what was being experienced on land as depicted by a smiling, perky weather girl.

It gave me a deep insight to the differences between what is real and what is on the news. Yes, there was coverage of the disaster of a regatta to the north. But no one seemed to be really talking about the storm as we were experiencing it at that very moment.

While we looked at the full-color weather maps on television, a coast guard rescue helicopter hovered directly overhead in the wailing wind, illuminating our decks with its searchlights. The radio crackled to life with an inquiry from the crew over our head as to whether we were secure. Larry and the captain waved them off to rescue somebody who needed it.

The wind blew for about twenty hours. A day and a night. To this day, I cannot explain that storm. At one point, the anemometer on our friend's boat was buried at eighty knots. On the television weather report, another reality prevailed. "Marine warnings were in effect," because of "rough weather" out in the Gulf.

They never reported how rough.

By afternoon the next day, the gale had calmed down considerably. I knew that we could not simply toss this trip and go back in. We still had our ice, we still had a partial catch, and we still needed the money. We needed a big catch to get out of the hole.

Larry had always wanted to try the fishing grounds up to the north where the regatta had met such a bad end the previous day. He conjectured that the storm would have stirred up the muddy bottom and the shrimp would have moved into those deeper waters to avoid being swept hither and thither. It sounded like a plan to me, even though I knew it would take the rest of the day to get there. We got out the charts, figured our position, calculated running time, and got underway.

We reached the designated fishing grounds not long after dark and dropped our nets. For several hours things went fine. Then the wind began to pick up again, now accompanied by rain falling in torrents that were actually sheets blowing sideways. Larry decided to anchor a couple miles up the ship channel that ran between a series of islands due east. If we could get on the lee side, at least the wind would be less violent even if we couldn't do anything about the rain. So we pulled in the nets, tied down the equipment, and headed to safe anchorage.

While we were running, since things seemed to be under control, I decided to take a shower and be ready for sleep when we dropped the anchor. After my shower, I put on my nightgown and a sleeveless, quilted jacket liner over it. The liner had buttonholes all around the edges that were used to secure it in a larger, heavier garment. When we reached the anchorage point, Larry pointed the bow in the wind and I went up the ladder, through the hatchway, and out on the front deck to slide the anchor over the side.

Just as the last of the chain portion of the line was sliding through my hands to the right, a big gust of wind blew the lower left flap of the jacket liner forward to catch on the clevis pin at the end of the chain. In the same instant, a big wave washed the boat.

I was thrown face down on the deck, right on the edge, with the huge anchor dangling from my jacket, pulling it tight around my throat, choking me. The length of rope behind me wrapped around my leg. As the bow of the boat dipped down, I slid forward on the wet deck. My head was over the edge and I was looking down into that black, icy water. I knew from the charts it was very deep. The only thing that kept me from being pulled completely over the side was a rope cleat on the edge of the deck against which my pelvis was painfully jammed.

There was nothing but wet deck in reach of my left hand. I tried to catch the anchor chain with my right arm, dangling over the side. I was just barely able to slip the heavy anchor over the side with both hands under ordinary circumstances, so it was a certainty that if I tried to pull it back in with one hand, the effort would do nothing but launch me into the water for sure. If I was pulled over with the rope around my ankle, even if I could shuck myself out of the jacket, I would be pulled very rapidly straight to the bottom with the anchor. Would I have sufficient air in my lungs to be able to disentangle myself and make it back to the top? How would I manage it in the dark when I couldn't see anything at all?

The odds were not good, to say the least.

My jaw was jammed against the deck by my resistance to the chokehold of the weight of the anchor pulling on that wonderfully made Army-issue jacket liner. Even if I could have made a sound, Larry wouldn't have heard me shouting over the sound of the wind and the engine.

The boat lifted and plunged a couple more times, and each time, I braced myself against that life-saving cleat pressing so painfully into my hip. Each time, I felt my body rolling right to the point that—with just a hair's more force—I would simply roll over the clevis and into the water, wrapped in the fatal spider's web of three hundred feet of anchor line.

Fortunately, by this time, Larry had figured out that I wasn't just lying there on the deck to pass the time of day while gazing soulfully into the water. We were in a precarious position. Without forward motion into the wind, we had no stability, but with forward motion and no one there to hold the wheel, we could instantly swing broadside to the wind and roll over completely with the top-heavy trawls tied to their metal frame bolted to the deck.

Larry put the engine in neutral, ran down the stairs from the steering cabin, through the main cabin to the ladder, up the ladder and out onto the deck where I was trapped by the anchor. He grabbed me, pulled me back enough that I was no longer dangling half over the side, and slipped the coils of rope from my leg. He then unhooked the anchor from my jacket, and let it go over the side. I slid myself backward to the hatch cover and backed down into it, waving my feet around to catch a rung of the ladder. Just as I did, another wave hit and I dropped through the hatch with my elbows spread out on either side like wings. I could almost hear the muscles tearing away from my shoulder blades. I nearly went unconscious from the pain.

Well, the rotator muscles in my shoulders had been torn—I was to be plagued for years with pain from this injury. We were sitting at anchor for two more days in the most miserable weather of my life. Nothing but wind and rain. Everything in the boat was damp and there was no way to get warm and dry. I was in pain, but I had to keep going because there was no way Larry could manage everything alone.

When the wind died down enough, Larry thought we might make it back to the docks. We headed out. Because we had used so much of our fuel just holding our position and keeping the electronics charged up, we had to make the run as directly as possible. This meant that we had to run "quarter" with the waves, an iffy prospect at best. I can tell you there were waves that were so tall they were like big buildings. They would come up at an angle to us in the rear, looking for all the world like they were going to swallow us whole. It was always a miracle when, instead of being swamped, the boat would lift up onto the wave, roll and plunge down into the trough, slamming violently against the water.

But this was a hard way to run. Over time, it could tear the boat apart. We had several hours of running before us. Larry decided to drop the trawls just barely into the water to stabilize the boat, to prevent the "slam dunk" of every wave. When they were up and out of the water and locked onto steel frame, it made us too top-heavy. But to run this way, under these conditions, Larry had to stay on deck to see to it they didn't slam against the side of the hull and smash a hole in the boat when we "hit bottom." This meant that I had to steer the boat.

I was alone in the cabin with nothing but the red glow of the instrument panel and the low rumble of the diesel engine under the floor—and my terror. I knew that, after this trip, I would never set foot on a boat again. This was sort of an admission that all was going down the tubes. I was struggling with my hurt and anger and bewilderment, praying fervently for understanding and compassion and love to fill my heart in spite of the apparent hopelessness of the situation. I wanted to be filled with the love of God. I wanted to subsume all of the experience into that single-pointed devotion that brings the peace that passes understanding. Over and over again I was repeating: "Help me, oh Lord! Help me!" The agony of the struggle was deeper than the mind can fathom or words can express.

The Apostle Paul describes it in Romans 8.26: *"... for we do not know what prayer to offer nor how to offer it worthily as we ought, but the Spirit Himself goes to meet our supplication and pleads in our behalf with unspeakable yearnings and groanings too deep for utterance."*

What we were experiencing had brought me face to face with just exactly what it was we were risking by following this venture of Mother's so stubbornly and persistently. In the face of death, all I could think about were my babies and how much I wanted to be there for them, to see them, to hold them, and to look after them and watch them grow. And how foolish it was to go after money so assiduously that not only were we never home with them, when we were, we were too exhausted to enjoy them. And when we were away from them, it was always a serious question whether we would even return. Every time we went out in that boat, our children were in danger of being orphaned. Now we were in danger of losing everything we had worked so hard for.

If living by faith was not working as it was claimed to work, what, exactly, was I doing wrong?

Well, the beginning of the verse in the book of Romans says: "So too the Spirit comes to our aid and bears us up in our weakness ..."

What happened next was a sensation of growing heat in my solar plexus, accompanied by a buzzing sound in my ears that soon became a sort of inaudible roaring which terminated in a resounding inner explosion: BOOM! Like being stone deaf and standing between two huge Chinese gongs while they were being struck simultaneously. It was soul-deep and resonated to a long, slow, and rhythmic internal oscillation that drew me in and enveloped me like a warm, comforting cloud.

Then there was the voice.

It was not audible, and not really in my head exactly, but it was a voice nevertheless. It emanated from some interior organ of spiritual hearing, rich and rapturously tender. This voice had the odd characteristic that it conveyed information more in the sense of concept than distinct words, though there seemed to be a process of translation going on in my mind simultaneous to receiving the "soul voice."

"You KNOW that I LOVE you, my child," the voice both said and conveyed in waves of ecstatic inner sound. "But until you remove the darkness from between us, I can do nothing."

The words vibrated and penetrated every cell in my body from a depth of being that is impossible to describe. The transference of the impression, of the idea of "love" as expressed from this source, rocked me to my very core. I understood there was no way that I, in this human body, could plumb that love. I was aware that to attempt to experience it in my flesh would result in instant death, because the human organism simply was not capable of carrying such energy. "Tasting" was all that humans could experience, and even that tasting carried risks of overwhelming the circuitry, like plugging a 110-volt appliance into a 220-volt outlet. In the same way, the term "darkness" was also unfathomable in its breadth and meaning.

My mind raced through all the aspects of my life. Like the proverbial moment before death when all of a person's deeds pass before their eyes, I reviewed my existence, enumerating all the ways I yearned to seek only to do the will of God. I couldn't find a single breach in this contract where one could think that evil would enter the picture. I enumerated all the ways in which I was living a Christian life as explicated in the terms of fundamentalist belief. I pointed out that we didn't just go to church and tithe; we made dedicated efforts to live the life fully and completely every moment of every day. And, I added, we did it in the face of often tremendous opposition! What more was there than living the life, building the faith, and teaching it to our children? "Just what," I demanded to know, "are we doing wrong?"

At this point, a response came, though not in words. It was like a holographic or experiential movie being run in my mind, soul, and awareness. I was shown my children in a series of vignettes that brought up the deep love and devotion I had for them. I was to understand that my love for my children, as great as it was, was merely a human love and could, in no way, equal the love of the Creator for his creation. I was being infused with this love in small, incremental amounts. It was consoling and warmly caressing to a level that is impossible to express with words. I was so lost in this feeling that I could have drifted in the waves of love washing over me forever. But the Voice had other plans.

The scene changed and I "experienced" myself admonishing my children to not play in ant beds. Fire ants were a big problem in our yard, and it was a common event that I pointed these places out to the children, warning them not to be tempted by the quiet and attractive exterior of the anthill. Inside, it was a boiling mass of stinging insects that could, under certain circumstances, kill a small child.

In the little experiential movie I was being shown, I saw that my children, as children will, did not listen to what I was saying. Their curiosity about the anthill led them to it, to observe and examine its perfect symmetry of structure and peaceful aspect of industry. Their lack of direct knowledge of ants coupled with their foolhardy, naive bravery caused them try to play with the ants, to force open the hill and see what was inside, how it was constructed, and what went on beneath that fascinating exterior.

The result was that they suddenly were covered with ants, biting and stinging them, and they were running to me, screaming for relief from the ants. And there I was, soothing them and brushing away the ants, and explaining that I could get rid of the ants, and I could put salve on the bites to soothe the pain, but it would do no good if they hadn't learned something from the experience about ants.

Sounds like a pretty simple little example, yes? I certainly didn't see how my life related to children playing in an ant bed! "What are the ants?" I asked. "What is the evil in my life?" And the voice came again, this time with overtones of regret and sorrow:

"Learn!"

The word reverberated away into inner silence as the sound of crashing waves and the diesel engine began to penetrate my awareness. I was floating on the sensation of the great infusion of love that had come with the first part of the "interaction." I call it that because it was hardly a vision in strict terms, though something happened of an internal visionary nature.

Even though the intensity of the experience could not be denied, I was uncertain as to its nature. Was this how God spoke to people? Is this what I had been hearing about all my life? If so, if God spoke to people in this way as regularly as they claimed, then they must be very powerful and lofty individuals to sustain such experiences on so regular a basis, as their claims suggested.

I was very anxious to share this event with the pastor of our church. I was certain that God had given me a message that I should share, that we should study and learn to navigate through our lives. Things were not what they appeared to be on the surface. Deeper meanings must be sought. Things seeming attractive and symmetrical and safe from the outside may not be so at all.

The voice had not said, "Have faith." It had said, "Learn!"

Well, I should have been prepared for the reaction of the pastor. I was told that it was impossible for God to speak to me because I hadn't received the Holy Ghost—I hadn't spoken in tongues. Besides, if I wanted to know about the love of God, all I had to do was come down to the altar at church on Sunday. And yes, God wanted us to learn: that's why they had Thursday night Bible class and preachers to tell us what we needed to know!

I was a bit nonplussed by this response. But it didn't diminish the inner sensations of expanding, rhythmic waves of love flowing through me endlessly. For weeks I was sustained by this love, and I certainly was going to need it.

By the time we made it to the dock, I never wanted to set foot on that boat again.

And I never did.

CHAPTER TWENTY-SIX

ANOTHER FACE AT THE WINDOW

Another thread of events that were running parallel with the overview given in Chapter 24 invovled my eldest daughter. She awakened in the night screaming in terror so intense she was almost completely unable to describe to us what was frightening her. Soothing and rocking (she was only in kindergarten) calmed her down sufficiently to get a coherent response.

There was, it seems, an alligator outside her window trying to come inside.

After a series of such nightly events, I could no longer brush it off as just a nightmare. Since my own experiences as a child had affected me so powerfully, I was not inclined to deny the validity of what she had experienced. From somewhere deep inside my soul, an alarm was sounding "Warning! Warning!" as if an ancient enemy had surfaced once again. There was a difference, however: I was no longer a child, and this was my own child under threat.

It was time to carefully re-examine the Face at the Window events for clues. Dealing with this as a possibly real phenomenon, even if only psychological, seemed to be the right approach. It never occurred to me, of course, that I might fail. My child was threatened as I had been so many years ago. There had been no one to protect me. But from this, at least, I could protect my child.

I pulled out several of my books on metaphysical subjects and found very little that was helpful except in the realms of different kinds of magic. Well, that was an area I didn't intend to go, but there was nothing else offered in these books. I closed them and decided to consult the pastor, but in an indirect, theoretical way. I most definitely didn't want to reveal such a problem in my household. And it's a good thing, too. I was told that such things did not occur in "Christian" families. If Jesus was in your heart, Satan could not enter your house. Period. And, even if he approached, the Bible said that if you "resist the devil, he will flee from you." The fleeing part was the key element. Any Christian with God and Jesus on his side was a guaranteed winner in any such contest. "If God is with you, who can be against you?"

That wasn't very helpful, in my opinion.

I knew that the Catholic Church had a rite of exorcism. While I didn't want to go that route precisely, thinking that it would be like shooting a mosquito with a cannon, it did occur to me that I could consult Sandra. She was Catholic. Perhaps she would ask her parish priest about any suggestions he might have.

In Sandra's family, Sicilian and Catholic, such subjects had come up before. In the "old country," they'd used the ninety-first psalm as a novena. Repeated nine times, Sandra assured me, it worked like a charm.

Well, I wasn't sure that "working like a charm" was at the root of any such effectiveness. I was already developing a theory about why anything might work at all and it had more to do with suggestibility and belief than anything else. A child felt powerless in the adult world. Perhaps this was at the root of such events as night terrors and other similar frightening events. The key, then, would be to give my daughter back her feeling of power in the situation. I also knew I needed to give it to myself. By dealing with her demon, I could also deal with my own.

And, if a prayer was the "magic charm," all the better.

I explained to my daughter that evening.

"I know a special way to make alligators at the window go away."

"You do?"

"Yes. It's a special prayer. It's very powerful."

I told her that the prayer could keep alligators away, and if they appeared, all she had to do was start to recite it, and they would go away. She was very anxious to learn it by heart.

So, at the age of five, my daughter memorized the ninety-first psalm and could recite it letter perfect in just a few days. Every night, when I tucked her into bed, we recited the psalm together, and it made us both feel better. I added my own prayers silently and stayed with her until she went to sleep. A good Christian mother couldn't do much more.

For a while, it seemed to work. Easy problem, easy solution, right?

ANOTHER FACE AT THE WINDOW

At this point, things took an even stranger turn. Again, my little girl woke us up with her screams, but this time, as we frantically struggled to wakefulness, Larry and I both saw the figure standing in the corner of the bedroom, and we both saw it fade or dissolve into a shimmery sort of atmosphere.

My daughter's screams reached a crescendo. We snapped out of our shock and flung ourselves out of bed and ran to her see what was going on. Her room was icy cold, even though it was summer. She informed us that the alligator was no longer outside the window; it had come into the house.

Well, no kidding!

We had planned an outing to a local island for a picnic the next day, a short hop in our bass boat. Mother was taking Grandma shopping, and we had a rare day for the children and didn't want to waste a minute of it. The island, called Horse Island, was reputed to have been the site of a buried pirate treasure that had been successfully recovered by some unknown person. I was curious to see the reported square pit that had been dug in the crushed-shell ground at some period still unknown.

We drove to the boat launch. No sooner had we put the boat in the water than I realized that I had left the second cooler with the drinks behind. Going anywhere with small children and no drinks was unthinkable, so they were going to fish and wait while I went back to fetch the drinks.

I pulled up behind the house and stopped the truck, looking toward the house as I did. The doors were still open as we had left them. We usually did, in complete safety. From the angle I was viewing the door, I could see in through the screen door, and then through the door between the dining room and the living room. My heart skipped a beat to see the same tall figure we'd seen in our bedroom pass from the dining room to the living room, but it had happened so fast. I shook my head to clear my eyes and brain and looked again. Surely it was just an effect of the shadows in the house cast by sunlight flowing in from other windows. Perhaps a cloud had passed over the sun and made me think it was a shadow moving in the house. Whatever it was, I had to go inside and get the drinks. My family was waiting at the boat launch.

My mouth was a bit dry as I got out of the truck and walked toward the house. I stepped inside the door quietly, listening for any sound at all. If anything, the house was more silent than usual. Inside, I couldn't even hear the normal traffic sounds of the growing housing development across the road. I quietly walked slowly through the house, looking for any sign of anything out of place. Everything seemed to be exactly as we had left it half an hour ago. It was only when I reached the hall that I felt anything at all.

Standing where I could see into my own bedroom as well as my daughter's, I felt an icy chill creeping up my neck with the intense sensation that there were eyes in the darkened corners of the narrow passage. Again I shook my head to clear the cobwebs from my brain, turned, and walked briskly back to the kitchen to pick up the cooler. When I arrived back at the boat launch, I was sure that I had imagined the whole thing.

That night, it was me who had the nightmare. I dreamed that I heard the screaming approach of low-flying jets flying in formation. As they flew over the house, someone just outside began shooting at them with an anti-aircraft gun that had been hidden in a clump of palmettos. I became hysterical because I knew that, by firing on the jets, attention had been alerted to our position, and we needed to get away before a retaliatory strike was launched.

In the dream, Larry laughed at my insistence that we wake the children and leave immediately. As he was arguing with me, we both heard a low roaring in the distance which, as it became louder and closer, I recognized as a whole squadron of low-flying airplanes—big bombers—approaching from out over the Gulf. Larry suddenly realized I'd been right, but it was now too late to get away safely. We grabbed the children and went out to our car. It wouldn't start because Larry had forgotten to fix something. We picked up the children out of the car and began to run for the road. There were houses some distance away, and when we came to one with a car in the driveway, Larry looked inside and found the keys were in it. We put the children inside, jumped in ourselves, and Larry cranked the engine. Just as we were pulling away, the bombs began to fall with horrible explosions all around us.

I woke up in a heart-pounding, sweating terror. The intensity of this dream was so severe that, for months afterward, any loud or sudden noise made me nearly jump out of my skin. That kind of dream was definitely not good for someone with a damaged heart! I spent most of the night sitting up until the sun began to lighten the sky, and then I went back to bed for a few hours of sleep before I had to get the children up and ready for church.

That Sunday morning was a momentous day for me, though I didn't know it while I was dressing my little children for church. In one of those strange synchronicities that have occurred throughout my life, I was about to come face to face with the very questions that had plagued me all my life, and which had been forcibly returned to my attention in the past few weeks.

There was a young couple visiting that morning. The young woman was the most skeletal being I had ever seen outside of photographs of the Holocaust. She was nothing but skin stretched over bones. How she was able to even walk passed my understanding.

It seemed that this young woman had been "plagued by a demon" and she had come to our church, reputed in the Church of God circuit for its holiness and zeal, to be delivered of her demon and saved by Jesus. She had been walking a path of darkness, and she had fallen into the snares of the devil, so now she was ready to be born again, and once that happened, the devil would flee and that would be that.

Well, don't that just beat all?

There she was: a real-life demoniac, sitting just two rows ahead of us. I could not take my eyes off of her. I was curious to know exactly what it was that made anyone think that she was possessed. Was it because of her skeletal appearance? Well, heck, that didn't seem too demonic to me. Maybe she was just ill. Why didn't they take her to a doctor instead?

Well, what was I thinking? There I was, member of a congregation that believed in faith healing. Where was my faith?

During the sermon the young woman got up and went out, followed soon after by her husband. He returned with her in tow, and I suspected that she had tried to excuse herself from the upcoming exorcism as being unnecessary. Apparently he had convinced her to try. She returned with a resigned or determined (it was hard to tell which) expression on her face.

After the service, the pastor called the visitors down to the altar and then called on all the deacons of the church as well. They gathered around the young woman, as they had around me when trying to "get me in the spirit." They all placed their hands on her while the pastor put both his hands on her head, front and back, and began to "pray the demon out."

Well, you never heard such praying! The girl began to twist and fight against them, and finally she fell on the floor practically foaming at the mouth. That didn't stop the pastor and the deacons. They were on their knees, keeping their hands on her while they ordered the demon to "leave our dear sister alone in the name of Jesus!" Again and again this demand was made, and each time, the poor girl jerked like a puppet responding to the yanking of the strings by the puppet master. Finally, with a horrible strangling sound, she arched her back and went rigid, followed by total collapse and limpness. The girl was asked if she accepted Jesus as her savior. She nodded and whispered yes.

Success! The pastor paced back and forth with his hands in the air thanking Jesus for the victory over the demon. More prayers and a veritable chorus of hallelujahs erupted from the congregation. Women were speaking in tongues; other women were dancing in the spirit. Members of the congregation were swaying from side to side with their arms raised in the air. "Thank you, Jesus!" I hadn't seen this much action at church since the last revival!

The young woman was helped to her feet and back to her seat, two rows ahead of me. I stared at the back of her head with great curiosity.

"What," I wondered, "could possibly be going through her mind after such an experience?"

No sooner had the thought been formed in my mind, as if in direct response, than the girl began to turn her head around in my direction until she stopped this strange, slow motion with her eyes directly on mine. Those eyes were not human. Not only that, they smoldered with inconceivably depraved and dangerous awareness and cunning that literally glistened from the black depths of her unnaturally enlarged pupils.

What do I mean? I have never seen this precise phenomenon again, though I have most definitely dealt with more horrifying things in my later work as an exorcist. But in this particular instance I had the visceral sensation that I was looking into the eyes of an ancient being, a timeless abomination looking out at me from this girl's physical structure. At some soul-deep level, I recognized—with sensations of bottomless horror and repulsion—something looking back at me that produced, above all, the impression that I was looking into the eyes of the enemy of mankind made manifest. I have long wondered about this sensation, but, at the time, I shook it off and denied such a foolish thought.

Did her eyes look like those of a serpent? Well, yes and no. Yes, they gave that impression in a cold and preternaturally predatory way, but no, there was no physical characteristic about them that I could point to and say that it was serpentine.

The eyes held mine and I felt my mind being probed. It is a sensation of deeper violation than being groped or insulted by a stranger because, at a very deep level, it was an attempt at rapacious appropriation that is so intensely repulsive that the body's own reaction is that of violent sickness. I was almost instantly overcome with nausea and the feeling of the gorge rising in my throat. I tore my eyes away from that hideously lazy gaze and demanded that Larry help me get the children out of there that very instant.

As we were leaving the church I suddenly realized that what I had seen in that young woman's eyes indicated not only that the so-called exorcism had failed, with all the holy members of the church contributing their exhortations and prayers, but also that an evil as old as time itself had been stirred to wakefulness. This was something that would have been better left alone. The gauntlet had been thrown down. I couldn't get away from there fast enough.

When I got home, I decided there would be no more messing around. I wasn't playing games with that creature out there stalking the planet. If a whole crowd of holy deacons and a church full of the Holy Spirit couldn't handle this, extreme measures were called for. Galvanized by the experience, not even bothering to sit and work my way through it rationally to discover any reasonable basis for what I was going to do, I took out the metaphysical books again and read the directions for erecting protective barriers for one's home. With my Bible and a large dish of salt over which I had recited—not nine, but seven—repetitions of the ninety-first psalm, I began the process of "cleaning" my house. My intention was to speak words into the atmosphere of my house, to announce my awareness of what was out there, and to definitely and completely refuse it permission, thereby changing the vibrational frequency. As I walked from room to room, reading the ninety-first psalm—followed by a clear statement, "I know what you are, and I demand you be gone!"—I scattered the salt as a holder of the energy of my words. With all my heart, I imbued my words with my intent, motivated by love for my child and a desperate desire to protect her and my family. There was a sense of outrage and violation that was driving me, and all of these emotions and intentions I directed into the structure of the house and the space inside and out.

Larry wasn't too sure about my behavior at that point. It was not entirely "Biblical," but I was certainly using prayer in an innovative way and he was willing to see if my improvised method had any results. At least he did not interfere.

That night, I dreamed of the dragon. In my dream, he actually very much resembled the animated dragon of the Disney feature *Sleeping Beauty*. But in my dream, he was all too real with his shiny scales and fetid breath, and the stench of sulfur emanating from every aperture of his body. The reality of the terror and unfathomable evil in the dream didn't have any cartoon characteristics, either.

He breathed fire at me. I fought him like the prince in the movie, right to the point where I was backed off a precipice and began to fall into endless blackness. As I tumbled head over heels into the abyss, sensations of futility overcame me, and a sense of grief and mourning for what could have been—what could have existed in the world—tore at my soul. I had lost and the dragon had won. The abject misery of this realization cannot even be conveyed in words. It was the grief of the Universe, not just a single soul.

As I fell in that bottomless pit of hopelessness and despair, from somewhere deep inside me the word "no" formed and I was surprised to feel my descent slow ever so slightly. I looked for the word and its meaning again, and found it: "No." It was imbued with deep meaning of *refusal of despair, refusal of the state of hopelessness*, and most of all, the *refusal of the domination of the fear and terror* evoked by the dragon combined with full awareness of its existence. I spoke it, and again my fall shifted and slowed.

That was interesting, so I began to reach deep inside me for this mind of awareness combined with refusal and to repeat over and over again, like a mantra, the word "no" encompassing this denial of subjection. As I chanted, I stopped falling and began to rise. I chanted "No!" louder and stronger, and my rise accelerated, and soon I was back on the level with the dragon, who seemed a bit surprised to see me again.

He looked as if he could devour me completely and finish the whole episode. His mouth was glistening with dripping, putrid slime. I stood my ground, uncaring of the fact that, in the next moment, I would be consumed. Looking straight into his eyes, full of righteous anger, fully aware of all his tricks and traps, I shouted "No!" over and over again, putting all the force of my will behind it. "No! Even if I die, you have not won because my soul is still mine!" There, with that hideous breath choking me, I exulted in the idea that even if he could destroy my body, he could never take away from me that denial of his power to make me afraid ever again.

And the strangest thing happened. Like a balloon, the dragon began to deflate and shoot and spurt and bounce from side to side, getting smaller with each *spfffft* sound, until nothing but an oily black object lay on the rocky ground of our battle, sinking into the rock from its own weight of evil.

Suddenly, I awoke. My heart was pounding with exertion and I was covered with perspiration. I felt exactly as if I had just actually fought against a fire-breathing dragon.

As soon as my breathing slowed, I got up and went in to check on my children. Their alabaster cheeks were radiant in the ambient moonlight of the bedroom. I breathed their fragrant breath as I brushed their little lips with feathery kisses. Sure, I hoped that there were guardian angels out there watching over them from somewhere. But I wasn't taking any chances.

CHAPTER TWENTY-SEVEN

THE NOAH SYNDROME OR THE LOST LOVE

As I described in overview in Chapter 24, my mother was going off like a loose cannon, supported by church members engaged by her sympathy ploys. My grandmother's cancer had metastasized after staying in remission for eleven years. My brother had betrayed me, taken in by Mother, even against his own grandmother. My cousin and my aunt were dead. There was a haunting and an encounter with pure evil within the church itself. This was the place I found myself, caught up in bizarre experiences, becoming less capable of meeting the family responsibilities on my shoulders, but somehow doing it all anyway.

In the end, it all culminated in Grandma's death. This was in October of 1984.

Within two weeks of her death, we had been evicted from our house by my mother.

We moved to a shack out in the woods on Larry's land, putting most of my furniture, books, and possessions in storage. The only luxury we kept at hand was my piano (which we eventually had to sell to pay bills during one of the endless episodes of Larry's unemployment and concurrent depression).

So: there we were, in a cabin in the woods with no electricity or running water, but we had a baby grand in the corner! Thank God for the piano.

At this point there was the daily struggle to see there was enough food for my small children so they would not have to go to bed hungry at night. Most of the time they didn't have decent shoes to wear, and it was only by charity they had clothes. We went from having two homes, investment property, and a business to literally nothing but a wild piece of land, practically a cardboard box to live in, and hope that we could make it all work by sheer force of will.

In my case, the spirit was willing, but the flesh was oh-so weak! I had the will, but the ability of my body to respond to that will was declining rapidly. I didn't know that I had an autoimmune condition that was progressing rapidly and no doctor I went to during those years ever diagnosed it correctly.

People who have tried living on the land soon find out it's a lot of work. When you have a hand pump in the yard about forty feet from the house, it is a daily ordeal to keep water available for all the normal uses of five people—especially when three of those people are small children. My already compromised physical condition was really not up to that level of work. I was determined to maintain as normal a standard of living as possible, so it was a question of determination and will to continue to do what had to be done against the deterioration of my body.

I was still operating on the idea that my faith was being tested and tried by fire. I often woke up at night in so much psychological and emotional pain at the loss of both my grandmother (actual) and my mother (virtual). The loss of the home of my childhood and my security in financial terms and overwhelming worries for the future of my children were so distressing that I would get up and pace in the darkness, wringing my hands and crying. I would often walk outside in the moonlight to find a quiet, private place and sit and rock and weep in the struggle to continue to find the "love in the moment," so that I could go on another day. During the day, I held such tight control over my emotions that I actually became something of a robot toward the children. I knew that if I gave in to my fears or my grief I would drown in the flood and somebody would have to come and lock me away. I was on the razor's edge of control and what's more, I knew it.

It has taken years for me to be able to articulate what was going on inside me at that point, and, in retrospect, I find that my grandmother's death was another gift, because it was the impetus for change.

When Grandma died, I was at the hospital and, even though they would not let me go to her side while they worked to prolong her life (a stupid thing, considering her age and condition, not to mention the fact that there was a duly signed and witnessed "do not resuscitate" order), I did have a glimpse of her in her last moments. When the fight was finally over, the nurse took me in and left me alone with her still body to say goodbye. I wept long and bitterly while holding her now motionless hand, growing perceptibly cold as I pressed it to my cheek. I understood deeply that this flesh that was my grandmother was no longer my grandmother, no matter how dear and familiar to me every molecule of her body was. Her mortal frame was like a glove that had been cast away after it was worn and threadbare. But her physical form was the only representation of her I had. She and I had interacted through this form. The dynamics of our lives together had been played out through this form. I knew this moment was the last I would look upon her in that structure, so I must look enough to last me the rest of my life.

Without animation, her beloved face was almost unrecognizable; her glorious, clear blue eyes were closed forever; but her hands were still the same hands that I remembered from my childhood. Those hands had never been still; they had been covered with flour from baking some special treat, or busy cleaning, sorting, folding, and washing all the material things in the environment of my childhood. Most of all, they had often been busy fanning me when it was too warm, covering me when it was cold, bathing my face when I was fevered. She was the one whose hands were always busy stroking away my hurts whenever I was sick or unhappy.

My grandmother's name was Lucy.

She had beautiful hands with long, graceful fingers and elegant nails. For a long time I sat in that cold room of the hospital, holding her hand in mine. Finally the nurse came and took me by the shoulders and said I ought to leave. I was so stricken that I allowed her to lead me from the room.

As I stood outside, I panicked and wanted to rush back inside, to throw myself onto her lifeless form, gather her in my arms, and take her with me. But the attendants already were taking her away.

I was then thirty-two years old and my grandmother had been an omnipresent part of my life. After a time, even if the wound is deep, it is covered with a scar, and the new "history" becomes the new way of being; the loss is no longer acutely painful. One becomes accustomed not to expect to hear a certain voice, to see a certain beloved face every day. And this new custom becomes the reality, as though the universe in which one now exists is not the same universe as the former one where the loved one was present.

The question that plagued me was what happens to the love between people when one of them dies. Where does it go?

How can it be that such a bond, one that may be assumed to exist in Platonic noumenal terms, yet which is expressed in physical manifestation, seems suddenly to end when the material body is sealed in the tomb? Why is there this dreadful veil that prevents our access to other realities in terms of certainty?

The *concept* of a chair or an apple or any concrete object is the only truly lasting thing about it. Was love therefore not real because the dynamic exchange ended? No! Every fiber of my being rejected that. Love and kindness, existing only as ideas, are more real in some realm of abstraction, but we have no access. But then, when the dynamic in which those abstractions exist in material terms ceases to be active, where does it go? In what realm does this world of ideas of engendered things exist, be they solid or only ideological?

In the simplest of terms, my thoughts were: *My grandmother is dead; how can I know she still loves me? What am I to do with the love I have to give her? What is the medium of exchange? Is it over?*

Is there no more? If so, then what's the point, damn it?

The answers offered by the Christian faith in which I was inured at that moment suddenly seemed not merely unsatisfactory, but downright insulting to the memory of my grandmother and the bond that had existed between us. The ideas of Spiritualism and the concepts of reincarnation were only slightly helpful. As far as I was concerned, there was no proof. There was a lot of so-called evidence and conjecture; but there was also another side: such evidence was declared to be a satanic delusion to lead us astray. Materialist explanations, based on picking and choosing evidence, are insulting to not only all life, but also the universe as a whole.

But the issue remained. For what purpose is love engendered, and where does it go when the interaction comes to an end?

It's easy to say "love never dies" and that love continues to exist between us and our loved ones who are no longer with us in some "astral" plane or place of the dead; or that we will meet the dear departed at some end-time resurrection. I was not satisfied with "The Lord gives and the Lord takes away; blessed be the name of the Lord." Even worse was: "It's not for us to understand God's ways; it's a Mystery!" And I most definitely wasn't going to have a séance and try to talk to my grandmother. To attempt to resurrect her that way felt blasphemous to the love I had for her, even worse than the idea she was lost to me until some final end-time resurrection.

THE NOAH SYNDROME OR THE LOST LOVE

My entire life as a seeker of truth was focused on the concept of eternal life and the dual pillars of salvation and faith, standing on the foundation of good versus evil.

I attended church one Sunday and listened to a stirring sermon based on the Book of Revelation from the New Testament. I listened carefully, trying to find some solace in this message about the Resurrection, but it seemed to be a fear-inducing rant designed to bring the Christian to his knees in supplication and self-abasement.

What did that have to do with love?

The pastor ended his diatribe with a quotation I am sure was intended to strike fear in the hearts of the congregation. On me, it had quite a different effect. The quote: *"But when the days come that the trumpet call of the seventh angel is about to be sounded, then God's mystery, His secret design, His hidden purpose, as He announced the glad tidings to His servants the prophets, should be fulfilled."*

Now, of course, the entire Christian perspective, in whatever denomination, teaches that the "mystery," this "secret design" or "hidden purpose," is the resurrection of the dead at the "end of time." But it struck me forcibly that, if this was so clearly known, why was John, the author of Revelation, saying quite clearly that there was something we were not being told? What would only be revealed "at the last trumpet"?

More than that, could it have anything to do with my question?

Hearing this was like being handed the end of the thread of Ariadne. I began to pull on it by asking questions and digging for answers, but only within the appropriate framework of the Bible—at least for the moment.

* * *

The child I was carrying at the time my grandmother died was born in the spring of 1985. The entire pregnancy was spent mourning for my grandmother. This was especially poignant because she would be the first baby I could not bring home and put directly in Grandma's arms for her to love and rock and sing to. She was the main member of my support team, and the organizer and leader of the "baby fan club" in our house. My babies were wonderfully enriched by her devotion to each of them.

It was an extremely difficult delivery for me and the new baby. My heart ached for my poor little one who had been injured in the birth process. When she was finally laid in my arms, right away I noticed her incredible little hands—exactly like my grandmother's. In fact, so much like them that I felt this was almost like a message from her.

Not only that, but the baby had a strawberry hematoma on her left ankle. My grandmother had broken her left ankle when I was a child, and it had required surgery to repair it. Ever afterward, it was swollen and red in exactly the same place that my baby's hematoma was situated.

My baby had also suffered a broken left collarbone during delivery, which made it impossible for her to use her tiny arm for several weeks. My grandmother had undergone a radical mastectomy on the left side that made it impossible for her to use her left arm for long periods of time.

Grandma had died of lung cancer (she never smoked), which meant that she essentially drowned in her own lung fluids. At birth, my baby had been unable to breathe or cry because her lungs were full of a thick, sticky fluid. It was a couple of very tense minutes while the hospital staff worked frantically to clean out her lungs and get her to breathe. Her lungs were so weak that her cry was like a little kitten mewing for months after her birth.

At about the same time, the collarbone healed, the strawberry hematoma disappeared, and her lungs improved, so I no longer sat up all night making sure she was breathing. Today, her hands are her own. But for that time, when I was most desperately grieving that my grandmother was no longer present to greet the new baby, I had received some small comfort from these signs of love that never dies.

Was my grandmother reincarnated into my fourth child? I don't know. Yes, they are very much alike in many ways—most notably in the desire to care for and see to the comfort and happiness of others—but I don't think about it anymore. She is who she is, a wonderful and extraordinary young lady with brains, talent, beauty, and, most important of all, a loving soul.

As a result of the injuries I had received during the delivery, I was bedridden for many months. There I was, living in the woods, isolated from family and friends; I had four little children to care for and I couldn't even walk. My oldest child was only six, and the responsibility for the care of her brother and sister, as well as her mother and the new baby, fell on her. She was smart, talented, and a real trooper, but it was clearly not a healthy situation.

On top of this soul-deep grief I was still unable to resolve, I was frustrated and irritable at not being able to do anything about my physical condition. Not only had I lost nearly everything I loved, I had now lost my health.

Since I could no longer maintain my very active participation in life in a physical way, I was forced—by the Universe, as it were—to find other outlets for my energy. I decided this would be the perfect time to master the art of meditation. Prompted by the little signs that appeared during this birth, I felt compelled to investigate this question of eternal life. I decided the only way I could accomplish this objective was to be able to truly open my heart to God, so He could infuse me with this "something" that obviously I so desperately lacked. Thus, the idea grew in me that I must still my own voice, both internal and external, so that I could hear daily the voice that betokens God's presence within.

I searched the Bible for clues. Having taught meditation, self-hypnosis, and other relaxation techniques, I knew all of these were ways many people claim to make contact with their "higher self." But, being on the faith trip, whatever I did had to be within the guidelines I had accepted for my life. I found a reference in Psalms: *"Let the words of my mouth and the meditations of my heart be acceptable unto thee, Oh Lord."*

Well, that clinched it for me! There it was, right in the Bible. I began to meditate using that very phrase as my mantra, since that seemed to be the acceptable way to do it by the rules. And it was at this point that things began to really happen.

Several years earlier I had found a book on a bargain table in a bookstore entitled *In Search of the Miraculous* by P. D. Ouspensky. The blurb on the cover said: *"The noted author of* Tertium Organum *combines the logic of a mathematician with the vision of a mystic in his quest for solutions to the problems of Man and the Universe."* Since it was a bargain and promised to reveal secrets about our world, naturally, I bought it immediately. When I got home with it and tried to read it, it proved to be rather dry, and I gave it up. It had lain on the shelf ever after.

I had continued, to a great extent, my reading habits through the past few years, though there had been considerable restriction on the time I was allowed to give to it. Larry resented the fact that I liked to read before going to sleep, and there were many nights when I sat up alone, shivering in the cold, to read what I considered to be my necessary daily allowance of intellectual input.

But now that I was bedridden, the door was wide open to reading as much as I liked. In that sense, it was a blessing. So, I remembered this book that I had put aside; it seemed that a book that promised insight to the issues I was struggling with—even a very dry book—didn't seem like such a bad idea when I could do nothing else. I asked for it, and soon it was located and brought to me.

I realized pretty quickly that this book would go to the top of the list of "forbidden works" according to the elders of our church, but I didn't care. After my experiences with the church over the past few years, my reliance on the pastoral care offered within Christianity was rapidly being undermined. I was still on guard against "evil ideas," but I was sure that I could filter out anything too "dangerous" in a work that promised insight on the issues for which I was seeking answers.

Everything was fine for about seventeen pages, and I was getting into the style of writing and found it to be deeply interesting and then—well—then this mysterious "G" (about whom I knew nothing) made a remark that completely knocked the wind out of my still mostly fundamentalist sails. In response to Ouspensky's speculation that, in the industrial age, humans were becoming more "mechanized" and had stopped thinking, Gurdjieff said:

"There is another kind of mechanization which is much more dangerous: being a machine oneself. Have you ever thought about the fact that all people themselves are machines? ... Look, all those people you see are simply machines—nothing more. ... You think there is something that chooses its own path, something that can stand against mechanization; you think that not everything is equally mechanical."

At this point, Ouspensky raised the very argument that was forming in my own mind: *"Why, of course not! ... Art, poetry, thought, are phenomena of quite a different order."*

Gurdjieff replied: *"Of exactly the same order. These activities are just as mechanical as everything else. Men are machines and nothing but mechanical actions can be expected of machines."*

I was so enraged that I snapped the book shut and threw it against the wall.

How dare he say such a terrible thing about human beings! How dare he deny the reality of the spirit, the sublimity of music and mysticism and the salvation of Christ! I'm surprised that steam didn't issue from my head. I was hot with outrage.

But, it had been said. The seed of the thought had been planted in my mind. After a while, my curiosity about such a concept came to the fore. I began to mull over the issue *in an attempt to find ways to disprove it*.

I mused over my own life, all my interactions with other people, significantly my own mother, and gradually, I began to realize that there was, indeed, something mysteriously "mechanical" about the interactions between human beings. I thought about the many people I had worked with therapeutically using hypnosis, and how mechanical the therapy was, and how the roots of most of their problems were rather like mechanical and conditioned reactions to their perceptions and observations. Generally, it seemed, these perceptions were erroneous, and it was the error of this mechanical thinking that created the problems in the first place.

But, over and over again, their problems and the ways they formed and operated, as well as the therapeutic solutions themselves, were, essentially, mechanical. It was like a formula. With just a few hints from the person, I could almost immediately see the whole dynamic of their past and the formation of their problem, as well as the mechanical way to solve it. I applied the technique, and just like changing the wires and spark plugs in a car, it made them start firing on all cylinders again.

Okay, so the guy had a point. But clearly, those people who were "saved" were saved from being mechanical, right? I wanted to find out if he had anything to say about that. I called one of the children to retrieve the book for me and I continued to read. The question was asked: "*Can it be said that man possesses immortality?*"

Gurdjieff's reply was fascinating:

"*Immortality is one of the qualities we ascribe to people without having a sufficient understanding of their meaning. Other qualities of this kind are 'individuality,' in the sense of an inner unity, a 'permanent and unchangeable I,' 'consciousness,' and 'will.' All these qualities can belong to man, but this certainly does not mean that they do belong to him or belong to each and every one.*

"*In order to understand what man is at the present time, that is, at the present level of development, it is necessary to imagine to a certain extent what he can be, that is, what he can attain. Only by understanding the correct sequence of development possible will people cease to ascribe to themselves what, at present, they do not possess, and what, perhaps, they can only acquire after great effort and great labor.*

"According to an ancient teaching, traces of which may be found in many systems, old and new, a man who has attained the full development possible for man, a man in the full sense of the word, consists of four bodies. These four bodies are composed of substances which gradually become finer and finer, mutually interpenetrate one another, and form four independent organisms, standing in a definite relationship to one another but capable of independent action."

Gurdjieff's idea was that it was possible for these four bodies to exist because the physical human body has such a complex organization that, under certain favorable conditions, a new and independent organism actually can develop and grow within it.

This new system of organs of perception can afford a more convenient and responsive instrument for the activity of an awakened consciousness.

"The consciousness manifested in this new body is capable of governing it, and it has full power and full control over the physical body. In this second body, under certain conditions, a third body can grow, again having characteristics of its own. The consciousness manifested in this third body has full power and control over the first two bodies; and the third body possesses the possibility of acquiring knowledge inaccessible either to the first or to the second body. In the third body, under certain conditions, a fourth can grow, which differs as much from the third as the third differs from the second, and the second from the first. The consciousness manifested in the fourth body has full control over the first three bodies and itself.

"These four bodies are defined in different teachings in various ways. The first is the physical body, in Christian terminology the 'carnal' body; the second, in Christian terminology, is the 'natural' body; the third is the 'spiritual' body; and the fourth, in the terminology of esoteric Christianity, is the 'divine' body. In theosophical terminology the first is the 'physical' body, the second is the 'astral,' the third is the 'mental,' and the fourth the 'causal.'

"In the terminology of certain Eastern teachings the first body is the 'carriage' (the body), the second is the 'horse' (feelings, desires), the third the 'driver' (mind), and the fourth the 'master' (I, consciousness, will).

"Such comparisons and parallels may be found in most systems and teachings which recognize something more in man than the physical body. But almost all these teachings, while repeating in a more or less familiar form the definitions and divisions of the ancient teaching, have forgotten or omitted its most important feature, which is: that man is not born with *the finer bodies. They can only be artificially cultivated in him, provided favorable conditions both internal and external are present.*

"*The 'astral body' is not an indispensable implement for man. It is a great luxury which only a few can afford. A man can live quite well without an 'astral body.' His physical body possesses all the functions necessary for life. A man without 'astral body' may even produce the impression of being a very intellectual or even spiritual man, and may deceive not only others but also himself.*

"*When the third body has been formed and has acquired all the properties, powers, and knowledge possible for it, there remains the problem of fixing this knowledge and these powers. Because, having been imparted to it by influences of a certain kind, they may be taken away by these same influences or by others. By means of a special kind of work for all three bodies the acquired properties may be made the permanent and inalienable possession of the third body.*

"*The process of fixing these acquired properties corresponds to the process of the formation of the fourth body.*

"*And only the man who possesses four fully developed bodies can be called a 'man' in the full sense of the word. This man possesses many properties which ordinary man does not possess. One of these properties is immortality. All religions and all ancient teachings contain the idea that, by acquiring the fourth body, man acquires immortality; and they all contain indications of the ways to acquire the fourth body, that is, immortality.*"

The book went flying again.

I was outraged. But this time, my indignation lasted only a very short time. Again, in thinking over the many clues about human beings I had been collecting all my life, including those derived from observing myself, I saw something very deeply true being said here. As much as I might not like it, I could not deny the fact it was certainly a hypothesis supported by observation.

Hints of these matters did occur in the Bible, though they were among the most obscure references. Preachers and theologians generally tended to leave them strictly alone. At least seventeen times in the New Testament, it's noted that Jesus taught his disciples in secret. The teachings of Jesus in the Bible itself consist only of his purported public discourses.

There was a lot missing, and Gurdjieff spoke as one with authority. What's more, it rang of truth.

The book was retrieved again. I was curious to see what further remarks might be made about Christianity. Ouspensky asked the same question I would have asked myself:

"For a man of Western culture, it is of course difficult to believe and to accept the idea that an ignorant fakir, a naïve monk, or a yogi who has retired from life may be on the way to evolution while an educated European, armed with 'exact knowledge' and all the latest methods of investigation, has no chance whatever and is moving in a circle from which there is no escape." Gurdjieff answered:

"Yes, that is because people believe in progress and culture. There is no progress whatever. Everything is just the same as it was thousands, and tens of thousands, of years ago. The outward form changes. The essence does not change. Man remains just the same. 'Civilized' and 'cultured' people live with exactly the same interests as the most ignorant savages. Modern civilization is based on violence and slavery and fine words.

"... What do you expect? People are machines. Machines have to be blind and unconscious, they cannot be otherwise, and all their actions have to correspond to their nature. Everything happens. No one does anything. 'Progress' and 'civilization,' in the real meaning of these words, can appear only as the result of conscious efforts. They cannot appear as the result of unconscious mechanical actions. And what conscious effort can there be in machines? And if one machine is unconscious, then a hundred machines are unconscious, and so are a thousand machines, or a hundred thousand, or a million. And the unconscious activity of a million machines must necessarily result in destruction and extermination. It is precisely in unconscious involuntary manifestations that all evil lies. You do not yet understand and cannot imagine all the results of this evil. But the time will come when you will understand."

And Gurdjieff was right.

He was speaking at the beginning of the first world war, in the opening rounds of a century of unprecedented warfare.

My copy of *In Search of the Miraculous* flew across the room at least a dozen more times. I fumed and raged inside each time I was confronted with an idea that, upon reflection and comparison to my observations and experiences, seemed a far better explanation of the dynamics of human existence than anything I had ever read in my life.

As for this "unconscious evil" that Gurdjieff mentioned, he explained in the Tale of the Evil Magician:

"*A very rich magician had a great many sheep. But at the same time this magician was very mean. He did not want to hire shepherds, nor did he want to erect a fence about the pasture where his sheep were grazing. The sheep consequently often wandered into the forest, fell into ravines, and so on, and above all they ran away, for they knew that the magician wanted their flesh and skins and this they did not like.*

"*At last the magician found a remedy. He hypnotized his sheep and suggested to them first of all that they were immortal and that no harm was being done to them when they were skinned. On the contrary, it would be very good for them and even pleasant. Secondly he suggested that the magician was a good master who loved his flock so much that he was ready to do anything in the world for them. In the third place he suggested to them that if anything at all were going to happen to them it was not going to happen just then, at any rate not that day, and therefore they had no need to think about it. Further, the magician suggested to his sheep that they were not sheep at all; to some of them he suggested that they were lions, to others that they were eagles, to others that they were men, and to others that they were magicians.*

"*And after this all his cares and worries about the sheep came to an end. They never ran away again but quietly awaited the time when the magician would require their flesh and skins.*"

Ouspensky wrote that theoretically, a man could awaken. But in practice this is almost impossible. As soon as a man awakens for a moment and opens his eyes, all the forces that caused him to fall asleep in the first place begin to act on him with tenfold energy. He immediately falls asleep again, very often dreaming that he is awake.

When I read this I immediately thought of the pastor who conducted that farcical effort to get me to speak in tongues and the so-called exorcism, the same pastor who'd been taken in by my mother's manipulations. Could it be possible that he was one of those described in Gurdjieff's tale as being hypnotized into believing that he was a magician? How many other people had I met who claimed to "know" things, but the evidence of their lives, their actions, did not support their claims?

I also thought about my study of the history of man in my search for the justification of God, and how I had come to see it as the biography of Satan.

I was beginning to realize that something was very wrong with the picture of the world that we are taught from the moment we are born and that is further implemented in our culture, our society, and most especially our religions.

I thought back over my life and realized that all the events that had gradually maneuvered me into my present position could most definitely be perceived as the "forces that act to keep a person asleep." It was a certainty that some tremendous pressure had been applied to stop me from observing, from analyzing, and most of all from thinking and learning.

The question was: who or what was the true nature of the evil magician?

Reading this book sort of jump-started my thinking processes, which had lain fallow for some time now. Unconsciously, I was establishing a regimen of deep and intense thinking, alternating with the stopping of thinking that was achieved during meditation. My meditations seemed to progress quite rapidly. I had heard that achieving just a few minutes of deep contemplation was difficult and often took years of practice, but it seemed that I rapidly achieved that point and soon was able to enter a rather "timeless" state for what proved to be somewhat extended periods of time.

After my regular meditation exercises, I would sit up in bed, surrounded by piles of books and notebooks, reading and writing notes on what I read. As I did so, I would stop and think about questions that occurred to me as I read. The instant these questions were framed in my mind, thoughts would simply pour into my head so fast that I was mentally leaping and jumping just to follow them. These thoughts always and only came in response to the questions that I would pose mentally about whatever I was considering at the moment in my studies. The urge to write these thoughts down was so overwhelming that I spent literally hours a day, filling page after page in longhand, until I felt completely drained mentally and physically. I still have these notebooks. Because these questions had little to do with matters of faith or religion, it didn't occur to me that I was "channeling" at the time. I was just "thinking."

But, there was a curious thing about this "thinking." If I didn't write the thoughts down, they would stay there, backing up like dammed-up water. As soon as I started to write again, it was as if there had been no break in the flow of thoughts whatsoever. They picked up right where they left off.

At some point, I decided that I must find out if these ideas that were coming to me had any basis in fact whatsoever. I most definitely needed more input. So the answers that came to me pointed me in the direction of certain studies that otherwise might not have been part of my experience. I was compelled by my rational and reflective nature to research each concept to discover if there was any way it could be supported scientifically and objectively.

I subscribed to a library service by mail and soon began ordering and reading book after book on subjects that ranged from geology to physics, from psychology to theology, from metaphysics to astronomy. As I read, I found many pieces that fit in the framework of the information that was pouring into my head relating to these very subjects. I was both surprised and energized to find that the ideas I was getting weren't so crazy after all!

While assembling my notes and ideas, I included notes from more mainstream sources that supported what I had written or expanded the idea, or, at the very least, gave it plausibility. If the idea I had was not supported by observation or scholarly opinion, if only indirectly, it had to be discarded. As it happens, the whole series of information streams did turn out to have a wide array of support, and I was forced to severely limit what I included for the sake of brevity.

During the entire time I was working on this project, Larry repeatedly criticized and ridiculed my efforts. He decided that if I could sit up and read and write, I was clearly able to do everything else. He was openly vocal in this way, in front of the children, telling me that it was obvious that I didn't want to be a wife and mother anymore or I would get well faster. This, naturally, led to terrible interactions between us, leaving me in a state of helpless frustration and terror that he would walk out and never come back. It wasn't so much the idea of his absence that made me afraid as it was the consequences of his absence: I knew that I was unable to take care of myself, much less the children. If Larry left, I would lose them, too.

At this point, I was still struggling to work within my faith, with a strong Christian perspective. I wasn't quite yet able to let go of the crutch of the church. That was soon to change, however.

* * *

One Sunday, after I had recovered most of my mobility, I was sitting in church during the pastoral prayer. I was praying hard along with the minister that God would send the Holy Spirit to me to help me understand all that I needed to understand. Suddenly, I heard a buzzing noise, or a crackling sound, similar to the sound of bacon sizzling in the pan. The voice of the pastor and the resonant "amens" from the congregation became very far away and metallic sounding, exactly as if I were hearing them broadcast from a loudspeaker under water.

This shocked me and my eyes snapped open to see if my vision was impaired. I thought I might be having a stroke. I was completely dismayed to see the minister, standing at the podium, gripping the stand with both hands, eyes closed and head thrown back in the profound drama of his praying, was overlaid with a shimmering, living image of a *wolf*.

The image of the wolf, in full color, was a sort of alter ego. All the expressions of the pastor were corrupted and twisted by the matching expressions of the wolf. When the minister moved his hands or shook his head, so did the wolf. Every move of the minister's mouth was exactly matched by the gaping jaws of the toothy figure from hell. Not a solid figure, it seemed more like a projection of light, so to speak.

I quickly looked around the sanctuary to see if this was a complete delusion, and was shocked to see similar overlays on all the people there. Many of them were sheep, but there were also pigs and cows and other creatures represented.

I was *horrified*. Considering the fairly recent experiences with the haunting and the demoniac woman at church, I was sure that the Devil had me now! Here I was, in the middle of church, seeing our beloved Minister in the guise of a *wolf*.

This was damnation for certain!

I closed my eyes and prayed harder. The sound anomaly continued. I opened my eyes to peek again. The wolf was still there, dramatizing the mellifluously intoned pastoral prayer.

I squeezed my eyes tightly shut and prayed and rebuked Satan and finally began to just repeat the Lord's Prayer to drive this image from my reality. Soon, it began to taper off and die away. When I opened my eyes again, the wolf was gone.

I was extremely relieved to win this battle with Satan.

A couple of Sundays later, we arrived a little late, expecting the services to be already started. We were surprised to see the congregation all gathered outside the church door, milling about like lost sheep. We discovered that our beloved pastor, the shepherd of the flock for a number of years now, the respected and erudite minister of the golden voice, along with his musically talented family had done a midnight flit, so to speak. Not only that, but they had left the church in a bad way, having embezzled a huge amount of money. There was even a bill for dock rent for a rather large yacht that the church was also paying for, unbeknownst to all. The expensive furnishings of the luxurious parsonage were gone, the mortgages on both buildings were on the verge of foreclosure, the electricity was about to be shut off … and the pastor and his family were gone to parts unknown.

I was stunned. I realized that my "vision" was exactly what I had been praying for: the Holy Spirit revealing the truth to me. I had rebuked it and cast it away!

The implications of this event were profound. When I put it together with all the other things that had occurred over the past few years, I saw a picture that was not pleasant to acknowledge.

There are those who would say that it didn't matter about the pastor being a fraud, that it is the faith of the individual and their own interaction with God through Jesus that really counts. And, I will agree. That is, in fact, my point. Because, in the end, following the prescribed pathway of a standard religion, praying in sincerity and faith, conducting my life in all the ways predicated upon being "born again," I was given a certain mandate to learn. In the process of trying to implement this mandate within my faith, I was then given a vision that proved correct. It was only reasonable to think that I was moving in the right direction—even if that direction was taking me straight out of organized, standard Christianity.

This resulted in a shift in my faith in my own ability to be in touch with God, or whoever was in charge of this universe. Clearly, I had been shown the truth under the surface, and my self-doubts and belief in the authority of others had interfered with my communion with Holy Spirit. This gave my studies a little boost. I understood an essential thing: if you truly pray for guidance, deeply and sincerely, that guidance will come. But it may not be what you want to hear or believe, and may go against what others say or teach—especially if what they say and teach is not supported by evidence and action. In later years, this ability to "see" the reality of individuals, the force behind them, has saved me from terrible mistakes, even if very often I am fooled at the beginning. I have accepted many people at their word, but when certain observational discrepancies begin to appear, I will "ask the question," and what I see always proves to be correct. But it only works when the question is asked. At this point in my life, the time of writing, I am finally learning to "ask the question" before I become involved with wolves in sheep's clothing.

I had faith, I prayed diligently and fervently, I struggled and strove for that love, that subsuming of all other emotions into an all-pervasive, comprehensive love of God—and it surely did something!

But this, of course, raises another question: If a number of people are claiming that the Holy Spirit is giving them revelations, and these revelations are contradictory to one another, how do we know who is being misled and who is truly receiving divine revelation?

Again, the answer was "Learn!"

* * *

In the early days of 1986 I was greatly troubled by a dream.

I found myself in a cold, barren landscape, accompanied by my children. We were viewing what seemed to be a most peculiar tornado at a great distance. It was a loosely curled cloud of smoke, more like a stretched-out bedspring than a funnel. I was puzzled because it did not touch the ground, yet I knew it was killing people. I felt very sad in the dream and I was overwhelmed by the bleakness of the landscape. In the dream, I was reminded of Poe's story "The Fall of the House of Usher." In the dream, I told my children there was no possibility of the tornado coming our way, but that we must pray for those we were seeing die.

On numerous other occasions during these years, I had dreamed flashes of disasters only to awaken and discover that something bearing strong similarity had occurred during the night somewhere around the globe. So, I expected to hear of a tornado striking somewhere and killing people, and I turned on the radio to catch the news. Apparently I was wrong. There were no disasters during the night, but I was pleased to hear that my urge to turn on the radio had informed me that I was up in time to view the shuttle launch.

The children and I trooped out into the cold with binoculars and began to search the sky over the tops of the winter bare trees in the woods surrounding our house. We saw a bright flash, which we assumed to be the staging of the rocket, and I focused the glasses on that area of the sky. What I saw was the peculiar curling cloud of my dream. At that moment I experienced an appalling sensation of sadness that I tried to shake off as silly, even though I had suddenly become aware of the likeness of the moment to the events of the dream.

I kept my eyes on the smoke as I listened to the radio announcer saying that some sort of problem was being experienced. We soon learned that the Challenger had exploded and all aboard were lost.

The only discrepancy between my dream and the actual event was the interpretation. I had interpreted my dream in terms of familiarity: a tornado, although I had been puzzled by the peculiar antics of this dream tornado. I had seen a powerful, moving, death-dealing force in the sky—with cloud-like effects—which did not make contact with the ground, and which did not threaten me or my household. What I saw was, in fact, what I got! But, I had never seen a rocket blow up—or, at least, did not consider that to be a possibility.

And, I might add, the central issue in the Poe story of the Usher family is *premature burial*. That element of the dream has always haunted me. Did our astronauts go to their watery tomb alive?

But even if I had understood the symbols of the dream and had rightly interpreted them, so what? What was I going to do? Call NASA and say, "Hey folks, I had this really weird dream ..." Of course they would pass me off to the nutcase desk or put me on permanent hold with Muzak. What about all the other purported "prophecies" which are sort of "close," or "stunningly accurate," or complete failures? What is the real principle behind this?

Again I went back to the Bible. I came across a most interesting story in II Chronicles, Chapter 18, which I would like to paraphrase:

Once upon a time there were two kings of two small kingdoms who were related by marriage. The first king decided to pay a visit to his brother-in-law, the second king. When he arrived for his visit, he was welcomed by the second king, who had prepared all sorts of goodies and entertainment.

After a great deal of feasting and merriment, the second king told his brother-in-law, the first king, that he was inclined to think of all of his possessions as mutual and he hoped the first king felt the same. This made the first king a bit nervous and he wondered what all of this was leading up to. He was not long in finding out. The second king wanted to make war against one of his neighbors and take territory and spoil, but in order to do this, he needed help. He knew that his brother-in-law had no such ambitions, and he and been softening him up to ask for his aid.

The first king was a bit taken aback at this request and asked if they could call in some prophets to find out if this plan was a wise course to pursue. The second king willingly called four hundred prophets. All of them, to a man, commended the plan and praised the acumen and ambition of their king. But the first king was still uneasy. He asked if there was not one more prophet to consult. As it turned out, there was, but the second king warned the first king not to expect much from this fellow. There was hatred between them and this bad feeling made the last prophet prejudiced against the second king. Having thoroughly assassinated the last prophet's character, he then called him in.

Sure enough, the last prophet contradicted all four hundred of the other prophets and told the second king that he would die if he went into battle. To punish this rudeness, the second king had the offending oracle cast into prison to think about his audacity until the return of the kings and the army. Insisting that his prophecy was true, the last prophet commented to the king that he would certainly be amazed if they returned.

But the wicked second king had a plan. Having persuaded his brother-in-law to accompany him, he arranged to go into battle dressed as a common soldier, while his relation went attired in his kingly robes.

As it turned out, enemy soldiers had been instructed to immediately seek out and kill only the second king. During the course of the engagement, the enemy soldiers chased after the only man attired as a king, and, finding him to not be the man they were after, they turned in rage and frustration and killed the nearest common soldier—who happened to be the evil second king.

Prophecy fulfilled.

Prophecy may be inexorable in some unknown terms unless fundamental alterations in activity and direction are made by knowing things that are not apparent on the surface. And a true prophecy very often manifests in the very same ratio depicted in this story: four hundred to one. A third, and no less important lesson: people seldom want to hear the truth. And, finally, the easiest way to avoid truth is to assassinate either the speaker or his character.

As I moved deeper into my research on the issues of "the great mystery of God" that is supposed to be revealed at the "end of time," I kept coming across references to a certain Immanuel Velikovsky, and a book entitled *Worlds in Collision*. Even though many of the commentaries written about this book were highly derogatory, because of the story about the four hundred prophets, I wanted to know what engendered so much outrage. I was fortunate to find my book at a sale at the library. Right on top, in the front stack of discards, was *Worlds in Collision*. I paid ten cents for a first edition.

I took my prize home and began to read. As I read, the scales fell from my eyes and the final pieces of the puzzle of the "mystery of God" fell into place.

* * *

These little supporting events that transpired through my seeking for answers showed me another thing about "asking." If a question is asked of the Universe, if it is asked deeply and honestly, the actual events of one's life begin to shape themselves to provide the tools with which one is enabled to obtain the answer. It's not free; it takes work. But for those who ask and keep on asking, those who knock and keep on knocking, it seems the door does, indeed, open.

I realized I was being taught a language of symbols and how God speaks to us in these symbols, and these symbols are our reality. Symbols reflect actual potentials, even though our interpretations may be skewed by personal experience. I began to realize that it must be in such terms that the ancient prophets and writers of religious myths understood the world. They described their visions and experiences in highly allegorical and culturally biased terms. Thus heavenly bodies became angels, archangels; cataclysmic events were deliberate "acts of God," and stupefying groanings and thunderings of nature became the voice of God. And, all things considered, who are we to say this perception of celestial beings and divinely inspired events is not more accurate than one would initially suppose?

As I pulled on the thread of Ariadne, it seemed the entire fabric of my religion, as it was taught, unraveled and there, concealed behind the metaphors of the Bible, supported by facts and ideas of science, was an idea so amazing that it took my breath away.

The idea was *Cosmic Metamorphosis in Quantum terms.*

How did I come to this when I started out trying to discover the noumenal existence of love and good and evil? Well, actually, it's quite simple. As I followed the thread through the labyrinth, going from the very large to the very small, it became clear to me that the Hermetic maxim "as above, so below" could be applied in any number of useful ways. In the end, the search for the true meaning of love was the same as the search for salvation and faith and, ultimately, the search for the meaning of eternal life.

The fact that the "great mystery of God" was to be revealed at the "time of the end" prompted me to gather together all I could on this eschatological theme.

In Matthew 24, Jesus gives a discourse on the end times, that period in which the last trumpet will sound and the mystery of God will be revealed. He remarks: *"... as were the days of Noah, so will be the coming of the son of man. For just as in those days before the flood they were eating and drinking, marrying and being given in marriage, until the day when Noah went into the Ark, and they did not know or understand until the flood came and swept them all away, so will be the coming of the Son of man."*

This event, the End, the time when *"God's mystery — His secret design, His hidden purpose — as He announced the glad tidings to His servants the prophets, should be fulfilled,"* was compared to the "days of Noah."

Well, what's so mysterious about a flood? What's so happy about most of the population of the planet being wiped out of existence? How can you call that "glad tidings"?

The key seemed to be held in the concept of the ark. My search for the true meaning of love, salvation, faith, and eternal life was, essentially, a search for the *meaning* of the ark. Metaphorically speaking, there is no better expression of this search than the story of Noah and the ark. All quests of life and love and existence can be expressed in this story of a man, faced with the destruction of his world—and in this case, it was literally destruction of the entire world, or so the story goes—who sets about *building an ark*.

Clearly, "building an ark" was considered to be an aberration in the time of Noah. His behavior was obviously looked upon askance by those around him. A syndrome is a group of signs and symptoms that collectively characterize or indicate a particular disease or abnormal condition. I thought about this in two ways. First, the signs and symptoms of our reality that tell us that the body of the cosmos is not well; and second, the signs and symptoms of those individuals who perceive this are, in a microcosmic way, reflecting the same syndrome.

In another sense, a syndrome can also describe certain insects who, when they have achieved a certain stage of growth, begin to manifest a group of signs and symptoms that cause them to build a cocoon in which metamorphosis takes place.

Those who feel that the reality is "right" or "well" naturally think those who believe otherwise are "diseased" in their minds or souls. And such "infected" people, who undertake to act in terms of "building an Ark," whether it is spiritual or material, will most definitely be seen as experiencing the syndrome of the cosmic disease in themselves. It will not be recognized that their extreme discomfort and dissatisfaction with the world is the syndrome that precedes cocooning. Thus, the Noah Syndrome characterizes the conditions of the planet as well as the experiences of those who sense the impending metamorphosis.

Exactly what is this process of metamorphosis, and exactly what constitutes an ark of safety?

I realized this was the question around which my thinking had revolved since I could remember: An ark, a place of safety, transformation and restoration of the Edenic state where there is direct communion with God.

I finished the research and notes for my book that I titled *The Noah Syndrome* on December 16, 1986. I went out and bought an old manual typewriter and began to type up my book from notes in longhand. By the time I was done with the manuscript, I was a real hotshot on that old manual typewriter!

As I typed, I began to have some very strange impressions. I could sense, or see with the mind's eye, a couple of very funny old men looking over my shoulder as I wrote, consulting with each other, telling me where I needed to make corrections or additions, and even chuckling with glee when I wrote certain comments. I knew that one of them somewhat resembled Albert Einstein, but it wasn't until quite a number of years had passed that I saw a photograph of Immanuel Velikovsky and recognized the other old gentleman.

To this day, I am not sure if they were simply figments of my overworked imagination, or if it was an actual experience with some form of discarnate guidance. All I know is they were hysterically funny in their remarks to one another as they oversaw my project, and they jovially clapped one another on the shoulder when I would finally "get it" in regard to a particular point.

After it was done, I sent it to a literary agent, paying $200.00 to have it read and evaluated. It was naturally rejected. I put my manuscript away for many years. And when the Internet became available to people around the world, I brought *The Noah Syndrome* into a new form. Now it has undergone a third metamorphosis. It became the starting point for an expanded work that has taken me far from my original quest: *The Secret History of the World and How to Get Out Alive*.

It is truly strange, in retrospect, that my efforts to "find my ark" ultimately led to being "found by my Ark" ... my husband, Arkadiusz. But, that is getting ahead of things ...

CHAPTER TWENTY-EIGHT

THE ARK IN MONTANA

When I think about the "Boat Ride to Damascus," it is exactly a metaphor for my life as a born-again Christian. The moment of truth, of course, was symbolized by the trap of the anchor that nearly pulled me to a watery grave. Moving out of that spiritual-psychological framework was exactly as problematical as the long and dangerous journey home, quartering the waves.

The year following my original work on *The Noah Syndrome*, and my emergence from the straitjacket of Christian fundamentalism I had donned, thinking it was a life-jacket, has to rank as one of the worst years of my life. It was actually so awful that I am not even sure of the sequence of events. But they are so important to later connections that I need to make some sense of it all. Please bear with me.

My research led me to the idea of a global holocaust in humanity's future. Certain people who had such awareness were inspired to act in faith by "building an ark," and so they survived the cyclical cataclysms of the planet down through the ages. Since I had this awareness, I searched for safe places and precisely what one must do in order to survive.

Larry had an old fishing buddy, Jim, who had joined the army as a career. His father had built a beautiful home out there in the woods, and occasionally we visited them, most often when Jim was home from Europe, where he was stationed for many years.

One day, unexpectedly, Jim came to see us. We were surprised to see him at home since he had been on leave not too long before. This trip was not a pleasure visit: his father had died of a sudden heart attack. Jim was home to help his mother take care of the estate. They were sorting through things so she could sell the house and move (apparently, she didn't like living so far away from everything), and he knew I liked to read, so would I like this trunk full of his father's books? Sure!

Based on the kinds of books in that trunk, Jim's father, a retired army major, was apparently interested in "government conspiracy." I will never forget the feeling that came over me when I read *None Dare Call it Conspiracy* by Gary Allen. Everything in this book just slotted into place with the teachings of Gurdjieff and Ouspensky that man is asleep and under the control of an evil magician.

I realized that the evil magician was a metaphor, at least in part, for political and historical control systems. This realization was, once again, devastating to my illusions. As Gary Allen suggests, without any intelligent control, 50% of the time events would occur in social, cultural, and political spheres leading to great benefit for all. Factoring in intelligent decisions to do good would bring this average up to about 70% of events. I could clearly see this wasn't reflected in our reality. Man hasn't stopped killing his brother; he has just developed more efficient and mechanical means of doing it.

Why? Who or what is influencing events to the negative?

Putting Allen's ideas together with Gurdjieff's, it seemed merely the result of certain mechanical laws of the universe that humans refer to as "good" and "evil." These laws were cyclical and could be better expressed in terms of physics. And that, of course, is the thread I followed to the idea of Cosmic Quantum Metamorphosis.

Naturally, an awareness of an impending global holocaust made me think about my relationships with others in somewhat different terms. I decided that I needed to make amends with my mother. I still loved her and certainly didn't want to think of her as being "left behind."

So, taking a copy of Noah in a box, we drove over to visit her. It was a somewhat uncomfortable encounter, but I gave the boxed manuscript to her, asked her to read it, and said I would visit again to discuss it.

I also decided to send a copy to Eva. She and I had kept up a correspondence by mail since my marriage to Larry, but she lived so far away now that it wasn't easy to visit.

When I sent Noah to Eva, I wanted her to understand so that we could think about plans for "building the ark." Her response was less than enthusiastic. While I'd been lost in the fundamentalist forest, Eva had become deeply involved in the work of Lama Sing and other New Age channeled sources. Most believed that earth changes were an easily avoidable problem if people just "harmonically converged" or "visualized love and light" surrounding the planet and, most of all, focused only on positive things. Thinking about negativity created it, and even learning about it was an act of creation of evil. So Eva had decided that not seeing anything in our reality that was unpleasant was the way to go. She called it "creating your personal myth."

It was easy to see this was just a variation on the fundamentalist approach of "Jesus Saves and we don't have to think." New Age religion taught that believing in the power of love and light was the ticket. In the end, the result was purported to be the same: salvation or ascension.

It was popularly posited, "those who do not believe in demons will not experience such things." In thinking back over my own experiences, it was clear that something "approached" me at a time and under circumstances that obviated any consideration of free will and belief. I was a very small child. And I seriously doubt that any of the members of my family, professed Christians though they were, actually believed in demons either. So I was having a bit of a problem with this idea that what you think about or what you believe creates your reality.

Contrary to popular New Age lore, the presence of evil does not require the permission or belief or thoughts of the host to exist or even to manifest in that person's life. What did seem to be true was that there was some sort of connection between belief and denial. When a person undertakes to believe something, there is a whole cosmos of other things that they are, by this act of belief, denying. Belief or non-belief seemed to have no bearing on the reality of these beings (if that is what they were). With limited knowledge, many people are left wide open to psychic intrusion.

I was deeply concerned that Eva was being led astray by such ideas. At the same time, Eva was convinced that I had created the suffering in my life by my endless questions about the nature of good and evil. She didn't catch the very important point that it was only when I had given up my questions and had plunged into the true-believer mode of existence that all other options seemed to have been closed off. In later years I became able to joke that when I gave up thinking in exchange for faith in Jesus, all hell broke loose. But at the time it wasn't very funny.

* * *

I had a somewhat different view. In thinking about the mechanical nature of the universe understood by the human mind as good and evil, I still had to deal with what I perceived as the "demon problem." There were clearly energies, whether actually conscious or not, or only mechanically so, that seemed to be concentrated essences of the negative polarity in terms of electrodynamics (possibly). That these essences existed at all levels was a logical extension of this idea. Gurdjieff had pointed out quite reasonably that "two very moral men may consider each other very immoral. The more moral a man is, the more immoral does he think other moral people."

This led me to think about missionary efforts of the Christian Church down through history, which were, essentially, massacres and destruction of indigenous cultures, histories, artifacts, and everything else that was considered to be immoral by Christianity. My side-trip in fundamentalism had given me an inside view of born-again-Christian thinking and its revivification in the New Age religions—which were, in fact, based on the same principles. A person who adopts a moral position that he is unequivocally right and has stopped asking questions because he has found a belief system, seems to follow this move by adopting the idea that he has to convert or fix or persuade by any number of tactics, including manipulation, other people to his view. If they refuse to agree with him, and refuse to be manipulated by him, he then begins to destroy by twisting and distorting and demonizing them. You can generally tell how subjective and probably erroneous a "right" position is by the zeal with which it is propagated.

In my efforts to come to some resolution about the deepest meaning of the teachings of Jesus, I had formulated some ideas about his real mission, assuming that he even existed at all. Every thought and saying of Jesus was directed and subordinated to one thing, a difficult concept to put into words today: the realization of the Kingdom of God upon the earth. This was Jesus' master idea. The term appears repeatedly in the Gospels—no less than thirty-seven times in Matthew alone, who usually calls it the Kingdom of Heaven or the Heavens, and thirty-two times in Luke. The New Testament is, quite simply, a virtual commentary on this one single idea.

For the Jews, living under the domination of the Romans after years of domination by the Babylonians, this idea had been projected onto a hope for a Messiah who would come as a conqueror to establish the Davidic Kingdom of God by force of arms. This materialistic view of the matter was later taken up by Christianity. The Kingdom of God became some literal place, even the kingdom on earth at the end of time.

However, in striking contradiction to his assurances of the imminence of the Kingdom, Jesus stated quite categorically on other occasions that the Kingdom was already here: *"If it is by the Spirit of God that I drive out the devils, then be sure the Kingdom of God has already come upon you."* Scholars point out that this statement is so alien to contemporary Jewish thought that it must be attributed to Jesus himself (or whoever the person was around whom this legend accreted) rather than to the Gospel writers or their sources.

However you look at it, the proclamation of the Kingdom of God, present and future, was the essential overriding feature of Jesus' preaching and instruction. His teaching was evidently brilliant (whomever the myth was formed around), but it was not primarily as a teacher of morals that he saw himself. The teaching of Jesus was entirely directed towards preparing people for that Kingdom and for its first fruits. And he proclaimed that he was creating that Kingdom.

This is the premise of every one of his moral injunctions: *"Set your mind upon his Kingdom and all the rest will come to you as well."*

As the scholars I admired pointed out, so predominant was the concept of the Kingdom of God in Jesus' thoughts that even his teachings on the abandonment of worldly hostilities was not motivated by gentleness or compassion or pacifism, but by his concentration on the Kingdom and the all-important task of securing admission to it. Additionally, and this may be surprising to many, Jesus' miracles were primarily and pre-eminently connected with and directed towards the *fulfillment* of the Kingdom.

And here we reach the crux of the matter: Jesus' prime intention was not to cure the sick, but to demonstrate how the "securing of the Kingdom" was to be accomplished. Every healing he performed moved us closer to the consummation of the Kingdom. Every exorcism he performed moved us further into the Kingdom. In other words, it was by directly dealing with those things we often call evil that the process of gaining entry to the Kingdom of God was effected.

The Gospels tend on occasion to distinguish between Jesus' two main activities of exorcism and healing, regarding them as related but separate. But these cures are directly linked and subordinated to the accompanying message of the divine Kingdom. His instructions to his apostles were: *"Heal the sick, raise the dead, cleanse lepers, cast out devils as you go. Proclaim the message: The Kingdom of Heaven is upon you."*

Such signs were not only symbols of what was happening, but also effectual signs that *caused what they signified*. Jesus' cures were not only symbolic seals of his mission but actual victories in the battle that had already been joined against the forces of evil.

"Believe my works if not my words."

"*If it is by the finger of God that I drive out the devils, then be sure the Kingdom of God has already come upon you.*"

These principles had become apparent to me as a result of the "Boat Ride to Damascus." The statement to me, by whatever the source of this vision, was that God cannot act in our lives as long as evil is in the way. I was most definitely putting my whole mind and soul into striving to live a holy life, and yet I was being told that evil existed in my life.

When I asked "what evil?" I was enjoined to "learn." That suggested to me that ignorance, itself, was evil.

* * *

And now, Eva was promoting these ideas as the cause for my own troubles—that I had thought too much about evil and darkness in my efforts to understand why bad things happen to good people. She forwarded to me a reading by Lama Sing, which was supposed to prove this point. However, what Lama Sing had to say about the matter was quite in line with my own thinking:

"*... The force of light is aligned with the Christ. The force of darkness is often aligned with the destructive or demonic.*

"*... The force of darkness lives on in the hearts and minds of mankind in a form or fashion in accordance to their acceptance and belief. There are pinnacles of light here and there in the Earth which give way to this darkness and which seek it out and replace it with light. But if there had not been the thought form or image within that entity which was not removed by some force, some action, where then might the light reside within them?*"

This last remark above is actually quite startling. In effect, Lama Sing is saying that certain souls are in the earth who have entered into existence for the very purpose of suffering the effects of the darkness in order to learn about it, and to then "seek it out and replace it with light." But the most important thing I noted was that those who are truly of darkness are those who expend their energy in destruction. They do not seem to create anything—they only seek to destroy that which is chosen by others.

"*Lama Sing: Evil is neither a living force, any more than the force of light is a living force. It is neither an entity nor a being, any more than the force of light is an entity or being. It is all God. ... Knowing then that this is all God, for all existence is God, then know as well that it is only the intent of minds of those who are a part of that same force who create the illusion of darkness, and by the use of the varying forces available to all perpetuate this illusion unto others, and thus this becomes then a continual experience which each must then use to make way for the in-flowing and indwelling of light.*

"*Q: So then, it's much the same as speaking of positive and negative. Both are necessary, and they are neither bad nor good; they are ...*

"*Lama Sing: That is quite accurate. ... The forces of light and the forces of darkness provide a sort of psychic flow of energy. If we remove the titles of light and dark, you would look at them totally differently, certain emotional reactions would be gone, and you would think of them in a more sterile or scientific demeanor.*

"*Q: Does the devil, Satan, exist? And if so, how did this being come about? Will this being ultimately return to be in harmony with God?*

"*Lama Sing: As a being this entity, this being, this personage or howsoever you might speak of this identity, does not exist. There is no question of that statement here. What does exist is the thought form which surrounds the epitome or pinnacle or some total of works of darkness or opposite polarity of the positive. ... For example, if you were to take ... statements of positive guidance, you would find an entity or group of entities who would oppose each and every positive statement, and if such entities were at the uppermost ranking of the forces of darkness, you might call these entities demonic in nature, totally destructive, and you might call the totality of them "Satan." And here then these entities build their thought form which exists as long as any entity contributes an energy, a force to it. When one violates the tenets of God, they are contributing to that thought form.*"

Here, Lama Sing has made a certain remark that he repeats a couple more times about the tenets of God. This was, for me, the crux of the matter: just what were the so-called tenets of God? At the beginning of his remarks he also commented that the forces of light often make use of the forces of darkness to do their work. In other words, as the saying goes, the devil is in the details. Now, back to Lama Sing:

"Some speak of the Fallen Angel, and the presence of this angelic host then to emerge as the leader of the dark forces is symbolic, for cannot God reach forth with a mighty thrust and return this, His own creation, unto Himself? Of course. But in His wisdom, then, there is the knowledge that the progression of all souls will relate to the understanding of this nature and to the experiencing of the forces which are pervaded by this understanding there can come a most beautiful and most logical progression."

Here Lama Sing has made a most remarkable statement that is so convoluted and veiled that one has to wonder at his cleverness in obfuscation. In talking about the "progression" of souls, he has said that this is accomplished by understanding the nature of, and experiencing the forces of, darkness. He then gives as an example the following analogy:

"Lama Sing: One does not force a child upon a pathway and anticipate that the reaching of the goal on the pathway shall be a joyous one. But how many are seen following a pathway freely chosen and the arrival and the discoveries, good or bad, to be joyous discoveries? Can your Father do less? See?"

Now, the questioner brings the matter into direct focus:

"Q: Does putting our attention upon the forces of darkness make them stronger?

"Lama Sing: If that intent is of the darkness, of destruction yes. If it is of the light, no; generally tends to diminish same."

And here we have a significant clue that relates to the remarks about the necessity of experiencing the darkness in order to be driven to learn about it, which then leads to the ability to focus on it and replace it with light. Putting our attention on the darkness with the intent of shining light on it, learning about it, exposing it to view for what it is, "generally tends to diminish same." But, of course, it's not as simple as that. Learning about something is not the same thing as acting on that knowledge. And the acting can often be problematical.

"Q: How can we best reduce vulnerability to the forces of darkness for ourselves and others?

"Lama Sing: Follow the tenets given by God to each and truly try to live them. Watch the intent, the thought, the attitude. The more so one can dwell and live in happiness, the less energy available to the forces of darkness, the forces of limitation."

Now we have a bit of a problem. Again, the "tenets of God" have been brought up. Additionally, we have an injunction to "watch the intent, the thought, the attitude." That doesn't seem to be too complicated, yet we realize from all that has been discussed as well as our observations of the real world, that there is some subtle difficulty here in knowing precisely how to apply this in practical terms. Lama Sing gives us the clue in his next remark:

"Then, too, to understand that the forces of darkness are the misuse of the forces of light and that the forces of darkness can be thought of as the potential for change [in] understanding ways of thinking, ways of living."

What greater "misuse" of the forces of light can there be than to persuade people to stop thinking, to stop analyzing, to stop learning and growing, whether it is by faith in the salvation of Jesus or by faith in the power of the personal myth that no evil exists unless you think about it? What greater misuse of the forces of creativity than to exert them to destroy another who has chosen a different belief system?

Indeed, it seems to be necessary to defend ourselves against such assaults to whatever extent necessary, but more importantly, our energy ought to be primarily devoted to creating, to building that which we have chosen. In the end, it doesn't seem to matter which system is most "right" or "wrong"; what matters is that the individual has devoted himself or herself to creating and expanding and growing in their chosen system, and has allowed others to do the same.

More than that, Lama Sing has said that these forces of darkness can be thought of as "potential for change" and this change is to be in "understanding ways of thinking, ways of living." Well, clearly that isn't going to happen if a person is fixated upon a single idea of faith or "you create your own reality by what you think about," and stubbornly refuses to observe the effects of this thinking in their lives, as I was being forced to do.

How many people, even in the face of similar events and experiences refuse to let go of the idea that their faith is being tested? All kinds of things happen in their lives that are distinctly unpleasant or even tragic and miserable, and they blithely go on thinking that they have to just work harder to either "endure" or to find the key that will unlock the right mantra or visualization in order to "create" the "right" reality. Or they become convinced that they have to destroy those who do not agree with them once they have encountered someone who simply refuses to participate in their reality. It's the same principle working in both contexts: a refusal to examine their thinking, attitudes, and intent. Lama Sing expounds on this a bit, but if the reader has lost the point of the previous sentence, what is said next will be completely misunderstood:

"*Lama Sing: It's not essential to command self to instantaneous perfection and then to fear each moment faltering or falling from this perfect state; but rather to think about life in general and to strive to make each aspect joyous, first within self, not to be angry with self and not to criticize self, not to quickly judge self, and to understand and be compassionate with one's own errors and one's own growth. Why?*

"*We do not give this that you would be centered then on self or that the ego would be builded, that self would become all-important; but because we know that each of you must have the experience of these compassionate and loving attitudes within yourselves in order that you can truly and fully give them to others. There are those of you who can reverse this and by intensely focusing these attitudes upon others in every aspect of your life can cause them to be reflected inwardly, every aspect of your life can cause them to be reflected inwardly, and those are very beautiful entities, very lovely souls indeed.*"

There is a very tricky point in the above remark: the attitudes a person focuses on others are what is reflected inwardly. In other words, if you focus "love and light" on others with the belief that they need to be fixed, that they are broken in some way, *that is what you will experience*. And that was my experience in fundamentalism. The belief that others needed to be saved, or that I needed to pray for them to get them saved, or that I needed to just love them and all else around me in order to save myself—all of this was predicated on the idea that something needed to be fixed, that there was lack in the universe, that God was under attack by the forces of darkness, so to speak.

What was it that Lama Sing said that we might focus on others? "*Compassion and loving attitudes; to think about life in general and to strive to make each aspect joyous, first within self, not to be angry with self and not to criticize self, not to quickly judge self, and to understand and be compassionate with one's own errors and one's own growth.*" Obviously, determining that someone else needs to be saved or needs to be surrounded with love and light, or even needs our prayers without being directly asked, is to deny the positive/negative nature of life, to be in a critical mode, to be judgmental, and to be intolerant of errors and the rate of growth in others. If we think we have to save others or transform them by focusing our love and light on them or their situations, then we are living in judgment and we are violating their free will.

The questioner addresses this issue directly:

"Q: *Some people have the idea of subduing or binding the forces of darkness. Some say that they will be transformed to the light. How will this come about?*

"*Lama Sing: These are indeed possible and do occur ofttimes. Being mindful that one cannot violate the laws of free will, the right of each entity to freely choose. But where an entity imposes forcibly a will, or attempts to impose same, upon self or others, they have, curiously, asked you to retaliate, and so you have the right to respond. Is this understandable?*"

Again, Lama Sing has made a statement at the beginning of a series of remarks that contains the key to all he says afterward. The question is about "subduing or binding the forces of darkness" in order to transform them to light. And Lama Sing clearly relates this to a violation of free will. He then notes that to impose one's own ideas of how things should be on another is literally an asking for retaliation. Of course, the way it is phrased is definitely obscure, and we have to question the motives for this.

What it amounts to is this: if I try to "change" someone else either by praying for their salvation, or sending love and light to surround or "bind" them, whether it is an individual or a specific situation which can be global, I have "asked" for retaliation. By the same token, if those of darkness seek to impose their will on me, they are, according to divine law, asking for me to retaliate or, at the very least, refuse this domination. I have the right to say no, and to say it in whatever way is necessary to achieve my freedom from domination.

"*Lama Sing: ... An entity violating your right of free will is initiating an action on the part of their free will, thus enabling you to function within the laws of God to respond. Hence, you can then use all those forces available to you, which are the forces of God ... to the extent that your belief allows you to muster this force. ... The result can be a binding force. The power of prayer to surround completely that entity, that being, can sever the source of the energy flow to that entity which is of darkness. In effect, consider that you are encapsulating that entity in light. Very often, then, if you can sufficiently sustain same, the entity will be borne out of darkness and into the light and you will find after this that [such a result was] the motivating force behind the entity's aggressive action towards you.*"

Unfortunately, the questioner did not approach the matter with sufficient openness to allow the point to be clearly delineated that this principle works both ways. The fact becomes apparent, when we consider the above remark, that when we attempt to save others because we have judged them to be in need of saving, or even if we attempt to save ourselves because we have judged ourselves to be imperfect, we literally are opening the door to, and inviting in, the forces of darkness.

But what is crucially important in the above remarks is that *"you can then use all those forces available to you, which are the forces of God ... to the extent that your belief allows you to muster this force ... The result can be a binding force ... you are encapsulating that entity in light. ... if you can sufficiently sustain same ..."* Now, of course, even doing this is predicated upon having been directly violated by the individual you wish to bind. It seems pretty clear that to do it on behalf of another who may not have asked for such assistance, or, even if they did ask with words, are not really asking in their hearts, is to invite disaster upon yourself. Moreover, if a human being—or even a group of human beings—seeks to act in this manner toward a very powerful being of darkness wherein there is no ability to either believe or sustain the belief, even greater disaster can ensue. But still, we have here a very interesting clue about the nature of universal law. Clearly, the pastor and the deacons who attempted to exorcise the demoniac woman I have already described did not have either the belief or the ability to sustain that belief sufficiently to do the job. And that brings us to the next, most important point: very powerful beings of darkness whom it is best to leave alone unless you are truly equal to them—which is not likely at this level of experience.

"Lama Sing: ... Understanding that all forces are generally striving to continue to exist, they cannot be destroyed, they can only be evolved. They can be blended, they can be changed in the sense of raising or lowering their vibrations."

Here, again, Lama Sing has made remarks with subtextual meanings that are missed by the reader who is not actively thinking. He has said, *"all forces ... cannot be destroyed, they can only be ... blended ... changed in the sense of raising or lowering their vibrations."*

The standard New Age believer or Christian fundamentalist who has been so convinced of the idea that higher vibrations can only mean good vibrations will miss this point entirely. Lama Sing is telling us that even the forces of darkness cannot be destroyed, but they *can* evolve, or be intensified, lessened, or even blended. The significance of this remark cannot be overstated. Yet, again, it has been mostly lost in the verbiage of the channel, in the obfuscatory nature of the delivery. Again, we ask why.

Perhaps because the questioner would not have been able to receive a clear answer.

"*Lama Sing: ... Great struggles, great conflicts have been won in realms unknown to you ... There is the continual action and reaction between the forces of light and the forces of darkness. There is the continual struggle to destroy and build; the continual effort to take, to remove, and to put and to build. In these realms ... it is recognized that ultimately there must be a merging and a purifying of these forces, that they can be in harmony.*"

The above is an interesting remark because it can easily be understood by a less perspicacious reader to be saying that, in our realm, there must be a "merging and purifying" of the battling forces. Yet, that is not what is being stated. Lama Sing is saying that such occurs in "realms unknown to you." So we understand that, at some point, in some realm, darkness and light *do* merge. Unfortunately, many people make the mistake of thinking that this is the function of *this* realm. And many channels promulgate such a teaching in more explicit terms, leading to much confusion and loss of energy in attempting to do that work which rightly belongs to other realms, other beings. Lama Sing even points this out for us:

"*Lama Sing: But when we speak of the forces of darkness and the forces of light as they relate to the Earth, we are not referring to the pure forces as used by the angelic host, the archangels and so forth, but rather those forces used by the mind of Man, either intentionally or subliminally. Here, at the levels of mind, at the levels of emotion, the forces of darkness do claim this as their own. This thought form, then, is real to the extent that it exists through the will of Man and through the perpetuation of carnal desires.*"

Lama Sing has now clearly told us that there is a distinct difference between realms, that the merging and purifying only occur at the levels of "angels" and "archangels." Further, he has stated quite boldly that the operation of the forces of darkness in opposition to the forces of light is the natural function of the realm of earth and mankind. He states explicitly that the forces of darkness claim the minds and emotions of mankind as their own because the "will of man" has chosen this. In other words, couching his remarks in terms that won't scare the bejeebies out of the readers, Lama Sing has said we are in a real situation here. The logical understanding of this leads us to the idea that, if it is the will of man—in the sense of the mass mind, mass emotion—that is controlled intentionally and subliminally by the forces of darkness, then for single individuals, or even small groups of individuals, to attempt to violate this will by imposing their ideas of salvation or transforming or destroying or doing away with this darkness, they are, in effect, just asking for retaliation by the very forces they are attempting to overcome. A real catch-22, you might say.

"*Lama Sing: ... There is, indeed, a conflict, and it is one which is in many aspects similar to a conflict in the Earthly sense, for those forces of darkness do not willingly give way that which has been their claim, their kingdom. [What darkness cannot possess, it seeks to destroy.]*

"*... The Earth is at a point of some considerable transition and has, just in the recent several earth years past, entered a new cycle, a new orb, and is located in terms of celestial alignments in a position of some rarity.*

"*... The struggles between the forces of light and darkness were foretold by those whom have gone before, and you are entering into that period of light whereupon the Earth can make itself aright again. And those who shall choose to dwell therein will be those who have chosen, those called in the sense of your Holy Book, the chosen ones. But they have done the choosing by their manner, by their work, by their intent, see?*"

In other words, there are creators and destroyers. We live in a world controlled by darkness due to some mass-mind choice in the distant past. We gave permission to the darkness to rule our minds. And they do not willingly give away that which has been their claim, their kingdom. The will of man, in the sense of the mass mind, mass emotion, is controlled intentionally and subliminally by the forces of darkness. The world is under the control of an evil magician.

In the end, after reading through Lama Sing's remarks on the subject juxtaposed against Eva's understanding of them and her belief in the necessity of erecting the "personal myth," I realized that she was not getting it in significant ways. Of course, to even think about it this way was an error on my part because I was so certain of a rapport between us that all I had to do was explain these things to her and she would come around to the "right" way of thinking. I was so easily falling into the programmed trap! I could see disaster in her future if she didn't open her eyes and mind to serious and dedicated searching for the subtle subtext in all these channeled pronouncements she was buying into.

As it turned out, I was correct in my predictions about her future, though I never voiced them to her directly. Eva subsequently developed cancer, followed by her husband developing cancer. Hers was successfully treated by surgery, but her husband died—not from the cancer, but from the weakening of his system by the treatment. Lama Sing was correct that people have to experience the results of living in darkness in order to learn. Nobody can teach what is not ready to be learned. And to try to destroy or change another person's choices or perspective or work or lessons is to align with the darkness. What a tightrope!

Learning this language of the world, the ways in which our lives and bodies and experiences speak to us, was the training I received during these days. We still have a few more years to go before I finally "got it," but it was most interesting the way it happened.

*　*　*

A few weeks after I had given Mother the manuscript of Noah to read, she came to visit. She wanted to know what I thought we ought to do if there was a real possibility of global catastrophe.

I wasn't sure. That part of the problem was still on the drawing board. After mulling over the issue at some length, I suddenly thought of the old Ouija board in the closet. Maybe we could get an answer that way? It had given interesting information in the past, warning that my father was going to die of a heart attack (which he did not long after), so maybe we could get an answer on where we ought to go to survive the coming earth changes.

During the course of the past few years I have received a lot of correspondence from people about my choice of "instruments"—the Ouija board. I will address these issues in some depth further on; suffice it to say that, at this point in time, I had done sufficient research to feel confident that my choice of "consciousness-tuning instruments" was correct. As a rule, I didn't trust channeled information that came directly into the mind. Even though I had just channeled the concepts behind *The Noah Syndrome*, I didn't think of that as channeling. I was just asking myself mental questions and thinking my way through them. It should be noted that my reaction to the ideas that came into my mind was to research them rather than just accept them as Holy Writ. *Noah* was a text based on science that had been discovered by inspiration.

That's the major difference between the mode of using the Ouija board and that of other channels. The Ouija board allows for a dialectic approach that does not effectively exist in other channeling procedures. It allows for a long period of thesis, antithesis, and finally synthesis. And, in a real sense, this was the process of *Noah*. The question was asked, the answer came, the research was done, and fuller and more valid understanding was achieved.

But I didn't fully realize that then. I still needed a tool that could be safely handled and monitored in a fully conscious state, and the only one that fit the bill was the Ouija board.

Mother and I got it out and placed it on the table between us. It began to move in slow circles after just a minute or two, and I asked if anyone was there. After the planchette indicated "yes," I asked for a name. After the name was obtained, I just launched into my questions.

First I asked if there were really going to be any major earth changes as so many prophets had suggested. The answer was "yes." Next, I asked if my interpretation of how they were going to manifest was accurate. The answer was "close." Then I asked if we should do anything to prepare. The answer was "move." I asked where. The answer: "Montana."

And that was about all we got from it. After that word was spelled, it seemed that the connection was dropped, and no more answers were forthcoming.

Montana. *Why Montana*, I wondered. *It's cold in Montana! It snows in Montana! Nobody lives in Montana! It's like the Outback or something! Nothing but sky and grass and maybe cows or wheat fields.*

Well, maybe that wasn't such a bad thing. Maybe Montana was destined to be a safe area and maybe, when everything was over, it would end up being more pleasant to live there than anywhere else.

Larry didn't like the idea of Montana, though he liked the idea of moving to some remote place. His dream had always been to move to Guyana and live in the jungle and fish. I pointed out all the disadvantages of trying to live in a jungle in another country where you don't even know the language, particularly with small children and their needs. Even though he reluctantly agreed that my points were valid, I sensed that those things that kept him from living out his dream were resented: me and the children.

Meanwhile, on the issue of moving to Montana, I approached it the same way I did everything else: research. Just because a suggestion was made by a so-called discarnate, didn't mean that I believed it. I sent off for maps, real estate brochures, and government publications. At the end of this phase, I was able to report to Larry that if we finished our house, we could sell it and have enough money to buy a sizeable farm in

Montana. He could hunt and fish all he wanted, and we could garden and basically do all the things he liked—just not in the tropics or on the ocean.

He agreed that my plan was sound enough. I felt we had a common goal: we would both work very hard to finish our building project and improve our property, so we could get top dollar for it.

Then we could "buy the ark," or the farm in Montana.

CHAPTER TWENTY-NINE

THE DREAM

No sooner did we have a plan and a shared goal that one would think could bring two people close together, something began to act on Larry in a strange and self-destructive way. First, he was fired from work. Then, every day, he managed to run into someone who needed his help. For ten or twenty dollars, he gave them his labor for an entire day, coming home with no job.

This continued for weeks. With the little money he'd pick up here and there in this deliberately desultory way, I was able to manage to keep enough food for the children, but it wasn't enough to feed all of us. When I pointed out to Larry that something had to be done because we couldn't keep food on the table, he jovially pointed out that he liked popcorn. We could fill up on that and we wouldn't be hungry.

Fine. The kids ate a lot of popcorn. In fact, I ate nothing but popcorn because I decided the kids needed what food we did have.

After a week or two of this, our VW bus broke down. We had no money to fix it. So we were stuck in the woods with very little food, no job, and no transportation.

Larry was actually having a good time. He was the "wilderness survivor," with his wits pitted against the wilds. He would take the children out in the woods to go berry picking or to fish or just wander around. When they would return, dirty and sweaty, needing extra baths for which I didn't have the energy, considering that all the water we used had to be carried in buckets, I was livid. Of course, my rage at Larry was diverted by him to the kids. Naturally, he looked like the "good guy" who just wanted to have fun with them. I was the bad guy because I wanted to spoil all their fun by making them stay clean, and demanding that Daddy go out and get a job. I was the wicked witch. I held back my frustration because I knew that if I went over the line, Larry would leave us. At this point, it wouldn't have mattered financially, but I was terrified of hurting the children.

As it happens, I am sensitive to corn. I didn't know it then, but after a steady diet of popcorn for several weeks, I awoke one night with a raging fever, nausea, and terrible knife-like pains in my lower abdomen. When it got to the point that I couldn't stand it, I told Larry to find a way to get me to a hospital. He left to walk to a neighbor's house, some distance away, and called an ambulance. It's a good thing I wasn't having a heart attack—I would have died before they got there. After they finally arrived and I was loaded on the stretcher, the driver actually got lost out in those sandy back roads. If you have never ridden in an ambulance over wood tracks meant to be traversed by horses or four-wheel-drive trucks, you just haven't lived. There were potholes in some of those roads big enough to bury a VW Beetle. It was especially interesting because every bump and jounce and sharp turn to avoid trees that leapt out in the darkness sent me into more spasms of pain. Thankfully, at some point, I went unconscious.

The doctor determined that I had appendicitis. I was put on IV antibiotics and surgery was scheduled for the morning. However, by the time morning came, all the symptoms were gone except the fever. Over and over again he poked and prodded and pressed and released. Nothing. He ordered more tests, and went out shaking his head.

My white blood count, elevated the night before, was normal. He told me that, quite frankly, he didn't know what was wrong. He would have sworn that my appendix needed to come out, but it was negative for surgery now. I was to be observed for several days, given antibiotics, and if there were no more signs of anything requiring hospitalization, I could go home.

Lying there alone in the hospital with no constant work staring me in the face, I realized that if I'd died at that precise moment, Larry and the children would have had a party to celebrate. I had absolutely no control over events outside of my sphere of influence, my house and children, so I had become obsessed with the little control I did have over my life. I saw this as a need to maintain certain standards, even though we were reduced to living in a hovel without modern conveniences. I drove the children to stay clean all the time. I drove them to help me keep their clothes washed, even though it entailed doing laundry by hand in a big tin washtub. I drove them to sweep and pick up their toys all the time, to rake the yard, to wash the dishes and keep their beds made. I was physically unable to do all this work myself, so the children had to help. I realized that I spent all my time telling them to "do this" or "do that."

Where had all the loving and happy interactions gone? There weren't any.

Larry complained. "You're just too damn picky. I couldn't please you if I hung you with a new rope," or "quit your bitchin', woman. You never had it so good!" He'd say this in front of the children repeatedly, so they had the perception that cleanliness was "my trip," that I was a "control freak," and that it was unfair and unreasonable for me to expect anyone else to do the work. Wives and mothers were supposed to be servants of husbands and children.

I was the one who was upset all the time, right? I was the one who thought that having a decent house to live in and regular meals and a few modern conveniences were necessities of life, right? And, as Larry pointed out, my demands for improvement were related to material things. I wasn't placing the proper value on spiritual things. Loving the children and being with them all the time, sharing woodland adventures, were the "real" values. What did it matter if they didn't have shoes to wear? They had love, right? And more than anything, I wanted to love and be loved by my children. I knew I had to change something, and the only thing I could really change was me. A new and intensified program of meditation and creative visualization was in order.

I began right there and then in the hospital, and for the next few days I visualized myself as being happy. Nothing else. No attempt to change the reality. Just seeing myself happy and at peace.

When I was finally back home, it was as though the Universe was supporting me in my decision. An old fishing friend of Larry's drove out to the house and offered him a job working on his commercial fishing boat. He made overnight fishing runs four nights a week. This paid very well. When Larry told him he had no transportation, he gave an advance on future earnings. Larry was able to fix the VW bus. Larry was happy to be back out on the water, and I was happy to be alone at night. It was a perfect arrangement for meditating. Trying to do this in the daytime with small children was impractical.

Mother had a big, blond German shepherd at the time who managed to have an encounter with her neighbor's Rhodesian Ridgeback one day.

A litter of gorgeous puppies resulted. Since we were out in the woods and Larry was gone at night, I decided to take a pair of them to raise as watchdogs. The kids loved those puppies and they were about the smartest dogs I have ever seen. We all just doted on them. They were about half-grown when disaster struck. Larry was coming up the long driveway early one morning, just before daylight, and as he came around the curve at the bottom of the hill, his headlights passed over the dogs lying on the ground about a hundred yards from the house. He came on up to the house and woke me up to tell me that something had "got the dogs" and we would have to take care of them before the kids woke up and found them.

A few hours later, when it was daylight, we went down to see if we could figure out what had happened. I'd heard no sounds of any kind of fight during the night and there was no indication of sickness in either of them. When I looked at them, I was completely stunned.

Whatever had happened to them, it had been brutal and terrible. It was also puzzling. Each one of them was missing an eye, an ear and part of their lower lip on one side. They also were missing their external sex organs and had huge holes in their rectums as though some sort of coring device had been used.

What in the name of God did something like that? There was no blood. No teeth marks. No ripping and tearing. No random mutilation. The only thing I could figure is that whatever had killed them both had done it somewhere else and had then dropped them where they lay.

Then I remembered that I had thrown away an almost empty container of rat poison. Maybe they had gotten into the trash and eaten it? That had to be the answer. Never mind that it was less than half a teaspoon. Maybe that was enough to kill both of them. I didn't know, but it was the only solution I could come up with. Maybe ants ate away the eyes and ears and lips? (There hadn't been a single ant on them.) Maybe the rectal condition was because the anal sphincter had simply relaxed when they died? I had heard that this happened, though I had never seen an example of it before, at least not an opening that was about the size of a half-dollar.

We buried them quickly so the children wouldn't see them, but we had to tell them later. They were heartbroken and I was devastated with guilt for being the probable cause of their death. Naturally, Larry announced to them that I had poisoned their dogs.

When I think about this incident in retrospect, it is so surprising to me now that I created and accepted such an explanation. I want to make it clear that both dogs had exactly the same wounds, in precisely the same configuration. They were both missing the same eye, the same ear, and the same lip. There were no other marks on them to indicate struggle, being bitten, or otherwise mauled. If the parts that were missing had been favored morsels by some scavenger, including the action of ants or beetles, the fact that said scavengers had so precisely selected those areas to mutilate them in identical ways was deeply troubling. It was also troubling that no scavenger had come to feed on the corpses nor were they even covered with ants, which would have been usual.

But such is the mind that if no rational, acceptable explanation exists, it will create one by patching together any theory that will do. Talk about your "personal myth"! As it turned out, I was going to need this ability to pull down the shades against reality quite a bit as the year progressed.

We decided to spend the Fourth of July with Larry's brother, who lived about forty miles north of us. Larry had the night off, and we planned to get an early start in the morning.

Our house was tiny, but I had arranged everything cleverly so there was some measure of privacy for everyone, using my tall chests of drawers as both storage and dividers. This was augmented with curtains so that Larry and I slept in a very tiny "room" in the southeast corner. The bed was pushed tightly against the corner walls. There was only enough space between the side of the bed and the two chests that were our "divider wall" for the drawers to open. You had to stand to the side of them to open them, or sit on the bed itself, because there was not enough room to stand in front of them and open them. At the foot of the bed was a curtain that separated the space where the baby crib stood. It was jammed tightly against the foot of our bed with the head of the crib against the foot of the bed. This meant that only a small part of the end of our bed was not enclosed. Essentially, it was closed in on three sides. I slept on the inside against the wall, and if I had to get up during the night, I had to wake Larry up not only to move, but also to help me since it was still difficult for me to get erect by myself.

I tried to meditate before going to sleep, as had become my habit, but soon realized that I could not stop thinking about all the things I wanted to remember for our trip the following day. I mentally packed a change of clothing for each of the children. I would get the house straightened up before we left. I'd been taught that you clean your house before you go anywhere. When you come home tired, you don't have to do anything.

Gradually my thoughts slowed down, and all I could hear in the tiny house were the occasional sleep sounds of the children and Larry's snoring. I finally fell asleep.

Something woke me up.

At first I wasn't sure what was going on. I felt overcome with confusion because there was so much outside activity going on that seemed to be rather sudden and unnatural. I opened my eyes and saw what seemed to be needles of light crisscrossing the interior of the house. I lifted my head from the pillow and noticed there was also a sort of roaring sound outside that seemed to come from all directions at once.

I thought perhaps the house was surrounded by a whole bunch of big trucks with their engines running, and all of them were facing the house shining their headlights on it. In fact, the light was so tremendously and intensely bright that I added to the theory by thinking that all these trucks must be those mud-bogging hunting trucks with banks of lights across the roofs, and these were being shined on the house also.

Having come up with a good explanation, I then decided Larry's friends had come to play a joke on him in the night. Thinking about it seemed to require great effort, and it also took a lot of effort to hold my head off the pillow.

I was overcome with wave after wave of sleepiness, and my last thoughts as I dropped my head back on the pillow were: *Well, let Larry take care of it! If he gets up and messes around tonight he will be exhausted on the drive tomorrow. But, tired or not, we are going. The kids are counting on it! He has to learn somehow. I'm not his mother, so I'm not going to point out the obvious to him! I'm going to get some sleep!*

The next thing I knew, I was waking up again in terrible pain. My back was killing me, and I realized that my position was contributing to this pain. I tried to shift myself and my face bumped against something strange: Larry's feet! How in the world? Had he gotten up and laid back down in the bed reversed? I felt almost drunk as I struggled to sit up so I could tell him that he was lying backward in the bed. As I reached out in the darkness to brace myself against the wall at the head of the bed, my hand touched the head of the baby crib at the foot of the bed.

I realized that I was the one who was turned around in the bed.

Confusion and puzzlement; I felt completely disoriented and disconnected from reality. It was impossible for me to be turned around. I am one of those people who will sleep an entire night in the same position.

And, if I do need to change my position, I have never, ever in my life, done it while sleeping. I always wake up to move. Always. Beyond that, however, was the fact that getting up from a horizontal position was still very difficult for me and I had to have help. If help was not available, I generally managed by pulling open a drawer in the dresser and using it to pull myself up. Additionally, there was the logistical problem of getting out of a bed that was enclosed on three sides by solid objects, and on the fourth by another person's body. Sure, theoretically, I could have pushed Larry's feet off the side of the bed and slid out the narrow space at the foot of his side of the bed. Even if I had been able to manage that—which was doubtful since I wasn't that agile—how did I get back in bed in reverse? I could, theoretically, have done a "human wheelbarrow" number and gotten down on my hands and knees and kicked my feet up onto the bed and walked on my hands, backing myself into the bed. No matter how I looked at it, I just became more and more confused.

I woke Larry up and asked him to help me get out of the bed. I was in so much pain that it took some maneuvering just to do that, and as I began to move, I was hit by another realization: my nightgown was wet. I was horribly embarrassed to think that I had wet myself while sleeping. I hadn't done that since I was a child and all the humiliation of such an event flooded through me. With Larry's help, I struggled to my feet and sort of tottered to the bathroom, a little "added on" room where Larry had installed a regular toilet and tub. (We had to fill the tank with buckets of water, but it worked.)

In the bathroom, I lit the kerosene lamp. My gown was wet only from the knees down. I was more confused and puzzled by the minute. I picked up the hem of my gown to smell it. It was not urine, it was water. What's more, it was covered with the little black seeds from the Bahia grass anthers.

How in the heck did I get turned around in my bed? How did my nightgown get wet from the knees down, covered with grass seed as though I had been out walking in the tall grass at the top of the hill on our property? Was I sleepwalking? Was my body capable of functioning in my sleep in ways that were impossible to me in the waking state? Just what in the name of God was going on?

I had no answers.

I decided that, yes, somehow I must have gotten out of the bed, in my sleep, without waking Larry, and had gone to the bathroom. While in the bathroom, I must have dipped my gown in the toilet. Then, with the wet gown, I must have gotten back in the bed in reverse somehow. What about the seeds all over my gown? Well, I just simply dismissed that item altogether. Since I had explained most of the problem to my own satisfaction, not having an explanation for that part of it wasn't so bad. I could easily just let that drop and sweep the whole thing under the rug.

And I did.

We made our day trip to Larry's brother's house and came home without incident.

The following morning my oldest daughter came to wake us up early, crying that something was wrong with her eyes. She couldn't open them. She had contracted a severe case of conjunctivitis. Both eyes were practically glued shut from pus forming under the eyelids. I heated water and soaked cotton balls and placed them on her eyes to soften up the encrusted matter so she could open them. No sooner had I cleared away all the pus and matter than it began to form again. It was forming so fast that, within a minute or two, her eyes were glued shut again.

Even worse, as each of the children awoke, I found that they were all in the same condition.

I decided that they had all contracted conjunctivitis from splashing in the wading pool at Larry's brother's house. I got all the kids dressed and ready to go to the doctor, stopping at each stage of the operation to soak their eyes so that they could keep them open long enough to dress and not bump into the walls.

Later, the children settled in their beds with ointment in their eyes, I suggested that Larry go to a phone and call his brother to check on the other kids who'd been swimming in the pool at the same time. Not a single one of them had any problem whatsoever.

Okay, swell. I guess that my kids were just susceptible.

The next day, my left ear began to bother me. It was really not much more than a "full" feeling, as though I'd gotten water in it while swimming. Having had a number of ear infections as a child—usually from swimming—I was very careful with my ears when I did go swimming. The only thing at this point was: I had not been swimming.

I ignored the ear. I had sick children to take care of. With the ointment the doctor had prescribed, they were improving rapidly.

Another day passed. It was actually beginning to hurt a bit. We went to bed that night, and I put some warm sweet oil in the ear with cotton

THE DREAM

to soothe it for sleeping. Sometime after midnight the pain awoke me and I knew it couldn't wait until morning.

The emergency room doctor came up beside me with a cotton swab and was going to insert it into the ear canal for a gentle swipe. The instant she touched it, the explosion of pain immediately transmitted itself to my arm and the reflexive blow nearly knocked her across the room. She understood immediately that when I said it was excruciatingly painful, I was not joking in the least. I knew very well the degrees of severe pain. In childbirth, one of my children required the separation of my pelvis to deliver—utter agony—and I never once raised my voice, uttered a single cry, or did anything more than groan discreetly. In my family, pain was endured with dignity, not complaint. One certainly didn't physically assault a doctor tending to the problem!

But this was unbearable.

I once read that Francis II, king of France, and husband of Mary, Queen of Scots, had died of an ear infection that quickly spread to his brain. Well, I can well understand how terrible an ordeal this must have been. It was one of the most painful experiences I have ever undergone while conscious. Of course, the ear infection I had while in boarding school was painful, but most of the time I was unconscious. What's more, since it happened when I was a child, I hardly remember it. I will never forget the pain of this one. It was like being repeatedly stabbed in the ear with an ice pick. The whole side of my head blew up like a balloon and I couldn't even close my mouth from the swelling of my jaw. The ear canal itself swelled shut so that there was no possibility of drainage. Some weeks after it was brought under control, I had a large ball of dried blood and matter removed from the ear.

For the next ten years I was to be plagued with regular recurrences of this problem. I lived with a standing prescription of antibiotic-cortisone drops on hand just to keep it under control. I have taken enough antibiotics for this ear problem to sink a battleship.

The curious thing about these chronic, regular blow-ups in my ear was that I had no warning. After the first incident, there was no slow building of a sensation of something being wrong. I would simply wake up with the side of my head swollen, in pain. It would develop, in the course of a single day, to a critical situation that required a trip to the emergency room.

As soon as the ear infection cleared, the headaches began.

These were not just ordinary headaches, nor were they, technically, migraines. They would start as a very slight feeling of tension at the top of the back of my neck, where the skull sits on it, and the area where the neck connects to the head would swell the size of a small orange cut in half. It usually began in the early morning when I awakened. By midmorning, I'd be squinting to block the light from my eyes and covering my ears to block out the ordinary sounds of the world around me. Everything that impinged on my system exacerbated the pain, like having a steel helmet tightened to the point where, with one more turn of a screw, my entire skull would collapse inward. Breathing hurt, light hurt, sound hurt, movement hurt, and the crushing hammer blows of my own heartbeat were unendurable.

I took aspirin, Tylenol, codeine, and several prescription drugs the doctors came up with. Nothing ever touched those headaches. Nothing. The only thing to do was to lie as still as possible with my eyes covered by a cold, wet cloth, and just try to survive until the pain ended. It usually took three to five days. After the first one, they came every month just like clockwork. I finally realized that they seemed to be directly related to my menstrual cycle and the headache came on schedule.

As I progressed through this period of time, another difficulty began to manifest. I was losing the feeling in my hands and arms.

This lack of feeling alternated with shooting pains that traveled down the backs of the arms and terminated in my ring and pinky fingers. Not only that, I was having more difficulty lifting my legs to walk.

I was sent to a specialist who decided that I had Buerger's Disease, otherwise known as thromboangitis obliterans. Basically, he said, the veins and arteries in my limbs were inflamed and would be "obliterated," resulting in gangrene. Consequently, I faced probable amputation within five years or so.

Well, swell! That's good news! Nothing like a losing a few body parts to make your day. Heck, they hurt anyway, so might as well cut 'em off now.

Seriously, however, his solution to this problem was to prescribe antidepressants. No kidding! I took them a couple of times and realized they affected my thinking. I didn't like that. If I was going to fade away and lose a part here and there as time went by, there was no point in starting with my brain. If it was the only part I could keep, might as well keep it working.

THE DREAM

Besides, I didn't trust doctors anyway. If I had listened to the first diagnosis when I was pregnant with my first child, she wouldn't exist and neither would any of the other children.

In August of 1987, after a week-long headache, my period was, undoubtedly, the closest thing to actual labor as anything could be and not produce a baby. For the next several months, following the headache, I would develop fever and chills and almost flu-like symptoms with each period. Finally, in December of 1987, my period started with this terrible ordeal, only it wouldn't stop. By the middle of January, after a month of heavy bleeding and passing of huge clots, day after day, I knew I needed to see the doctor.

I was sent to the hospital for a D&C and a laparoscopy. That's a procedure where they make an incision to insert a camera to examine all the internal organs. It was a day-surgery event, though it included general anesthesia, and after I had recovered sufficiently to be released, Larry drove me home and helped me to bed.

Of course, I was in pain at the site of the incisions (there were two), and I was sore on the inside from the D&C, but what really was bothering me was a deep, burning pain on my backside right where I sat. It was so painful, in fact, that I thought I must be developing a boil or something. I asked Larry to have a look.

He was as puzzled as I have ever seen him when he described what he found on my bottom: two matching circles of missing flesh—one on each cheek like a mirror image—exactly round, about an eighth of an inch deep, that looked like someone had just used a cookie cutter on me.

I couldn't imagine what he was talking about so I asked him to get me a mirror so I could look myself. I did. He was right. Damndest thing I ever saw. What's more, I could not figure out how in the world I had received such wounds. Obviously, since they weren't there in the morning before Larry had taken me to the hospital, and were now there right after we returned, I had acquired them during the surgery. It was a puzzle I tucked away to ask the doctor about later.

When I did ask, the doctor looked at me like I had either lost my mind or decided to create some case for a malpractice suit. I even offered a possible solution. Maybe that new "surgical super glue" had been used and someone spilled a couple of drops on the operating table, gluing my bottom to the table without knowing it, and when they moved me to the stretcher, maybe it had just torn perfectly circular hunks of my flesh away. The doctor assured me that he had done the surgery and there was no surgical glue employed in the operating room.

In the end, it is a mystery that has not been solved.

I did feel much better after surgery. The gynecologist prescribed a new medication for my headaches: naproxen sodium, a prostaglandins inhibitor. It seemed to work well enough if I took it at the beginning of the headache; if I waited until it was already going strong, nothing would touch it. The doctor also recommended that I schedule a hysterectomy as soon as possible as my condition, endometriosis and adenomyosis, would not get better; a D&C was only a temporary fix.

Whatever was wrong with me, I knew I needed to get better for the sake of the children, but I was not ready to do any more major surgery. As long as I could function, I decided to put it off.

* * *

I need to say something about the children here. When I discovered I was pregnant with the first one, I went out and bought or borrowed books on child psychology, baby care, and whatnot. I never took another drink of alcohol for many years (until all of my children were well out of diapers). I ate carefully through every pregnancy. I read only uplifting literature while pregnant, I listened to only classical music; in short, I completely devoted my whole body, mind, and soul to providing an optimum environment for the growth and development of the child.

After my first was born, I suppose I became something of a fanatic about cleanliness. I also was extremely protective in the sense that I wanted to anticipate anything and everything that might pose a problem or danger to my child and worked very hard to eliminate such potential hazards. I didn't want to dampen creativity or curiosity, so things that might be harmful were simply removed to safe, high storage, and everything that was at child level was then permitted to the child to handle. I absolutely did not believe in spanking a child. I believed that artful distraction to interesting and permitted things was preferable to an endless series of "no," "don't touch," or "don't do this or that." In short, I had amalgamated a whole series of ideas from various schools of thought and was attempting to implement them as the "perfect mother."

I also didn't have my children to farm them out. Except for one trip to the hospital, for over ten years I never left any of my children with a babysitter. I never went anywhere that I could not take them or when they could not be watched by their father.

When Larry entered our lives, he had quite different ideas about discipline, though he was in total agreement with the "no babysitters" rule, but obviously for different reasons than my own. He was of the school that held "spare the rod and spoil the child" as the rule of thumb though certainly it was never applied that often. Since it was Biblical and was presented as the means of salvation at many levels, I gradually came to accept it as what was right, even though it went totally against my original thinking on the subject. But, I had discarded my earlier thinking, because my life, which had been based upon that thinking, had proven to be so disastrous that it seemed only right to discard all vestiges of it, including my ideas about child rearing. Of course, at that time, I didn't realize that the adoption of the fundamentalist ideation was going to be even more disastrous.

I decided that Larry and I ought to discuss and codify what "the rules" were. They should then be fairly dealt with in every case, considering the age and development of the individual child. The only things I could think of that were truly important to enforce in any way were that we should not allow physical aggression against persons or property. It seemed logical that acts of physical aggression should be met by some consequential physical response so that the children—if they became aggressive in such ways—would quickly learn that you get back what you give. I then decided that I would like to find a way to teach the children that lying was not a positive thing. I knew that fear of punishment might make a child lie to protect herself, so it was agreed that telling the truth might result in some kind of restriction, but not a spanking. I also believed that striking a child in anger was not a good thing, so that any physical punishment ought to be administered in a cool state, moderately, and only on the child's well padded bottom. Finally, I believed firmly that a child should be allowed to express their feelings without fear of judgment or retribution. I wanted to make it clear that they could think or say anything they wanted that came from inside them, even if they felt that they hated me or one of their siblings and wanted to say it; they just couldn't *act* on it. This excluded labeling or calling names. It was okay to say "I don't like you," but it was not okay to say "you're stupid." Labeling and calling names was, in my mind, a sort of verbal violence. In short, I was trying to find a way to support Larry's views, with sufficient modifications so that my own ideas could be implemented. However, once again, my intentions were soon thwarted and twisted.

The first spanking my oldest child ever had was because she refused, at the age of three, to use the potty. She would hold it until she became constipated and, after several episodes of having to use suppositories because the poor little thing was so miserable, Larry decided that the only solution was to spank her if he caught her holding her bowels. I was terribly upset by this. All the received wisdom from the different schools of psychology claimed that making an issue over potty training was very damaging psychologically. Larry patiently explained to me that if the child kept doing something that was detrimental even to their own health, then a judicious shock—a swat on the behind—applied in response to the incident would condition the child to not do it.

Fine, only we aren't talking about dogs here. Nevertheless, the spanking over the bowel problem was mild, and seemed to work, so I accepted the idea of physical punishment being a possibility. And, as time passed, it became a norm—even if it was rare. The only problem was that, as time went by, the only time Larry administered such discipline was when the child did something that upset *him*, specifically, and often had nothing to do with genuine misbehavior or infractions of the so-called rules.

What's more, he never stood behind any of the rules or requests that came from me and, in fact, would support the children against me in deliberate breaking of the rules we had established between us. The end result was that they learned, unconsciously, to do those things that broke the rules of order that were normal and natural in such a way that Larry would back them up against me. I would be provoked into a sense of helpless fury at being treated like a slave, servant, or worse—invisible, not even a human being—by both my husband and my children. Even though I could clearly see that Larry was responsible, that he was not fulfilling his role as a moderate and fair disciplinarian as we had agreed, I knew that I had to make it clear to the children that such behavior was not acceptable. It was not healthy for a child to have contempt for their mother and what was right and to think that they could just run to Daddy and get away with things. And I couldn't spank Larry. When I told him he was encouraging the very behavior that we had agreed was unacceptable, and that he should act in ways to support respect for their mother, he said he just didn't have the heart to punish them. When I pressed the issue, he declared, "Okay, YOU do the discipline since my input isn't wanted!"

There was no united front of parental authority with logical, reasonable rules that were not so mutable that they changed every day. My only solution was to spank them to make it clear that what they were doing was not acceptable, would not be tolerated, even if Larry either promoted it or permitted it.

Yes, in retrospect, that was pretty sick. This was a gradual development, over time, and like the frog in the pan of water, I didn't realize that the heat was being turned up on me. I was driven to behave in ways that were totally contrary to my inner nature, my intentions, and my wishes.

At the same time, if one of the children did something that particularly upset Larry, like using something that belonged to him and not putting it back, he would erupt in fury and the punishment was all out of proportion to the deed. If one of the children did something in public to embarrass him, he would similarly overreact. He became verbally abusive if one of them contradicted him, and he constantly told them their ideas were wrong. My objections prompted him to withdraw completely from any family participation and sulk for days. I begged, I pleaded, I reasoned, I cajoled—trying to establish a parental relationship between us that was united, healthy, and fair. It was like spitting in the wind.

I admit that my worries about the children were excessive. I think that this was partly because of the constant overshadowing presence of the Face at the Window and the lack of stability of my own childhood. I was almost pathologically paralyzed whenever the children were out of my sight or hearing, terrified that something terrible would happen to one of them and I would not be there to prevent it. The only times the children were ever physically hurt was when they were in Larry's care and I was otherwise occupied. This amounted to several broken bones, a severe scalding injury to my second child that put her in the hospital for two weeks and nearly killed her, and assorted other injuries that made me grow to distrust Larry as a guardian of the children.

To be fair, there were a couple of injuries that occurred when they were under my eye, but in both cases, I had an intuition that I ignored. I soon learned to listen to this inner voice. Larry never had an inner voice, or he never listened to it. He used my fears for the safety of the children as a means of tormenting me. He would take them somewhere, tell me that he would be back at a certain time, and then stay gone several hours longer than he indicated. He knew that if they weren't back at the appointed time, or he didn't call, that I would suffer extreme panic and anxiety, but he brushed it off as something that I needed to "get over." Well, no kidding! I knew it, he knew it, but shoving my face in it wasn't the way to go about it.

It was only in the unfolding of the events of my life, the emerging awareness of other lives and other experiences, that I was able to come to terms with my crippling need to keep my children as close as possible at all times; my terror that something terrible would happen to them if they were not in my sight.

For many years I have kept an on-again, off-again dream journal, and fortunately, this is among the dreams that were recorded. Before I describe the dream, however, I need to explain the context in which it occurred.

By the time I had finished the initial research for The Noah Syndrome, I was very nearly convinced of the idea that World War II and the Holocaust had been "created" events—and the finger pointed directly at elements of a secret power within the government. By following the paper trail, by examining the facts dispassionately, by simply observing humanity and the world at large, I was gradually brought to that conclusion. It hurt me a lot. I'm a person who cries when the flag passes in a parade or when the Star-Spangled Banner is played at a ballgame. As a child, I was proud to stand up every morning before class, place my hand over my heart, and say the Pledge of Allegiance. It never stopped bringing a lump to my throat. To see that elements of the authorities in the good old U.S. of A. could possibly have been responsible, even if only partly, for that obscenity we now call the Holocaust, was personally devastating.

Once I had come to some sort of peace about it, realizing that very often people within government do nasty things that have nothing to do with the people they govern, I still realized that there was some element of this that still escaped my understanding. The Holocaust was something else altogether. It was Evil with a capital "E" raised to an incredible order of magnitude. I was obsessed with it. I told myself that I had to look into the face of this Evil, to search the eyes of its victims for some sort of reflection of what they saw, how they experienced what they did, and how, in the name of God, any of them survived with their sanity intact. In the end, I suppose, I had some sort of unarticulated idea that if anything of truth and love could survive such an event, it would have to be of such intensity and purity that nothing, not even the gates of hell, could stand against it. And I needed to know that this existed.

THE DREAM

Day after day, week after week, I poured through the books, examining every face in every photograph, every withered and emaciated limb, every haunted pair of eyes, every tender and precious babe, child, husband, wife, parent, tossed in heaps like so much cordwood for the furnaces of Eastern Europe. Page after page I turned, reading stories, personal accounts of horrors too dreadful to be spoken aloud, much less committed to writing. And as I moved through it, the horror mounted inside me like a volcano building up to explode. I realized that I was looking for a face. Not just any face. A face I would know.

And I wept.

And then, the dream:

September 11, 1987—Dreamed I was the wife of a "dark" (complexion) man who was going on a trip. I was upstairs in our apartment, on the balcony, waving goodbye. We had four children—one was a teenaged boy and one was a little baby. My husband was somehow a "foreigner." As he was leaving, he blew kisses and called to me that he loved me. I answered very softly because I was aware that there was some sort of dangerous prejudice around against "foreigners" and I didn't want to exacerbate already hostile feelings of the neighbors. But two men in the courtyard below overheard me and saw to whom I was saying "I love you," and they became enraged at expressions of love between me, a "white" woman, and this dark foreigner. They rushed at him with big guns and killed him—blew his face away right before my eyes and bits of his blood and flesh spattered on me.

Apparently, I must have committed suicide and was watching the action from the astral realms because the rest of the dream seemed to center around the fact that I was not there to care for my children. Some powerful men came and killed the murderers of my husband, but they let our children be adopted out because they were just as prejudiced against me for being white! They didn't want the shame of half-white children.

As I awoke, that "voice" that speaks without sound announced to me: "This is the dynamic of your last life!"

I was crying because I loved this husband I had lost so much it was almost impossible to bear the grief. He was The One, and I knew it. I knew him so deeply in my soul that his absence was the greatest burden I had ever faced. He was the one I was looking for every time I had awakened feeling lost and out of place. I also realized that it was this loss that had haunted me all my life; it was this hole in my heart that I had been seeking to fill for all these years.

I had never before awakened crying—that is, in the act itself, with tears already soaking my pillow—but now I was sobbing uncontrollably and Larry wanted to know why.

I couldn't tell him.

CHAPTER THIRTY

A KNIGHT IN ARMOR

I called Eva. I wanted to tell her about my dream of the former life and my conviction that I'd committed suicide. After I finished, Eva became was very quiet for a long moment.

"Yes, I already knew that," she said finally.

"How?"

"When Lama Sing did the reading for you, years ago, the last time you'd almost …"

"Almost killed myself."

"Yes. Well, there was other information he gave. We held it back from you."

"What!"

"Al Miner's wife called me right after that," Eva said. "Al told her Lama Sing came through to him, saying this was one of the primary issues you were dealing with in this life. He said that you had committed suicide in your immediate past life. The emotions at the moment of death are, apparently, some sort of pattern overlay on the subsequent life."

This was a surprise. "What context was this information presented in, Eva?" I wanted to know.

"Al's wife didn't know very much. She just thought it would be best if we kept this information away from you then."

It had either not been recorded on the tape, or had been erased, Eva said, and now there was no way of knowing if any specifics had been given.

I don't know if it would have helped or made things more difficult to know at the time. It's hard to gauge something like that. But I had confirmation of a sort that the information coming through in my dreams was accurate—or at least close. Eva thought I would benefit from some guided meditation tapes. I was agreeable to try it, but I knew that her purpose was to divert me from any further thinking about the possibility that an evil magician ruled the world.

I wrote to Eva:

"December, 1987—About the 'Journey Into the Light' tape you sent—it was very interesting and not unfamiliar or dissimilar to previous personal experiences of my own. But, I want to comment that, years ago, I interviewed a number of people who had taken mescaline. It seems they had all experienced fantastic "inner voyages." It is, it seems, a total alteration of perception; they 'see' sounds and 'hear' colors and movement. Most of them described, laying over the whole experience, 'waves of reality.' They traveled into 'other realms' and perceived other beings—even very frightening areas of darkness and despair. They describe a disintegration of reality that includes the self. For most of them, this 'loss of identity' is terrifying.

"In my own experiences with meditation, I have experienced 'transfer of information,' most of which is kept buried and which I have never shared with anyone. Until I can find confirmation of it in some other source, I will continue to hold it inside.

"The point is: the mescaline experience—including other hallucinogens—is purely chemical—or, at least, chemically induced. Since the brain is capable of such incredible 'voyages' as a result of chemicals, how can we assert with absolute certainty that similar self-induced 'flights' or even acts of 'channeling' are not also merely chemical reactions within the physical brain? How do we know we are not merely manifestations of the imagination of some slumbering Cosmic Being? Or the toys or whatever of a group of celestial adversaries? (For I cannot doubt some foundation for our existence other than mere accident).

"Now, I suppose that what has happened to me is that my faith—once so strong and impervious to external assault—has succumbed to a sort of 'devil's advocate' mode of thinking. For so long I maintained the 'proper' attitudes—performed the proper acts—to 'create' a reality more in line with what I felt would provide the environment for creative productivity and simple happiness ...

"Well, hope springs eternal, as they say. I will continue to do those things which should lead to 'enlightenment.' I will water the shriveled plant of my faith and withhold judgment. But I cannot lie and pretend all is at peace in me or that I find my life, up to this point, at all what I would have hoped.

"I am now at the age you were when I met you. You are now past 50—and so little time has passed! I thought we would be young and adventurous and carefree forever, or at least until we died. As Rose said: I expect to be dead someday, but I don't plan to spend any time dying. Yet, my mortality has never weighed so heavily upon me as now. Maybe I'm going through 'the change.' I feel crazy as hell sometimes ..."

Eva wrote back:

"Try to keep a positive mind—you sounded a bit pessimistic—and send a note to the Lama Sing prayer group. I am using my crystal to pray for you also & holding positive, healing images, light etc."

Of course I was putting into practice every known and possible "remedy" for my situation—most especially the conditions of my mind. Perhaps it is a flaw to always seek the solution to problems in one's own attitude and thinking, but it is certainly a greater difficulty for those who never consider that they could be wrong about anything.

Even in my state of doubt, I continued to meditate. I had the idea that if I could produce the required changes in myself—even if it was only acceptance—that would enable me to pass through this rough period. Most particularly, I wanted a change in my marriage. I needed Larry's acceptance of me as a questioning, intelligent human being—not merely a cook, housekeeper, sex object, babysitter, and doormat. I knew that he had been wounded, that he had insecurities, that perhaps his behavior was simply designed to drive me away, to manifest some self-fulfilling prophecy he had about himself that no woman could love him or stand by him. I knew that, if anybody could do it, I could. And the goal was, of course, to heal myself so that Larry would be healed. Then, if we were both en rapport, our children would benefit, and all would be right with the world.

My meditation practice rapidly progressed. After only a few months of practice, I found myself "zoning out" for up to three hours at a time, coming to myself feeling as though no time at all had passed. The only problem was: I never seemed to bring anything back with me. I had no idea what had been going on, where my mind had been. I did note that I was far more peaceful and able to cope with the difficulties of my life, but it was still frustrating not to obtain something a bit more concrete from all of this endeavor.

These complete blackouts were explained partly by Gurdjief, as recorded by Ouspensky in *In Search of the Miraculous*:

"Man number one means man in whom the center of gravity of his psychic life lies in the moving center. This is the man of the physical body, the man with whom the moving and the instinctive functions constantly outweigh the emotional and the thinking functions.

"Man number two means man on the same level of development, but man in whom the center of gravity of his psychic life lies in the emotional center, that is, man with whom the emotional functions outweigh all others; the man of feeling, the emotional man.

"Man number three means man on the same level of development but man in whom the center of gravity of his psychic life lies in the intellectual center, that is, man with whom the thinking functions gain the upper hand over the moving, instinctive, and emotional functions; the man of reason, who goes into everything from theories, from mental considerations.

"Every man is born number one, number two, or number three. ...

"In order to understand the work of the human machine and its possibilities, one must know that, apart from these three centers and those connected with them, we have two more centers, fully developed and properly functioning, but they are not connected with our usual life nor with the three centers in which we are aware of ourselves.

"The existence of these higher centers in us is a greater riddle than the hidden treasure which men who believe in the existence of the mysterious and the miraculous have sought since the remotest times.

"All mystical and occult systems recognize the existence of higher forces and capacities in man although, in many cases, they admit the existence of these forces and capacities only in the form of possibilities, and speak of the necessity for developing the hidden forces in man. This present teaching differs from many others by the fact that it affirms that the higher centers exist in man and are fully developed.

"It is the lower centers that are undeveloped. And it is precisely this lack of development, or the incomplete functioning, of the lower centers that prevents us from making use of the work of the higher centers. ...

"As has been said earlier, there are two higher centers: The higher emotional center, working with hydrogen 12, and the higher thinking center, working with hydrogen 6. "If we consider the work of the human machine from the point of view of the 'hydrogens' which work the centers, we shall see why the higher centers cannot be connected with the lower ones.

"The intellectual center works with hydrogen 48; the moving center with hydrogen 24.

"If the emotional center were to work with hydrogen 12, its work would be connected with the work of the higher emotional center. In those cases where the work of the emotional center reaches the intensity and speed of existence which is given by hydrogen 12, a temporary connection with the higher emotional center takes place and man experiences new emotions, new impressions hitherto entirely unknown to him, for the description of which he has neither words nor expressions. But in ordinary conditions the difference between the speed of our usual emotions and the speed of the higher emotional center is so great that no connection can take place and we fail to hear within us the voices which are speaking and calling to us from the higher emotional center.

"The higher thinking center, working with hydrogen 6, is still further removed from us, still less accessible. Connection with it is possible only through the higher emotional center. It is only from descriptions of mystical experiences, ecstatic states, and so on, that we know cases of such connections. These states can occur on the basis of religious emotions, or, for short moments, through particular narcotics; or in certain pathological states such as epileptic fits or accidental traumatic injuries to the brain, in which cases it is difficult to say which is the cause and which is the effect, that is, whether the pathological state results from this connection or is its cause.

"If we could connect the centers of our ordinary consciousness with the higher thinking center deliberately and at will, it would be of no use to us whatever in our present general state. **In most cases where accidental contact with the higher thinking center takes place a man becomes unconscious. The mind refuses to take in the flood of thoughts, emotions, images, and ideas which suddenly burst into it. And instead of a vivid thought, or a vivid emotion, there results, on the contrary, a complete blank, a state of unconsciousness. The memory retains only the first moment when the flood rushed in on the mind and the last moment when the flood was receding and consciousness returned.** But even these moments are so full of unusual shades and colors that there is nothing with which to compare them among the ordinary sensations of life. This is usually all that remains from so-called 'mystical' and 'ecstatic' experiences, which represent a temporary connection with a higher center. Only very seldom does it happen that a mind which has been better prepared succeeds in grasping and remembering something of what was felt and understood at the moment of ecstasy. But even in these cases the thinking, the moving, and the emotional centers remember and transmit everything in their own *way, translate absolutely new and never previously experienced sensations into the language of usual everyday sensations, transmit in worldly three-dimensional forms things which pass completely beyond the limits of worldly measurements; in this way, of course, they entirely distort every trace of what remains in the memory of these unusual experiences. Our ordinary centers, in transmitting the impressions of the higher centers, may be compared to a blind man speaking of colors, or to a deaf man speaking of music.*

"In order to obtain a correct and permanent connection between the lower and the higher centers, it is necessary to regulate and quicken the work of the lower centers."

The only thing I can say is that I was doing this zoning out regularly and, as Gurdjieff described, brought nothing back with me. As a matter of practicality I generally meditated lying on the bed. Some people cannot do this because they tend to fall asleep, but that was never a problem for me. I could zone out in meditation, "come to" some time later, and then go to sleep easily at night. I was generally so uncomfortable in any position that getting to sleep was problematical if I didn't meditate first.

So, I went to bed and waited for Larry to go to sleep. If he thought I wanted quiet for meditation, he would manage to just have to make some sort of noise or disruption, apologize, and then do it again.

After he was asleep, I began my breathing exercises. This part of the process I had borrowed from my hypnotherapy training and was extremely useful. Of course, I later learned that it had been "borrowed" for hypnotherapy from certain meditation systems. (The practices I used at this time are now being made available and taught in the Éiriú Eolas program. You will be able to read here about the amazing experiences I had with this practice.)

At this point, I don't know what happened. All I remember is starting the breathing phase, which came before the contemplative phase of the exercise. But then I made some kind of big "skip."

The next thing I knew, I was jerked back into consciousness by a sensation that can only be described as a boiling turbulence in my abdomen. It was so powerful that, at first, it felt actually physical—like there was a boiling agitation in my organs that was going to erupt upward in some way.

I was frantically holding my throat, because I could feel a tightening of the muscles in the throat area, as wave after wave of energy blew upward like the precursors of steam blasts from a volcano before it erupts. I struggled out of the bed, holding the wall with one hand and my throat with the other, clenching my teeth so whatever it was would not come gushing out of me and disturb Larry or the children. For all I knew, I was just going to be violently sick.

I rushed outside to the porch Larry had recently built onto our little house, where there was a lawn sofa, and collapsed onto it just as the outpouring began.

I wish I could describe this in better words, but there are simply none that apply other than ordinary descriptions which don't come close to the essence and intensity of the event. What erupted from me was a shattering series of sobs and cries that were utterly primeval and coming from some soul-deep place that defies explanation. Accompanying these cries, or actually, embedded in them, were images—visions—complete scenes with all attendant emotional content and implied context conveyed in an instant. Again, it was like the idea of your life passing before your eyes. But, in this case, it was not scenes from this life. It was lifetime after lifetime. I knew that I was there in every scene, in these vignettes of other lives. I was experiencing myself as all these people.

And the tears. My God! The tears that flowed. I had no idea that the human physiology was capable of producing such copious amounts of liquid so rapidly.

Now, if this had been just an hour-long crying jag or something like that, it would have to pass into history as "just one of those things," maybe like PMS. But, this activity had a life of its own. It went on, without slowing or stopping, for *more than five hours*. If I attempted to slow it down, stop it, or "switch" my mind in another direction, the inner sensation of explosive eruption rapidly took over, all the muscles in my body would begin to clench up and I was no longer in control. I could only sit there as a sort of instrument of grief and lamentation, and literally sob my heart out for every horror of history in which I had seemingly participated or to which I had possibly been a witness. I think that there were even some that I was simply aware of without my direct participation. And some were truly horrible scenes.

Plague and pestilence and death and destruction. Scene after scene. Loved ones standing one moment, crushed or lying in bloody heaps the next. Rapaciousness, pillaging, plundering; rivers of blood and gore; slaughter, carnage, and butchery in all its many manifestations passed before my eyes; holocaust and hell. Rage and hot anger, bloodlust and fury, murder and mayhem, all around me, everywhere I looked. Evil heaped on evil like twisted, dismembered bodies. And the grief of centuries, the unshed tears of millennia, the guilt, remorse, and penitence flooded through me; melting, thawing, and dissolving the burdensome shell of stone that encased my petrified heart; washing away the pain with my tears. An ocean of tears.

As this release of the worlds of accumulated guilt and grief of many lifetimes went on, the voice-that-was-not-a-voice in the background, ever soothing, ever calming, repeated:

"It's not your fault. There is no blame. It's not your fault. You didn't know."

And I came to understand something very deep: I understood that there is no original sin. I understood that the terrors and suffering mankind experiences here in life on earth are not caused by some sort of flaw or error or aberration from within. It is not punishment. It is not something from which one can be saved.

I understood that every scene of terrible suffering and heart-rending cruelty was the result of IGNORANCE. And each experience was the gaining of knowledge.

It is easier to see this idea when you consider the Crusades or the Inquisition. You can trace the path of twisted reason, leading from the idea of the love of God to imposing that view on others "for their own good, " ending in torture and mass murder. Forget for a moment about those who just viciously used such philosophies for their own gain and political maneuvers. Think for a moment about the sincerity of the philosophies behind such events. But it is based on IGNORANCE.

Those who were seemingly out for gain and self-aggrandizement were operating out of ignorance—fear and hunger of the soul that cannot be satisfied. It is only a matter of degrees, but in the end, it is only ignorance.

When the flow of energy, images, and tears finally began to subside, I felt a sensation of warm, balmy liquid, almost airy in its lightness, and so sweet that to this day, I can still remember the piercing quickening of the fire of love for all of creation. It was ecstatic, rapturous, and exultant all at the same time. I was lost in wonder, amazed and at the same time bewildered at this vision of the world.

Well, the result of this event was a state of prolonged elevation or loving peace that persisted for a very long time. You could even say that the effects reverberate to the present. Never again was I able to condemn—

act against with intent to destroy what they choose to believe—another, no matter how wicked their deeds. I could see that all so-called evil and wickedness was a manifestation of ignorance. No person, no matter how holy and elevated they may think they are in this life, has not reveled in the shedding of another's blood in some other time and place. And no person who chooses ignorance and wickedness and destruction in this life is "wrong." Yes, I had the right to avoid them, to defend myself against them, to understand what they were doing; but it was not my place to go on a campaign to change their mind.

The significant point is this: Ignorance is a choice, and one made for a reason: to learn and to grow.

And that realization led to another: to learn how to truly choose. To be able to learn, at this level of reality, what is and isn't of ignorance, what is of truth and beauty and love and cleanliness. I understood the saying of Jesus that some things are bright and shining on the outside, but inside they are filthy and full of decay. And I don't mean that I was seeing this negativity as something to be judged. I clearly understood its reason and place as modes of learning, but I was deeply inspired to seek out all I could learn about this world to best manifest what was of light.

I was so excited by this revelation that I wanted to tell everybody.

At that point, members of the church we had attended were still coming by occasionally to find out why we had sort of dropped out. These visits gave me the opportunity to talk about my spiritual experiences. In every single case, I was literally rebuked as having been duped by Satan.

I thought about that a lot. I wondered if it could be so, if the whole drama of the visions, the actions of the minister who had been a wolf in sheep's clothing, could have been set up and dramatized just to deceive me. Perhaps my soul was in peril. But, if they were wrong, what did that make of the whole basis of Christianity? How could anything they had built on this basic error be right?

This distressed me. I was most definitely "adjusting" my Christian position, but I was not quite prepared to toss the whole thing out the window. I mean, after all, through all the years of study and investigation, Christianity had been my background. When, as a child, I began questioning the existence of a god at all, that was altogether different. But, now, *making the decision to believe that Christianity was foundationally wrong—if there was no original sin from which to be saved, there was no necessity for a savior—this amounted to making a choice.*

It was a matter that took a number of years to resolve. What is important is that, from this experience forward, I was never again able to see sin in quite the same light. When I read about murderers and deeds of mayhem, I knew these were things that I had done also in times past, in my ignorance. When anyone did something that hurt me, I knew that I had done such things as well. I could no longer feel any judgment or criticism because I knew, at some place and time, it was myself I was judging. All my lifetimes had been for learning. I grew from each experience. I learned what not to do by doing it. And, in a very real sense, this is the reason for pain and suffering. It is like an automatic guidance system that keeps a person on the path of learning. But the trick is to be able to discern the difference between choosing a path that gives immediate physical comfort, and then leads to great psychic or soul pain, and a path that may be physically uncomfortable temporarily, that leads to peace of the heart.

Of course, this principle was not automatically perfectly enacted in my life. I had the idea, now it was just a matter of learning how to apply it. And I made mistakes, and still make mistakes. Most of these mistakes relate to the fact that this world is run by an evil magician who seeks to control everything and everybody with truly devious manipulations. And it seems that anyone who seeks to escape this control becomes a target of even greater and more subtly devious manipulations through "agents" of the Control System.

What is more, if a person seeks to share this information by merely putting it out there for others to consider, the levels of attack and attempts to destroy increase exponentially. And always, they come in the guise of "love and light," and claims that "I'm only doing this for your own good; I really want only to help you."

Had I not had the need to care for my children, I might have simply withdrawn from the world to spend the rest of my life in studious contemplation and repetition of ecstatic exercises. What actually happened in the real world can be looked at in a more miraculous light. We might even say that these events were a direct reflection of the shift in my perspective as a result of direct contact with the higher centers as described by Gurdjieff and being able to bring something back.

Larry found a job that paid better wages and began working days, so our schedule was more normal. Eva's husband, who owned a fleet of trucks, decided to get new ones, and offered to sell us one (with very low mileage) for less than a fifth of its market value. With more income, were able to add onto the "cabin"—more than tripling our living space—install electricity and plumbing, and basically return to the real world. Of course, by this time I had already had to sell my piano, and I mourned its absence for a very long time. I resumed doing hypnotherapy, which had been abandoned during the "faith trip," and began to do past-life therapy. I didn't do this by going out and opening an office and hanging out a shingle. It actually came about in a strange way.

When my second daughter was born, I went to great lengths to make sure that my first child didn't have any experiences that would lead to so-called sibling rivalry. I made sure my older child did not suffer from any lessening of attention, allowing her to hold and help with the new baby, and so forth. I thought I had accomplished this fairly well until an incident occurred that took the wind right out of my sails.

Not long after we had moved out to Larry's property in the woods, he had just finished building the septic tank a short distance from the little house. There was a mound of clean, white sand I decided we ought to just keep for the children to play in rather than rake it out and disperse it.

The girls were outside in the sand pile, and I was resting on the bed and listening to them play, checking on them every few minutes through the window. They weren't aware that I was watching them.

Since I was just listening to their voices and not the specific words, I can't say how the discussion between them was progressing, but suddenly I was shocked to hear my oldest say: "I hate you! I wish you were dead!"

I looked out the window and there they were, my little angels, the older one holding a cement trowel against the stomach of her little sister, pressing the point of it into the flesh dangerously, and saying: "Ever since you came, I've hated you! If I could get away with it, I'd kill you!"

Well! Talk about shattering of illusions! From my point of view, both of them were absolutely perfect and gorgeous and smart and talented and *angelic*. I had worked so very hard to ensure that they would have no reason for jealousy or rivalry between them, and here, clearly, I had missed something. I couldn't be angry with either of them because I realized there was an issue here that was clearly deeper than anything I had ever heard of or read about. The immediate situation had to be handled cleverly because, if my oldest daughter felt this way, most of all I needed to know why. Shaming her or berating her would not open communications between us.

I made some "stirring about" noises and went to the door and called the girls, acting as though I had seen and heard nothing. I began to watch them closely, to try to take corrective actions so that both of them felt equally loved and cherished.

It didn't help. As time went by, my older daughter became more morose and resentful and often came running to me to demand that I order her sister not to follow her around, to go away and let her play alone, or to otherwise disappear from her world in some way.

Everything her sister did annoyed and irritated her to the point of wanting to explode. She hated it when her little sister, who absolutely worshipped her, would try to dress the same way, or wear her hair the same, or use the same expressions, or any of the other imitative things that little children do when they admire someone.

I pointed out that this imitation was a form of love and showed how much her little sister respected her. It didn't help. She admitted that she knew this was true; she knew her feelings had no cause, no rhyme or reason. In the end, she just knew that she deeply hated her sister and wanted to see her dead.

Well, we had a problem. I was glad that she felt that she could share her feelings with me, that she was able to look at it logically and see that it wasn't rational (she was nine by this time), but when she burst into tears and began shaking, saying that she really wanted me to help her because she was afraid she would do something really bad, I knew I had to find a solution.

I hadn't done any hypnosis for a number of years, and the girls had been mostly shielded from my "spiritual quest" activities. Until I was certain of which way things would fall, I saw no point in upsetting their belief system formed by Larry and the church. It was okay for me to ask questions and experiment, but I didn't feel I had the right to upset them by just saying one day, "Oops! Well, you know all that stuff we told you about God all your life? Well, it's wrong! Sorry!"

They knew nothing about ideas of reincarnation, metaphysics, and other philosophies. They had also spent nearly their entire lives without television or movies or other "forbidden" activities. They had been protected from exposure to anyone who drank alcohol (even just a beer!), or swearing, or dancing and so on. They were, in effect, totally "pure" according to the church teachings, but also totally ignorant of the real world. (That's another thing that was going to come back and bite me later.) I knew for certain that nothing obvious in their lives or experience up to that point could have generated such a problem. I also knew that sometimes, seemingly minor events of life, as seen from the perspective of an adult, could be very influential in the mind of the child. This had come up repeatedly in many hypnotherapy sessions I had conducted. Had one of us said or done something inadvertently that she perceived as a reason to hate her sister?

My daughter was just barely old enough for hypnosis, and this was most assuredly the type of issue that hypnotherapy was touted to cure. When she cried and asked me to help her, I responded that yes, I might know a way. Did she want to try it?

"Yes," she pleaded. "I'm going to go crazy if I can't stop feeling this way!"

As always, I didn't want to contaminate my work with leading questions. After I had put her under, I simply said, "Go to the place and time where this feeling of hatred toward your sister first began." That was it. No suggestion that it might be another life or that her sister might be a different person. And, with her complete lack of knowledge of such things, I really expected to have some minor incident revealed that I would then help her to process and gain a broader understanding so that the issue would be resolved easily.

No such luck!

In a voice that was stronger and more adult than that of a nine-year-old little girl, my daughter began to describe a mad ride on horseback through a forest. She was a soldier, a volunteer for a dangerous journey to deliver a message that would bring reinforcements to a besieged fortress full of family, friends, and comrades at arms. The lives of hundreds of people depended on her achieving her mission.

Suddenly an enemy soldier appeared in her path and her horse shied and she was knocked to the ground by an overhanging limb. The blow nearly knocked her senseless, and as she was finally able to gather her wits, she saw the enemy standing over her, contemptuously lifting his visor to show his face before driving the sword into the weak place in the armor. The last thought of the dying soldier was the knowledge that she had failed in her mission and now all she loved was lost. Hatred for the one who was, in effect, the cause of so much death and destruction was frozen in her heart at the instant of death.

Well. It's not a good idea to do this kind of therapy with people you are close to: the bonds of love make you vulnerable to their experiences in an almost direct way. I was stunned, to say the least. Of course, it could also be true that such dramas were created by the mind as a means of symbolically expressing a conflict that the conscious mind did not want to acknowledge. I was inclined to think that it may have been a real experience, but it could have been a psychodrama presented by the subconscious mind. It was also possible that she had read stories about knights in armor and chose this one to dramatize her emotions.

It didn't really matter, however. I knew that the objective was to work with what was given. I guided her to the between-life state where she could look back on the incident with a greater perspective and, hopefully, forgive the enemy she realized had become her sister in this present life.

No dice. She wasn't ever going to forgive her. She had killed her in other lives already and it had brought no peace, and even though she knew she couldn't kill her in this life, she would certainly never forgive her.

I suggested that, perhaps, this event might have been an interaction that was predicated upon an even earlier dynamic, and perhaps we should look for that?

"Yes," she admitted. "I already killed her a long time ago."

"Before this time?"

"Yes."

She had killed her sister in an even earlier period and this event between the soldiers was merely a reversal of the former event. But still, the condition existed that so many other people she loved had been killed as a result of her failure to obtain reinforcements. The two acts were not equal. She still couldn't forgive because of that.

We went around and around with no resolution.

"Well, your former enemy, who is now your sister, must have resolved this situation in her heart," I told my daughter.

"Why do you say that?"

"She loves and admires you so much now," I said. "This is her way of seeking your forgiveness."

Grudgingly my daughter admitted this might be so.

Finally, I moved to direct suggestions for forgiveness, understanding, love, and peace in her heart toward her sister. It was all I could do, and I could only pray that it would do the job. There did seem to be an improvement. After several months of anxious observation, I relaxed and began to breathe a bit easier.

A KNIGHT IN ARMOR

* * *

My friend Sandra was excited to get me back into working with hypnosis. She promoted, scheduled, and provided the environment for me to resume a small hypnotherapy practice, though it could hardly be called that. After such a long break, I found that my skills had not diminished, and my experiences had brought new depth to my understanding of the problems people faced. I studied past-life therapy and began to employ it experimentally.

In the beginning, I had some idea that I ought to collect facts that could be checked, but as often as not, the subject just simply was not able to provide them in a consistent way, and I was not really in a position to check them. There were some "maybes" on a few situations, but no solid hits. In the end, I decided that it didn't really matter if I was going to be able to prove reincarnation. Others had tried and what proof they had obtained did not convince those who didn't want to be convinced, and those who believed already didn't need to be convinced. The only thing that mattered was that the therapy worked.

Naturally, just doing it at all was problematical. Larry was gradually moving into the position that all I did in such directions smacked faintly of satanic pursuits. He was ready to give up the specific church, but unwilling or unable to give up his beliefs. Larry's own beliefs were becoming quite fanatical and had embraced all kinds of government conspiracy ideas that Christians were soon to be objects of dire persecution. I ended up having a lot of "lunches" with Sandra. While he could complain about this, he didn't say too much, because Sandra always gave me extra money during these lunches and Larry had no problem with what he thought was charity from my friend. That I was working for this money never occurred to him. That anyone would pay for hypnotherapy also never occurred to him.

Thus it was that a knight in armor armed a different "Knight" and sent her off on a mission. But, as we will see, the price was high.

CHAPTER THIRTY-ONE

THE CLEFT IN THE ROCK

In 1988 I decided that a garden would help me to exercise and strengthen my muscles, ease pain, and assist a gradual return to full mobility. It was still difficult to walk. I had to put pants on sitting down because I couldn't lift my feet high enough; I couldn't exert enough control to insert them into the right leg.

Little by little, my garden became one of the few truly enjoyable aspects of my life. Of course, Larry very subtly demeaned it as useless and a waste of time. Growing flowers didn't produce food for the table. Well, that was true, but when I'd helped him start a vegetable garden, there was so much conflict and criticism about everything I did that I left him alone with his beans and squash. What's more, if we were going to sell the place, making sure it looked attractive was productive work to my way of thinking.

So I ignored his rants about the time I was wasting on grass and flowers. I took three Tylenol three to four times a day and worked away in the garden. Pain was easier to bear in summer air with the plants, seeing them grow and respond to my care in ways that clearly didn't work with my family. Eventually, even Larry appreciated my efforts after other people complimented me on my glorious roses and beds of giant marigolds. It was there that I prayed and "talked to God."

One day, crawling around on all fours pulling weeds, covered with dirt, I realized suddenly exactly where I was and what I was doing. With startling clarity, I saw that nothing I had ever thought about my future had come to pass.

We were in no position to send our children to college, they had never been to a summer camp, had very few friends and even fewer material comforts. I sat back against a tree and looked up at the sky and asked why.

I wanted God to tell me: *Why create a mind with the spirit of a mystic and the will of a bulldog, only to confine it to the prison of poverty and total obscurity?*

By this time, I'd learned how to hear the voice of God in the world around me. I saw all my glorious flowers, I saw my beautiful children playing across the yard. I realized the only thing that would matter in a hundred or a thousand or a million years was the satisfaction I'd experienced in growing my roses and loving my children. Maybe the only thing that existed eternally was the love we give away. Imperfect as I was, God only knows, I loved deeply and fully, with all my being. Those I loved, I would gladly give up my life for.

And perhaps I had. "Okay, God," I sighed. "I get it. I'll grow where you've planted me. Just show me what to do next."

Not very long after this, in a rather comical way, I had an out-of-body experience for the first time.

Meditating before going to sleep on a very warm night, I'd pulled my nightgown up above my knees and was lying on the bed without even a sheet to cover me so I'd be cool as possible. I began my breathing exercises and suddenly heard a sort of crackling or buzzing sound in my head. Then there was a sort of "whooshing" sound like an internal cosmic-whisper effect, and a word reverberated through me: *"Shekina!"*

Well, I quickly ran through my memory banks and pulled up the notion that this word meant "forerunner of the presence of God."

Wow! That was heavy!

My reaction to this was a sort of panicked feeling that I was "indecent" and that I ought to pull the sheet up to be more modestly arranged for whatever was going to happen now. I reached down and tugged my nightgown down decorously, pulled the sheet up, and folded my hands prayerfully. Next thing I knew, I badly had to go to the bathroom. So, I rolled to my side and reached out to brace myself as to stand up.

My hand went right through the wall.

Well, that was startling, but I really had to go, so I leaned forward to sort of lunge out of bed, and the upper half of my body went right through the wall into the bathroom.

Whoa! I stopped moving and looked around me. I realized with a start that I now had 360-degree vision. Not only that, I could see through everything. It wasn't that things were transparent, but rather that they were like living, colored light.

Everything was alive, and so colorful. I thought quickly about the children, and instantly I was there, hovering over them—all of them at once!—seeing them in their beds as they slept. That was impressive, so I decided to try thinking about something a few miles away. I thought of The Farm. Whoosh! There it was. A thought of anything brought me in direct contact. At the same time, focusing on any single thing did not eliminate the view of everything else around me in all directions at once.

Then I suddenly wondered, *What if I'm dead?!* I panicked at the thought of leaving the children unprotected. The instant I felt this panic, I snapped back like a rubber band. It was almost painful, like a sharp sting. I realized I was in my body, the sheet was still down, and I had never arranged my nightgown as I was sure I had.

Whatever had happened to me, wherever I had been, it had begun with the *cosmic whisper*. Everything after that had been in another realm.

* * *

In August of that year, Eva decided that I needed to get away from it all for a little break. I had never been away from my children more than a few days—generally in the hospital—and I felt uncomfortable with the idea.

But the vacation Eva had in mind was hard to resist.

Eva and her husband had a cabin in North Carolina. A Lama Sing symposium was planned near there. At this point, Eva had just completed treatment for her colon cancer and she hoped going up to the mountains would be restful and healing. She planned for us to spend a few days in Maggie Valley at the symposium, and then drive to their cabin for another seven days to hang out, meditate, poke around the mountains a bit, and rest and read.

The symposium was organized by a physician and his wife, close friends of Lama Sing's channel, Al Miner. Lectures, group meditations, dinners, and so on sounded like a lot of fun, and possibly a path to something new. Putting aside my fears about being away from the children, I agreed to go.

The talks proved lively and interesting. During the breaks, people walked around claiming to be seeing auras, ecstatic expressions on their faces, pronouncing sagely on the "wonderful energy present." Everybody told about their psychic experiences in much the same way fundamentalists speak in tongues and dance in the spirit. I wasn't saying much, just observing and feeling a bit put off by the lack of evidence to back up these stories. It seemed little different from the "testifying" in churches around the world.

I guess, in a sense, I had become a true skeptic. I wasn't going to believe anything or anybody without some corroborating evidence of at least the circumstantial kind if nothing else was available. I was even a little worried about Eva because she seemed to be completely taken in by all the claims and was turning into a true believer in the New Age religion.

On the next-to-last day of the symposium, the doctor's wife who'd helped sponsor the event gave a talk about the many people who were coming forward at that time with reincarnation memories of the Holocaust.

When she began to read from personal accounts of recovered memories, this produced in me an uncontrollable spell of crying. Again, it started as the boiling sensation in the pit of my stomach, and I had to leave the room and hide in a stall in the ladies' lavatory until I was able to gain control of myself. I really thought I was losing my grip. Nothing had ever affected me that way in public. It was one thing to have such an event occur as a result of prolonged meditation exercises, but something else altogether to have this reaction stimulated by words read from a podium. What was wrong with me that I felt so raw and vulnerable?

The next day, group meditation was scheduled as a closing ceremony. When Eva left to go, I stayed behind in the darkened motel room with cold towels and ice on my head.

At breakfast the next morning, a lady at our table remarked that the dress I had been wearing at the meditation the previous day was very lovely. I looked at her in surprise and said that I hadn't gone because I had been ill. She looked back at me and said, "I saw you clearly. No, I am not mistaken!" Eva laughed and assured her that I had been in bed. After an awkward silence, the chatter began again. But I was puzzled by this.

At the symposium, we had met two elderly ladies, very spry and hugely entertaining and interesting in a Dickensian sort of way. One of them claimed to have had some training in hypnosis and advanced meditative techniques, which she had taught at various times. Eva and I were interested in this, so we quickly discussed whether she ought to invite them back to the cabin with us for some experimentation. Eva approached them with the proposal and they quickly agreed. We decided that our stay at the cabin could be a lot of fun. In addition to meditation experiments, we could go digging for rocks at one of the local public crystal mines, and just generally have a hen party.

After driving half a day through the mountains, we arrived at the cabin, isolated at the end of an old logging road on the edge of the Nantahala National Forest. It was completely peaceful and delightful, perfect for our "experimental" meditations.

Our new friend June agreed to direct a guided meditation accompanied by musical tones on tape. We all found comfortable places, and the instructions began. I remember following the breathing part, and tuning in to the musical tones, but from that point, it seems my inner consciousness had plans of its own.

The next thing I knew, I felt myself lift out of my body and—"*shoooop!*"—I was suddenly hovering before a rock face on the side of a tall mountain. There was a crack, or cleft, in the rock. I knew that only very few people could pass through this narrow opening, and attempting it without being "one of those who can" would result in a shock that might be physically destructive. I decided to try. I aimed for it with volitional intent, and the next thing I knew I was emerging on the other side at the edge of a beautiful valley. There were meadows of green grass and wildflowers of deep luminescence and liveliness. The grasses were waving back and forth in the breeze, so it would seem, though this breeze was a conscious caressing of the grass and the waving of the grass was a conscious response to the caress, the way a cat purrs when stroked.

I found myself in a sort of body, and began to walk through this grass, which received my steps, caressing my feet and legs as I merged with it at every step. It passed me along, rather than me walking through it.

There was a striped tent a short distance before me with banners flying from the posts in the "consciously caressing" breeze, but it was on the other side of a small river. I knew this tent was where I was going, though there was no sensation of obligation. I was curious how it was going to feel when I stepped into the water of the river.

I looked at the water, crystal clear and sparkling in the bright sunlight, though there did not seem to be a sun in the sky, exactly. You could say that the jumping and dancing light on the water was a conscious interplay between this ambient, intense light and the water itself.

I stepped into the water, noticing that my feet were bare and that I seemed to be wearing a white under-robe with a striped over-robe that I hoisted out of the water with my hands. I was surprised to feel the current moving so swiftly, yet giving the sensation of a *merging* with my feet. The feeling can only be described as delicious to my feet. I was fascinated by the glittering, jewel-like stones at the bottom of the river. They were smooth, yet constantly flashing with the movement of the water across them. I walked across the river. This was an intense experience of deep significance. When I reached the other side, I was glad that I had passed a test, but regretful that the experience was over.

I approached the tent. Two men sat under an outer tent flap, open-sided like a porch, on a carpet spread on the grass. They were also dressed as I was. The tent was striped in the same pattern as the stripes of the over-robes, and the colors of the stripes were red, white, and black with a constantly repeating thin border to each stripe of lapis blue.

One of the men spoke to me: "We have been waiting for a long time. There is joy in seeing you again." Curiously, though I had the impression he was speaking, I was also aware this was an intentional whole-thought transfer.

For some reason, this didn't strike me as unusual. I had the feeling this meeting had been arranged a very long "time" ago. I bowed and acknowledged the greeting.

Then, the other man said: "He is inside." I felt overwhelming love and happiness that I would see "him" again after so long and weary an absence.

I ducked my head to enter the tent. An old man with young skin like iridescent porcelain stood inside. His expression on seeing me was absolute happiness and satisfaction. He embraced me strongly and kissed me on both cheeks, tears coming to his eyes. "We will break bread first," he said. We sat down on the carpeted ground inside the tent around a small table. The two men came in with bowls of milk. There was a golden goblet on the table already filled with something like wine. A large loaf of bread on the table was broken into equal pieces by the old man. Each of us was handed a piece. We dipped it in the milk and ate. Then the goblet was taken up by the old man, who passed his hands over it, blew on it, drank from it, and passed it to me. At that moment, I became aware that they were all watching me. I knew that drinking was another test. I drank and expressions of happiness were evident on all their faces.

Then the old man stood up and went through a door into an inner room in the tent. I knew that I was also supposed to follow. In this room was a golden chest about the size of a large breadbox. He went to it and opened it, taking out a large necklace.

Now, this necklace was about the strangest thing I have ever seen. It was made up of a series of balls of gold that were graduated like a strand of pearls. The smallest was about the size of a playing marble and the largest, in the center, was about the size of a golf ball. Suspended at the center was a figured-gold object set with a large stone. The figure of the piece consisted of two curved horns similar to rams' horns, mounted to the side of the flat surface on which the stone was fixed. The flat surface was both circular *and* triangular. How it could be both, I cannot say, but it was. The circular part seemed to be a function of the stone, which was rounded like a golfball cut in half. The stone fascinated me. Imagine a combination between a diamond and an opal and you have some idea of what it was like. It was milky, yet crystalline; flashing fire and colors like an opal, yet brilliant and transparent like a diamond. The *living nature* of this stone was apparent, and I was in awe of it.

The old man turned to me and looked at me long and carefully, searching my eyes for something. He held the necklace in both hands, suspended in air as he did so, and finally said: "You understand?" The understanding that was instantly "opened" to my mind was that, if I accepted the stone, there were responsibilities and consequences. Any manifestation of falseness in me would turn on me and destroy the instrument in which I was operating: the physical body of my present incarnation. It didn't matter if falsehood was unintended. I was being charged to seek out and speak only truth with no latitude for subjective wishful thinking. It could even be said that the necklace itself represented a sort of new circuit through which energies might be transmitted. By accepting the necklace, I was undertaking a process of seating something in my current physical body that had rarely, if ever, been manifested in the world of physical existence. I replied: "Yes."

With the acceptance of these conditions in full comprehension, I felt the mantle of enormous responsibility and risk I was accepting settle down upon my being. It was sobering, awe-inspiring, and even a little frightening. But the fear passed quickly. "You accept?" the old man asked, as if to fully confirm my acceptance of the conditions. "I do," I replied and bent my head to receive the stone. He placed the necklace carefully around my neck, adjusting the fit at the shoulders so that the stone should rest exactly at the base of my breastbone.

I was embraced again. The old man held on to me tightly for a moment as if in fear for my safety, kissed me again on both cheeks, and we turned and passed out of the inner room to the outer where the two other men were waiting. When they saw the stone, their faces lit up with joy and they clasped their hands together and bowed as I passed. I signaled them with my eyes as I did so, *knowing that I could no longer speak in that realm.*

The next thing I knew, I could hear June's voice calling my name at a great distance. Like a rocket, I shot through the cleft in the rock and found myself over the mountain where the cabin stood that held my mortal body, and then I was in the body, coming back as though emerging from a dark tunnel into the light of this world. I opened my eyes.

My friends were looking at me and laughing that I had gone to sleep.

I tried to say that something very extraordinary had happened, but words failed me. I found that I could not really describe this experience in anything but the most prosaic terms. They were making great fun of me, so I decided that I shouldn't talk and kept it to myself. They did ask what the stone was when I tried to describe it.

"It's called the Speaking Stone," I said.

* * *

There was another curious thing about my meditation practice. Not too long after I had begun, strange anomalies began to occur around me. Things would break in my presence with no apparent cause—fragile things, like drinking glasses or kerosene lamp chimneys. Objects disappeared and reappeared mysteriously, often in the exact places I had searched. To make sure my mind wasn't playing tricks, I even had Larry or one of the children search with me. When the object would reappear where we all knew it had not been, none of us could explain what was going on.

The breaking of objects was, naturally, more disturbing. I had attempted to try to explain this as rapid shifts in temperature that occur when you pour boiling water into a glass, but that didn't really work in the summer time, when there was nothing in the glass, and the lamp chimney had been sitting unused all day. In the end, it became just another anomaly to shove under the rug.

Now, however, on the trip down from the mountains on the way home, I was thinking about the Stone and how I was going to cope with this condition on my existence in my relations with Larry. At that very instant, the back window in my friend's new car exploded with a loud noise like a shot from a cannon. Eva was so startled that she slammed on the brakes. She looked in the rearview mirror with a startled expression. The back window was all milky-looking with the thousands of tiny fractures that appear in tempered glass as it breaks into little balls. Obviously, something had struck the window hard enough to make the noise and shatter it, but not hard enough to penetrate the glass.

There wasn't another car in sight and no apparent place that a missile could have come from. In fact, there didn't seem to be any impact point. The whole window was still in one piece, but completely covered with those lines of fracture. It was impossible to see through.

Swell! There we were, driving along with about five or six hundred miles to go, with a shattered rear window and a pile of luggage and souvenirs in the back seat! Not only that, it started raining. The window seemed to be holding, so Eva started off again and we kept moving slowly. At some point Eva came to a closed gas station, so we turned in. The instant we hit the bump on the end of the pavement, the whole window fell in on the seat in a pile of thousands of little glass balls.

The damage was eventually replaced, but the mechanics were completely baffled. They could come up with no explanation why the window would suddenly shatter.

*   *   *

We had a new bedroom built onto our "cabin," which had now become a house, and the room was lined on two sides with large plate-glass windows that measured four feet by six. The house was in the middle of a grove of trees, like having the outdoors inside. The head of the bed was against one of the walls of glass. I really enjoyed this room, especially when it rained.

I was meditating on the bed when Larry came into the house, forgetting to catch the screen door to prevent it from slamming shut with the force of the spring attached to it. When it slammed, I felt an internal jerking and the next thing I knew, the window at the head of the bed exploded, exactly as Eva's back window had done before. Again, it was tempered glass, and it was a moment before the balls began to start falling, slowly at first, then all at once, collapsing in a pile on top of me.

I spent days after this event walking around the property trying to figure out if some sort of missile could have been directed at the house. Maybe a hunter out in the woods had fired in the wrong direction? Of course, a new house had been built across the road on top of the hill there, and it was actually impossible for an errant bullet to have arrived from that trajectory. In fact, there really was no angle from which a bullet could have come, unless it was from someone standing directly at the front of our property at the bottom of the hill. There were too many trees, barriers, and hills to have prevented it.

Nevertheless, I was not ready to believe that it was really I doing this. Of course, everyone around me was becoming convinced that, in every instance, the "event" occurred in relation to some distress inside me. If this was psychokinesis, I had absolutely no awareness of how it operated, and definitely no control over it.

Needless to say, at that point, Larry became just a bit more cautious in actions designed to jerk my chain. He was already wary of the dozen or so shattered glasses and lamp chimneys that had gone before, but this was taking it to a new level. Heck, who knows? Maybe he was thinking I was some kind of witch. But this frightened him. I was moving into territory where he could not or would not follow.

I have to admit I was sometimes a bit frightened myself. Well, to be completely honest, sometimes I was utterly terrified. I didn't know what was happening to me.

I was on some sort of *path*.

I could only do as I did, because to do otherwise was, in a strange way, impossible. I thought of it as walking on water. In my mind, I was out in the middle of a vast ocean. There was a certain path for me, but each step was an act of faith as well as judicious consideration of probabilities.

I had a pretty good idea where the supports were hidden just under the surface of the water, but I was not allowed to see before I put my foot forward for the next step. I knew at any moment I might find that my step was not met by the support structure, and I would plunge into the waves.

And nobody was telling me what to do. I was having to figure it out myself based on the clues around me.

CHAPTER THIRTY-TWO

MOVING TO MONTANA

There were five named tropical storms in September after Eva and I made the trip to North Carolina in August. Tropical storm Keith, the last storm of the 1988 hurricane season, moved up through the Gulf of Mexico before crossing central Florida right over our heads. Keith brought more than wind and rain: the storm was the harbinger that signaled the beginning of my work as an exorcist. Again it was my daughter who opened the door.

Tropical storm Keith churned its way to our back door on November 19th. Keith was a minor storm in a sense, but gusting winds at fifty to sixty miles per hour and threatening to intensify into a hurricane before it made landfall. Most people weren't taking chances.

We had neighbors by now, though the term "neighbors" is relative when everyone lives on lots four to eight acres in size. Next to us there lived a young couple with a six-year-old son and a new baby, and they weren't too sure the mobile home they lived in while building their house would be safe in such winds. Larry told them they ought to come and wait out the storm with us, which is a fairly common practice in Florida during such weather. The sturdiest house becomes the safe house, and generally serves as hurricane shelter for small groups of friends and neighbors. By this time our house had tripled in size and was very sound, even if it could have used some expert finish work. We had installed tempered plate-glass windows all around. I was actually looking forward to sitting out the storm with a good view.

My neighbor's husband and Larry were soon engrossed in a fishing and hunting discussion, occasionally taking a break to put on their slickers and go outside to check on the neighbor's goats. After several hours of playing together with the wind howling outside, the children were definitely getting cranky. Suddenly, my older daughter came running out to tell us that the neighbor's little boy had said something really naughty. His mother was mortified and demanded that he come to her immediately and sit beside her where he could be watched. We were all in a stressful situation and I didn't think that too much ought to be made of it, so I suggested that maybe my children ought to all go to their beds and the little boy could sleep on my bed for the duration. Gratefully, she agreed, and we got them all situated.

After the children were all snug in bed, my young neighbor began to open up and confide that this was only one of many incidents that had been a source of concern for some time. She said that there was a significant problem with their little boy: he seemed not to be himself. She described all sorts of behavior clearly not normal for a six-year-old. As I probed for details, her descriptions became chilling indications that there was definitely something amiss here. The boy had developed an obsessive and very adult interest in sexuality that should have been absolutely beyond his possible knowledge base. What was more, when she questioned him about it, she remarked that he alternated between being a normal, sweet six-year-old and an old, jaded pervert.

Her words were: "He looks at me with eyes that are not his!"

I thought back to my own experiences with such eyes and wondered: just what kinds of possibilities were we looking at here?

My neighbor knew that I was doing hypnotherapy. She begged me to see if I couldn't find out what was troubling her son. He was a bit young, in my opinion, for any such therapy, but she was so desperate I agreed to give it a try at some point in the future. But it seems that fate had other plans.

We had been so engrossed in our conversation that we didn't even notice that the boy had been standing in the shadows at the door to my bedroom. Now he stepped forward.

"I brought the storm," he said, "and I hope that you all die!"

A frisson of fear ran up my backbone. The eyes looking at me out of that child's face were not his eyes. They were ancient and cunning and evil. I thought I was seeing things, imagining things, overwrought with the storm and the endless wind and rain. Maybe the child was just overtired or upset, his schedule upset. A hundred thoughts raced through my mind in an instant.

I had seen the same eyes looking out at me from the ravaged face of the demoniac woman in church. There was a deep silence between us as I stared into those eyes, hard and cold abysses of cruelty.

Finally I decided to take it as a game. He said he brought the storm, so I asked him, "Who are you?"

I don't know what I expected a six-year-old child to say. It seemed safe enough to ask, without going over the line into some paranoid freak-out, where a lunatic woman assumes that a child is possessed by the devil and starts ranting and raving.

Silence.

"Who are you," I asked again, a bit more demanding. "Tell me your name."

"We are many."

This is not sounding good, I thought to myself. The skin on my arms was prickling and the hair on my neck was practically standing on end. *I am really not competent to do this sort of thing. What do I do next?* It seemed reasonable to continue the pretense that it was a sort of game of make-believe, so I asked, "Well, if you are many, where is Kevin?" (Not his real name.)

Whatever I expected him to say, it wasn't what I heard next.

"I am the one who stalks you," he hissed. "I have come to destroy you. No matter what I have to do, no matter how long it takes, I will do it!"

The feeling of cold hate that literally emanated from that child took my breath away. What was even more frightening was that the voice that came from the little child, whose normal voice was really a normal, high-pitched child's voice, produced the odd effect of both deeper tones as well as multiple, layered voices. It was subtle enough that I wasn't sure yet if this was merely an effect of perception.

But something else happened. As I looked into the innocent face of that child, I knew that this "thing" looking at me and hissing evil words at me was not the child himself. His mother, clutching my arm in terror, wanted her son back.

"What have you done with my son?" she asked in a panicked voice.

"Oh, he's here. He's just sleeping a bit. It's so easy to put this one to sleep."

And the word "sleep" was pronounced like a protracted hissss ...

I heard, as if from a great distance, the low voices of Larry and our neighbors talking in the next room and the children still talking back and forth in their beds. The wind was blowing the hardest it had all day, and the hour was late and we were all tired. It seemed as if the fury of nature was peaking over our heads in the raging wind.

I knew that, of all things on this earth, protecting my children, and the children of others, was at the top of the list. I would do anything for them, even give up my own life. If there was such a thing as a real demon, if he was really after me, then let him take me on. Just leave the children alone.

Something inside me cried out for help. With the resounding crash of a falling tree outside, I felt a surge of force enter the top of my head, a baptism of fire, and I knew what to do. I took both the child's hands in mine, overcoming his resistance and struggle. Looking into those eyes, transformed into pools of blackness that drew all they looked upon into a swirling nothingness, I ordered this thing to release the child, to return to whatever bottomless pit of hell it had issued from.

"Leave this child NOW! Before I really get angry!"

I have no idea what force was in me at that moment. I did not know how I called it forth. But as the child twisted in an agonized attempt to tear his hands away from mine, and to withdraw his eyes from my glare, I held my gaze and held my ground. I wasn't letting go. What's more, I wasn't afraid.

"Go!" I commanded again. "Go!"

I felt a supreme struggle of wills and the weakening of the "other." Rage and fury was directed at me as the invader began to lose its grip. Whatever it was, it went. The little boy went limp, and I grabbed him and pulled him into my arms. And just as if he were waking from sleep, he opened his sweet eyes and looked up and inquired curiously, "How did I get here?"

I was flabbergasted. Was it possible for a six-year-old child to put on a performance like that to excuse naughty behavior? Had he engaged in a drama with me to act out some psychological pas de deux whose dynamics I'd never read about in all the literature?

I didn't know. But what did this mean? "He's just sleeping a bit. It's so easy to put this one to sleep ..." With all the so-called spiritual training this child was receiving in a Christian home, why wasn't it working? Where was the opening? What was the weakness? How did children so young become so vulnerable? I knew that Kevin's parents were very much like us. They were trying very hard to raise their child in a Christian environment.

My mind was drawn back to certain events of the past year. I did have a clue to what makes children vulnerable, however small it might be. Not long after the hypnosis session with my daughter, when she revealed the past life source of antagonism toward her sister, I decided to encourage her to get away for a little vacation all her own. I talked to Eva, and she proposed to take my daughter for a couple weeks for a visit.

Eva came to pick my daughter up. The child was so excited to be going somewhere on her own, and I was happy to think she'd have a good time. Eva seemed the right one to handle whatever might come up with discretion. I hoped the two of them could form a bond that would bring mutual happiness.

But the visit turned out to be a disaster. Within less than a week, our neighbor, whose phone we often used, came over and delivered a message from Eva to call her immediately. Of course I did. Eva's voice was a bit tense. I was puzzled to hear that "something had come up" and they were not going to be able to keep my daughter for the full two weeks after all. Eva would bring her home the next day. She assured me that everything was fine, they had a great time, but I felt strongly there was something wrong, and Eva wasn't telling me.

Next, I spoke to my daughter. She went on and on about what a wonderful and luxurious house Eva had, how she had her own bedroom and bathroom, how they had gone to so many places and done so many things. She just was having the time of her life. When I told her that Eva would be bringing her home soon, she burst into tears and said, "No! I don't want to come home!"

I was hurt. But I couldn't blame her. Compared to life at Eva's, what did she have to come home to? Well, except for her family … The only clue I ever got from Eva was that my daughter was "a bit bossy" and a "very assertive young lady."

Now, mulling it over in comparison to this present situation, I realized there must have been a distinct conflict with very subtle roots. My daughter had never in her life experienced an environment at the level of luxury that Eva accepted as normal. Eva had a beautiful home—well beyond the ordinary. Her husband made a lot of money. They owned racehorses and their own private plane. They ate at fine restaurants as casually as other people go to the refrigerator for a glass of milk. We didn't even have a refrigerator!

My poor child was thrust into an overwhelming environment, with all the luxuries Larry constantly described as "the lures of Satan." Larry ruled the emotional atmosphere in our home and established an airtight reality. Against his pronouncements, in stentorian tones, about God, the Bible, sweat of the brow, the sinfulness of having anything that wasn't slaved for—and even then, it ought to be as little as possible—the daily contributions of my own attempts to balance his views faded into obscurity.

Larry's pressure on us to conform to his beliefs was so relentless that this sensitive, careful, and caring child worked tirelessly to seek his approval. The anxiety she expressed toward her sister may have been simply a mode of expressing this constant mental assault. She resisted, fought, even cried, but then she felt even more confused.

It is now excruciatingly evident that my daughter, at the age of nine, and six-year-old Kevin had come to believe that they did not have the right to exist. The natural, loving, and giving self of the child had been twisted all out of its natural conformation.

A child who is continually warned about a dire end if they eat of the forbidden fruit of luxury and comfort has been impregnated with the rejected and "sinful" desires of the parent. Larry's constant rejection of a normal lifestyle, his rants against the life of sinners, his assertion that no godly person desired a comfortable life, money, or even happiness, had been impressed upon my daughter as truth from her earliest memories. She worshipped and adored Larry. So he must be right. The same was true of little Kevin. Only Kevin was, apparently, more vulnerable to psychic invasion.

If our girls expressed interest in material things, Larry told them they were their mother's children, subject to hellfire and damnation. Any girl or woman who was "delicious" would "end up in the gutter." Being beautiful and sexy and enjoying life meant unholiness. And so, my daughter felt rejected. She was thrust out of Eden. The illusion of her internal worthlessness had frozen into place. And just like her grandmother and just like Larry, my daughter built a second self to protect this wounded little girl inside: she became self-centered with the compulsive need to be right.

After this visit to Eva's, my daughter didn't want to go shopping with us. She was embarrassed to be part of a family with so many children. And when we went out, she told me: "people looked at us strangely," as if they knew a secret: we were poor and of no account.

She had been proud of her ability to go shopping for me while I was bedridden. At the age of six, she had been able to write a list, go to the market, and shop for the best buys like an adult. Now, she no longer felt proud of her own abilities and felt shamed by our real circumstances.

Like Larry, who moved into his illusion of "wilderness man," my daughter had gone to sleep in her own narcissist's dream of a world where she was perfect. Her anger and resentment against her family for being unable to match her dream began to grow. Her capacity for lying to herself to sustain her illusions grew with each passing day. And clearly this was what was meant by "it's so easy to put this one to sleep ..."

My daughter, like Kevin, was only a child, in no way responsible for the environment into which she was born. Meanwhile, Larry and I, Kevin's parents, and even Eva, dreamed on, each one wrapped in the illusion that we were all doing our best. And in the end, we find this essence of mundane evil to be, at its core, the very track that we can follow to fuller knowledge and awareness of what is truly behind the system of our reality that promotes and perpetuates this darkness. As Gurdjieff said: *"People are machines. Machines have to be blind and unconscious, they cannot be otherwise, and all their actions have to correspond to their nature. Everything happens. ... And what conscious effort can there be in machines? ... It is precisely in unconscious involuntary manifestations that all evil lies."*

And so it began. I was launched on a path of study that Eva predicted would bring the fires of hell down on my head. *"Don't you know that what you think about becomes your reality?"* Well, it was certainly already a part of my reality, and I needed to learn as quickly as possible how to close the doorway that permitted its entry.

My reaction to facing such evil on the night of the storm was an intense need for comfort and safety, and with Larry, there was only one way to get that. It seems that I conceived my fifth child that night.

A couple of weeks later I experienced the worst premenstrual cramping of my life. I knew it was now time to schedule the hysterectomy the doctor had said I would need. It had been nearly a year since the D&C, and I had bought that much time, but I was no longer willing to suffer two weeks of complete incapacitation every month. So, in December of 1988, I waited for the results of the lab tests done as pre-op work for the surgery. The results were stunning: I was pregnant.

"This will kill me," I told the doctor.

"Yes, it is not an ideal situation. The risks are very high, and you will have to be closely monitored."

I started to cry. I couldn't have another baby. I was too old, I was too sick, and most of all I was too tired.

"Can't we just forget about the pregnancy test and schedule the surgery?" I pleaded.

He looked at me with sympathy and said kindly, "No, I can't do that. But I can send you to another doctor who can take care of you safely. You can come back and we'll schedule the surgery." He wrote a name and number on his prescription pad, handed it to me, and passed the box of tissues. I blew my nose, sniffled my way out, and went home. It was just before Christmas. I was given an appointment date of January 3rd, 1989, for an abortion.

I was miserable all through Christmas. My condition was so bad that even Larry agreed that I couldn't have another baby. We both knew it would kill me.

It was a very depressing Christmas even though we tried to make it as cheerful as possible for the children. The January 3rd date loomed in my mind as more like an execution than anything else, and I wept for this poor child who simply could not be born.

On the day of the appointment, we took the children over and left them with my mother at The Farm. Larry drove me to the doctor.

With me on the table in the famous stirrup position women know so well, the doctor began his work, poking and prodding. The sweat began to bead on his forehead. Nothing was going on but more poking and more prodding. Finally he dropped his instruments on the tray, pulled his gloves off with a snap and dropped them, made some unintelligible remark to the nurse, and walked out of the room.

The nurse patted me and said she would be right back. She rushed after the doctor, and in a few minutes returned and told me that I could get up and go home. There wasn't going to be an abortion.

"What?" I was desperate.

"The doctor is unable to anchor the cervix. It keeps moving. The procedure will have to be done in the hospital under general anesthesia. You can make an appointment with the receptionist." She patted me comfortingly on my shoulder as I finished dressing, and I left the room.

That was enough for me. As far as I was concerned, that was as close to a sign from God as I needed. Whatever it took, if it killed me, this baby would be born.

* * *

I had made a momentous decision based on coincidence. Finally, I knew I needed rest and decided to read myself to sleep. I went to the bookcase to select something that wasn't too demanding, and found an old edition of *Edgar Cayce on Reincarnation*.

Settling in bed, I began to read the introduction by Hugh Lynn Cayce, the same standardized intro that appeared in most of the Cayce books I'd read.

Then I came to the phrase: *"When Edgar Cayce died on January 3rd, 1945 ..."*

I realized with a start that I was reading this exactly forty-four years to the day after the event. According to numerology, which I had researched while writing *Noah*, that equaled an eight. Number eight signified "reincarnation." It was the beginning of a new cycle of the octave of creation. After seven, which was completion, the eight was the equivalent of the number one of the next higher sequence.

Cayce himself had predicted that he would be born again in 1989 as a liberator for humanity, though I didn't remember the precise terms. Naturally, my heart began to beat a little faster. I wondered if it was possible that this child was special in some way.

Was this how the Universe conveyed that information to me?

Well, all mothers have such fantasies or similar ones, so I didn't take it too seriously. Whoever or whatever child came to me would be special.

As it turned out, that was the easiest pregnancy I had. If anybody was being reborn by it, it was me. For the third time, though, I had a ten-month baby. She also had her own plans about what day she was going to be born. When the first contraction came late in the afternoon on August 17th, we made it to the hospital in record time. After six hours of labor, it was obviously time to deliver. The doctor did a final exam before I was taken to the delivery room. A troubled look came over his face and, after removing his gloves, he came around the bed, put one arm around me, took my hand in his, and said gently: "You're going to have to hold it for awhile until we can get an anesthesiologist in here. We have to do a caesarean. The baby is presenting sideways. She cannot be delivered this way."

To say I was a bit distraught to have to "hold it" when my body was convulsing and screaming to "do it now!" is an understatement. But, somehow I managed. I watched the clock as the minutes ticked by like hours of agony, and finally they came to take me to surgery. It was just after midnight. My fifth child and fourth daughter was born at seventeen minutes after midnight on 8/18/89. You will notice that, numerologically, that is an eight. Funny place, this universe we live in.

* * *

Backing up a bit, Larry's father had become ill and couldn't live alone anymore. (Larry's mother had divorced him long ago, and Larry had been raised by his stepfather.) He wasn't happy staying with his daughters, Larry's half-sisters, and he just showed up at our door one day practically on the verge of collapse. He had paid a neighbor to drive him all the way to our house, about a hundred and fifty miles, and the neighbor told us that he found him wandering senseless outside. The family needed to do something.

Well, I took one look at him and put him in the hospital. His belly was bloated with what I supposed was a liver disorder. It turned out that I was right: he had hepatitis. Because I was pregnant, I was forbidden by his doctor as well as my own from being in a room with him without gloves and a mask. That meant, of course, that I couldn't take care of him as Larry wanted.

We put him in a nursing home, but after my first visit to him there, I told Larry that I simply could not reconcile myself to doing that to anyone. They tied him in his bed and he was lying in his own excrement.

At almost the same time, the man whom Mother had hired to run her boat drove it across a big rock pile out in the Gulf. It sank. Even after it was salvaged, with the huge hole in the hull it was declared a total loss. She didn't have insurance. Well, Mother was in a fix with that big mortgage to pay and no income other than her social security, so it seemed the obvious solution that she could take care of Larry's father, and we would pay her out of his income. Meanwhile, we had to take care of his father's property, and it seemed like the best thing to do to sell it since it was too far away to manage at that distance.

Just a few days after the new baby was born, Larry's father suffered a stroke and died a few hours later in the hospital. I felt bad that I had not been able to visit with him, even though I hardly knew him, but I also knew that we had done the best thing for all concerned. He had lived his last months in peace and tranquility, Mother had survived a period of near disaster, and we had experienced an improvement in our own situation with the income from the sale of his property.

Things were not so positive for Mother at this point, however. When she finally let it be known that she was going to lose the place very soon, I extracted all the details from her. I was shocked at the amount of money she had borrowed. Even if we sold it, after the note was paid off there wouldn't be much left. I looked around me at the decay and decline of the property I had loved so much and had put so much work into maintaining on my own, and despair flooded me. What, in the name of God, had she done with all that money? There was nothing—nothing!—to show for it. I knew what had to be done. I turned to face her and said: "You sign the deed over to me and I'll bail you out of this one. But don't you ever question what I am doing, and don't stand in my way."

She didn't have much choice. Neither did I. The Farm was on land now officially protected as wetlands. No one could subdivide or build on it. As a potential investment for real estate, it was virtually worthless now. But I got a referral to an attorney who specialized in real estate law. She found an investor just panting to part with his money and willing to take on state regulators and federal environment agencies. Fine, where do I sign?

It broke my heart.

We needed to find Mother a house to live in that she could afford to make payments on. I most definitely did not want her living with us. There was enough money to cover half the cost of a nice little house, but the remainder would have to be financed and we couldn't help her make payments more than just occasionally.

So I set about the search for a house by doing library research on buying and selling real estate. I didn't want any financial surprises. Mother didn't qualify for a real estate loan, so that limited my selection to sellers willing to hold a note. Every day I went through the ads in the two local papers and made a list of potential properties. Then I called and asked the "right questions," according to the books. I discovered that it was actually a lot of fun to walk through empty houses and imagine them with all kinds of different decorating schemes. I realized that if I had a lot of money, I would probably just buy houses to decorate them and then re-sell them.

House after house, and nothing was quite right. I had learned a lot about the various neighborhoods, the utilities that served them. One day I found a new ad with the right price, the right terms, and even the right neighborhood. I made an appointment to meet the owner and look at it. It was even the right color.

I explained my terms to the owner. He said: "You must have been reading a book about buying real estate!" I laughed and admitted I had. He was a young guy from South America. I strongly suspected he was laundering drug money from the amount of gold he had all over him, as well as his flashy car. But, that wasn't an issue for me. I was looking to buy the right house for the right terms.

He agreed to my terms and we made an appointment with the real estate attorney to draw up the papers. I guess it's a good thing she was booked into the next week, considering what happened next.

Having found the right house, I discovered that looking at houses had become sort of an addiction. There I was, the first morning after striking the deal, with no ads to read, no lists to make, no houses to look at. Well, heck, why not look just to see if there's a good one that got away!

Actually, there was an interesting ad, though it certainly wasn't for a house that would suit my mother. In fact, it was for a house that would suit us and our five children. It was a five-bedroom, two-story house. "Handyman Special: Come expecting the worst and be pleasantly surprised." Gee, who could resist an ad like that? But I wasn't shopping for another house.

I put the paper away. An hour or so later, a small voice inside my head whispered, *What would be the harm in just looking? Just a peek to see what they meant by that curious ad? After all, walking around in empty houses was a lot of fun.*

Okay, I gave in. I opened the paper back up, found the ad, and called the realtor. I told him I really didn't want to waste his time to show it to me since I wasn't buying, but I did want to just drive by and look at it. He gave me the address: it was on *Montana* Avenue.

I drove by the house and thought, *Gee! That's a pretty big house! It looks really good, too. What do they mean, a "handyman special"?* I admit my curiosity got the better of me. I drove into a convenience store to call

The house on Montana Avenue.

the realtor to see if it was at all possible to have a look inside. As it happened, he was free and agreed to meet me there in ten minutes.

When I walked inside, I knew why it was a handyman special. It would take two weeks to clear all the junk out and get it clean. The downstairs was finished, but apparently, no one had ever finished the upstairs. There were partitions for bedrooms, and someone had dropped the ceilings to an unpleasant height, but basically, it was as livable as the house we were living in and in some ways better. What's more, it was twice, or even three times, as big.

Okay, I had my fun. I went home. All night long I kept waking up and thinking about that house. It was so big and so charming and had such possibilities that I couldn't get it out of my mind. But, of course, it would be impossible to buy it because I had already committed my money for Mother's house.

Then I thought about selling the house we had built. This led to the idea that if we did sell the current property and bought this bigger house, it would be very easy to make some inexpensive improvements and re-sell it for a much larger profit than we hoped to make from our present house. That would mean we could move to Montana much sooner than we had planned.

The next day, I decided I really had to go and look at it again just to make sure that all the possibilities I had thought of the night before were really there and I wasn't just fooling myself. Maybe I hadn't looked hard enough for the flaws. Besides, what would it hurt? If there was a real possibility of buying it as an investment, then not going to look at it would be walking away from money we could put to good purpose for our "ark in Montana."

I went. There were two couples already there looking at it and discussing possible improvements and renovations. It was better than I remembered it, and I examined it even more closely. As I was wandering through, several other couples arrived to look and suddenly I was in a panic that someone would buy it and all our chances of getting to Montana would go down the drain.

Without even thinking about it more than the length of time it took to realize what I needed to do, I made the decision and left to drive straight to the realtor's office.

"I want that house," I told him. "I have no idea if I can get the money to buy it, but I at least want a chance to try."

For some reason, I guess he wanted me to have the house too. Even though he was the seller's agent, he sat down and wrote up an offer for the most ridiculously low price you could even imagine. It was just about half of what was being asked for the house, which was already a bargain. I signed it, wrote a check for the "earnest money," and went home. I knew I had a problem: explaining to Larry that I had made an offer for a house without consulting him first. Never mind that it was one of those decisions that couldn't wait. I knew he would be furious.

I decided that maybe I ought to break it to him gently. If I could get him to go with me to look at the house, I was sure he would see a good investment and a big improvement over where we were living. It even had a washer and dryer and dishwasher. I knew the kids were sick of doing laundry and endless dishes, and so was I.

Reluctantly, Larry agreed to go look at the house. I called the realtor the next morning to make another appointment. Larry and I met him there. We went inside, and I was anxiously watching Larry's face to see how he reacted to the house. I could see that he was impressed with the big fireplace in the living room. The realtor was yakking away as we walked through the room, and he headed straight for the stairs and started up. I followed and Larry came behind me. The guy yakked on until he reached the top of the stairs, at which point he stopped, turned around and said, "Oh, by the way, the owner accepted your offer." I could feel Larry's eyes burning a hole in my back as he asked, "What offer?"

"Oh, well…" I laughed. "I sort of made an offer on the house. I just knew you'd love it and it's too good an investment to pass up and it won't take much to get it into shape to sell, and I knew if I didn't make an offer right away, it would be gone in nothing flat … so I just—made an offer …"

It wasn't working. He was furious.

When we got home, we had the biggest fight of our marriage. Only this time, I didn't take the blame, I didn't back down, and I ended up saying: "If you don't want to help me, fine. I'm buying that house with you or without you. The kids and I will live there with you or without you." And I meant it. Larry knew I meant it, too.

Now I was faced with figuring out how I was going to pay for it. I went to the bank—several, in fact—but none of them would lend on a house built in 1925. It was just too old. Never mind that it was built out of heart pine and was a better house than all the little tract houses that had been built since the real estate boom in the '50s and '60s—the bank said no.

I was practically in despair. I had been so certain that this was the way to get to Montana, and now it was just going to slip out of my hands. Suddenly I thought of the guy who was selling me the house for my mother. He had given me his card and it had said "real estate investments." Okay, maybe it means he lends money?

He did, and he actually seemed to want to help me sort out my situation. He pointed out that buying a house for my mother did not really make sense. She could just as happily, and even more conveniently, live in an apartment in one of the many communities set up for elderly people. She didn't need the headache of maintaining a home, and we didn't need to be hassled with taking care of it for her. His idea was that he could simply rescind the agreement we had made on the small house for my mother, I would put the money I had on the big house, and he would lend me the balance.

Everything he said made sense. I was surprised that he was willing to give up a sale, but, in the end, it was six of one, half a dozen of the other to him. There was always somebody tomorrow who would buy the other house. The end result: with the large down payment we were able to make on the house, we actually ended up paying for more than half of it up front; and we were getting it so cheap, due to the amazing fact that the seller had accepted my ridiculously low offer, again, suggested by the realtor because of some internal nudging, it would seem. There was absolutely no doubt in my mind that there were forces at work that wanted me to have this house.

But I still had a problem to work out: how to sell our unfinished house. Not an easy task, to say the least. In fact, just to assure myself that I was truly following the guidance of the Universe, I made a deal with myself that I would put both of the houses we now owned on the market. If I sold the one we just bought at my asking price, I would still make money. If we sold the one we were living in, then we could pay off the note on the new one. This way, the Universe could make a clear declaration of intent. Believe it or not, we sold the house and acreage on the first day my ad came out. The Universe had answered the question.

Because I was so focused on moving to Montana, I didn't even realize that I had already done it. There was the street sign right out front: Montana.

Whoever is in charge of this world sure does have a sense of humor!

CHAPTER THIRTY-THREE

SYNCHRONICITY CITY

We moved into the new house on my birthday: February 12th. Although the interior still needed cosmetic improvements, it was like moving into a palace after five years in the shack-becoming-a-house in the woods. Sandra came on moving day, bringing a feast and a cake. We all celebrated our return to the "real world." All except Larry, that is.

We purchased materials for improvements on the house to prepare it to sell, so we could make our big quantum leap to the state of Montana. But Larry was fired from his job. I knew there was a gradually building antagonism between Larry and his boss, but that didn't ease the blow when it came. The only thing I could do was to work as fast as possible to get the house into saleable condition. Larry was far too depressed to help, so I got a job.

I went to work for an attorney who was among the first to realize the potentials of the "age of information." He had created a human resources service for large corporations. The resources and skills of a private investigator were employed to create dossiers on potential employees. The litigious nature of our society had made such a service almost mandatory to protect a potential employer from lawsuits claiming various types of exclusion. If a hard file of facts justified refusal of employment, such litigation was easily answered. By the same token, employees who might not be fit, and who might later be a cause for suit by a client, were also able to be excluded. Finally, the best candidates for any position, from simple clerks to CEOs, could be identified. The benefits to their dossiers of such validation of experience, expertise, and references were considerable. A fully vetted candidate could be placed at the head of the line for consideration.

The company handled mostly large corporate accounts where hundreds and thousands of dossiers were compiled. After a short time as a sort of glorified clerical worker, my employer decided I had potential, and I was trained in the law and assigned to handle the accounts of several major airlines. My specialty soon became "pilot dossiers." Some airlines wanted to collect certain "psychological" facts about candidates for pilot positions without the obvious psychiatric examination, so I was further trained in certain psychological assessment techniques. I soon developed an interviewing style designed to elicit very deep information relating to these issues. The company was pleased with my work. My thoughts and opinions were valued, my skills were praised, and I learned many new things—most especially, about computers, and fell in love with them almost instantly—and for the first time in many years began to experience myself as a valued human being.

Larry felt threatened by my new job. His response was rather strange. Instead of finding a "real" job, as he could easily have done with his intelligence and skills, he took a job driving a parking lot vacuum truck on the night shift. He took our children to accompany him on his rounds and collect the garbage while he swept the lots.

I was extremely unhappy for my children to be out at night bagging garbage from public trashcans. Aside from health considerations, the demeaning, soul-killing aspect troubled me deeply. His view was that it was a "noble and worthy service." As a good Christian, the "sweat of the brow" deal was almost mandatory in his mind, and the more "humble" the work, the greater the crown of glory he would receive. Clearly, if we were going to enjoy a big new house, there was a price to be paid for it. Naturally, the children were not asked whether they wanted a crown of glory. It did put them alone in his company for many hours at a time; I believe he did his damnedest to convince them I was not only on a path to damnation, but crazy to boot.

Two months into this routine, me working days and Larry working nights, an event of terrifying significance occurred.

I was sleeping—alone—and I was awakened by a series of noises. The drawers of Larry's chest were pulled open and the contents rifled through. I thought Larry had stopped off to pick something up and was just doing it in the dark to avoid turning on the lights and waking me up. I lifted my head and saw that it wasn't Larry. A strange man was in my bedroom, going through the top drawer in the dresser.

Maybe I had awakened in a different life! A life where I was married to someone else, and that man stood here in my bedroom. But I sort of did a reality check and quickly realized this wasn't the answer. I was in this life, and not another; I was married to Larry, and not this strange man whose back was still to me as he continued to search for something.

My next thought was that Larry had brought someone home with him—a helper, perhaps. Maybe he had sent the guy into the bedroom to get something for him while he made coffee in the kitchen. I discarded that idea immediately because Larry would never send a strange man into the bedroom where I was sleeping to get anything. The only obvious solution: Larry wasn't home and this strange man had come into the house illegally.

Now, of course, all this happened rather quickly and when the final conclusion was drawn, my heart nearly stopped.

I decided that pretending to be asleep would give me an edge if I needed one. I dropped my head back on the pillow and quickly pulled my hair over my face to hide the fact that my eyes were open and I was watching. The man turned and looked at me, thought I was still sleeping, and tiptoed out of the room. In horror I saw that he was carrying a knife.

I rolled over to reach the phone under the bed and managed to find the zero in the darkness. As soon as an operator answered, I whispered, "There is a strange man in my house and he's armed!"

The operator connected me with 911. I repeated my whispered declaration. Quickly, they took my address and told me to stay on the line. They asked if I could shut the door and lock myself in the room. Well, I could have, if Larry hadn't taken the doors off the hinges in his desultory efforts to work on the house.

As I whispered "no" to the dispatcher, I realized with a growing sense of terror that the drawer the man had been going through was full of only one thing: boxes of bullets of various sorts that went to the rack of guns on the wall outside my room. And my children were sleeping in the house. I think that, at that moment, I nearly lost it. I hissed to the dispatcher that the guy might now be armed with a high-powered rifle.

Within five minutes, I could hear the distinct sounds of police cars approaching from all directions, pulling into the side street, the alley, and in front of the house. The dispatcher asked me if I knew where the man was now. I thought he was in the dining room, judging by the sounds. I was told to stay put.

Well, they came in like gangbusters for sure! K-9 troops and all. And as they came in the front door, the burglar flew out the back door. Apparently he jumped the fence to the neighbor's yard, where he ditched his cap, jacket, and weapons. But it was too late. The dogs were after him. He ended up face down in the street about a block away, surrounded by probably more cops than he had ever seen in his life.

They brought him around in a squad car for me to identify, and the whole adventure was over.

The children never even woke up.

The "bust" made the papers two days later and I was toasted by my employers and fellow workers as a veritable heroine who kept her cool.

Larry's hound dog had been out roaming around. It was time to get a dog who knew his job. We acquired a half-Chow, half-Labrador puppy and the kids named her Isis.

* * *

I was growing in awareness. I knew this relatively mundane incident had a deep message for me. This was a clue from the Universe that I needed to learn something fast. If I didn't, I was in danger. I was coming to the idea that the world around us is a very accurate mirror of what we refuse to acknowledge. No matter what happened in our lives, if we took the time and trouble to examine our thinking and our attitudes, and to compare them to the symbols of reality, we could isolate and identify the lessons pointing the way toward change. That way we would not need to experience the lesson again. It seemed to be so that it was not what we thought that created our reality, but what we ignored consciously and what our subconscious mind was observing and trying to bring to our attention.

It was clear that my powers of subconscious manifestation had achieved an all-time high with this one. I wasn't making glasses and windows break anymore. Now I was manifesting dramas of full materialization, including human actors!

But what was it? What doorway was open in my life that made me vulnerable to being robbed and possibly even killed? What was I not seeing? What observation was my subconscious mind making that my conscious mind was refusing to acknowledge?

I proposed this idea to Larry, and he went off on an absolute rant that I was really losing it. He said, "Do you mean to tell me that you think that whatever happens in our lives, all our experiences, are lessons?"

"Yes," I said.

"If I walk in the room here and somebody has spilled a box of pins and I step on one of them, it's a lesson?" he inquired contemptuously.

"Yes," I said, less sure of my ground.

"You are suggesting that every time we have an injury or suffer an illness, or experience an event, there is something we are supposed to learn from it? It's a 'message' or a clue of some sort to a spiritual reality?"

"Yes," I replied—certain that it was so, but unable to articulate how or why I was sure, or even how to make these interpretations of reality.

"Then if that is the case," he said, smiling like the cat that ate the canary, "what's wrong with YOU? Why have you experienced so much sickness?"

I believed my experiences of the past ten years had been the result of my own attitudes borne in the fundamentalist trap of ignoring these very things: the lessons of life. I pointed out that, as soon as I had effected some changes, as soon as I had begun to be aware of things, our reality had changed.

Larry wasn't buying it. He simply couldn't see any causal relationship between the changes I had experienced and what had manifested in our lives. God either gave or took away, and it had nothing to do with us except, perhaps, in the context of whether or not we were good Christians.

Finally, he said, "Well, if your theory is right, then it's obvious. You have the problem, because I wasn't even home when the guy broke in." Triumphantly, he left the room.

He had a point.

* * *

In the fall of 1990, our youngest child, the baby, became ill. I had had to stop nursing when I went back to work, and I sorely missed the constant closeness I had been able to create with each of my other babies. Mother was living with us, on the waiting list for an apartment in a retirement community, and she watched the children while I was at work.

My baby had received a tentative diagnosis of cystic fibrosis, and at a certain point, it seemed to be obvious that she was going to die. I resigned from my job to stay home so I could be with her as much as possible for whatever time we might have. It was a terrible time: seven months of terror and emergency hospital trips, sometimes in the middle of the night, when the baby stopped being able to breathe. I was a wreck.

Mother came home from the chiropractor one day and announced that he could help our child. In fact, after she had described the situation to him, he was so confident that he could cure her, he offered to do it at no charge.

I was willing to try anything. As it turned out, he was right. He thought there had been some glitch in her delivery that "subluxated" her spine at the point where the nerves to the lungs exit. It was a situation just waiting for the right conditions to exacerbate it, possibly when I stopped nursing and put her on infant formula. It was true that she had been jammed sideways in the womb while I held back delivery for over forty-five minutes, waiting for the anesthesiologist to arrive at the hospital the night she was born. Being squeezed by hard labor for that period of time, in that position, was probably enough to subluxate anybody's spine!

After six adjustments, taking her off all cow's milk products, and putting her on raw goat's milk, I was able to take her off all medication, and she began to thrive.

* * *

As soon as the baby was better, I felt again that I ought to be doing more toward getting us on stable financial footing to sell the house and move to Montana. I was seeing hypnotherapy clients through contacts Sandra made for me. At this point, she was a supervisor of a large state agency that managed cases where people had been extremely traumatized and the state was paying for treatment. Many of my clients cane to me through Sandra when standard psychotherapy had not proved effective. I fully realized the risks I was taking in agreeing to talk to these people. Sandra had consulted with the legal expert in her office and advised me to obtain religious ordination, have legal release drawn up for each client to sign, and accept donations rather than charge a set fee.

I told Sandra I felt like a fraud being ordained by mail, but she was so certain that what I was doing was a necessary service that she always found ways to talk me out of my objections. Sandra, herself, had many inner conflicts about the Catholicism of her background. I think that my work, which I always discussed with her, was her way of getting questions answered that plagued her as much as they did me. Of course, her interest and overt activity had to be kept secret from her family and co-workers.

Because of her position and contacts, these encounters became subjects in our search for answers about the true nature of life and death, good and evil, and most of all: the nature of our reality itself. However, more often than not, those who needed therapy the most were unable to pay more than a token amount.

I was becoming adept at applying the past-life-therapy techniques to good benefit. Issues could be carried from one life into the next, causing problems that ordinary psychotherapy did not even attempt to address. That, of course, raised the significant question about life itself.

Nearly everything we are taught about life, cradle to grave, seemed to be a deliberate system of lies built to protect the edifice of the religious teachings of One God, the monotheism of Christianity, Judaism, and Islam.

These were dangerous systems, designed to keep people ignorant and distinctly vulnerable to Evil with a capital "E." Of course, my idea about who was behind it all ran along the lines of just simple greed for money and power being used to control gullible human beings. After all, it wasn't possible for this to be deliberately imposed from "above." Was it?

Even if mankind had distorted the "word of God" and had twisted it in the Bible, or promulgated fraudulent versions of it, it was still possible to find the threads of truth in all religions and, by gathering them together, to find what was really of truth and beauty and goodness in the earth, wasn't it?

Well, I wasn't sure. It was time to begin an in-depth study of demonic possession, exorcism, and the nature of Darkness. For this, I needed books. For books, I needed money.

Hypnotherapy was not a moneymaker for sure, even if the information I was acquiring was utterly priceless. I tried various "work at home" schemes and read the employment advertisements daily in hopes of finding the perfect "work at home" deal in the same way I had found the perfect house.

Which reminds me: there was another unusual thing about this house: it was right down the street from the house that had belonged to Grant's mother. Yes, the Grant of my first "love." Not only that, but his mother had died, leaving him the house, and he now lived there, just a few blocks away.

I came by this knowledge by walking down our new street one day to get the feel of the neighborhood. On the corner of Lincoln and Montana, there stood a house with the complicated Polish name that I knew so well on the mailbox. I went home and looked the name up in the phone book and found that it was, indeed, the same person. What a surprise!

On an impulse, I called Grant just to see how his life had progressed since last I saw him. He launched into a pathetic tale of woe. He'd been in a car wreck not long after marrying the woman who had answered the phone and accused me of destroying his life. He received a large settlement from this accident and invested in a motorcycle dealership in partnership with his best friend. His wife then fell in love with this friend and ended up divorcing him, acquiring in the divorce settlement not only his house, but also his business. He said she took him for everything he had.

At the end of this recitation, I admit that I was less than holy in my response. The only thing I said was: "There IS a God!"

Apparently he didn't hear me, or couldn't hear me, because then he proceeded to reminisce about how much he had loved me, how much he had missed me all these years, how "great and glorious" a passion we had shared.

I replied: "That wasn't love, it was sickness."

He didn't hear me. On and on he went, hinting subtly and then overtly that we ought to meet and possibly pick up where we left off.

I wasn't even tempted. As many difficulties as I could see in my marriage, there was no way on God's green earth that I would allow emotional hooks ever to hurt people again. I managed to evade any suggestions and finally worked my way to ending the conversation. When I hung up, I thought, *Whew! I can't believe I was ever taken in by that nonsense!*

But, thinking about "old times" reminded me about Keith again. More than anything, I wondered how he had gotten on these many years. As crazy as he had been, I still had a soft spot for his suffering. We had parted under such unpleasant circumstances, I was sure he'd never want to hear from me again, so I merely mulled it over for a few days. In the end, I felt that resolution of the issue was better than constantly questioning.

He turned out to be ecstatic to hear from me. In fact, he wanted me to come and visit him as he had "many things" to tell me about what he had learned in the past seventeen years. I made a date to come up, bringing a couple of my children with me, and we had a very nice visit. He had changed in many ways, but he was still the same way about being unable to exert any control over his emotions whatsoever.

Keith was still writing, and I was surprised that he had not modernized and gone to a computer. He was interested in the idea and, with his secretary's help, we came up with a plan to find a good system. He generously offered to buy one for me, too.

So I had my first computer, courtesy of Keith Laumer.

My options for working at home were now significantly expanded. I obtained a good astrology program for doing horoscopes. In my late teens I'd learned how to cast a chart the hard way, doing all the math and interpretations by hand. How much easier to have the computer do the chart erection, and I'd just need to type up the text.

Then I thought, *Why not make money doing what I enjoyed: writing?*

I was reading the employment ads daily when suddenly, one day, there was a new one: scriptwriter for a television producer who made infomercials.

What an interesting thing! I had never heard of any film company in the area. In the end, it was more curiosity about who was behind the ad than any real anticipation I might get the job that prompted me to call.

And that is how I met Francis Grant Scott. He became my friend Frank, and meeting him changed my life.

I mention the attitude of non-anticipation because it has turned out to be a clue to activation of universal potentials. I have learned that when I act in the "mind of a child," without emotional attachment or any anticipation of a given outcome, the Universe has a marvelous way of responding with all and everything that is needed. But I didn't really know that then. I was getting a lot of hints, realizing that the Universe speaks to us in the events of our lives as symbols of deeper truths, but I was still, essentially, just "walking on water."

As it happened, my work experience interested Frank enormously and, after finishing up basic talk about the job, we moved on to discuss metaphysics. He was particularly interested in astrology and wanted me to do his chart. He gave me the necessary data, including his birthplace: Ypsilanti, Michigan.

During the course of this conversation, we discovered that we had read many of the same books and held many of the same opinions about various phenomena, and so on. What was most bizarre was the combination of factors. Frank had the famous (or infamous, depending on how you look at it) middle name "Grant." He also had a cousin with the same name as mine, including my middle name, and who was also the mother of five children. The only difference in the name was a single-letter difference. He also had a sister who had a daughter born in the same year and had the same name as my youngest child. Again, the only difference in the name was a single-letter difference.

That was quite a strange list of synchronicities, and I wondered if these were signs and symbols of the Universe speaking. Well, they could have been: the question was, were they signs of good things, or warnings? I decided to keep my own counsel; only time would tell.

We ended the conversation with a date for Frank to pick up the horoscope, and that was that. As far as the job was concerned, I figured I was out of the running, but I didn't mind. Within two minutes after I hung up the phone, it rang again. It was a wrong number, but the crazy thing was that it was a woman calling long distance trying to contact her relatives in Florida, and she wanted me to help her find their number. She mentioned, without prompting, that she was calling from Ypsilanti, Michigan. Needless to say, I did a double take.

The Universe was definitely trying to get my attention.

At the appointed time, Frank arrived to pick up his horoscope. I had an impression of him from his voice that he would be a very large, portly man. But, he was, on the contrary, exceptionally tall and thin.

We began a series of conversations, unlike any that I had before, that continued on for several months. He made it a habit to visit at least once a week. He also made sure that I got the job as the scriptwriter.

I didn't know it then, but Initiation had begun in earnest.

CHAPTER THIRTY-FOUR

THAT'S HOLLYWOOD!

As mentioned, when Frank arrived at my door, I was surprised at his appearance. His deep baritone voice on the phone gave the impression of a large, portly—and most especially, very masculine—man. Frank was very tall and gangly, and most definitely gave an almost immediate impression of androgynous character. He reminded me, more than anything, of an oversized child who, having just experienced a recent growth spurt, had not yet learned to manage his limbs gracefully. It seems, in retrospect, to have been merely an impression of a lack of comfort in his own physical structure. Yet Frank was an attractive young man with his blond hair, strong square chin, symmetrical features, and generally pleasing proportions. The attractiveness of his face was diminished slightly by small, close-set eyes and a mouth that formed a natural frown when in repose. I had always heard that one should not trust a person with such narrowly placed and proportionately small eyes, and Frank most definitely had them. I was immediately on guard.

However, Frank had a very engaging manner. I don't mean that one was "engaged" by being charmed, but rather that he exerted himself considerably to engage me in conversation by asking many questions to which he listened attentively and nodded understandingly at the appropriate junctures. The feeling of being understood was amplified by occasional comments. The impression given was that he was most definitely en rapport.

I had the idea that he was a healthy young man, while I was a middle-aged *hausfrau* with five children, and he certainly ought to be going out on weekends and socializing with friends his own age. But, apparently, he didn't have that many friends, or if he did, he was not motivated to have a "good time" in those ways. He seemed to be perfectly happy to come to my house and sit and talk for hours on end.

Very early on, I shared the manuscript of *Noah* with Frank.

"It's fascinating," he said. "Brilliant. I couldn't put it down."

"Great!"

"But there's only one problem."

"What's that?" I asked.

"You failed to include the UFO and alien phenomenon."

"No I didn't," I insisted. "It's right there in the chapter about the Rapture!" I had alluded to the New Age belief, shared in part by some fundamentalist Christians, of miraculous rescues off the planet during some end-time event.

"There is nothing on the planet more important and worthy of study than the alien problem. Trust me, I've been studying it for years!"

"Nonsense!"

Frank responded with a long monologue about aliens that gave me serious doubts about the stability of his intellect. It was so hard to reconcile his brilliant expositions on so many subjects with this silly, childish belief in "little green men."

I was, I admit, a flaming skeptic about aliens. I had spent so much time poking around in people's heads in therapeutic ways, that, with only a cursory examination of the issue, I'd decided that sightings and claims of abductions were strikingly similar to past-life dramas. After reading Whitley Strieber's gothic book *Communion* and Ruth Montgomery's patently ridiculous *Aliens Among Us*, I refused to give any serious consideration to the subject.

The stories were so crazy I simply could not consider them to be real in any context other than as useful metaphors that the subconscious cooks up to explain unhappy events in childhood.

I was trying to keep an open mind from a clinical and scientific viewpoint. I wasn't sure that our whole existence, as we perceived it, wasn't simply a series of chemical reactions in the brain of the Cosmic Dreamer.

In short, stories of aliens and abductions seemed an archetypal drama of the subconscious mind. I called it the "millennial disease," and saw it as a form of mass hysteria. I attributed the physical scars and traces of abduction to stigmata-like effects, or poltergeist-type events. Clearly, there was very little about UFOs and aliens that couldn't be explained by these theories.

So, when Frank wanted to discuss the alien business as a reality, we fell into disagreement. We were at an impasse on this subject. I even became contemptuous and sarcastic when referring to it as "the alien rapture theory." I held it to be about as reasonable as the various pre-tribulation, mid-tribulation, and post-tribulation Rapture theories of the fundamentalist Christians. Frank was not deterred by my rejection of the subject.

* * *

Frank had interceded on my behalf to get me the job as scriptwriter for his employer, the television producer. This turned out to be a most entertaining and instructive experience. We'll just call Frank's boss "Dane."

I was very surprised to discover that Frank literally hated Dane. He unashamedly expressed his dislike of the man. One day we were driving up to Dane's home and studio for a meeting. Frank suddenly expressed all his resentment and anger at Dane for years of unspecified abuse of some kind. As we got closer to Dane's, Frank said he was literally getting sick to his stomach at the thought of being in Dane's company. (Shades of Keith Laumer!)

"I go through this every day," Frank said. "Some day I won't be able to take it any more and I'll just snap!"

"Well, Frank, if you really feel that way," I said, "wouldn't it be easier to quit your job?"

Frank launched into a long monologue why that was impossible, and how the job working for Dane was so ideal for him and his "special nature."

This "special and unique disposition" was a regular subject of Frank's discourse. He was, it seems, convinced that fate, destiny, or whoever was in charge of deciding who has to be incarnated, had most definitely made a mistake in his case. He cited reason after reason he was simply not suited to this world, this environment of human failings and foibles. Most of these reasons related, in some way, to his conviction that he was a "higher being" or "didn't belong" with the rest of the *hoi polloi* on the planet. And, of course, because of this, he was most definitely regularly and repeatedly victimized by those of less delicate and refined sensibilities. He was "too good" for this gross and materialistic world where a person was expected to earn a living and put up with the slings and arrows of outrageous fortune. But, based on what he told me, Frank had never really suffered anything serious.

This led, inevitably, to his consideration of suicide as the ultimate solution for his misery in this life. He spent hours telling me all the logical and reasonable ways he had thought his way through it and had come to the conclusion that it was, indeed, the correct action in his case.

"The religious and mystical literature claims no one is born by accident," I reminded him. "Some even say we actually choose our parents and the circumstances of our lives for the very lessons that we, ourselves, have decided to study in the school of earth."

Frank buttressed his arguments with scholarly references and citations proving he was right and my cited sources wrong. He seemed enormously invested in my agreement with his assessment of the issues. This discussion continued for months with neither side willing to give in. Even if I ran out of arguments to convince him that suicide was not the solution, I insisted if he was patient and open-minded, the Universe would reveal a purpose to him and he would inevitably realize that I was right on this one. I pointed out that I had once been in so much despair that I had wanted to end my life, though for a somewhat different reason.

I was, of course, quite impressed by his endless scholarly references and allusions, though I was a bit put off by his need to be the center of attention. He brooked no interruption in his outpouring of words. It was, in the end, a very unequal exchange.

By this time in my life, having had some experience with my mother and her campaigns against so many people, I was not inclined to take Frank's word about Dane, but rather thought that I would try to form my own opinion. In fact, Dane was quite intelligent and charming, and I enjoyed talking to him immensely. In private, Frank warned me direfully about the fact that I was being taken in by Dane as everyone else had been, to their sorrow. He endlessly, and in great detail, described Dane's exploits in the world of con artistry, beginning with the kidnapping of his own son from the country of his origin. This nefarious deed was intended to use his son as a cover and to garner sympathy from women who were, in the end, his chief targets. Dane's most heinous sin: he had later brought his own parents to this country and had lived on their pensions for years—even after they had been long dead! Frank nearly crowed with delight at being able to produce this clear evidence of decidedly criminal behavior.

Hearing all this, I was ready to just walk away from the whole project. Frank begged me to stay. I was the person, he claimed, who could make it all work. He recognized in me that "drive and dedication" which could make a success.

Would I stick with it for his sake?

Put that way, I couldn't refuse. Frank assured me that, with his guidance, I would be able to navigate the tricky waters of Dane's cunning and underhandedness. He, Frank, would protect me and ensure my interests were looked after.

I went to work on the assignment and produced a script. I submitted it to Frank, who went over it with Dane.

"Not quite what we wanted, Laura. Can you give us a rewrite?"

I was a bit surprised. I had most certainly fulfilled every outlined requirement we had discussed at length, right down to the timing.

Frank shook his head sadly. He said I was embarked on my first lesson of what a rotten guy Dane really was. He most certainly would ask for rewrites a dozen times and finally reject the whole thing. Then I would learn, to my sorrow, just what a skunk Dane was.

I was not in a position to spend weeks and weeks working on something and not get paid for my effort. I was perfectly outraged this man had the nerve to treat anyone that way.

"I'm calling Dane this very moment," I said. "I am just simply telling him he can get another writer!"

Frank calmed me down. "Be patient. I'll work everything out."

He was prepared for the occasion. He'd already written a check that very day from the company expense account to make good all the time I'd put into the script. Dane didn't know. This would be our secret. I was very grateful, and my doubts about Frank receded. Frank was clearly the good guy in this drama!

Enter Nancy.

Frank and I both met Nancy at a metaphysical discussion-group meeting at the home of another hypnotherapist. Nancy quickly attached herself to us and—being divorced and without family obligations to restrict her, and very much interested in discussing any and all aspects of metaphysical things—began to hang out with us during our Friday or Saturday night discussions. These visits were becoming quite regular.

If Larry was jealous of my friendships, it was not in the ordinary way. He would frequently make disparaging remarks about my "fruity" friends, but I could see that he also welcomed my little weekend "salon" because it gave him an excuse to spend more and more time fishing. Additionally, even if he always made some remark that diminished the fact, he was glad that I was making money while still being at home to cater to him when he made his erratic appearances.

As the project for the infomercial proceeded, Frank, Dane, and I had a planning meeting one night and decided that we needed an actress who was not an actress and who could project that "freshness" on camera. Frank suggested Nancy. I agreed that she was a possible, and Dane wanted to meet her. We confirmed the plan with Nancy and made a date for a dinner meeting at the usual out-of-the-way restaurant. Frank pointed out that Dane always selected such places to eat or meet because he was constantly avoiding the people he had defrauded in other schemes.

Whether or not he was a scam artist, Dane had made a great deal of money on his numerous selling-on-TV projects, and Frank was determined to see this success repeated. He intended to be cut in on the profits after working like a dog on the last one. This time, Dane wasn't going to get away with treating him like dirt. And, of course, if I stuck with him, I would surely become quite well off myself.

At the meeting, Frank and I noticed an instant physical attraction between Dane and Nancy. Before we knew it, they were ordering more wine, laughing, and moving closer in the booth until, finally, Dane walked Nancy to her car. Frank and I, walking in the other direction to our cars, noticed they ended up in an embracing lip-lock in the dark. Whether they thought we couldn't see them or not, I don't know, and whether or not they cared if we did, I don't know. I was rather pleased to see Dane and Nancy expressing interest in one another. Both of them seemed singularly lonely.

Frank, on the other hand, was perfectly livid when he saw Dane kissing Nancy. "I can't believe him! He's never done this before! Has he lost his mind? She's a slut!" and so forth. It was like witnessing a child having a fit because his single parent has found romance and his own place as the parent's beloved is threatened.

Well, by now the reader is sure that I am being sucked into some sick melodrama, and that assessment is exactly right. I couldn't imagine what was so bad about a little romance between Dane and Nancy, but I knew it was deeply disturbing to Frank. In our next discussion, I probed gently to attempt to discover what terrible thing had happened in his life to make him so sour about human relations, particularly the relations between men and women.

Well, to Frank, romance of any kind was utterly and totally revolting. His disparaging remarks about the carnal desires of human beings, the "hot and sweaty absurdity of copulation," made me question my own human nature! Again, with scholarly incisiveness, Frank managed to present arguments that demonstrated his own superiority as a "higher being." He was completely beyond such lusts of the flesh.

I was confused at this point and the only other person to talk to was Nancy. So, I discussed the nature of spirituality and carnal lusts. During the course of the conversation, I told her what Frank had said about such things and the sources he had cited. "Piffle!" she said. "There's more to that than meets the eye!"

I asked her what she meant.

"It ought to be obvious!"

"What do you mean?" I asked.

"Obviously Frank is gay and he's in love with Dane."

I was shocked at the very thought and immediately defended Frank, sure that Nancy had misjudged him.

"We'll see," she replied.

I wasn't sure what she meant. I was soon to find out. One day soon after, Nancy and I drove to Dane's house for a business meeting. Nancy smoothly asked how Dane's relationship with Frank had come about. Dane explained how Frank had attached himself as a friend of his son's (they attended the same school) and Dane had given him a little job taking orders and shipping. After that, he said woefully, it was impossible to get rid of him. Frank had told him he wished Dane was his father because his own parents had been so abusive. After that, Dane said, he never had the heart to send Frank packing, even if he was "as useless as tits on a nun."

I was very, very confused. If Dane was telling the truth, then what happened to all of Frank's claims about Dane as an evil and manipulative monster? Could it be true that he was in love with Dane, or, at the very least, working in some subversive way designed to isolate and control Dane? If so, what did he want? Dane's money?

Then Nancy suggested that if Frank had been just a hanger on at the beginning, he must be quite valuable now, since Dane was paying him so generously. Dane looked at her in a puzzled way. "He doesn't get paid, you know, though I've promised him a percentage of the income from the new show."

"Oh!" Nancy said. "From the way he spends money, he must have made a bundle working for you!"

"Yes, I was very generous with Frank. Besides," he waved his hand nonchalantly, "he lives alone and has no expenses. He doesn't go out with women, you know!"

On the drive home, Nancy announced to me that Dane was being had by Frank.

"What do you mean?" I asked.

"Just my intuition," she said.

Nancy was, in the end, no match for Frank. By moving in on Frank's declared territory, Nancy became the enemy. In the end, I think she wisely decided not to pursue a relationship with Dane, overshadowed with the constant presence of Frank. Nancy became a casualty. That should have warned me this was a war, though a very subtle one. But I thought I was clever enough to navigate this minefield. Hah! Famous last words.

After Nancy had moved on to new territory, we needed to find a new star for our program. Dane wanted a well-known, but older actor of some considerable repute. Negotiations were underway to obtain his services. I was required to do some rewrites with this man in mind, and the whole project took on a new flavor and life of its own. But, this actor died suddenly and Dane was apparently desolate at this blow to his plans. He felt it was just a sign from God that the whole project ought to be shelved.

Frank was utterly frantic. He saw the promises Dane made about his future wealth and success dissolving before his eyes. Frank could not endure any more repeats of Dane's formula: Dane would start projects, Frank was promised that he would become wealthy, Dane would just suddenly drop it.

But, he assured me, he knew Dane. Dane couldn't function without Frank. He'd taken over all the detail work Dane hated to do. If Frank just holed up in his apartment and stayed away, soon Dane would beg him to come back. This time, he would refuse, until Dane gave absolute proof, in writing, that the project would be finished and he, Frank, would benefit significantly.

By this time, I was so disgusted with the whole thing that I didn't care if the script ever made it to film or not, and I said so to both of them.

All in all, it seemed pretty sick to me. But, again, Frank's lengthy explanations and interpretations of everything he perceived, backed up by citations of events and proofs that he was correct, persuaded me of at least one thing: he needed help. Whatever was going on here, he needed someone who would not abandon him.

At this point, Dane asked what I knew about Frank's financial situation. He definitely wanted to reward him for faithful service, he didn't want to leave him hanging, but since Frank wouldn't talk to him, would I please act as go-between? If Dane were to present Frank with a nice reward for faithful service, then they would be able to move forward through this barrier to their friendship. I was convinced that, even though he had much anger toward Dane, Frank truly loved him as a friend and mentor, and healing the breach between them seemed to be a worthy goal for me to assist in any way I could.

The answer, when it came, shocked me to my core. For years, Frank had been manipulating Dane's bank account in order to pay not only himself, but also Dane's son—who was apparently in on the fraud. Dane had tormented them with promises of future projects, while they were expected to dance attendance on him and give endlessly of their time and effort, for an occasional lunch at a low-class restaurant or a tank of gas for all their running around. They had managed, between the two of them, to set up a situation in which Dane trusted Frank (though he would not trust his own son in this way) enough to make him a signer on the business account. The two of them had been literally embezzling funds sufficient to have a reasonably comfortable lifestyle all this time, unknown to Dane who truly didn't wish to be bothered with the details of how and when the bills were paid as long as somebody else took care of it.

Nancy had been right.

Frank pointed out that neither of them had been greedy—they hadn't been buying cruises or fine art or taking trips to the Riviera—merely paying themselves reasonable salaries for their time. Well, actually, Frank was doing it, but he was being helped to cover it up by Dane's son.

What was I going to do? This was clearly the item that acted between them to prevent any progress in either the relationship or any possible work that might have been accomplished.

Finally, I came to a decision. If Dane truly had Frank's best interests at heart, Frank would be able to resolve the issue only with full disclosure. I urged Frank to confess. He was utterly panicked at the very suggestion: Dane would seek him out and destroy him!

I believed the only resolution was the truth.

I dialed the phone and when Dane answered, I took a deep breath and explained to him why Frank was shutting him out, and how terrified he was that Dane would destroy him.

Dane assured me that what I was telling him was something he already knew, and his major concern was that Frank be assured they could work this out. He was sorry that Frank had felt he had to be deceptive about the matter—all he had to do was ask and everything Dane could do for him, he would do. His only request was that I convey to Frank that he did, indeed, know and understand the situation.

Well, what a relief.

I called Frank and told him about my conversation with Dane, that his secret was not really a secret. He became utterly hysterical. I tried to calm him down, pointing out how reasonable Dane had been about it and that he certainly had nothing to fear.

Dane attempted over and over again to get Frank to talk to him, but Frank stubbornly refused. He holed up in his apartment in terror of the imagined wrath of Dane. This behavior may have been what created the fulfillment of what he feared. On the one hand, Dane was telling me how understanding he was, while on the other, in the background, he had been seeing an attorney with the clear intention of destroying Frank. The only question is: did he do this because Frank refused to communicate with him or would he have done it no matter what? Frank said that Dane had every intention from the beginning of destroying him. Whatever the motivations were, Dane seemed to be sincerely trying to work out the matter, and Frank seemed to be the one refusing to work things out.

Dane had his attorney send a letter to Frank, which demanded all funds he had "stolen," or face further legal action. Since Dane had told me he wanted to work things out with Frank, this upset me. I called Dane and suggested that he had been using me to try to destroy Frank. Dane reasonably pointed out that he was just trying to get Frank to show his good intentions by facing him and talking to him. As far as he could see, Frank had no good intentions. He had deliberately and maliciously embezzled funds, and his malicious intent was evident in the fact that he wouldn't talk to Dane. I pointed out to Dane that Frank had worked for him for five years or longer. Did he reasonably expect to have that time for free? At this point, Dane revealed what he really wanted: he wanted Frank to return to the fold in exchange for dropping the embezzlement charges.

What a dreadful muddle. Now what was I supposed to do? Frank was literally suicidal. He called me one night, half drunk on whiskey, and declaimed Hamlet's lament in modern terms. He was sitting there with a loaded pistol in his lap. As soon as he finished getting completely drunk, he was going to put a period to his existence.

I was perfectly terrified. What's more, it would be all my fault! Or at least, I perceived it to be so. I begged him to not do anything. I would see what I could do to sort the whole thing out. "Just give me a day or so."

Dane said he wanted his money back. That was it. Money was Dane's god. If Frank could pay him off, Dane would go away and leave him in peace. (Or, Frank could restore the relationship, which he declared he could never do.) Frank would be saved if his father would agree to pay Dane back the money.

The only problem was, Frank's father did not believe that paying Dane back was the solution. Frank's father thought Frank ought to face the music (which was actually not unreasonable). So Frank renewed his threat to shoot himself. I felt it was my job to rescue Frank.

"Don't do it, Frank," I pleaded. "I'll talk to your father. I'll explain to him that Dane is a dangerous and cunning man. I'll find a way to convince him that your way is the only way to handle it! Just give me some time!"

"You will?" he asked incredulously. "You'll talk to him? Oh, if only you would! It's the only answer!"

And I did, even if Frank had, indeed, been mostly to blame by his own desire to make something work in his life in a certain way. Dane's approach was evidence that he was just as dysfunctional in his own way, and this translated into a desire to destroy Frank that was all out of proportion to the crime. Compared to Dane's wealth, the amount of money was paltry, and Dane wouldn't even agree to a series of payments. It was all or nothing. Clearly, destroying Frank was Dane's objective by now. But then, as noted, that was because Frank acted the way he did, which seemed designed to create the fulfillment of his own prophecy about Dane.

I called Frank's father and explained to him that Frank was in the clutches of a conscienceless manipulator whose only agenda was to destroy him. I tried to stick to the facts as best I could, though, in the end, I merely parroted Frank's spin on them. I hoped with all my heart that Frank was correct and that, by accepting his version as the truth, I was making the correct decision.

His father listened carefully to all I said and merely thanked me in an embarrassed, but courtly way. "I'll take care of it," was what he said.

An attorney was consulted to act as go-between, the money was paid, Dane signed a waiver of prosecution, and Frank decided not to kill himself after all.

I didn't realize, however, that with the words I spoke to Frank's father, pleading for him to save his son, I was destroying forever any hopes he had held in his heart for his son to be successful in life, to be a real man.

CHAPTER THIRTY-FIVE

THE CRANE DANCE

According to the latest researches in cognitive science, we do what we do to survive because we have little choice in the matter. Gurdjieff was right and modern-day psychological studies repeatedly demonstrate that he was a pioneer in the matter.

We are programmed, conditioned, set up to be targets in some celestial sideshow. I knew from my experiences with hypnotherapy that few people ever have any deliberate intentions to hurt others, to create dramas in their lives that drive their loved ones away, or produce situations in which everyone is miserable, tragedies occur, and hearts are broken. Yet that was the state of the world. The "noonday devil" of stalking mundane evil was alive and well. We were all in its grip. (Of course, at the time all this was being written, I had not yet embarked on my studies in psychopathy, so the reader ought to take that into consideration.)

So when I saw Frank going through the dreadful experience he had created for himself, knowing the dreadful experiences I had created for myself, I had nothing but sympathy for him. I wanted to help him, to heal him, to make him whole. I realized that, more than anything, he needed someone who accepted him as he was, with all his unique talents and quirks and brilliance and very human foibles.

And that brings us back to the "family planet" as the environment in which we grow and evolve. We all have some idea of what a "normal" and "healthy" family is supposed to be. But really, has anybody ever seen such an entity?

According to researchers in child psychology, the ideal family is supposed to be the haven of support, where our personalities grow and develop the same way plants grow and develop in a garden. In our families, we are supposed to find a place of rest from emotional burdens, nurtured by its caring and loving members. In the ideal family, a child feels safety in sharing experiences and feelings and thoughts without having to be defensive. Ideally, the response will be open and accepting. The family, as the first and the most important source of identity and of emotional support, is a greenhouse where a child feels loved, accepted, and secure.

We learn to share the tasks of the family, promoting its survival. The family responds to us with material sustenance. Here, we learn what is considered moral and acceptable. Here, we develop our mode of absorbing, processing, and using information.

Psychological growth seems to be the result of a sort of dance, an interaction of inner nature with external environment. When the inner self reaches out to the environment and encounters an obstacle to its needs, desires, or will, growth may be arrested to some extent, or it may merely be redirected. This redirection may be similar to pruning a plant, or training a vine to grow where it ought to be, rather than running amok all over the ground. But it seems that, like trees, the human soul is designed to grow no matter what. A tree that is planted in suitable soil with the proper area for growth has the ability to grow straight and strong. If it receives adequate moisture and light, it will grow full and abundant. If it is properly pruned and trimmed when needed, it can be a thing of great beauty and usefulness to those seeking shade or birds needing homes.

But a tree that is planted in the wrong soil, with insufficient area for growth, with many obstacles to growth in the way such as barriers of concrete or other overshadowing trees that block the light, or various restrictions on straight and healthy growth, will still grow. Just as a tree can send out shoots that twist and turn around obstacles, ever-expanding, resulting in the crumbling destruction of the mightiest structures of mankind, so does the soul send its roots out into the soil of the universe, and its branches out to seek the light, no matter how many obstacles are in place. And, just as a tree that encounters these obstacles to growth can be stunted or become twisted and distorted in its growth, so can human souls become deformed and ugly, or destructive and diseased.

This "force of growth" compels the individual to continue to grow in the face of an obstacle or "disturbance in the force," and then the personality literally twists and turns, deforming itself, to reach functionality in the world. Psychological development follows the rule of all life: adaptation above all, growth at any price—straight or deformed. It seems the force of soul is stronger than any hindrance. Human beings develop personalities on the outside of their souls that are best suited to their needs for survival, based upon the fundamental constraints of childhood combined with their individual temperament. Such a person may be, indeed, abnormal.

But where there is life, there is hope.

We can go in any number of directions with the tree analogy, coming back to the idea of the family planet where the conditions for potential growth are initially established. We have looked at my own family planet and seen certain atmospheric aberrations, but basically, the soil was good and rich and there was a consistent sort of pruning, even if we might think that it was definitely overdone. In another sense, instead of twisting around obstacles, whatever was growing inside me literally pushed obstacles out of the way. I've talked about the family planet in which Larry grew and developed. Again, the soil was adequate, and there was pruning of another kind that allowed growth in some directions and not others. These situations are fairly standard even if we would not call them ideal.

Perhaps the metaphor can be extended to include different kinds of trees representing the different temperaments. We were all, in the beginning, different kinds of trees.

So, we come to Frank. Here we find another tree with certain growth adaptations we might easily assume are similar to those I experienced, that Larry experienced, that most of the human population on the planet experience. But in Frank's case, the results were quite extraordinary due to his genetically determined temperament.

I spent quite a number of years in a very close interaction with Frank, engaged in thousands of hours of conversation, and interacted with his family. Frank's father was a physician. During his childhood they lived in Chicago. He was brought up in an upper-middle-class neighborhood where he never, then or since, suffered lack or deprivation of any material sort. His family environment placed great emphasis on logic, monetary value, and scientific transactional approaches to life. In his family, cerebral and academic excellence was an expression of superiority—a means to an end. And the "end" was generally to live well, be rich, or even to be famous.

Frank's mother was the child of immigrants from a Scandinavian country. She had experienced a very unhappy first marriage, which produced a daughter, and after a bitter divorce had married Frank's father, who was quite a bit older. She was artistically gifted in a conventional way.

Frank's father was quite set in his ways at the time he married a divorcee with a young child. As a man of scientific background, Frank's father was steeped in the child-rearing theories of his own generation rather than the more modern conceptions of nurturing the psyche. His ideas related to hardening the body, toughening the will, and cultivating the mind.

Frank's mother, with her immigrant background, supported the same concepts since they were a part of her heritage, but she had also been brought up to serve and support the will of her husband and children. She was, in this drama, the slave to her husband, as well as the slave of her children, and that is a situation that can lead to great conflicts when the natural manipulations of children go against the will of the husband.

I don't think that Frank was ever physically abused in any serious way, though he did claim on a number of occasions that his father "knocked me across the room." Such incidents were, I think, rare.

What Frank complained about most was the fact that his father, finally having a son, needed so desperately for his son to be strong, to be manly, and to be the all-American boy. This included not just academic and moral strength, but also athletic excellence. To this end, Frank said he was subjected from a very early age to various programs designed to produce this paragon of American virtue. But Frank was not the least bit inclined to want to play baseball, go camping with a scout troop, or exert himself in activities demanding interaction with the world at large.

As infants and toddlers, we all feel that we are the center of the universe, that we are omnipotent and omniscient beings. In the beginning, we perceive our parents as merely extensions of ourselves in the sense that when we are uncomfortable in any way, these shadowy figures, the landscape of our universe, act on our behalf. Thus it is that, at the earliest stages of development, the "response of the universe" to our needs becomes our deepest belief about life itself—a belief inculcated before verbal skills are developed, and therefore, hardly amenable to psychiatric exploration in the ordinary sense.

If, when we are hungry or cold or too warm, or lonely and in need of touching and comfort, the universe-as-mother responds immediately with the appropriate solution; our earliest and deepest sense of existence tells us that the universe is safe, that it is good, that it is responsive to us. This becomes the fundamental platform from which we operate throughout our lives. We have learned that the universe is safe, that it is good to us, that we can reach out or cry out and the universe and all within it will provide.

When a child is treated, at the very earliest stages, as an object to be molded and shaped by regimentation, a dreadful crime against the essential self, at the deepest levels of being, is committed. A child who is left hungry because it is not the scheduled feeding time will be conditioned to believe the universe does not provide nourishment in response to his cries. A child who is not picked up and comforted when he is frightened, startled, or simply lonely and in need of being touched, is conditioned to believe that there is no point in reaching out or interacting with the universe in any way. So it is that a child raised according to the Cartesian "man as machine" model has no sense of safety or sufficiency.

An infant subjected to abrupt and arbitrary schedules, promoted by parents who, convinced by medical and psychiatric theories, believe they are doing the right thing, end up producing intense injuries to the infant's tender, budding self-esteem. Such injuries can be severe and irreversible.

The empathic support of our primary objects, the parents, is crucial at these early stages. In its absence, our sense of self-worth and self-esteem in adulthood tends to fluctuate wildly between over-valuation of ourselves by regressing to the infantile narcissistic mode, or devaluation of ourselves as the helpless child slave of a sadistic, even if well-meaning, parent.

As the experts note, such a child can grow up with a heavy sense of bitter disappointment and radical disillusionment with the universe as a whole. They are often unable to accept self-limitations, disappointments, setbacks, failures, criticism, or disillusionment with grace and tolerance. Their self-esteem is inconstant and negative. There is a tendency to believe everything that happens to them is the result of outside events, or that everything is their fault, in some way. In my own case, Larry took the former approach, and I took the latter. A child may think that if they only give more or do more, or find the flaw in themselves, they will be able to "fix everything." Such a view is growth inducing. If they cannot tolerate the stress of the feeling of being wrong, they often choose a growth-denying mode of reversion to the narcissistic phase of infancy. This was my mother's choice, Larry's choice, and Frank's choice. And that was due to genetic temperament.

Since his father, aided and abetted by his mother, worshipped the external self, how Frank appeared to others became a chief concern. The constant pressure to be a certain way, which is essentially artificial, by default convinces the child that what is inside him is not acceptable. His parents believed, in a peculiar mix of the child as a "blank slate" and the "natural child," that a child was a dirty and ignorant animal in need of training. In short, as a soul with specific inclinations and tendencies requiring delicate handling, Frank never had a chance.

Frank's experiences as a child were, in many respects, similar to my own, though certainly what happened to him occurred much earlier in his life, and he didn't have grandparents, as I did, to fill in as careful and devoted nurturers. His father, supported by his mother like a Greek chorus in the background, put him down and disregarded him and his feelings. The most poignant story he told me about his childhood concerned a time when he was left, before he was two years old, with an uncaring babysitter while his parents went on a two-week vacation. Frank's father was certain that a child so young couldn't possibly have any awareness of a caretaker or any capacity to feel more than basic instinctive drives and programs. It was his father's intention to toughen and condition Frank. Unfortunately, Frank was not only cognizant of what was being done; he never forgot it.

At the same time, Frank was being tormented by more than a "Face at the Window." He was being regularly and repeatedly "visited" by what he came to know as "aliens." He believed that he was regularly taken by them, and tortured by them, and all his efforts to communicate this to his parents were ignored and disregarded. He lived under siege with no one to turn to for protection.

He was utterly terrified to be left with strangers (not a surprise). On one occasion, he discovered that his mother had left him with a children's playgroup without telling him, in a moment when he'd been distracted. He cried so bitterly that the teacher forced him to stand up in the middle of the group and tell his name. He was naturally paralyzed and incapable of doing so. Frank remembered all the other children staring at him in his misery, laughing and pointing at him.

The next day, when he realized he had to go back again, he resisted and delayed getting dressed and ready. Finally in the car and on the way, in desperation he grabbed the door handle and told his mother that if she didn't stop the car and turn around and take him home, he would jump out that very instant and kill himself. He was only four years old.

Frank's mother stopped and turned around. Frank had learned the secret of controlling others to do his will. His mother's submission was probably the first time in his short life that he felt any power in his environment at all. This became a seed later to bear bitter fruit for all of them.

I have most definitely experienced that feeling of being paralyzed and unable to act. More than once. But in thinking these things over, I realize my own good fortune in the fact that my choice in every such situation has been to take some sort of definitive action to solve the problem, and that I am basically fearless in all cases. So, somebody must have done something right when I was an infant. Whatever it was, it wasn't done for Frank. Plus, I simply have a different genetic temperament.

In the end, it seems that Frank's efforts to deal with the "unfriendly universe" created by his parents had failed repeatedly and consistently. My own experiences had been similar in some respects, but I had learned a different way to cope. I wanted to help Frank break out of his loop also.

The contrast between the fantasy world of the omnipotent four-year-old who threatened his mother with suicide to obtain relief from external pressures, and the real world in which he was continuously frustrated, was clearly too painful to deal with. At that age, or perhaps even earlier, this dissonance may have caused him to make an unconscious decision to live in the fantasy world, where he was omnipotent and omniscient. In his private world, he felt special and entitled to things for which he had not worked nor put forth the effort expected of ordinary human beings.

And it was from this platform that the next interesting phenomenon developed.

As he grew older, Frank learned a curious "trick." He discovered that a sort of rhythmic dancing (more like the shuffling steps of a Native American ritual) and creation of vibratory sounds and sensations enabled him to enter and sustain this fantasy existence to an extraordinary degree. In this trance, he was the only occupant of the universe and he was entitled to all its secrets and lore. The way he did this was to perform a sort of "crane dance" while beating the ground with a stick. He once demonstrated this for me and it was, as close as I can describe it, a shamanic performance of pure instinct.

The soothing effect of retreating into this trance state was so effective that, in the same way some people become addicted to other things, Frank became addicted to being in a trance. He had discovered the ultimate means of retreating into what was, effectively, a pre-birth state of non-existence.

It is likely that the first time he achieved this state, it was accidental. He described it as having occurred after one of the episodes where he reached out to his parents for love and acceptance and, instead, received a lecture that included a list of all his faults and failings. He went out to the backyard and picked up a stick and began to pound the ground with it. As he did so, he became fascinated by both the vibratory sensation traveling up the stick from the impact, as well as the sound itself. He then began to experiment with different rhythms, most likely in an idle way, and then found himself entranced. At that point, the trance dancing began.

Thus he learned a trick that provided comfort.

Frank began to stimulate the trance state habitually in order to derive pleasure and gratification in a world that was friendly to his real self in opposition to the real world. The fact that this self-gratification was so easy to produce, rapidly conditioned him to prefer it. This, of course, produced another effect: laziness. But, this was not laziness in the ordinary sense of the word. Frank became lazy in the psychological sense because he learned that fantasyland was preferable to investing efforts in reality, where failure was assured. Frank became just like a rat with an electrode implanted in the pleasure center of the brain, repeatedly pushing the button that induced ecstasy in preference to real life.

And here we have an important clue as to how and why Frank also developed highly specific abilities that enabled certain results to transpire in my interactions with him.

Frank told me that he was performing this ritual stick dance so often that his parents became concerned and, at a very early age, they labeled him as sick and called in a psychiatrist.

This shamed his father terribly and only added to the demands being made on Frank to "toughen up" and "be a man." Frank reacted by intensifying his ritualistic behavior and time spent in a trance, though he learned to hide it better.

Frank had acquired the gift of the Crane Dance. At what cost, we can only guess.

CHAPTER THIRTY-SIX

HAILING THE UNIVERSE

We come at last to the crux of the matter: the Cassiopaean Experiment. How, in heaven's name, did it come about, considering that it was initiated by two such damaged individuals as Frank and me? More importantly, what was the end result for both of us? The reader will discover that this, like everything else, was a function of temperament.

The fact that we were damaged and knew it was, as far as I can see now, part of the impetus, the maneuvering of the Cosmos that brought us to this crossroads of action. I had always needed to find what prevented me from feeling at peace in the world and to resolve emotional issues that might act as barriers between me and my communion with God. I wanted to see clearly that which was within and release any hindrances to my ability to live each moment with a fresh and loving view of the universe and all within it.

Frank, on the other hand, wanted to discover what it was "out there" that had caused him so much suffering. He wanted to obtain validation of his view that he was utterly perfect and innocent unless he was "attacked" or manipulated by outside forces.

Two very different attitudes.

Nevertheless, we were both equally invested in discovering the truth that we thought was important, though we came at the question from totally opposing perspectives.

Frank had, by this time, described to me his Crane Dance trances and claimed that during these states he channeled incredible information that he was simply unable to express. I had the feeling it was more that he was unwilling to put the effort into it than anything. As he had grown up, he had graduated from the dancing mode of entrancement to other repetitive actions that produced the same result, such as juggling balls or any group of small objects.

Frank was very anxious for me to use hypnosis to bring forth and record his "channeling." I realize now that part of his motivation was that he hoped it would be published and he would take his place among the "stars" of the metaphysical world with a string of books, speaking engagements, and adulation from devoted disciples. Naturally, I would be the one who did all the work since he was, after all, The Channel. He would say: "The one thing I CAN do is channel. I do it all the time."

I decided to test this claim, and he demonstrated with automatic writing. I was not impressed. It was the same cosmic word salad that's been around for years. I suggested he needed to "tune" properly, so he settled down and agreed to listen to what I had to say.

Part of the theory I hammered out was that the reason other sources proved, in the end, in case after case, to be so human and fallible was because an initial error was made in the thinking of the various individuals who acted as channels or mediums. They assumed that a higher source could just be dialed up on the phone, so to speak, and that was that. I theorized, from the few flashes of light I could discern in the vast body of material I had studied, that an occasional truly higher source would manage to connect momentarily, or in a skewed or corrupted way, but that, for the most part, it was either discarnates who didn't know a whole lot more than humans did, or that the phenomenon was produced by psychopathology. I studied the matter from a number of directions trying to discover a clue as to what the obstruction was, if higher sources did, in fact, exist. (I was assuming that for the sake of experiment.)

The chief obstruction seemed to be this very cloud of theoretical lower-level beings and thoughts that apparently surrounded our realm like a curtain. My research into this area led me to the work of Dr. William Baldwin, Dr. Edith Fiore, Dr. Carl Wickland, and others who had worked directly with possession and exorcism and related therapeutic techniques. Since studying these matters had long been on my agenda of things to do, it seems that it manifested in my life at precisely the right moment.

There are many half-baked hypnotherapists who write lengthy books describing the afterlife as a place of great beauty and spiritual delight. The "journeys" and "destinies" of souls are explicated by recounting the most blatantly leading hypnotic sessions I have ever read. I would be ashamed to present material that exposed me as such a mind manipulator! Nevertheless, such books become wildly popular because they cater to the human need for existential comfort.

But, aside from leading questions and mind manipulation by the hypnotist, it most certainly seems that there are a lot of "dead dudes" (we'll call it that since we can't prove one way or the other what they are) who will come forward in various ways, including using the vocal instruments of a medium, who make such pronouncements, and who describe things in glowing and ephemeral terms. But, upon deeper inspection, it seems that there is a very great deal more to the matter than that.

The numbers of texts that have been written on the subject of the problems with the positivist channeled messages are considerable, most of them produced by research and not channeled information itself or philosophical conjecture. Many of the researchers in the field have been either professionals—psychologists, psychiatrists, medical doctors—or priests with medical or psychological training.

I began my own experimental work in this area with a major attitude of skepticism. That was good because, as it turned out, having started as a skeptic, I was quite taken aback to discover the reality that the so-called astral planes are a veritable jungle. Even though I conducted my sessions with extreme care to avoid any possibility of contaminating my subjects, over again, I discovered that all was not well in the "higher" realms.

That led, of course, to the question as to why so much nonsense is propagated by so-called channeled sources who are clearly, in many instances, lying? In other cases, they are, at the very least, guilty of such serious lack of attention to these matters that it amounts to a horrifying crime of omission. In my opinion, at this point in time, the lack of knowledge about this single issue is one of the chief reasons that it continues to build and perpetuate, increasing and amplifying the sufferings of humanity. How "good" are channeled sources that do not inform us of these conditions? If anything, the so-called New Age movement has been so heavily inculcated with the idea that one must not ever think about such negative things, that they, above all other people, are most subject to its predations. If you don't know about something, you cannot defend yourself against it. It was becoming apparent that there was something or someone "out there" who didn't want us to know something. (Gurdjieff's evil magician?)

Yes, I know that this just flies in the face of most religious doctrine, and most definitely it contradicts standard New Age philosophies. But let me just say that, over and over again, this has been proven to be so in the clinical experience of a sufficient number of trained researchers that before anyone rejects the premise, they ought to give it consideration as a working hypothesis to be tested. If it's wrong, no harm can be done by having considered it. If it's right, it could save our lives.

In *Spirit Releasement Therapy*, William Baldwin writes: "*With limited, if any, knowledge and distorted perceptions of the nature of the spirit world, the non-physical reality, many people leave themselves open and create their own vulnerability as part of creating their own reality.*"

This remark contains within it the description of the trap into which millions upon millions of human beings have been imprisoned for millennia. I would like to point out that they are, essentially, the philosophical foundations of faith as taught by the three major monotheistic religions, as well as the New Age religion. In other words: Faith, as understood and practiced by most human beings is merely another word for denial. And denial constitutes living a lie. And a lie, by the definitions of those very religions involved, is "satanic."

It is fashionable today to channel the "higher self" or "spirit teachers," to send love and light without having a specific request to do so (thereby opening a bi-directional portal where the negative energies one is seeking to transform can rebound on the sender), and so forth. Without knowledge and an ability to discern, one is then subject not only to the vagaries of any passing entity who hears the call, but also to cosmic laws of which most of humanity are abysmally ignorant.

Some surround themselves with light, or pray and specify "for my highest good" in their invocations. What they do not realize is that this actually constitutes permission and invitation to any discarnate spirit who truly believes that it is acting "for your highest good" in its realm of wishful thinking and earthbound ego fixation. (See Baldwin, quoted above.)

Keep in mind that we are not talking about demonic possession here. That is an entirely different kettle of fish, though it follows the same rules. We are talking about your garden-variety, well-meaning dead dudes wandering in the lower astral planes due to ignorance or some sort of affinity to the earth. As Edgar Cayce remarked: *A dead Presbyterian is just that: a dead Presbyterian!*

In coming face to face with all of this material and experience, I have to admit that I attempted to formulate a rationalist theory to explain it all. I could see that the jungle-like nature of the astral realms might be merely another psychological drama invented by the endlessly creative mind as a means of sorting through some current life issue. But, in the same way that I have never really cared if reincarnation was real or not, I didn't really care if the fact that there seemed to be higher-level negative beings on the astral planes was real or not; *I only cared that the therapeutic applications worked.*

And work it did—consistently and remarkably. One of the most amazing things about it was the consistency of the symbolic or archetypal language of the subconscious.

Subject after subject, from all walks of life, with all different levels of education and intellectual development, from different religions and belief systems, all of them, *when asked the same series of questions, responded with the same types of symbols relating to similar issues and relationships.*

Whether they were actually discarnate beings, or some split-off aspect of human personality, or energy constructions of an etheric sort, which could be detected and symbolically assigned personality and history, didn't matter to me; I knew that the mind is infinitely creative and I was reluctant to take a hard and fast position on the subject; I neither believed nor disbelieved. I continued to work with the concepts, constantly on the lookout for new data that might help me to refine, prove, or disprove my theory. To remain as open as possible to new information, my working hypothesis was that it was very likely that all that existed was an artifact of consciousness; the only thing to which I was giving a high probability was that consciousness could and did exist independently of matter. Consciousness could be positive or negative. But whether it was, in all cases, or even in most cases, consciously conscious, I didn't know.

Part of the difficulty presented by this work with exorcism-type activities (though that is a misnomer for the usual procedure, which amounts to "discarnate counseling") indicated that most activity that passed for channeling could be immediately dispensed with as being merely the production of the so-called astral realms (leaving aside the issue of whether the astral realms were artifacts of consciousness). I began to wonder if there was anything truly "higher," and if so, what it was and how "high" could one really go?

This led to the formulation of the idea of the second obstruction to achieving possible high-level contact; I called it the "transducing factor." This hypothesis suggested that it was evidential that a truly higher-level source—defined as such by whatever criteria—simply could not make a full and secure connection with consciousness that was embodied in the physical state, because it would be like trying to run a 110-volt appliance on 220-volt current. If it were a higher source, by definition, its energy would so overwhelm any human recipient that it could not be sustained.

Actually, I formulated this idea based on reading case histories. There were many that supported this hypothesis, and there were even examples of people who clearly had lost their minds after contact with higher sources. Like meteorites, they flashed across the sky of our collective psychological and spiritual domains, brief illuminators of the landscape, only to crash and burn in ignoble descent. For the most part, it was clear that such efforts posed many dangers as explicated in extensive readings in ancient literature, occult writings, and various Eastern mystical teachings.

There was another reason that I formulated this idea, and it was based on the observations of nature. The one thing we observe consistently in the world around us is growth. What's more, we observe that growth occurs in cycles. Human consciousness begins to grow from the moment of conception. Whether or not this is the result of a merging of an external consciousness with a developing neurological/physical system, or whether it is merely the result of the "ghost in the machine" effect, consciousness grows. Let's take that as an observable given principle.

At the beginning of life, when there is less apparent consciousness, the being sleeps a great deal. In the prime of life, when the consciousness is most apparent and active, the time spent sleeping (within wide variation, which may depend on richness of consciousness) is less.

At some point, consciousness begins to recede from the body in old age (again, with wide variation depending on unknown factors, possibly richness of consciousness), and the body again reverts to longer periods of sleep. The important thing is: we might think that this sleep and consciousness ratio is evidence of merging and emerging and receding stages of consciousness. In other words, a seed consciousness is planted in a newly conceived or born human being; it grows according to the richness of the environment and the potentials of the DNA parameters that are present in the body. When it reaches optimum growth, maximizes all it can do with the available medium, it begins receding. The important thing to understand is that consciousness apparently recedes because it has grown to the maximum and it no longer "fits"—its mandate is to grow, and it can't in that particular environment. It has achieved its fullest expression in that body, utilizing the available neurological/physical construct. We might conjecture that when this upper limit, or critical mass, has been achieved, then movement out of the body proceeds by stages.

This movement into the body by stages, and movement out of the body by stages, suggested to me that the death process was a sort of birth into a higher or richer and denser state of being that was not sustainable by the physical construct. Had it been sustainable at a higher level, or at greater density and richness, the death process might not have been stimulated to begin at that point. That this might have something to do with genetic considerations occurred to me. Just as different plants and creatures have certain and definite genetic parameters that determine their configuration, function, learning potentials, and life expectancy, so do individual humans, within certain ranges, have similar configurations, functions, learning potentials, and life expectancy. That these potentials could relate in a symbiotic way to consciousness occurred to me as a strong possibility. In other words, consciousness can only grow to a certain limit that is determined by the genetic constraints of the body it occupies.

Thus, it seemed that it was logical to pursue this line to the tentative conclusion that a truly higher being, or one that has achieved great density and richness of consciousness, could not, by the very constraints of the genetic configurations of function and potential in the human body, actually enter into the human consciousness energy field and put on somebody else's body like a glove for the purposes of direct interaction, unless it was of similar configuration and potential as the host body itself. It had grown and would no longer "fit."

The logical deduction then would be that if a consciousness that was external was, in fact, able to enter or merge with a human being, or connect in a direct way, it could only be one that was not any more advanced than the normal consciousness potential of that human being, though without the constraints of space and time. This last consideration might give a different perspective to such a consciousness, but that didn't attest to its advancement in philosophical or spiritual terms.

In other words, a dead Presbyterian is just that: a dead Presbyterian. If the consciousness can use your body as its own, it can't be much different from your own.

I noted in going through the literature on channeling and spirit mediumship that there were certain very interesting cases where it could be thought that the possessing entity (because, despite claims to the contrary, trance channeling *is* possession) was, at the very least, a consciousness a small order of magnitude more dense and rich than the medium him- or herself, who may or may not have achieved their consciousness/genetic potential.

The curious thing about such cases was that there seemed to be a direct relationship between such potentials and body mass. In other words, mediums who seemed to be capable of making limited connection to seemingly higher (though only slightly) beings were rather large (not always, but generally). Not only that, but when subjected to scientific controls and measurements, as some of them were in the nineteenth and early twentieth centuries, it was learned that such mediums could lose up to fifteen pounds of body mass in an hour or two of such contact. Eusapia Palladino is a case in point.

Considering such things made me think, naturally, of the very ancient Goddess images found all over the world, where She is nearly always represented as a very fat woman. Well, I was definitely a qualified applicant for the job! The only thing was, I was not at all satisfied with the levels of contact achieved even in those cases described above.

There were also stories of yogis and shamans who, in states of meditation or shamanic ecstasy where they claimed to have made some sort of "cosmic connection," lost incredible amounts of weight due to the "heat of the state." That this was a heat that did not necessarily register on a thermometer was clear, but heat of a certain kind was definitely present in these cases, as well as significant fluctuation in body mass.

This led me to the idea that, in terms of channeling truly higher beings, the mode itself presented significant problems. Relative to the theorized "high voltage" of such higher sources, I proposed that the only way to make such a contact was to combine the energies of two or more people as a "receiver," and then to attempt to "tune" the receiver with repeated acts of intent.

As I puzzled over the problem, I realized that the only real way to combine energies as a human bio-cosmic receiver was to use some form of communication that required more than one person and which also provided an immediate feedback checking mechanism. The obvious answer was a spirit board–type instrument.

Well, in my younger days I most definitely had experienced modest success "playing" with such an instrument, though I had given it up as possibly dangerous or just merely childish. It was slow, tedious, and I wasn't exactly sure of the source of the replies, never mind how accurate they were. Nevertheless, now I was looking at it in a different way and considering the possibilities that it was a potential means of coordinating focus and intent as well as proximity of energetic biopsychic fields, with the added feedback loop for tuning. I knew that I needed to research it to discover if, theoretically, it would suit the purpose.

There are two main theories about how the spirit board is supposed to work. The first is called *automatism*. Automatism is also supposed to be the means by which dowsing, pendulums, table tipping, automatic writing, and other movement of physical objects by purported spiritual forces is supposed to take place. What this means is that the participants may not realize that they are responsible for the movements of the indicator, but they are still doing it themselves. Conscious or unconscious expectations can signal nerves to fire thereby causing tiny, imperceptible motions of the fingers, which produce the "answers." In this theory, the use of the "talking" board is similar to theories of automatic writing that claim such messages originate in the conscious or unconscious mind of the medium. Defined within this context, the talking board is merely a bypass of the conscious mind, and a shortcut between the unconscious mind and the neuromuscular control system. "Collective automatism" would occur when more than one person is operating the board.

So we see that, psychologically speaking, automatism allows the subconscious mind temporary control of some part of the body without the interference of the conscious mind. At the same time, it leaves the conscious mind conscious for checking the feedback, monitoring the activity, and basically balancing the effort within the controls of experimental protocols. It's not a bad system for finding out what is going on in your subconscious if you can restrict it to that alone. In that sense, it's not much different from Freudian psychoanalysis.

Some "experts" claim that having a healthy unconscious mind is the key to protection, since opening such a door without due care could most certainly trigger psychosis in certain individuals. I have a slightly different view. I don't think that bypassing the conscious mind in this way can trigger psychosis. What I do think is that it can open a door to reveal psychosis that already exists within the mind and which, if careful analysis is undertaken, will be seen to have been present all along, manifesting in many symptoms of the body and life of the individual.

The issue of whether or not using a board, or any other type of unconscious accessing tool, can "invite" possession is rather like asking which comes first, the chicken or the egg. Dr. Baldwin brings this issue up in an interesting way. Even though he has reasonably assessed so many other things, on this issue he demonstrates that he, too, has fallen under the spell of the movie *The Exorcist* and draws illogical conclusions. The evidence, as Baldwin describes it himself, tells us that the state of possession probably already exists in any given individual, and the use of the conscious bypass only allows it to "speak" and reveal itself. But that presents its own set of problems. *Obviously, anyone who is not trained in the techniques of spirit release should never open such a door.* By the same token, based on reasonable assessment of the situation, *an individual who has no knowledge of these techniques, who has not spent a considerable period of time learning about them and working with them, ought never to attempt to channel either in any context.* To do so is to invite disaster. And that, of course, brings up the obvious question as to why channeling has become such a popular sport.

The spiritualist theory, of course, declares that the messages that may come via a spirit board clearly originate from "outside." Spirits or forces are contacted and channeled through the board. The spiritualist theory posits that the communicants are discarnate spirits or other ethereal beings who have a purpose for contacting the living. Nevertheless, even the spiritualist theory depends upon the theory of automatism for actual operation. The discarnate spirit is able to connect to the operator via the subconscious or unconscious mind and take control of the ideomotor responses, bypassing the conscious mind, and generating movement of the indicator via stimulation of nerve impulses. Naturally, this theory posits that, as soon as the communication has ended, the spirit leaves, and all is well and good. The evidence, however, indicates that if certain knowledge is not available, and certain actions are not taken, the spirit does not leave. It merely withdraws into the "interstitial" spaces of the energy field of the host and becomes quiescent, continuing to drain psychic life force for its own sustenance.

One of the more interesting theories I came across was developed by Barbara Honegger, said to be the first person in the United States to obtain an advanced degree in experimental parapsychology. Honegger suggested that automatism was the result of stimulation of the right hemisphere of the brain so that it could overcome the suppression of the left hemisphere. It was never entirely clear what was doing the stimulating, however, and I could obtain no further information on her research.

The Chinese seem to have been the first to use spiritual automatism in the form of a "writing planchette." The Chinese device was called a chi and it was a sort of divining or dowsing rod used to write. It was said that the spirits came down into it, moving it, and the object of the activity was to use it to spell out the gods' messages on paper or in sand.

It seems that all "primitive" or preliterate cultures had some form of codified communication between spirits and the living. This phenomenon seems to be universal in the ancient world and only came under condemnation with the inception of monotheism around 1000 BC. When Yahweh spoke to, or through, his channels, they were called prophets and the activity was "divine inspiration." When anybody else did it, it was necromancy or demonic possession, or even just out-and-out deception. This was because, obviously, since Jehovah/Yahweh was the only god (according to him), those other "gods" did not exist; therefore, anyone who claimed to be channeling them was lying. Of course that begs the question as to why people were put to death for lying about communicating with gods that were claimed not to exist. If they did actually exist and were actually communicating, as Yahweh was also, then what does that suggest about Yahweh's status, since he was the one who claimed to be the only god and that this was true simply because Yahweh said so via channeling? Most curious.

In the sixth century BC the Thracian Dionysiac cults were known to be using shamans as trance channels to communicate with the spirits, or what were then known as *theoi* or gods: discarnate immortal beings with superhuman powers. Some scholars suggest that rationalist philosophy was born out of the Dionysiac, Orphic, and Eleusinian mystery cults devoted to the channeling of these gods; certainly much ancient Greek philosophy, especially that of Pythagoras, Heraclitus, and Plato, was saturated with these mysteries.

This brings up the question, of course, as to how channeled information could have been the basis of the rationalist philosophy that there was nothing to channel. Could it be merely a progression of the idea of Yahweh that there was only one god, and he was it? Just another step in stripping away any spiritual support from the lives of human beings?

In Plato's *Theages* Socrates confesses, "By the favour of the Gods, I have since my childhood been attended by a semi-divine being whose voice from time to time dissuades me from some undertaking, but never directs me what I am to do." Apparently, they didn't do much in the way of protecting Socrates from the backlash since, in the end, he was condemned to death for his activities. Again, most curious.

The Greek oracles at Dodona and Delphi and other sites would prophesy by sinking into a trance during which they were possessed by discarnate spirits, some of the famous ones by a single spirit, or what we would today call a "spirit guide." Oracles often lived in caves and thought of the spirits they channeled as coming up to them from the underworld through fissures in the rock.

The most interesting item of all is the fact that Pythagoras used something like a spirit board—or a planchette, actually—as early as 540 BC: a "mystic table" on wheels moved around and pointed toward signs that were then interpreted by the philosopher himself or his pupil Philolaus. Even down to the present day, the mysteries of the Pythagoreans are subjects of intense interest to scientists and mystics alike. And here there seems to be evidence that the advanced knowledge of Pythagoras may have been obtained via a Ouija board!

By the time the Romans had conquered Greece, the rationalist movement was turning against spirit-channeling. Cicero, the Roman rationalist whom the early Church Fathers highly revered, railed against spirit-channeling or necromancy on the grounds that it involved ghastly pagan rituals. But, as noted above, eventually, rationalism bit the hand that fed it and began to devour its father, monotheism, by further extending the argument to the idea that there is no God, there are no spirits, nothing survives the death of the physical body, there is really nobody for us to talk to on the "other side," so why bother? Science took the view that the whole thing was a con game, and that's pretty much the current mainstream scientific opinion of the phenomenon today.

After working with spirit attachment issues, I had a lot of questions. As I have already said, there was an open possibility in my mind that such "spirits" were merely fragments of the personality of an individual, sort of like little broken-off circuits in the brain running in repetitive loops, created by trauma or stress. (Cf. Martha Stout's *The Myth of Sanity*.) Perhaps an individual, when faced with a difficulty, entered a narcissistic state of fantasy, created a dream, which was imprinted in the memory of the brain. If they then emerged from this state back into dealing with their reality, but not having dealt with the issue itself, it might become locked away in a sort of cerebral file drawer, sitting there, waiting to be triggered by the electricity or neurochemicals of the brain in some random unconscious scan or a similar situation or feeling that put them back in the same dream over and over again. The same could be said for so-called past-life memories: they were merely self-created memory files generated in a state of narcissistic withdrawal due to stress. Such neurological files could then be downloaded and read by using the conscious bypass method of either automatism or simply allowing the conscious mind to "step aside," as in trance channeling. As noted, simple psychotherapy could be considered channeling in these terms. Conscious channeling via possession is more problematic because it suggests a definite pathological condition in which spirit attachment or multiple personality may play a part. In such cases, the alter ego, as either an alternate personality or an actual attached entity, is strong and well entrenched enough to establish a far stronger hold on the body of the host than those which can only manifest via automatism or trance and can take over whenever it chooses.

Professor Douglas Robinson at the University of Mississippi suggests that an analogy can be drawn between the function of a translator and the channel or medium. It is their purpose to step aside and allow the original author of a work in another language to speak through them. It is their profession to convey the fullest intention of the original author to a new audience that otherwise, not knowing the language, would not have access to the material. In the ordinary sense, translation is done merely across linguistic or cultural barriers. In the sense of channeling, it is done across temporal, consciousness, or even hyperspatial barriers.

The crucial thing about both translating and channeling is the necessity for the mediator not to convey to the target audience his or her own ideas, meanings, arguments, or images. The translator must be a neutral conduit to the target audience of the ideas and meanings of the original author.

In Professor Robinson's words: *"The analogy suggests both (a) that the source author has the power to initiate communication with the target audience through the translator (the author is active, the translator is passive, or at the very most active only in the act of surrendering his/her activity to that of the author), and (b) that the translator possesses some means of gaining access to the author's voice and meaning, of reliably 'opening up' to the intentional speaking of a person who is almost invariably other. Sometimes translators translate source texts they wrote themselves, but usually the source author is another person, most often distant in time and place, and not infrequently dead."*

In the present day, under the influence of rationalist Western technology, the idea that anyone can just sit down and begin to channel is very similar to the idea that translation can be done by machines with no human interface. This is a very subtle point. In terms of a computer program that translates from one language to another, and most channels, we see that the program attempts to execute an algorithm or series of algorithms that consists of gathering intelligence, charting a course of action, giving a series of commands, and carrying them out. The results are only as good as the algorithms. And we see from the literature that the channeling phenomenon as it is widely practiced *omits reason from the algorithm*. There is no feedback mechanism and thus no possibility of accurate tuning. This means that it does not allow for an algorithm that can handle the fact that there may be competing forces inside the channel's head. Excluding reason and the possibility of competing forces results in the algorithm: "I am the Lord your God and there is no other because I said so! And if you don't believe me, then it will be all the worse for you!" Not very productive, to say the least.

The fact is, machine translation researchers despair of ever programming a machine to produce a translation of professionally usable quality without human assistance. In the same way, it is likely impossible to produce channeled material of any usable quality without full consideration for the competing forces as well as the application of reason in dealing with them. Without application of knowledge and direct, rapid feedback, there is little possibility that anything other than useless psychobabble will emerge; and such seems to be the case. But of course, that excludes the narcissistic delusionals, the deliberate frauds, and the pathological cases of multiple personality. They are all out there in New Age Land, and it's a jungle!

In the end, those machine translation systems that do work are, effectively, cyborg translation systems: they all require a human—machine interface.

In science fiction movies we often see a "machine translator" that enables the space traveler to just plug himself into a gadget via some brain electrode, and open his mouth and automatically speak in the language of the planet he is visiting. The words may start out in his brain in his own language, but by the time the come out of his mouth, the machine has altered the nerve impulses to the organs of speech causing them to produce correct words in the unknown tongue. Apparently, the machine also works in reverse, and the space traveler may hear words spoken in the unknown language, but he experiences them in his own. What is interesting to me is the fact that *it is a prosthetic device* that turns the space traveler into a sort of cyborg translator who becomes able to "channel" foreign speech.

The point I am trying to make is that by the use of prosthetics, we are in a position to employ an algorithm that includes reason and feedback. Reason, when properly employed, posits an entire army of what Adam Smith called "invisible hands," which shape, direct, regulate, and control translation. And that leads us to the most interesting conclusion that *reason itself can be an invisible hand.*

"*Reason is an internalized form of ideological mastery.*" Just as the spirit seizes or possesses the channel and speaks or otherwise operates through the channel's willing body in the same way a text in a foreign language is fed into a computer to be translated (often quite ineptly), so too does ideology and its agents—including reason—seize or possess the ideological subject and wield that subject's body as virtually its own. And in this sense, we discover that the channel, as a "translation machine," can become something far more interesting.

An individual who, via long and intensive study, comes to the idea that there is a possibility of communicating with higher consciousnesses, formulates a hypothesis of how to do it, and then experiments with that hypothesis, adjusting and modifying throughout the process, is, in a sense, being guided by invisible hands, or forces of the cosmos. But it is clearly a source of some greater complexity and deep need to communicate complex and new concepts that *prepares* such a translator. In terms of ordinary lower-level channeling, we find that the spirits of such activities "hail" the channel through whom he or she wishes to speak by appearing before the clairvoyant, or welling up like verbal pressure inside the head begging to be released for the clairaudient. Sometimes the channel falls into unconsciousness and wakes up to find that something or somebody else has been using their organs of speech.

In the same way does the cosmos-at-large, via reason and knowledge and a questing spirit planted in a human form hail a potential channel/translator of truly higher realities. The words "translate," "transfer," and "transduce" all have the same Latin root. *It is in the role of translator that we discover that just "plugging in and turning on the machine" is not enough.*

Translators must be trained; they must not only know the other language, they must know how to regulate the degree of fidelity with the source text, how to tell what degree and type of fidelity is appropriate in specific use contexts, how to receive and deliver translations, how to find help with terminology, and so on. All of this suggests *a long period of training and preparation.*

A translator–channel is someone who has studied these things, who knows these things, and who, most importantly, governs their channeling–translating behavior in terms of this knowledge. This knowledge is ideological. It is controlled by cosmic ideological norms. To know, via reason, what those cosmic norms prescribe and act upon them is to submit to control by them. To become a translator–channel of truly higher Cosmic Consciousness is to be hailed as a translator by the invisible hand of the Universe.

If you want to become a translator–channel, you must submit to the translator's role of learning the language in an expert way (and such learning is via life experiences); you must submit to being directed by what the cosmic ideological norms inform you is the true spirit of the source author and to channel that spirit unchanged into the target language.

Thus it was, with all of these considerations in mind, I finally settled on the board-type instrument as the best mode of dealing with these issues. It is a prosthetic device that allows constant feedback between the algorithm of "machine translation" of the subconscious/ unconscious and the human interface of the conscious mind, which must constantly employ reason for tuning. This is possible only with a board due to the fact that the channel is using the conscious bypass for reception, while at the same time is able to maintain constant conscious integrity. By being, at all times, in full possession of their own mind and having the ability to observe, control, and direct acceptance or rejection of any material or sensation at any time, reason is brought in as part of the algorithm. In other words, used correctly by an individual who is knowledgeable in the subjects under discussion, as well as the clinically demonstrated realities of other realms, this is one of the finest tools available for developing contact with the subconscious, the higher self, and benevolent entities which wish to make telepathic contact. And that is the key word: telepathic. This type of device allows one to create a separate line, so to speak, a "switchboard" where a new circuit is established through a minute thread of consciousness without giving up control in anyway.

Due to the influence of the movie *The Exorcist*, the device has acquired a negative reputation. Yet, this was not always the case. Funny how an entire doctrine can be created by Hollywood and then people accept it as gospel.

Some so-called experts will claim that being a medium is okay, but using a board or automatic writing as a medium or even trance channeling can only bring in lower-level entities. They base this wholly illogical statement on the claim that "no spirit of an advanced degree of spirituality, no ascended master or guardian spirit, would ever stoop to abusing the writing or speaking talents of another person, living or dead." Let me get this straight: it's okay to do any of the above as long as you call yourself a medium, but if you call yourself a channel, or if you establish protocols whereby you are in constant, conscious control, you are, by definition, only in contact with lower-level entities? Most peculiar. Also most abysmally ignorant.

Contrary to the above "expert" opinion, one part of my hypothesis, based on years of research, was that sustained contact with true higher-level sources had rarely, if ever, occurred *in the entire history of channeling*. At least not the type of sources I theorized to exist at truly higher levels of existence. Thus, no one really "knew the language." It was absurd to think that one could just sit down, from their present human condition, download, and translate something that, evidentially, had almost never been encountered before.

At this point in time, I hypothesized that the universe-at-large, or the "source" I wished to contact, did, in fact, have the power to initiate communication with the target audience—humanity—because it was evident, through all the experiences of my life up to that point, that the Universe speaks to us via the events of our lives. The many remarkable synchronicities in evidence, as well as close observation of the dynamics of my life itself and the lives of other people I had observed could only be interpreted as deliberate actions from some ultra-cosmic reality attempting to teach me the language of symbols. I felt that I had, most definitely, been hailed by the Universe, which was asking me to undertake the task of learning the language and acting as translator-channel. Whether or not a more direct mode of communication could be established via myself as such a translator, I was not entirely certain. But I was most definitely anxious to make the attempt to gain access to the voice of the Universe by hailing back via a long process of building a circuit into and possibly even through the deep unconscious mind.

Since it was clear that these interactions involved some level of being of which most of us are unaware, and to which we have little access, I realized that this amounted to the fact that I had to learn the language at some as-yet-unknown level of my being. Not only was I proposing to learn this language that had never before been systematically studied, I knew that I had to learn how to *"regulate the degree of fidelity with the source text, how to tell what degree and type of fidelity is appropriate in specific use contexts, how to receive and deliver translations, how to find help with terminology, and so on."* This was the reasoning, or "ideological state apparatus," I was setting up as the protocol for the return "signal."

Reading through the literature on channeling, it was evident that the most respected and trustworthy material in the history of channeling had either come through a board-type instrument or had been initiated by a board-type instrument. That it was a means of learning a new language in some internal place in the mind, like plugging in a translation matrix device, was evident. With the added information at my disposal regarding spirit attachment, multiple personality disorder, and other pathological conditions, as well as the means of dealing with them effectively that I had learned over years of practice as a hypnotherapist, I realized that, if I was correct in my hypothesis, I could possibly take channeling to a level never before achieved—or at least, only very rarely—maybe once every thousand years or so.

But, of course, it all depended on a long period of training and applying the algorithm. And this meant a possibly very long period of using a board-type instrument to channel not only one's own subconscious fragments through their series of dramas, but possibly an endless number of frequency-related discarnates before all the loops had been played out and dealt with and brain synchrony was achieved.

In the end, I decided that even if that was all that we accomplished in the process, it was still a worthwhile activity. Purifying the mind by healing its fragments in whatever terms they manifest could only be good! The important thing I realized was to not give up using the board too soon. That would be like assuming one had a good mastery of a language just because one could use it for everyday purposes. To be a true translator, one must master a new language at the most subtle and refined levels imaginable.

At this point, I thought I had a pretty good theory and it was time to put it into the test phase; so, we began. Frank and I met every week to sit and "hail the Universe." I have notebooks that record every motion of the indicator for over two years prior to the appearance of the Cassiopaean connection. In the end, this material does, indeed, support my theory. We waded through endless loops of the unconscious mind, endless purported discarnate entities or past-life scenarios, endless lost souls wandering in the astral realms seeking release into the light. At one point I realized that if any of this material had any factual basis, the board was an excellent tool for effecting spirit release, contrary to the opinions of Dr. Baldwin.

In the end, we were both quite fascinated with the parade passing before us, and we joked that it was better than going to the movies, watching television, or going to parties. In full consciousness, we could peer into endless realms of otherworldly activity—dramas of tragedy and hope, despair and joy—and do it all while drinking coffee, eating cookies, and taking time out to chat. But what was really going on at other levels of being would prove to be more fascinating and mysterious than anything I had hypothesized.

CHAPTER THIRTY-SEVEN

MISSING CHILD, MISSING TIME

As our experiment in channeling proceeded, we discussed the many possible ways that a true higher source might be identified. We both thought that a higher source, by virtue of greater and more inclusive cosmic perspective, would be able to make absolutely stunning predictions that would hit the mark every time. But, in a short-term feedback loop of testing, how to validate such a hypothesis?

Frank came up with a solution: the lottery. Well, that seemed reasonable enough. We could ask for a lotto prediction from every entity, then grade them based on their ability to predict. Since there were daily games, we concentrated on these.

Now, while I have been known to buy an occasional lotto ticket or two based on a dream or just an impulse, and to win when I do, I have never been a real gambler. If I had the money to buy a soft drink and, instead, decided to give up the drink in favor of a lottery ticket, I felt that this was no more than I would spend on the minimal amount of junk food I ordinarily consumed—a few soft-drinks denied, and there was a movie ticket—and for me that was all it was: entertainment. If I won, it was fun. If I didn't, I hadn't lost any more than I would have wasted otherwise. I never considered buying a lottery ticket as a way of getting out of any financial difficulty. If I was in a situation where I could not justify buying even a candy bar because money was that tight, I didn't buy a lottery ticket either.

For me, the "lotto test" was theoretical. *I* wasn't going out and buying tickets; I was just noting the numbers down and checking them with the posted results. It was only later that I discovered that Frank was. Not only that, he seemed particularly devoted to this aspect of the experiment.

Doing it as a test was one thing, but doing it with intent to profit was somewhat disturbing to me.

In actual fact, we did have a few hits in that regard. They usually came up on a different day than predicted, sometimes even as long as several weeks after they were given. Frank claimed to have made money this way, but I reminded him that his overall expenditure on tickets ought to be deducted from his winnings to get a real picture.

* * *

In January of 1993, my old friend Keith Laumer died. I had driven up to see him some months earlier and he looked terrible. It had been twenty years—almost to the day—since I had sat in his house and watched him brandish a gun with the ostensible purpose of putting a period to his existence. During my last visit with him, Keith seemed tired and broken. He told me that if he had a switch on the wall to turn out the lights of his life the same way he could bring darkness to his room before sleeping, though he desperately wanted to, he wasn't sure he'd have the courage to do it. "I realize at long last what a coward I have always been," he said. The bitterness in his voice nearly undid me. Whether it was a new manipulation or just a sad statement of fact, borne of great struggle in his life, I will never know.

When his secretary called to tell me he had passed away during the night of the 23rd, I felt as though a door had closed on an entire thread of my life. In his honor, I put on a tape of Puccini. It actually wasn't too bad.

A few weeks later, a local twelve-year-old girl was reported missing. I was very shaken by it because, when her photo was displayed on the television, she looked so much like my number-two daughter that I almost began to cry. I was surprised by my emotional reaction, and even more surprised when, watching the news report, I "saw" in my mind's eye that the girl was dead, naked, wrapped in what looked like saran wrap, lying in a stand of pine trees. I even had a "sensation" of the general location.

The vision came to me as if remembering an intense experience from my own past. In my mind the heat shimmered at the edges of the shade in a pinewoods. Mottled shadows moved slightly as the rising air softly rushed between the pine needles. I could actually smell the pinesap. The body lay nearly face down with an arm tucked under the side. Flies droned sickeningly as they reconnoitered the rapidly putrefying flesh. I didn't know exactly where this place was, but I knew I was seeing the missing girl.

I forced my normal awareness back into place, much like pulling a shade down over a window, and continued to listen to the details about the child. She had only been missing since the day before, and, under normal circumstances, no investigation of any kind would be launched for at least twenty-four hours. But, in this case, the family was close to a high-ranking member of the sheriff's department. From his personal knowledge of the situation and the persons involved, he determined that foul play must be strongly suspected. A full-scale investigation had been launched within just a couple of hours of when she was due home.

The name of the sheriff's department official was given in the report as "Henry Smith" (a pseudonym). Good old Henry. Son of a friend and former employer of my mother; two years ahead of me in high school. As I watched the newscast, I wanted to tell them there was no point in looking for a living child. The child was already dead.

There had been a number of occasions in my life when I just "knew" things about crimes I would read or hear about. It was always an initial flash of insight which, if I try to push it further, sort of disappears. It actually became a sort of side hobby to make predictions about who may have done a crime just to test myself. On the occasions when I did get an initial impression, I was always right. But I never had an opportunity to provide the information to anyone who could do anything about it. In fact, I probably would not have told anyone if I had the chance, because I had no taste for being labeled a psychic.

The point is, I keep score with myself. It's a game I play and I win only if I am right on every point and it is certain that I could have no way of knowing what I know by normal means. When I get the information, it is good, but there are times when I get nothing at all. It is as though some people and some situations are simply on another channel.

But this case was one I could tune in to more clearly than others. I had a twelve-year-old daughter of my own who was so similar in appearance. The newscaster described a child very much like my own. It seemed that the missing girl, the perfect child, had gotten off the school bus and disappeared. No physical evidence of any kind was found. She disappeared with books, purse, and clarinet. No one saw anything at all unusual, except that the other kids on the school bus seemed to remember a blue truck in the vicinity. The details on the blue truck were vague, and there seemed to be nothing else to go on. So, I watched the case with interest.

On the following day Marcia Matthews called. (This is not her real name.) Marcia is a local self-proclaimed psychic, hypnotherapist, western dancer, and general wise woman. She didn't waste any time getting to the point.

"Have you heard anything about the little girl that's missing?"

I acknowledged that I had.

"Well, I just came from over there and I just want to run some things by you to get your reaction."

"What do you mean you just came from over there?" I asked.

"Well, not exactly *there*. We were at the county fair, you know, and it seems the girl's parents have been working with some group over there. The cops were all over the place. So I decided to see if I could get some feelings ... There's a van they were checking out ... and I tell you, when I got near that van, my flesh just crawled! I mean, there is some nasty stuff there! And I just know she's alive but she doesn't have much time. I HAVE to find her! She's cold and in a dark place and she's hanging on for dear life ... and I'll tell you, if some of these bastards don't listen to me they're going to have that girl's death on their hands!"

"Slow down, Marcia!" I was used to Marcia getting all wound up. I knew if I was going to make any sense of the conversation I was going to have to make her stop and start at the beginning.

"You and Bennie went to the fair, right? How did you get involved with the cops? Did they just come up to you and ask you if you knew anything?"

"Well, not exactly. We saw the posters they were putting up all over, you know, the pictures of the little girl, and I went up and introduced myself and offered to help. I told them I'm a psychic and, I was surprised, they didn't seem turned off at all! In fact, they invited me over to see if I could pick up anything from a van parked behind the fair. They think that maybe one of the fair people had something to do with it."

"Why do they think that?" I asked patiently.

"Because the girl's parents belong to some organization doing something here at the fair and the kid has spent a lot of time in the past few days hanging out here. The cops think that maybe one of the carnies found out where she lived and abducted her."

"So tell me about this van," I prompted.

"Well, I wanted you to tell me what you get."

"It's white, full of junk, and has something blue on the engine cover," I replied promptly. I have no idea where it came from, but then, I never do.

"Yes," she urged, "but what is the blue thing."

"I have no idea." I was getting impatient. I knew the van had nothing to do with the missing girl, and I could feel another one of Marcia's wild-goose chases coming on.

"It's a Bible," she announced breathlessly. "A Bible! Can you figure that! And I can just see the girl on the floor in the front curled into a ball with rags thrown over her and this son of a bitch driving her down the road. He raped her, man, he tortured her … she's a mess and I've got to find her before its too late!" Marcia was starting to wind up again, so I stopped her with a question.

"Where do you think she is? "

"I'm not sure, but I know it is near her house. I get a well house—a shed, something to do with water. Oh man, she's in pain!" I could see the conversation was going nowhere so I decided to tell her the truth.

"She's dead, Marcia. She's been dead since yesterday."

"No, I don't agree. She's out there calling to me. I'm going to look. This cop named J. D. gave me her card and I am going to go and look. There's a road I noticed on our way in here. I had a funny feeling about that road and I just know she's down there. If I can't get them to look, I'll do it myself. I have to find her! When I find the spot, I'll call this J. D. and get her to get some men out there. I gotta go, I'll talk to you later."

"Sure, keep me posted." I hung up the phone wondering just what kind of cosmic drama was being played out with this event. Marcia had probably called every psychic person she knew, gotten their impressions, and was now unable to distinguish between true intuition and all the interference she was picking up. The only problem was that most of the so-called psychics around town were shrewd cold-readers with very little true ability. Oh, they had an occasional flash now and then, but generally they failed miserably. Because of "psychics" like that, I didn't want to be numbered as part of their group.

Over the next few days I kept my own counsel. Marcia called with frequent updates of her wild-goose chase. She told me another friend of ours, Danielle, worked with the missing girl's stepfather at the local resource recovery plant. I called Danielle to pick up any information I could. All she could tell me was a reprise of Marcia's insistence that the girl was alive and that, as far as she could see, the family was a normal happy one.

I told Danielle I was sure that the child was dead. She totally rejected the idea. But she did say that the child's stepfather was at the plant at the time of the girl's disappearance.

The media appealed for information on the missing child, keeping up an onslaught of endless stories about the family and how normal and upstanding they were. For some reason, I had no further insights. On the night the family appeared before the TV cameras to beg for the return of their daughter, I watched in horrified fascination. I couldn't help but put myself in their shoes. They asked for every resident of the county to search every building they owned, every shed, every pump house—I could see Marcia's hand at work—to leave no trail un-walked and no stone unturned. There was something odd about the interview, though. I just couldn't put my finger on it. The stepfather did all the talking while the mother sat stony faced and silent. It made me wonder. But it's easy to criticize. What I would be doing myself, I couldn't know. I couldn't go that far in my imagination. It was too terrible.

I called Sandra, who was by now a bigwig at the state social services agency. Sandra was also extremely intuitive. As I expected, she had already done a little poking around through the family services files. The scuttlebutt within the agency was that the family had some problems with the girl. There were signs of rivalry between the new stepfather and the girl's natural father. There were whispers that the child had tried to run away before to go to her father. Sandra was putting her money on the stepfather. She was convinced that sexual abuse was rampant in that house and that a confrontation on the subject had led to the child's death. Like me, Sandra also knew the girl was dead. I shared with Sandra the information I had gotten from Danielle, that the stepfather could not have been a party to the fact the child was missing because he was at work with a lot of witnesses at the time. We both pondered the matter, but nothing else came up. It was most definitely a curious case.

I wondered about what Sandra had discovered. It was likely that the sheriff's department was already privy to the information there had been problems in the home. So why had they launched a full-scale crime investigation into what must have looked, at first glance, like a simple runaway?

Something wasn't adding up.

That night, I tried to meditate and clear my mind of all conflicting ideas and information. I knew the torture I would feel not knowing where my child was or if she was dead or alive, certain that every moment I would be thinking the worst and that the burden of those thoughts would drive me mad. Just thinking about it was more than I could bear. I began to cry. I silently sent a summons to the universe to "bring that little girl home!" Over and over I repeated it: "Just bring her home." Suddenly, I felt a flood of peace wash through me and knew that events would soon begin to move.

The following day I was as tense as if my own daughter was missing. It seemed as if the whole county, all of nature, was holding its breath. The missing girl had become everyone's child. I was still frustrated because I had no further impressions. But I continually "asked the question." The only thing I could see was an old road I used to drive as a teenager—a road with hills and curves and fields of hay and cattle. I knew she was there, somewhere in the vicinity of that road.

I picked up the children from school. They were excited with news that the missing girl had been found. Their source seemed to be a schoolteacher whose daughter worked for the newspaper. The kids' story was confirmed by a bulletin on television almost as soon as we arrived home. A body had been found off P___ Road, the very road I had been seeing in my mind. No positive identification had been made.

But everyone knew who it was.

The evening news put a period to the speculation. The missing child had been positively identified but no further details would be forthcoming until an autopsy was performed. We could all breathe again but we did so with tears and trepidation. There was obviously a killer on the loose.

The appeals to apprehend the killer intensified. Everyone was now looking for a blue truck that some of the children on the school bus thought they remembered seeing. I paced the floor in anguish, realizing that the only way I would be able to get the answer would be if someone connected to the case "asked me the question."

This was another thing I had noticed about my "abilities." Just as the process of channeling the inspiration for *Noah* had occurred only in response to mental questions, very often I have no insight into what is not my business until someone whose business it is asks me about it. When they do, the answer simply comes to me.

Finally, unable to just close my mind to the affair, I sat down to write a letter. I addressed the letter to the sheriff's department official close to the family: Henry Smith. I asked him to please not share with anyone what I was going to say. You just never know who else might work down at the sheriff's office and, of all things, I didn't want to get a reputation as a weirdo.

I told Henry what I had seen so far, which had been accurate, and that I felt I might be able to see more if only I were asked. I intended to use astrological charts on the subject as the method of focusing. I had the idea that it was possible, in this way, to identify the killer, or at least some things about him to produce a rather specific profile. What I was offering, however, might not be any better than nothing, and I said so. But, I was willing to have a go at it.

I really did not expect a response except a polite "thank you, but we have all the leads we can handle." I certainly did not expect Henry himself to call me the very next day after I mailed the letter! But he did. He told me that he had consulted the family and, on their behalf, and as a friend of the family and not as a public official, he was asking me to look into the matter.

The type of chart I was going to do is called horary astrology. Horary means "of the hour." The idea is that when a question is asked in seriousness and sincerity, the answer is inherent in the moment of asking. I recorded the time of the question as well as the birth data he gave me for the astrological charts.

During the course of the conversation, he confirmed my vision: the body had been stripped, had been hosed to remove all traces of evidence, and was wrapped in plastic sheeting. I pointed out that this indicated someone who was familiar with forensic procedures and who intended, most definitely, to remove all traces of fibers or other microscopic elements that might have served to at least identify where the murder occurred. Not only had all evidence been thoroughly removed, the body was left just over the line in the adjacent county which most definitely confused investigative issues. Henry agreed with this assessment.

"Would you go out to the site with me and see if you could sense anything else?" he asked me.

"Henry, this really is not my forte!"

"We need your help, Laura. Isn't that standard psychic procedure to go to the scene and …"

"But I probably only had the original insight because of my emotional reaction to seeing her face," I told him. "It was just so similar to my own daughter's. I'm sure I would get better results by working on the astrological charts."

"I understand. But for the family's sake, could you just give it a try?"

It was about twenty miles to the location where the body was found. That's not a great distance, but it included a lot of driving around the area where the girl lived and frankly, my health was in such a bad state that I budgeted my time very carefully. Any driving other than just around town to run a few errands left me totally exhausted, not to mention the swelling of my legs. But still, under the circumstances I couldn't refuse.

I don't know what made me think of doing it the way I did, but that's what I did. My objective was to see everything through the mind of the killer and get into his thought processes.

Well, that was a big mistake. Yes, I got impressions. Yes, I later did all the charts. Yes, I believe I solved the crime, and insiders on the subject are also convinced that my solution is the correct one. But there is not one single, solitary shred of real evidence on which to justify an accusation, much less an arrest. It is also very unlikely that the individual will ever kill again. But if he does, someone is watching. I also cannot give those details due to issues of possible defamation. But that's not what is important here.

As a result of all this traipsing around and putting on that "mind of the killer," the stress nearly killed me. My body swelled with what the doctor called ascites, speculating that I had damaged my liver by taking nine Tylenol a day for the past seven years or so. My heart was backflushing constantly, my kidneys had shut down, and I was as close to death as I have ever been.

The doctor wanted to admit me to the hospital, but I refused. I remembered the horror of my grandmother's death, which could have been peaceful with me at her side. I remembered how the hospital personnel deprived me of those last few moments with their absurd resuscitation efforts. If I was going to die, I wanted to do it at home.

My doctor shook his head in near despair at my stubbornness, ordered me to bed for complete rest for two weeks or longer, and prescribed medication. He was sure I would give in and he would see me at the hospital by the next day at the latest. I was just as sure he wouldn't. I had Larry get me home to bed. I almost couldn't walk.

After a few days of feeling on the verge of death, declining all medicine, eating nothing, drinking only distilled water, I began to feel just a tiny bit better. My thought processes had almost completely stopped working from the build-up of toxins in my body. But as I began to recover, I soon began to feel the need for new activity. Obviously I couldn't move from the bed, so I called Frank and asked him to bring me something good to read.

Frank arrived with a big grocery sack full of UFO and alien abduction books!

I was furious.

"Frank, I am NOT going to read them, so you just take them back!"

He set the bag down. "In case you change your mind, I'll just leave them anyway." He grinned with sadistic satisfaction.

"I assure you that I am not that desperate!"

"Suit yourself," said Frank, and left me with the bag of lurid paperbacks.

After a while, the boredom became pretty severe.

I reached into the bag and pulled out a book.

Hmm. *Missing Time* by Budd Hopkins. I was pretty amazed as I read. This was not the flaky flim-flam of Ruth Montgomery or the gothic existential angst of Whitley Strieber. It was actually an attempt at serious research! I was surprised.

More disturbing, I recognized many events that I'd shoved under the rug in my own life, clearly evident in the lives of the people interviewed for this book. They had reached a point of exploring these anomalies and talking about them and retrieving memories under hypnosis.

But, after some consideration, I brushed their "alien abduction" explanations away. I could think of a dozen other solutions. Besides, it was too soon to draw conclusions: I needed more data.

I read on. Book after book.

The Interrupted Journey. The Andreasson Affair. The Alien Agenda.

There were people claiming we had been being visited by aliens since archaic times. There were others who claimed we had been visited a few times, but they were gone now, nothing to worry about! Another group claimed that we had "let them in" by setting off the atomic bomb; they were here to make sure we didn't blow ourselves up along with the rest of the universe. Some claimed they were good guys who were just a little weird because they had followed a different path of evolution, or were further along than we were. Others claimed they were demons from hell and we had better get ourselves back to church if we expected to survive the invasion.

Sheesh! The only thing certain was that people were seeing and experiencing something singularly strange. Secret government projects? Secret aliens-in-cahoots-with-the-government? By the time I finished I was sure of one thing and one thing only: there was a LOT of smoke!

But smoke obscures the source of the fire even if, underneath, there might only be a smoldering mess. I wasn't sure if this was a manipulation by the government to make people think aliens existed, or if aliens did exist and were trying to make the government look guilty.

What a morass of confusion!

Not to be intimidated by unexplained phenomena of any sort, I started working on a new theory to explain the UFO/alien abduction phenomenon. There was little in these stories that could not be explained by mass hallucination and hysteria, psychokinesis, stigmata, repressed memories of physical or sexual abuse, psychosis, schizophrenia—heck, just a whole cornucopia of tricks of the mind to choose from.

I worked on the problem, discussed it with Frank, and demonstrated how every event in every case he cited could be explained by some aspect of my new "rationalist rheory of UFOs." He was practically foaming at the mouth in frustration with my stubborn refusal to see anything other than what could be classified, categorized, and explained by any number of currently established scientific perspectives, even if some of them were a little far to the left of "normal." I was actually pretty proud of my fiendishly clever solution.

This was in March of 1993.

Pride goes before a fall, you know. The Universe, it seems, had a big hole just waiting for me to fall into. Things were just getting warmed up!

CHAPTER THIRTY-EIGHT

FLYING BLACK BOOMERANGS

Not long after I had been released from my sickbed and the inundation of UFO books, I went to the supermarket one morning, and there was a stack of pink flyers with flea-market–type ads. I was looking for some additional computer equipment, so I picked one up and tucked it in my pocket. When I got home, I read over it and noted an ad for exactly what I wanted.

I called the number and talked to the woman. We began to chat about computers in general and specific. She asked, conversationally, what programs I used. I mentioned my astrology programs, which piqued her interest. This led to questions, which led to a series of remarks about my hypnosis work. *That* really piqued her interest.

She began to probe a bit about the subject and then asked about scheduling a session because something really strange had happened to her back in 1987, and it *still* bothered her and she wanted to know why, or at least get relief from the internal anxiety it had caused.

The story was that she had been to the funeral of an aunt, accompanied by her sixteen-year-old son, and they were returning home to Maryland and were driving on the Pennsylvania Turnpike. (I don't remember where the funeral was.)

It began to snow, and she saw a very bright light ahead, off to the side of the road, sort of bluish white, and she thought that it was a light that had come on to illuminate a billboard since the snow had made things a bit dark.

She then said that what happened next was so strange that, even in remembering it, she felt strange and uneasy. She said that she felt a paralysis come over her hands and arms as though someone had taken control of the car.

I immediately recognized the purported prodromal signs of a "missing time" experience as described by Budd Hopkins, so I casually asked what happened next.

She said that this was the crazy part, because she couldn't remember. After seeing the light and feeling the paralysis, the next thing she remembered was sitting at a traffic light fifty or sixty miles down the road. She did not remember making the turn off the main highway, and her son had just cut his finger on a tin of cookies he was trying to open. He was bleeding, and she "came to herself" saying "there's a towel in the back seat." To further add to her dismay, she arrived home much later than she should have, but, at the same time, still had an almost-full tank of gas.

Certainly everyone has had the experience of dissociating while driving, running on autopilot, and suddenly coming back to themselves with no memory of going from point A to point B. I mentioned an experience of this type that I had myself, earlier in this book. What was unusual then was that I don't have such experiences as a matter of habit like other people do. But I am aware that it happens to many and for some of them, quite often. The only difference between events of that sort and what this woman was describing was the emotional content. She was extremely distressed.

She was sure that it had been her aunt attempting to contact her psychically and she really needed to have an answer. What had her aunt been trying to tell her?

Well, the fact that she made no mention or claim about aliens made the whole thing far more interesting to me. And, of course, I did not want to even suggest anything about aliens, as I wanted to try to prove my theory about alien abductions being psychodramas in the same manner as past lives. I just told her that we could certainly clear the problem up quickly with hypnosis!

She made an appointment. I decided to make a videotape of this session rather than the usual audiotape. I wanted a record of my proof that the alien abduction phenomenon had another explanation!

* * *

On the evening of the appointment (she was caring for an ill husband and needed to come at a time when her kids would be home to look after his needs), it began to storm terribly. I was sure she would not come out in such rain and expected a cancellation. But she showed up.

We went through the normal pre-session interview, and then talked a bit about the event again. I wanted to get the times and details down about her general life situation, so I would have clues about areas of possible family conflicts that might be at the root of such a drama.

She was a real estate agent and also owned a medical reports business working under government contract. She talked a bit about her children and her disabled husband, who was dying. I was sure the stress of caring for him was an exacerbation of her problems.

Nothing was said about aliens at any point whatsoever. I carefully inquired about her interests. She had never been interested in metaphysics, much less aliens though she was certainly curious about astrology. She was a former devout Catholic who was now in a state of doubt about her religion. She was sure that I was not going to be able to hypnotize her.

She was a good subject and quickly went under.

I never transcribed this session or even viewed it from the time it occurred until I handed the videotape over to Tom French for his *St. Pete Times* article. Since he is the one who has viewed it over and over again and transcribed it for his own research, as well as having interviewed the subject afterward (and hasn't returned the tape), I am going to quote from the *Times* version of it here. You will get some idea of my hypnosis techniques by reading carefully.

* * *

"I wish that damn light would change," said the woman on the couch.

Her eyes were shut, her body stretched out under a blanket. Her hands were folded above the blanket, making tiny movements. In her mind, she was still at the wheel.

Laura, sitting in her chair a few feet away, did not understand.

"What?"

"I'm just waiting for the light to turn green," the woman said. Suddenly her voice changed. "Oh my God, Patrick! What did you do?"

Something was wrong. They had gone through it all together, Laura and the woman. Laura had gotten her to close her eyes and slow her breathing, and then the woman had gone under and resurfaced back inside that night out on the turnpike. She had already told Laura what happened.

Now, still under hypnosis, she was telling it again, letting it run in her head, like a scene in a movie.

She and her teenage son, Patrick, were returning from a funeral in Pittsburgh. It was snowing. There was fog and ice. They took a detour onto another highway, trying to find better weather. Then the woman sees the light in front of the billboard. The light is an iridescent blue, a pale oval of baby blue, and the oval is hanging there in front of the billboard, it makes no sense, and the woman thinks she is imagining it, she is rubbing her eyes, but it isn't working, the light doesn't go away, it just keeps getting bigger, and so she asks Patrick if he sees it, but he doesn't, only he does say something about electricity, and then she feels something taking control of the car, now she's not driving it anymore, something else is, and the light is still growing.

Then the skip.

Suddenly she and her son are somewhere down the road. Now they are in a little town called Waynesboro, off the highway, just north of the Maryland state line. Something has happened. Fifty miles have ticked by on the odometer, and they do not know where the miles have gone. All they know is that they are sitting at a traffic light in Waynesboro. The woman is at the wheel, waiting for the light to change, and her son is beside her, trying to open a tin of cookies someone gave them after the funeral. But he can't open them, so she tells him to look in the glove box, there's a penknife, and he gets the knife, and he works at the cookie tin, and he cuts himself. Now he is bleeding. They are at the light, and Patrick's hand is bleeding.

"Oh my God, Patrick!" *the woman was saying.* "What did you do? There's a towel in the back seat. Get it."

Still in her chair, Laura studied the woman carefully. [Frank], a friend of Laura's, was watching, too, videotaping the session from the corner.

By this point the woman had grown agitated. Something was upsetting her, and not just the cut on her son's hand. She was breathing faster. She had raised her arms to her chest and crossed them, as though she was trying to protect herself.

Laura told the woman everything was fine. She reminded her that she and her son were safe. But they needed to go back to the beginning, back to the turnpike, and start over.

"Let's go through it again," Laura said. "A little more slowly this time."

It was the night of Thursday, April 15, 1993. Laura and Frank and their subject were working in Laura's living room in her home in New Port

Richey, there on Montana Avenue. Outside it had been storming. Inside, all was quiet, except for the interplay between Laura's voice, soothing yet insistent, and the woman's voice, confused and edgy. Occasionally there were the chirping sounds of the family's cockatiels; there were also murmuring noises as Frank whispered a few words to Laura.

Now here she was, lying in Laura's living room with her eyes closed, driving again through that night. Every time she replayed it for Laura, it came out the same. She and her son would be driving on the turnpike, and they would take the detour, and then she was seeing the blue light. Then the skip. The same skip, every time. Suddenly they would be at that traffic light in Waynesboro, 50 miles down the road, and her son was opening the tin of cookies with the knife and cutting his hand.

Laura was determined to find out what had happened during those 50 miles. Frank, videotaping from the corner, already thought he knew. That was why he was so excited.

"This is an alien abduction," he told Laura.

Frank was big on UFOs. He was well aware, as was Laura, that a growing number of Americans—the exact number remained unclear—had come forward in recent years with stories of disturbing encounters with creatures that had traveled here from other planets. Many of these people believed, or claimed to believe, that aliens had abducted them from their cars or bedrooms, somehow rendered them helpless, then taken them aboard a spacecraft of one kind or another, subjected them to medical or scientific experiments, then returned them to their lives with all memories of the abductions blocked from their minds. When these people would try to recall what had happened, they would simply draw a blank; their recollections of the aliens typically surfaced later, often under hypnosis.

Frank believed these people's stories demanded attention. So did others who followed the phenomenon, including John Mack, a Harvard psychiatrist who had interviewed some of the alleged abductees.

Laura was not so sure. At Frank's urging, she had been reading about the abduction accounts but had found them unconvincing. Laura was open to believing in many things; her whole life was devoted to considering possibilities in the universe that others found ludicrous. Still, she had trouble believing that little gray men were stealing people away by the hundreds or even thousands and playing doctor with all of them on some fancy mothership in the sky. If it was happening to so many, why was there no proof? Why could no one produce a single indisputable snapshot of one of these aliens or even one of their ships? Where was the video? Why weren't these aliens appearing on Geraldo?

Like many others, Laura found it far more likely that these people had undergone some serious trauma—possibly sexual abuse, suffered during childhood—and that now they were subconsciously transforming their buried memories of these experiences into encounters of another kind. Perhaps it was easier for them to imagine an alien illicitly entering their bedroom and violating them, rather than to confront the fact that it was really their stepfather or their mother's boyfriend.

Laura thought she detected an element of mass hysteria in the proliferation of abduction accounts. With the approach of 2000, maybe these people were simply going a little nuts. "Millennial disease," she called it.

All of which explained why Laura was taking such pains to find out precisely what had happened to the woman she was working with this night. Before hypnotizing her, Laura had asked the woman about her childhood, probing for any sign of abuse or family problems or anything suggesting emotional or mental instability. But she had found nothing to account for the missing time in the woman's story.

Laura was undeterred. She decided to take the woman under even deeper, getting her to slow her breathing even more and replay that night yet again. This time, the woman remembered a parking lot. She could see the blue light growing, and feel the car leaving the highway, and now she and her son were stopped in the parking lot of a diner, just off the road, not far from the billboard where she'd first seen the light.

"What happened next?" said Laura.

"I wish that damn light would change," said the woman.

Back to the skip. Whatever it was, it had happened somewhere between the moment in the parking lot and the moment when her son cut his hand.

So Laura tried again, taking the woman as deep as she knew how. Speaking softly, she asked her subject to imagine herself sitting inside a favorite room. Maybe the family room at her home; maybe a study. Anyplace where the woman felt safe. Inside this room she was asked to imagine a recliner. She was sitting in the recliner, resting comfortably, and in front of her was a television. On that television, she was to project the scene from that night, unfolding on the screen, and describe what she saw.

Laura told the woman she had a remote in her hand and could manipulate the action before her. She could fast forward, rewind, turn it off. Whatever she needed to do to feel safe and in control.

Back onto the highway went the woman, her son at her side. They were taking the detour. The billboard was coming up.

Slow it down, Laura told her. Use your remote, and hit pause, and let the tape advance one frame at a time.

The light. She saw the blue light. It was in front of the billboard. It was growing. She was losing control of the car. It was leaving the road. Then they were in the parking lot. They were in the lot, outside the diner. They did not know why. Wait. Someone was coming. Someone was approaching the car.

Laura asked her to describe who it was.

"I can't," said the woman. She was getting agitated again. She was hyperventilating; her upper arms were twitching; she was rubbing her hands, as though she were in pain.

"What do you mean, you can't?" said Laura.

"Because **they** won't let me."

Laura pressed the woman to tell her what was going on. Who was she talking about? Who was stopping her from saying?

The woman just shook her head.

"I can't tell," she said. "I can't."

That evening, when the woman on the couch grew so upset, Laura decided to end the session. She wanted to keep probing, but for the moment it was too traumatic. So Laura brought the woman out of hypnosis and told her that they would try again, in another session. Laura was left to consider the implications of what her subject had revealed. Was Frank right? Had this woman and her son been abducted by aliens?

At first, Laura remained skeptical. Then, in the weeks that followed, something happened that chipped away at her doubts. The newspaper and TV were reporting multiple sightings of UFOs in the area. From mid to late April in 1993, more than a dozen people in Pasco, Hernando and Pinellas counties said they had seen a large, boomerang-shaped craft moving across the sky. One of the witnesses, a Hernando County sheriff's deputy, said the craft carried no markings, was adorned with blue lights and had a wingspan of at least 200 feet. He watched it for several minutes, he said, before it accelerated away from him at a speed that would have been impossible for any human-made craft.

"Based on what I know now, no, I don't think it's from this planet," the deputy told a *St. Petersburg Times* reporter. "Nothing on Earth could hover and haul ass like that."

Reading the accounts in the newspaper, Laura was startled to discover that the first alleged sighting of the boomerang-shaped object had been made in New Port Richey on the evening of Thursday, April 15, the same night she was conducting her hypnosis session with the woman in her living room. The person who had seen the object that night lived only six blocks or so from Laura's house; she said she had seen the craft through her bedroom window after 10 p.m. that evening, after L.A. Law came on.

As Laura read the details of the account, she realized something else. The witness claimed that she had seen the giant boomerang at the exact time Laura was deep into her session; in fact, she said she'd seen it hovering over Laura's own neighborhood.

To Frank, this was all more proof that the woman with the missing time had been telling them something dangerous that night, something the aliens didn't want her to share. That's why her memory block was so strong, he said; that explained what she'd meant when she said "they" wouldn't allow her to continue with the story.

Laura still was not ready to buy Frank's theories. As far as she was concerned, the rash of sightings was just another outbreak of millennial disease. One person claimed to have seen the giant boomerang, and the rest had probably heard the claims, then gotten excited and imagined seeing the same object. If there were so many spaceships out there, carrying all these aliens and snatching all these poor earthlings, where was the proof?

"Where's the evidence?" she asked Frank. "Show me a damned alien, for God's sakes."

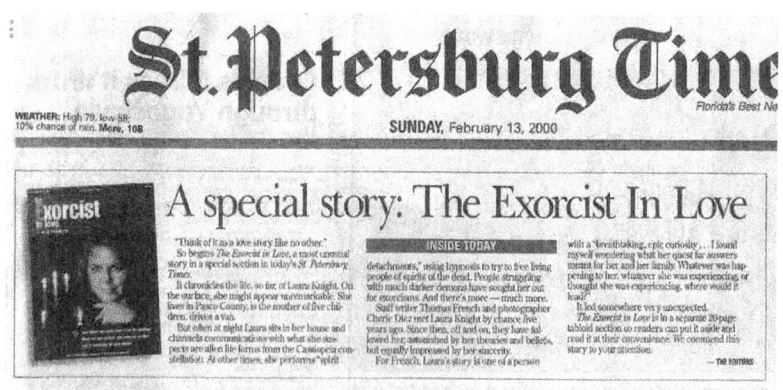

The front page of the *St. Pete Times* on Feb 13, 2000, inviting the reader to check out the special section.

As it turned out, no more evidence was forthcoming from the woman with the missing time that night in Pennsylvania. After the first session with Laura, she called and said she'd changed her mind. She would not be returning for another session. (Excerpted from Thomas French's "The Exorcist in Love," St. Petersburg Times, Feb. 13, 2000.)

* * *

Yes, I admit freely that my intent was to expose the alien abduction phenomenon as a fraud; as the psychodrama I believed it to be. Having the videotape to work from, Tom described the session probably better than I would have.

If ever there was proof that a hypnotherapist with a pre-formed belief cannot influence the recall of a subject, this case is a classic in that regard. I am ashamed to admit my assumptions now, and I freely admit that it was not the proper approach to the problem, but then again, the subject was not claiming to have been abducted by aliens—at least not consciously. And I was going to be very careful not to lead in any way, so the "experiment" would be uncontaminated.

To say that I was puzzled and frustrated is an understatement. I had never encountered a blocked memory that I could not find some way to access. This was one of my specialties. I could find the "back door" of the mind, ease the pain, and get to the root of the problem. But try as I would, nothing worked. She repeated: "I can't! I can't!" So, in frustration I asked why, and her answer raised the hair on my head and chilled me to the bone: "Because they won't let me!"

For a few moments I was completely nonplussed. I had never encountered a "they" who could so effectively block memory and cause pain and suffering when attempts were made to access it.

I realized that I was clearly dealing with a deeply repressed trauma. I wanted to believe that it related to something in childhood, or perhaps even a past life, but I couldn't shake the eerie sensation that washed over me when she cried "THEY won't let me!"

I knew that I could not lose professional control, and I decided that perhaps she just needed to be in a deeper trance to access this information. But, I was not going to push any further at this moment. Sometimes a subject must be conditioned, over time. So I started the suggestions that would make her feel good, make her like hypnosis, make her want to do it again, and help her to go into a trance more easily in the future so that a deeper state could be achieved and we could deal with this thing. Then, I brought her out.

We discussed a future appointment and she agreed that she would like to try again, and that was that, except for the fact that she called and cancelled on the day of the next appointment.

Okay, fine. End of story? Nope.

The reports of the black boomerangs that came in conjunction with this session did not make me happy. In fact, it gave me the absolute creeps!

It also made me think.

If we conjecture that this "alien phenomenon" is part of some deep government conspiracy designed to experiment on people—perhaps to make them think that they are being abducted by aliens so that they will assiduously seek greater controls and protection from "Big Brother"—we have a curious problem with this case. The problem becomes: how could such a hypothesized group engineer the response to this session that did, in fact, manifest?

I was very careful not to mention the word "alien" or "abduction" to the woman on the phone prior to the session. If phone conversations are being monitored, how did this one get selected for special attention? Such monitoring, even for keywords that would trigger a need for personal attention, suggests a conspiracy of such vast and complex proportions that the logistics of it stagger the mind.

Well, suppose it is a government conspiracy. Suppose that they do have such monitoring capabilities, that they are monitoring my phone, the woman's phone, or the phones of everybody by computer. As a result, suppose they knew I was going to hypnotize her and sent out a flotilla of stealth aircraft to beam some wave at her (or something like that) that would prevent her from talking to me.

Why would they go to all that trouble?

It seems to me that it would be easier to just send one of those nice white-panel trucks we see in the movies to park a block away from my house for their wave-beaming activities.

Well, okay; maybe they just thought it was a handy time to create a UFO flap at that moment for general purposes: to get everyone all excited, to reinforce the "alien phenomenon" scenario they are creating.

We are still looking at logistics that stagger the mind.

The next question we have to ask is this: since this woman appeared in my life at precisely the moment I had been familiarized with the phenomenon sufficiently to recognize the symptoms, how do we deal with that synchronicity? If it is a government conspiracy that was aiming at taking me in by gradual degrees, by creating a series of events in my life that would lead me to give up my rational explanations of the phenomenon, what kind of surveillance and management does that suggest?

Again, it boggles the mind.

Thinking these thoughts produced a strange feeling in me of being watched in ways hard to describe. It was so strange a synchronicity that I couldn't help but think that the appearance of these craft related to our activities. I tried to sweep this thought under the rug, but it kept coming back.

Well, there was a final article in the *Times* about this series of sightings, and this last article was designed to put it all to rest; it was a suggestion that what had been seen was a stealth bomber.

It was all just a strange coincidence. My comfort zone was reestablished and I could rest at night.

For a while.

CHAPTER THIRTY-NINE

FLYING BLACK BOOMERANGS REDUX

At this point, again, health issues moved to the forefront. All my life, it seemed when I recovered by sheer force of will from one assault, another would arrive seemingly out of nowhere.

I was most definitely looking at this as a symbol of my inner state and constantly made adjustments in my relationships with others. I struggled to discover what lurked in my subconscious attitudes or beliefs. I was sure, at some level, that we do, indeed, create our own reality or, at the very least, interact with it in a dynamic way. It was becoming rather clear that our preoccupations didn't manifest as reality in any consistent way. More often, the things we denied or sought to shove under the rug grew larger and confronted us.

My ability to keep going was rapidly falling short of the challenges presented. I was able to walk limited distances no longer than five minutes. Standing soon became excruciatingly painful. Meanwhile, the numbness, tingling, and bone-deep aching in my left arm nearly drove me crazy. The doctor diagnosed it as angina, related to my damaged heart, and suggested that I lose weight and get exercise.

Well, how do you get exercise when you can neither stand nor walk for more than a few minutes? Thyroid medication I had taken for years seemed to have no effect on my weight and only exacerbated the heart problem. I truly could eat almost nothing and still gain weight. I joked that I could just look at a glass of water and get fat.

But it wasn't a joke.

I looked in the mirror one day and realized that the pattern of weight distribution had changed over the past few years. I appeared very much like a person who had adrenal problems. I figured, *It's no wonder. I worry day and night how we are going to pay our bills and provide for our children, and whether we are going to be on the verge of losing everything the next time Larry takes us through months of depression and not working.*

I needed to be able to work for the sake of the children.

At this point, I was seeing three or four hypnotherapy clients a week. This was so draining that the entire day following a session was employed in recovery. Each day I had to make a choice on how to engage my limited ability to function. Each choice meant a whole list of other things I couldn't do.

If I agreed to see a client and asked Larry to cook dinner so I could conserve my strength, he loudly proclaimed to the children that I clearly didn't want to be a wife and mother anymore. So, I cut back on the schedule to satisfy him. When I did, he simply left to go fishing! After trying various adjustments, it became clear that he did not really want to spend time with me and the children but merely resented that I spent time with anyone else. He wanted me to be available to do what he wanted, when he wanted, because he wanted it.

I don't think it ever occurred to him that I detested my inability to accomplish all the things I wanted to do. Here was this interesting puzzle to be solved, and I didn't have the stamina to do the research I needed, much less to perform the basic functions of a wife and mother.

I remember lying on the bed one day in so much pain that I had to clench my teeth to endure it. I knew the house was a mess, I knew that laundry was waiting to be done, I knew that it would be nice if I could just tear into all the chores and get them done. I asked the children to help so I would have the energy to cook dinner.

However, Larry had decided at that moment to hold me up as an example of a really bad mother. He did it, of course, in a "Christian" context, but that didn't erase the cruelty of his comments on my inadequacies and physical problems. The children should not be asked to do anything.

"They're just kids! It's your job to do those things! You seem to be able spend your time reading or sitting at that table entertaining your friends. Why don't you spend some time taking care of your family?" As he said these things, I felt the pain in my arm mount to the point that I thought I would scream.

I quickly swallowed three or four aspirin and fled to the privacy of the bedroom to cry alone.

Now, I could hear them gaily making popcorn and settling down to watch a video with Larry, the "good guy." They had driven the wicked witch out of the room.

* * *

Pain is an abstract concept to anybody who is not experiencing it. Larry was athletic and active and always had been, even after the surgery on his back. While he was in pain, he was a complete baby, but he got over it so quickly that it was soon forgotten. He attributed his health to his active lifestyle. He told me that if I would just get out and walk and do things, I would be healthy too! Problem was, after my fourth child, when my pelvis had been damaged, I couldn't walk at all for months, and what mobility I had recovered was accompanied by constant pain.

So, there I was, lying in a bedroom that was never allowed to be "mine." It was full of Larry's stuff, including the constant smell of oils and chemicals he used to keep his gun collection clean and in working order. There they were, racked high on the walls: instruments of death and destruction.

I thought how easy it would be to just end all the pain.

Instantly, I was overwhelmed with shame at the thought. The very image of my children hearing a loud noise in the bedroom and rushing to see what it was, and discovering my body with blood and brains splattered everywhere, was enough to horrify me at the total selfishness and destruction to others involved in such an act. The little one was only four years old. I was instantly "in" her mind and emotions, realizing how such acts destroy others far more thoroughly than they ever destroy those who commit them.

No, that wasn't the answer. For my children, I would endure the pain and keep going no matter what.

The doctor had suggested that mild aquatic exercise would strengthen my heart without further stressing it. The only place to go for such therapy was a stressful thirty-minute drive away, and my legs swelled terribly after just ten or fifteen minutes of riding in the car.

The obvious solution was a swimming pool.

I began to think about how I might get one and even spent some time visualizing a pool and myself in a healthy condition splashing in the water. I realized that there was just simply no way that we could manage such a project. It was a hopeless fantasy in terms of our present situation. I would have to think of another way. Perhaps the beach or the public pool. But, just to make my point, I said out loud to the empty room: "God, a swimming pool would help!"

As I have already said, I am not a gambler. But Larry seemed to have a definite tendency in that direction, never forgetting to buy his weekly lottery tickets. Since I saw nothing wrong in spending a couple of dollars a week on such entertainment, I didn't object to his habit.

One night, my number-two daughter asked her father if she could pick the numbers as he was going out the door to buy his lottery tickets. He laughed and said, "Sure!"

She picked them, and we won. Fifteen grand. We had the pool.

Of course, having learned very conservative habits where spending money is concerned, I was not able to just order a fancy in-ground pool. An above-ground pool would serve my needs just as well, leaving plenty of money left over for a new computer, things for the children and the house, and a decent used truck for Larry.

The pool wasn't ready until August. I thought it was appropriate that the children and I could "baptize" the pool by floating on our rubber rafts and watching the Perseid meteor shower.

* * *

August 16, 1993: In the subtropics, it gets dark about nine o'clock in the evening, so it would not be until a couple of hours later that viewing conditions would be optimal. The children were excited to stay up late and watch a meteor shower in the pool. They had rushed out at about ten o'clock, while I stayed in and struggled to clean up the kitchen before going out to join them at eleven. Three of the five children were out there with me. My eldest daughter was on a date, and the baby was in bed.

The back of our house showing the side of the pool from which the UFOs were sighted.

I slid into pool for the very first time and was so happy and grateful to have it. I walked to the far side to lean my head against the ledge and float, looking in the direction the meteors were supposed to be found. The viewing conditions were favorable: no moon, clear sky with only a slight upper-level haze from the humidity, and the ambient light was minimal.

Suddenly, my twelve-year-old daughter cried out, "Look! Up there!"

This was no meteor. It was a 300-foot-wide black boomerang, emanating a faint reddish glow, moving so slow and low that I knew if I had been standing on the roof of my two-story house, I could have reached up and touched it. We had plenty of time to observe it and note the brushed-matte-black-metal appearance of its underside.

We watched as it moved ever so slowly overhead, utterly silent, seeming to float more than anything else. It continued south, seeming to skim the treetops.

We were looking at each other and all saying at once, "What was that?!" when my son shouted, "Another one!" and, sure enough, just to the west of the path of the first one, there was another. Every detail was identical: altitude, speed, reddish glow, and utter silence. I was, at this point, in sufficient possession of my senses to try to hear something. Dead silence. That struck me as odd, since there are normally all kinds of night sounds: crickets, night birds, frogs, and so forth. But there was no sound, no vibration, no hum. Nothing.

We stood there in amazement for a few frozen moments and then the kids began to shout for their dad to come out. He came to the door.

"What's all the excitement about?"

The kids were saying, all at once, "We saw a UFO!"

"That's nonsense," he said.

I will never be able to explain why I said this, but what came out of my mouth was: "Oh, it was just a flock of geese! I guess we are going to have bad weather because the geese are flying douth early this year!"

And I laughed as I shoved it under the rug.

He looked at me like I was an idiot. "Geese," he said sarcastically, "do not fly south in August. And anyway, we are south!"

Hearing a logical refutation had a strange effect on me: I became very upset and confused all out of proportion to the event. The only thing I could think of to do was to go inside and call Frank.

Frank was absolutely ecstatic, crowing with delight.

"Finally you'll believe me! You saw a real UFO!"

"Now look, Frank! Just because something is a UFO doesn't mean it's an *alien* UFO!"

Frank's enthusiasm was not to be dampened. He had an ace to play. He had just gotten home a short time before I called, and there was a message on his answering machine that he wanted me to hear. He rewound it and played it for me over the phone. Dane's son had called him to describe having seen the exact same thing an hour earlier. He had been out in his driveway at ten o'clock to see a few meteors. He'd been overflown by the big black boomerang, with his neighbor as a witness. If it was a secret government aircraft, why was it cruising our neighborhood so repetitiously, and why was it that he happened to know two of the very people to whom it had "shown" itself?

Well, that didn't seem like a great mystery to me. No doubt many people had seen it.

Nevertheless, logic was crumbling inside me no matter how I tried to reason. At this point, I became so upset that I had to go in my bedroom and sit and consider the matter. It was clear to me that if I could not find a rational explanation for this thing, there was only one thing to think: either they were real, or I had contracted the millennial disease and was losing my mind.

This was certainly not a stealth bomber. The newspaper article had described them pretty thoroughly when the previous flap had occurred. The writer had assumed that when people say they are seeing a boomerang-shaped object, they are really saying a *triangular* object. The description of the stealth bombers included a fuselage that the object we had seen simply did not have. It had been a boomerang shape. Not a triangle, not a diamond, a boomerang without any sort of "body." But how could I know this for sure? Maybe there were stealth bombers that were newer or different models?

Did anybody else see it besides Frank's friend and his neighbor and the kids and me? I wanted to get a consensus of descriptions. I wanted to know that I was not crazy. And I wanted an explanation. That meant, of course, that with the weight of evidence from others, I would be able to consult with authorities and confirm that it was, indeed, a secret government craft. Problem solved, case closed.

So, the next day, trying to act very casual in spite of my embarrassment at even asking such a question, I called a couple of the local television stations to inquire if there had been any reports of strange objects in the sky. One woman was very nasty and informed me that of course there had been strange objects in the sky; it was called a meteor shower! Well, I was not talking about lights flashing across the sky, and I certainly knew a meteor from a 300-foot-wide black boomerang, but damned if I was going to even utter those words! All I wanted to know was if there had been any reports of anything from all the meteor watchers that could not be explained.

The results were less than helpful. I was treated like a lunatic for even asking the question. That only served to heighten my dismay, but I wasn't ready to give up yet.

I received similar treatment from various other media sources I contacted in my effort to get some information. I was not comfortable enough to make a report of my own, so I was really trying to talk about the subject without even using the term "UFO." In retrospect, my reluctance to even say it is comical.

There didn't seem to be any information to be obtained until Frank called and told me that the weatherman on one of the television stations had mentioned that one of the community weather observers had reported several flocks of geese the previous night. Since I had tried to explain it to myself in these same terms, I thought that this might be a hit. But that was all I was going to get from the standard sources.

I was frustrated at being blown off and treated like an idiot. This frustration only added fuel to the fire burning in me, driving the need to discover what it was I had seen. As I considered my options, I remembered an organization that collected reports of such things: MUFON. Maybe they would know. Even if they were somewhat to the left of rational in their belief that some sightings of strange craft were "alien," they were said to be trying to sort the real ones from the false reports. Perhaps they could help me confirm that I had seen an aircraft that was known, or conjectured to be, part of a secret government project?

I looked in the back of one of Frank's books and found the phone number for the national headquarters of MUFON. The person who answered gave me the number for the local chapter. An answering machine picked up. The director was going to be on vacation for the next two weeks. I hesitated, but finally left my name and number and the fact that I wanted some information about a "possible UFO sighting." I was using "UFO" in the literal sense of the word: it was unidentified, and I was seeking identification in a rational sense, not a confirmation of alien visitations and more mumbo jumbo.

It was well into September before anyone from MUFON called me back, with an apology for taking so long. Since the monthly meeting was the next day, they said, perhaps I would come and give the report in person. Well, that was pushing me just a bit too far, too fast. I was not ready to hang out with geeks who believed in little green men and who probably wore plastic pocket protectors, coke-bottle glasses, and kept Mad magazine rolled up in their back pockets.

I mean, get real!

The day of the MUFON meeting, I was definitely not going to go. I was going to drop the whole subject. But, as the clock rolled around, the kids disappeared to various activities, the baby went off with Larry, and I was left at home alone. The need to know had not lessened one bit, and I tried to come up with any rational excuse not to go. Surprisingly, my usual state of exhaustion was at a minimum and, with no other apparent reason to hinder me, I thought that maybe, just maybe, I would go and check this MUFON bunch out. If it was creepy, or if I became too tired, I could always come right home. It was only a ten-minute drive away.

I was surprised. There were no geeks. Not a single pocket protector. And these folks were certainly too old for Mad magazine!

I entered quietly, took a seat at the back of the room and listened to a discussion in progress. I was amazed at how extremely intelligent and rational these folks were—more so than average, in my opinion, and certainly brighter than the run-of-the-mill New Age groupie. No one was ranting a spittle-flecked monologue about being visited by Venusians, taken aboard their craft, and transported to LooneyLand. Nobody was talking about aliens-as-God, here to "serve mankind." In fact, it was a rather technical discussion of possible propulsion systems of UFOs, based on observed behavior by creditable witnesses whose stories were cited, along with some impressive documentation and credentials.

At the break, I was asked to sign a guest sheet. The director recognized my name and asked me to talk about my sighting.

After the break I stood in front of the group and, with extreme embarrassment, began to tell my little story about the Black Boomerang. As I was getting warmed up, the door opened (this was a public meeting room in a local library), and a big, burly, bearded man came in. I stopped talking while he got seated and the director introduced him to me. I was surprised at his name, which is an unusual Welsh one that happened to be a family name. As I finished, all sorts of questions were asked. I made a drawing on a blackboard and that was that. I had said my piece and I sat down.

A discussion followed. The earliest sighting of the Black Boomerang-type object, as I had drawn it on the chalkboard, was in Albuquerque in 1951. They were also seen in Lubbock, Texas, and became famous as the Lubbock Lights. It was noted, as a point of interest, that these early sightings also occurred in the month of August, which I thought was peculiar. What was most interesting to me was the fact that the same design was seen over forty years previously. That sort of cancelled out my idea of a new design. No change in model in forty years? Those boys in black ops are really slipping—no imagination at all!

There were also extensive reports of these types of craft being sighted repeatedly in the Hudson Valley of New York in a famous series of events that included all kinds of anomalous phenomena among the hundreds of witnesses. A scientist had been involved in that situation, a Dr. Hynek. I had never heard the name before, but I was soon to hear it quite a lot. I would also come to respect his work and opinions.

Long after these events and discussions, I did more research on the "Black Boomerang" matter and discovered some very disturbing connections in an article in the book series "Mysteries of Mind, Space and Time," written by Hamish Howard and Toyne Newton, edited by Peter Brookesmith, UK:

"*Clapham Wood is a small densely-treed area nestling in the shelter of the South Downs in West Sussex, England. ... this is an area of mystery and intrigue and UFO sightings ... Stunted trees, a large crater where nothing grows, and mysterious little clearings containing ruins of old cottages [are found there.]*

"*Several hundred years ago, an aged resident of Clapham reported that she had seen a 'bright round shape like the full Moon' float down into the woods and disappear into the bushes. The woods were 'filled with fumes that stinketh of burning matter' and the people of the town were afraid to go there afterwards. Since that time, there have been many more UFO sightings in this small area.*

"*In October 1972, a telephone engineer saw a large saucer shaped object in the sky above the woods. It hovered for some time before making a* circle of the area, then veered off. At the same time, a couple were walking near the main road and thought they saw Jupiter or Venus low in the western sky—until it started to move very quickly due north, keeping in line with a ridge as it came toward them. Suddenly, when the object was over Clapham Wood, a beam of light descended vertically from it, and then rapidly withdrew, and the object shot away north-eastward at great speed.

"Paul Glover of the British Phenomenon Research Group was walking along the downs toward Clapham Wood one clear starlit night in the summer of 1967. At about 10 p.m., both men suddenly became aware of a huge black mass low in the sky blotting out the stars as it moved very quickly toward them. The object was boomerang shaped and made no sound. As it passed overhead the displacement of air was so great they ducked into the bushes for safety. They vehemently denied it could have been a cloud, for it retained its shape, was on a definite course, and there was no wind to drive it. Minutes later, they saw two bright objects high in the sky, which they watched for several minutes. One of the UFOs released a smaller object that traveled across to the second object, seemed to enter it, and then re-emerged and veered off, disappearing from sight. An hour later, on their return in the opposite direction of their walk, [apparently] two yellow lights descended in the region of the woods, followed just a few seconds later by two more, and then a final pair, making a total or three groups of two. Then at the point where they seemed to have dipped down into the woods, two white beams of light shot out horizontally—quite unimpeded by the contours of the downlands—followed by the next two beams and then the final two, all traveling very fast, before disappearing into the night sky. No craft of any kind could be seen behind the lights.

"During that same year, in the village of Rustington a few miles westwards along the coast, two schoolboys, Toyne Newton and John Arnold, who had never even heard of Clapham Wood, had a strange story spelled out to them **on a Ouija board**: that Clapham Wood was a base for spacecraft, and that one had landed recently to fetch supplies of sulphur and other chemicals.

"No one believed the boys, of course, but nearly 10 years later an investigation was carried out when soil samples were taken from the woods. From the report given in BBC-TV's Nationwide program at the time, it seems there was more than a grain of truth to the sulphur story. The investigation had been triggered by reports of dogs disappearing in the woods in 1975.

"According to a local paper, the 'Worthing Herald,' Wallace, a 3 yr. old chow belonging to Mr. and Mrs. Peter Love of Clapham, disappeared, as did a 2 yr. old collie belonging to Mr. John Cornford. Apparently the collie, although normally obedient, suddenly rushed off into a small copse between two trees in an area known locally as the Chestnuts, and was never seen again. The mystified owner searched thoroughly!

"Mrs. H.T. Wells, who lives at nearby Durrington, said that when her collie gets near the woods, it becomes 'desperate,' and a golden retriever belonging to Mr. E.F. Rawlins of Worthing ran into the woods one day and returned 'very distressed.' Shortly afterwards it became paralyzed and had to be destroyed.

"Another dog owner, who wished to remain anonymous, reported that when she took her dog to this area it ran around in circles, foaming at the mouth, with its eyes bulging as if in great pain."

The account goes on to say that a horseman (who also wished to remain anonymous, but his report was verified) tied his horse to a tree and stepped back a ways to have a pit stop. When he stepped back out of the bushes, he was amazed to find his horse missing. Although he searched the area extensively and made exhaustive enquiries, the horse was never found.

Several people have reported the feeling of being "pushed over by invisible forces" in this area and other have had spells of faintness.

"Two men walking through the wood reported that both were afflicted at the same moment: one doubling over in internal agony and the other clutching his head and screaming that his eardrums were 'being pulled out of his head.' They both staggered about 50 yards further and the effects ceased.

"The body of a missing man was found two weeks after he went missing, but in an extremely advanced state of decomposition. Forensic evidence showed that the rate of decomposition had been greatly accelerated due to 'unknown factors.'

"A skeptical investigator, Dave Stringer of the Southern Paranormal Investigation Group, visited the area with a Geiger counter in August [there is that month again] 1977. The woods were silent and the air still. Everything appeared normal, but, as he pushed through heavy undergrowth, he had to lift the machine above his head. When he did so, it began to register an alarming high level. Mr. Stringer stopped and looked back at the area he had just passed through. He saw a dark shape about 12 feet in height; while not being distinctive in outline, it was very definitely not smoke and he could only describe it as a 'black mass.' Seconds later a large white disk shot out from behind nearby trees at a 45 degree angle and disappeared into the sky. Simultaneously, the dark mass disappeared. Stinger retraced his steps [braver than I!] and found at the spot where the form had appeared, an imprint of a four toed footprint similar to one found at a place called Devils' Dyke near Brighton, where there was known to be a black magic 'coven.'

"Stringer made a quick sketch of the footprint. It was unknown to him at the time, that it matches a footprint reproduced in Collin de Plancy's 'Dictionaire infernal' published in 1863, and that this footprint is supposed to be that of the 'Demon Amduscias.'

"UFO sightings continued at Clapham into 1978 and 1979. The spate of strange reports at that time concluded with the disappearance of the Reverend Neil Snelling, vicar of Clapham church. One morning after shopping at Worthing, he decided to walk back to his Steyning home through Clapham Wood. He has not been heard of since and an exhaustive search of the area revealed nothing.

"Paul Glover and Dave Stringer and another man went to Clapham to see if they could spot any UFOs. There was no activity. They decided to go home and as they were walking out of the woods, all three of them simultaneously had a feeling of intense cold. They hurried on and the feeling ceased. They decided to go back and check it out again. They did this three times, and each time experienced the sensation of a sudden and unnatural drop in temperature. Glover pointed his camera at the area of the cold, even though nothing was apparently visible. When the film was developed, it showed an uncanny white mass in the unmistakable image of a goat's head." (Newton, et al.)

All in all, I was coming to an awareness that this phenomenon was not only strange; it was possibly dangerous. Just how strange and dangerous I would discover soon enough.

But, back to the account of the MUFON meeting. It seems that synchronicity was rapidly becoming my middle name.

The gentleman who had arrived late was, apparently, well known by the group as an expert on the theories of Zecharia Sitchin. I was intrigued by the historical connections to UFO sightings, though I discounted the precise interpretation put on the Sumerian writings by Dr. Sitchin.

At the end of the meeting, I asked this gentleman where he came from and told him that his name was also in my family. He turned out to be my second cousin once removed. The only reason I had never known of him or met him was, according to him, there had been a "religious" schism in the family. (Somebody who was Methodist converted to Baptist!)

Nevertheless, here I was, talking to a long lost cousin because I had seen a purported UFO.

We decided to have lunch. We exchanged phone numbers and he promised to call and visit and continue our discussion. It was completely strange to meet this man who had so strong a family resemblance to me, and who was wonderfully intelligent, articulate, informed. Let's call him Sam.

I told Sam about our channeling experiment and joked about the lotto number test that clearly wasn't working, though we had won a decent prize *without a prediction* from the board. This item seemed to interest Sam a great deal, and I ended up inviting him to join Frank and me for our next session.

* * *

Meanwhile, two most disturbing things were taking place.

My dog went into a decline that nothing I could do seemed to help. The vet was completely baffled, and everything we tried failed. In the end, he could only suggest a congenital heart defect leading to cardiac insufficiency. Within three months of the Black Boomerang, he died with his head in my lap on the kitchen floor. Dannyboy was a gorgeous tricolor collie, the most gentle and affectionate dog I have ever had, and he was only three years old. I was heartbroken. (Yes, it was quite startling when I discovered the article quoted above some years after this event and noted the effects on animals described therein. But, at this point in time, I was making absolutely no connection between the Black Boomerang and Dannyboy's death.)

At the same time, my own physical condition, instead of getting better, had gotten worse from that first night in the pool. I was constantly sick. I had terrible

Dannyboy with his favorite person: my youngest daughter.

rashes, hives, and welts. All the mucous membranes of my body kept swelling to the point that my throat and nose would almost shut completely. The undersides of my eyelids were so irritated they oozed yellowish, sticky fluids constantly. My ears itched deep inside which nearly drove me crazy.

These symptoms were always the precursor to a sort of attack. This began with severe nausea. I felt as though a fence post had been driven through my chest. My breathing was labored and painful. I broke out in a cold sweat. My doctor sent me to an allergist. This doctor was equally baffled, but finally suggested that I was suffering allergies that exacerbated my already compromised cardio-pulmonary system. It was decided that I must have reached a sort of critical mass of allergen exposure at some recent time. I had some relief from Benadryl, but that was not a long-term solution. My body simply did not seem to be able to handle the toxins anymore. The doctor wanted to run extensive allergy tests and begin a course of treatment designed to more or less desensitize me to whatever was affecting my system. But again, we could not afford such treatment.

The symptoms were worse at night, starting at about 11:00 p.m. I reasoned this must be the time of critical mass of the day's exposure to whatever allergen was active at the moment.

One night, around this time, Sandra had come by to visit. We were just chatting when my eyes started burning and I felt the slight tingling sensation in my lower lip that presaged the whole syndrome. I had told Sandra about the problem, trying to figure out what it might be I was allergic to, and I don't think she really understood how it worked. As she sat there watching, before her eyes, my lips slowly swelled until they were almost inside out; my eyes became slits, oozing fluid that I had to constantly wipe away with tissues.

Sandra was completely shocked. "We need to get you to an emergency room right now!"

I laughed it off, went to the kitchen to get some Benadryl, and told her that there wasn't much the doctors could do. They'd observed the swelling, the hives, and the inflammation of my eyes. The fence-post-in-the-chest just simply did not cooperate with being put under a microscope, and if they couldn't catch it in the middle of manifesting, they couldn't know what it was. Tests done when there were no symptoms told nothing.

I explained to Sandra that, on two occasions when the symptoms began to manifest, Larry had driven me to the hospital, and by the time we arrived, the heart symptoms had gone away entirely, leaving only the surface manifestations. This was puzzling in the extreme, and Larry took it as proof that there was absolutely nothing wrong with me except in my mind.

I, on the other hand, was thoroughly frightened at what was happening to me. Larry's attitude was not only hurtful; it left me feeling entirely alone and unable to talk about anything at all to him. If the person you are married to doesn't believe you, who will?

I was living on aspirin and Benadryl, but I was not getting relief. I reduced my schedule to a bare minimum. I would rest all day when Frank and I "sat for the contact," and often he and Sam would come to visit and talk while I was unable to sit upright at all. I was so weak sometimes that I could barely lift my head. But, I could think and talk, and these visits gave me something to look forward to.

One night with the two of them, discussing ancient cultures and the possibility of otherworldly interactions in those distant times, there seemed to be a flash of light that startled me. I had been resting my eyes under a cool compress. This flash of light came so fast that I couldn't be certain it was not some random neuron firing in my brain, lighting up my optic nerves. However, this was immediately followed by the strangest thing.

Suddenly Sam was speaking to Frank in a very hostile tone, saying, "If you light that cigarette, this discussion is over!"

What in the world is going on? I thought.

I jokingly told Frank that yes, we ought to open the door and turn on the central fan in the house to air things out since we both did smoke a lot and poor Sam was a non-smoker. I emphasized the "both" as a subtle reminder to Sam that it was my house and I was a smoker too. He knew it before he came through the door. I always tried to make guests who were non-smokers moderately comfortable, but just as I deferred to the wishes of non-smokers in their homes, so did I expect the same deference to me in my home.

The uncomfortable moment passed, but Sam soon left.

Frank asked me if I had experienced anything strange just before Sam's change in demeanor.

"Like what?" I asked cautiously.

"Like a flash of light," Frank replied.

We had no idea what it was.

The next day Sam called me on the phone and informed me that I had better watch out where Frank was concerned. It was Sam's considered opinion that Frank was manipulating me in some way, "playing you like a Stradivarius."

What a puzzling situation.

* * *

I continued to force myself to function by sheer will. I knew I would die, because the will that kept me going was gradually being eroded away by constant pain. I still needed assistance in and out of chairs, in and out of bed, in the bathroom, in and out of the tub, and so on. If I was in another room and couldn't do something on my own, I would call Larry to please come and help me. He would say, "In a minute," and those minutes became longer and longer. Sometimes, I would sit half an hour until he decided to come and give me assistance.

However, as long as I was sitting still and didn't try to move, the pain was tolerable. And my brain hadn't died, so I continued to read and study to divert my mind. I also kept a schedule of hypnosis sessions. Larry pointed to this as proof that I could do what I "liked to do," but I wasn't doing anything for him to attend to his physical needs. I was stung and deeply hurt. Without reading and my work, I would have felt completely useless. I would have had no life at all.

The pain in my left arm was so constant a condition that I actually had fantasies of a madman with an axe breaking into the house and chopping my arm off, thereby giving me some relief. Sandra suggested that I should go to a different doctor, even going so far as to walk me through the process of getting the state to pay for a rehabilitative procedure.

The new doctor decided that I didn't have angina after all, or if I did, it was not the primary cause of the pain I was suffering in my left arm. He did a series of neurological tests and determined that nerve signals just simply were not being transmitted in my arms in a normal way. I had nerve damage and needed carpal tunnel surgery. Naturally, he didn't really explain why the pain was in the upper arm and chest area, and only on the left side, but go figure. I was desperate for relief. If it could be done as day surgery, and I didn't have to check into the hospital for an overnight stay, and as long as the state was paying for it, I didn't see that I had any other real option. I could swallow my dislike of hospitals and do it.

I asked the doctor very seriously if I would be able to play the violin after this surgery.

He looked at me with a startled expression. "Of course!"

"That's marvelous!" I exclaimed with a straight face. "I never played one before!"

He didn't have a sense of humor.

When I woke up after surgery that was supposed to have been on my left wrist, both hands were bandaged up like huge boxing gloves with little vials taped to the outside, which were connected to rubber tubes that were still inserted into my wrists to drain any fluids. I was completely horrified. How was I going to do anything with *both* hands like that? And the pain was close to the worst I had ever experienced. It was worse than having a baby. This pain was in the same category as the headaches and ear infections. I was not prepared for that. And it didn't go away as the doctor said it would. The surgery also hadn't done anything to relieve the arm pain. So I was worse than before, almost completely helpless.

Larry was waiting when they released me from the recovery room to go home. I was still partially asleep, but I could feel every bump and bounce as we drove the fifteen miles home, like bombs exploding in my hands.

I didn't fully realize the complications I was going to face. Think about it a minute. I was as effectively without hands as if they had been amputated. How would I go to the bathroom? There were no fingers emerging from the bandages that I could even hook onto my panties. How was I going to get a drink of water? How could I open a door? How could I pick up the phone?

I thought I had just better go to bed. The doctor had given a prescription for pain pills, and Larry went off to get it filled. I stood there trying to figure out how I was going to move the pillows on the bed so I could pull the covers down and get in. Finally, I just laid down on top of everything and kicked my shoes off.

Larry brought the prescription back and announced that, since I was going to be sleeping, and since the kids were at my mother's, it was an ideal time for him to go fishing. I didn't have the strength to argue. I asked him to just help me get into a nightgown, pull the bedclothes down, put a glass of water with a straw by the bed, and leave the pills close at hand.

I got into bed and he started to walk out of the room. I stopped him and asked if he would please pull the covers up for me. This time, he didn't even try to mask his impatience. What was more, he deliberately jerked them sideways and chuckled that now I would not be able to fix the bed! (This was a reference to the fact that I have always been particular about sleeping in a bed that is "straight." If the covers slip sideways during the night, I will get up and straighten them. Yes, I know that's compulsive, but it was one of the few things in my life I could control. I felt that I had a right to sleep the way I liked.)

So, with that last dig, Larry went fishing.

I dozed off but soon woke up with the throbbing pain in my hands reaching a new level of agony. Where were those pain pills? Oh, there they were … on the night table … all secure in that nice childproof container which I could not open, and there was no one there to help me.

Well, we can draw the veil over that episode.

After it was all over and the tubes and stitches had been removed, I was worse than before the surgery. For a year I didn't have strength in my hands to turn a doorknob or take the lid off a jar or hold a potato to peel it. I couldn't lift a pot from the stove. I still can't hold a pen or pencil for longer than a minute or two without being gripped by an agonizing spasm that ends with my hand turning into a quivering, spastic claw right out of a horror movie. Forget playing the piano. (Never mind the violin!)

That was pretty depressing. What was worse, Larry took some sort of perverse pleasure in torturing me with the situation. I was constantly reminded that if I wanted anything done, I'd just have to figure out how to do it myself.

Okay, I would.

CHAPTER FORTY

ALIENS, DEMONS, AND VAMPIRES

In January of 1994, the Frank & Dane debacle (already described) unfolded and I understood why Frank had been so desperately interested in using the board to predict lottery numbers. After his father bailed him out of trouble, Frank was so humble and contrite, declaring he'd learned the most important lesson of his life, I was confident we'd made significant progress.

The forces of our lives clearly demonstrated the importance of our living as cleanly and honestly as possible. This event seemed proof that great strides had been made in that direction. There was simply no point in ever bringing it up again. Such a secret had been a very great barrier between us. Now that it was gone, we could proceed at a more intense level of psychic and mental purification. From my own point of view, criticizing Frank for any difficulties in his life would have been calling the kettle black. I just hadn't realized how serious the issues might be in Frank's case. And so we continued.

After we had thoroughly discussed his experiences, and his certainty that his own nature was a result of some sort of "attack" from psychic sources, Frank turned the focus on me and enumerated the string of strange, synchronistic, and miraculous events that had brought me to this moment. He cited point after point through my life history, right up to the past few years when the bizarreness had increased to the extent that I felt like I was living in a madhouse where normal reality no longer held sway. The formerly solid earth of my reference system slowly crumbled beneath my feet. With each point he made, I felt like another wave was washing over my foundation of sand. I seemed to be sinking into the mire of complete lunacy.

How can you deal with a life that has gone completely over the edge in terms of strangeness that you neither wish to experience, nor wish to perpetuate?

As Frank pointed out, even though I was most definitely a "non-believer," as soon as I had gained some knowledge about the alien phenomenon, I encountered my first "alien abductee" case. Didn't I think this was unusual? And wasn't it a fact that UFOs had accompanied that first abduction session I'd conducted? Didn't I think this was an unusual phenomenon? Not everyone who might be an abductee under hypnosis attracts a whole flap of UFOs.

The question was, of course: was it the abductee or the therapist in whom the denizens of UFO-land were interested?

I didn't like the way the conversation was going.

Frank then pointed out the obvious (to him) connection between my deteriorating physical state and my own UFO encounter. When I protested there may be no relation at all, he pointed out how my dog had suffered and died within a very short time after this exposure, and how my symptoms always seemed to peak at exactly the time of night the UFO had come along. What was my explanation for that little item?

I had none. I was distressed for him even to put it in words. As long as it was unspoken, I could continue to ignore it.

He kept pressing his points: what about the Face at the Window? What about the kidnapping when I was a child by an individual who had been connected to the Navy in some mysterious way? What about the light outside at boarding school? What about the incident when I awakened reversed in the bed? What about all the gynecological mishaps I had suffered? On and on he went, and as he ticked off each item, I felt more and more nauseated.

Frank's theory was that the whole UFO drama of recent times—a series of events spread across several counties, including dozens of witnesses, most of whom I didn't even know—was staged to get my attention, to wake me up. What was more, even our meeting was obviously a destined event if one factored in the name synchronicities, topped off by the Ypsilanti wrong number.

I did not like what Frank was saying. Like the incidents of the wet nightgown and the strange lights, I was really struggling to ignore the anomalies in my life. I did not like the connotation Frank was putting on my experiences. In the first place, I had studied too much, seen too much, and worked with too many troubled people to overlook the myriad ways the mind can deceive itself, not to mention the dangers of ego leading one in those directions. When anyone starts to think they are "special," that God is "talking" to them, it's a sure sign of descent into delusion and magical thinking.

Nevertheless, I had read many cases by that time of strange events similar to my own that were attributed to aliens, and that was the problem. Who or what were they? Were they literally visitors from deep space? Or were they the perceptions of victims of some vast government mind-control experiment? Most terrifying of all: were they demons?

Why would anyone or anything go to so much trouble to set up so many bizarre things to get my attention if I wasn't supposed to do something about it? And if I was supposed to do something, they had certainly picked the wrong person, because it was becoming pretty clear that I was probably not going to live a lot longer.

Considering this UFO business had another effect on me: I was grieving. I mourned the years I'd spent studying and digging for answers, only to have it all trashed in one night by a stupid black boomerang.

"Why me?"

"That's what you need to figure out," Frank said.

I detected the signature of an intelligence working in my life and my experiences, and it was difficult to tell if it was to awaken me, or an effort to either destroy or divert me from something. If they were evil beings and had the power to interfere in my life with malicious intent, even when I was deeply involved in a life that included regular prayer and meditation—which one would suppose should act as a defense—what protection did anyone have? Were we, the human race, defenseless against these creatures?

The words of Gurdjieff came back to haunt me. Were the belief systems of metaphysics and religion useless drivel promulgated by an evil magician to convince people they were lions, men, eagles, or magicians instead of sleeping sheep?

What kind of madhouse had I opened my eyes to see? Was the fact that I had seen it the very source of its existence? Was I, by noticing evil, more vulnerable to attack? Surely not: the evidence of the presence of evil threaded its way through the lives of others who denied all the clues. I saw clearly the mechanical or accidental nature of the universe that Gurdjieff talked about. But now I realized that our own programmed refusal to see reality, our ignorance, was the chief door in our lives through which evil and suffering entered.

Was it possible, as Gurdjieff suggested, to become free of this? To awaken? To see the projector behind the slide show of our lives? And, more important, to see who was running the projector and why?

I struggled with my thoughts and emotions for days. I was truly passing through the valley of the shadow of death. I had thoroughly convinced myself that UFOs and aliens could not possibly exist. In fact, even after the flap surrounding the hypnosis session with Pam, I had contemptuously declared that the millennial disease was spreading. Upon seeing the thing itself with my own eyes, I had pronounced it to be a flock of geese, in the same way I had rationalized the wet nightgown and grass seeds on the night I woke up reversed in my bed.

All those times, and the night I saw the strange light in the snow at boarding school, the events had been followed by protracted illnesses. If there were other incidents preceding any of my other physical disturbances, I certainly didn't remember them. But by now, from studying the literature, I was aware that many people might remember nothing at all.

To consider the idea of malevolent beings in control of our world that could prey on us at will, behind our ordinary reality, was utterly soul shattering.

I began to see the possibility of an interpenetrating reality of more or less physical solidity that interacted with humans as we may interact with wildlife in a forest: the hunters and the hunted. What was clear to me was the paranormal nature of the UFO phenomenon.

Down through the ages people have been visited by all sorts of strange beings. Some of these creatures have been utterly fantastic in description as well as activity. By far the most common type, however, have been humanoid—having some semblance to the human physical configuration—although their powers have been distinctly superhuman.

I had read stories going back hundreds of years that told of these humanoid beings.

A creature with strange, glowing or compelling eyes comes in the night and somehow drains the energy, blood, or life force from a victim unable to call out for help and paralyzed in body and mind. Their presence often is heralded by unusual lights or freezing temperatures. The strange beings have powers that include the ability to disappear, to fly, to control weather, to direct the behavior of animals, to change into the form of animals, to pass through solid objects. The beings can produce hybrid offspring by having sex with their victims.

This belief in supernatural beings is to be found in every society around the world, a common theme in all religions as well as folklore. The reports are as frequent in our own day as they have ever been. And the numbers and types of visitors are legion. I realized that this historical assessment was quite consistent with the UFO and alien abduction situation.

Katharine Briggs's *Encyclopedia of Faeries* (1976) gives many examples of fairy abductions. They show a startling similarity between fairy abductions and UFO abductions. People who reported interactions with fairies generally had marks on their bodies consistent with marks that were claimed to be physical proof of alien abductions. Fairy abductions and UFO abductions also exhibit striking similarities to the activities of incubi and succubi. Almost always a thick drink is given to the abductee, who is then paralyzed and levitated away. The fairies traveled in circular globes of light also commonly reported in UFO abductions.

In the end, many so-called fairies and aliens look and act a lot like historic descriptions of demons.

I was seeing, finally, a tradition of otherworldly beings abducting humans and their children stretching back probably thousands of years.

Along with most rationalists, I had always considered these stories to be psychodramas, or "artifacts of consciousness." The study of anomalous experiences, the paranormal, and related psycho-spiritual fields has occupied many of the brightest minds of our race for millennia. Endless theories and their variations have been proposed to explain them and, for the most part, such ideas are even behind most of the world's religions. Jacques Vallee's control-system hypothesis is interesting in this regard. In *Dimensions* (1988), he writes:

"I believe there is a system around us that transcends time as it transcends space. The system may well be able to locate itself in outer space, but its manifestations are not spacecraft in the ordinary 'nuts and bolts' sense. The UFOs are physical manifestations that cannot be understood apart from their psychic and symbolic reality. What we see in effect here is not an alien invasion. It is a control system which acts on humans and uses humans."

The very idea that this might be a reality that dominated or controlled our own was staggering. What made the problem so terrifying was the fact that my studies and experiences in spirit attachment and demonic possession were reflected in the so-called UFO and alien phenomena. They had the same taste, the same dynamic.

The fact that modern alien abductions mirror demonic infestation and vampirism is part of a historical pattern. This, according to Vallee, implies a pattern maker. But who or what that pattern maker is, or for what purpose it is operating the control system, Vallee will not or cannot say.

There are certainly striking parallels. The first thing I noticed in deeply studying this phenomenon was that some encounters with entities seem accidental, but others clearly are directed at a specific person. This led me to wonder whether the seemingly accidental encounters were as accidental as they appeared to be. In such a case, I had to ask again: did the manifestation occur in response to some hidden need, a psychological state that calls for outside intervention of some kind?

French ufologist Jean-Francois Boeded, in his book *Fantastiques recontres au bout du monde* (1982), suggests that UFO sightings start long before the actual experience. He noted many cases in which the witnesses had premonitions that something was about to happen, or for some reason they went home by a different route or took an unaccustomed walk. Somehow, it seems, the witnesses were being prepared for the experience they were about to undergo. In many cases, the abductee claims there is a sensation of a presence before an actual encounter takes place.

I can't say that any such premonition occurred in my experience, but that may simply be due to a lack of sensitivity or awareness to certain subtle clues. Perhaps my rational approach acted as a barrier?

However, Boedad has a point. Many so-called attached entities I conversed with during spirit-release hypnosis claimed that their host was chosen "before he was born." In most cases, a line of contact and the gradually building assault can be traced back to childhood. It can be said, in general, that the process of possession has already begun before the target or those around him are aware of the signs.

Again, this flew in the face of many religious and philosophical teachings.

In any case of psychic vampirism or actual possession, there is usually an actual entry point, the point at which the spirit enters into a relationship with the individual. A decision is made by the victim to allow that contact. This often occurs simply because the victim is not aware of the significance of the event. It seems to be a minor event and may come as the result of tiredness, mental excitation, frustration, or pain. These beings, whether demons, vampires, or aliens, have the ability to control our thoughts to a certain extent, our physical bodies, the weather, and events in our lives, to the point that we can be worn down under such attack and give in to control by another. In the case of alien abductions, repeated incidents may be a process of wearing down the victim as much as an energy-stealing interaction.

The famed Betty and Barney Hill case describes a simulated medical test in which a long needle is inserted into the navel. A fifteenth-century French calendar, the *Kalendrier des bergiers*, illustrates the tortures inflicted by demons on the people they have taken. The demons are depicted piercing their victims' abdomens with long needles.

Jacques Vallee supposes that literally millions of similar incidents may occur, many unreported for fear of ridicule, others forgotten under the pressure of mind-control techniques. Vallee doubts that a civilization with space- and time-travel capabilities would come in such numbers to do stupid things like abduct people and perform primitive experiments or examinations on them.

Many people report that their abductors were benevolent beings. These stories seem designed to perpetuate a dangerous and cunning lie. In my examination of the standard religions as well as the many and varied New Age teachings, I saw these systems being used as the very means of propagating such a lie. I could see individuals with no extensive knowledge of historical metaphysics being fooled by a belief in the "benefits" of alien abduction. We repeatedly see terms describing "light" or related phenomena. This tends to make the percipients regard the experience as good. Gurdjieff was right: mankind is asleep. One of the conditions of this sleep is the absence of an active "BS meter."

Are people asleep because they choose to be, or are they asleep because they are so cleverly deceived by "false light" which induces acquiescence and resultant hypnosis?

Many people reporting abductions, when the surface or screen memories have been probed in a competent way, reveal memories of events so chilling in their implications that the first interpretation must be looked at carefully. The fear evoked in these experiences is tangible. Yet, these other beings somehow convince that all they do is for "the good of the planet" or "the enhancement of our race" or because "you agreed."

Even the esteemed John E. Mack, M.D., professor of psychiatry at Harvard, seemed to have been taken in by such a view. He writes in *Abduction* (1994):

"*The idea that men, women, and children can be taken against their wills from their homes, cars, and schoolyards by strange humanoid beings, lifted onto spacecraft, and subjected to intrusive and threatening procedures is so terrifying, and yet so shattering to our notions of what is possible in our universe, that the actuality of the phenomenon has been largely rejected out of hand or bizarrely distorted in most media accounts.*

"*... My own work with abductees has impressed me with the powerful dimension of personal growth that accompanies the traumatic experiences ... especially when these people receive appropriate help in exploring their abductions histories.*

"*... Let us suppose that [cosmic intelligence] ... is not indifferent to the fate of the Earth, regarding its life forms and transcendent beauty as one of its better or more advanced creations. And let us imagine that the imbalance created by the over growth of certain human faculties ... were diagnosed ... as the basic problem. What could be done as a corrective? The two natural approaches of which we can conceive would be the genetic and the environmental. Is it possible that through a vast hybridization program affecting countless numbers of people, and a simultaneous invasion of our consciousness with transforming images of our self-destruction, an effort is being made to place the planet under a kind of receivership?*"

This view is rooted in emotional beliefs that cling desperately to any straw offered that those more powerful than we are "good."

As I waded through the literature, I came across many controversial accounts said to originate from military intelligence officers, physicists hired to work on secret projects, and others claiming inside knowledge of a vast government cover-up. Some matched the reports of increasing numbers of people who have recalled, consciously or under hypnosis, scenes of unparalleled horror and abuse at the hands of some of the so-called alien visitors.

Why would such participants be motivated to come forward? Are they part of a vast mind-control experiment designed like a monstrous crazy-making drama, where the government secretly promotes a belief in aliens while publicly denying it? As they've penetrated deeper into the veil of secrecy, have they become horrified witnesses whose consciences prompted them to talk? Perhaps those in power began keeping their arrangements secret, only to discover they had a tiger by the tail and couldn't let go. Maybe they began sending agents out to "reveal" fragments of the truth, while the possibility of forced exposure looms ever closer?

The book *Clear Intent* (1984) by Lawrence Fawcett and Barry J. Greenwood provides evidence based on the government's own documents that the highest-ranking public officials and the elite of the U.S. security and intelligence organizations deliberately and persistently lied about aliens and UFOs for the last fifty years.

I began to think: *The Alien presence on our planet is real. Those who choose to close their eyes to this reality do so at their own peril.* And I was terrified.

If there is a psycho-spiritual or even literally physical invasion taking place before our very eyes, under our very noses, represented in the symbolic system of our lives and experiences, interacting with this control system at some deep level, what kind of protection do we have?

Well, in thinking about it deeply, it does appear that these beings—whatever they turn out to be—can plunder our world, our lives, and our very minds at will. But I also have observed that they seem to be going to an awful lot of trouble to conceal their activities and to confuse observers with hundreds of crazy stories of different races and groups of semi-mythological good guys and bad guys.

Many people who think they are psychic, have prophetic dreams or visions, channel "space brothers," people who are contacted by beings who are here to "help" us or to "save" us if only we will let them, or who have other psychic experiences are, in fact, being regularly visited by aliens who literally program these ideas into their minds. These stories are spread around, increasing the level of confusion. But the greatest deception of all is the idea that negative higher forces do not exist, and that even if negative forces did exist, there's no need to worry. If we just think nice thoughts, meditate regularly, and repeat our affirmations, nothing icky will ever enter our reality.

We are not dealing with materialistic, earth-based technology here. For God's sake, these guys seem to be able to walk through walls, float people out of their bodies, and control minds—the abilities we have historically attributed to angels or demons or vampires.

In the past, we dealt with ghosts and gods and demons. We are dealing with the same entities now, only we are calling them aliens. They probably always were aliens!. And maybe they want to be gods again.

One thing I knew for sure from doing the spirit-release work: evil insinuates itself into our lives in the guise of goodness and truth. This problem is made even worse by the acceptance of the New Age teaching that evil simply does not exist unless an individual creates it in their reality. Evil follows the line of erosion of our spirituality through the erosion of knowledge. What better way to protect evil activities than to deny that they exist?

The New Age types say that putting one's attention on these ideas gives them energy. This is true only if one focuses in this way with the intention of participation. However, a comprehensive understanding of these forces is absolutely necessary in order to know how to give them less energy. Intent is everything.

It was a stunning and grotesque prospect for me to consider that humanity, as a whole, has been used and cunningly deceived for millennia. I realized that the UFO and alien business was truly nothing new. We have historical records of these phenomena stretching back thousands of years. But that raises an interesting question: If these beings could get what they want simply by moving in and taking it, would they spend so much time creating terror and confusion? Alternatively, perhaps the terror and confusion is exactly what they want to generate because they feed on it? But that makes me also wonder why they are going to so much trouble to persuade us to accept their total control if they could take it at will? These guys would not be spending so much time wearing us down and terrorizing us and trying to sneak in the back door if it were possible for them to walk in directly. There is something we have that they want. There is some power we have that they don't want us to discover.

The act of facing the pattern of activity behind the events of my own life that bespoke such a hidden reality was absolutely soul searing and mind-numbing. It acted as a conflict between my internal integrity, intellectual acuity, and all my emotional beliefs in a kind and loving God—Him for whom I had been seeking all my life. I was reminded of what I had been told: "I cannot act until you remove the evil from between us." And when I asked "what evil?" the answer was "LEARN!"

Well, I was most definitely learning. But I didn't like what I was learning. You could even say that, of all people who never wanted to know anything at all about UFOs and aliens, I deserve a place at the head of the line. Yet, there it was.

Standing back from my life in overview, there were the hints of some sort of pattern maker, and it wasn't God in any sense that I had ever conceived of Him. Yes, I could see both positive actions and negative actions—a dynamic interplay of forces that related in some direct way to my own thinking, seeking, and growth—but exactly what it was, and precisely how it operated, I couldn't tell yet. It was like a shadow show where the shadows are produced by certain angles of light behind objects that, when finally revealed, may bear no resemblance whatsoever to the form of the shadow. A balled-up fist could as easily be interpreted as a bird or a dog, or—when expanded to its full shape—a hand. Just what was I seeing? What's more, why did it seem that I was being challenged to see it? Why me?

I struggled until I was exhausted in my soul.

I remember clearly sitting on my bed one night at the end of this struggle, thinking about these strange "hints" that there was something deeper to our reality than I might have supposed in my years of research and work—something really, really big, that I had simply chosen to overlook and ignore. The only problem was, as I pointed out wearily to God, I was too sick to do anything. "You blew it, Buckwheat!" I told him. "If there was ever anything you wanted me to do, you let me suffer too much for too long."

There I was, as non-functioning as a human being can be and still appear to be functional. But an overwhelming sensation of purposefulness swept over me. If all these things were orchestrated to get my attention, it had surely worked. But I was too far gone to pick up the ball and run with it. "If I am supposed to DO anything, you gotta fix me up here," I said. "As I am, I can do nothing."

Within two weeks I found Reiki. Or Reiki found me.

CHAPTER FORTY-ONE

AUNT CLARA

The *very day after* my little "talk with God," a letter arrived in my mother's mail, and she called excitedly to tell me. A local organization for retired people offered a course in home health nursing. To my mother, it sounded too good to be true. All supplies, uniforms, and transportation were provided without cost.

About a week into this course, Mother told me a lady in her class had invited her to an open house on the following Wednesday. She needed me to drive her to this evening affair. Well, after my surgery, my hands didn't work very well, but I told her I could manage. Driving was painful, but after all, doing for others was what I was trained to do. I was happy to see my mother "get a life." I planned to make every effort to rest so I could accompany her to this social event.

When we arrived, about fifteen people stood with their hands resting on patients lying on three massage tables. There was incense burning and New Age music playing in the background. Some folks were standing with their eyes closed in meditative tranquility. I wasn't sure if I had stepped into a new version of the fundamentalist "laying on of hands" deal or what.

I usually try to find a balance between good manners and my curiosity, which sometimes makes for funny situations, I can tell you! So I settled in a chair after the introductions and asked, "What exactly, are ya'll doing here? What is the idea behind it? What precise procedures are you following?" No reason to beat around the bush! I expected something like "we are praying" or "we are meditating on wellness" or something like that.

But instead, the answer was "we are channeling Reiki."

Okay ... sure you are!
"What is Reiki?"

The story of a certain Dr. Usui was recounted to me by various participants as they stood with their hands on the patients. Every move and placement of the hands was explained. As it went on, I became more and more skeptical. I mean, of all the healing methods I had heard or read about or tried, this was truly the most nebulous and least likely. It seemed patently ridiculous that someone could initiate or attune another person to increase their ability to channel energy. I expected them to say next that Reiki could help you walk on water!

I was urged to give it a try, but managed to decline gracefully. I would have felt perfectly silly on that table with five people laying their hands on me for forty-five minutes or so. Wasn't gonna happen!

But I was working at being polite and gentle in my skepticism. Soon the conversation turned to astrology—safe ground for me—and I mentioned in passing that I had a computer program that did pretty good charts. The woman holding the Reiki open house offered me a trade: three Reiki treatments in exchange for an astrological chart.

I started to wonder how bright this gal could be. She was offering me several hours of her time and effort in exchange for a few minutes of data entry and printing. Didn't seem too fair to me. I figured if she was silly enough to be convinced that she could channel healing energy to me through her hands, and was willing to go to that length to do it, I was game for the test. I also had the thought that maybe it was her way of getting a chart done that she otherwise could not afford. So, I agreed. An appointment was made for the following day, and sure enough, she showed up.

So, there I was, in such lousy condition that I actually had to be assisted to lie down on the massage table that was set up in my living room. And more embarrassing, I fell asleep during the treatment. When she had put her hands on me all I could really feel (and I was paying close attention with a *lot* of skepticism) was warmth little more than the normal heat that's evident when one person puts their hands on another.

But the real surprise was to come when I got *off* the massage table at the end of the treatment. I could barely stand! I was so dizzy it was quite literally like being drunk. When I tried to walk I had to hold on to the furniture and walls to keep from falling down.

I collapsed in bed and closed my eyes, but that didn't help. I had the exact same sick, spinning sensation that comes with having had a bit too much to drink. When I opened my eyes and tried to focus on the ceiling and walls, they spun dizzyingly as though I had been a child spinning in circles who falls to the ground to watch the sky and clouds keep moving.

I was really concerned that something was going completely berserk with my system, and I hoped it would pass. I was nauseated and felt a creeping tingling, just like being drunk. I just tried to breathe deeply and stop the spinning into the void in my head and soon fell asleep.

That night I slept better than I had in the past ten years or longer. But it wasn't until well into the next day, as I was unloading the clothes dryer, when I suddenly realized that my back didn't hurt. Not only that, but I realized I had already done a lot more of my housework than I had been capable of doing in a very long time. Without even thinking about it, I had just started tackling one chore after another, moving from one to the next, without noticing anything unusual. It wasn't until I'd been working for several hours that I came to the startling realization that something was very different.

There was something missing here: the long-familiar debilitating pain.

For years I had learned to function with pain, developing ways to maneuver through life accommodating its constant assault. I actually sat down and began to mentally go over my body to discover if I didn't feel some little familiar twinge here or there.

There was *no pain*.

I was sure that, at any moment, I was going to get slammed with it again. I got up very carefully and continued with my work, constantly monitoring myself for the return of the pain. Actually, I think I even wanted the pain to return because otherwise, I would have to think that Reiki had worked. And we certainly could not be believing that sort of nonsense. What a dilemma!

Now, the clear thing here is this: I did not expect the Reiki to work. Further, I expected the pain to return. But something objective was going on that I didn't understand. I was still thinking in the programmed way that expectations led to your experiences and that faith was an integral part of healing. I was still working on digging up whatever might be buried in my own subconscious that was responsible for my suffering. That prevented me from having the faith to effect a healing. And on and on in a circle.

But here I was again, experiencing a positive result without exerting faith of any kind. My skepticism about Reiki was rather deep rooted. Reiki had worked anyway. Or so we might think. What other explanation could there be?

What about UFOs? That was something that I not only didn't believe in, but about which I was absolutely contemptuous and dismissive. What about the complete collapse of the "faith trip" I had already experienced? These thoughts flashed quickly through my mind, but it was way too much to think about at that moment when I was suddenly, after years of suffering, free of pain.

I actually began to cry with gratitude. Only those who have suffered long and constant physical agony can understand how I felt to not be in pain.

But, I was still on guard. Even though I had momentary relief, I expected the pain to return.

I had to go pick my daughter up. While we were driving home I told her about the pain being gone and that I thought the Reiki had done it. She laughed at me and said it only worked because I believed it would work. I pointed out to her that my belief had been exactly the opposite, and since that was the case, I was wondering now exactly what this Reiki business was.

After two more treatments and the passing of a week, I was convinced that whatever was happening was working. I went to the open houses regularly after this. Not only was I healed of the back pain, the angina attacks lessened almost to nonexistence, the swelling of the eyes and throat stopped entirely, my energy level increased. I was able to see more clients and be more active. This suited me fine!

Still, I was thinking that it wasn't the Reiki itself, but merely a transference of energy that anyone could accomplish if they just stood around for forty minutes with their hands on another person. So, even though I was receiving benefits, I had my own theory. Surely it was an absurdity to think that someone could "confer" this almost magical ability on another in some way. And, to make this point, I was anxious for the Reiki master who had initiated my new Reiki friends to come to town for a scheduled class.

That seemed to be the point of the open house: to attract new students.

I was going to bring all my powers of observation and skepticism to this new investigation. If there was anything to this Reiki business, I was going to find out. I had no intention of believing it unless there was more or less objective proof.

When the day arrived for the first initiation, I was loaded for bear, actively looking for some sort of hocus pocus or mumbo jumbo that would reveal the truth. I figured that people were being charged large sums of money to be made to think they could channel Reiki, when the real effect was merely a natural energy flow that was available to all who had the patience to stand around with their hands on another person. The only thing I felt during the attunement process was a generalized "rush" of heat from my abdomen up through my head and a little "popping" sound in my head. But it was so nebulous that I considered it to be discountable as a subjective observation.

But, what happened later that night was surprising. We were told that, after the attunements, the body would experience some symptoms of adjustment such as excessive thirst and urination or even diarrhea. But I didn't expect this: when I put my hands near any of my children I felt a clear and distinct rush of heat against my palms exactly like the sensation of a blow dryer. This rush would be felt before the hand was close enough to be able to detect the normal heat exchange between bodies. This occurred at about six inches away. There was a distinct "magnetic" feeling to this heat, similar to the pulling you feel when you hold two magnets close enough together to act on one another.

The first time it happened, I jerked my hand back as if I'd been burned. And then I began to experiment with moving my hand closer until I could distinctly identify the point at which the sensation occurred, the attraction was felt. I moved my hand closer by very small degrees to feel the effect at every stage of nearness. It was definitely there. No question about it. And the kids could feel it also.

Later that evening I was sitting on the sofa and my son came to sit on the floor in front of me and leaned back against my legs. As soon as he did, I could feel the heat begin to pass from my legs to his body exactly like the blow-dryer effect. Apparently this was not just restricted to the hands: it was a whole-body thing going on here! Both of us soon became so hot from this minimal contact, in an air-conditioned room, that he complained, "Mom! It's hot in here!" and moved away. By this time, we were both dripping with perspiration.

It proved to be several months before this effect dissipated where the children were concerned. It continues to this day when I touch anyone who has an energy deficit. But I suspect that, after a time, the children became energized, and so no longer pulled energy as strongly. Of course, if one of them is ill, there is a drawing of energy, but nothing like the time of the Reiki initiation. (Some time later when I took the Master-level attunements, my palms actually blistered and peeled for several weeks.)

There seem to be objective realities in which no belief is necessary or required. This was a stunning realization.

* * *

This Reiki group was a pretty funny collection of people. They all attended the local metaphysical/spiritualist church, and had brought the Reiki Master in as one of many program presentations.

Apparently, they also arranged seminars of other teachings, including Hawaiian Huna, psychic surgery, Kabballah, Tarot, meditation, channeling, Native American shamanism, sweat lodges, in a veritable supermarket of New Age goodies!

I had never been much of a joiner or a "group" person. But the Reiki crowd that met every Wednesday night was so wonderful and fun, and had such a profound healing effect on me, I knew that it was time to get over this little "loner glitch" in my personality. After all, I had found "my group," or so it seemed.

I shared a little bit about my spirit-release work with the group. They nodded sagely that they knew all about such problems. Their minister down at the metaphysical church had told them they had only to surround themselves with love and light and they were okay. I pointed out that some serious clinical research did not support this idea, but they assured me it was true. People only had attachments if they were not sufficiently adept at surrounding oneself with love and light.

The only way to do that was, of course, to learn the proper techniques from the Great Reverend Rita down at the church. Reverend Rita also seemed to be an expert on about everything else, so I was pretty interested in meeting such a paragon. Not only that, but the Reiki attunements were supposed to "set the direction of energy flow" so that no negative energy could enter a person's "auric field." So, I no longer had to worry about attachments and so forth. I had become a veritable "light being" and any problems in my deep psyche or any idea of darkness in the outer world could not survive in such light. Wow! What a deal! I even had the idea that all future clients who came to me for spirit release should have the Reiki attunements to keep them protected from that point on. Heck,

I wanted to give the whole planet Reiki. Having such a healing sure does get a person all fired up!

I was invited to the church. Reverend Rita, the "Maven of Mystery," was introduced to me by one of the Reiki group. I was a bit surprised at the adoring devotee manner that all of the Reiki people took on once they had entered the environs of the church. And, I didn't quite know what to make of Reverend Rita sitting there *in her wheelchair*. But I felt a frisson of something cold when I looked in her eyes, and it almost seemed there was something else in there for a moment looking back at me before it quickly retreated. Again, I doubted my perception. Surely the teacher of all these wonderful, loving people with whom I was now associated could not be less than holy. After all, hadn't she been the shepherd of the church group that made it possible for me to learn about Reiki?

Just as in an ordinary church, the service included singing hymns. Well, that's fine! I'm a hymn singer from way back—always my favorite part of going to church. The problem here: the selection was a song no one had ever heard before. Not only that, it was evident that the organist who selected it had never heard it either. To make the matter worse, the organist had only the most rudimentary skills with the instrument and took so long to place her fingers on the keys in response to reading the notes that the tempo was something akin to a funeral procession mired in quicksand.

The congregation—mostly women—was waiting for each note to sound in order to be able to follow. The note would come, obscured in a bass chord that was a lot like the bellowing of a rutting elephant, and the voices all trembled into action trying to match the identified pitch … only to have the organist suddenly decide she had hit the wrong key, fumble to the right one, and then all the congregation would jerk their voices in mid-warble to the amended note. *At least nobody was gonna be hypnotized by **this**! I thought.*

Fortunately, my sense of humor did not desert me, even though my aesthetic sensibilities were being savaged to the point that it was actually painful. Since I could not only read music, but also sing fairly decently, I decided to help the situation out a bit by singing the correct notes, at the correct tempo, just loud enough so that the people around me could catch on and follow. I was hoping that this would help both the organist and the congregation to make it through this performance, bringing it to an earlier conclusion than the next ice age.

That part worked well enough, and soon everyone was getting it and singing along. The organist still lagged behind, though, and the singers were leaving her in the dust. The song was finished with grace and aplomb while the organist kept plodding along to her ill-timed and tardy finish.

The congregation struggled to suppress giggles. The final chord was tortured out of the poor instrument (the rutting elephant "scored"), and everyone sat down in relief, in the perfect mood to get "in the spirit." I sat down and glanced around to find Reverend Rita glaring at me with all the friendliness of a coiled rattlesnake. So much for humor!

The sermon was being delivered by a woman we will call "Hillary," who channeled somebody or other who was supposed to be something like an Ascended Master or a dead dude (I have forgotten which). Hillary was a very sweet elderly lady with blue hair and wearing a print silk dress, looking for all the world like anyone's grandma. She just radiated grandmotherly comfort as she talked. She started off in a silvery, tremulous voice talking about love and opening the heart center and so on. There were overtones of Helena Blavatsky and Alice Bailey in her descriptions of planes and bodies of the individual soul. As she got warmed up, her eyes began to glow with subtle power. Her voice became stronger and more urgent and the message turned to saving the world with this love that was supposed to manifest when one's heart center was opened and connected via these planes and bodies, which were to be activated through certain activities that were not clearly defined as yet. As she talked, she began to walk back and forth in an animated way. Every part of her was being involved in the action—the words—the message. She was talking with her whole body.

Now the strange thing happened ... as she was walking across the little dais in this animated delivery of love and light, she suddenly stopped, frozen for a moment, and sort of trembled slightly and then snapped to attention. Actually, her head snapped up so fast and hard that it made me think she was not as fragile as she appeared. She looked around the room at all the breathless, expectant faces—a cool-eyed assessment in the midst of the feverish anticipation of the audience. Her head suddenly rolled back and her "control" was in *full* control. Hoo boy! Time to rock and roll!

I don't know who this guy she was channeling was, but I can say that he was really good. He must have been a Pentecostal preacher in his last life. It was like being at an old-time Southern Revival at its best. Hooting and hollering and drama. Strutting and stomping and pounding on the podium. The only thing was ... the message had changed ever so subtly. Most of the people in the room were hypnotized at this point by the drama they had been drawn into and didn't realize what was going on, but I was remembering the church Larry and I had attended, where I had been exposed to so many preachers of this type. Having been inoculated against this sort of thing, I knew it was just showmanship and the old "wolf in sheep's clothing" syndrome. I could see that here we were dealing with the same hypnotic factors at work in most fundie Christian churches.

The message had gone from love and light and opening the heart, to guilt and chastisement for not being successful in giving enough love and light or opening the heart sufficiently, and this was to be rectified, of course, by more attendance of classes and meditation sessions, more giving of time, resources, and most especially money. Attend church, give money, take classes, get salvation. Simple formula. Nothing terribly unusual. Same song, different verse.

After the sermon was over, a couple of the people who were in Reverend Rita's channeling classes were going to demonstrate their powers. One of these was Trudy. I was watching with great interest to see how effective these classes might be.

Trudy put her hand to her head à la Karnak the Magnificent and tried to "tune in."

"There is someone here who has just received unhappy news ..." she began. And, of course, in any group that is a pretty good guess; so the person who had just received an "unhappy" phone call raised her hand excitedly and said, "Yes, yes! Me! Me!" So, Trudy "tuned in" to her further and made a series of pronouncements that either evinced a nod or a puzzled look, at which point Trudy made the proper adjustment in the direction indicated.

It was a pretty poor performance of cold reading. I had been inoculated against this sort of thing also, many years ago when I spent so much time and money checking out all the psychic readers in the area. I had quickly learned their form of reading cues in the face or response of the person to gradually weed out what did not apply, enabling them to make a final, definite, and "amazing" pronouncement of the facts that were bothering the individual at the end of this exercise in subtle probing.

Of course, to be fair, I had noticed that sometimes things were received which were clearly out of the cold-reading loop, and quite accurate, but it was statistically no more or less amazing than two friends who have the same thought at the same time. No special rating as a psychic is needed. And my estimation was that everyone was psychic, to one extent or another, so no cigar.

The problem arises when the subject of a reading gives away the anticipated answer in their voice or the phrasing of the question. This enables the reader to know what the client wants to hear, and they feed this wishful thinking. The reader makes "predictions" based on what the client wants to hear, and because it is the desired thing, the person seeking the information feels en rapport with the reader and then ascribes to them all sorts of powers and abilities that simply are not there. The strange part of this scenarios is that, when the predictions do not transpire as described, the individual is by this time so invested in their belief of the powers of their chosen reader that they will go to all kinds of ridiculous extremes to excuse the failed prediction.

This is a very common situation. These failures are the clues we are given as little alerts to the larger picture, but we tend to ignore them, to cover them up, to excuse them; to continue to believe what we like rather than what is true simply because it matches our preconceived notions of how things would be if we were creating our own reality. What's more, if we pay money it has to be right. Either that, or we were duped. It's difficult for many people to admit they've been hornswoggled.

After Trudy was done with her rather embarrassing demonstration, another student got up to do readings. For some reason, she picked me—probably because I was a new and unfamiliar face. I had long ago schooled myself to be able to keep a poker face and a flat voice when checking out readers, so I kept my face a blank while at the same time providing ambiguous feedback such as "maybe," or "it could be described that way," and so on. At the same time, I was inwardly open to contact. If there was a real talent going on here, there would be no deliberate blocking. I was trying not to hinder the "tuning in" or give anything away externally at the same time.

But this reading was worse than could have been accomplished by just random guessing. I was not impressed by the graduates of Reverend Rita's classes.

After this non-event, a healing circle was formed where everyone gathered around Reverend Rita and her assistant, laying on hands, praying and giving "love and light" and energy. It was pretty much like any laying on of hands in a Pentecostal church. The only difference: Reverend Rita seemed to sort of swell from the contact. I wasn't sure if my eyes were deceiving me, but everyone else was perfectly exhausted after the service, so something was draining them. Again I was wondering why a service that was supposed to feed and energize a given flock was actually doing the opposite.

On the drive home, I heard nothing but the praises of Reverend Rita and her great works. And now, since I was considered to be more a part of the group—everyone assuming, I guess, that I'd been taken in by the recent performance—a new thing was revealed to me. Apparently Reverend Rita had a secret circle that admitted only those who had proved themselves worthy or had passed certain tests administered in her many classes. The members of this inner group were promised that Reverend Rita was going to give them many great secrets. My hostess had already signed up for the next series of lessons and sessions with the Great One.

I said nothing, but I knew I didn't want to go back. That church made me feel ill at ease and was clearly a waste of time. I couldn't understand how the members of the Reiki group, which seemed to be so much more rational than other metaphysical mumbo-jumbo groups I had encountered in past, could be so taken in by that drivel. But, on the other hand, maybe I had the problem. It certainly seemed that everyone involved in the Reiki group was certainly full of love and benevolence and good intentions.

* * *

The Reiki group was a gathering of people of many ages and backgrounds. "Louise," the woman who had approached my mother with the initial invitations, was an older lady, of retirement age (otherwise she would not have been in the class), but she physically appeared much younger: she didn't look a day over thirty-five! She had a knockout figure and such a charming and feminine presence that you just had to be in awe of her ability to control by seeming not to do so. She had a breathy, Marilyn Monroe type of voice, gorgeous red hair, and alabaster skin. She was the one who had brought the idea of the original Reiki class to Reverend Rita. She'd learned about Reiki in Virginia Beach and spent some time with the A.R.E. crowd up there. It was impressed upon us that we were so fortunate to have our initiations from one of Takata's original students, since Reiki had later split and been corrupted after Takata's death, but that's another story.

Then there was "Trudy" and her husband "George," who were also past retirement age. Trudy was a tall, rangy woman, more like a man in many of her characteristics than a woman. In the beginning, I thought she was very funny and engaging with her snappy comebacks and wry humor. But, as time went by, I began to see a certain element of cruelty in her remarks, especially when addressing or talking about her husband. I wrote it off as the great familiarity of people long married. And who was I to say that he hadn't done things to invite such remarks? Maybe that was their way of showing affection? George was a retired owner of a boat-building factory. His wife had been his secretary when they met, divorced their respective mates, and married each other. They were considered to be the wealthiest members of the group and thus had some status.

Then there was the younger contingent, my age or younger. The most active were "Candy" and "Sandy."

Sandy had been awakened to spiritual issues by the death of her fiancé. After her awakening, she decided to go to school to become a massage therapist. Among the others in the group, a young man named Tim seemed to be very spiritually knowledgeable. It was unusual to see someone his age so devoted to helping others. He stated his religious affiliation as Wiccan, and this later proved to have some interesting repercussions, to say the least.

Since Reiki really doesn't require meditative focus or any kind of mumbo-jumbo–type concentration, on Reiki nights we were all basically free to do two things at once—Reiki and talk. These conversations, while we were all standing around the massage table with our hands on whomever, really ran the gamut when talking about our different experiences with spiritual development. I was a bit reluctant to talk about many of my own, but after a while, I felt more comfortable sharing some with the others, and we were able to begin to form what seemed to be a real bond of closeness.

I very quickly brought the Reiki group up to date on my ideas about channeling and the experiment going on with Frank. One of the ladies from the older group pronounced balefully upon our selection of the board as an instrument, citing the movie *The Exorcist* as proof of its direful consequences. I countered with the facts of the real case on which the movie was based. There had been no indication that a board was the main player in the alleged demonic possession. Also, most of the greatest material in the history of channeling has come through a board instrument or began with one.

Everyone began asking more and more questions about the experiment, so I told them all I could. That led to discussions about my hypnosis work. I told about my recent experience with the Black Boomerang, which had, in a sense, set me up to be led to the Reiki crowd to begin with.

Everyone had a really good laugh that I had to be chased by aliens before I found Reiki.

Before I went home that night, I mentioned that if anyone wanted to participate in our experiment, they were welcome to come on Saturday nights when we "sat" for contact. Four or five of them were excited and agreed that they wanted to try it out.

The next day, Candy called. "There is something I have to tell you and I don't really know how, but you had better beware of Trudy."

"What do you mean?" A serpent in Reiki Eden?

Candy explained: After I had left the previous evening, Trudy made nasty remarks about me being a know-it-all, and anybody who participated in anything I suggested was definitely being taken in and led down the primrose path to destruction. Words to that effect, anyway. This hurt, because I don't preach, but describe my experiences and the research of others who are far more qualified to give opinions.

"But you have to understand," Candy continued. "Trudy is like a mother to the rest of us. She's just being protective. She means well, but she's from the old school. She grew up with Cayce and all that. *She likes the robes and rituals and things.* Reverend Rita is even saying that she is sort of preparing Trudy to take over the church, so of course she feels responsible for all of us like we were her own children."

The upshot of the whole conversation was that Candy wanted me to be careful what I talked about to Trudy and the others because they were old fashioned and narrow minded, even if they meant well. It was a maneuver designed to spare their feelings. At the same time, Candy wanted to participate in our experiment and have some hypnosis sessions done to speed up her spiritual advancement, since she had in mind that she was destined to be the next Jeane Dixon. Of course, she didn't want Trudy or any of the older crowd to know about her participation.

As it turned out, it seems that Reverend Rita had told Candy that she could never be a channel, because of some flaw in her background. It didn't make much sense to me, as Candy explained it, and we just agreed that it must be just more of the "old-fashioned narrow mindedness" of the older crowd who weren't part of the new paradigm of very advanced souls in young bodies. They just didn't understand how fast people were able to progress in the present "urgent" time.

I wasn't sure that I agreed with her all the way on her idea that she was supposed to move so rapidly, but I reserved judgment until some work could be done. But at least there was a reasonable explanation for the undercurrent that I had sensed at the church—the "old fashioned" attitude of the older folks as opposed to the younger ones. It made perfect sense. I could finally get some rest from the worrisome little glitches. I didn't know what to make of the "robes and rituals" remark, because I hadn't really seen anything of that specific nature, but I let it pass.

Candy wanted to be my friend and have a much closer friendship than just the once-weekly Reiki meeting. She was a lot of fun, laughing and joking and mimicking other people's foibles in funny portrayals of everyone's egotistical hang-ups. This was always prefaced by "you know I love so-and-so, but …"

Sometimes I did wonder, though. Would she make similar jokes about me to them? Of course not! Candy was my friend. We had a special rapport.

The next Reiki night, I noticed a distinct tightness in Trudy's face when I walked in the room and said hello. She was distant and cool in her manner. Because I had been primed by Candy to be more patient and understanding, I tried to defer to her ideas and keep my own opinions to myself.

Meanwhile, Trudy and George seemed to be having problems. George stopped coming to Reiki, and Trudy spent entire sessions telling us all how dreadful her marriage was. Later on, George would tell Louise, Candy, and me terrible tales of how Trudy had turned from a sweet, devoted wife to an abusive monster who had even physically threatened him. George was afraid she would kill him to have access to his money. She had some sort of power, and he was helpless in the face of it. I asked George if he had ever considered getting a divorce if he truly feared for his life.

This led to a significant misunderstanding in which Trudy made me her avowed enemy for suggesting such a thing to her husband, and Louise and Candy refused to come to my defense. Finally, we all set up a luncheon meeting to iron out the problem.

At that meeting, I met Jeannie, an elderly woman with a reputation as a gifted psychic.

"You have the light in you," Jeannie told me afterwards. "Those people hate you for that. When the light comes into the middle of darkness, it exposes things. They can't stand the light. You have to be careful. There are things out there that can really hurt you. I know! They've been trying to kill me all my life. Now they are trying to kill you! And beware of Louise! Did you see how she didn't say a word in your defense? Well, that's because she's one of them! And Candy, too. You need to be on your guard."

Well, after a declaration like that, I was sure that Jeannie was like "Aunt Clara" on the old TV series *Bewitched*. What she was saying just did not make sense. It was crazy talk. But she was so sweet and sincere and urgently concerned that I assured her I would take the greatest care. I promised to keep in touch. I told Candy what she had said and we agreed that the poor dear may have been a good psychic (as Louise assured us) but she was obviously over the hill now.

I was wrong.

CHAPTER FORTY-TWO

GREEN SLIME

A few weeks went by after the "Trudy affair," we continued with our Reiki nights, and things were better.

But there was still an undercurrent of dis-ease. I did my best to put as much love and light around the situation as I could and keep myself in a "bubble" of light so all my words and actions would issue from a deep place of love and understanding in my heart. I was terribly grieved that Trudy had been so hurt, and I did all I could to make it up to her. But she began changing in some way. Even her appearance changed, and she began to get heavier. At the same time, her husband just seemed to be wasting away to nothing. He whined and complained, and Trudy rolled her eyes in exasperation.

Meanwhile, Candy and several others were coming to our sittings on Saturday nights, and even if all we did at this point was chat with dead dudes, we still had fun with it. All of them wanted to go through the spirit-release process, so we set up hypnosis sessions.

One day Candy told me that Rev. Rita was becoming very upset because I was "stealing" her congregation. I was shocked. I wasn't stealing anybody. In no way, shape, form, or fashion did I wish to interfere with her conducting her services and classes and whatever else she had going on in her little church. Just because I was doing hypnosis and spirit-release work on a small handful of her congregants was definitely not an act of "stealing" anybody. What we were doing was more social than anything else.

How could she accuse me of stealing her people?

I wanted to know how Candy knew this. "I can't say," she answered mysteriously. "Just be on guard."

AMAZING GRACE

* * *

At this time, events began to converge rapidly in a strange synchronicity. Random threads from the past, in the space of a few weeks, began weaving together in a coherent design in ways that astonished me.

The phone rang one day with a call from my private investigator friend. We'd cooperated on the 1993 child murder investigation described in an earlier chapter. He had a question about something unrelated to that case. At the end of our exchange, he asked me about a conversation I had with a certain law enforcement employee. Well, this conversation had never happened.

"What are you talking about?"

"I called you back in October when he was here in the office with me," my friend said, "and one of your kids said you were in the hospital. I left his number and a message that you should call him. I was sure you had by now."

I never got the message. The kids must have forgotten. I called the number and left a message.

Now here I am going to have to use pseudonyms, which will not fully reflect the meaning conveyed in the names, but I'll try to get as close as possible. I'll call the police detective "Marion Wilbore." I knew that "Marion" was fairly common as a man's name in the past, but it was unusual now, so I thought it odd. Also, Wilbur was the name of both my brother and my grandfather.

Two days later, Marion Wilbore returned my call. I thought it was most curious this guy should call on my grandfather's birthday, February 11th. Two "Wilburs."

Then the phone rang again just a few minutes later. This time, it was "Marion Wilson," the owner of a local secondhand bookstore, calling to tell me that she had a copy of Velikovsky's *World's in Collision* that I could have for seven dollars. I was so excited that I told her to put a sold tag on it and I would be right down. I'd been searching for this book without success for two years after my copy had been borrowed and never returned.

It wasn't until I hung up that I realized the pattern. "Marion Wilbore? Marion Wilson? Two Marions? Two Wilburs? What is going on here?!"

The phone rang again. I was going out the door and almost didn't answer it, but decided I'd better. It was Sam, my cousin, whom I'd met for the first time at the MUFON meeting. Sam is the one whose name is my grandfather Wilbur's middle name. He, too, was calling to announce that he had just found a copy of Velikovsky's *Worlds in Collision* in a box of books in his garage. He knew I had been looking for it, and it was mine if I wanted it.

Well, that was just too much! Two "Marions," two Wilburs on Wilbur's birthday, two last names beginning with "Wil," two copies of Velikovsky after two years of searching, one of them from a guy who had Wilbur's middle name as a last name.

All within about half an hour. Come on, skeptics, figure the odds of that!

I mean, what were the chances of two completely unrelated people named Marion, with their last names beginning with "Wil"—for God's sake!—calling me within a few minutes of each other? And what were the odds, within the same few minutes, of having two people offer me a specific book after two years of trying to locate it, with the name connections (and the date) all running together?

I shook my head to clear the cobwebs, sure that I was being taken over by magical thinking. I knew things were getting weird, I just didn't know how weird they were gonna get.

* * *

It was Wednesday—Reiki night.

When I arrived for the Reiki session, several people were sitting on the patio outside. As I got closer, I was surprised to see Reverend Rita. There was a big redheaded woman, and a man dressed all in white—white shorts, white shirt, white socks, and even white shoes—with a heavy gold chain around his neck that disappeared inside his partly unbuttoned shirt, and wearing heavy gold chains on his wrists. I spoke to them cordially as I went in the house, but their responses seemed to be somewhat less than friendly. I just mentally sent love in their direction and closed the door.

The woman who was "up" when I found my place at one of the tables was a hospice nurse who had been suffering from a lot of physical problems that were probably related to the stress of her job. I had never seen her before. I figured she'd been invited by one of the other practitioners. I was given the head position, and when I put my hands on her, it was like two powerful magnets suddenly connecting—*BAM!*—in a way and with a strength that I had not ever experienced before. And the energy began to pour.

Now, the only way I have ever been able to describe my personal sensation of channeling Reiki energy is that it really feels almost like the sensation of nursing a baby. The instant contact is made, it feels like the milk "lets down," only it is in the arms and not the chest. But it is a distinct sensation. I can feel and monitor the flow constantly exactly as I felt and monitored the flow of milk when I was nursing my five children through the years.

This particular woman, the hospice nurse, was pulling energy so hard it was actually painful. My wrists began to ache like an abscess that needed to be lanced. I knew this might relate to the surgery I had on my wrists; there were obviously some "short circuits" or something, but I'd been able to deal with this discomfort. In this instance, I could hardly stand the pain. I disconnected for a few minutes and shook my hands and rested them a few moments before I put them back. Same thing. This poor woman was sure exhausted of all reserves, and I was glad to be able to help her in this way, even if it was somewhat uncomfortable. It took awhile, but eventually the flow began to slow down, the pain eased, and the magnetic sensation released. I knew that she was "finished" for that treatment.

I was going to take a break and have some punch and let somebody else have my spot, but just then the man in white from outside came in. "Don't go yet," he said. Louise introduced him as a friend of Reverend Rita's who had come to try out the Reiki for phlebitis. He hopped on the table with such spryness I could hardly believe he had any problems at all.

I went back to my position at the head as requested.

There was nothing unusual about this man in terms of energy consumption. In fact, he didn't seem to be drawing at all. I did smell whiskey on his breath. Alcohol and Reiki do not mix. I have seen people get violently sick if they drank too soon before or after a Reiki treatment. I thought I would mention that it would be better to refrain for a few hours, but I never got the chance.

As soon as the five of us took our hands away, the man sat up and jumped to his feet, swinging around to face me. "This is for you," he said. He reached inside his shirt, where an object dangled from the end of the heavy gold chain. Before I had time to react, he had traced some sort of figure on my forehead with his finger.

It was as if everyone in the room froze for a few, almost imperceptible, moments, and everyone remained frozen until he had walked out the door and we were startled back to awareness by the sound of car doors slamming, a motor starting, and a car driving away.

At that instant, as though someone had turned everyone back "on" from their frozen posture of staring at me, they all began to talk at once. "What was *that* all about?" or "What *did* he *do*?" or "Who is that man?" or "How *dare* he touch you without your permission?"

The last was the main issue. It was pretty standard in Reiki classes that no one touches anyone without their permission. It was repeated over and over again to us, and we took it seriously.

I asked Louise who the guy was, and she claimed not to know any more than the fact that Reverend Rita and her friend had brought him. Candy and the others were all exclaiming in outrage and examining the greasy smudge on my forehead to see if they could make out what had been drawn there.

Nobody knew who the man was. Nobody knew the meaning of his actions. Nobody knew what was going on with the sudden visit of Reverend Rita and friends. That was the consensus.

After all the hubbub died down, we all settled back to our work, and I was surrounding myself with love and light, certain that whoever the man was, and whatever the purpose of his strange behavior, it couldn't penetrate my shield.

That night, at about midnight, I woke up in so much pain that I knew I was having a heart attack. There was not only an elephant sitting on my chest; there was a fence post driven through my breastbone *and* I was encased in an iron maiden that was slowly squeezing the breath out of me. I woke Larry. He took me to the emergency room.

The doctor said I would have to be admitted for tests and kept under observation for a few days. At this point, I was so frightened I was willing to overcome my dislike of hospitals and let the doctor handle this one. Needless to say, I was pretty terrified at this sudden activation of a condition that I believed to have been cured by Reiki. I had not suffered a single episode for months.

When the nurse wheeled in the cart with the IV setup, a voice as clear and powerful as anything I can ever remember spoke in my head: *If I let them put that needle in my arm, it would be used to kill me.*

My rational conscious mind immediately countered with *That is utter nonsense! You are paranoid! You've been reading too much weird stuff for too long.*

Then a wave of heat washed over me and "knowing" I would die if I stayed in the hospital surged forward again, drowning out the conscious argument. I felt totally schizoid for a moment. I mean, how do you say, "thanks for trying to save my life, but no thanks!" to something like that? I was between a rock and a hard place of overwhelming proportion. There seemed to be no way out.

I tried to convince the nurse that an IV wasn't necessary. She simply brushed my objections away and said it was standard procedure and needed to be done. There was no option.

I then told her quite simply, "No, I don't want the IV."

She ignored me, stripped away plastic wrapping, and laid out the instruments.

Perhaps I was having a heart attack, and it could be a precursor to the "big one." But, on the other hand, it could also be something to do with that man at the Reiki meeting.

If I was perceiving accurate information on how things could work at psychic or unseen levels, then maybe what was happening to me was designed to get me in the hospital. And maybe it was being done so that somebody at the hospital could then be activated to "get to me" and "accidentally" do something stupid that would result in my death.

That was so egotistical a thought that I immediately discarded it. I was a nobody. What difference would it make in cosmic terms if I lived or died?

When I asked myself that question, an answer immediately presented itself: the nonlinear nature of the universe. The idea that the flapping of a butterfly's wings in China could start a chain of events that would lead to a hurricane in Boston was not lost on me. Nobody that I was, there still might be some small thing I was supposed to do, similar to the butterfly that started a storm.

But, no matter what, it was still a choice I had to make without visible proof. I could go with the "surface" or "standard" interpretation of events—I needed to be in the hospital because I might be having a heart attack, which entailed taking the risk of dying either naturally or unnaturally. Or I could go with the subtle, spiritual interpretation, based on knowledge I had accumulated by study, observation, experience, and most important of all: *reason at an absolutely abstract level*. By using this mode of assessment, I could make a choice to take the responsibility for my life into my own hands, do something significant based on knowledge without proof.

At that moment, I felt just as I had years before in the dream of battling the dragon. The same denial of fear, the same crazy courage swept over me. Right or wrong, for once in my life, I had to listen to my inner impressions. If I was wrong and I died, so be it. It would not be for lack of courage!

I decided.

A great calmness descended over me. I told the nurse firmly that she could put the kit away; I was not going to be admitted. At first, I don't think she believed me, but when I got off the gurney and began to put my clothes on, she said, "Let me get the doctor," and dashed off in a great panic.

The doctor came in and gave me the "you are making a big mistake here!" talk. I would have to sign release of liability forms and all that. "I'll sign. I have nothing against the hospital or you or anything, but I am not going to stay here and I am not going to have needles and drugs pumped into my system." And, just for good measure, I said, "It's against my religion."

Well, that must have been the right thing to say, because they had the forms ready by the time I got to the desk. I signed, went out to the waiting room, and told Larry to take me home.

Larry thought I had completely lost my mind. So did I. But I just simply could not argue with the inner conviction that was compelling me to leave that place.

I went home, shivering with the implications of what I'd done. I had opposed and defied all normal convention. I had gone against all the programming of my life to be under one kind of control or another—to be a "good girl" and let "the doctor," or whoever, make the decisions about what happened to me. After the fact, I was assailed by so many doubts it's a wonder I didn't have the "big one" there and then!

But through it all, I clung to that slender thread of "rightness" and my courage never left me, even if doubts plagued me about whether I was right or not.

The next day I was feeling very bad. I was weak and felt "on the edge" of something deep and dark. The fence-post-effect was ever present, and the elephant on my chest seemed to have gained weight. I was functioning, but only barely.

When I went to the kitchen to get a drink of water, I looked out and saw that the pool was green. It had turned into "pea soup" overnight.

This distressed me even more. I asked Larry to have the water tested and fix it. He did. Two days later, it was still—pea soup.

Somehow I knew that this condition of the water in the pool represented my psychic environment. There was an "invasion" of psychic "slime."

Candy was very anxious to help. She chose this moment to inform me that she had received extensive training in various schools of magic, including Wicca and Native American shamanic systems. She came over armed with sage and candles and salt and crystals and a whole raft of metaphysical accoutrements and set to work.

She "cleared" a place in the study and set up an "altar" with candles, bowls of herbs, stones that had been "charged," and all sorts of things. She went around the house with burning sage, opened all the doors and windows to air the place out, carried a drum around, beating on it, chanting, and so on and so forth. She had me stand in a loose gown while she "saged" my entire body and then waved incense all around, incense guaranteed to get rid of any negative energies or your money back!

I was certain it would work because—heck—even I wanted to leave after smelling it!

I didn't really object to this because, after all, I had done some little rituals of my own making years before, when my daughter had been threatened by the "alligator at the window." *Who knows? Maybe such herbs have an effect in terms of reversing atomic polarities?* I was already working on a theory.

After she was done, Candy packed up all her paraphernalia except for the little altar and candles she had left burning. I wasn't to touch them, and by the time they went out, everything would be as right as rain. As she left, Candy said she'd try to find out more about the man at the Reiki session. She would call me back later to report.

The candles finally reached the end. Nothing happened. As much as I relied on these rituals to be able to fight fire with fire, I still felt the elephant on my chest. The sensation of depression and constant pressure was still there.

* * *

Meanwhile, Tim—the young Wicca guy from the Reiki group—called me and wanted to talk about the incident at the Reiki session. He was as distressed about it as I was. He also had many suggestions for "cleaning" my psychic environment that he had learned from his Wiccan friends, and he offered to come over and try them. He also wanted to see the pool situation for himself.

Sure! Why not? If they were convinced these things would work, I was most definitely open to the experiment. And, since Candy had her shot at it, why stop now? Maybe this was a double-header situation and would take two times at the bat to make it to home?

I said, "Come on over."

Tim came and had a look at the pool and then did his selection of guaranteed-to-work rituals, which were not much different from Candy's, though he used a lot more salt. I was vacuuming salt up for weeks after.

Tim's candles on the altar created by Candy burned away over the course of the day and night. The next morning, nothing had happened. The elephant was still sitting on my chest, and my pool was still growing green slime.

Larry went for more chemicals.

* * *

Candy was very clever in getting information out of Reverend Rita's assistant, and it seems that our gentleman of the Reiki open house was an alleged adept in ritual magick, the "Highest Initiate Big Banana" of magickal mumbo jumbo in the whole state. He knew all the Enochian, Golden Dawn, O.T.O., Aleister Crowley stuff, it seems.

Swell. That didn't make me feel any better. In fact, I was downright depressed thinking about people who would do something so nasty and hurtful when I hadn't ever done anything to them.

Clearly we had a problem with the "love-and-light shield" business. It didn't work.

The next day, the pool was still pea soup. I sent Larry down to get more chemicals. We dosed the 15,000-gallon pool with enough chlorine and algae killer to clean an Olympic-sized pool four or five times as big. We ran the pump constantly, cleaned the filter over and over again, ran it again, cleaned it, and so on for another twenty-four hours.

Over a hundred dollars' worth of chemicals later—pea soup. It was even developing "body." I could just see it spewing out of the kid's mouth in *The Exorcist* movie, as her head spun like a top. The pool guy said it looked like we were going to have to drain the pool and start over with fresh water. He had never seen such a case in all his years tending pools.

* * *

Day after day I struggled to function against the physical attack, which soon became a form of horrible oppression in my mind. I felt as if I were wounded and a pack of wolves were slowly circling, getting closer and closer, sniffing and testing, waiting for the weakness to take away all powers of resistance. Then they would spring forward and destroy me.

Day after day there was pea soup in the pool. Chemicals in the pool. Rituals, prayers, and "cleansing" actions in the house and around myself. Hours were spent erecting "psychic" barriers of love and light around me, the house, and so on.

We tried psychic mirrors, cutting psychic connections—you name it, we tried it. Nothing happened. Frank, Candy, Tim, and I discussed it up one side and down the other with no resolution.

During the many hours I was laid up in bed, an inkling of a solution came to me. I had some clues from the spirit-release work. The problem might be an "etheric cord" of some sort, kept in place by association with certain people. I knew from the claims of such entities that attachment very often resulted from simply being close to specific individuals who usually don't even realize that they are carriers or instruments of connection. It was rather like the idea of a psychic Typhoid Mary.

Since I couldn't exactly see who the carrier was, I'd have to experiment. First of all, break with the crowd at the Reiki sessions until I was strong enough to experiment with each one to see who was the carrier of attack.

This was hard. I really liked these people, and we had a very good time together. Of course, the incident with Trudy made it possible she was the conduit of attack, but that meant anyone who associated with her and then with me could carry the infection by proxy.

I tried to explain my thinking to Candy, suggesting that, as an experiment, we should all cease any association with the group until we could make some tests. Candy was appalled at the idea. This was an idea that went blatantly against the love-and-light philosophy of acceptance and unconditional love. It also went against compromise and "working to get along," and so on.

But, at this point, based on what I had learned and experienced in spirit-release work, it was the logical extension of that information. I mentally closed off connections to all those people until I could find out more about what was going on.

I reluctantly told Candy that, since she did not have any desire to cease association with that group, I would have to include her in the moratorium.

She sounded hurt when I said this, and I regretted most painfully what I was doing, but it was the only thing I could see that I hadn't tried. I apologized and told her that if I were wrong, I would admit it.

But I didn't think I was wrong.

I also talked to Tim, explaining my position to him. He agreed that it sounded reasonable and volunteered to join me in the experiment. I was grateful for the support.

That night I had a dream.

In the dream there was the pool. Somebody evil had driven a car into the pool. I was trying to figure out how I was going to get the car out. There were two people in the car, and I was trying to save them, but I couldn't. A woman suddenly arrived on the scene who seemed to be a relative. She told me not to worry.

"This will be as easy as pie to manage," she told me. She had a wrecker waiting that pulled the car out. Then she drained the pool, hauled all the other debris out, scrubbed away the mud and oil and gas, and then waved her hand in the air.

With this motion, a wave came from the nearby ocean and refilled the pool with sparkling water.

I woke up and wondered what the dream might mean. It had given me a positive feeling, and I got out of bed feeling much better. The pressure was gone, and my breathing was much easier. I went to the kitchen and looked out the window.

The pool was clear.

I stood there staring at it in disbelief. For the previous few days, we had put no more effort into trying to clear it. We gave up, decided the pool guy was right and the only solution was to drain it.

And now, there it was: just as clear and sparkling as the pool in my dream.

At that moment, Tim knocked at the door.

"You won't believe it," I told him. "The pool's clear. Come and look."

He stood there staring at the sparkling water, shaking his head and saying over and over again, "I can't believe it! I can't believe it!"

Tim had helped with chemical applications, filter cleaning, and so on, along with "spiritual cleansing" activities, so he was amazed at the sudden turnaround. I told him about the dream, but I was uncertain about its meaning, or the identity of the woman relative who had come to help me.

At that moment, Candy called with news of her own. A metaphysical church member told her that Reverend Rita's red-headed assistant and the Big Banana Magickal Mojo guy had been in an automobile accident during the night. They were both in the hospital in critical condition. Prayers were being requested for them by Reverend Rita.

Candy felt this accident proved I was right in my assessment of Big Mumbo Jumbo Banana. I told Candy how bizarre this accident news seemed in connection with my dream about a car being driven into my pool. Now the pool was clear, and the elephant had finally gotten off my chest.

What were the connections between the dream, the clearing of the pool, the relief from the "attack," and my decision to terminate contact with the group and taking action on this intention?

* * *

There is a point in the life of a person who seeks knowledge when events no longer seem to happen in a simple, straightforward, consecutive way. Linear time seemed too limited to hold the trajectories of meaning that began to surround my life. My work began to occur on several levels of meaning at once.

Was the relative in the dream a higher aspect of myself that was being activated—by activation of principles in my physical life that were derived from higher perception—thereby establishing a link between the higher self and the physical reality?

Was a key being revealed? *The connection to the higher self is activated by choosing to act based on a spiritual perception that is a result of reading the subtle clues in the environment.*

These clues were put together with what I had learned about darkness, rather than choosing to act according to the rules with which we are conditioned. Even the so-called teachings of metaphysics, which were supposed to be based on "spiritual" perceptions, are still part of the control system.

This brought me face to face with several ideas: the idea that surrounding oneself with love and light might not be as effective as was touted, especially in certain circumstances. It might be something that people are told for the express purpose of leaving them vulnerable, to prevent them from understanding how much knowledge they must acquire, and most of all, that they need to apply this knowledge in their lives.

What was apparent was that even the Major Mojo worker of certain high occult practices had no clout against such an activation of knowledge.

Wow! What a concept.

Could it be that the belief in the "bubble of love and light" as well as the belief in the powers of magick were both some sort of inhibitor of knowledge, of growth, of progression?

People who were living in such cocoons of belief were exactly as likely to be attached—to be used by dark forces or dead dudes—as anyone else. Maybe even more likely, because they did not believe it was possible, they believed they were "protected." They were unable to realize that it was probably happening to them without their knowledge!

"*The only thing necessary for the triumph of evil is for good men to do nothing.*" Here we had a perfect example of this statement. Without knowledge, nobody was doing anything except continuing to perpetuate the same beliefs that clearly belonged to that mechanical universe described by Gurdjieff.

When a person is locked in a belief system, they cannot see what is really happening in an objective way. They do not question their observations or experiences and seek knowledge to explain them, but rather interpret them according to their a priori belief system, with no options for other explanations. Square pegs that don't fit in the round holes are ignored or swept under the rug.

I knew this mode well, having been a past master at the sweeping under the rug activity.

It also seemed that a lot of people were presenting themselves as "light workers" who were not, in fact, of such a nature. Maybe they truly believed they were. But without knowledge, they were simply passing on the contagion of lies and ignorance. It was becoming highly probable, in my estimation, that at some deep level, something was going on that really required fresh study and observation to discern. Little by little I was being guided to discover a hypothesized "other level" of reality, and step by step, I was facing repeated struggles between whether or not I could accurately "read" it and act based on that reading, or accept the standard teaching.

Again, the words of Gurdjieff came back to me:

"In order to be able to speak of any kind of future life there must be a certain crystallization, a certain fusion of man's inner qualities, a certain independence of external influences. If there is anything in a man able to resist external influences, then this very thing itself may also be able to resist the death of the physical body. But think for yourselves what there is to withstand physical death in a man who faints or forgets everything when he cuts his finger?"

What is there in people that is able to overcome the action of negative influences in their life if they ignore everything that points to such things and close their eyes to its existence by pulling down the shades of their "personal myth"?

It seemed more and more likely that learning about these things and facing them was crucial to overcoming them.

Gurdjieff wrote:

"... What may be called the astral body is obtained by means of fusion, that is, by means of terribly hard inner work and struggle.

"Fusion, inner unity, is obtained by means of 'friction,' by the struggle between 'yes' and 'no' in man. If a man lives without inner struggle, if everything happens in him without opposition, if he goes wherever he is drawn or wherever the wind blows, he will remain such as he is. But if a struggle begins in him, and particularly if there is a definite line in this struggle, then, gradually, permanent traits begin to form themselves, he begins to 'crystallize.'

"But crystallization is possible on a right foundation and it is possible on a wrong foundation. 'Friction,' the struggle between 'yes' and 'no,' can easily take place on a wrong foundation. For instance, a fanatical belief in some or other idea, or the 'fear of sin,' can evoke a terribly intense struggle between 'yes' and 'no,' and a man may crystallize on these foundations. But this would be a wrong, incomplete crystallization. Such a man will not possess the possibility of further development. In order to make further development possible he must be melted down again, and this can be accomplished only through terrible suffering."

I had suffered and I had achieved this inner will; I had grown a sort of crystallized self—but it was on the wrong foundation. I had spent years and years of my life searching and sorting and categorizing and analyzing, and I really thought I had a handle on things. And remember, I was not doing it from the perspective of materialist existence. I was pretty open to all kinds of theories of consciousness and philosophies and metaphysical stuff of every form and sort. I even had the idea that there might be some usefulness to the magickal operations of some groups ... that ritual was a valid means of producing results.

But this was a *wrong* crystallization.

And when Gurdjieff talks about being "melted down" through terrible suffering, he isn't kidding! There is nothing more terrible than facing the destruction of a belief system.

I thought again of Gurdjieff's description of the "four bodies" of man: the physical body, the astral body of feelings and desires, the spiritual body of the mind, and the divine body of consciousness. It seemed that some sort of development of a higher body was taking place in me as a result of these struggles between the "conditioned" view of the universe—even though my view was based on far broader categories than the views of most people—and this new "seeing" of the pattern behind the symbols of life.

Make no mistake about it: this was a struggle.

I had spent years struggling with my body; striving to develop will to overcome the weaknesses of the flesh. In like manner, I had struggled to exert will over my emotions. Up to this point, I had used the knowledge base that was generally available to anyone who took the time to seek it out. Now it was clear that this wasn't enough. I was now struggling with a different level of knowledge that seemed to be the path to truly achieving mastery over the body and emotions. At this point, I was vaguely beginning to understand my position, knowing that I lacked certain essential information that would guide me to "crystallize" the "third body."

More than this, I was beginning to realize that, exactly as Gurdjieff had proposed, such work on the self was *against nature*, or at the very least against some sort of control system that was imposed on humanity—the nature of which I was not entirely certain. I began to realize how true it is that *"Strait is the gate and narrow the way and few there be that enter therein ..."*

As Gurdjieff pointed out, in everyday life there exist small, almost imperceptible phenomena that contain within them the "instructions" for development of hidden and higher possibilities. Following these clues is opposed to the general pursuit of everyday life as we are conditioned to believe in it. In fact, following these clues is opposed to nearly all religious and philosophical treatments of how a person ought to live their life. I was seeing that following the rules of life as we are taught them—even including the New Age view—is the "wide way" that leads to death.

It was becoming clear to me that our lives and the conditions of our lives and our experiences correspond to what we are. Becoming cognizant of these symbols, learning to read them, learning to respond to them appropriately according to a higher vision of reality is the crystallization of the third body, the acquiring of knowledge that must accompany being.

I needed more data. What's more, I needed more proof.

It was soon to come.

CHAPTER FORTY-THREE

HUNGRY ALIENS, STINKY DEMONS, AND THE RETURN OF KEITH

All through the early months of 1994 while the dramas of the Reiki crowd were playing out, we had continued our weekly sittings. Sam had stopped attending—ostensibly because of his *contretemps* with Frank—but I think that the real reason was that none of the lottery numbers won him any money.

This may have been the basis for his opinion that Frank was playing me like a Stradivarius. He didn't understand that it was a process, and that asking for lottery numbers was the smallest part of it. We also regularly tested various entities with questions about weather, earth changes, politics, news items of various sorts, asked for predictions about this or that person, and, admittedly, asked all kinds of snoopy questions just to see what would bounce back.

The point was to establish a feedback loop designed to access deep levels of consciousness at the least, or to tune the bio-cosmic receiver, at most. Candy, Tim, and some of the other younger members of the Reiki crowd came and went, but most had neither the patience nor the motivation to continue in anything that did not provide instant gratification. They wanted to be able to just "turn on, tune in and channel now!" Working at it was too much like—well—like work!

Sandra sat with us frequently. The addition of her energy to the mix was always interesting, often resulting in psychokinetic activity around the room that was distracting, to say the least. After a candelabrum flew off a shelf half-way across the room one night, she declined to participate any further and would only sit on the side and watch.

* * *

When I had first met Candy, she wanted me to work with her using hypnosis to develop her channeling abilities. She actually had another agenda going on that she wasn't telling me about in the beginning—she believed she had been abducted by aliens.

After dealing with Pam the night of the flying Black Boomerangs, I wasn't too anxious to dive into that arena without due consideration. Just because I was a good hypnotist and had good techniques and ideas in the more or less normal range of problems, didn't mean that I knew beans from apple butter about alien abductions. Reading mass-market books about it wasn't going to give me the education I needed to handle it, either.

Well, naïve bozo that I sometimes am, I thought it would just be a matter of making some calls to find who to go to for advice or training. I started at the logical place to begin: call the local psychologists and psychiatrists for guidance.

It wasn't a very good idea. Nobody in our semi-backwater area would even consider such an idea, much less touch it with a ten-foot pole!

Okay. I called a couple of people at MUFON. Some names of psychologists in distant cities weren't going to do me any good. There also were MSWs specializing in "experience counseling," and even more with diploma-mill Ph.D.'s or Th.D.'s offering their services for nice fees.

Didn't anybody in the legitimate scientific fields think this phenomenon deserved investigation? Even if the phenomenon was bogus, what about the people claiming such experiences? Weren't they human beings deserving of counseling?

As I continued to make calls on Candy's behalf, the enormity of the problem began to overwhelm me. From what I could determine, many, many thousands of people—a cross section of humanity—were coming forward and saying that they had experienced contact with aliens from other worlds. In all my reading of history and social phenomena, I had never encountered anything quite like this. The general response that they get from others, including professionals who are supposed to be providing help and support, is *ridicule*.

In reviewing the cases available to me, I noted that the typical victim was almost frantically worried about a "loss of time," and some vague memory of being restrained or trapped. The person becomes almost hyperactive in their irritability, suffers from loss of concentration and short-term memory. An abductee is generally hypersensitive to loud noises, claims to hear things no one else can hear, and to see things no one else can see, including getting feelings about others that are impossible to explain or quantify in normal ways.

One of the more disturbing aspects of the phenomenon is that there are often physical traces—scratches, puncture wounds, bruises—and even missing segments of skin, generally in perfectly round configuration as though removed by a cookie cutter.

This last item, naturally, disturbed me a great deal when I remembered the two missing circles of flesh from my bottom after my surgery some years before.

However, as far as I could tell, I had certainly never suffered as Candy was suffering. She was almost hysterical in her desperation to find an answer to what was going on in her life. It was clear that she felt almost abandoned by her husband and friends in this matter, because it was so strange and out of keeping with the other, utterly normal, aspects of her life. It was clear that she was suffering from severe anxiety, and a very real fear of being alone for even a short while.

No matter what the explanation for their experiences, these people needed to be taken seriously; they needed to be validated; and most of all they needed a support system.

Basically, I had three choices to consider in regard to Candy.

She was creating a hoax, no abduction occurred and she knew it did not occur.

An abduction really occurred by persons or beings unknown.

No abduction occurred, but Candy believed it did.

I was rapidly giving up the idea that abduction stories were concocted for fame and glory. For most, the event was one of great shame, and they most certainly didn't want anybody to know about it. That they were so desperate for help that they overcame tremendous reluctance indicates how severely they were traumatized.

The question of the lack of sanity of people claiming to have been abducted was also rapidly being answered in the negative. If millions of people believed that a guy, two thousand years ago, died on a cross and arose three days later, and were considered sane, then people claiming abductions, with far more direct experience and evidence, were undoubtedly sane also. Yes, that's "relative sanity," but that's what you get in our culture!

Each individual case has to be considered separately. To assume anything from the beginning was not ethical. To begin an investigation of such an event meant that the only thing I would be dealing with was Candy's memory—either conscious or unconscious. Thus, a consideration of her life history was necessary. I was going to be far more thorough with Candy than I had been with Pam.

* * *

Candy was about thirty-five years old, the wife of a doctor, owner of her own fashion boutique, and mother to two girls. She had been born and raised in a very strict religious family, but, chafing at the restrictions, had left home at an early age to stay with a brother who worked in a designer clothing shop. There, she also began working in the same business and ended up marrying the owner. This man died, leaving her with a small child and a large inheritance.

A beautiful young widow with a baby and a lot of money does not remain on the marriage mart very long. With her new husband, the doctor (the spitting image of Dudley Do-Right), she moved to Florida where they had a second child together. The object was to get away from the unhappy memories of the loss of her first husband and start a new life. The boutique she left in the care of her brother, who managed the business on her behalf.

After her youngest child started school, Candy became bored and decided to go to work for a different doctor in the large medical complex where her husband also had his offices. She took an administrative position and settled into her role with ease. She was very intelligent, charming, and attractive.

At the same time, Candy began to attend the local metaphysical/spiritualist church I've already described, probably more out of curiosity than anything else, but soon became deeply involved in the spiritualist beliefs and practices.

At this point, strange things began to happen. She claimed that strange things had happened to her all her life, but she just had managed to suppress most of it.

First, she kept encountering a man in the building where she worked. He was employed by a practice on a different floor, so she only saw him in the elevators, the parking lot, and the local eateries. But, every time she did encounter him, she was conscious of a strange electricity between them. Soon they were exchanging brief pleasantries.

One evening, Candy and a co-worker, her friend Edith, went out for drinks together when Candy's husband was at a medical convention. The man coincidentally appeared in the same bar and stopped by their table. They invited him to sit down, and soon were involved in a conversation on metaphysical topics. The man said he knew the location of an old Indian mound, apparently a place of great power. He offered to show both ladies where it was. Feeling secure with a female companion, Candy wanted to see this Indian mound, and they all went together in the man's car. Keep in mind that it was well past dark when they made this plan. When they arrived at the location, a swampy, wooded area on the Gulf of Mexico coast, they all got out and proceeded to hike through the underbrush to this purported Indian mound.

Now, aside from the absurdity of the picture presented here—three adults in their business clothing, hiking out in the muddy swamps after dark—there is the consideration of what, in the name of all good sense, would have sent anyone off on such a hike?

Nevertheless, that is, apparently, what they did. Three professional adults of allegedly impeccable good sense decided to go stomping in the tidal swamps on the Florida coast at night. At some point, Edith was left behind and lost, and something happened to frighten Candy, but afterward she couldn't say what it was, only that she was very confused. She demanded to be taken home. The man cheerfully obliged, they located Edith wandering in the bushes, and he drove them back to their cars and off they went home.

The only problem was, when Candy got home, it was almost midnight. She had "lost" well over two hours.

I went over this point with her carefully, going over the exact chronology of that night. She should have been home no later than 9:30 at the outside. Yet, it was just a few minutes before midnight when she made it home. She was surprised because her children were already in bed sleeping, and the house was quiet and dark. When she saw the time, she became almost hysterical at the very thought that she had been gone so long. What might her children have thought?

At that point Candy's life began to fall apart. She was suddenly so emotional that she couldn't stay on an even keel from one minute to the next. She became almost uncontrollably obsessed with the man in the building, believing he was her soulmate one minute and that he was a government spy the next. She felt that somehow she must find ways to be with him. Then she felt he was watching her and she had better avoid him.

Immediately following this event, her husband was in an auto accident with another woman in the car. Candy's marriage began to disintegrate. It was at this point that I first met her at the Reiki gathering. In other words, she must have made her trip to the swamps at almost the exact time my mother received her invitation to attend the home health classes for seniors.

Candy apparently knew the abduction-encounter scenario from things people had told her at various local metaphysical meetings. She thought she had experienced some sort of encounter with "space brothers." She was convinced that she had been given a message during her encounter and that it was important for her to remember it to share with mankind.

Trying to get the story out of her in a linear way was like pulling teeth. The subject was so laden with emotion that it was difficult to make anything out of it without stopping her repeatedly, backing her up, and having her describe things in a sequential way. I didn't want to jump to any conclusions, because I still held out for the possibility of other explanations. Based on the series of events, I thought it was also possible that she had been given some kind of date-rape drug by this man who took her to the Indian mound.

But Candy held firmly to the idea that the man had hypnotized her or in some way, she had been mind-controlled, that he was a government agent, and that the government was watching her because she was "chosen" by the aliens to deliver a message. Why or how he would be involved in her abduction if he were a government agent wasn't exactly clear, and certainly didn't make any sense. Candy knew it. She agreed with a rueful laugh that she knew she sounded crazy, and it was clear that she was close to the edge. She most definitely needed help, and if I couldn't find someone competent to send her to, or to instruct me, we might just have been on our own with this one.

It also seemed to me to be important to find out how much Candy had actually read about alien abductions.

She claimed that she had never read anything about it, that what she knew was just gossip and word of mouth, but I wasn't too sure. If she had spent a lot of time reading about the subject, she was, in my opinion, contaminated as a true test subject. I could help her to deal with the trauma, but I could never consider her statements under hypnosis to be evidence of anything.

After several weeks of putting her off while I tried to find a legitimate psychologist to help her and trying to just let her talk about it to see if that would ease her anxiety, I realized that I wasn't going to find any real help. I scheduled a hypnosis session with plans to do the spirit-release work first, before considering anything else. Candy agreed this was the approach she wanted to take as well.

During this session, an attached entity identified himself as "Thomas." His story was that he had been a practitioner of Voodoo in Haiti and had been killed by a rival Voodoo doctor in 1945. The real shocker was when he claimed that he had been induced or commanded by a magician to attach to Candy as a "control conduit."

A magician?

He would not identify the "who," and it was clear that he was terrified of punishment if he betrayed his "master," but he did say that this had occurred in the previous few weeks and that Candy did know this individual. Our best guess afterward was connected with Rev. Rita and her Big Banana doing their black magick juju number on me. Candy was very distressed to think that she had been used this way and she was also very apologetic toward me, though I assured her that it most definitely wasn't her fault. The question was: had the things I had said about the matter influenced her thinking and created this scenario in her mind?

There was another alleged entity that had attached to Candy via marital relations with her husband, but that one was rather glad to be sent to the light and gave no trouble.

There were two suicides who had attached to the first "frequency-available" host, Candy, in their fear of having violated a religious taboo in killing themselves. This is not uncommon in the spirit-release scenarios that people reveal under hypnosis. Apparently, one of the biggest reasons for spirit attachment is the ignorance of the individual about what really happens after death. A strong religious belief can be as detrimental as no belief in an afterlife at all.

There was also an automobile accident victim, and a victim of a shooting. I never did find out if that particular entity was involved in a crime or if it was just an accident because he or she left almost immediately to go into the light. This entity followed the process with the previous ones, learning from what was being exchanged with them.

If there are multiple attachments, they seem to be influenced by the actions of each other in their shared host/home. (And we are keeping in mind that all of these alleged entities may very well be merely psychodramas in the person's mind created to explain or dramatize emotions.)

As might be expected, in Candy's subconscious mind, there were abductions galore. Candy was a veritable "chosen child" of the friendly Gray aliens. However, certain elements came up in her sessions that startled her. The abduction process was decidedly not as friendly as she'd thought.

Here are some extracts:

> Q: *Okay. What's happening to you next?*
> A: *I see this bright light and I'm alarmed ... I see fingers like suction cups on the end of them ...*
> Q: *What do they do?*
> A: *They're like touching my face ...*
> Q: *How many individuals are there with you?*
> A: *Oh God, this is weird. (Sigh) It's almost like I see a dinosaur or something. With little short arms ... and it's, um ... it's got funny skin ... it's like, it's like ... brownish, slickish ... it's got a real funny face ... it's like a skull but the front of the skull is like going out, real far out ...*
> Q: *Like a snout?*
> A: *Yeah.*
> Q: *How tall was it?*
> A: *Um ...*
> Q: *Taller than you?*
> A: *Oh yeah, it looked bigger than me. It's just funny.*
> Q: *What's funny?*
> A: *Nothing, it's gone.*
> Q: *Where did it go?*
> A: *I don't know. It disappeared.*
> Q: *What do you mean it disappeared?*
> A: *I don't know. It's almost like an image. And then it just vanished.*
> Q: *How many other beings are there with you?*
> A: *Um ... they're all busy all over.*
> Q: *About how many are there?*
> A: *Um ... five or six.*

Q: What do they look like? Do they all look the same?
A: Oh, they're funny looking ... they're almost like, um ... they remind me of the baby dinosaur ... how puffy his face was with the eyes were like ... smaller ... not big eyes like him ... like squinty eyes ...
Q: What color are their eyes?
A: Um ... I don't know ... when I look at their eyes I see a green circle that keeps swirling ...
[...]
Q: What is happening to you?
A: Um. (Sigh) It's hard to breathe.
Q: Do you smell something?
A: No. I see a little— It's almost like a little gold scorpion. It's right by my nose ... my face ...
Q: What is it doing?
A: I don't know. They have it on the end of some tweezers.
Q: Where is the scorpion going?
A: (Signs of distress) Uh, this is weird ... it's almost like it goes in my mouth ... the back of my ... my, um, throat ...
Q: How does it get there?
A: They put it there.
Q: How do they put it there?
A: Um ... it's almost like I see a machine with an arm on it. Almost like a dentist's arm ... I don't know ...
Q: What is it for?
A: I don't know ... television comes to my mind ...
Q: Did they tell you what it was for?
A: No, they don't tell me.
Q: Is it in place now?
A: Um ... They're working on it. They're moving my head ... I hear ringing in my ears.
Q: What happens next?
A: Um ... the back of my neck hurts!
Q: Why does the back of your neck hurt?
A: I don't know, its like ... I have these headaches ...
Q: Where are you now?
A: I'm on the table.
Q: What are they doing to you?
A: They're rubbing my arms.

Q: Has the scorpion been put in?
A: Um hmm.
Q: Did it hurt?
A: Um-hmm.
Q: It did?
A: I don't know ... it's just ... I got a headache now...
Q: Where did they put it into?
A: Well, you know, it's like ... in the back of my neck ... it's through my mouth into the back of my neck ... and my ears ... I hear my ears ringing ... they're like clogged up ... and I feel ... I don't know ... like shh ... shocks or ... I don't know ...
Q: Shocks?
A: Pain shooting through my head.
Q: Pain? What is the pain from?
A: It's like nerve something ... I don't know ...
Q: Okay. You have a small mark above your ear ... where did you get that mark?
A: I don't know, it's like, um ... I don't know ... I see this ... I see a little tiny, um ... metal box ... I'm just gonna say what I see ... I don't know ...
Q: That's connected to the mark above your ear?
A: Yeah. It's almost like I feel like I'm being bit by an ant or something ...
Q: Well, were you being bit by an ant?
A: Hm. When I thought ... When you said that I see uh, um, it's almost like an ant made out of metal ...
Q: Okay.
A: With the stingers.
Q: What does it do?
A: What, the ant?
Q: Um-hmm.
A: It has ... I'm seeing a needle on it ...
Q: Long needle, short needle ...
A: Uh, I see a needle ... its like it connects to something ...
Q: What does it do?
A: Goes in and it connects to something ... I don't know ...
Q: Did this happen at the same time that the scorpion was put in your neck through your throat?
A: No ... (Distress)

Q: Let's go back to where you are on the table and they have just put the little scorpion in the back of your neck through your throat ... Now, you said this hurt ... Did it hurt when they put it in? Or did it begin hurting after they put it in?
A: After they put it in. I had a headache ... I have a headache ...
[...]
Q: Okay. How long have you been connected with this group?
A: Um ... I just see a face in front of me ...
Q: What does the face look like?
A: Um ...
Q: Is it one of them?
A: Um-hmm ... it has real sad eyes ... it doesn't want me saying anything ...
[...]
Q: Do they have any future plans?
A: I hear something saying yes.
Q: Do you know when?
A: No.
Q: Do you know what's in store ... what will happen? Are you in cooperation with them?
A: Umm ... I don't know ... I don't feel good.
Q: What are you feeling right now?
A: I don't know ... I'm feeling kind of sick to my stomach.
Q: Take a real deep breath and the nausea will pass. I am going to count from five to one and on the count of one you will be more deeply relaxed than you have ever been before ... (Countdown)
A: Oh, God! (Sighs)
Q: Now, Candy I'm here and I'll take care of you. You know we discussed beforehand that we want to know at the deepest level we can understand. Are these beings working with you with your permission?
A: Umm ... No.
Q: Is there action you can take, or that you can perceive in a broad way, to prevent this kind of action or activity?
A: Umm ... I don't know what this is I'm seeing ... a tunnel ...
Q: You're seeing what, a tunnel?
A: A tunnel with like webs all on it ... I don't know what it is ... it's ... (Long pause, signs of distress)
Q: A tunnel with webs in it?

A: Yeah ... it's not a nice place ... (Signs of extreme nausea and distress) Mmmm ...
Q: If the tunnel could speak, what would it say?
A: You don't want to be here.
Q: Where is here?
A: It's almost like "where we can put you if we want you."
Q: What is there?
A: Bad stuff.
Q: What kind of bad stuff.
A: Ah ... this is weird ... it's almost like see a crayfish eating like a red glob ... but the crayfish has a mouth ...
Q: If the crayfish could talk, what would it say?
A: They don't talk. (Signs of nausea and distress)
Q: What is the red glob?
A: I don't know ... (Gagging)
Q: All right, take a deep breath now ...
A: I don't like this ...
Q: All right, I am going to count from five to one, and on the count of one you are going to move to your highest level of consciousness ... a place of pure light and knowledge. (Countdown) How do you feel now?
A: Okay.
Q: Now, do you see the light?
A: Um-hmm.
Q: All right. I want you to merge with the light and the knowledge that is in the light. Is there any means by which you can stop these events or protect yourself? The knowledge will be there, you can access it easily.
A: (Long pause) It's almost like I'm hearing a voice say that we have something beautiful that they will never ever have.
Q: We as humans?
A: Um-hmm.
Q: Is this what they wish to acquire?
A: Um ... I don't know ... they're just like, I would guess, parasites, or something like that.
[...]
Q: What's going on around you?
A: I'm just going to tell you what I see ... it's kind of weird. Umm ... I see all these little white guys, they're like children ... they're running

around ... a bunch of 'em ... umm ... I see this woman with gray umm ... I don't know if I can see her ... (Distress) You know, it's like I'm trying to see and it's slipping. She's there but I can't see her.

Q: Take a real deep breath. I am going to count to three and on the count of three any blocks to your memory, any impediments, any distortions will dissolve away and you will see clearly and completely everything that occurred to you at that point in space time and forward. (Countdown) What do you see? Look at this woman. What does she look like?

A: Umm ... I'm in a different room. This room is a round room and it has almost like a glass dome over the top of it ... ummm ... I'm, uh ... it's like a city I'm seeing. This is strange ...

Q: Stop a minute ... stop and take a real deep breath. Back up. Back up to the woman you couldn't see. On the count of three she will appear on the screen and you will be able to describe her clearly. (Countdown)

A: Umm... oooh... I see this woman ... she's got long wiry white hair ...

Q: What about her eyes?

A: I'm just going to tell you what I see. When I look in her eyes they are like circle green ... circling green ... spiraling ... on one picture I see her as ugly but then I see a beautiful woman's face ... I see her one way and when I look there is like a shadow over the face ... it looks like a beautiful woman but when I first looked at her it wasn't but ... when I look at it again it looks like a beautiful woman ...

Q: What sensation do you get from this woman?

A: I just want to say she's hateful.

Q: Does she say anything to you?

A: No. It's like she's watching me real careful.

Q: What does her body look like?

A: Umm ... real thin and tall ... really thin, thin, thin arms and long fingers.

Q: How many fingers?

A: I want to say four. She's real, real tall. Real skinny. But this big head with this wiry hair

Q: Describe the head.

A: It's a triangle but kind of rounded on the edges.

Q: Does she have big ears or little ears?

A: No, I'm seeing little curves on the side of her head.

Q: What about her mouth?

A: Rows of teeth.
Q: What about a nose?
A: I'm seeing two little curves, real small ... two holes, just holes.
Q: Does she say anything to you?
A: No. She's watching me though. Watching me as I'm walking by with these, these ... she dislikes me for some reason.
Q: Okay, you're walking by, what happens next?
A: We're sitting down.
Q: We who?
A: I'm sitting down and there is a small woman next to me and there's a man next to me. And this woman's like, right around behind me, standing up.
Q: Which woman is behind you?
A: The one with the, uh, the woman I don't like. She's bossy.
Q: Is she in charge?
A: Unh-uh. But she's got— I don't know... she has a certain function or something ... But, umm ... I don't know, she's just not nice.
Q: I want you to try a little experiment. I am going to count to three and on the count of three I want you to tap into her mind and see what she is thinking. (Countdown) Connect and describe what she feels and thinks. How does she perceive what's going on?
A: (Distress) What I'm feeling right now is really hungry.
Q: Is that how she feels?
A: Um-hmm.
Q: Hungry for what? What is she hungry for?
A: (Sigh) She feeds off of us.
Q: How does she feed off of us? What does she do when she feeds? What is it she is wanting to do?
A: She feeds off of us ... I don't know.
Q: What does she do physically? Does she just stand next to someone and breathe the air?
A: It's like she puts her mouth over you and sucks something ... like your air out or something ... and her eyes, you know what I mean? It's, you know ... she drains you.
Q: And she is one of this group that you're with?
A: She's like lurking in the back. She isn't in charge, but she's, um, in the background. She's watching me.
A: It's funny because this isn't the way the dream happened.

Naturally, after reviewing these experiences, Candy had a whole different perspective on the abduction phenomenon. She became obsessed with reading everything about it she could find. In this respect, we were certainly on the same path.

When we talked on the phone, there were strange clicks and buzzes on the line. I laughed at the thought of anybody tapping my line to see what we knew about aliens, because it was a certainty that we knew very little.

But Candy was convinced that she had something they were after—that the objective of any surveillance was herself. Her conviction that the man who had taken her out to the mounds was a government agent became somehow intertwined with that bizarre conviction that he was also her soulmate. He was being used to lure her into some kind of government conspiracy and it was her job to rescue him in some way by the strength and purity of her love.

I knew that it was going to take a lot more work to peel away the screens and false memories, not to mention the emotional programs that were still driving Candy.

* * *

One night, at about this time, I received a phone call from Tim. (I was at Candy's house and he had called my house and found out where I was.) He was in a complete panic. He had been trying a particular ritual, and something had gone terribly wrong. He had run hot water in his tiny bathroom to make it like a sauna and then did some sort of "calling forth" ritual while staring in the mirror. (Seems to me that he would have had to be constantly wiping the steam off the glass to even do this!) Well, the upshot was that a horrible demonic face had appeared in the mirror and had told him that it was his companion and was now going to have fun tormenting him or feeding on him or something.

Tim had the feeling of pressure on his chest, his heart started beating like crazy, and he thought he was going to die. He was actually calling from the hospital. They'd given him a sedative and told him that nothing was essentially wrong with him except a stress reaction. He was terrified to go home because the demon was there. What should he do?

I tried to calm him down and told him to come right over and I was sure we could fix him up pretty quick.

It was a long wait before Tim arrived, and when he did, he was in a terrible state. He told us that on his way over, he had actually been in an accident—another car had sideswiped him and spun his car around and into a ditch. He was certain that it was the demon doing it, and his terror had practically gone through the roof.

We got him up on Candy's massage table and started giving him Reiki just to calm him down. As we did, there were all kinds of strange things going on with his body. Muscles would jump and jerk in a way that was definitely not normal.

Tim said he could actually feel something slithery (as he described it) moving around inside him.

Well, we were sort of freaking out too. A can of hairspray ought to be part of the standard equipment of an exorcist! But my experience in many spirit-release sessions had schooled me to remain calm and in control of the situation. I asked Tim to recount exactly everything that was done and said. He began to breathe more normally and calmed down.

As soon as he was stable, I put him under hypnosis and proceeded to begin a differential diagnosis. It was clear from the start this was not going to be a standard session. Whoever or whatever was hanging out in Tim's "space," it was not happy that I was addressing it and demanding answers.

As I repeated my questions, poor Tim alternately swelled and diminished by expulsion of the most horrid gas imaginable. This was definitely not a case of finding a poor, lost, departed dead dude who needed to be counseled to go into the light. This critter had no intention of going anywhere. He had been "invited," and he liked his new "home," and there wasn't gonna be an eviction!

Well, I had a different opinion of the matter and was equally determined that he was going to depart rather quickly, so it was pretty much a matter of who was going to prove to be the strongest in the dispute.

I did the usual calling on the "guides" and "light workers" of the astral planes to come and assist in the freeing of the victim, followed standard procedures and so forth.

No dice.

I did the "in the name of Jesus" routine, which can work *depending on the religious affiliation* of the victim.

Didn't work. The critter actually sneered and laughed at that one.

The entity was making poor Tim jerk and jump on the table, constantly swelling with gas and expelling it in quantities that were simply abnormal by any pathological criteria. When I directed Tim to join with Candy and myself in visualizing light to encapsulate the entity, it began to complain that it was "hot" and "burned" and for us to just stop and leave it alone. It started to whine and moan that we ought to have sympathy and compassion because that was the philosophy we were espousing in the love-and-light New Age trend, wasn't it? It was actually a caricature of the recent machinations of both Trudy and George, and I was not fooled one bit.

Apparently, this approach was weakening the entity. Finally I told it that I was not going to leave it alone, I was not going to stop harassing it with heat and light, and that if I had to, we would stay there all night and all the next day and however many days it took. That seemed to have an effect because Tim became suddenly very still. All was quiet for a moment. I decided that now must be my chance. I gathered my will together and directed it with intent.

I demanded that the entity leave NOW!

With a last blowup of Tim's abdomen, followed by a particularly noisy expulsion of the most horrible sulfurous stench, the entity left. Tim was finally peaceful.

This was definitely a whole new level of nastiness, one that, apparently, even Bill Baldwin hadn't encountered. If he had, he most definitely hadn't described it well at all. His reliance on the Christian approach was clearly misleading.

I knew that already from the demoniac at church, so I was prepared. I shuddered to think what might happen to other practitioners who did not realize the limitations of Christian beliefs.

I brought Tim out of hypnosis. Unlike your standard dead dude, this entity had been singularly uncommunicative. I realized that the whining had been an act that was designed to take me in with pity, and that the significant thing about this entity was its inability to respond to questions at all. This told me something about the nature of the beast, a level of negativity so contractile that the act of communication was impossible. It could only feed and manipulate.

It was our guess that it had been initially attracted to Tim at one of the coven meetings, where a whole host of such entities might congregate, selecting their prey, and then hang around, waiting for the opportunity to connect in a more permanent way. Based on the available literature, such entities can actually influence the individual to perform certain acts that facilitate entry, and even though the individual thinks these ideas are their own, they are not. Apparently, enough mind contact can be made to plant thoughts and ideas to do this or that (including attempts at channeling) that will lead to fuller possession.

Now, I am not saying that is true of Wicca because it is Wicca. I was hypothesizing at that point based on clinical references. A later case, even more severe than Tim's (which I actually refused to handle because the victim was simply not ready to employ her own will to assist), indicated that demonic possession, whether an artifact of consciousness or not, can and does occur in Christian churches. It seems that religious gatherings of all kinds, if they are based on certain illusions, are literal feasts for discarnate entities. I shuddered to think of what had been hanging out all those years in the fundamentalist church we had attended. Anyone who is a member of the Wiccan path ought not to take this as a criticism of that religion. It seems to be so that rituals and acts of blind belief are weaknesses in the spiritual armor.

The end result was that Tim was certainly cured of his interest in religion, Wicca or otherwise.

* * *

At this point, we had been sitting with our board experiment for almost two years. We were chatting with a lot of interesting and even funny dead dudes, and, for the most part, we used the board to counsel them and send them into the light. But always, before we did, we would ask if they had any messages for us or predictions to make.

One night, as we were getting ready to sit at the board, I had the idea that music might be nice. For some reason, I wanted to listen to my Puccini tape. We sat down and began with the usual formula: "Is anyone with us?" The answer was "yes." What is your name? "The Sea."

Q: *I don't understand. What do you mean you are "the sea"?*
A: *Mythic Momma said she felt like she needed a bath after me. Who am I?*
Q: *That's what I'm asking you. Who are you?*
A: *I'm the sea. Laura you are slipping. The C.*
Q: *I'm afraid that I am completely lost and you are making no sense whatsoever.*

> A: OK here's the last clue (pause) Mortality Drop.
> Q: What the heck does that mean?
> A: Clue.
> Q: Are we supposed to guess who you are?
> A: That's what I said.
> Q: Does your name begin with "s"?
> A: Wrong. One more clue (pause) Coachman Road Meat Purchase.

And I got it. Keith Laumer.

> A: Finally!

I was completely stunned. In the twenty years since the incident at the meat market with Keith, not only had I never told anyone about it (just too embarrassing), I had also forgotten it myself. And now that I was being reminded, I wasn't even sure of the name of the road the meat market had been on.

(The following day I checked; not only was this the correct name of the road, the meat market was still there!)

The clues now made sense: The Sea was the translation of Keith's French name into English: Laumer—*la mer*. "Mortality Drop" was a clue to one of the novels Keith had written, of which he had been especially proud: *Deadfall*. It was, in fact, the only book of his that I still had in my possession.

Well, there was nothing to do but continue the dialogue to find out if I was really chatting with Keith.

> Q: Is that really you, Keith?
> A: Yeah, baby! (Typical Keith-type answer)
> Q: Are you stuck in the earth plane?
> A: Lighten up!
> Q: Do you have a message for me?
> A: Yes. Write book.
> Q: What about?
> A: UFOs. Larry will give you flak ... jealous.
> Q: Can you give me any advice about that?
> A: Advice is not my place on the board; the board does not answer all life's problems.

> Q: *Keith, when you died you owed me five thousand dollars! Does it bother you?*
> A: *I gave at the office!*

(Typical Keith remark! Keith and I had made a bet and I won—he picked the amount and swore that he really meant it and was going to pay me. I didn't push it and he died before we ever talked about it again.)

> Q: *Since you are in a different position, do you see things differently?*
> A: *Yes.*
> Q: *Can you tell us if the works of Zecharia Sitchin are factual?*
> A: *Sitchin wrote for money.*
> Q: *Well, so did you!*
> A: *At least I did mine as a labor of love. Sitchin Fiction. Some truth by coincidence.*
> Q: *What about UFOs and aliens? What do you know about them?*
> A: *I never believed but now I know.*
> Q: *What do you know?*
> A: *A lot of things.*
> Q: *When you were alive, you were pretty narrow minded about such things.*
> A: *Well, that is a little harsh, Laura. Tired now.*
> Q: *Well, good night then. Sleep well.*
> A: *Yes.*

To say that I was startled by this exchange is putting it mildly. Up to this moment in time, I could say that what we were doing was just an experiment that might include the real possibility we were talking to genuine discarnates, but I really hadn't assigned a really high probability to it. It was a working hypothesis, following a formula that worked, but it wasn't necessary to believe in it for it to work. It was as likely, in my mind, that such encounters were merely an artifact of consciousness. I tended to assign a higher probability to that than to the idea that an individual consciousness no longer in a body could communicate with the living.

I never really cared if any of the theories about reincarnation or spirit release or aliens or demons were true. I only cared that the therapies worked. It was fascinating, a subject of endless experiment and speculation, and here I was looking at a possibility that I had actually communicated with an old friend who was now no longer in the body. The style and flavor of the communication was entirely characteristic of Keith.

I also had to wonder about the urge I had felt to listen to Keith's favorite music. Was this a sign of his presence and intent to communicate?

No one else at the table knew the story but Keith and me. That eliminated any deliberate movement of the planchette by Frank. It was also curious that the incident was one I had completely forgotten. If it was being telepathically read by Frank, it was read from my subconscious mind. It didn't occur to me at the time that this was a clue that would later be important.

The name of the road where the meat market was located was another issue. That was something I never knew consciously at all. When I'd driven Keith there, twenty years before, I had merely followed his directions to "turn here, turn there." The name of the road could have been buried deeply in my subconscious mind. Perhaps I had noted it on a street sign at the time. Even so, the event suggested that if this was all coming out of my subconscious mind, then we had, at least, penetrated to a deep level of awareness.

If my theory was correct, we didn't have far to go to access "Universal Consciousness." Again, whatever was being read was in my unconscious mind, not Frank's.

In any event, I was pleased to communicate with Keith, to know that he was all right, and to think, even if it was only a nice illusion, that he still had his great sense of humor.

Either way, we were making progress.

CHAPTER FORTY-FOUR

COMETS AND CASSIOPAEANS

Keith never dropped in to visit again. My best guess, based on my working hypothesis, was that he was "in the light." We had finally passed through all the lower-level entities of the earthbound astral planes and were dealing directly with those who were not in need of spirit release or similar assistance. I cannot, of course, prove that this idea was correct, but the evidence seems to support it because the character of the communication changed. No longer were we chatting with lost souls seeking counsel; now they were just souls of all sorts with all kinds of views and perspectives.

Interspersed with the dead dudes were the "space brothers." One identified himself as "Jordan," and claimed to be on a ship near Mars, having just arrived there from an orbit around Neptune. He then went on to answer all kinds of questions that confirmed many of the theories of Zecharia Sitchin, claimed that he was a member of a "sister race" to mankind, and just generally performed like your standard space brother. I was not impressed.

Jordan seemed to want to be a regular visitor, but after doing a differential diagnosis, I decided he was just wasting our time and I sent him on his way.

The notebook for that period is full of earth changes and disaster prognostications, the kinds of questions everyone was interested in asking. Just skimming through it I can note such things as:

Earthquake in the Bahamas.
Tsunami east coast—200 feet high.
Raising of Atlantis April 23 1994. (That one was a loser for sure!)

> *Hurricane 8/21/94 barometric pressure 21.00, winds gusting at 600 mph, landfall Boston (another loser).*
> *Earthquake California, 10/23/94, the big one, 8.9 Richter (another loser).*
> *Economic collapse stock market drop 500 points in one day on 12/4/94.*
> *Pole Shift 9/9/99.*
> *Extraterrestrial contact.*
> *AIDS will mutate to airborne virus, will be also transmitted by fleas; and so on and on.*

Obviously, like the many prognostications about photon belts and Hale Bopp from so many popular sources, it was just nonsense piled upon nonsense. I don't think the entities were deliberately lying to us, nor do I think that they were evil. I just think that Cayce was right: a dead Presbyterian is just a dead Presbyterian. If a person dies with strong beliefs formed in the crucible of life on earth, they take those beliefs with them. And it seems that souls congregate with other souls of similar "frequency" or belief. In this way, they support one another in their illusions and become convinced that what they experience is the whole banana. In this way, they can communicate with the living, absolutely convinced that what they are saying is truth, with the best of intentions; and in the end, it can be all lies.

I didn't want lies, however well intentioned the source. I didn't want to hear the same tired old illusions that humankind has been fed for millennia which have never done anything to help us change our status on earth and in the cosmos. I wanted one thing and one thing only: the objective truth, *if* it existed. I wanted to know how to "go home." Like a person playing blind man's bluff, I was groping for answers.

*　　*　　*

Candy frequently joined us, and we spent many hours discussing the "alien business." We were also attending MUFON meetings fairly regularly to see what kind of information we could pick up. That's where I met Terry and Jan, editors and publishers of the area MUFON newsletter. It was a clever and nicely done little publication, and reading it gave me a good opinion of their analytical skills. I was surprised to discover that Jan didn't believe in anything having to do with the UFO business, but she participated in the meetings and newsletter in support of her husband, Terry.

Terry witnessed several sightings, but he was open to the idea that they could have been secret aircraft rather than off-world vehicles. I found that I was most definitely uncomfortable with hard-shell debunkers or fanatical true believers. Remarkably—and thankfully—Terry and Jan didn't fit in either category.

They drove forty miles from their home once or twice to sit with us in the early days, but it became too tedious and non-productive to make such a drive worthwhile more than once or twice. Nevertheless, we stayed in contact by phone and Jan kept me updated on all the MUFON news and scuttlebutt.

* * *

As I studied, the questions inside me grew larger and larger. By this time I had read a few dozen books on UFOs and aliens, but their arguments were so contradictory and confusing that I despaired of ever making any sense of it all.

Frank and I had watched several videos starring Al Beliek and Bob Lazar, and all their supposed "answers" raised more questions than gave answers. Sure, it was fine and dandy for Bob Lazar to say that he worked on alien craft at Area 51 and that endless reports of the phenomenon existed from thousands of years ago. But were the lights in the skies and the stories of fairy abductions the same phenomena that happened here and now in our world? If that was so, what about the alleged alien craft that Lazar claimed existed at Area 51? The claims of cover-up and conspiracy had a certain appeal. I really got the creeps thinking about alien critters with bug eyes and B.O.

One anonymous writer claimed that until he had hard evidence that it was not the CIA or some maverick secret government experimenting on human beings, he would continue to deny that it could be aliens. This person wrote:

"THE INTELLIGENCE APPROACH TO UFOs

"*Risking reproach from a number of UFOlogists, I prefer to begin any analysis of the phenomena with the premise that it is being orchestrated by governments rather than off-world beings in fantastic lightships.*

"That is not to say that we are not being visited now or will not be visited in the future. I simply have seen no concrete evidence of it and, until I do, I will continue to believe first that the military and particularly the intelligence agencies are behind much of the UFO phenomena. They have the money and the motives to both create the hoax and to keep it going for years.

"Despite revealing videos such as that produced by Mr. Lazar, we still don't have any proof that the USAF or CIA has sequestered alien disks at S4 or anywhere else. Much to Mr. Lazar's credit, he acknowledges the fact that he has no solid proof to substantiate his claims that he worked on alien disks for the government."

As badly as I want to believe the drawings in the video represented alien craft, I fear I cannot simply because I found nothing during the presentation to explain how the saucers operate while in earth's atmosphere or why they appear as extremely bright balls of light when floating over our cities or preparing to land in our meadows.

According to Mr. Lazar, the saucer should appear as something similar to a comet standing on its tail until it becomes fully energized, at which time it should become invisible as it jumps into another dimension or star cluster such as Zeta Reticuli or Proxima Centauri or even to the dark side of the moon. All that is wonderful narrative but it doesn't tell us what glowing balls of light are flying the skies of this planet.

"Until someone kills a real alien and lays its cadaver on my doorstep, I will continue to believe 'Grey Aliens' are USAF or CIA personnel dressed up in funny costumes. I will continue to believe that our comrades are being abducted and murdered by government agencies [and] that telepathic contact experiments are being conducted by the same government agencies. If aliens are not humans in costumes, they are at least darklings built by human DNA tinkerers in some of those secret underground laboratories.

"I have a great deal of trouble accepting the story that aliens have been conducting genetic experiments on humankind for 10,000 years. That would suggest that we are really little more than their livestock, they actually 'own' us, just as we believe we 'own' beasts of the field and fish of the seas and birds of the air. It also suggests they have an extremely long attention span unless they are moving through time and aren't really 'going anywhere!'

"We tag sea turtles in the North Atlantic and track them by satellite to see which way they go. We tag birds and fish and elephants to follow their migrations. Are we supposed to believe creatures from Zeta Reticuli are doing the same to humans?

"Friends! Why would beings who can travel sixty-six zillion light years through space and time in any direction at any time, want to concern themselves with something as stupid and boring as tagging and following the migration and sexual behavior of humans (who would be the equivalent of primeval slugs to them)? What is the point?

"To capture, examine, impregnate and tag human females to carry their crossbred children? If they are as wonderful and advanced as some say, they should be able to grow their children in canning jars on their own planet!

"To cultivate us as food? If they are twenty billion years more advanced than we, why haven't they figured out how to grow synthetic protein in culture dishes in their own labs on their own planet in their own star cluster?

"If we are nothing more than experiments of an advanced race of beings, no more than bacteria on a cosmic glass slide, that means there is no God, no law, no rules, no leaders, no followers. ...There should be no trials or punishment for "crimes" because the concept of crime and punishment would be null and void if we belong to funny-looking grey creatures from Zeta Reticuli.

"If we have no more rights than a common housefly, then we'll have to do away with ownership of property as well. If we believe that, we'll have to do away with governments and public minions, dismantle the military and let anarchy reign supreme, laying about until one of the owners comes round to lop off an arm or leg for dinner or grind us into sausage and stir us up in a big vat somewhere in Nevada, USA.

"But wait! Why would creatures who can jump from Earth to Zeta Reticuli in a heartbeat keep their food supply in Nevada? Why don't they take it with them? "If you were able to jump from one town to another or one state to another by thinking it, and you wanted to paint a house in say, Texas, would you keep the paint bucket in New York and jump back and forth every time you had to load the brush just because you could jump back and forth? If you could jump to the grocery store, would you jump forty times to buy forty items or would you get everything in one jump so you wouldn't have to bother?

"People! That's why we have refrigerators and pantries! So we don't have to get in the car (flying saucer) and drive to the store (Nevada) every day! I can't believe we're more intelligent than our grey owners! They must be humiliated.

"But if all this nonsense is being orchestrated by an agency of Earthlings who wants you to believe in UFOs and funny-looking grey aliens, then it all makes sense, doesn't it? Humans are being abducted for medical experiments. Humans are being contacted telepathically to sort out the ESPers. Human females are carrying the seeds of a future race of cosmonauts. They may be producing embryos which are sent into space aboard the shuttle to see if they live or die in a weightless environment, the evidence of which will be applied to the technology of future manned excursions to the planets of this solar system and beyond.

"Lab rats simply won't provide the needed information, you see." (Unknown author)

The above is, in a nutshell, the view of the hard-shell skeptics. Putting aside the hyperbole and evangelistic style of writing, the guy has a point.

So, such an argument sounds pretty reasonable at first glance. It was only when I thought about it a bit longer that I realized the problem with such an idea. If the government is behind all the abductions, surely they would have screwed up at least once in forty-five years and we would know that fallible human beings were doing it. The fact that not one single incident, not one single abduction, not one single purported kidnapping event has ever resulted in a screw-up that led to anyone seeing the man behind the curtain—not one—should give us pause to think.

This guy expects me to believe that the US government can pull off an enterprise of this kind, with evidence of worldwide activity, for over fifty years, involving possibly millions of individuals, the logistics of which make the machinations of WWII look like the planning for a Sunday afternoon picnic? I'm sorry. I can't buy that. And so, even though he has many points about the phenomenon that beg for explanation, I think that we have to look for a hypothesis that explains and predicts the phenomenon better than what he has suggested. And part of that hypothesis may be that the ideas he is proposing are deliberately planted in the mind of the public for the very purpose of producing certain behavior, or hiding a dreadful and sinister secret, or both.

We can also see that, if the government is not involved, then public officials would be most interested in maintaining the cover-up. As the guy pointed out: to admit certain possibilities could lead to worldwide chaos and anarchy. If we are, as Charles Fort was wont to say, "property," if we "belong" to some race of advanced beings who use us for food and resources, then there is no point to anything we believe in at all. It is all a lie; a sham; a grand illusion; an enormous cosmic fraud. Who can live with that thought?

So there was no answer. Only clues to be followed.

* * *

Following the clues, based on my work with spirit release and exorcism, I had an idea about why the purported aliens really wanted human beings. It had nothing to do with regenerating their race by stealing embryos or using human beings in their version of Hamburger Helper. From reading the cases, from the information about Candy's supposed alien abductors, and a few other cases I dealt with, I had the idea that their food was a type of energy: the energy of negative emotions.

The stories told about a gazing process, where the abductee was subjected to a sustained and intense eye contact that generated a form of life review. This drew forth extreme emotional response as the chief feature of the experience. And afterward, the victim often became ill, feeling drained or depleted in a significant way.

But this did not explain certain other reports filtering out here and there about aliens feeding on human blood, or bathing in ghastly vats of body fluids and parts to absorb nutrients. If they were creatures that fed on energy, what were they doing partaking of material nourishment, no matter how the process was accomplished?

Again, there were more questions in my mind than answers.

* * *

On July 16, 1994, at our weekly Saturday evening sitting, we were all a bit excited at the latest news from space. Fragments of Comet Shoemaker-Levy 9 were soon to begin a series of collisions with the planet Jupiter, an extremely rare cosmic event. The impacts were supposed to continue for the next seven days, and I was very interested to see if this would have any noticeable effect on earth as some rumormongers were suggesting.

We had added a new element to our experiment: Reiki symbols. Candy had recently taken her second-level attunements and had brought the printed symbols. They reminded me of certain elements in crop circles. For a long time I had thought about the crop circle phenomenon in terms of printed circuitry similar to computer chips. What if we placed these symbols under the board itself? Would it be like installing a chip that expanded the function of our computer interface? One of the Reiki symbols was designated an "ether tube connector," and another was said to "increase power." Well, that sounded like the right circuit combination to me! I decided to add a little RAM and processing speed to the process.

I drew the symbols on a piece of paper with a black marker and slipped them into place aligned to the north. The three of us sat around the table. Candy told us that we were supposed to speak the names of the symbols to activate the energy. Supposedly, this sounding would imprint the energy circuit in the frequency field of the body. It also occurred to me that sound vibration could play a part in brain entrainment, and by doing this, we would be linking our brain energies, which might amplify them to penetrate the veil. We chanted away while visualizing a spiraling energy tube passing through the darkness into the blazing light of truth.

After a few minutes we were out of breath and feeling pretty silly. Obviously, nothing was going to happen. We sat back and relaxed, drinking coffee and dunking cookies and spilling drops on the board. I was verbally puzzling over Bob Lazar's statement on video that the aliens refer to humans as "containers." What did this mean?

We were just sitting there with our fingers lightly on the planchette, the "question" inside me growing larger and larger, when suddenly the planchette began to move in slow, deliberate circles in a way we had never before experienced.

We jerked our fingers away.

I asked Frank, "Did you just do that?"

"No," he replied indignantly. "Put your fingers back. Let's see what's going on!"

A funny pinching feeling and a tingle started at the back of my head that ran down my arm. The planchette began to move again slowly in a spiral. Spiral in and spiral out. We did the usual thing and said, "Hello!"

Slowly, the planchette precisely and deliberately spelled "Hello."

That was not exactly usual. The usual response to "hello" was for the planchette to go to "yes." It always took a bit for each entity to get warmed up and be able to move comfortably around the board.

As unusual as that opening was, we were not prepared for what was about to happen.

We were not recording either. In the transcript that follows, the questions are reconstructed from memory. The answers, however, were written down as received.

Q: *Do you have any messages for us?*
A: *Keep doing what comes naturally.*
Q. *(L) In what respect?*
A: *Study.*
Q: *(L) What is your name?*
A: *Mucpeor.*

This was an unusual name. Up to this point in time, the names we had been given had all been, more or less, familiar. Names like "Dave" or "John" or "Mary" were not uncommon with the dead-dude crowd. Some of them even used archaic, but still familiar, names like "Agamemnon" or "Aquila." So, a completely unfamiliar name with no known connection was another first. However, part of the name was familiar to me: "Peor." It is the name of a mountain in the Bible, and is related to the "Heresy of Peor." Baal Peor was a divinity who was worshipped at that mountain peak.

If Peòr is connected to the Hebrew stem *p'r* ('open'), used both of mouth and bowels, it might mean 'opening' and so Ba'al Peòr could mean 'Lord of the Opening.' Despite the fact that the Bible attempts to portray Peor in as bad a light as possible, there are curious remnants of the worship in the Song of Solomon where it says: *"My beloved put in his hand by the hole of the door, and my bowels were moved for him."* (King James Bible Cambridge Ed.)

The line of the Aaronic priesthood was justified in the Bible by the actions of Phinehas, grandson of Aaron. A man—the Israelite Zimri, the son of Salu—brings a Midianite woman into the camp in the sight of Moses (whose wife was also a Midianite and whose father-in-law, a Midianite priest, apparently was the source of Moses' great knowledge), where the people are weeping because of a plague. The story that was created by the writers of the Bible has Phinehas rising up with a spear, following the man into the chamber and thrusting the spear through both the man and woman, who were evidently in the act of copulation. According to the Bible (which was polemic against literally everything that wasn't under the control of the psychopathic Yahweh) tells us then that the plague, from which 24,000 had died, then ended, and the Aaronic line of priests was justified by this "holy" act of Phinehas. Of course, from the point of view of the writers of the Bible, Baal Peor is evil and has been further reviled in disgusting ways in rabbinic literature. That poses the interesting possibility that Peor may have been a very positive influence. An ancient Aramaic inscription, found at Dier Alla, identifies Balaam as a prophet of Shamash, a Semitic sun-god, and consequently, it could well be the case that the unidentified Baal of Peor is Shamash. If Peor's connection to Pi-Hor is factual, then the Baal of Peor may be the Egyptian god Horus. It was also identified as the Moon Goddess in some areas.

So, all in all, this name provided some interesting speculation for me. Now, back to the exchange. Since we had already been visited by a spate of space brothers, the next logical question was:

Q: (L) Are you an alien from another planet?
A: Alien from your perspective, yes.

That was a funny answer. They were not aliens, but were "alien" *from our perspective*. Well, Jordan and the other space brothers had belonged to one alien group or another. The Cosmic Confederation or the Galactic Brotherhood or whatever. So the next natural question was:

Q: (L) What is your group called?
A: Corsas.
Q: (L) Where are you from?
A: Cassiopaea.
Q: (L) Where is that?
A: Near Orion.
Q: (L) I heard that the Orions are the "bad guys." Are the Orion group bad?
A: Some bad.

The word "corsas" was odd too. The only thing I ever found on that was that it is a genus of moths from the *Noctuidae* or owlet family. Many moths from this family have the unique ability to be able to eat and thrive on poisonous plants that would kill other species.

I had read so much about different purported groups of aliens, most of whom pointed the finger at a slew of them from somewhere in Orion who were here to do all kinds of nasty things. So this was certainly a test question. The fact that the Cassiopaeans did not jump on the Orion-bashing bandwagon was interesting, though they did say that *some* were "bad."

Candy had recently read a book on the channeled *Ra Material*, which explained a concept of determining "good guys" from "bad guys." This consisted in asking if the entity served self or others. So, that was the next logical question:

Q: (L) Do you serve self or others?
A: I serve both.
Q: Are you bad or good, in our terms?
A: Good.
Q: (L) What is your philosophy?
A: One.
Q: (L) What are you here for tonight?
A: Prophecy.
Q: (L) What prophecies?
A: Tornadoes Florida—several.
Q: Where else?
A: Also Texas and Alabama.
Q: (L) When?
A: Sun is in Libra.
Q: (L) What planet are you from?
A: Carcosa. [Misspelled in the notes, scratched out and re-written]

The term "Carcosa" was another sign that we were dealing with something a bit different here. Up to this point, none of the discarnate entities we had dealt with had been able to read our minds. But here, there was a funny reference to a word that had been playing through my mind all day. I was a bit startled by this remark. It was from Jacques Vallee's book, *Revelations*. At the beginning of each section, there are quotes from "Cassilda's Song" in *The King in Yellow*, Act 1, Scene 2, by Robert W. Chambers. After the session, I opened the book to re-read the quotes. The Song goes:

Strange is the night where black stars rise,
And strange moons circle through the skies,

But stranger still is ... Lost Carcosa.
Songs that the Pleiades shall sing,
Where flap the tatters of the King,
Must die unheard in ... Dim Carcosa.
Along the shore the cloud waves break,
The twin suns sink behind the lake,
The shadows lengthen ... In Carcosa.

It was rather haunting and had been playing through my mind all that afternoon.

More interesting still, to those already familiar with the Cassiopaean material, is the reference to the "twin suns" that appears in this little poem.

Q: *Where is that?*
A: 2 DILOR.

The planchette had begun to move very fast and we were not able to keep up. The last remark was lost and only a few of the letters written down. "DILOR" is only part of that response.

Q: *What was that again?*
A: *You pay attention.*
Q: *(L) What else do you have to tell us?*
A: *Seattle buried; Japan buckles; Missouri shakes; California crumbles; Arizona burns.*
Q: *[Unknown question.]*
A: *Go to Denver airports.*
Q: *(L) When is all this going to happen?*
A: *Scandal—Scandal—Denver Airport.*
Q: *(L) What about the Denver airport?*
A: *Scandal.*
Q: *I don't understand.*
A: *New Denver airport.*
Q: *I don't understand.*
A: *Pay attention.*
Q: *Okay, we are paying attention. What are you trying to tell us?*
A: *Denver new airport big big big big scandal.*

Q: (L) What kind of scandal?
A: Government.
Q: (L) Specifically what?
A: You will see Dallas airport is secret base Orlando too Miami too.
Q: (L) What about Denver airport and how does it relate to prophecies?
A: Denver reveals the government Look for it Pay attention.
Q: (L) What else do you have to tell us?
A: Montana: Experiment with human reproduction All people there— rays—radon gas.
Q: (L) How are they doing this?
A: Compelled—Don't trust Don't ignore too strong urges sinister plots.
Q: (L) What do you mean? I don't understand?
A: Strong urge is directed by sinister plot.
Q: Plot by whom?
A: Consortium.
Q: (L) Who are the members of the consortium? Aliens? The government?
A: All.
Q: (L) All who?
A: Government and other.
Q: (L) Who is the other?
A: Unknown.
Q: (L) Why can't you tell us who is the other?
A: You know who.

Well, all this was very interesting. Finally, an entity that could spell and didn't spend any time wandering around looking for the letters. Now was my chance, so I decided to ask the question that had been bugging me all day.

Q: (L) Bob Lazar referred to the fact that aliens supposedly refer to humans as containers. What does this mean?
A: Later use.
Q: (L) Use by who? How many?
A: 94 per cent.
Q: (L) 94 per cent of what?
A: Of all population.

Q: (L) What do you mean?
A: All are containers 94 per cent use.
Q: I don't understand.
A: Will be used 94 percent.
Q: (L) Used for what?
A: Total consumption.
Q: (L) What do you mean by consumption? Ingested?
A: Consumed for ingredients.
Q: (L) Why?
A: New race Important 13 years about when happens.
Q: (L) Why are humans consumed?
A: They are used for parts.
Q: (L) We don't understand. How can humans be used for parts?
A: Reprototype Vats exist Missing persons often go there and especially missing children.

At this answer, I was in shock. What kind of being was telling us such things? What kind of awful reality must such information proceed from? I was torn between terminating contact that very instant, and working my way through it to find some resolution.

Q: (L) Do we have any protection?
A: Some.
Q: (L) How can we protect ourselves and our children?
A: Inform them Don't hide the truth from children.
Q: (L) How does truth protect us?
A: Awareness protects Ignorance endangers.
Q: (L) Why tell children such horrible things?
A: Need to know.
Q: I don't know how knowing this helps. This is awful. Why tell children such things?
A: Must know—ease pain with meditation.

Well, the very suggestion of frightening my children with such horror stories practically sent me into a fit! But, again, I was torn. More than anything I was curious as to what kind of being would be saying such dreadful things. The negative entities I had encountered most definitely had never said such things; in fact, they always presented themselves as really good but misunderstood and persecuted. Finding excuses for their evil was the hallmark of beings of darkness. Were we now addressing a different kind of dark being, one that was so dark it didn't care how many awful things it said?

Or, were they telling me things designed to galvanize me—me, the mother of five children—to ask more questions designed to protect our children?

Q: *Why are you telling us this? It's awful!*
A: *We love you.*

Swell. But what kind of love would tell us such awful things, I wondered. And then, immediately I realized that I was always warning my children about dangers. Even if I didn't like to admit that the world was a dangerous place, I knew that I had to tell them such things in order for them to be aware—to preserve them. Why? Because I loved them and wanted them to survive in a dangerous world.

Q: *Are we supposed to tell others?*
A: *Don't reveal to public. You would be abducted.*

That was a reasonable answer and certainly didn't suggest that they had an agenda for us to go around scaring people. I was curious about the so-called project mentioned as being completed in about thirteen years, for which this being was saying so many terrible human sacrifices were made. Even if it was an evil being, maybe I could get enough information in a hurry that I could tell others and maybe it would make sense to some of those who were more familiar with such details. (As to whether anything that gives a sign of some completed project in 2007, thirteen years after this statement was made, might be noted in the events of that year, that is still open.)

Q: *(L) What is the purpose of this project?*
A: *New life here.*

Since I had formulated my idea that the aliens feed on human emotion, I decided on this for a test question. An alien who fed on us would very likely deny it unless, as I already thought, we were being addressed by a being of such insouciant darkness that we had never encountered its ilk before.

> Q: (L) Are the aliens using our emotions and energies?
> A: Correct; and bodies too. Each earth year 10 percent more children are taken.

They weren't going to let that missing children issue alone. It was too horrible to contemplate. Why did they keep saying something that upset me so? I was a bit distraught, as a mother, and in a shaking voice I asked:

> Q: (L) Do they suffer?
> A: Some.
> Q: (L) Do they all suffer?
> A: Some.
> Q: What happens to souls? Is this physical only?
> A: Physical—souls recycled.
> Q: Where do the souls go?
> A: Back here—most.
> Q: Do some go elsewhere?
> A: And go out of planet human.

Again, just in case this monstrous story was true, I wanted details—something I could check.

> Q: Who is responsible for this?
> A: Consortium.
> Q: (C) This is totally sick! I don't want to do this any more!
> A: Sick is subjective.
> Q: (L) But what you are telling us is so awful!
> A: Understand, but all does not conform to your perspective.

And with that answer, I realized that what we were being told, as crazy as it sounded, just might be the truth. But again, what kind of being tells such truths?

> Q: Why is this happening to us?
> A: Karma.

Q: (L) What kind of karma could bring this?
A: Atlantis.
Q: (L) What can protect us?
A: Knowledge.
Q: (L) How do we get this knowledge?
A: You are being given it now.
Q: (L) What knowledge do you mean?
A: You have it.
Q: (L) How does the knowledge of what you have told us help us?
A: Gives great defense.
Q: (L) What knowledge gives defense?
A: Just gave it.
Q: (L) What specifically?
A: Don't ask that not important.
Q: We don't understand.
A: Knowing about it gives psychic defense.
Q: How do we tell other people? And who should we tell?
A: Inform indirectly only.
Q: (L) How?
A: Write.
Q: Should we use hypnosis to uncover such memories?
A: Open.
Q: (L) Have any of us been abducted?
A: Yes.
Q: Who of us sitting here?
A: All.
Q: (L) How many times?
A: Frank-57; Candy-56; Laura-12.
Q: (L) Why has Laura not been abducted as much? (Laura laughs)
A: It is not over.
Q: (Candy laughs)
A: Candy was abducted last month. Laura—33—[years of age or years ago?]
Q: (L) Who is abducting us?
A: Others.
Q: (L) What is the name of the group?
A: Different names.
Q: (L) Are we all abducted by the same group?

A: *Mostly.*
Q: *(L) What did they do to us?*
A: *Gave false memories. Made you inhibited child—headaches—sick at school.*
Q: *(C) Where is my implant?*
A: *Head.*
Q: *Frank?*
A: *Same.*
Q: *Laura?*
A: *Same.*
Q: *(L) What are the implants for?*
A: *Study device.*
Q: *(L) To study what?*
A: *Soul composition.*
Q: *(L) Do any of the rituals we perform provide protection against further abduction?*
A: *Don't need protection if you have knowledge.*
Q: *(L) How do we get this knowledge?*
A: *Deep subconscious.*
Q: *(L) When did we get it?*
A: *Before birth.*
Q: *(L) Is there anything else we can do for protection?*
A: *Learn, meditate, read.*
Q: *(L) Are we doing what we need to be doing at the present?*
A: *So far. Need awaken. Must go now. Out of Energy. I must go.*

I didn't know what to think. But, indeed, again there was that injunction to learn.

I was traumatized by the information given; that was a certainty. How was I supposed to process that? Over the years I had become so sensitive to the sufferings of others that I had to look away if we were forced to pass an auto accident. I had to leave the room if there was a sad story on the news. If a movie became sad, I couldn't continue watching it. If I read a story about an ill or abused child, I would become depressed for days afterward.

I had five beloved children of my own, and I was a sort of vicarious mother to every child on the planet. I didn't see grubby little boys as bratty kids; I saw them as the beloved child of their mother; and I identified with all mothers. I would take as much care for the child of a stranger as for my own and would be grateful for any other mother to feel the same about my children. My children were my life. So why did they push this issue about children being taken and experimented upon? Was this designed to hurt me specifically so that I would feel bad and the entity, whoever he was, could feed on the energy of my suffering? Or was I being driven to learn something important, something crucial for all humanity?

There was only one thing to do: get some facts.

I thought it would be a relatively easy thing to buy a world almanac and discover what the statistics on missing children were: how many were missing, how many were successfully returned to their families.

Nope. Not that simple, apparently.

Okay, plan B. I made calls to local law enforcement agencies. What government department kept track of such statistics? I was passed from one to the other and back again.

How about plan C? I called agencies and said I was a freelance news reporter doing an article. In this country, that's a fair way to get public information. No special credentials are required.

But it didn't matter. No one knew much about missing children. Nobody could give me the answers I needed.

There are now dozens of organizations and agencies that are devoted to missing and exploited children. The only problem is, you still can't get a straight, single answer to a simple question: how many children go missing every year and how many are returned safely, and where's the proof? Everywhere you look you get a different figure, though, over time, a sort of standard figure has evolved. But getting any kind of hard copy on hard statistics with data to back it up is, as far as I have been able to tell, impossible. Nobody wants to talk about it in those terms.

And I began to ask myself why.

What's more, during that week of trying to get answers to this one particular issue, I began to get a feeling that something was definitely not right with our world. Something was horribly wrong and nobody was admitting it, much less talking about it. I had no proof that what the communication from the board had told me was true. Yet I most definitely had been obstructed in trying to prove it to be false.

Maybe he or she was telling a simple truth, and wasn't that what I was after? Even though I was asking for truth, like everyone else, I still had the idea that truth ought to be "nice." The fact that it might not be all sweetness and light was not lost on me even if I still had that prejudice that "higher beings" would say only "lofty" things.

* * *

The next session, on the last day of the Comet Shoemaker-Levy impacts with Jupiter, the barrier between realms collapsed, quite literally, with a thunderous crash. It was July 22nd.

We were a bit curious whether the strange communicant from the previous week would return. Again, Candy and I were quietly pronouncing the words of the Reiki symbols to create a circuit in the frequency of the body for an "etheric connection."

The planchette spelled out: "Frank say it too." So, Frank joined us in the gentle repetition of these "energy words."

Suddenly, we heard three very loud and very close thunderclaps—crashing sounds—directly above the house, so strong they made the building shake. It sounded like a plane exploding right over the top of us. Fearing imminent destruction, we dashed madly to the door to see what was happening in the skies overhead.

The sky was completely clear, stars twinkling, nothing. After looking around and listening for a bit, we decided this must be one of those "out of the blue" lightning strikes we had heard about, even if there had been no flash of light accompanying it. We would have noticed the light with the windows open.

We returned to the table and began to sit again, talking about this strange thunder and paying little attention to the board at all. Again, the planchette began to move in slow, deliberate spirals. And again, I said, "Hello!"

> A: Hello.
> Q: Is anyone with us?
> A: Listen, Look. Learn. Stop eating. [Candy was having a snack.]
> Q: What is the problem with eating?
> A: Not good connection.
> Q: (L) What is your name?
> A: Ellaga.

Another unusual name; I was intrigued.

Q: (L) Are you discarnate from earth?
A: No.
Q: Are you from the same group we communicated with the other night?
A: Yes.
Q: (L) Are you from another galaxy?
A: No.
Q: (L) Where are you from?
A: Cassiopaea.
Q: (L) Is this the constellation we know as Cassiopaea?
A: Yes.
Q: (L) What can we do for a better connection?
A: Less noise.

There was distracting activity in the next room because the children were in there. We shut the door.

Q: (L) Do you have information for us this evening?

With this question, the planchette took off, and I started calling out the letters for Candy to write, trying desperately to keep up. They were delivered in one long string with no word breaks so that we had to study them after to divide them into words. It was impossible to try to follow word by word, putting the letters together in the mind, so I gave up and just pronounced each one as the planchette dashed around the board.

> *A: Space invasion soon Four to six years. Battle between forces good and evil Wait near Look far Listen Mexico fall Ethiopia quake September both New Near January Paris bomb London Blizzard 109 die Plane down Tahiti Cholera Montana January 1995 government US behind California quakes Three soon Oklahoma political abduction February 95 Big news.*

The curious thing about this last remark is that on February 25, 1995, we were given a warning of a terrorist bomb attack within a month. Connect that to Oklahoma "political abduction," the word February followed by "big news," and we find a curious relationship to the April 19, 1995, Oklahoma bombing of a federal building in which at least 168 people lost their lives. Later convicted in the bombing, Timothy McVeigh, a Gulf War veteran, told reporters he was under the control of an implant in his hip, and that he believed he had been abducted and programmed by the government.

Q: (L) What is causing the earth changes?
A: Electromagnetic wave changes.
Q: (L) Can you be more specific?
A: Gap in surge heliographic field.
Q: (L) I don't understand.
A: Put Frank on processor channel open.
Q: Do you mean that Frank can channel on the computer?
A: Yes. Do it now.

I thought this was an attempt at sidetracking the process. I had the feeling that such a request was coming from Frank—who was not very enamored of the board process, though he patiently went along with me—or from some other source that would have very much liked to divert us from our method. We had certain feedback-loop tuning control. From wherever the request came, I was determined not to accede to any requests and just said "no" and pushed on.

Q: (L) Is a meteor or comet going to hit earth?
A: Open.
Q: (L) What are the effects on us of the comet striking Jupiter?
A: Further field imbalance.
Q: (L) Was that comet meant for earth as some psychics are saying?
A: Open.

Internet rumors at the time of the Comet Shoemaker-Levy impacts on Jupiter held that this comet had been meant to hit earth, but a certain group of aliens, and I don't remember which one, had decided to save the earth by redirecting these comet fragments to strike Jupiter instead. Naturally, all of mankind was supposed to be grateful to this particular group for saving our buns from the fire.

Q: [Unknown question, probably relating to missing children. I think I had brought the subject up again to test and see if we couldn't get a

more "nice-nice" answer. Well, if that was what I was expecting, that was not what I got!]
A: Bits childrens organs removed while wide awake—kidneys crushed—then next feet—next jaw examined on table—tongues cut off—bones stress tested—pressure placed on heart muscle until burst.
Q: Why are you saying these awful things?!
A: Must know what consortium is doing.
Q: What children are they doing this to?
A: Done mostly to Indian children.
Q: Why am I getting this horrible feeling while you are telling us this?
A: Because subject is distressing.
Q: Why do we need to know these things?
A: Very big effort on behalf of Orions and their human brethren to create new race and control.
Q: (L) Where are you from?
A: Cassiopaea.
Q: (L) Where do you live specifically?
A: Live in omnipresence.
Q: (L) What does that mean?
A: All realms.
Q: (L) Can you tell us what your environment is like?
A: Difficult.
Q: (L) Well take a stab at it.
A: What stab?
Q: (L) Do you serve self or others?
A: Both. Self through others.
Q: (L) Candy wants to know the details of her abductions.
A: Do you?
Q: (C) Yes.
A: Are you sure?
Q: (C) Yes.
A: Soon, vibrations not right at this time.
Q: (L) Does this mean Candy's vibrations are not right to receive this information?
A: Right.
Q: Why was information about our abductions given last time?
A: Was not I.

Q: And who are you?
A: Ellaga.

This last response only became clear later. We were soon to learn that each session brought forth a different "entity." As each "moment" in space-time was totally unique, so were the energies surrounding us and our questions. Thus a different name of the communicating entity designated a different frequency relating to something like an "information field"; we were told that there were really no "separate" entities communicating. Each session was unique in its question–answer energy exchange.

Since my cousin Sam had been so devoted to the ideas of Zecharia Sitchin's *12th Planet*, I decided that a couple of questions along that line might be interesting. Sitchin claims in his books that a superior race of alien beings once inhabited our world. He claims that they were travelers from the stars, that they arrived eons ago and genetically engineered mankind to serve as their slaves. He claims that the "Sons of Anak" mentioned in the Bible are the Annunaki, and also that they are the same as the Biblical Nefilim. They are a race of gold-seeking giants from a renegade planet in our own solar system, known to the Sumerians as the "Planet of the Crossing." This planet crosses the plane of the ecliptic every 3,600 years, and when it gets close enough, these beings make a hop to earth to check up on their creation. Supposedly, this will happen again soon. The title comes from the fact that Sitchin proposes twelve houses of the zodiac for twelve "planets." He includes the sun and moon in his count because they are zodiacally significant. But, in actuality, it is really a tenth planet, excluding the sun and moon. He also fails to note that the earth is excluded from zodiacal considerations due to the fact that astrology is geocentric. Since Sam was so sold on the Sitchin scenario of ancient astronauts, and I was equally convinced that it was a theory that was full of errors, I thought that this would be another good test question.

Q: (L) Is there a tenth planet as described by Zecharia Sitchen?
A: No. [Okay, no point in pursuing that!]
Q: (L) Was Venus ejected from Jupiter?

This was proposed by Immanuel Velikovsky as an explanation why ancient astronomers and myth-makers claimed that Venus was born from Jupiter.

The reader will most certainly wish to read *Worlds in Collision*, because it is one of the most rational books ever written. Even if Velikovsky was wrong about some of the conclusions he drew regarding myth and legend, his observations and proposals of a new way at looking at the cosmos have yet to be fully appreciated. And, according to the Cassiopaeans, he was, at least, partly correct. But, in response to the question—was Venus ejected from the planet Jupiter—the answer was:

A: No.
Q: (L) Did Venus follow a cometary orbit for a time as theorized by Velikovsky?
A: Yes.
Q: (L) Did Venus appear in our solar system, from the area of Jupiter, coming from deep space as suggested by Velikovsky?
A: That is correct.
Q: (L) Was Venus the pillar of smoke by day and fire by night as seen by the Jews during the Exodus?
A: No.
Q: (L) What was seen by the Jews?
A: A Guideship.
Q: (L) Were Sodom and Gomorrah destroyed by nuclear weapons?
A: Yes and no.
Q: (L) How were they destroyed?
A: EMP
Q: (L) What is "EMP"?
A: Electromagnetic pulse.

This remark about "electromagnetic pulse" energy was made long before any of us at the table were aware of anything called EMP. It was later described in some detail by Col. Corso in his book *The Day After Roswell*. But that was a few years ahead of us at this point in time.

Unfortunately, after the previous two years of mostly nonsense spirit interactions, we were not yet in the habit of taping and we did not know if this communication was a fluke or not. So, we only have notes from the first half-dozen or so early sessions.

After a couple of weeks of repeated contact and apparent strengthening of the communication, I bought a special tape recorder to tape the sessions.

From this point on, we began what I intended to be a far more rigorous testing phase of the communication. This consisted in rapid questions that jumped from one subject to another across a broad range of categories. I was checking consistency, trying to confuse the source, and also trying to determine range and limits. I was most especially interested in questions relating to "unsolved mysteries" and spent days going through books looking for particular mysteries to ask about.

In one sense, this was a good thing, and in another it was not so good. One thing that became very evident during this process was that there was no way possible for any of the information to have been "beamed" into our heads from any human source. The questions were so random, and the answers were so rapid, many of them checking out after later research. We had to really dig for the answers that invariably confirmed that the Cassiopaeans could tell us things that were most definitely not part of our own subconscious minds. More than this, if the information had been beamed via a satellite, whoever was there reading our minds in zero time, or tuning in to our questions, must have had the fastest "look-it-up-quick" crew on the planet.

The Cassiopaeans were fast on the draw, and they soon began doing their own punctuation, accurately I might add, so that if anyone was beaming information into our heads, they were a stickler for grammar, as well as the fastest at looking up answers in the world's biggest library.

The very bad thing about my testing phase is the fact that there is almost no part of the material where the subjects do not just jump all over the place. Indeed, we would come back and ask follow-up questions at later times, but any one session could jump from higher cosmic realms to the perception of house cats.

Nevertheless, even though I was taking the experiment a bit more seriously, I still had no idea what I had done here.

* * *

This was the beginning of what has become known as the Cassiopaean Transmissions. It was also the beginning of the manifestation of Amazing Grace in my life to such an extent that if it had not happened to me, if someone else had told me such a story about their lives—as mine proceeded from this point onward—I would simply find it impossible to believe. I had no idea that the events during that seven-day period would bring me together with a mainstream European scientist with a thirty-year career in mathematics and physics, who, like me, had been looking all his life for The One. I did not realize that all my dreams and impressions of Nazi Germany were past-life drivers that compelled me to keep searching, to keep working to overcome obstacles that ultimately led to being reunited with my husband from that time, my lost love, my other half in most literal terms.

I did not realize that, by virtue of remaining true to an Ideal in the face of all evidence to the contrary, by asking and continuing to ask, by knocking and continuing to knock at the door, it was being opened to me, and the Guardian at the Door had beckoned me to enter. Over the next two years I was initiated into realms of knowledge that few people ever encounter. All of my life up to this point was a preparation for this understanding, a test to determine if I truly loved truth enough to continue to ask for it, and to recognize it when it was presented to me. I began my own experimental work in this area with a major attitude of skepticism. That was good because, as it turned out, having started as a skeptic, I was quite taken aback to discover the reality that the so-called astral planes are a veritable jungle. Even though I conducted my sessions with extreme care to avoid any possibility of contaminating my subjects, I discovered that all was not well in the "higher" realms. That led, of course, to the question: Why is so much nonsense propagated by religion and so-called channeled sources who are clearly in many instances lying? In other cases, they are at the very least guilty of such serious lack of attention to these matters that it amounts to a horrifying crime of omission.

The lack of knowledge about the true nature of our reality is one of the chief reasons for the sufferings of humanity. How "good" is a religion or a channeled source that does not inform us of these conditions? Religious believers have been indoctrinated with the idea of faith without question as the answer to all problems, and the so-called New Age movement has been heavily inculcated with the idea that one must not ever think about negative things. As a result, they are, above all other people, most subject to the predation of evil.

It is in identifying the true evil magician who controls this world, and the ways and means to escape this control, that the Cassiopaeans have been invaluable—initiating us into these deepest secrets of the universe. In the process of testing and validating what the Cassiopaeans have told us, has it been possible to get close to the original teachings of Christianity, considering the millennia of corruption, distortion, destruction of material, and brainwashing of the masses of people?

Indeed, there are many clues. In the Gnostic Gospel of Thomas, the disciples ask Thomas what Jesus told him when he withdrew and "told him three things." Thomas said to them: *"If I tell you even one of the things he told me, you will pick up rocks and stone me. Then fire will come forth from the rocks and devour you."*

What in the world was so controversial about what Jesus was saying in private that even some of his closest followers could not be told?

At another point, Jesus says to his disciples, following a rendition of the parable of the sower: *"This is also how you can acquire the kingdom of heaven. If you do not acquire it through knowledge, you will not be able to find it."*

Repeatedly throughout the Gnostic texts, the seeking of knowledge being opposed to belief in salvation from a "god out there" was emphasized. That was truly heretical in those days. In fact, it is heretical now. But even in the canonical gospels, these truths bleed through. If "three-day deaths and resurrections" of savior gods were so commonplace throughout the Middle East, why was Jesus saying the following:

"You miserable people! You unfortunate ones! You pretenders to truth! You falsifiers of knowledge! You sinners against the spirit! Why do you continue to listen when from the beginning you should have been speaking? Why do you sleep when from the beginning you should have been awake, that the kingdom of heaven might receive you? I tell you the truth: it is easier for a holy person to sink into filth, and for an enlightened person to sink into darkness, than for you to reign."

At one point, in the Gospel of Thomas, Jesus makes a rather astounding comparison:

"They saw a Samaritan carrying a lamb and going to Judea. He said to his disciples, 'Why is he carrying the lamb around?' They said to him, 'So that he may kill it and eat it.' He said to them, 'He will not eat it while it is alive, but only after it has been killed and has become a carcass.' They said, 'it cannot happen any other way.' He said to them, 'So also with you: seek a place of rest for yourselves, that you may not become a carcass and be eaten.'"

I persisted in my search through obstacles that would have destroyed the mind and will of many people. And there were many more obstacles to come. Some of them nearly cost me my life during the first two years of initiation via the Cassiopaeans. It was clear that forces opposed this initiation, and it was entirely up to me and my exercise of will to overcome these forces. The Cassiopaeans could give me the knowledge to do this, but they could not directly interfere.

And in the end, when the first stage was completed, when I had passed many tests and Amazing Grace manifested in my life in so many wonderful ways, I realized that I had begun to experience the removal of the hindrance, or the revealing of the mystery of God in my own life.

For now, let us just say that at this point, *"Through many dangers, toils and snares we have already come. T'was Grace that brought us safe thus far, and Grace will lead us home."*

Amazing Grace.

NOTE: This is the end of the original version of *Amazing Grace*. The reader may now wish to begin reading *The Wave* or *Adventures with Cassiopaea* series, also published by Red Pill Press and available on our website, cassiopaea.org. As for *Amazing Grace*, I think I should continue it, because the reader who has traveled through all that pain and suffering (and I skipped a lot of details) really deserves to get to the part where it's all made clear and one learns that knowledge really does protect and there is a light at the end of the tunnel, and Love is everlasting ... and it was all worth it.

ACKNOWLEDGMENTS

*Thanks to Kristine Rosemary for "ironing" the text.
Any reader who finds the book readable and enjoyable ought to thank Kristine also.
Thanks to Donna for hauling Kristine and me out of the pit of grammatical and copy errors.
Thanks to Jonathan Metcalfe for the beautiful artwork on the cover.
Thanks to my son, Jason, for the graphic design of the cover.
Thanks to my girls, Amelia and Arielle, for running the house while Mommy was writing.
And most of all, thanks to my Ark for being my ark.*

www.ingramcontent.com/pod-product-compliance
Lightning Source LLC
Chambersburg PA
CBHW060906300426
44112CB00011B/1364